WOMEN'S
DEVOTIONAL
NEW TESTAMENT
WITH PSALMS & PROVERBS

WOMEN'S
D E V O T I O N A L
N E W   T E S T A M E N T
WITH PSALMS & PROVERBS

NEW INTERNATIONAL VERSION

Zondervan

> You will be pleased to know that a portion of the purchase price of your new NIV
> Bible has been provided to International Bible Society to help spread the gospel of
> Jesus Christ around the world!

CONTENTS

INTRODUCTION
NIV WOMEN'S DEVOTIONAL

Welcome to the NIV Women's Devotional New Testament! Are you ready to embark on an exciting journey through God's Word? You say you're too busy to take on any new adventures this year? This Bible is designed just for *you*—one of today's women who wants to step out into God's Word to discover encouragement and comfort, and yet who feels tugged in a hundred different directions.

Written for, by and about today's woman, the NIV Women's Devotional New Testament will reach you right where you are. But it won't leave you there! With God's Word and the sensitive and insightful reflections of many godly women, this Bible will transport you step by step on a journey to Christian maturity.

Several features make the NIV Women's Devotional New Testament an exceptional devotional guide:

The Bible

The NIV Women's Devotional New Testament features the text of the New International Version. This version's readability and accuracy make it the most popular modern translation available today. Included here are the books of the New Testament as well as the books of Psalms and Proverbs.

The Devotions

All of the daily and weekend devotions are written by women—women who have experienced both the joys and struggles of Christian living and who are willing to share those triumphs and trials with you. Each devotion is located within the text, in close proximity to the Scripture passage on which it is based.

The Introductions

The introduction to each Bible book succinctly highlights that book's practical themes. Each introduction gives you interesting facts and helpful background information to aid your understanding as you read that particular book and the accompanying devotional meditation.

Ease of Use

If you are like most women today, your life is full—you may even say sometimes that your life is too full. There are so many things to do, so many demands on your time. So we've designed the NIV Women's Devotional New Testament to give you a quick and easy Bible reading/devotional meditation plan to help you walk the road to maturity and growth.

The devotions in the NIV Women's Devotional New Testament take a distinctive pattern following the days of the week: Monday, Tuesday, Wednesday, Thursday, Friday. In recognition of your need for something different on the weekend, we've developed "Weekending"—combining one provocative devotional thought with short Scripture readings for both Saturday and Sunday.

No matter what day of the week you begin your reading, you simply turn to a devotion for that day. Then for the next day, look to the bottom of the devotion for the page number on which you'll find the next day's devotion. For example, if you start on a Monday, you could turn to the first devotion in the book of Matthew, page 5. Glance at the bottom of Monday's devotion and you will see the page number where Tuesday's devotion will be found—and so on as you keep walking on through Friday.

Friday's devotion will direct you to a "Weekending," which will provide you with a reflective insight for your weekend and a Scripture reading for both Saturday and Sunday. The bottom of the "Weekending" will send you to the next Monday devotion. And you are well on your way—through a year of spending precious time in God's Word and growing closer to him.

Reading Plans

On page 558 you'll find a plan to help you read through the New Testament and the books of Psalms and Proverbs in one year. God's Word has a wonderful continuity and many treasures that you'll discover as you read it through chapter by chapter and book by book.

Author Biographies

You will most likely recognize the names of many of the women who contributed to the NIV Women's Devotional New Testament. The author index, found on page 565, gives you some interesting information about each woman, as well as a list of the pages where her devotions appear.

Subject Index

You've had a tough day as a mom; you've just started a new job; you struggle with a serious illness; you're consumed with guilt. Whatever the circumstances that confront you, the subject index will help direct you to just the right words to encourage and motivate you. Look up a wide variety of subjects in this index on page 570, and turn to the listed page number for a devotion that fits your need.

So come on along. You're invited to open the pages of the NIV Women's Devotional New Testament and start along the pathway to a growing maturity. The treasures of God's Word await you at every step along the way, and the meditations of the women who have shared a bit of themselves will give the encouragement you need to keep moving ahead. And as you go, we pray you'll become all that God intends you to be as a woman of God in today's world.

THE NEW INTERNATIONAL VERSION is a completely new translation of the Holy Bible made by over a hundred scholars working directly from the best available Hebrew, Aramaic and Greek texts. It had its beginning in 1965 when, after several years of exploratory study by committees from the Christian Reformed Church and the National Association of Evangelicals, a group of scholars met at Palos Heights, Illinois, and concurred in the need for a new translation of the Bible in contemporary English. This group, though not made up of official church representatives, was transdenominational. Its conclusion was endorsed by a large number of leaders from many denominations who met in Chicago in 1966.

Responsibility for the new version was delegated by the Palos Heights group to a self-governing body of fifteen, the Committee on Bible Translation, composed for the most part of biblical scholars from colleges, universities and seminaries. In 1967 the New York Bible Society (now the International Bible Society) generously undertook the financial sponsorship of the project—a sponsorship that made it possible to enlist the help of many distinguished scholars. The fact that participants from the United States, Great Britain, Canada, Australia and New Zealand worked together gave the project its international scope. That they were from many denominations—including Anglican, Assemblies of God, Baptist, Brethren, Christian Reformed, Church of Christ, Evangelical Free, Lutheran, Mennonite, Methodist, Nazarene, Presbyterian, Wesleyan and other churches—helped to safeguard the translation from sectarian bias.

How it was made helps to give the New International Version its distinctiveness. The translation of each book was assigned to a team of scholars. Next, one of the Intermediate Editorial Committees revised the initial translation, with constant reference to the Hebrew, Aramaic or Greek. Their work then went to one of the General Editorial Committees, which checked it in detail and made another thorough revision. This revision in turn was carefully reviewed by the Committee on Bible Translation, which made further changes and then released the final version for publication. In this way the entire Bible underwent three revisions, during each of which the translation was examined for its faithfulness to the original languages and for its English style.

All this involved many thousands of hours of research and discussion regarding the meaning of the texts and the precise way of putting them into English. It may well be that no other translation has been made by a more thorough process of review and revision from committee to committee than this one.

From the beginning of the project, the Committee on Bible Translation held to certain goals for the New International Version: that it would be an accurate translation and one that would have clarity and literary quality and so prove suitable for public and private reading, teaching, preaching, memorizing and liturgical use. The Committee also sought to preserve some measure of continuity with the long tradition of translating the Scriptures into English.

In working toward these goals, the translators were united in their commitment to the authority and infallibility of the Bible as God's Word in written form. They believe that it contains the divine answer to the deepest needs of humanity, that it sheds unique light on our path in a dark world, and that it sets forth the way to our eternal well-being.

The first concern of the translators has been the accuracy of the translation and its fidelity to the thought of the biblical writers. They have weighed the significance of the lexical and grammatical details of the Hebrew, Aramaic and Greek texts. At the same time, they have striven for more than a word-for-word translation. Because thought patterns and syntax differ from language to language, faithful communication of the meaning of the writers of the Bible demands frequent modifications in sentence structure and constant regard for the contextual meanings of words.

A sensitive feeling for style does not always accompany scholarship. Accordingly the Committee on Bible Translation submitted the developing version to a number of stylistic consultants. Two of them read every book of both Old and New Testaments twice—once before and once after the last major revision—and made invaluable suggestions. Samples of the translation were tested for clarity and ease of reading by various kinds of people—young and old, highly educated and less well educated, ministers and laymen.

Concern for clear and natural English—that the New International Version should be idiomatic but not idiosyncratic, contemporary but not dated—motivated the translators and consultants. At the same time, they tried to reflect the differing styles of the biblical writers. In view of the international use of English, the translators sought to avoid obvious Americanisms on the one hand and obvious Anglicisms on the other. A British edition reflects the comparatively few differences of significant idiom and of spelling.

As for the traditional pronouns "thou," "thee" and "thine" in reference to the Deity, the translators judged that to use these archaisms (along with the old verb forms such as "doest," "wouldest" and "hadst") would violate accuracy in translation. Neither Hebrew, Aramaic nor Greek uses special pronouns for the persons of the Godhead. A present-day translation is not enhanced by forms that in the time of the King James Version were used in everyday speech, whether referring to God or man.

For the Old Testament the standard Hebrew text, the Masoretic Text as published in the latest editions of *Biblia Hebraica*, was used throughout. The Dead Sea Scrolls contain material bearing on an earlier stage of the Hebrew text. They were consulted, as were the Samaritan Pentateuch and the ancient scribal traditions relating to textual changes. Sometimes a variant Hebrew reading in the margin of the Masoretic Text was followed instead of the text itself. Such instances, being variants within the Masoretic tradition, are not specified by footnotes. In rare cases, words in the consonantal text were divided differently from the way they appear in the Masoretic Text. Footnotes indicate this. The translators also consulted the more important early versions—the Septuagint; Aquila, Symmachus and Theodotion; the Vulgate; the Syriac Peshitta; the Targums; and for the Psalms the *Juxta Hebraica* of Jerome. Readings from these versions were occasionally followed where the Masoretic Text seemed doubtful and where accepted principles of textual criticism showed that one or more of these textual witnesses appeared to provide the correct reading. Such instances are footnoted. Sometimes vowel letters and vowel signs did not, in the judgment of the translators, represent the correct vowels for the original consonantal text. Accordingly some words were read with a different set of vowels. These instances are usually not indicated by footnotes.

The Greek text used in translating the New Testament was an eclectic one. No other piece of ancient literature has such an abundance of manuscript witnesses as does the New Testament. Where existing manuscripts differ, the translators made their choice of readings according to accepted principles of New Testament textual criticism. Footnotes call attention to places where there was uncertainty about what the original text was. The best current printed texts of the Greek New Testament were used.

There is a sense in which the work of translation is never wholly finished. This applies to all great literature and uniquely so to the Bible. In 1973 the New Testament in the New International Version was published. Since then, suggestions for corrections and revisions have been received from various sources. The Committee on Bible Translation carefully considered the suggestions and adopted a number of them. These were incorporated in the first printing of the entire Bible in 1978. Additional revisions were made by the Committee on Bible Translation in 1983 and appear in printings after that date.

As in other ancient documents, the precise meaning of the biblical texts is sometimes uncertain. This is more often the case with the Hebrew and Aramaic texts than with the Greek text. Although archaeological and linguistic discoveries in this century aid in understanding difficult passages, some uncertainties remain. The more significant of these have been called to the reader's attention in the footnotes.

In regard to the divine name *YHWH*, commonly referred to as the *Tetragrammaton*, the translators adopted the device used in most English versions of rendering that name as "Lord" in capital letters to distinguish it from *Adonai*, another Hebrew word rendered "Lord," for which small letters are used. Wherever the two names stand together in the Old Testament as a compound name of God, they are rendered "Sovereign Lord."

Because for most readers today the phrases "the Lord of hosts" and "God of hosts" have little meaning, this version renders them "the Lord Almighty" and "God Almighty." These renderings convey the sense of the Hebrew, namely, "he who is sovereign over all the 'hosts' (powers) in heaven and on earth, especially over the 'hosts' (armies) of Israel." For readers unacquainted with Hebrew this does not make clear the distinction between *Sabaoth* ("hosts" or "Almighty") and *Shaddai* (which can also be translated "Almighty"), but the latter occurs infrequently and is always footnoted. When *Adonai* and *YHWH Sabaoth* occur together, they are rendered "the Lord, the Lord Almighty."

As for other proper nouns, the familiar spellings of the King James Version are generally retained. Names traditionally spelled with "ch," except where it is final, are usually spelled in this translation with "k" or "c," since the biblical languages do not have the sound that "ch" frequently indicates in English—for example, in *chant*. For well-known names such as Zechariah, however, the traditional spelling has been retained. Variation in the spelling of names in the original languages has usually not been indicated. Where a person or place has two or more different names in the Hebrew, Aramaic or Greek texts, the more familiar one has generally been used, with footnotes where needed.

To achieve clarity the translators sometimes supplied words not in the original texts but required by the context. If there was uncertainty about such material, it is enclosed in brackets.

Also for the sake of clarity or style, nouns, including some proper nouns, are sometimes substituted for pronouns, and vice versa. And though the Hebrew writers often shifted back and forth between first, second and third personal pronouns without change of antecedent, this translation often makes them uniform, in accordance with English style and without the use of footnotes.

Poetical passages are printed as poetry, that is, with indentation of lines with separate stanzas. These are generally designed to reflect the structure of Hebrew poetry. This poetry is normally characterized by parallelism in balanced lines. Most of the poetry in the Bible is in the Old Testament, and scholars differ regarding the scansion of Hebrew lines. The translators determined the stanza divisions for the most part by analysis of the subject matter. The stanzas therefore serve as poetic paragraphs.

As an aid to the reader, italicized sectional headings are inserted in most of the books. They are not to be regarded as part of the NIV text, are not for oral reading, and are not intended to dictate the interpretation of the sections they head.

The footnotes in this version are of several kinds, most of which need no explanation. Those giving alternative translations begin with "Or" and generally introduce the alternative with the last word preceding it in the text, except when it is a single-word alternative; in poetry quoted in a footnote a slant mark indicates a line division. Footnotes introduced by "Or" do not have uniform significance. In some cases two possible translations were considered to have about equal validity. In other cases, though the translators were convinced that the translation in the text was correct, they judged that another interpretation was possible and of sufficient importance to be represented in a footnote.

In the New Testament, footnotes that refer to uncertainty regarding the original text are introduced by "Some manuscripts" or similar expressions. In the Old Testament, evidence for the reading chosen is given first and evidence for the alternative is added after a semicolon (for example: Septuagint; Hebrew *father*). In such notes the term "Hebrew" refers to the Masoretic Text.

It should be noted that minerals, flora and fauna, architectural details, articles of clothing and jewelry, musical instruments and other articles cannot always be identified with precision. Also measures of capacity in the biblical period are particularly uncertain (see the table of weights and measures following the text).

Like all translations of the Bible, made as they are by imperfect man, this one undoubtedly falls short of its goals. Yet we are grateful to God for the extent to which he has enabled us to realize these goals and for the strength he has given us and our colleagues to complete our task. We offer this version of the Bible to him in whose name and for whose glory it has been made. We pray that it will lead many into a better understanding of the Holy Scriptures and a fuller knowledge of Jesus Christ the incarnate Word, of whom the Scriptures so faithfully testify.

The Committee on Bible Translation

June 1978
(Revised August 1983)

Names of the translators and editors may be secured
from the International Bible Society,
translation sponsors of the New International Version,
P.O. Box 62970, Colorado Springs,
Colorado,
80962-2970 U.S.A.

NEW TESTAMENT

MATTHEW writes this gospel to emphasize how Jesus fulfills God's promises from the Old Testament. He includes numerous sayings of Jesus about living as one of his disciples and as a member of the church, concluding with the command of Jesus to make disciples of all nations. As you read this book, ask yourself whether you are living as a disciple of Jesus, as well as how you can tell others the story of Jesus.

MATTHEW

The Genealogy of Jesus

1 A record of the genealogy of Jesus Christ the son of David, the son of Abraham:

²Abraham was the father of Isaac,
Isaac the father of Jacob,
Jacob the father of Judah and his brothers,
³Judah the father of Perez and Ze-rah, whose mother was Tamar,
Perez the father of Hezron,
Hezron the father of Ram,
⁴Ram the father of Amminadab,
Amminadab the father of Nah-shon,
Nahshon the father of Salmon,

⁵Salmon the father of Boaz, whose mother was Rahab,
Boaz the father of Obed, whose mother was Ruth,
Obed the father of Jesse,
⁶and Jesse the father of King David.

David was the father of Solomon, whose mother had been Uriah's wife,
⁷Solomon the father of Rehoboam,
Rehoboam the father of Abijah,
Abijah the father of Asa,
⁸Asa the father of Jehoshaphat,
Jehoshaphat the father of Jeho-ram,
Jehoram the father of Uzziah,
⁹Uzziah the father of Jotham,

Jotham the father of Ahaz,
Ahaz the father of Hezekiah,
[10]Hezekiah the father of Manasseh,
Manasseh the father of Amon,
Amon the father of Josiah,
[11]and Josiah the father of Jeconiah[a]
and his brothers at the time of
the exile to Babylon.

[12]After the exile to Babylon:
Jeconiah was the father of Sheal-
tiel,
Shealtiel the father of Zerubbabel,
[13]Zerubbabel the father of Abiud,
Abiud the father of Eliakim,
Eliakim the father of Azor,
[14]Azor the father of Zadok,
Zadok the father of Akim,
Akim the father of Eliud,
[15]Eliud the father of Eleazar,
Eleazar the father of Matthan,
Matthan the father of Jacob,
[16]and Jacob the father of Joseph,
the husband of Mary, of whom
was born Jesus, who is called
Christ.

[17]Thus there were fourteen generations
in all from Abraham to David, fourteen
from David to the exile to Babylon, and
fourteen from the exile to the Christ.[b]

The Birth of Jesus Christ

[18]This is how the birth of Jesus Christ
came about: His mother Mary was
pledged to be married to Joseph, but before they came together, she was found to
be with child through the Holy Spirit.
[19]Because Joseph her husband was a righteous man and did not want to expose her
to public disgrace, he had in mind to divorce her quietly.

[20]But after he had considered this, an
angel of the Lord appeared to him in a
dream and said, "Joseph son of David, do
not be afraid to take Mary home as your
wife, because what is conceived in her is
from the Holy Spirit. [21]She will give birth
to a son, and you are to give him the name
Jesus,[c] because he will save his people
from their sins."

[22]All this took place to fulfill what the
Lord had said through the prophet:
[23]"The virgin will be with child and will
give birth to a son, and they will call him

Immanuel"[d]—which means, "God with
us."

[24]When Joseph woke up, he did what
the angel of the Lord had commanded
him and took Mary home as his wife.
[25]But he had no union with her until she
gave birth to a son. And he gave him the
name Jesus.

The Visit of the Magi

2 After Jesus was born in Bethlehem in
Judea, during the time of King Herod,
Magi[e] from the east came to Jerusalem
[2]and asked, "Where is the one who has
been born king of the Jews? We saw his
star in the east[f] and have come to worship him."

[3]When King Herod heard this he was
disturbed, and all Jerusalem with him.
[4]When he had called together all the people's chief priests and teachers of the law,
he asked them where the Christ[g] was to
be born. [5]"In Bethlehem in Judea," they
replied, "for this is what the prophet has
written:

[6] " 'But you, Bethlehem, in the land of
Judah,
are by no means least among the
rulers of Judah;
for out of you will come a ruler
who will be the shepherd of my
people Israel.' [h] "

[7]Then Herod called the Magi secretly
and found out from them the exact time
the star had appeared. [8]He sent them to
Bethlehem and said, "Go and make a
careful search for the child. As soon as
you find him, report to me, so that I too
may go and worship him."

[9]After they had heard the king, they
went on their way, and the star they had
seen in the east[i] went ahead of them until it stopped over the place where the
child was. [10]When they saw the star, they
were overjoyed. [11]On coming to the
house, they saw the child with his mother
Mary, and they bowed down and worshiped him. Then they opened their treasures and presented him with gifts of gold
and of incense and of myrrh. [12]And having
been warned in a dream not to go back to
Herod, they returned to their country by
another route.

---

[a]11 That is, Jehoiachin; also in verse 12   [b]17 Or Messiah. "The Christ" (Greek) and "the Messiah"
(Hebrew) both mean "the Anointed One."   [c]21 Jesus is the Greek form of Joshua, which means the
LORD saves.   [d]23 Isaiah 7:14   [e]1 Traditionally Wise Men   [f]2 Or star when it rose   [g]4 Or
Messiah   [h]6 Micah 5:2   [i]9 Or seen when it rose

The Escape to Egypt

¹³When they had gone, an angel of the Lord appeared to Joseph in a dream. "Get up," he said, "take the child and his mother and escape to Egypt. Stay there until I tell you, for Herod is going to search for the child to kill him."

¹⁴So he got up, took the child and his mother during the night and left for Egypt, ¹⁵where he stayed until the death of Herod. And so was fulfilled what the Lord had said through the prophet: "Out of Egypt I called my son."ᵃ

¹⁶When Herod realized that he had been outwitted by the Magi, he was furious, and he gave orders to kill all the boys in Bethlehem and its vicinity who were two years old and under, in accordance with the time he had learned from the Magi. ¹⁷Then what was said through the prophet Jeremiah was fulfilled:

¹⁸"A voice is heard in Ramah,
    weeping and great mourning,
Rachel weeping for her children
    and refusing to be comforted,
because they are no more."ᵇ

The Return to Nazareth

¹⁹After Herod died, an angel of the Lord appeared in a dream to Joseph in Egypt ²⁰and said, "Get up, take the child and his mother and go to the land of Israel, for those who were trying to take the child's life are dead."

²¹So he got up, took the child and his mother and went to the land of Israel. ²²But when he heard that Archelaus was reigning in Judea in place of his father Herod, he was afraid to go there. Having been warned in a dream, he withdrew to the district of Galilee, ²³and he went and lived in a town called Nazareth. So was fulfilled what was said through the prophets: "He will be called a Nazarene."

John the Baptist Prepares the Way

3 In those days John the Baptist came, preaching in the Desert of Judea ²and saying, "Repent, for the kingdom of heaven is near." ³This is he who was spoken of through the prophet Isaiah:

"A voice of one calling in the desert,
'Prepare the way for the Lord,
    make straight paths for him.' "ᶜ

⁴John's clothes were made of camel's hair, and he had a leather belt around his waist. His food was locusts and wild honey. ⁵People went out to him from Jerusalem and all Judea and the whole region of the Jordan. ⁶Confessing their sins, they were baptized by him in the Jordan River.

⁷But when he saw many of the Pharisees and Sadducees coming to where he was baptizing, he said to them: "You brood of vipers! Who warned you to flee from the coming wrath? ⁸Produce fruit in keeping with repentance. ⁹And do not think you can say to yourselves, 'We have Abraham as our father.' I tell you that out of these stones God can raise up children for Abraham. ¹⁰The ax is already at the root of the trees, and every tree that does not produce good fruit will be cut down and thrown into the fire.

¹¹"I baptize you withᵈ water for repentance. But after me will come one who is more powerful than I, whose sandals I am not fit to carry. He will baptize you with the Holy Spirit and with fire. ¹²His winnowing fork is in his hand, and he will clear his threshing floor, gathering his wheat into the barn and burning up the chaff with unquenchable fire."

The Baptism of Jesus

¹³Then Jesus came from Galilee to the Jordan to be baptized by John. ¹⁴But John tried to deter him, saying, "I need to be baptized by you, and do you come to me?"

¹⁵Jesus replied, "Let it be so now; it is proper for us to do this to fulfill all righteousness." Then John consented.

¹⁶As soon as Jesus was baptized, he went up out of the water. At that moment heaven was opened, and he saw the Spirit of God descending like a dove and lighting on him. ¹⁷And a voice from heaven said, "This is my Son, whom I love; with him I am well pleased."

The Temptation of Jesus

4 Then Jesus was led by the Spirit into the desert to be tempted by the devil. ²After fasting forty days and forty nights, he was hungry. ³The tempter came to him and said, "If you are the Son of God, tell these stones to become bread."

⁴Jesus answered, "It is written: 'Man does not live on bread alone, but on every word that comes from the mouth of God.'ᵉ"

⁵Then the devil took him to the holy city and had him stand on the highest

---

ᵃ15 Hosea 11:1   ᵇ18 Jer. 31:15   ᶜ3 Isaiah 40:3   ᵈ11 Or in   ᵉ4 Deut. 8:3

point of the temple. 6"If you are the Son of God," he said, "throw yourself down. For it is written:

" 'He will command his angels
      concerning you,
   and they will lift you up in their
      hands,
so that you will not strike your foot
      against a stone.'ᵃ "

7Jesus answered him, "It is also written: 'Do not put the Lord your God to the test.'ᵇ "

8Again, the devil took him to a very high mountain and showed him all the kingdoms of the world and their splendor. 9"All this I will give you," he said, "if you will bow down and worship me."

10Jesus said to him, "Away from me, Satan! For it is written: 'Worship the Lord your God, and serve him only.'ᶜ "

11Then the devil left him, and angels came and attended him.

Jesus Begins to Preach

12When Jesus heard that John had been put in prison, he returned to Galilee. 13Leaving Nazareth, he went and lived in Capernaum, which was by the lake in the area of Zebulun and Naphtali — 14to fulfill what was said through the prophet Isaiah:

15"Land of Zebulun and land of
      Naphtali,
   the way to the sea, along the
      Jordan,
Galilee of the Gentiles—
16the people living in darkness
   have seen a great light;
on those living in the land of the
      shadow of death
   a light has dawned."ᵈ

17From that time on Jesus began to preach, "Repent, for the kingdom of heaven is near."

The Calling of the First Disciples

18As Jesus was walking beside the Sea of Galilee, he saw two brothers, Simon called Peter and his brother Andrew. They were casting a net into the lake, for they were fishermen. 19"Come, follow me," Jesus said, "and I will make you fishers of men." 20At once they left their nets and followed him.

21Going on from there, he saw two other brothers, James son of Zebedee and his brother John. They were in a boat with their father Zebedee, preparing their nets. Jesus called them, 22and immediately they left the boat and their father and followed him.

Jesus Heals the Sick

23Jesus went throughout Galilee, teaching in their synagogues, preaching the good news of the kingdom, and healing every disease and sickness among the people. 24News about him spread all over Syria, and people brought to him all who were ill with various diseases, those suffering severe pain, the demon-possessed, those having seizures, and the paralyzed, and he healed them. 25Large crowds from Galilee, the Decapolis,ᵉ Jerusalem, Judea and the region across the Jordan followed him.

The Beatitudes

5 Now when he saw the crowds, he went up on a mountainside and sat down. His disciples came to him, 2and he began to teach them, saying:

3"Blessed are the poor in spirit,
   for theirs is the kingdom of heaven.
4Blessed are those who mourn,
   for they will be comforted.
5Blessed are the meek,
   for they will inherit the earth.
6Blessed are those who hunger and
      thirst for righteousness,
   for they will be filled.
7Blessed are the merciful,
   for they will be shown mercy.
8Blessed are the pure in heart,
   for they will see God.
9Blessed are the peacemakers,
   for they will be called sons of God.
10Blessed are those who are persecuted
      because of righteousness,
   for theirs is the kingdom of heaven.

11"Blessed are you when people insult you, persecute you and falsely say all kinds of evil against you because of me. 12Rejoice and be glad, because great is your reward in heaven, for in the same way they persecuted the prophets who were before you.

Salt and Light

13"You are the salt of the earth. But if the salt loses its saltiness, how can it be

ᵃ6 Psalm 91:11,12   ᵇ7 Deut. 6:16   ᶜ10 Deut. 6:13   ᵈ16 Isaiah 9:1,2   ᵉ25 That is, the Ten Cities made salty again? It is no longer good for anything, except to be thrown out and trampled by men.

¹⁴"You are the light of the world. A city on a hill cannot be hidden. ¹⁵Neither do people light a lamp and put it under a bowl. Instead they put it on its stand, and it gives light to everyone in the house. ¹⁶In the same way, let your light shine before men, that they may see your good deeds and praise your Father in heaven.

The Fulfillment of the Law

¹⁷"Do not think that I have come to abolish the Law or the Prophets; I have not come to abolish them but to fulfill them. ¹⁸I tell you the truth, until heaven and earth disappear, not the smallest letter, not the least stroke of a pen, will by any means disappear from the Law until everything is accomplished. ¹⁹Anyone who breaks one of the least of these commandments and teaches others to do the same will be called least in the kingdom of heaven, but whoever practices and teaches these commands will be called great in the kingdom of heaven. ²⁰For I tell you that unless your righteousness surpasses that of the Pharisees and the teachers of the law, you will certainly not enter the kingdom of heaven.

Murder

²¹"You have heard that it was said to

MONDAY

VERSE FOR THE DAY:	*AUTHOR:*	*PASSAGE FOR THE DAY:*
Matthew 5:16	Charlotte Stemple	Matthew 5:13–16

Keep Shining

THIS verse was dramatically illustrated when we were missionaries in Vietnam during the war. While our husbands were away from home, a missionary friend and I were invited by a Korean general to an important military ceremony. The only women amidst thousands of Korean, Vietnamese and American troops, we sat on the reviewing stand with the three-nation generals to watch the elaborate ceremonies and observe the presentation of medals to individuals and units. Later, after hors d'oeuvres, we were among the guests selected to receive lovely gifts.

Still thoroughly mystified as to why we had been invited, we were conducted to the general's mess where we ate a sumptuous meal on crested china and gold-plated flatware.

Finally, at the end of the meal, the Korean general called for his interpreter and, after polite opening conversation on both sides, said to me, "I am sure you are wondering why I invited you here today!" He continued with this remarkable comment: "When I was a small boy in Korea, an American lady missionary led me to Jesus Christ, and I never had an opportunity to thank her. So wherever I go, I look up the missionaries and honor them!"

There are no doubt many who have illuminated our paths through this life. As we are obedient to his command there will be those whose lives we may brighten. Let your light so shine!

Additional Scripture Readings:
Philippians 2:12–16; 1 Thessalonians 1:6–9

Go to page 8 for your next devotional reading.

the people long ago, 'Do not murder,[a] and anyone who murders will be subject to judgment.' [22]But I tell you that anyone who is angry with his brother[b] will be subject to judgment. Again, anyone who says to his brother, 'Raca,[c]' is answerable to the Sanhedrin. But anyone who says, 'You fool!' will be in danger of the fire of hell.

[23]"Therefore, if you are offering your gift at the altar and there remember that your brother has something against you, [24]leave your gift there in front of the altar. First go and be reconciled to your brother; then come and offer your gift.

[25]"Settle matters quickly with your adversary who is taking you to court. Do it while you are still with him on the way, or he may hand you over to the judge, and the judge may hand you over to the officer, and you may be thrown into prison. [26]I tell you the truth, you will not get out until you have paid the last penny.[d]

Adultery

[27]"You have heard that it was said, 'Do not commit adultery.'[e] [28]But I tell you that anyone who looks at a woman lustfully has already committed adultery with her in his heart. [29]If your right eye causes you to sin, gouge it out and throw it away. It is better for you to lose one part of your body than for your whole body to be thrown into hell. [30]And if your right hand causes you to sin, cut it off and throw it away. It is better for you to lose one part of your body than for your whole body to go into hell.

Divorce

[31]"It has been said, 'Anyone who divorces his wife must give her a certificate of divorce.'[f] [32]But I tell you that anyone who divorces his wife, except for marital unfaithfulness, causes her to become an adulteress, and anyone who marries the divorced woman commits adultery.

Oaths

[33]"Again, you have heard that it was said to the people long ago, 'Do not break your oath, but keep the oaths you have made to the Lord.' [34]But I tell you, Do not swear at all: either by heaven, for it is God's throne; [35]or by the earth, for it is

his footstool; or by Jerusalem, for it is the city of the Great King. [36]And do not swear by your head, for you cannot make even one hair white or black. [37]Simply let your 'Yes' be 'Yes,' and your 'No,' 'No'; anything beyond this comes from the evil one.

An Eye for an Eye

[38]"You have heard that it was said, 'Eye for eye, and tooth for tooth.'[g] [39]But I tell you, Do not resist an evil person. If someone strikes you on the right cheek, turn to him the other also. [40]And if someone wants to sue you and take your tunic, let him have your cloak as well. [41]If someone forces you to go one mile, go with him two miles. [42]Give to the one who asks you, and do not turn away from the one who wants to borrow from you.

Love for Enemies

[43]"You have heard that it was said, 'Love your neighbor[h] and hate your enemy.' [44]But I tell you: Love your enemies[i] and pray for those who persecute you, [45]that you may be sons of your Father in heaven. He causes his sun to rise on the evil and the good, and sends rain on the righteous and the unrighteous. [46]If you love those who love you, what reward will you get? Are not even the tax collectors doing that? [47]And if you greet only your brothers, what are you doing more than others? Do not even pagans do that? [48]Be perfect, therefore, as your heavenly Father is perfect.

Giving to the Needy

6 "Be careful not to do your 'acts of righteousness' before men, to be seen by them. If you do, you will have no reward from your Father in heaven.

[2]"So when you give to the needy, do not announce it with trumpets, as the hypocrites do in the synagogues and on the streets, to be honored by men. I tell you the truth, they have received their reward in full. [3]But when you give to the needy, do not let your left hand know what your right hand is doing, [4]so that your giving may be in secret. Then your Father, who sees what is done in secret, will reward you.

---

[a]21 Exodus 20:13   [b]22 Some manuscripts *brother without cause*   [c]22 An Aramaic term of contempt   [d]26 Greek *kodrantes*   [e]27 Exodus 20:14   [f]31 Deut. 24:1   [g]38 Exodus 21:24; Lev. 24:20; Deut. 19:21   [h]43 Lev. 19:18   [i]44 Some late manuscripts *enemies, bless those who curse you, do good to those who hate you*

Prayer

5"And when you pray, do not be like the hypocrites, for they love to pray standing in the synagogues and on the street corners to be seen by men. I tell you the truth, they have received their reward in full. 6But when you pray, go into your room, close the door and pray to your Father, who is unseen. Then your Father, who sees what is done in secret, will reward you. 7And when you pray, do not keep on babbling like pagans, for they think they will be heard because of their many words. 8Do not be like them, for your Father knows what you need before you ask him.

9"This, then, is how you should pray:

" 'Our Father in heaven,
hallowed be your name,
10your kingdom come,
your will be done
on earth as it is in heaven.
11Give us today our daily bread.
12Forgive us our debts,
as we also have forgiven our
debtors.
13And lead us not into temptation,
but deliver us from the evil one. a '

14For if you forgive men when they sin against you, your heavenly Father will also forgive you. 15But if you do not forgive men their sins, your Father will not forgive your sins.

Fasting

16"When you fast, do not look somber as the hypocrites do, for they disfigure their faces to show men they are fasting. I tell you the truth, they have received their reward in full. 17But when you fast, put oil on your head and wash your face, 18so that it will not be obvious to men that you are fasting, but only to your Father, who is unseen; and your Father, who sees what is done in secret, will reward you.

Treasures in Heaven

19"Do not store up for yourselves treasures on earth, where moth and rust destroy, and where thieves break in and steal. 20But store up for yourselves treasures in heaven, where moth and rust do not destroy, and where thieves do not break in and steal. 21For where your treasure is, there your heart will be also.

22"The eye is the lamp of the body. If your eyes are good, your whole body will be full of light. 23But if your eyes are bad, your whole body will be full of darkness. If then the light within you is darkness, how great is that darkness!

24"No one can serve two masters. Either he will hate the one and love the other, or he will be devoted to the one and despise the other. You cannot serve both God and Money.

Do Not Worry

25"Therefore I tell you, do not worry about your life, what you will eat or drink; or about your body, what you will wear. Is not life more important than food, and the body more important than clothes? 26Look at the birds of the air; they do not sow or reap or store away in barns, and yet your heavenly Father feeds them. Are you not much more valuable than they? 27Who of you by worrying can add a single hour to his life b? 28"And why do you worry about clothes? See how the lilies of the field grow. They do not labor or spin. 29Yet I tell you that not even Solomon in all his splendor was dressed like one of these. 30If that is how God clothes the grass of the field, which is here today and tomorrow is thrown into the fire, will he not much more clothe you, O you of little faith? 31So do not worry, saying, 'What shall we eat?' or 'What shall we drink?' or 'What shall we wear?' 32For the pagans run after all these things, and your heavenly Father knows that you need them. 33But seek first his kingdom and his righteousness, and all these things will be given to you as well. 34Therefore do not worry about tomorrow, for tomorrow will worry about itself. Each day has enough trouble of its own.

Judging Others

7 "Do not judge, or you too will be judged. 2For in the same way you judge others, you will be judged, and with the measure you use, it will be measured to you.

3"Why do you look at the speck of sawdust in your brother's eye and pay no attention to the plank in your own eye? 4How can you say to your brother, 'Let me take the speck out of your eye,' when all the time there is a plank in your own eye?

a13 Or from evil; some late manuscripts one, / for yours is the kingdom and the power and the glory forever. Amen.   b27 Or single cubit to his height

⁵You hypocrite, first take the plank out of your own eye, and then you will see clearly to remove the speck from your brother's eye.

⁶"Do not give dogs what is sacred; do not throw your pearls to pigs. If you do, they may trample them under their feet, and then turn and tear you to pieces.

Ask, Seek, Knock

⁷"Ask and it will be given to you; seek and you will find; knock and the door will be opened to you. ⁸For everyone who asks receives; he who seeks finds; and to him who knocks, the door will be opened.

⁹"Which of you, if his son asks for bread, will give him a stone? ¹⁰Or if he asks for a fish, will give him a snake? ¹¹If you, then, though you are evil, know how to give good gifts to your children, how much more will your Father in heaven give good gifts to those who ask him! ¹²So in everything, do to others what you

TUESDAY

VERSE FOR THE DAY:
Matthew 6:27

AUTHOR:
Beth Donigan Seversen

PASSAGE FOR THE DAY:
Matthew 6:25–34

Those Baby Monitors!

WORRY and exhaustion were creeping up on me. My daughter Kate was ten days old and asleep in her crib on the second floor of our small Cape Cod home. I had neglected to ask my husband to instruct me in the use of our new baby monitor and was certain it was quite beyond me. "What did mothers do before the invention of baby monitors?" I asked myself as I ironed in the basement.

The doctor had given me strict instructions due to the trauma of Kate's birth: "One trip up and down the stairs a day, for two weeks!" Yet, there I was, running up two flights of stairs in between each garment I ironed, leaning breathlessly over the crib rail to assure myself that my helpless little babe was still breathing. On the trip back to the basement I would scold myself harshly for being this silly. But, once again, while I was bending over the ironing board, fearful thoughts relentlessly teased, "What if crib death steals my baby away or what if she chokes and I'm not there?" So, back up the stairs I tread.

After one of those completed round trips, the question I'd asked earlier interrupted my fretting. What did mothers do before baby monitors? The still small voice residing in my heart replied, "They trusted in the Lord far more, worried far less, and got a lot more accomplished!" My thoughts were drawn next to Matthew 6:25,27: "Therefore I tell you, do not worry about your life . . . . Who of you by worrying can add a single hour to his life?" I knew then it was time to pause and confess: "Thank you, Father, that little Kate is of great value to you and that she is under your constant watch. I am ashamed of my worries. Please forgive me and help me to trust her life to you. Amen."

Additional Scripture Readings:
Ezra 8:21–23; Psalm 94:17–19

Go to page 12 for your next devotional reading.

would have them do to you, for this sums up the Law and the Prophets.

The Narrow and Wide Gates

13"Enter through the narrow gate. For wide is the gate and broad is the road that leads to destruction, and many enter through it. 14But small is the gate and narrow the road that leads to life, and only a few find it.

A Tree and Its Fruit

15"Watch out for false prophets. They come to you in sheep's clothing, but inwardly they are ferocious wolves. 16By their fruit you will recognize them. Do people pick grapes from thornbushes, or figs from thistles? 17Likewise every good tree bears good fruit, but a bad tree bears bad fruit. 18A good tree cannot bear bad fruit, and a bad tree cannot bear good fruit. 19Every tree that does not bear good fruit is cut down and thrown into the fire. 20Thus, by their fruit you will recognize them.

21"Not everyone who says to me, 'Lord, Lord,' will enter the kingdom of heaven, but only he who does the will of my Father who is in heaven. 22Many will say to me on that day, 'Lord, Lord, did we not prophesy in your name, and in your name drive out demons and perform many miracles?' 23Then I will tell them plainly, 'I never knew you. Away from me, you evildoers!'

The Wise and Foolish Builders

24"Therefore everyone who hears these words of mine and puts them into practice is like a wise man who built his house on the rock. 25The rain came down, the streams rose, and the winds blew and beat against that house; yet it did not fall, because it had its foundation on the rock. 26But everyone who hears these words of mine and does not put them into practice is like a foolish man who built his house on sand. 27The rain came down, the streams rose, and the winds blew and beat against that house, and it fell with a great crash."

28When Jesus had finished saying these things, the crowds were amazed at his teaching, 29because he taught as one who had authority, and not as their teachers of the law.

The Man With Leprosy

8 When he came down from the mountainside, large crowds followed him. 2A man with leprosy*a* came and knelt before him and said, "Lord, if you are willing, you can make me clean."

3Jesus reached out his hand and touched the man. "I am willing," he said. "Be clean!" Immediately he was cured*b* of his leprosy. 4Then Jesus said to him, "See that you don't tell anyone. But go, show yourself to the priest and offer the gift Moses commanded, as a testimony to them."

The Faith of the Centurion

5When Jesus had entered Capernaum, a centurion came to him, asking for help. 6"Lord," he said, "my servant lies at home paralyzed and in terrible suffering."

7Jesus said to him, "I will go and heal him."

8The centurion replied, "Lord, I do not deserve to have you come under my roof. But just say the word, and my servant will be healed. 9For I myself am a man under authority, with soldiers under me. I tell this one, 'Go,' and he goes; and that one, 'Come,' and he comes. I say to my servant, 'Do this,' and he does it."

10When Jesus heard this, he was astonished and said to those following him, "I tell you the truth, I have not found anyone in Israel with such great faith. 11I say to you that many will come from the east and the west, and will take their places at the feast with Abraham, Isaac and Jacob in the kingdom of heaven. 12But the subjects of the kingdom will be thrown outside, into the darkness, where there will be weeping and gnashing of teeth."

13Then Jesus said to the centurion, "Go! It will be done just as you believed it would." And his servant was healed at that very hour.

Jesus Heals Many

14When Jesus came into Peter's house, he saw Peter's mother-in-law lying in bed with a fever. 15He touched her hand and the fever left her, and she got up and began to wait on him.

16When evening came, many who were demon-possessed were brought to him,

---

a2 The Greek word was used for various diseases affecting the skin—not necessarily leprosy.   *b3* Greek *made clean* and he drove out the spirits with a word and healed all the sick. [17]This was to fulfill what was spoken through the prophet Isaiah:

"He took up our infirmities
    and carried our diseases."[a]

The Cost of Following Jesus

[18]When Jesus saw the crowd around him, he gave orders to cross to the other side of the lake. [19]Then a teacher of the law came to him and said, "Teacher, I will follow you wherever you go."

[20]Jesus replied, "Foxes have holes and birds of the air have nests, but the Son of Man has no place to lay his head."

[21]Another disciple said to him, "Lord, first let me go and bury my father."

[22]But Jesus told him, "Follow me, and let the dead bury their own dead."

Jesus Calms the Storm

[23]Then he got into the boat and his disciples followed him. [24]Without warning, a furious storm came up on the lake, so that the waves swept over the boat. But Jesus was sleeping. [25]The disciples went and woke him, saying, "Lord, save us! We're going to drown!"

[26]He replied, "You of little faith, why are you so afraid?" Then he got up and rebuked the winds and the waves, and it was completely calm.

[27]The men were amazed and asked, "What kind of man is this? Even the winds and the waves obey him!"

The Healing of Two Demon-possessed Men

[28]When he arrived at the other side in the region of the Gadarenes,[b] two demon-possessed men coming from the tombs met him. They were so violent that no one could pass that way. [29]"What do you want with us, Son of God?" they shouted. "Have you come here to torture us before the appointed time?"

[30]Some distance from them a large herd of pigs was feeding. [31]The demons begged Jesus, "If you drive us out, send us into the herd of pigs."

[32]He said to them, "Go!" So they came out and went into the pigs, and the whole herd rushed down the steep bank into the lake and died in the water. [33]Those tending the pigs ran off, went into the town and reported all this, including what had happened to the demon-possessed men. [34]Then the whole town went out to meet Jesus. And when they saw him, they pleaded with him to leave their region.

Jesus Heals a Paralytic

9 Jesus stepped into a boat, crossed over and came to his own town. [2]Some men brought to him a paralytic, lying on a mat. When Jesus saw their faith, he said to the paralytic, "Take heart, son; your sins are forgiven."

[3]At this, some of the teachers of the law said to themselves, "This fellow is blaspheming!"

[4]Knowing their thoughts, Jesus said, "Why do you entertain evil thoughts in your hearts? [5]Which is easier: to say, 'Your sins are forgiven,' or to say, 'Get up and walk'? [6]But so that you may know that the Son of Man has authority on earth to forgive sins. . . ." Then he said to the paralytic, "Get up, take your mat and go home." [7]And the man got up and went home. [8]When the crowd saw this, they were filled with awe; and they praised God, who had given such authority to men.

The Calling of Matthew

[9]As Jesus went on from there, he saw a man named Matthew sitting at the tax collector's booth. "Follow me," he told him, and Matthew got up and followed him.

[10]While Jesus was having dinner at Matthew's house, many tax collectors and "sinners" came and ate with him and his disciples. [11]When the Pharisees saw this, they asked his disciples, "Why does your teacher eat with tax collectors and 'sinners'?"

[12]On hearing this, Jesus said, "It is not the healthy who need a doctor, but the sick. [13]But go and learn what this means: 'I desire mercy, not sacrifice.'[c] For I have not come to call the righteous, but sinners."

Jesus Questioned About Fasting

[14]Then John's disciples came and asked him, "How is it that we and the Pharisees fast, but your disciples do not fast?"

[15]Jesus answered, "How can the guests of the bridegroom mourn while he is with them? The time will come when the

---

[a]17 Isaiah 53:4   [b]28 Some manuscripts Gergesenes; others Gerasenes   [c]13 Hosea 6:6

bridegroom will be taken from them; then they will fast.

16"No one sews a patch of unshrunk cloth on an old garment, for the patch will pull away from the garment, making the tear worse. 17Neither do men pour new wine into old wineskins. If they do, the skins will burst, the wine will run out and the wineskins will be ruined. No, they pour new wine into new wineskins, and both are preserved."

A Dead Girl and a Sick Woman

18While he was saying this, a ruler came and knelt before him and said, "My daughter has just died. But come and put your hand on her, and she will live." 19Jesus got up and went with him, and so did his disciples.

20Just then a woman who had been subject to bleeding for twelve years came up behind him and touched the edge of his cloak. 21She said to herself, "If I only touch his cloak, I will be healed."

22Jesus turned and saw her. "Take heart, daughter," he said, "your faith has healed you." And the woman was healed from that moment.

23When Jesus entered the ruler's house and saw the flute players and the noisy crowd, 24he said, "Go away. The girl is not dead but asleep." But they laughed at him. 25After the crowd had been put outside, he went in and took the girl by the hand, and she got up. 26News of this spread through all that region.

Jesus Heals the Blind and Mute

27As Jesus went on from there, two blind men followed him, calling out, "Have mercy on us, Son of David!"

28When he had gone indoors, the blind men came to him, and he asked them, "Do you believe that I am able to do this?"

"Yes, Lord," they replied.

29Then he touched their eyes and said, "According to your faith will it be done to you"; 30and their sight was restored. Jesus warned them sternly, "See that no one knows about this." 31But they went out and spread the news about him all over that region.

32While they were going out, a man who was demon-possessed and could not talk was brought to Jesus. 33And when the demon was driven out, the man who had been mute spoke. The crowd was amazed and said, "Nothing like this has ever been seen in Israel."

34But the Pharisees said, "It is by the prince of demons that he drives out demons."

The Workers Are Few

35Jesus went through all the towns and villages, teaching in their synagogues, preaching the good news of the kingdom and healing every disease and sickness. 36When he saw the crowds, he had compassion on them, because they were harassed and helpless, like sheep without a shepherd. 37Then he said to his disciples, "The harvest is plentiful but the workers are few. 38Ask the Lord of the harvest, therefore, to send out workers into his harvest field."

Jesus Sends Out the Twelve

10 He called his twelve disciples to him and gave them authority to drive out evil*a* spirits and to heal every disease and sickness.

2These are the names of the twelve apostles: first, Simon (who is called Peter) and his brother Andrew; James son of Zebedee, and his brother John; 3Philip and Bartholomew; Thomas and Matthew the tax collector; James son of Alphaeus, and Thaddaeus; 4Simon the Zealot and Judas Iscariot, who betrayed him.

5These twelve Jesus sent out with the following instructions: "Do not go among the Gentiles or enter any town of the Samaritans. 6Go rather to the lost sheep of Israel. 7As you go, preach this message: 'The kingdom of heaven is near.' 8Heal the sick, raise the dead, cleanse those who have leprosy,*b* drive out demons. Freely you have received, freely give. 9Do not take along any gold or silver or copper in your belts; 10take no bag for the journey, or extra tunic, or sandals or a staff; for the worker is worth his keep.

11"Whatever town or village you enter, search for some worthy person there and stay at his house until you leave. 12As you enter the home, give it your greeting. 13If the home is deserving, let your peace rest on it; if it is not, let your peace return to you. 14If anyone will not welcome you or listen to your words, shake the dust off your feet when you leave that home or town. 15I tell you the truth, it will be more

---

a1 Greek *unclean*   *b8* The Greek word was used for various diseases affecting the skin—not necessarily leprosy.

bearable for Sodom and Gomorrah on the day of judgment than for that town. [16]I am sending you out like sheep among wolves. Therefore be as shrewd as snakes and as innocent as doves.

[17]"Be on your guard against men; they will hand you over to the local councils and flog you in their synagogues. [18]On my account you will be brought before governors and kings as witnesses to them and to the Gentiles. [19]But when they arrest you, do not worry about what to say or how to say it. At that time you will be given what to say, [20]for it will not be you speaking, but the Spirit of your Father speaking through you.

[21]"Brother will betray brother to death, and a father his child; children will rebel against their parents and have them put to death. [22]All men will hate you because of me, but he who stands firm to the end will be saved. [23]When you are persecuted in one place, flee to another. I tell you the truth, you will not finish going through the cities of Israel before the Son of Man comes.

[24]"A student is not above his teacher, nor a servant above his master. [25]It is enough for the student to be like his teacher, and the servant like his master. If the head of the house has been called Beelzebub,[a] how much more the members of his household!

[26]"So do not be afraid of them. There is

a25 Greek *Beezeboul* or *Beelzeboul*

WEDNESDAY

VERSE FOR THE DAY:
Matthew 10:8

AUTHOR:
Phyllis Hobe

PASSAGE FOR THE DAY:
Matthew 10:1–16

The Gift of Understanding

SOMETIMES, when we love someone, we feel we just can't give them enough. We may even do without things we need ourselves. I think most parents feel that way about their children. Love makes us generous.

But generosity is more than giving.

If anyone could have showered gifts on those he loved, it was Jesus Christ. But he didn't. He provided for their basic needs; he saw to it that they had shelter and enough to eat. He watched them counting coins when he could have filled their laps with riches.

Jesus gave something more precious and more lasting than gifts. He gave understanding. He knew how hard it is to live in this world. He felt what others felt and couldn't put into words. And out of his understanding he gave what people truly need, such as forgiveness for Zacchaeus's guilt, hope for the cynical woman at the well, recovery for a dying child.

The next time you want to give a gift to someone you love, don't worry about how much you can afford to spend or how big the present ought to be. Consider, instead, what generosity really means: *understanding.* That's something each of us can afford to give—all the time.

Additional Scripture Readings:
Proverbs 20:5–6; John 4:10–14

Go to page 14 for your next devotional reading.

nothing concealed that will not be disclosed, or hidden that will not be made known. [27]What I tell you in the dark, speak in the daylight; what is whispered in your ear, proclaim from the roofs. [28]Do not be afraid of those who kill the body but cannot kill the soul. Rather, be afraid of the One who can destroy both soul and body in hell. [29]Are not two sparrows sold for a penny[a]? Yet not one of them will fall to the ground apart from the will of your Father. [30]And even the very hairs of your head are all numbered. [31]So don't be afraid; you are worth more than many sparrows.

[32]"Whoever acknowledges me before men, I will also acknowledge him before my Father in heaven. [33]But whoever disowns me before men, I will disown him before my Father in heaven.

[34]"Do not suppose that I have come to bring peace to the earth. I did not come to bring peace, but a sword. [35]For I have come to turn

" 'a man against his father,
    a daughter against her mother,
a daughter-in-law against her
        mother-in-law—
[36] a man's enemies will be the
        members of his own
        household.'[b]

[37]"Anyone who loves his father or mother more than me is not worthy of me; anyone who loves his son or daughter more than me is not worthy of me; [38]and anyone who does not take his cross and follow me is not worthy of me. [39]Whoever finds his life will lose it, and whoever loses his life for my sake will find it.

[40]"He who receives you receives me, and he who receives me receives the one who sent me. [41]Anyone who receives a prophet because he is a prophet will receive a prophet's reward, and anyone who receives a righteous man because he is a righteous man will receive a righteous man's reward. [42]And if anyone gives even a cup of cold water to one of these little ones because he is my disciple, I tell you the truth, he will certainly not lose his reward."

Jesus and John the Baptist

11 After Jesus had finished instructing his twelve disciples, he went on from there to teach and preach in the towns of Galilee.[c]

[2]When John heard in prison what Christ was doing, he sent his disciples [3]to ask him, "Are you the one who was to come, or should we expect someone else?"

[4]Jesus replied, "Go back and report to John what you hear and see: [5]The blind receive sight, the lame walk, those who have leprosy[d] are cured, the deaf hear, the dead are raised, and the good news is preached to the poor. [6]Blessed is the man who does not fall away on account of me."

[7]As John's disciples were leaving, Jesus began to speak to the crowd about John: "What did you go out into the desert to see? A reed swayed by the wind? [8]If not, what did you go out to see? A man dressed in fine clothes? No, those who wear fine clothes are in kings' palaces. [9]Then what did you go out to see? A prophet? Yes, I tell you, and more than a prophet. [10]This is the one about whom it is written:

" 'I will send my messenger ahead of
        you,
    who will prepare your way before
        you.'[e]

[11]I tell you the truth: Among those born of women there has not risen anyone greater than John the Baptist; yet he who is least in the kingdom of heaven is greater than he. [12]From the days of John the Baptist until now, the kingdom of heaven has been forcefully advancing, and forceful men lay hold of it. [13]For all the Prophets and the Law prophesied until John. [14]And if you are willing to accept it, he is the Elijah who was to come. [15]He who has ears, let him hear.

[16]"To what can I compare this generation? They are like children sitting in the marketplaces and calling out to others:

[17]" 'We played the flute for you,
        and you did not dance;
    we sang a dirge,
        and you did not mourn.'

[18]For John came neither eating nor drinking, and they say, 'He has a demon.' [19]The Son of Man came eating and drinking, and they say, 'Here is a glutton and a

---

[a]29 Greek an assarion   [b]36 Micah 7:6   [c]1 Greek in their towns   [d]5 The Greek word was used for various diseases affecting the skin—not necessarily leprosy.   [e]10 Mal. 3:1

drunkard, a friend of tax collectors and "sinners." ' But wisdom is proved right by her actions."

Woe on Unrepentant Cities

²⁰Then Jesus began to denounce the cities in which most of his miracles had been performed, because they did not repent. ²¹"Woe to you, Korazin! Woe to you, Bethsaida! If the miracles that were performed in you had been performed in Tyre and Sidon, they would have repented long ago in sackcloth and ashes. ²²But

I tell you, it will be more bearable for Tyre and Sidon on the day of judgment than for you. ²³And you, Capernaum, will you be lifted up to the skies? No, you will go down to the depths. *a* If the miracles that were performed in you had been performed in Sodom, it would have remained to this day. ²⁴But I tell you that it will be more bearable for Sodom on the day of judgment than for you."

Rest for the Weary

²⁵At that time Jesus said, "I praise you,

a23 Greek *Hades*

VERSE FOR THE DAY:
Matthew 10:34

AUTHOR:
Jill Briscoe

PASSAGE FOR THE DAY:
Matthew 10:32–42

The Hate Principle

JESUS cared about the family. But he knew that ministry would bring its own strains. One day he was talking to his people and he said, "If anyone comes to me and does not hate his father and mother, his wife and children, his brothers and sisters—yes, even his own life—he cannot be my disciple" (Luke 14:26). This has been called the "hate" principle. Jesus obviously did not mean we are to hate those people in our families who are closest to us. He had already told us to love God with all our hearts and our neighbors as ourselves.

Terms used to define the emotions and affections were frequently comparative. Jesus was saying that "natural affection is to be, as compared with the Christian's devotedness to Christ, as if it were hate" (*Oxford NIV Scofield Study Bible*, p. 1074). Christ illustrated this principle in his own person when talking of the new relationships of the kingdom: "Pointing to his disciples, he said, 'Here are my mother and my brothers. For whoever does the will of my Father in heaven is my brother and sister and mother'" (Matthew 12:49–50).

Jesus knew the coming of the gospel would bring division within families—it brought it in his own. But this did not mean that Jesus was not firmly in favor of "family." He cared for his mother from his cross, appeared to his oldest brother James after the resurrection, and united his family in ministry in Jerusalem. The gospel will bring reactions and responses—even from within our families. Disciples must be ready for them.

Additional Scripture Readings:
Mark 7:9–13; John 19:25–27

Go to page 16 for your next devotional reading.

Father, Lord of heaven and earth, because you have hidden these things from the wise and learned, and revealed them to little children. ²⁶Yes, Father, for this was your good pleasure.

^{27d}"All things have been committed to me by my Father. No one knows the Son except the Father, and no one knows the Father except the Son and those to whom the Son chooses to reveal him.

²⁸"Come to me, all you who are weary and burdened, and I will give you rest. ²⁹Take my yoke upon you and learn from me, for I am gentle and humble in heart, and you will find rest for your souls. ³⁰For my yoke is easy and my burden is light."

Lord of the Sabbath

12 At that time Jesus went through the grainfields on the Sabbath. His disciples were hungry and began to pick some heads of grain and eat them. ²When the Pharisees saw this, they said to him, "Look! Your disciples are doing what is unlawful on the Sabbath."

³He answered, "Haven't you read what David did when he and his companions were hungry? ⁴He entered the house of God, and he and his companions ate the consecrated bread—which was not lawful for them to do, but only for the priests. ⁵Or haven't you read in the Law that on the Sabbath the priests in the temple desecrate the day and yet are innocent? ⁶I tell you that one^a greater than the temple is here. ⁷If you had known what these words mean, 'I desire mercy, not sacrifice,'^b you would not have condemned the innocent. ⁸For the Son of Man is Lord of the Sabbath."

⁹Going on from that place, he went into their synagogue, ¹⁰and a man with a shriveled hand was there. Looking for a reason to accuse Jesus, they asked him, "Is it lawful to heal on the Sabbath?"

¹¹He said to them, "If any of you has a sheep and it falls into a pit on the Sabbath, will you not take hold of it and lift it out? ¹²How much more valuable is a man than a sheep! Therefore it is lawful to do good on the Sabbath."

¹³Then he said to the man, "Stretch out your hand." So he stretched it out and it was completely restored, just as sound as the other. ¹⁴But the Pharisees went out and plotted how they might kill Jesus.

God's Chosen Servant

¹⁵Aware of this, Jesus withdrew from that place. Many followed him, and he healed all their sick, ¹⁶warning them not to tell who he was. ¹⁷This was to fulfill what was spoken through the prophet Isaiah:

¹⁸"Here is my servant whom I have chosen,
    the one I love, in whom I delight;
I will put my Spirit on him,
    and he will proclaim justice to the nations.
¹⁹He will not quarrel or cry out;
    no one will hear his voice in the streets.
²⁰A bruised reed he will not break,
    and a smoldering wick he will not snuff out,
till he leads justice to victory.
²¹ In his name the nations will put their hope."^c

Jesus and Beelzebub

²²Then they brought him a demon-possessed man who was blind and mute, and Jesus healed him, so that he could both talk and see. ²³All the people were astonished and said, "Could this be the Son of David?"

²⁴But when the Pharisees heard this, they said, "It is only by Beelzebub,^d the prince of demons, that this fellow drives out demons."

²⁵Jesus knew their thoughts and said to them, "Every kingdom divided against itself will be ruined, and every city or household divided against itself will not stand. ²⁶If Satan drives out Satan, he is divided against himself. How then can his kingdom stand? ²⁷And if I drive out demons by Beelzebub, by whom do your people drive them out? So then, they will be your judges. ²⁸But if I drive out demons by the Spirit of God, then the kingdom of God has come upon you.

²⁹"Or again, how can anyone enter a strong man's house and carry off his possessions unless he first ties up the strong man? Then he can rob his house.

³⁰"He who is not with me is against me, and he who does not gather with me scatters. ³¹And so I tell you, every sin and blasphemy will be forgiven men, but the blasphemy against the Spirit will not be forgiven. ³²Anyone who speaks a word

---

^a6 Or *something*; also in verses 41 and 42   ^b7 Hosea 6:6   ^c21 Isaiah 42:1-4   ^d24 Greek *Beezeboul* or *Beelzeboul*; also in verse 27

His Rest

DO you ever feel as though you have nothing to give? That so many demands are made of you that you've become depleted . . . empty . . . exhausted?

Do you have an automatic signal when your posterior hits the bottom of a chair—immediately a voice from the farthest room in the house calls "MOTHER . . . " as if the house were on fire?

If you answered a hearty "amen" to the above, congratulations. You're a bonafide member of twentieth-century motherhood. One of the conditions of membership is that you exchange your calm and orderly life for upheaval, busyness and whirlwind activity.

We entered motherhood so eagerly—babes in our arms and stars in our eyes. So cuddly and cute, these wee ones took hold of our hearts and lives. We didn't know the gentle thump, thump, thump of their hearts was the ticking of a time bomb, ready to explode with the energy of an atomic bomb at any minute. As parents, we are the managers and harnessers of this energy, so we fill our days with clever schemes and fancy plans to keep our children occupied. Soon we find ourselves caught in the great car pool of life. We pick up and drop off miniballerinas, soccer players, piano virtuosos and future NFL champions until life is little more than a blur.

If ever anyone needed rest, it's today's mother. And I have great news. There is rest for us—a rest more rejuvenating than a long and leisurely nap, and more soothing to frayed nerves than a Brahms concert. This rest reaches into the depths of our souls and claims us from within.

This special promise of rest comes from Jesus' words in Matthew 11:29: "Take my yoke upon you and learn from me . . . and you will find rest." The yoke spoken of in this passage is fashioned of discipline and discipleship; its lining is love. Rather than bringing restriction, it brings refreshment. Through this yoke he calls us to learn of himself and find quietness and blessed rest.

Rest for the soul is the most desirable rest. It affects not only our spiritual health, but our emotional and physical health as well. The only way to receive this rest is to sit at Christ's feet and hear his word, to take the time to learn more about who he is and what he is like.

Additional Scripture Readings:
Exodus 33:12–14; Mark 6:30–31

Go to page 20 for your next devotional reading.

against the Son of Man will be forgiven, but anyone who speaks against the Holy Spirit will not be forgiven, either in this age or in the age to come.

³³"Make a tree good and its fruit will be good, or make a tree bad and its fruit will be bad, for a tree is recognized by its fruit. ³⁴You brood of vipers, how can you who are evil say anything good? For out of the overflow of the heart the mouth speaks. ³⁵The good man brings good things out of the good stored up in him, and the evil man brings evil things out of the evil stored up in him. ³⁶But I tell you that men will have to give account on the day of judgment for every careless word they have spoken. ³⁷For by your words you will be acquitted, and by your words you will be condemned."

The Sign of Jonah

³⁸Then some of the Pharisees and teachers of the law said to him, "Teacher, we want to see a miraculous sign from you."

³⁹He answered, "A wicked and adulterous generation asks for a miraculous sign! But none will be given it except the sign of the prophet Jonah. ⁴⁰For as Jonah was three days and three nights in the belly of a huge fish, so the Son of Man will be three days and three nights in the heart of the earth. ⁴¹The men of Nineveh will stand up at the judgment with this generation and condemn it; for they repented at the preaching of Jonah, and now one[a] greater than Jonah is here. ⁴²The Queen of the South will rise at the judgment with this generation and condemn it; for she came from the ends of the earth to listen to Solomon's wisdom, and now one greater than Solomon is here.

⁴³"When an evil[b] spirit comes out of a man, it goes through arid places seeking rest and does not find it. ⁴⁴Then it says, 'I will return to the house I left.' When it arrives, it finds the house unoccupied, swept clean and put in order. ⁴⁵Then it goes and takes with it seven other spirits more wicked than itself, and they go in and live there. And the final condition of that man is worse than the first. That is how it will be with this wicked generation."

Jesus' Mother and Brothers

⁴⁶While Jesus was still talking to the crowd, his mother and brothers stood outside, wanting to speak to him. ⁴⁷Someone told him, "Your mother and brothers are standing outside, wanting to speak to you."[c]

⁴⁸He replied to him, "Who is my mother, and who are my brothers?" ⁴⁹Pointing to his disciples, he said, "Here are my mother and my brothers. ⁵⁰For whoever does the will of my Father in heaven is my brother and sister and mother."

The Parable of the Sower

13 That same day Jesus went out of the house and sat by the lake. ²Such large crowds gathered around him that he got into a boat and sat in it, while all the people stood on the shore. ³Then he told them many things in parables, saying: "A farmer went out to sow his seed. ⁴As he was scattering the seed, some fell along the path, and the birds came and ate it up. ⁵Some fell on rocky places, where it did not have much soil. It sprang up quickly, because the soil was shallow. ⁶But when the sun came up, the plants were scorched, and they withered because they had no root. ⁷Other seed fell among thorns, which grew up and choked the plants. ⁸Still other seed fell on good soil, where it produced a crop—a hundred, sixty or thirty times what was sown. ⁹He who has ears, let him hear."

¹⁰The disciples came to him and asked, "Why do you speak to the people in parables?"

¹¹He replied, "The knowledge of the secrets of the kingdom of heaven has been given to you, but not to them. ¹²Whoever has will be given more, and he will have an abundance. Whoever does not have, even what he has will be taken from him. ¹³This is why I speak to them in parables:

"Though seeing, they do not see;
  though hearing, they do not hear or
    understand.

¹⁴In them is fulfilled the prophecy of Isaiah:

" 'You will be ever hearing but never
    understanding;
  you will be ever seeing but never
    perceiving.
¹⁵For this people's heart has become
    calloused;
  they hardly hear with their ears,

---

a41 Or *something;* also in verse 42   *b43* Greek *unclean*   *c47* Some manuscripts do not have verse 47.

and they have closed their eyes.
Otherwise they might see with their
     eyes,
hear with their ears,
understand with their hearts
and turn, and I would heal them.'[a]

16But blessed are your eyes because they see, and your ears because they hear. 17For I tell you the truth, many prophets and righteous men longed to see what you see but did not see it, and to hear what you hear but did not hear it.

18"Listen then to what the parable of the sower means: 19When anyone hears the message about the kingdom and does not understand it, the evil one comes and snatches away what was sown in his heart. This is the seed sown along the path. 20The one who received the seed that fell on rocky places is the man who hears the word and at once receives it with joy. 21But since he has no root, he lasts only a short time. When trouble or persecution comes because of the word, he quickly falls away. 22The one who received the seed that fell among the thorns is the man who hears the word, but the worries of this life and the deceitfulness of wealth choke it, making it unfruitful. 23But the one who received the seed that fell on good soil is the man who hears the word and understands it. He produces a crop, yielding a hundred, sixty or thirty times what was sown."

The Parable of the Weeds

24Jesus told them another parable: "The kingdom of heaven is like a man who sowed good seed in his field. 25But while everyone was sleeping, his enemy came and sowed weeds among the wheat, and went away. 26When the wheat sprouted and formed heads, then the weeds also appeared.

27"The owner's servants came to him and said, 'Sir, didn't you sow good seed in your field? Where then did the weeds come from?'

28" 'An enemy did this,' he replied.

"The servants asked him, 'Do you want us to go and pull them up?'

29" 'No,' he answered, 'because while you are pulling the weeds, you may root up the wheat with them. 30Let both grow together until the harvest. At that time I will tell the harvesters: First collect the weeds and tie them in bundles to be burned; then gather the wheat and bring it into my barn.' "

The Parables of the Mustard Seed and the Yeast

31He told them another parable: "The kingdom of heaven is like a mustard seed, which a man took and planted in his field. 32Though it is the smallest of all your seeds, yet when it grows, it is the largest of garden plants and becomes a tree, so that the birds of the air come and perch in its branches."

33He told them still another parable: "The kingdom of heaven is like yeast that a woman took and mixed into a large amount[b] of flour until it worked all through the dough."

34Jesus spoke all these things to the crowd in parables; he did not say anything to them without using a parable. 35So was fulfilled what was spoken through the prophet:

"I will open my mouth in parables,
     I will utter things hidden since the
          creation of the world."[c]

The Parable of the Weeds Explained

36Then he left the crowd and went into the house. His disciples came to him and said, "Explain to us the parable of the weeds in the field."

37He answered, "The one who sowed the good seed is the Son of Man. 38The field is the world, and the good seed stands for the sons of the kingdom. The weeds are the sons of the evil one, 39and the enemy who sows them is the devil. The harvest is the end of the age, and the harvesters are angels.

40"As the weeds are pulled up and burned in the fire, so it will be at the end of the age. 41The Son of Man will send out his angels, and they will weed out of his kingdom everything that causes sin and all who do evil. 42They will throw them into the fiery furnace, where there will be weeping and gnashing of teeth. 43Then the righteous will shine like the sun in the kingdom of their Father. He who has ears, let him hear.

The Parables of the Hidden Treasure and the Pearl

44"The kingdom of heaven is like treasure hidden in a field. When a man found it, he hid it again, and then in his joy went

---

[a]15 Isaiah 6:9,10   [b]33 Greek three satas (probably about 1/2 bushel or 22 liters)   [c]35 Psalm 78:2

and sold all he had and bought that field.

45"Again, the kingdom of heaven is like a merchant looking for fine pearls. 46When he found one of great value, he went away and sold everything he had and bought it.

The Parable of the Net

47"Once again, the kingdom of heaven is like a net that was let down into the lake and caught all kinds of fish. 48When it was full, the fishermen pulled it up on the shore. Then they sat down and collected the good fish in baskets, but threw the bad away. 49This is how it will be at the end of the age. The angels will come and separate the wicked from the righteous 50and throw them into the fiery furnace, where there will be weeping and gnashing of teeth.

51"Have you understood all these things?" Jesus asked.

"Yes," they replied.

52He said to them, "Therefore every teacher of the law who has been instructed about the kingdom of heaven is like the owner of a house who brings out of his storeroom new treasures as well as old."

A Prophet Without Honor

53When Jesus had finished these parables, he moved on from there. 54Coming to his hometown, he began teaching the people in their synagogue, and they were amazed. "Where did this man get this wisdom and these miraculous powers?" they asked. 55"Isn't this the carpenter's son? Isn't his mother's name Mary, and aren't his brothers James, Joseph, Simon and Judas? 56Aren't all his sisters with us? Where then did this man get all these things?" 57And they took offense at him.

But Jesus said to them, "Only in his hometown and in his own house is a prophet without honor."

58And he did not do many miracles there because of their lack of faith.

John the Baptist Beheaded

14 At that time Herod the tetrarch heard the reports about Jesus, 2and he said to his attendants, "This is John the Baptist; he has risen from the dead! That is why miraculous powers are at work in him."

3Now Herod had arrested John and bound him and put him in prison because of Herodias, his brother Philip's wife, 4for John had been saying to him: "It is not lawful for you to have her." 5Herod want-ed to kill John, but he was afraid of the people, because they considered him a prophet.

6On Herod's birthday the daughter of Herodias danced for them and pleased Herod so much 7that he promised with an oath to give her whatever she asked. 8Prompted by her mother, she said, "Give me here on a platter the head of John the Baptist." 9The king was distressed, but because of his oaths and his dinner guests, he ordered that her request be granted 10and had John beheaded in the prison. 11His head was brought in on a platter and given to the girl, who carried it to her mother. 12John's disciples came and took his body and buried it. Then they went and told Jesus.

Jesus Feeds the Five Thousand

13When Jesus heard what had happened, he withdrew by boat privately to a solitary place. Hearing of this, the crowds followed him on foot from the towns. 14When Jesus landed and saw a large crowd, he had compassion on them and healed their sick.

15As evening approached, the disciples came to him and said, "This is a remote place, and it's already getting late. Send the crowds away, so they can go to the villages and buy themselves some food."

16Jesus replied, "They do not need to go away. You give them something to eat."

17"We have here only five loaves of bread and two fish," they answered.

18"Bring them here to me," he said. 19And he directed the people to sit down on the grass. Taking the five loaves and the two fish and looking up to heaven, he gave thanks and broke the loaves. Then he gave them to the disciples, and the disciples gave them to the people. 20They all ate and were satisfied, and the disciples picked up twelve basketfuls of broken pieces that were left over. 21The number of those who ate was about five thousand men, besides women and children.

Jesus Walks on the Water

22Immediately Jesus made the disciples get into the boat and go on ahead of him to the other side, while he dismissed the crowd. 23After he had dismissed them, he went up on a mountainside by himself to pray. When evening came, he was there alone, 24but the boat was

WEEKENDING

RECHARGE

Lord, when my soul is weary
and my heart is tired and sore,
and I have that failing feeling
that I can't take it any more;
then let me know the freshening
found in simple, childlike prayer,
when the kneeling soul knows surely
that a listening Lord is there.
— *Ruth Bell Graham*

RESTORE

For a busy woman, time alone with yourself and
with God may be almost impossible to find. But
the busier you are the more you need it.

REVIVE

Saturday: Matthew 14:22–23; Mark 6:45–46
Sunday: Isaiah 40:27–31

Go to page 24 for your next devotional reading.

already a considerable distance[a] from land, buffeted by the waves because the wind was against it.

[25]During the fourth watch of the night Jesus went out to them, walking on the lake. [26]When the disciples saw him walking on the lake, they were terrified. "It's a ghost," they said, and cried out in fear.

[27]But Jesus immediately said to them: "Take courage! It is I. Don't be afraid."

[28]"Lord, if it's you," Peter replied, "tell me to come to you on the water."

[29]"Come," he said.

Then Peter got down out of the boat, walked on the water and came toward Jesus. [30]But when he saw the wind, he was afraid and, beginning to sink, cried out, "Lord, save me!"

[31]Immediately Jesus reached out his hand and caught him. "You of little faith," he said, "why did you doubt?"

[32]And when they climbed into the boat, the wind died down. [33]Then those who were in the boat worshiped him, saying, "Truly you are the Son of God."

[34]When they had crossed over, they landed at Gennesaret. [35]And when the men of that place recognized Jesus, they sent word to all the surrounding country. People brought all their sick to him [36]and begged him to let the sick just touch the edge of his cloak, and all who touched him were healed.

Clean and Unclean

15 Then some Pharisees and teachers of the law came to Jesus from Jerusalem and asked, [2]"Why do your disciples break the tradition of the elders? They don't wash their hands before they eat!"

[3]Jesus replied, "And why do you break the command of God for the sake of your tradition? [4]For God said, 'Honor your father and mother'[b] and 'Anyone who curses his father or mother must be put to death.'[c] [5]But you say that if a man says to his father or mother, 'Whatever help you might otherwise have received from me is a gift devoted to God,' [6]he is not to 'honor his father[d]' with it. Thus you nullify the word of God for the sake of your tradition. [7]You hypocrites! Isaiah was right when he prophesied about you:

[8] "'These people honor me with their lips,

but their hearts are far from me.
[9]They worship me in vain;

  their teachings are but rules taught
      by men.'[e]"

[10]Jesus called the crowd to him and said, "Listen and understand. [11]What goes into a man's mouth does not make him 'unclean,' but what comes out of his mouth, that is what makes him 'unclean.' "

[12]Then the disciples came to him and asked, "Do you know that the Pharisees were offended when they heard this?"

[13]He replied, "Every plant that my heavenly Father has not planted will be pulled up by the roots. [14]Leave them; they are blind guides.[f] If a blind man leads a blind man, both will fall into a pit."

[15]Peter said, "Explain the parable to us."

[16]"Are you still so dull?" Jesus asked them. [17]"Don't you see that whatever enters the mouth goes into the stomach and then out of the body? [18]But the things that come out of the mouth come from the heart, and these make a man 'unclean.' [19]For out of the heart come evil thoughts, murder, adultery, sexual immorality, theft, false testimony, slander. [20]These are what make a man 'unclean'; but eating with unwashed hands does not make him 'unclean.' "

The Faith of the Canaanite Woman

[21]Leaving that place, Jesus withdrew to the region of Tyre and Sidon. [22]A Canaanite woman from that vicinity came to him, crying out, "Lord, Son of David, have mercy on me! My daughter is suffering terribly from demon-possession."

[23]Jesus did not answer a word. So his disciples came to him and urged him, "Send her away, for she keeps crying out after us."

[24]He answered, "I was sent only to the lost sheep of Israel."

[25]The woman came and knelt before him. "Lord, help me!" she said.

[26]He replied, "It is not right to take the children's bread and toss it to their dogs."

[27]"Yes, Lord," she said, "but even the dogs eat the crumbs that fall from their masters' table."

[28]Then Jesus answered, "Woman, you have great faith! Your request is granted."

---

[a]24 Greek *many stadia*   [b]4 Exodus 20:12; Deut. 5:16   [c]4 Exodus 21:17; Lev. 20:9   [d]6 Some manuscripts *father or his mother*   [e]9 Isaiah 29:13   [f]14 Some manuscripts *guides of the blind*

And her daughter was healed from that very hour.

Jesus Feeds the Four Thousand

[29]Jesus left there and went along the Sea of Galilee. Then he went up on a mountainside and sat down. [30]Great crowds came to him, bringing the lame, the blind, the crippled, the mute and many others, and laid them at his feet; and he healed them. [31]The people were amazed when they saw the mute speaking, the crippled made well, the lame walking and the blind seeing. And they praised the God of Israel.

[32]Jesus called his disciples to him and said, "I have compassion for these people; they have already been with me three days and have nothing to eat. I do not want to send them away hungry, or they may collapse on the way."

[33]His disciples answered, "Where could we get enough bread in this remote place to feed such a crowd?"

[34]"How many loaves do you have?" Jesus asked.

"Seven," they replied, "and a few small fish."

[35]He told the crowd to sit down on the ground. [36]Then he took the seven loaves and the fish, and when he had given thanks, he broke them and gave them to the disciples, and they in turn to the people. [37]They all ate and were satisfied. Afterward the disciples picked up seven basketfuls of broken pieces that were left over. [38]The number of those who ate was four thousand, besides women and children. [39]After Jesus had sent the crowd away, he got into the boat and went to the vicinity of Magadan.

The Demand for a Sign

16 The Pharisees and Sadducees came to Jesus and tested him by asking him to show them a sign from heaven.

[2]He replied,[a] "When evening comes, you say, 'It will be fair weather, for the sky is red,' [3]and in the morning, 'Today it will be stormy, for the sky is red and overcast.' You know how to interpret the appearance of the sky, but you cannot interpret the signs of the times. [4]A wicked and adulterous generation looks for a miraculous sign, but none will be given it except

the sign of Jonah." Jesus then left them and went away.

The Yeast of the Pharisees and Sadducees

[5]When they went across the lake, the disciples forgot to take bread. [6]"Be careful," Jesus said to them. "Be on your guard against the yeast of the Pharisees and Sadducees."

[7]They discussed this among themselves and said, "It is because we didn't bring any bread."

[8]Aware of their discussion, Jesus asked, "You of little faith, why are you talking among yourselves about having no bread? [9]Do you still not understand? Don't you remember the five loaves for the five thousand, and how many basketfuls you gathered? [10]Or the seven loaves for the four thousand, and how many basketfuls you gathered? [11]How is it you don't understand that I was not talking to you about bread? But be on your guard against the yeast of the Pharisees and Sadducees." [12]Then they understood that he was not telling them to guard against the yeast used in bread, but against the teaching of the Pharisees and Sadducees.

Peter's Confession of Christ

[13]When Jesus came to the region of Caesarea Philippi, he asked his disciples, "Who do people say the Son of Man is?"

[14]They replied, "Some say John the Baptist; others say Elijah; and still others, Jeremiah or one of the prophets."

[15]"But what about you?" he asked. "Who do you say I am?"

[16]Simon Peter answered, "You are the Christ,[b] the Son of the living God."

[17]Jesus replied, "Blessed are you, Simon son of Jonah, for this was not revealed to you by man, but by my Father in heaven. [18]And I tell you that you are Peter,[c] and on this rock I will build my church, and the gates of Hades[d] will not overcome it.[e] [19]I will give you the keys of the kingdom of heaven; whatever you bind on earth will be[f] bound in heaven, and whatever you loose on earth will be[f] loosed in heaven." [20]Then he warned his disciples not to tell anyone that he was the Christ.

---

[a]2 Some early manuscripts do not have the rest of verse 2 and all of verse 3.   [b]16 Or Messiah; also in verse 20   [c]18 Peter means rock.   [d]18 Or hell   [e]18 Or not prove stronger than it   [f]19 Or have been

Jesus Predicts His Death

²¹From that time on Jesus began to explain to his disciples that he must go to Jerusalem and suffer many things at the hands of the elders, chief priests and teachers of the law, and that he must be killed and on the third day be raised to life.

²²Peter took him aside and began to rebuke him. "Never, Lord!" he said. "This shall never happen to you!"

²³Jesus turned and said to Peter, "Get behind me, Satan! You are a stumbling block to me; you do not have in mind the things of God, but the things of men."

²⁴Then Jesus said to his disciples, "If anyone would come after me, he must deny himself and take up his cross and follow me. ²⁵For whoever wants to save his life*a* will lose it, but whoever loses his life for me will find it. ²⁶What good will it be for a man if he gains the whole world, yet forfeits his soul? Or what can a man give in exchange for his soul? ²⁷For the Son of Man is going to come in his Father's glory with his angels, and then he will reward each person according to what he has done. ²⁸I tell you the truth, some who are standing here will not taste death before they see the Son of Man coming in his kingdom."

The Transfiguration

17 After six days Jesus took with him Peter, James and John the brother of James, and led them up a high mountain by themselves. ²There he was transfigured before them. His face shone like the sun, and his clothes became as white as the light. ³Just then there appeared before them Moses and Elijah, talking with Jesus.

⁴Peter said to Jesus, "Lord, it is good for us to be here. If you wish, I will put up three shelters—one for you, one for Moses and one for Elijah."

⁵While he was still speaking, a bright cloud enveloped them, and a voice from the cloud said, "This is my Son, whom I love; with him I am well pleased. Listen to him!"

⁶When the disciples heard this, they fell facedown to the ground, terrified. ⁷But Jesus came and touched them. "Get up," he said. "Don't be afraid." ⁸When they looked up, they saw no one except Jesus.

⁹As they were coming down the mountain, Jesus instructed them, "Don't tell anyone what you have seen, until the Son of Man has been raised from the dead."

¹⁰The disciples asked him, "Why then do the teachers of the law say that Elijah must come first?"

¹¹Jesus replied, "To be sure, Elijah comes and will restore all things. ¹²But I tell you, Elijah has already come, and they did not recognize him, but have done to him everything they wished. In the same way the Son of Man is going to suffer at their hands." ¹³Then the disciples understood that he was talking to them about John the Baptist.

The Healing of a Boy With a Demon

¹⁴When they came to the crowd, a man approached Jesus and knelt before him. ¹⁵"Lord, have mercy on my son," he said. "He has seizures and is suffering greatly. He often falls into the fire or into the water. ¹⁶I brought him to your disciples, but they could not heal him."

¹⁷"O unbelieving and perverse generation," Jesus replied, "how long shall I stay with you? How long shall I put up with you? Bring the boy here to me." ¹⁸Jesus rebuked the demon, and it came out of the boy, and he was healed from that moment.

¹⁹Then the disciples came to Jesus in private and asked, "Why couldn't we drive it out?"

²⁰He replied, "Because you have so little faith. I tell you the truth, if you have faith as small as a mustard seed, you can say to this mountain, 'Move from here to there' and it will move. Nothing will be impossible for you.*b*"

²²When they came together in Galilee, he said to them, "The Son of Man is going to be betrayed into the hands of men. ²³They will kill him, and on the third day he will be raised to life." And the disciples were filled with grief.

The Temple Tax

²⁴After Jesus and his disciples arrived in Capernaum, the collectors of the two-drachma tax came to Peter and asked, "Doesn't your teacher pay the temple tax*c*?"

²⁵"Yes, he does," he replied.

When Peter came into the house, Je-

---

a25 The Greek word means either *life* or *soul*; also in verse 26.   *b20* Some manuscripts *you. 21But this kind does not go out except by prayer and fasting.*   *c24* Greek *the two drachmas* sus was the first to speak. "What do you think, Simon?" he asked. "From whom do the kings of the earth collect duty and taxes—from their own sons or from others?"

²⁶"From others," Peter answered.

"Then the sons are exempt," Jesus said to him. ²⁷"But so that we may not offend them, go to the lake and throw out your line. Take the first fish you catch; open its mouth and you will find a four-drachma coin. Take it and give it to them for my tax and yours."

The Greatest in the Kingdom of Heaven

18 At that time the disciples came to Jesus and asked, "Who is the greatest in the kingdom of heaven?"

²He called a little child and had him stand among them. ³And he said: "I tell

| MONDAY |

VERSE FOR THE DAY:
Matthew 16:24–25

AUTHOR:
Catherine Marshall

PASSAGE FOR THE DAY:
Matthew 16:21–28

Happiness Is . . .

AS I've been pondering the subject of happiness this morning—an elusive and seemingly unattainable state for so many—I am led to these words of Jesus:

> If anyone would come after me, he must deny himself and take up his cross and follow me. For whoever wants to save his life will lose it, but whoever loses his life for me will find it (Matthew 16:24–25).

I believe the secret of happiness lies imbedded in those words, painful though they appear to be. How else explain radiant people like the young man who sat in our living room and described how his six-year-old boy had died in his arms from leukemia. Today this man finds fulfillment in giving himself totally to helping college students. Or the woman I visited recently whose husband had turned out to be a homosexual and demanded a divorce. Some years later, this woman also lost her eyesight. Yet she is a cheerful, loving person, fully self-supporting.

You might say that such people almost have a right to be unhappy. That they are not, lies in the way they spend themselves for others.

I have observed that when any of us embarks on the pursuit of happiness for ourselves, it eludes us. Often I've asked myself why. It must be because happiness comes to us only as a dividend. When we become absorbed in something demanding and worthwhile above and beyond ourselves, happiness seems to be there as a by-product of the self-giving.

Additional Scripture Readings:
Luke 10:30–37; Acts 2:42–47

Go to page 26 for your next devotional reading.

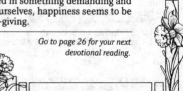

you the truth, unless you change and become like little children, you will never enter the kingdom of heaven. [4]Therefore, whoever humbles himself like this child is the greatest in the kingdom of heaven.

[5]"And whoever welcomes a little child like this in my name welcomes me. [6]But if anyone causes one of these little ones who believe in me to sin, it would be better for him to have a large millstone hung around his neck and to be drowned in the depths of the sea.

[7]"Woe to the world because of the things that cause people to sin! Such things must come, but woe to the man through whom they come! [8]If your hand or your foot causes you to sin, cut it off and throw it away. It is better for you to enter life maimed or crippled than to have two hands or two feet and be thrown into eternal fire. [9]And if your eye causes you to sin, gouge it out and throw it away. It is better for you to enter life with one eye than to have two eyes and be thrown into the fire of hell.

The Parable of the Lost Sheep

[10]"See that you do not look down on one of these little ones. For I tell you that their angels in heaven always see the face of my Father in heaven.[a]

[12]"What do you think? If a man owns a hundred sheep, and one of them wanders away, will he not leave the ninety-nine on the hills and go to look for the one that wandered off? [13]And if he finds it, I tell you the truth, he is happier about that one sheep than about the ninety-nine that did not wander off. [14]In the same way your Father in heaven is not willing that any of these little ones should be lost.

A Brother Who Sins Against You

[15]"If your brother sins against you,[b] go and show him his fault, just between the two of you. If he listens to you, you have won your brother over. [16]But if he will not listen, take one or two others along, so that 'every matter may be established by the testimony of two or three witnesses.'[c] [17]If he refuses to listen to them, tell it to the church; and if he refuses to listen even to the church, treat him as you would a pagan or a tax collector.

[18]"I tell you the truth, whatever you bind on earth will be[d] bound in heaven, and whatever you loose on earth will be[d] loosed in heaven.

[19]"Again, I tell you that if two of you on earth agree about anything you ask for, it will be done for you by my Father in heaven. [20]For where two or three come together in my name, there am I with them."

The Parable of the Unmerciful Servant

[21]Then Peter came to Jesus and asked, "Lord, how many times shall I forgive my brother when he sins against me? Up to seven times?"

[22]Jesus answered, "I tell you, not seven times, but seventy-seven times.[e]

[23]"Therefore, the kingdom of heaven is like a king who wanted to settle accounts with his servants. [24]As he began the settlement, a man who owed him ten thousand talents[f] was brought to him. [25]Since he was not able to pay, the master ordered that he and his wife and his children and all that he had be sold to repay the debt.

[26]"The servant fell on his knees before him. 'Be patient with me,' he begged, 'and I will pay back everything.' [27]The servant's master took pity on him, canceled the debt and let him go.

[28]"But when that servant went out, he found one of his fellow servants who owed him a hundred denarii.[g] He grabbed him and began to choke him. 'Pay back what you owe me!' he demanded.

[29]"His fellow servant fell to his knees and begged him, 'Be patient with me, and I will pay you back.'

[30]"But he refused. Instead, he went off and had the man thrown into prison until he could pay the debt. [31]When the other servants saw what had happened, they were greatly distressed and went and told their master everything that had happened.

[32]"Then the master called the servant in. 'You wicked servant,' he said, 'I canceled all that debt of yours because you begged me to. [33]Shouldn't you have had mercy on your fellow servant just as I had on you?' [34]In anger his master turned him over to the jailers to be tortured, until he should pay back all he owed.

[35]"This is how my heavenly Father will

---

[a]10 Some manuscripts *heaven.* [11]*The Son of Man came to save what was lost.*   [b]15 Some manuscripts do not have *against you.*   [c]16 Deut. 19:15   [d]18 Or *have been*   [e]22 Or *seventy times seven*   [f]24 That is, millions of dollars   [g]28 That is, a few dollars

VERSE FOR THE DAY:
Matthew 18:19

AUTHOR:
Rosalind Rinker

PASSAGE FOR THE DAY:
Matthew 18:18–20

The Secret of Power

JESUS teaches us to pray together in dialogue prayer in order to release God's power to bind evil and release good. Dialogue prayer is simply conversational prayer, two people praying back and forth. The audible words are necessary for agreement and for giving love. This prayer-power requires the presence of our risen Lord and our cooperation in audible prayer. This changes us and the situations for which we pray.

We abandon clichés and use short childlike sentences that are honest, specific and personal. In a nutshell: pray to Jesus, our risen Lord, from the child in your heart. This enables the child we each keep silent in our hearts to pray with others and together find love, freedom and joy.

Here are four subjects to guide you: 1. *Jesus is here* (worship). 2. *Thank you, Lord* (for gifts given: spiritual, physical, material, for people, and for the good earth). 3. *Forgive me, Lord* (confession, using "I" not "we"). 4. *Help my sister/brother* (intercession).

Experience has taught us that first worship, and then thanksgiving, open our hearts and mouths. Confession, the third point, is necessary because without it, we do not easily receive the Spirit's guidance for intercession.

Here's an example of confession: "Lord, help us to love others more than we do." But when urged to be personal, honest and specific, the woman's confession becomes: "Lord, help me to love that person I work with."

This then leads into the prayer partner's intercession, when she can pray, "Lord, you promised forgiveness when we confess (1 John 1:9). Now show her what next she should do in her life," or similar comforting words blended with thanksgiving.

In this way we share one another's joys and burdens and become living members of our risen Lord, who teaches us to love one another as he loves us.

Additional Scripture Readings:
Colossians 4:2–4; James 5:13–16

Go to page 35 for your next devotional reading.

treat each of you unless you forgive your brother from your heart."

Divorce

19 When Jesus had finished saying these things, he left Galilee and went into the region of Judea to the other side of the Jordan. ²Large crowds followed him, and he healed them there.

³Some Pharisees came to him to test him. They asked, "Is it lawful for a man to divorce his wife for any and every reason?"

⁴"Haven't you read," he replied, "that at the beginning the Creator 'made them male and female,'ᵃ ⁵and said, 'For this reason a man will leave his father and mother and be united to his wife, and the two will become one flesh'ᵇ? ⁶So they are no longer two, but one. Therefore what God has joined together, let man not separate."

⁷"Why then," they asked, "did Moses command that a man give his wife a certificate of divorce and send her away?"

⁸Jesus replied, "Moses permitted you to divorce your wives because your hearts were hard. But it was not this way from the beginning. ⁹I tell you that anyone who divorces his wife, except for marital unfaithfulness, and marries another woman commits adultery."

¹⁰The disciples said to him, "If this is the situation between a husband and wife, it is better not to marry."

¹¹Jesus replied, "Not everyone can accept this word, but only those to whom it has been given. ¹²For some are eunuchs because they were born that way; others were made that way by men; and others have renounced marriageᶜ because of the kingdom of heaven. The one who can accept this should accept it."

The Little Children and Jesus

¹³Then little children were brought to Jesus for him to place his hands on them and pray for them. But the disciples rebuked those who brought them.

¹⁴Jesus said, "Let the little children come to me, and do not hinder them, for the kingdom of heaven belongs to such as these." ¹⁵When he had placed his hands on them, he went on from there.

The Rich Young Man

¹⁶Now a man came up to Jesus and asked, "Teacher, what good thing must I do to get eternal life?"

¹⁷"Why do you ask me about what is good?" Jesus replied. "There is only One who is good. If you want to enter life, obey the commandments."

¹⁸"Which ones?" the man inquired.

Jesus replied, " 'Do not murder, do not commit adultery, do not steal, do not give false testimony, ¹⁹honor your father and mother,'ᵈ and 'love your neighbor as yourself.'ᵉ"

²⁰"All these I have kept," the young man said. "What do I still lack?"

²¹Jesus answered, "If you want to be perfect, go, sell your possessions and give to the poor, and you will have treasure in heaven. Then come, follow me."

²²When the young man heard this, he went away sad, because he had great wealth.

²³Then Jesus said to his disciples, "I tell you the truth, it is hard for a rich man to enter the kingdom of heaven. ²⁴Again I tell you, it is easier for a camel to go through the eye of a needle than for a rich man to enter the kingdom of God."

²⁵When the disciples heard this, they were greatly astonished and asked, "Who then can be saved?"

²⁶Jesus looked at them and said, "With man this is impossible, but with God all things are possible."

²⁷Peter answered him, "We have left everything to follow you! What then will there be for us?"

²⁸Jesus said to them, "I tell you the truth, at the renewal of all things, when the Son of Man sits on his glorious throne, you who have followed me will also sit on twelve thrones, judging the twelve tribes of Israel. ²⁹And everyone who has left houses or brothers or sisters or father or motherᶠ or children or fields for my sake will receive a hundred times as much and will inherit eternal life. ³⁰But many who are first will be last, and many who are last will be first.

The Parable of the Workers in the Vineyard

20 "For the kingdom of heaven is like a landowner who went out early in the morning to hire men to work in his vineyard. ²He agreed to pay them a denarius for the day and sent them into his vineyard.

ᵃ4 Gen. 1:27   ᵇ5 Gen. 2:24   ᶜ12 Or *have made themselves eunuchs*   ᵈ19 Exodus 20:12-16;
Deut. 5:16-20   ᵉ19 Lev. 19:18   ᶠ29 Some manuscripts *mother or wife*

³"About the third hour he went out and saw others standing in the marketplace doing nothing. ⁴He told them, 'You also go and work in my vineyard, and I will pay you whatever is right.' ⁵So they went.

"He went out again about the sixth hour and the ninth hour and did the same thing. ⁶About the eleventh hour he went out and found still others standing around. He asked them, 'Why have you been standing here all day long doing nothing?'

⁷" 'Because no one has hired us,' they answered.

"He said to them, 'You also go and work in my vineyard.'

⁸"When evening came, the owner of the vineyard said to his foreman, 'Call the workers and pay them their wages, beginning with the last ones hired and going on to the first.'

⁹"The workers who were hired about the eleventh hour came and each received a denarius. ¹⁰So when those came who were hired first, they expected to receive more. But each one of them also received a denarius. ¹¹When they received it, they began to grumble against the landowner. ¹²'These men who were hired last worked only one hour,' they said, 'and you have made them equal to us who have borne the burden of the work and the heat of the day.'

¹³"But he answered one of them, 'Friend, I am not being unfair to you. Didn't you agree to work for a denarius? ¹⁴Take your pay and go. I want to give the man who was hired last the same as I gave you. ¹⁵Don't I have the right to do what I want with my own money? Or are you envious because I am generous?'

¹⁶"So the last will be first, and the first will be last."

Jesus Again Predicts His Death

¹⁷Now as Jesus was going up to Jerusalem, he took the twelve disciples aside and said to them, ¹⁸"We are going up to Jerusalem, and the Son of Man will be betrayed to the chief priests and the teachers of the law. They will condemn him to death ¹⁹and will turn him over to the Gentiles to be mocked and flogged and crucified. On the third day he will be raised to life!"

A Mother's Request

²⁰Then the mother of Zebedee's sons came to Jesus with her sons and, kneeling down, asked a favor of him.

²¹"What is it you want?" he asked.

She said, "Grant that one of these two sons of mine may sit at your right and the other at your left in your kingdom."

²²"You don't know what you are asking," Jesus said to them. "Can you drink the cup I am going to drink?"

"We can," they answered.

²³Jesus said to them, "You will indeed drink from my cup, but to sit at my right or left is not for me to grant. These places belong to those for whom they have been prepared by my Father."

²⁴When the ten heard about this, they were indignant with the two brothers. ²⁵Jesus called them together and said, "You know that the rulers of the Gentiles lord it over them, and their high officials exercise authority over them. ²⁶Not so with you. Instead, whoever wants to become great among you must be your servant, ²⁷and whoever wants to be first must be your slave— ²⁸just as the Son of Man did not come to be served, but to serve, and to give his life as a ransom for many."

Two Blind Men Receive Sight

²⁹As Jesus and his disciples were leaving Jericho, a large crowd followed him. ³⁰Two blind men were sitting by the roadside, and when they heard that Jesus was going by, they shouted, "Lord, Son of David, have mercy on us!"

³¹The crowd rebuked them and told them to be quiet, but they shouted all the louder, "Lord, Son of David, have mercy on us!"

³²Jesus stopped and called them. "What do you want me to do for you?" he asked.

³³"Lord," they answered, "we want our sight."

³⁴Jesus had compassion on them and touched their eyes. Immediately they received their sight and followed him.

The Triumphal Entry

21 As they approached Jerusalem and came to Bethphage on the Mount of Olives, Jesus sent two disciples, ²saying to them, "Go to the village ahead of you, and at once you will find a donkey tied there, with her colt by her. Untie them and bring them to me. ³If anyone says anything to you, tell him that the Lord needs them, and he will send them right away."

⁴This took place to fulfill what was spoken through the prophet:

5"Say to the Daughter of Zion,
'See, your king comes to you,
gentle and riding on a donkey,
on a colt, the foal of a donkey.' "*a*

6The disciples went and did as Jesus
had instructed them. 7They brought the
donkey and the colt, placed their cloaks
on them, and Jesus sat on them. 8A very
large crowd spread their cloaks on the
road, while others cut branches from the
trees and spread them on the road. 9The
crowds that went ahead of him and those
that followed shouted,

"Hosanna*b* to the Son of David!"

"Blessed is he who comes in the
name of the Lord!"*c*

"Hosanna*b* in the highest!"

10When Jesus entered Jerusalem, the
whole city was stirred and asked, "Who is
this?"

11The crowds answered, "This is Jesus,
the prophet from Nazareth in Galilee."

Jesus at the Temple

12Jesus entered the temple area and
drove out all who were buying and selling
there. He overturned the tables of the
money changers and the benches of those
selling doves. 13"It is written," he said to
them, " 'My house will be called a house
of prayer,'*d* but you are making it a 'den
of robbers.'*e*"

14The blind and the lame came to him
at the temple, and he healed them. 15But
when the chief priests and the teachers of
the law saw the wonderful things he did
and the children shouting in the temple
area, "Hosanna to the Son of David," they
were indignant.

16"Do you hear what these children are
saying?" they asked him.

"Yes," replied Jesus, "have you never
read,

" 'From the lips of children and
infants
you have ordained praise'*f*?"

17And he left them and went out of the
city to Bethany, where he spent the night.

The Fig Tree Withers

18Early in the morning, as he was on his
way back to the city, he was hungry.
19Seeing a fig tree by the road, he went up

to it but found nothing on it except
leaves. Then he said to it, "May you never
bear fruit again!" Immediately the tree
withered.

20When the disciples saw this, they
were amazed. "How did the fig tree wither
so quickly?" they asked.

21Jesus replied, "I tell you the truth, if
you have faith and do not doubt, not only
can you do what was done to the fig tree,
but also you can say to this mountain,
'Go, throw yourself into the sea,' and it
will be done. 22If you believe, you will receive whatever you ask for in prayer."

The Authority of Jesus Questioned

23Jesus entered the temple courts, and,
while he was teaching, the chief priests
and the elders of the people came to him.
"By what authority are you doing these
things?" they asked. "And who gave you
this authority?"

24Jesus replied, "I will also ask you one
question. If you answer me, I will tell you
by what authority I am doing these
things. 25John's baptism—where did it
come from? Was it from heaven, or from
men?"

They discussed it among themselves
and said, "If we say, 'From heaven,' he
will ask, 'Then why didn't you believe
him?' 26But if we say, 'From men'—we
are afraid of the people, for they all hold
that John was a prophet."

27So they answered Jesus, "We don't
know."

Then he said, "Neither will I tell you by
what authority I am doing these things.

The Parable of the Two Sons

28"What do you think? There was a man
who had two sons. He went to the first
and said, 'Son, go and work today in the
vineyard.'

29" 'I will not,' he answered, but later
he changed his mind and went.

30"Then the father went to the other
son and said the same thing. He answered, 'I will, sir,' but he did not go.

31"Which of the two did what his father
wanted?"

"The first," they answered.

Jesus said to them, "I tell you the truth,
the tax collectors and the prostitutes are
entering the kingdom of God ahead of
you. 32For John came to you to show you
the way of righteousness, and you did not

a5 Zech. 9:9　　*b9* A Hebrew expression meaning "Save!" which became an exclamation of praise; also
in verse 15　　*c9* Psalm 118:26　　*d13* Isaiah 56:7　　*e13* Jer. 7:11　　*f16* Psalm 8:2

believe him, but the tax collectors and the prostitutes did. And even after you saw this, you did not repent and believe him.

The Parable of the Tenants

[33]"Listen to another parable: There was a landowner who planted a vineyard. He put a wall around it, dug a winepress in it and built a watchtower. Then he rented the vineyard to some farmers and went away on a journey. [34]When the harvest time approached, he sent his servants to the tenants to collect his fruit.

[35]"The tenants seized his servants; they beat one, killed another, and stoned a third. [36]Then he sent other servants to them, more than the first time, and the tenants treated them the same way. [37]Last of all, he sent his son to them. 'They will respect my son,' he said.

[38]"But when the tenants saw the son, they said to each other, 'This is the heir. Come, let's kill him and take his inheritance.' [39]So they took him and threw him out of the vineyard and killed him.

[40]"Therefore, when the owner of the vineyard comes, what will he do to those tenants?"

[41]"He will bring those wretches to a wretched end," they replied, "and he will rent the vineyard to other tenants, who will give him his share of the crop at harvest time."

[42]Jesus said to them, "Have you never read in the Scriptures:

" 'The stone the builders rejected
     has become the capstone[a];
the Lord has done this,
     and it is marvelous in our eyes'[b]?

[43]"Therefore I tell you that the kingdom of God will be taken away from you and given to a people who will produce its fruit. [44]He who falls on this stone will be broken to pieces, but he on whom it falls will be crushed."[c]

[45]When the chief priests and the Pharisees heard Jesus' parables, they knew he was talking about them. [46]They looked for a way to arrest him, but they were afraid of the crowd because the people held that he was a prophet.

The Parable of the Wedding Banquet

22 Jesus spoke to them again in parables, saying: [2]"The kingdom of heaven is like a king who prepared a wedding banquet for his son. [3]He sent his servants to those who had been invited to the banquet to tell them to come, but they refused to come.

[4]"Then he sent some more servants and said, 'Tell those who have been invited that I have prepared my dinner: My oxen and fattened cattle have been butchered, and everything is ready. Come to the wedding banquet.'

[5]"But they paid no attention and went off—one to his field, another to his business. [6]The rest seized his servants, mistreated them and killed them. [7]The king was enraged. He sent his army and destroyed those murderers and burned their city.

[8]"Then he said to his servants, 'The wedding banquet is ready, but those I invited did not deserve to come. [9]Go to the street corners and invite to the banquet anyone you find.' [10]So the servants went out into the streets and gathered all the people they could find, both good and bad, and the wedding hall was filled with guests.

[11]"But when the king came in to see the guests, he noticed a man there who was not wearing wedding clothes. [12]'Friend,' he asked, 'how did you get in here without wedding clothes?' The man was speechless.

[13]"Then the king told the attendants, 'Tie him hand and foot, and throw him outside, into the darkness, where there will be weeping and gnashing of teeth.'

[14]"For many are invited, but few are chosen."

Paying Taxes to Caesar

[15]Then the Pharisees went out and laid plans to trap him in his words. [16]They sent their disciples to him along with the Herodians. "Teacher," they said, "we know you are a man of integrity and that you teach the way of God in accordance with the truth. You aren't swayed by men, because you pay no attention to who they are. [17]Tell us then, what is your opinion? Is it right to pay taxes to Caesar or not?"

[18]But Jesus, knowing their evil intent, said, "You hypocrites, why are you trying to trap me? [19]Show me the coin used for paying the tax." They brought him a denarius, [20]and he asked them, "Whose portrait is this? And whose inscription?"

[21]"Caesar's," they replied.

Then he said to them, "Give to Caesar

---

[a]42 Or cornerstone   [b]42 Psalm 118:22,23   [c]44 Some manuscripts do not have verse 44.

what is Caesar's, and to God what is God's."

²²When they heard this, they were amazed. So they left him and went away.

Marriage at the Resurrection

²³That same day the Sadducees, who say there is no resurrection, came to him with a question. ²⁴"Teacher," they said, "Moses told us that if a man dies without having children, his brother must marry the widow and have children for him. ²⁵Now there were seven brothers among us. The first one married and died, and since he had no children, he left his wife to his brother. ²⁶The same thing happened to the second and third brother, right on down to the seventh. ²⁷Finally, the woman died. ²⁸Now then, at the resurrection, whose wife will she be of the seven, since all of them were married to her?"

²⁹Jesus replied, "You are in error because you do not know the Scriptures or the power of God. ³⁰At the resurrection people will neither marry nor be given in marriage; they will be like the angels in heaven. ³¹But about the resurrection of the dead—have you not read what God said to you, ³²'I am the God of Abraham, the God of Isaac, and the God of Jacob'ᵃ? He is not the God of the dead but of the living."

³³When the crowds heard this, they were astonished at his teaching.

The Greatest Commandment

³⁴Hearing that Jesus had silenced the Sadducees, the Pharisees got together. ³⁵One of them, an expert in the law, tested him with this question: ³⁶"Teacher, which is the greatest commandment in the Law?"

³⁷Jesus replied: " 'Love the Lord your God with all your heart and with all your soul and with all your mind.'ᵇ ³⁸This is the first and greatest commandment. ³⁹And the second is like it: 'Love your neighbor as yourself.'ᶜ ⁴⁰All the Law and the Prophets hang on these two commandments."

Whose Son Is the Christ?

⁴¹While the Pharisees were gathered together, Jesus asked them, ⁴²"What do you think about the Christᵈ? Whose son is he?"

"The son of David," they replied.

⁴³He said to them, "How is it then that David, speaking by the Spirit, calls him 'Lord'? For he says,

⁴⁴ 'The Lord said to my Lord:
  "Sit at my right hand
until I put your enemies
  under your feet." 'ᵉ

⁴⁵If then David calls him 'Lord,' how can he be his son?" ⁴⁶No one could say a word in reply, and from that day on no one dared to ask him any more questions.

Seven Woes

23 Then Jesus said to the crowds and to his disciples: ²"The teachers of the law and the Pharisees sit in Moses' seat. ³So you must obey them and do everything they tell you. But do not do what they do, for they do not practice what they preach. ⁴They tie up heavy loads and put them on men's shoulders, but they themselves are not willing to lift a finger to move them.

⁵"Everything they do is done for men to see: They make their phylacteriesᶠ wide and the tassels on their garments long; ⁶they love the place of honor at banquets and the most important seats in the synagogues; ⁷they love to be greeted in the marketplaces and to have men call them 'Rabbi.'

⁸"But you are not to be called 'Rabbi,' for you have only one Master and you are all brothers. ⁹And do not call anyone on earth 'father,' for you have one Father, and he is in heaven. ¹⁰Nor are you to be called 'teacher,' for you have one Teacher, the Christ.ᵈ ¹¹The greatest among you will be your servant. ¹²For whoever exalts himself will be humbled, and whoever humbles himself will be exalted.

¹³"Woe to you, teachers of the law and Pharisees, you hypocrites! You shut the kingdom of heaven in men's faces. You yourselves do not enter, nor will you let those enter who are trying to.ᵍ

¹⁵"Woe to you, teachers of the law and Pharisees, you hypocrites! You travel over land and sea to win a single convert, and when he becomes one, you make him twice as much a son of hell as you are.

ᵃ32 Exodus 3:6   ᵇ37 Deut. 6:5   ᶜ39 Lev. 19:18   ᵈ42,10 Or Messiah   ᵉ44 Psalm 110:1
ᶠ5 That is, boxes containing Scripture verses, worn on forehead and arm   ᵍ13 Some manuscripts to.
¹⁴Woe to you, teachers of the law and Pharisees, you hypocrites! You devour widows' houses and for a show make lengthy prayers. Therefore you will be punished more severely.

16"Woe to you, blind guides! You say, 'If anyone swears by the temple, it means nothing; but if anyone swears by the gold of the temple, he is bound by his oath.' 17You blind fools! Which is greater: the gold, or the temple that makes the gold sacred? 18You also say, 'If anyone swears by the altar, it means nothing; but if anyone swears by the gift on it, he is bound by his oath.' 19You blind men! Which is greater: the gift, or the altar that makes the gift sacred? 20Therefore, he who swears by the altar swears by it and by everything on it. 21And he who swears by the temple swears by it and by the one who dwells in it. 22And he who swears by heaven swears by God's throne and by the one who sits on it.

23"Woe to you, teachers of the law and Pharisees, you hypocrites! You give a tenth of your spices—mint, dill and cummin. But you have neglected the more important matters of the law—justice, mercy and faithfulness. You should have practiced the latter, without neglecting the former. 24You blind guides! You strain out a gnat but swallow a camel.

25"Woe to you, teachers of the law and Pharisees, you hypocrites! You clean the outside of the cup and dish, but inside they are full of greed and self-indulgence. 26Blind Pharisee! First clean the inside of the cup and dish, and then the outside also will be clean.

27"Woe to you, teachers of the law and Pharisees, you hypocrites! You are like whitewashed tombs, which look beautiful on the outside but on the inside are full of dead men's bones and everything unclean. 28In the same way, on the outside you appear to people as righteous but on the inside you are full of hypocrisy and wickedness.

29"Woe to you, teachers of the law and Pharisees, you hypocrites! You build tombs for the prophets and decorate the graves of the righteous. 30And you say, 'If we had lived in the days of our forefathers, we would not have taken part with them in shedding the blood of the prophets.' 31So you testify against yourselves that you are the descendants of those who murdered the prophets. 32Fill up, then, the measure of the sin of your forefathers!

33"You snakes! You brood of vipers! How will you escape being condemned to hell? 34Therefore I am sending you prophets and wise men and teachers. Some of them you will kill and crucify; others you will flog in your synagogues and pursue from town to town. 35And so upon you will come all the righteous blood that has been shed on earth, from the blood of righteous Abel to the blood of Zechariah son of Berekiah, whom you murdered between the temple and the altar. 36I tell you the truth, all this will come upon this generation.

37"O Jerusalem, Jerusalem, you who kill the prophets and stone those sent to you, how often I have longed to gather your children together, as a hen gathers her chicks under her wings, but you were not willing. 38Look, your house is left to you desolate. 39For I tell you, you will not see me again until you say, 'Blessed is he who comes in the name of the Lord.'ᵃ"

Signs of the End of the Age

24 Jesus left the temple and was walking away when his disciples came up to him to call his attention to its buildings. 2"Do you see all these things?" he asked. "I tell you the truth, not one stone here will be left on another; every one will be thrown down."

3As Jesus was sitting on the Mount of Olives, the disciples came to him privately. "Tell us," they said, "when will this happen, and what will be the sign of your coming and of the end of the age?"

4Jesus answered: "Watch out that no one deceives you. 5For many will come in my name, claiming, 'I am the Christ,ᵇ' and will deceive many. 6You will hear of wars and rumors of wars, but see to it that you are not alarmed. Such things must happen, but the end is still to come. 7Nation will rise against nation, and kingdom against kingdom. There will be famines and earthquakes in various places. 8All these are the beginning of birth pains.

9"Then you will be handed over to be persecuted and put to death, and you will be hated by all nations because of me. 10At that time many will turn away from the faith and will betray and hate each other, 11and many false prophets will appear and deceive many people. 12Because of the increase of wickedness, the love of most will grow cold, 13but he who stands firm to the end will be saved. 14And this gospel of the kingdom will be preached in the whole world as a testimony to all nations, and then the end will come.

ᵃ39 Psalm 118:26   ᵇ5 Or Messiah; also in verse 23

15"So when you see standing in the holy place 'the abomination that causes desolation,'[a] spoken of through the prophet Daniel—let the reader understand— 16then let those who are in Judea flee to the mountains. 17Let no one on the roof of his house go down to take anything out of the house. 18Let no one in the field go back to get his cloak. 19How dreadful it will be in those days for pregnant women and nursing mothers! 20Pray that your flight will not take place in winter or on the Sabbath. 21For then there will be great distress, unequaled from the beginning of the world until now—and never to be equaled again. 22If those days had not been cut short, no one would survive, but for the sake of the elect those days will be shortened. 23At that time if anyone says to you, 'Look, here is the Christ!' or, 'There he is!' do not believe it. 24For false Christs and false prophets will appear and perform great signs and miracles to deceive even the elect—if that were possible. 25See, I have told you ahead of time.

26"So if anyone tells you, 'There he is, out in the desert,' do not go out; or, 'Here he is, in the inner rooms,' do not believe it. 27For as lightning that comes from the east is visible even in the west, so will be the coming of the Son of Man. 28Wherever there is a carcass, there the vultures will gather.

29"Immediately after the distress of those days

" 'the sun will be darkened,
    and the moon will not give its light;
the stars will fall from the sky,
    and the heavenly bodies will be
        shaken.'[b]

30"At that time the sign of the Son of Man will appear in the sky, and all the nations of the earth will mourn. They will see the Son of Man coming on the clouds of the sky, with power and great glory. 31And he will send his angels with a loud trumpet call, and they will gather his elect from the four winds, from one end of the heavens to the other.

32"Now learn this lesson from the fig tree: As soon as its twigs get tender and its leaves come out, you know that summer is near. 33Even so, when you see all these things, you know that it[c] is near, right at the door. 34I tell you the truth, this generation[d] will certainly not pass

away until all these things have happened. 35Heaven and earth will pass away, but my words will never pass away.

The Day and Hour Unknown

36"No one knows about that day or hour, not even the angels in heaven, nor the Son,[e] but only the Father. 37As it was in the days of Noah, so it will be at the coming of the Son of Man. 38For in the days before the flood, people were eating and drinking, marrying and giving in marriage, up to the day Noah entered the ark; 39and they knew nothing about what would happen until the flood came and took them all away. That is how it will be at the coming of the Son of Man. 40Two men will be in the field; one will be taken and the other left. 41Two women will be grinding with a hand mill; one will be taken and the other left.

42"Therefore keep watch, because you do not know on what day your Lord will come. 43But understand this: If the owner of the house had known at what time of night the thief was coming, he would have kept watch and would not have let his house be broken into. 44So you also must be ready, because the Son of Man will come at an hour when you do not expect him.

45"Who then is the faithful and wise servant, whom the master has put in charge of the servants in his household to give them their food at the proper time? 46It will be good for that servant whose master finds him doing so when he returns. 47I tell you the truth, he will put him in charge of all his possessions. 48But suppose that servant is wicked and says to himself, 'My master is staying away a long time,' 49and he then begins to beat his fellow servants and to eat and drink with drunkards. 50The master of that servant will come on a day when he does not expect him and at an hour he is not aware of. 51He will cut him to pieces and assign him a place with the hypocrites, where there will be weeping and gnashing of teeth.

The Parable of the Ten Virgins

25 "At that time the kingdom of heaven will be like ten virgins who took their lamps and went out to meet the bridegroom. 2Five of them were foolish and five were wise. 3The foolish ones took

a15 Daniel 9:27; 11:31; 12:11   b29 Isaiah 13:10; 34:4   c33 Or he   d34 Or race   e36 Some manuscripts do not have nor the Son.

their lamps but did not take any oil with them. [4]The wise, however, took oil in jars along with their lamps. [5]The bridegroom was a long time in coming, and they all became drowsy and fell asleep.

[6]"At midnight the cry rang out: 'Here's the bridegroom! Come out to meet him!'

[7]"Then all the virgins woke up and trimmed their lamps. [8]The foolish ones said to the wise, 'Give us some of your oil; our lamps are going out.'

[9]" 'No,' they replied, 'there may not be enough for both us and you. Instead, go to those who sell oil and buy some for yourselves.'

[10]"But while they were on their way to buy the oil, the bridegroom arrived. The virgins who were ready went in with him to the wedding banquet. And the door was shut.

[11]"Later the others also came. 'Sir! Sir!' they said. 'Open the door for us!'

[12]"But he replied, 'I tell you the truth, I don't know you.'

[13]"Therefore keep watch, because you do not know the day or the hour.

The Parable of the Talents

[14]"Again, it will be like a man going on a journey, who called his servants and entrusted his property to them. [15]To one he gave five talents[a] of money, to another two talents, and to another one talent, each according to his ability. Then he went on his journey. [16]The man who had received the five talents went at once and put his money to work and gained five more. [17]So also, the one with the two talents gained two more. [18]But the man who had received the one talent went off, dug a hole in the ground and hid his master's money.

[19]"After a long time the master of those servants returned and settled accounts with them. [20]The man who had received the five talents brought the other five. 'Master,' he said, 'you entrusted me with five talents. See, I have gained five more.'

[21]"His master replied, 'Well done, good and faithful servant! You have been faithful with a few things; I will put you in charge of many things. Come and share your master's happiness!'

[22]"The man with the two talents also came. 'Master,' he said, 'you entrusted me with two talents; see, I have gained two more.'

[23]"His master replied, 'Well done, good

and faithful servant! You have been faithful with a few things; I will put you in charge of many things. Come and share your master's happiness!'

[24]"Then the man who had received the one talent came. 'Master,' he said, 'I knew that you are a hard man, harvesting where you have not sown and gathering where you have not scattered seed. [25]So I was afraid and went out and hid your talent in the ground. See, here is what belongs to you.'

[26]"His master replied, 'You wicked, lazy servant! So you knew that I harvest where I have not sown and gather where I have not scattered seed? [27]Well then, you should have put my money on deposit with the bankers, so that when I returned I would have received it back with interest.

[28]" 'Take the talent from him and give it to the one who has the ten talents. [29]For everyone who has will be given more, and he will have an abundance. Whoever does not have, even what he has will be taken from him. [30]And throw that worthless servant outside, into the darkness, where there will be weeping and gnashing of teeth.'

The Sheep and the Goats

[31]"When the Son of Man comes in his glory, and all the angels with him, he will sit on his throne in heavenly glory. [32]All the nations will be gathered before him, and he will separate the people one from another as a shepherd separates the sheep from the goats. [33]He will put the sheep on his right and the goats on his left.

[34]"Then the King will say to those on his right, 'Come, you who are blessed by my Father; take your inheritance, the kingdom prepared for you since the creation of the world. [35]For I was hungry and you gave me something to eat, I was thirsty and you gave me something to drink, I was a stranger and you invited me in, [36]I needed clothes and you clothed me, I was sick and you looked after me, I was in prison and you came to visit me.'

[37]"Then the righteous will answer him, 'Lord, when did we see you hungry and feed you, or thirsty and give you something to drink? [38]When did we see you a stranger and invite you in, or needing clothes and clothe you? [39]When did we

[a]15 A talent was worth more than a thousand dollars.

VERSE FOR THE DAY:
Matthew 25:24–25

AUTHOR:
Hope MacDonald

PASSAGE FOR THE DAY:
Matthew 25:14–30

Burying Our Talents

THIS is a parable of God's call for faithfulness in the use of our talents. It is also a parable of warning and promise.

Not long ago, I was sitting in a small group. The discussion centered around evangelism. One of the members breathed a sigh of relief and said, "Well, that's just not my gift." With that statement he buried his God-given talent to share the love of Jesus with others. How many of us have buried our talents in search of that "special" gift?

Today we often expect our talents to come completely developed, neatly labeled, and tied with a shining red ribbon. If they don't, then we proclaim, they aren't "my gifts." The result is that we limit God—he is put in a box—and we restrict our potential for service. I wonder how many neglected opportunities slip by because of this kind of thinking? Gordon Fee refers to these self-imposed limitations as "hardening of the categories"!

We forget in this day of instant satisfaction that none of our talents come full-grown. It's only as we cultivate them that they begin to mature and multiply. The more we use them, the more others are blessed through them. Soon we discover that God has given us a multitude of gifts and equipped us with endless resources.

God is calling each of us to a life of adventure. Remember, an adventure is not an adventure unless there is some risk involved. Are we willing to take risks in our walk with Jesus? Are we willing to look a little foolish from time to time as we seek to develop new talents? If we are, God will continue to bring us new opportunities of service.

The warning of this parable is this: God holds us responsible for our lives and what we do with them.

The joyful reward is this: One day we will stand before our great God and hear him say, "Well done, good and faithful servant!" (Matthew 25:21).

Additional Scripture Readings:
Exodus 4:10–12; Ephesians 3:14–21

Go to page 37 for your next devotional reading.

see you sick or in prison and go to visit you?'

40"The King will reply, 'I tell you the truth, whatever you did for one of the least of these brothers of mine, you did for me.'

41"Then he will say to those on his left, 'Depart from me, you who are cursed, into the eternal fire prepared for the devil and his angels. 42For I was hungry and you gave me nothing to eat, I was thirsty and you gave me nothing to drink, 43I was a stranger and you did not invite me in, I needed clothes and you did not clothe me, I was sick and in prison and you did not look after me.'

44"They also will answer, 'Lord, when did we see you hungry or thirsty or a stranger or needing clothes or sick or in prison, and did not help you?'

45"He will reply, 'I tell you the truth, whatever you did not do for one of the least of these, you did not do for me.'

46"Then they will go away to eternal punishment, but the righteous to eternal life."

The Plot Against Jesus

26 When Jesus had finished saying all these things, he said to his disciples, 2"As you know, the Passover is two days away—and the Son of Man will be handed over to be crucified."

3Then the chief priests and the elders of the people assembled in the palace of the high priest, whose name was Caiaphas, 4and they plotted to arrest Jesus in some sly way and kill him. 5"But not during the Feast," they said, "or there may be a riot among the people."

Jesus Anointed at Bethany

6While Jesus was in Bethany in the home of a man known as Simon the Leper, 7a woman came to him with an alabaster jar of very expensive perfume, which she poured on his head as he was reclining at the table.

8When the disciples saw this, they were indignant. "Why this waste?" they asked. 9"This perfume could have been sold at a high price and the money given to the poor."

10Aware of this, Jesus said to them, "Why are you bothering this woman? She has done a beautiful thing to me. 11The poor you will always have with you, but you will not always have me. 12When she

poured this perfume on my body, she did it to prepare me for burial. 13I tell you the truth, wherever this gospel is preached throughout the world, what she has done will also be told, in memory of her."

Judas Agrees to Betray Jesus

14Then one of the Twelve—the one called Judas Iscariot—went to the chief priests 15and asked, "What are you willing to give me if I hand him over to you?" So they counted out for him thirty silver coins. 16From then on Judas watched for an opportunity to hand him over.

The Lord's Supper

17On the first day of the Feast of Unleavened Bread, the disciples came to Jesus and asked, "Where do you want us to make preparations for you to eat the Passover?"

18He replied, "Go into the city to a certain man and tell him, 'The Teacher says: My appointed time is near. I am going to celebrate the Passover with my disciples at your house.' " 19So the disciples did as Jesus had directed them and prepared the Passover.

20When evening came, Jesus was reclining at the table with the Twelve. 21And while they were eating, he said, "I tell you the truth, one of you will betray me."

22They were very sad and began to say to him one after the other, "Surely not I, Lord?"

23Jesus replied, "The one who has dipped his hand into the bowl with me will betray me. 24The Son of Man will go just as it is written about him. But woe to that man who betrays the Son of Man! It would be better for him if he had not been born."

25Then Judas, the one who would betray him, said, "Surely not I, Rabbi?"

Jesus answered, "Yes, it is you."*a*

26While they were eating, Jesus took bread, gave thanks and broke it, and gave it to his disciples, saying, "Take and eat; this is my body."

27Then he took the cup, gave thanks and offered it to them, saying, "Drink from it, all of you. 28This is my blood of the*b* covenant, which is poured out for many for the forgiveness of sins. 29I tell you, I will not drink of this fruit of the vine from now on until that day when I

---

a25 Or "You yourself have said it"　　*b28 Some manuscripts the new* drink it anew with you in my Father's kingdom."

³⁰When they had sung a hymn, they went out to the Mount of Olives.

Jesus Predicts Peter's Denial

³¹Then Jesus told them, "This very night you will all fall away on account of me, for it is written:

" 'I will strike the shepherd,
    and the sheep of the flock will be
        scattered.'ᵃ

³²But after I have risen, I will go ahead of you into Galilee."

³³Peter replied, "Even if all fall away on account of you, I never will."

³⁴"I tell you the truth," Jesus answered,

ᵃ31 Zech. 13:7

| THURSDAY |

| VERSE FOR THE DAY: | AUTHOR: | PASSAGE FOR THE DAY: |
| Matthew 26:12 | Sue Richards | Matthew 26:6–13 |

A Gift

SHE came bearing a gift of love, probably without invitation, and certainly without forewarning. We are told that while Christ was reclining at table at the home of Simon the Leper, she came and poured a very expensive perfume on his head. The disciples, Christ's specially chosen men, became indignant when they saw her anoint the Lord in this manner. " 'Why this waste?' they asked. 'This perfume could have been sold at a high price and the money given to the poor.' " But Christ said to them, "Why are you bothering this woman? She has done a beautiful thing to me . . . . When she poured this perfume on my body, she did it to prepare me for burial" (Matthew 26:8–9).

She was obviously a very sensitive woman, wanting to give something special to the Lord before he was taken away. She had a great deal of spiritual discernment as well. She had heard of Christ's coming execution, and believed it. Even so, her gift and her basis for giving it were not understood even by these special men, the leaders of the early church. But Jesus understood. He appreciated her outpouring of love and made a promise like no other in Scripture. Christ said, "Wherever this gospel is preached throughout the world, what she has done will also be told, in memory of her" (Matthew 26:13).

Just as this woman's gift was misunderstood by the leaders of the early church, many churches today criticize women for trying to share their special gifts. It's comforting to know that our gifts are acceptable, accepted and appreciated by the Lord when given in love. He understands our motivations; he accepts what we bring.

Father, help us to give cheerfully and to accept graciously.

Additional Scripture Readings:
Luke 21:1–4; Romans 14:6–8

*Go to page 39 for your next
devotional reading.*

"this very night, before the rooster crows, you will disown me three times."

³⁵But Peter declared, "Even if I have to die with you, I will never disown you." And all the other disciples said the same.

Gethsemane

³⁶Then Jesus went with his disciples to a place called Gethsemane, and he said to them, "Sit here while I go over there and pray." ³⁷He took Peter and the two sons of Zebedee along with him, and he began to be sorrowful and troubled. ³⁸Then he said to them, "My soul is overwhelmed with sorrow to the point of death. Stay here and keep watch with me."

³⁹Going a little farther, he fell with his face to the ground and prayed, "My Father, if it is possible, may this cup be taken from me. Yet not as I will, but as you will."

⁴⁰Then he returned to his disciples and found them sleeping. "Could you men not keep watch with me for one hour?" he asked Peter. ⁴¹"Watch and pray so that you will not fall into temptation. The spirit is willing, but the body is weak."

⁴²He went away a second time and prayed, "My Father, if it is not possible for this cup to be taken away unless I drink it, may your will be done."

⁴³When he came back, he again found them sleeping, because their eyes were heavy. ⁴⁴So he left them and went away once more and prayed the third time, saying the same thing.

⁴⁵Then he returned to the disciples and said to them, "Are you still sleeping and resting? Look, the hour is near, and the Son of Man is betrayed into the hands of sinners. ⁴⁶Rise, let us go! Here comes my betrayer!"

Jesus Arrested

⁴⁷While he was still speaking, Judas, one of the Twelve, arrived. With him was a large crowd armed with swords and clubs, sent from the chief priests and the elders of the people. ⁴⁸Now the betrayer had arranged a signal with them: "The one I kiss is the man; arrest him." ⁴⁹Going at once to Jesus, Judas said, "Greetings, Rabbi!" and kissed him.

⁵⁰Jesus replied, "Friend, do what you came for."ᵃ

Then the men stepped forward, seized Jesus and arrested him. ⁵¹With that, one of Jesus' companions reached for his sword, drew it out and struck the servant of the high priest, cutting off his ear.

⁵²"Put your sword back in its place," Jesus said to him, "for all who draw the sword will die by the sword. ⁵³Do you think I cannot call on my Father, and he will at once put at my disposal more than twelve legions of angels? ⁵⁴But how then would the Scriptures be fulfilled that say it must happen in this way?"

⁵⁵At that time Jesus said to the crowd, "Am I leading a rebellion, that you have come out with swords and clubs to capture me? Every day I sat in the temple courts teaching, and you did not arrest me. ⁵⁶But this has all taken place that the writings of the prophets might be fulfilled." Then all the disciples deserted him and fled.

Before the Sanhedrin

⁵⁷Those who had arrested Jesus took him to Caiaphas, the high priest, where the teachers of the law and the elders had assembled. ⁵⁸But Peter followed him at a distance, right up to the courtyard of the high priest. He entered and sat down with the guards to see the outcome.

⁵⁹The chief priests and the whole Sanhedrin were looking for false evidence against Jesus so that they could put him to death. ⁶⁰But they did not find any, though many false witnesses came forward.

Finally two came forward ⁶¹and declared, "This fellow said, 'I am able to destroy the temple of God and rebuild it in three days.'"

⁶²Then the high priest stood up and said to Jesus, "Are you not going to answer? What is this testimony that these men are bringing against you?" ⁶³But Jesus remained silent.

The high priest said to him, "I charge you under oath by the living God: Tell us if you are the Christ,ᵇ the Son of God."

⁶⁴"Yes, it is as you say," Jesus replied. "But I say to all of you: In the future you will see the Son of Man sitting at the right hand of the Mighty One and coming on the clouds of heaven."

⁶⁵Then the high priest tore his clothes and said, "He has spoken blasphemy! Why do we need any more witnesses? Look, now you have heard the blasphemy. ⁶⁶What do you think?"

"He is worthy of death," they answered.

ᵃ50 Or "Friend, why have you come?"ᵃ   ᵇ63 Or Messiah; also in verse 68

⁶⁷Then they spit in his face and struck him with their fists. Others slapped him ⁶⁸and said, "Prophesy to us, Christ. Who hit you?"

Peter Disowns Jesus

⁶⁹Now Peter was sitting out in the courtyard, and a servant girl came to him. "You also were with Jesus of Galilee," she said.

⁷⁰But he denied it before them all. "I don't know what you're talking about," he said.

⁷¹Then he went out to the gateway, where another girl saw him and said to the people there, "This fellow was with Jesus of Nazareth."

⁷²He denied it again, with an oath: "I don't know the man!"

⁷³After a little while, those standing there went up to Peter and said, "Surely

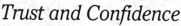

FRIDAY

VERSE FOR THE DAY:
Matthew 26:39

AUTHOR:
Carol L. Baldwin

PASSAGE FOR THE DAY:
Matthew 26:36–46

Trust and Confidence

PICTURE Jesus. Alone in the Garden of Gethsemane, deserted by even his closest disciples, he is preparing to face the painful death of crucifixion. Not only will he die an innocent man; he will experience a bitter separation from his heavenly Father and the agony of bearing the punishment for the sins of his people.

How does our Lord respond at this moment of tremendous trial and testing?

His simple yet powerful response pricks our consciences as he speaks the ultimate prayer of trust and confidence: "My Father, if it is possible, may this cup be taken from me. Yet not as I will, but as you will" (Matthew 26:39). Can there be a more graphic demonstration of trust in God? Can there ever be a better example of submission to our heavenly Father's will?

Jesus' actions and attitude provide a model to all believers of how we are to face the difficult tasks, and the emotional, spiritual or physical struggles that God ordains for us.

Scripture reminds us that we are not to be surprised when suffering and trials come into our lives (1 Peter 1:6–7; 4:12–13); rather we are to rejoice that God is refining in us the precious jewel of faith, which is of far greater worth than gold.

Every problem with our children, each disagreement with our husbands, each stressful assignment at our jobs provides an opportunity to call on God to strengthen our faith, to develop our perseverance, to build our character and to ground our hope deeper in him (Romans 5:3–4).

May God grant us an increase in our trust in him, even as Jesus displayed. May he build in us precious Christian character, refined in the furnace of his discipline and love.

Additional Scripture Readings:
Daniel 3:13–19; James 1:2–4

Go to page 41 for your next devotional reading.

you are one of them, for your accent gives you away."

[74]Then he began to call down curses on himself and he swore to them, "I don't know the man!"

Immediately a rooster crowed. [75]Then Peter remembered the word Jesus had spoken: "Before the rooster crows, you will disown me three times." And he went outside and wept bitterly.

Judas Hangs Himself

27 Early in the morning, all the chief priests and the elders of the people came to the decision to put Jesus to death. [2]They bound him, led him away and handed him over to Pilate, the governor.

[3]When Judas, who had betrayed him, saw that Jesus was condemned, he was seized with remorse and returned the thirty silver coins to the chief priests and the elders. [4]"I have sinned," he said, "for I have betrayed innocent blood."

"What is that to us?" they replied. "That's your responsibility."

[5]So Judas threw the money into the temple and left. Then he went away and hanged himself.

[6]The chief priests picked up the coins and said, "It is against the law to put this into the treasury, since it is blood money." [7]So they decided to use the money to buy the potter's field as a burial place for foreigners. [8]That is why it has been called the Field of Blood to this day. [9]What was spoken by Jeremiah the prophet was fulfilled: "They took the thirty silver coins, the price set on him by the people of Israel, [10]and they used them to buy the potter's field, as the Lord commanded me."[a]

Jesus Before Pilate

[11]Meanwhile Jesus stood before the governor, and the governor asked him, "Are you the king of the Jews?"

"Yes, it is as you say," Jesus replied.

[12]When he was accused by the chief priests and the elders, he gave no answer. [13]Then Pilate asked him, "Don't you hear the testimony they are bringing against you?" [14]But Jesus made no reply, not even to a single charge—to the great amazement of the governor.

[15]Now it was the governor's custom at the Feast to release a prisoner chosen by the crowd. [16]At that time they had a no-

torious prisoner, called Barabbas. [17]So when the crowd had gathered, Pilate asked them, "Which one do you want me to release to you: Barabbas, or Jesus who is called Christ?" [18]For he knew it was out of envy that they had handed Jesus over to him.

[19]While Pilate was sitting on the judge's seat, his wife sent him this message: "Don't have anything to do with that innocent man, for I have suffered a great deal today in a dream because of him."

[20]But the chief priests and the elders persuaded the crowd to ask for Barabbas and to have Jesus executed.

[21]"Which of the two do you want me to release to you?" asked the governor.

"Barabbas," they answered.

[22]"What shall I do, then, with Jesus who is called Christ?" Pilate asked.

They all answered, "Crucify him!"

[23]"Why? What crime has he committed?" asked Pilate.

But they shouted all the louder, "Crucify him!"

[24]When Pilate saw that he was getting nowhere, but that instead an uproar was starting, he took water and washed his hands in front of the crowd. "I am innocent of this man's blood," he said. "It is your responsibility!"

[25]All the people answered, "Let his blood be on us and on our children!"

[26]Then he released Barabbas to them. But he had Jesus flogged, and handed him over to be crucified.

The Soldiers Mock Jesus

[27]Then the governor's soldiers took Jesus into the Praetorium and gathered the whole company of soldiers around him. [28]They stripped him and put a scarlet robe on him, [29]and then twisted together a crown of thorns and set it on his head. They put a staff in his right hand and knelt in front of him and mocked him. "Hail, king of the Jews!" they said. [30]They spit on him, and took the staff and struck him on the head again and again. [31]After they had mocked him, they took off the robe and put his own clothes on him. Then they led him away to crucify him.

The Crucifixion

[32]As they were going out, they met a man from Cyrene, named Simon, and

---

[a]10 See Zech. 11:12,13; Jer. 19:1-13; 32:6-9.

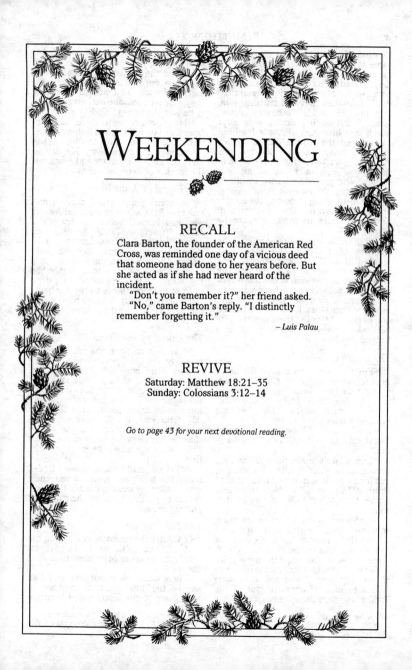

WEEKENDING

RECALL

Clara Barton, the founder of the American Red Cross, was reminded one day of a vicious deed that someone had done to her years before. But she acted as if she had never heard of the incident.

"Don't you remember it?" her friend asked.

"No," came Barton's reply. "I distinctly remember forgetting it."

– Luis Palau

REVIVE

Saturday: Matthew 18:21–35
Sunday: Colossians 3:12–14

Go to page 43 for your next devotional reading.

they forced him to carry the cross. ³³They came to a place called Golgotha (which means The Place of the Skull). ³⁴There they offered Jesus wine to drink, mixed with gall; but after tasting it, he refused to drink it. ³⁵When they had crucified him, they divided up his clothes by casting lots.ᵃ ³⁶And sitting down, they kept watch over him there. ³⁷Above his head they placed the written charge against him: THIS IS JESUS, THE KING OF THE JEWS. ³⁸Two robbers were crucified with him, one on his right and one on his left. ³⁹Those who passed by hurled insults at him, shaking their heads ⁴⁰and saying, "You who are going to destroy the temple and build it in three days, save yourself! Come down from the cross, if you are the Son of God!"

⁴¹In the same way the chief priests, the teachers of the law and the elders mocked him. ⁴²"He saved others," they said, "but he can't save himself! He's the King of Israel! Let him come down now from the cross, and we will believe in him. ⁴³He trusts in God. Let God rescue him now if he wants him, for he said, 'I am the Son of God.' " ⁴⁴In the same way the robbers who were crucified with him also heaped insults on him.

The Death of Jesus

⁴⁵From the sixth hour until the ninth hour darkness came over all the land. ⁴⁶About the ninth hour Jesus cried out in a loud voice, *"Eloi, Eloi,ᵇ lama sabachthani?"*—which means, "My God, my God, why have you forsaken me?"ᶜ

⁴⁷When some of those standing there heard this, they said, "He's calling Elijah."

⁴⁸Immediately one of them ran and got a sponge. He filled it with wine vinegar, put it on a stick, and offered it to Jesus to drink. ⁴⁹The rest said, "Now leave him alone. Let's see if Elijah comes to save him."

⁵⁰And when Jesus had cried out again in a loud voice, he gave up his spirit.

⁵¹At that moment the curtain of the temple was torn in two from top to bottom. The earth shook and the rocks split. ⁵²The tombs broke open and the bodies of many holy people who had died were raised to life. ⁵³They came out of the tombs, and after Jesus' resurrection they went into the holy city and appeared to many people.

⁵⁴When the centurion and those with him who were guarding Jesus saw the earthquake and all that had happened, they were terrified, and exclaimed, "Surely he was the Sonᵈ of God!"

⁵⁵Many women were there, watching from a distance. They had followed Jesus from Galilee to care for his needs. ⁵⁶Among them were Mary Magdalene, Mary the mother of James and Joses, and the mother of Zebedee's sons.

The Burial of Jesus

⁵⁷As evening approached, there came a rich man from Arimathea, named Joseph, who had himself become a disciple of Jesus. ⁵⁸Going to Pilate, he asked for Jesus' body, and Pilate ordered that it be given to him. ⁵⁹Joseph took the body, wrapped it in a clean linen cloth, ⁶⁰and placed it in his own new tomb that he had cut out of the rock. He rolled a big stone in front of the entrance to the tomb and went away. ⁶¹Mary Magdalene and the other Mary were sitting there opposite the tomb.

The Guard at the Tomb

⁶²The next day, the one after Preparation Day, the chief priests and the Pharisees went to Pilate. ⁶³"Sir," they said, "we remember that while he was still alive that deceiver said, 'After three days I will rise again.' ⁶⁴So give the order for the tomb to be made secure until the third day. Otherwise, his disciples may come and steal the body and tell the people that he has been raised from the dead. This last deception will be worse than the first."

⁶⁵"Take a guard," Pilate answered. "Go, make the tomb as secure as you know how." ⁶⁶So they went and made the tomb secure by putting a seal on the stone and posting the guard.

The Resurrection

28 After the Sabbath, at dawn on the first day of the week, Mary Magdalene and the other Mary went to look at the tomb.

²There was a violent earthquake, for an angel of the Lord came down from heaven and, going to the tomb, rolled back the

---

ᵃ35 A few late manuscripts *lots that the word spoken by the prophet might be fulfilled: "They divided my garments among themselves and cast lots for my clothing"* (Psalm 22:18)   ᵇ46 Some manuscripts *Eli, Eli*   ᶜ46 Psalm 22:1   ᵈ54 Or *a son* stone and sat on it. ³His appearance was like lightning, and his clothes were white as snow. ⁴The guards were so afraid of him that they shook and became like dead men.

⁵The angel said to the women, "Do not be afraid, for I know that you are looking for Jesus, who was crucified. ⁶He is not here; he has risen, just as he said. Come and see the place where he lay. ⁷Then go quickly and tell his disciples: 'He has risen from the dead and is going ahead of you into Galilee. There you will see him.' Now I have told you."

⁸So the women hurried away from the tomb, afraid yet filled with joy, and ran to tell his disciples. ⁹Suddenly Jesus met them. "Greetings," he said. They came to him, clasped his feet and worshiped him. ¹⁰Then Jesus said to them, "Do not be

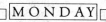

MONDAY

VERSE FOR THE DAY:
Matthew 28:19

AUTHOR:
Janice Kempe

PASSAGE FOR THE DAY:
Matthew 28:16–20

Dandelions

DANDELIONS! No matter how carefully I try to pull one up, I never get the whole thing. The root stays deep in the ground, threatening to grow up and blossom again.

But despite their bad reputation, dandelions are pretty little flowers with their yellow strands all tucked neatly into the center. And truly they are the most beautiful of all flowers when presented clutched in a child's dirty little hand. No one gets yelled at for picking them. Perhaps they grow only to be used and enjoyed by children.

Dandelions are ignored or attacked, never nurtured or cared for, and yet they always bloom profusely. They demand no pampering or special attention to yield their bright blossoms; they pop up in fields, in lawns, and between cracks in the sidewalk, even in the best neighborhoods. Can you imagine trying to grow them in a garden? They'd sneak through the boundaries and pop their sunny yellow faces up in the surrounding lawn. They would never stay put!

Christians should be more like dandelions. Our sunny yellow faces should be a reminder that simple faith has deep roots that are impossible to dislodge. Our vast number would show the world that even though we are not fancy or pampered we are evident everywhere, even in the best neighborhoods.

We should be as easily accessible as a dandelion. Jesus was. We need to get out of our gardens and jump across the boundaries that keep us where people expect to find us. We need to show our sunny yellow faces in all the spots that need a little brightening up—the crack in the sidewalk or the lawn of a country club.

Additional Scripture Readings:
Acts 8:1–4; Colossians 2:6–7

*Go to page 47 for your next
devotional reading.*

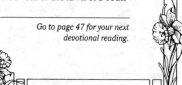

afraid. Go and tell my brothers to go to Galilee; there they will see me."

The Guards' Report

11While the women were on their way, some of the guards went into the city and reported to the chief priests everything that had happened. 12When the chief priests had met with the elders and devised a plan, they gave the soldiers a large sum of money, 13telling them, "You are to say, 'His disciples came during the night and stole him away while we were asleep.' 14If this report gets to the governor, we will satisfy him and keep you out of trouble." 15So the soldiers took the money and did as they were instructed.

And this story has been widely circulated among the Jews to this very day.

The Great Commission

16Then the eleven disciples went to Galilee, to the mountain where Jesus had told them to go. 17When they saw him, they worshiped him; but some doubted. 18Then Jesus came to them and said, "All authority in heaven and on earth has been given to me. 19Therefore go and make disciples of all nations, baptizing them in*a* the name of the Father and of the Son and of the Holy Spirit, 20and teaching them to obey everything I have commanded you. And surely I am with you always, to the very end of the age."

---

a19 Or *into*; see Acts 8:16; 19:5; Romans 6:3; 1 Cor. 1:13; 10:2 and Gal. 3:27.

MARK writes this gospel to tell the basic story about Jesus. He recounts miracles, parables and other sayings of Jesus. Almost half of his book deals with the final week of Jesus' life, ending with his death on the cross and his resurrection from the dead. As you read this book, notice how full of life and emotion Jesus is and how caring he is. Note too why he came into the world—to give his life for you (Mark 10:45). God wants you to accept his Son Jesus as your own personal Savior and Lord.

MARK

John the Baptist Prepares the Way

1 The beginning of the gospel about Jesus Christ, the Son of God.[a]

[2] It is written in Isaiah the prophet:

"I will send my messenger ahead of
      you,
   who will prepare your way"[b] —
[3] "a voice of one calling in the desert,
   'Prepare the way for the Lord,
      make straight paths for him.' "[c]

[4] And so John came, baptizing in the desert region and preaching a baptism of repentance for the forgiveness of sins. [5] The whole Judean countryside and all the people of Jerusalem went out to him. Confessing their sins, they were baptized by him in the Jordan River. [6] John wore clothing made of camel's hair, with a leather belt around his waist, and he ate locusts and wild honey. [7] And this was his message: "After me will come one more powerful than I, the thongs of whose sandals I am not worthy to stoop down and

untie. [8]I baptize you with[a] water, but he will baptize you with the Holy Spirit."

The Baptism and Temptation of Jesus

[9]At that time Jesus came from Nazareth in Galilee and was baptized by John in the Jordan. [10]As Jesus was coming up out of the water, he saw heaven being torn open and the Spirit descending on him like a dove. [11]And a voice came from heaven: "You are my Son, whom I love; with you I am well pleased."

[12]At once the Spirit sent him out into the desert, [13]and he was in the desert forty days, being tempted by Satan. He was with the wild animals, and angels attended him.

The Calling of the First Disciples

[14]After John was put in prison, Jesus went into Galilee, proclaiming the good news of God. [15]"The time has come," he said. "The kingdom of God is near. Repent and believe the good news!"

[16]As Jesus walked beside the Sea of Galilee, he saw Simon and his brother Andrew casting a net into the lake, for they were fishermen. [17]"Come, follow me," Jesus said, "and I will make you fishers of men." [18]At once they left their nets and followed him.

[19]When he had gone a little farther, he saw James son of Zebedee and his brother John in a boat, preparing their nets. [20]Without delay he called them, and they left their father Zebedee in the boat with the hired men and followed him.

Jesus Drives Out an Evil Spirit

[21]They went to Capernaum, and when the Sabbath came, Jesus went into the synagogue and began to teach. [22]The people were amazed at his teaching, because he taught them as one who had authority, not as the teachers of the law. [23]Just then a man in their synagogue who was possessed by an evil[b] spirit cried out, [24]"What do you want with us, Jesus of Nazareth? Have you come to destroy us? I know who you are—the Holy One of God!"

[25]"Be quiet!" said Jesus sternly. "Come out of him!" [26]The evil spirit shook the man violently and came out of him with a shriek.

[27]The people were all so amazed that they asked each other, "What is this? A new teaching—and with authority! He even gives orders to evil spirits and they obey him." [28]News about him spread quickly over the whole region of Galilee.

Jesus Heals Many

[29]As soon as they left the synagogue, they went with James and John to the home of Simon and Andrew. [30]Simon's mother-in-law was in bed with a fever, and they told Jesus about her. [31]So he went to her, took her hand and helped her up. The fever left her and she began to wait on them.

[32]That evening after sunset the people brought to Jesus all the sick and demon-possessed. [33]The whole town gathered at the door, [34]and Jesus healed many who had various diseases. He also drove out many demons, but he would not let the demons speak because they knew who he was.

Jesus Prays in a Solitary Place

[35]Very early in the morning, while it was still dark, Jesus got up, left the house and went off to a solitary place, where he prayed. [36]Simon and his companions went to look for him, [37]and when they found him, they exclaimed: "Everyone is looking for you!"

[38]Jesus replied, "Let us go somewhere else—to the nearby villages—so I can preach there also. That is why I have come." [39]So he traveled throughout Galilee, preaching in their synagogues and driving out demons.

A Man With Leprosy

[40]A man with leprosy[c] came to him and begged him on his knees, "If you are willing, you can make me clean."

[41]Filled with compassion, Jesus reached out his hand and touched the man. "I am willing," he said. "Be clean!" [42]Immediately the leprosy left him and he was cured.

[43]Jesus sent him away at once with a strong warning: [44]"See that you don't tell this to anyone. But go, show yourself to the priest and offer the sacrifices that Moses commanded for your cleansing, as a testimony to them." [45]Instead he went out and began to talk freely, spreading the news. As a result, Jesus could no

---

[a]8 Or in   [b]23 Greek unclean; also in verses 26 and 27   [c]40 The Greek word was used for various diseases affecting the skin—not necessarily leprosy.

longer enter a town openly but stayed outside in lonely places. Yet the people still came to him from everywhere.

Jesus Heals a Paralytic

2 A few days later, when Jesus again entered Capernaum, the people heard that he had come home. ²So many gathered that there was no room left, not even outside the door, and he preached the word to them. ³Some men came, bringing to him a paralytic, carried by four of them. ⁴Since they could not get him to Jesus because of the crowd, they made an opening in the roof above Jesus and, after digging through it, lowered the mat the paralyzed man was lying on.

⁵When Jesus saw their faith, he said to the paralytic, "Son, your sins are forgiven."

⁶Now some teachers of the law were sitting there, thinking to themselves, ⁷"Why does this fellow talk like that? He's blaspheming! Who can forgive sins but God alone?"

⁸Immediately Jesus knew in his spirit that this was what they were thinking in their hearts, and he said to them, "Why are you thinking these things? ⁹Which is easier: to say to the paralytic, 'Your sins are forgiven,' or to say, 'Get up, take your mat and walk'? ¹⁰But that you may know that the Son of Man has authority on earth to forgive sins . . . ." He said to the

TUESDAY

VERSE FOR THE DAY: AUTHOR: PASSAGE FOR THE DAY:
Mark 1:31   Jill Briscoe   Mark 1:29–34

A Must, Not a Maybe

WHEN you have a heart for God you have a heart for ministry. The two go hand in hand. When Jesus captured a life, healed a sick body or soul or mind, the recipient of those blessings invariably began to minister. Only on two occasions did Jesus have to tell them to do so. When Jairus's daughter was brought back from the dead, Jesus told her parents to "give her something to eat" (Mark 5:43), and when the Lord appeared first to Mary Magdalene after his resurrection, he told her to go tell the disciples that she had seen the Lord (John 20:17–18).

When you meet the Master, ministry naturally follows. Jesus forgave a sinful woman "her many sins," and she began to love him much (Luke 7:47). Having been forgiven much you begin to love much, and ministry is the natural outcome.

Martha and Mary, greatly loved by Jesus, loved him back by serving him, each in her own way. The mother of the disciple James, along with others, served the Lord by preparing his body for burial (Luke 24:10), while Joanna supported Jesus out of her own means (Luke 8:3). Even the woman at the well, having met Jesus, began at once to share her discovery with the people in her town (John 4:28–29).

You do not need to twist arms once you have had a personal encounter with the Christ of Galilee. Ministry is not then a maybe—it's a must.

Additional Scripture Readings:
Mark 2:14–15; John 1:43–46

Go to page 52 for your next devotional reading.

paralytic, [11]"I tell you, get up, take your mat and go home." [12]He got up, took his mat and walked out in full view of them all. This amazed everyone and they praised God, saying, "We have never seen anything like this!"

The Calling of Levi

[13]Once again Jesus went out beside the lake. A large crowd came to him, and he began to teach them. [14]As he walked along, he saw Levi son of Alphaeus sitting at the tax collector's booth. "Follow me," Jesus told him, and Levi got up and followed him.

[15]While Jesus was having dinner at Levi's house, many tax collectors and "sinners" were eating with him and his disciples, for there were many who followed him. [16]When the teachers of the law who were Pharisees saw him eating with the "sinners" and tax collectors, they asked his disciples: "Why does he eat with tax collectors and 'sinners'?"

[17]On hearing this, Jesus said to them, "It is not the healthy who need a doctor, but the sick. I have not come to call the righteous, but sinners."

Jesus Questioned About Fasting

[18]Now John's disciples and the Pharisees were fasting. Some people came and asked Jesus, "How is it that John's disciples and the disciples of the Pharisees are fasting, but yours are not?"

[19]Jesus answered, "How can the guests of the bridegroom fast while he is with them? They cannot, so long as they have him with them. [20]But the time will come when the bridegroom will be taken from them, and on that day they will fast.

[21]"No one sews a patch of unshrunk cloth on an old garment. If he does, the new piece will pull away from the old, making the tear worse. [22]And no one pours new wine into old wineskins. If he does, the wine will burst the skins, and both the wine and the wineskins will be ruined. No, he pours new wine into new wineskins."

Lord of the Sabbath

[23]One Sabbath Jesus was going through the grainfields, and as his disciples walked along, they began to pick some heads of grain. [24]The Pharisees said to him, "Look, why are they doing what is unlawful on the Sabbath?"

[25]He answered, "Have you never read what David did when he and his companions were hungry and in need? [26]In the days of Abiathar the high priest, he entered the house of God and ate the consecrated bread, which is lawful only for priests to eat. And he also gave some to his companions."

[27]Then he said to them, "The Sabbath was made for man, not man for the Sabbath. [28]So the Son of Man is Lord even of the Sabbath."

3 Another time he went into the synagogue, and a man with a shriveled hand was there. [2]Some of them were looking for a reason to accuse Jesus, so they watched him closely to see if he would heal him on the Sabbath. [3]Jesus said to the man with the shriveled hand, "Stand up in front of everyone."

[4]Then Jesus asked them, "Which is lawful on the Sabbath: to do good or to do evil, to save life or to kill?" But they remained silent.

[5]He looked around at them in anger and, deeply distressed at their stubborn hearts, said to the man, "Stretch out your hand." He stretched it out, and his hand was completely restored. [6]Then the Pharisees went out and began to plot with the Herodians how they might kill Jesus.

Crowds Follow Jesus

[7]Jesus withdrew with his disciples to the lake, and a large crowd from Galilee followed. [8]When they heard all he was doing, many people came to him from Judea, Jerusalem, Idumea, and the regions across the Jordan and around Tyre and Sidon. [9]Because of the crowd he told his disciples to have a small boat ready for him, to keep the people from crowding him. [10]For he had healed many, so that those with diseases were pushing forward to touch him. [11]Whenever the evil[a] spirits saw him, they fell down before him and cried out, "You are the Son of God." [12]But he gave them strict orders not to tell who he was.

The Appointing of the Twelve Apostles

[13]Jesus went up on a mountainside and called to him those he wanted, and they came to him. [14]He appointed twelve — designating them apostles[b] — that they might be with him and that he might send them out to preach [15]and to have authori-

---

[a]11 Greek *unclean*; also in verse 30   [b]14 Some manuscripts do not have *designating them apostles*.

ty to drive out demons. 16These are the twelve he appointed: Simon (to whom he gave the name Peter); 17James son of Zebedee and his brother John (to them he gave the name Boanerges, which means Sons of Thunder); 18Andrew, Philip, Bartholomew, Matthew, Thomas, James son of Alphaeus, Thaddaeus, Simon the Zealot 19and Judas Iscariot, who betrayed him.

Jesus and Beelzebub

20Then Jesus entered a house, and again a crowd gathered, so that he and his disciples were not even able to eat. 21When his family heard about this, they went to take charge of him, for they said, "He is out of his mind."

22And the teachers of the law who came down from Jerusalem said, "He is possessed by Beelzebuba! By the prince of demons he is driving out demons."

23So Jesus called them and spoke to them in parables: "How can Satan drive out Satan? 24If a kingdom is divided against itself, that kingdom cannot stand. 25If a house is divided against itself, that house cannot stand. 26And if Satan opposes himself and is divided, he cannot stand; his end has come. 27In fact, no one can enter a strong man's house and carry off his possessions unless he first ties up the strong man. Then he can rob his house. 28I tell you the truth, all the sins and blasphemies of men will be forgiven them. 29But whoever blasphemes against the Holy Spirit will never be forgiven; he is guilty of an eternal sin."

30He said this because they were saying, "He has an evil spirit."

Jesus' Mother and Brothers

31Then Jesus' mother and brothers arrived. Standing outside, they sent someone in to call him. 32A crowd was sitting around him, and they told him, "Your mother and brothers are outside looking for you."

33"Who are my mother and my brothers?" he asked.

34Then he looked at those seated in a circle around him and said, "Here are my mother and my brothers! 35Whoever does God's will is my brother and sister and mother."

The Parable of the Sower

4 Again Jesus began to teach by the lake. The crowd that gathered around him was so large that he got into a boat and sat in it out on the lake, while all the people were along the shore at the water's edge. 2He taught them many things by parables, and in his teaching said: 3"Listen! A farmer went out to sow his seed. 4As he was scattering the seed, some fell along the path, and the birds came and ate it up. 5Some fell on rocky places, where it did not have much soil. It sprang up quickly, because the soil was shallow. 6But when the sun came up, the plants were scorched, and they withered because they had no root. 7Other seed fell among thorns, which grew up and choked the plants, so that they did not bear grain. 8Still other seed fell on good soil. It came up, grew and produced a crop, multiplying thirty, sixty, or even a hundred times."

9Then Jesus said, "He who has ears to hear, let him hear."

10When he was alone, the Twelve and the others around him asked him about the parables. 11He told them, "The secret of the kingdom of God has been given to you. But to those on the outside everything is said in parables 12so that,

" 'they may be ever seeing but never
        perceiving,
    and ever hearing but never
        understanding;
otherwise they might turn and be
        forgiven!'b "

13Then Jesus said to them, "Don't you understand this parable? How then will you understand any parable? 14The farmer sows the word. 15Some people are like seed along the path, where the word is sown. As soon as they hear it, Satan comes and takes away the word that was sown in them. 16Others, like seed sown on rocky places, hear the word and at once receive it with joy. 17But since they have no root, they last only a short time. When trouble or persecution comes because of the word, they quickly fall away. 18Still others, like seed sown among thorns, hear the word; 19but the worries of this life, the deceitfulness of wealth and the desires for other things come in and choke the word, making it unfruitful. 20Others, like seed sown on good soil,

a22 Greek Beezeboul or Beelzeboul   b12 Isaiah 6:9,10

hear the word, accept it, and produce a crop—thirty, sixty or even a hundred times what was sown."

A Lamp on a Stand

21He said to them, "Do you bring in a lamp to put it under a bowl or a bed? Instead, don't you put it on its stand? 22For whatever is hidden is meant to be disclosed, and whatever is concealed is meant to be brought out into the open. 23If anyone has ears to hear, let him hear."

24"Consider carefully what you hear," he continued. "With the measure you use, it will be measured to you—and even more. 25Whoever has will be given more; whoever does not have, even what he has will be taken from him."

The Parable of the Growing Seed

26He also said, "This is what the kingdom of God is like. A man scatters seed on the ground. 27Night and day, whether he sleeps or gets up, the seed sprouts and grows, though he does not know how. 28All by itself the soil produces grain—first the stalk, then the head, then the full kernel in the head. 29As soon as the grain is ripe, he puts the sickle to it, because the harvest has come."

The Parable of the Mustard Seed

30Again he said, "What shall we say the kingdom of God is like, or what parable shall we use to describe it? 31It is like a mustard seed, which is the smallest seed you plant in the ground. 32Yet when planted, it grows and becomes the largest of all garden plants, with such big branches that the birds of the air can perch in its shade."

33With many similar parables Jesus spoke the word to them, as much as they could understand. 34He did not say anything to them without using a parable. But when he was alone with his own disciples, he explained everything.

Jesus Calms the Storm

35That day when evening came, he said to his disciples, "Let us go over to the other side." 36Leaving the crowd behind, they took him along, just as he was, in the boat. There were also other boats with him. 37A furious squall came up, and the waves broke over the boat, so that it was nearly swamped. 38Jesus was in the stern, sleeping on a cushion. The disciples woke him and said to him, "Teacher, don't you care if we drown?"

39He got up, rebuked the wind and said to the waves, "Quiet! Be still!" Then the wind died down and it was completely calm.

40He said to his disciples, "Why are you so afraid? Do you still have no faith?"

41They were terrified and asked each other, "Who is this? Even the wind and the waves obey him!"

The Healing of a Demon-possessed Man

5 They went across the lake to the region of the Gerasenes.a 2When Jesus got out of the boat, a man with an evilb spirit came from the tombs to meet him. 3This man lived in the tombs, and no one could bind him any more, not even with a chain. 4For he had often been chained hand and foot, but he tore the chains apart and broke the irons on his feet. No one was strong enough to subdue him. 5Night and day among the tombs and in the hills he would cry out and cut himself with stones.

6When he saw Jesus from a distance, he ran and fell on his knees in front of him. 7He shouted at the top of his voice, "What do you want with me, Jesus, Son of the Most High God? Swear to God that you won't torture me!" 8For Jesus had said to him, "Come out of this man, you evil spirit!"

9Then Jesus asked him, "What is your name?"

"My name is Legion," he replied, "for we are many." 10And he begged Jesus again and again not to send them out of the area.

11A large herd of pigs was feeding on the nearby hillside. 12The demons begged Jesus, "Send us among the pigs; allow us to go into them." 13He gave them permission, and the evil spirits came out and went into the pigs. The herd, about two thousand in number, rushed down the steep bank into the lake and were drowned.

14Those tending the pigs ran off and reported this in the town and countryside, and the people went out to see what had happened. 15When they came to Jesus, they saw the man who had been pos-

a1 Some manuscripts Gadarenes; other manuscripts Gergesenes　　b2 Greek unclean; also in verses 8 and 13 sessed by the legion of demons, sitting there, dressed and in his right mind; and they were afraid. [16]Those who had seen it told the people what had happened to the demon-possessed man—and told about the pigs as well. [17]Then the people began to plead with Jesus to leave their region.

[18]As Jesus was getting into the boat, the man who had been demon-possessed begged to go with him. [19]Jesus did not let him, but said, "Go home to your family and tell them how much the Lord has done for you, and how he has had mercy on you." [20]So the man went away and began to tell in the Decapolis[a] how much Jesus had done for him. And all the people were amazed.

A Dead Girl and a Sick Woman

[21]When Jesus had again crossed over by boat to the other side of the lake, a large crowd gathered around him while he was by the lake. [22]Then one of the synagogue rulers, named Jairus, came there. Seeing Jesus, he fell at his feet [23]and pleaded earnestly with him, "My little daughter is dying. Please come and put your hands on her so that she will be healed and live." [24]So Jesus went with him.

A large crowd followed and pressed around him. [25]And a woman was there who had been subject to bleeding for twelve years. [26]She had suffered a great deal under the care of many doctors and had spent all she had, yet instead of getting better she grew worse. [27]When she heard about Jesus, she came up behind him in the crowd and touched his cloak, [28]because she thought, "If I just touch his clothes, I will be healed." [29]Immediately her bleeding stopped and she felt in her body that she was freed from her suffering.

[30]At once Jesus realized that power had gone out from him. He turned around in the crowd and asked, "Who touched my clothes?"

[31]"You see the people crowding against you," his disciples answered, "and yet you can ask, 'Who touched me?'"

[32]But Jesus kept looking around to see who had done it. [33]Then the woman, knowing what had happened to her, came and fell at his feet and, trembling with fear, told him the whole truth. [34]He said to her, "Daughter, your faith has healed you. Go in peace and be freed from your suffering."

[35]While Jesus was still speaking, some men came from the house of Jairus, the synagogue ruler. "Your daughter is dead," they said. "Why bother the teacher any more?"

[36]Ignoring what they said, Jesus told the synagogue ruler, "Don't be afraid; just believe."

[37]He did not let anyone follow him except Peter, James and John the brother of James. [38]When they came to the home of the synagogue ruler, Jesus saw a commotion, with people crying and wailing loudly. [39]He went in and said to them, "Why all this commotion and wailing? The child is not dead but asleep." [40]But they laughed at him.

After he put them all out, he took the child's father and mother and the disciples who were with him, and went in where the child was. [41]He took her by the hand and said to her, *"Talitha koum!"* (which means, "Little girl, I say to you, get up!"). [42]Immediately the girl stood up and walked around (she was twelve years old). At this they were completely astonished. [43]He gave strict orders not to let anyone know about this, and told them to give her something to eat.

A Prophet Without Honor

6 Jesus left there and went to his hometown, accompanied by his disciples. [2]When the Sabbath came, he began to teach in the synagogue, and many who heard him were amazed.

"Where did this man get these things?" they asked. "What's this wisdom that has been given him, that he even does miracles! [3]Isn't this the carpenter? Isn't this Mary's son and the brother of James, Joseph,[b] Judas and Simon? Aren't his sisters here with us?" And they took offense at him.

[4]Jesus said to them, "Only in his hometown, among his relatives and in his own house is a prophet without honor." [5]He could not do any miracles there, except lay his hands on a few sick people and heal them. [6]And he was amazed at their lack of faith.

Jesus Sends Out the Twelve

Then Jesus went around teaching from village to village. [7]Calling the Twelve to him, he sent them out two by two and gave them authority over evil[c] spirits.

[8]These were his instructions: "Take

---

[a]20 That is, the Ten Cities   [b]3 Greek *Joses,* a variant of *Joseph*   [c]7 Greek *unclean*

VERSE FOR THE DAY:	AUTHOR:	PASSAGE FOR THE DAY:
Mark 5:34	*Wanda K. Jones*	*Mark 5:25–34*

Touch the Lord

MARK 5:25–34 speaks of a woman who had been bleeding for twelve years. She had seen many doctors but none were able to make her well. And while she spent all her money seeking a cure, her condition only grew worse.

Then she heard about Jesus and believed that if she could get to him and just touch him she would be healed. What a testimony to her persistence!

Imagine the scene: "A large crowd followed and pressed around him" (Mark 5:24). Some were blind, some deaf, some were mothers carrying children. And no doubt the day was hot and the road dusty. But this particular woman determined that in spite of the crowd she was going to touch Jesus and be healed. And she was!

Jesus responded to faith's touch by asking, "Who touched my clothes?" (Mark 5:30). The woman fell at his feet and told him her problem. How characteristic of the Master to respond in a comforting voice when he said, "Daughter, your faith has healed you. Go in peace and be freed from your suffering" (Mark 5:34).

Jesus is just as interested in your need as he was in this woman's need many years ago. Whatever your situation, whatever your problem, he stands ready to help you.

About two years ago I had the opportunity to witness about my faith to a woman who was near death. At the same time I had the privilege to hear her reaffirm her faith in Jesus Christ. She sang many of the hymns she had loved as a young girl, including "Blessed Assurance" and "What a Friend We Have in Jesus." We prayed together, and the next day she went to heaven with a smile on her face. She had touched the Lord on earth, and now she would be with him in heaven.

You may be looking for answers because you're in a faltering marriage. Or you may be hurting because you have been abused or neglected. Remember the woman of Mark 5. She sought Jesus and was determined to find him. When she did, he met her needs. He will meet yours. Ask him.

Additional Scripture Readings:
John 20:24–29; Hebrews 4:14–16

Go to page 55 for your next devotional reading.

nothing for the journey except a staff—no bread, no bag, no money in your belts. [9]Wear sandals but not an extra tunic. [10]Whenever you enter a house, stay there until you leave that town. [11]And if any place will not welcome you or listen to you, shake the dust off your feet when you leave, as a testimony against them."

[12]They went out and preached that people should repent. [13]They drove out many demons and anointed many sick people with oil and healed them.

John the Baptist Beheaded

[14]King Herod heard about this, for Jesus' name had become well known. Some were saying,[a] "John the Baptist has been raised from the dead, and that is why miraculous powers are at work in him."

[15]Others said, "He is Elijah."

And still others claimed, "He is a prophet, like one of the prophets of long ago."

[16]But when Herod heard this, he said, "John, the man I beheaded, has been raised from the dead!"

[17]For Herod himself had given orders to have John arrested, and he had him bound and put in prison. He did this because of Herodias, his brother Philip's wife, whom he had married. [18]For John had been saying to Herod, "It is not lawful for you to have your brother's wife." [19]So Herodias nursed a grudge against John and wanted to kill him. But she was not able to, [20]because Herod feared John and protected him, knowing him to be a righteous and holy man. When Herod heard John, he was greatly puzzled[b]; yet he liked to listen to him.

[21]Finally the opportune time came. On his birthday Herod gave a banquet for his high officials and military commanders and the leading men of Galilee. [22]When the daughter of Herodias came in and danced, she pleased Herod and his dinner guests.

The king said to the girl, "Ask me for anything you want, and I'll give it to you." [23]And he promised her with an oath, "Whatever you ask I will give you, up to half my kingdom."

[24]She went out and said to her mother, "What shall I ask for?"

"The head of John the Baptist," she answered.

[25]At once the girl hurried in to the king with the request: "I want you to give me right now the head of John the Baptist on a platter."

[26]The king was greatly distressed, but because of his oaths and his dinner guests, he did not want to refuse her. [27]So he immediately sent an executioner with orders to bring John's head. The man went, beheaded John in the prison, [28]and brought back his head on a platter. He presented it to the girl, and she gave it to her mother. [29]On hearing of this, John's disciples came and took his body and laid it in a tomb.

Jesus Feeds the Five Thousand

[30]The apostles gathered around Jesus and reported to him all they had done and taught. [31]Then, because so many people were coming and going that they did not even have a chance to eat, he said to them, "Come with me by yourselves to a quiet place and get some rest."

[32]So they went away by themselves in a boat to a solitary place. [33]But many who saw them leaving recognized them and ran on foot from all the towns and got there ahead of them. [34]When Jesus landed and saw a large crowd, he had compassion on them, because they were like sheep without a shepherd. So he began teaching them many things.

[35]By this time it was late in the day, so his disciples came to him. "This is a remote place," they said, "and it's already very late. [36]Send the people away so they can go to the surrounding countryside and villages and buy themselves something to eat."

[37]But he answered, "You give them something to eat."

They said to him, "That would take eight months of a man's wages[c]! Are we to go and spend that much on bread and give it to them to eat?"

[38]"How many loaves do you have?" he asked. "Go and see."

When they found out, they said, "Five—and two fish."

[39]Then Jesus directed them to have all the people sit down in groups on the green grass. [40]So they sat down in groups of hundreds and fifties. [41]Taking the five loaves and the two fish and looking up to heaven, he gave thanks and broke the loaves. Then he gave them to his disciples

---

[a]14 Some early manuscripts *He was saying*   [b]20 Some early manuscripts *he did many things*
[c]37 Greek *take two hundred denarii*

to set before the people. He also divided the two fish among them all. [42]They all ate and were satisfied, [43]and the disciples picked up twelve basketfuls of broken pieces of bread and fish. [44]The number of the men who had eaten was five thousand.

Jesus Walks on the Water

[45]Immediately Jesus made his disciples get into the boat and go on ahead of him to Bethsaida, while he dismissed the crowd. [46]After leaving them, he went up on a mountainside to pray.

[47]When evening came, the boat was in the middle of the lake, and he was alone on land. [48]He saw the disciples straining at the oars, because the wind was against them. About the fourth watch of the night he went out to them, walking on the lake. He was about to pass by them, [49]but when they saw him walking on the lake, they thought he was a ghost. They cried out, [50]because they all saw him and were terrified.

Immediately he spoke to them and said, "Take courage! It is I. Don't be afraid." [51]Then he climbed into the boat with them, and the wind died down. They were completely amazed, [52]for they had not understood about the loaves; their hearts were hardened.

[53]When they had crossed over, they landed at Gennesaret and anchored there. [54]As soon as they got out of the boat, people recognized Jesus. [55]They ran throughout that whole region and carried the sick on mats to wherever they heard he was. [56]And wherever he went—into villages, towns or countryside—they placed the sick in the marketplaces. They begged him to let them touch even the edge of his cloak, and all who touched him were healed.

Clean and Unclean

7 The Pharisees and some of the teachers of the law who had come from Jerusalem gathered around Jesus and [2]saw some of his disciples eating food with hands that were "unclean," that is, unwashed. [3](The Pharisees and all the Jews do not eat unless they give their hands a ceremonial washing, holding to the tradition of the elders. [4]When they come from the marketplace they do not eat unless they wash. And they observe many other traditions, such as the washing of cups, pitchers and kettles.[a])

[5]So the Pharisees and teachers of the law asked Jesus, "Why don't your disciples live according to the tradition of the elders instead of eating their food with 'unclean' hands?"

[6]He replied, "Isaiah was right when he prophesied about you hypocrites; as it is written:

" 'These people honor me with their
        lips,
    but their hearts are far from me.
[7]They worship me in vain;
    their teachings are but rules taught
        by men.'[b]

[8]You have let go of the commands of God and are holding on to the traditions of men."

[9]And he said to them: "You have a fine way of setting aside the commands of God in order to observe[c] your own traditions! [10]For Moses said, 'Honor your father and your mother,'[d] and, 'Anyone who curses his father or mother must be put to death.'[e] [11]But you say that if a man says to his father or mother: 'Whatever help you might otherwise have received from me is Corban' (that is, a gift devoted to God), [12]then you no longer let him do anything for his father or mother. [13]Thus you nullify the word of God by your tradition that you have handed down. And you do many things like that."

[14]Again Jesus called the crowd to him and said, "Listen to me, everyone, and understand this. [15]Nothing outside a man can make him 'unclean' by going into him. Rather, it is what comes out of a man that makes him 'unclean.'[f]"

[17]After he had left the crowd and entered the house, his disciples asked him about this parable. [18]"Are you so dull?" he asked. "Don't you see that nothing that enters a man from the outside can make him 'unclean'? [19]For it doesn't go into his heart but into his stomach, and then out of his body." (In saying this, Jesus declared all foods "clean.")

[20]He went on: "What comes out of a man is what makes him 'unclean.' [21]For from within, out of men's hearts, come

a4 Some early manuscripts pitchers, kettles and dining couches   b6,7 Isaiah 29:13   c9 Some
manuscripts set up   d10 Exodus 20:12; Deut. 5:16   e10 Exodus 21:17; Lev. 20:9   f15 Some early
manuscripts 'unclean.' 16If anyone has ears to hear, let him hear.

VERSE FOR THE DAY:
Mark 6:46

AUTHOR:
Elisabeth Elliot

PASSAGE FOR THE DAY:
Mark 6:45–52

Meeting God Alone

A VERY tall man, wrapped in a steamer rug, kneeling alone by a chair. When I think of my father, who died in 1963, this is often the first image that comes to mind. It was the habit of his life to rise early in the morning—usually between 4:30 and 5:00 A. M. to study his Bible and to pray. We did not often see him during that solitary hour (he purposed to make it solitary), but we were used to seeing him on his knees.

My father, an honest and humble disciple of the Lord Jesus, wanted to follow his example: "Very early in the morning . . . Jesus got up, left the house and went off to a solitary place, where he prayed" (Mark 1:35).

Christians may (and ought to) pray anytime and anywhere, but we cannot well do without a special time and place to be alone with God. Most of us find that early morning is not an easy time to pray. I wonder if there is an *easy* time.

The simple fact is that early morning is probably the *only* time when we can be fairly sure of not being interrupted. Where can we go? We may need to find a literal closet or a bathroom or a parked car. We may walk outdoors and pray. But we must *arrange* to pray, to be alone with God sometime every day.

The Bible is God's message to everybody. We deceive ourselves if we claim to want to hear his voice but neglect the primary channel through which it comes. We must read his Word. We must obey it.

When we have heard God speak, what then shall we say to God? In an emergency or when we suddenly need help, the words come easily: "Oh, God!" or "Lord, help me!" During our quiet time however, it is a good thing to remember that we are here not to pester God but to adore him.

All creation praises him all the time—the winds, the tides, the oceans, the rivers, move in obedience; the song sparrow, the molecules in their cells, the stars in their courses, and the burning seraphim do, without protest of slovenliness, exactly what their Maker intended, and thus praise him.

We read that our heavenly Father actually looks for people who will worship him in spirit and in reality. Imagine! God is looking for worshipers. Will he always have to go to a church to find them, or might there be one here and there in an ordinary house, kneeling alone by a chair?

Additional Scripture Readings:
Isaiah 55:6–11; John 4:23–24

Go to page 58 for your next devotional reading.

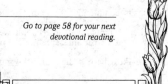

evil thoughts, sexual immorality, theft, murder, adultery, 22greed, malice, deceit, lewdness, envy, slander, arrogance and folly. 23All these evils come from inside and make a man 'unclean.' "

The Faith of a Syrophoenician Woman

24Jesus left that place and went to the vicinity of Tyre.ª He entered a house and did not want anyone to know it; yet he could not keep his presence secret. 25In fact, as soon as she heard about him, a woman whose little daughter was possessed by an evilᵇ spirit came and fell at his feet. 26The woman was a Greek, born in Syrian Phoenicia. She begged Jesus to drive the demon out of her daughter.

27"First let the children eat all they want," he told her, "for it is not right to take the children's bread and toss it to their dogs."

28"Yes, Lord," she replied, "but even the dogs under the table eat the children's crumbs."

29Then he told her, "For such a reply, you may go; the demon has left your daughter."

30She went home and found her child lying on the bed, and the demon gone.

The Healing of a Deaf and Mute Man

31Then Jesus left the vicinity of Tyre and went through Sidon, down to the Sea of Galilee and into the region of the Decapolis.ᶜ 32There some people brought to him a man who was deaf and could hardly talk, and they begged him to place his hand on the man.

33After he took him aside, away from the crowd, Jesus put his fingers into the man's ears. Then he spit and touched the man's tongue. 34He looked up to heaven and with a deep sigh said to him, "Ephphatha!" (which means, "Be opened!"). 35At this, the man's ears were opened, his tongue was loosened and he began to speak plainly.

36Jesus commanded them not to tell anyone. But the more he did so, the more they kept talking about it. 37People were overwhelmed with amazement. "He has done everything well," they said. "He even makes the deaf hear and the mute speak."

Jesus Feeds the Four Thousand

8 During those days another large crowd gathered. Since they had nothing to eat, Jesus called his disciples to him and said, 2"I have compassion for these people; they have already been with me three days and have nothing to eat. 3If I send them home hungry, they will collapse on the way, because some of them have come a long distance."

4His disciples answered, "But where in this remote place can anyone get enough bread to feed them?"

5"How many loaves do you have?" Jesus asked.

"Seven," they replied.

6He told the crowd to sit down on the ground. When he had taken the seven loaves and given thanks, he broke them and gave them to his disciples to set before the people, and they did so. 7They had a few small fish as well; he gave thanks for them also and told the disciples to distribute them. 8The people ate and were satisfied. Afterward the disciples picked up seven basketfuls of broken pieces that were left over. 9About four thousand men were present. And having sent them away, 10he got into the boat with his disciples and went to the region of Dalmanutha.

11The Pharisees came and began to question Jesus. To test him, they asked him for a sign from heaven. 12He sighed deeply and said, "Why does this generation ask for a miraculous sign? I tell you the truth, no sign will be given to it." 13Then he left them, got back into the boat and crossed to the other side.

The Yeast of the Pharisees and Herod

14The disciples had forgotten to bring bread, except for one loaf they had with them in the boat. 15"Be careful," Jesus warned them. "Watch out for the yeast of the Pharisees and that of Herod."

16They discussed this with one another and said, "It is because we have no bread."

17Aware of their discussion, Jesus asked them: "Why are you talking about having no bread? Do you still not see or understand? Are your hearts hardened? 18Do you have eyes but fail to see, and ears but fail to hear? And don't you remember? 19When I broke the five loaves

---

ª24 Many early manuscripts *Tyre and Sidon*   ᵇ25 Greek *unclean*   ᶜ31 That is, the Ten Cities for the five thousand, how many basketfuls of pieces did you pick up?"

"Twelve," they replied.

20"And when I broke the seven loaves for the four thousand, how many basketfuls of pieces did you pick up?"

They answered, "Seven."

21He said to them, "Do you still not understand?"

The Healing of a Blind Man at Bethsaida

22They came to Bethsaida, and some people brought a blind man and begged Jesus to touch him. 23He took the blind man by the hand and led him outside the village. When he had spit on the man's eyes and put his hands on him, Jesus asked, "Do you see anything?"

24He looked up and said, "I see people; they look like trees walking around."

25Once more Jesus put his hands on the man's eyes. Then his eyes were opened, his sight was restored, and he saw everything clearly. 26Jesus sent him home, saying, "Don't go into the village.*a*"

Peter's Confession of Christ

27Jesus and his disciples went on to the villages around Caesarea Philippi. On the way he asked them, "Who do people say I am?"

28They replied, "Some say John the Baptist; others say Elijah; and still others, one of the prophets."

29"But what about you?" he asked. "Who do you say I am?"

Peter answered, "You are the Christ.*b* "

30Jesus warned them not to tell anyone about him.

Jesus Predicts His Death

31He then began to teach them that the Son of Man must suffer many things and be rejected by the elders, chief priests and teachers of the law, and that he must be killed and after three days rise again. 32He spoke plainly about this, and Peter took him aside and began to rebuke him. 33But when Jesus turned and looked at his disciples, he rebuked Peter. "Get behind me, Satan!" he said. "You do not have in mind the things of God, but the things of men."

34Then he called the crowd to him along with his disciples and said: "If anyone would come after me, he must deny himself and take up his cross and follow me. 35For whoever wants to save his life*c* will lose it, but whoever loses his life for me and for the gospel will save it. 36What good is it for a man to gain the whole world, yet forfeit his soul? 37Or what can a man give in exchange for his soul? 38If anyone is ashamed of me and my words in this adulterous and sinful generation, the Son of Man will be ashamed of him when he comes in his Father's glory with the holy angels."

9 And he said to them, "I tell you the truth, some who are standing here will not taste death before they see the kingdom of God come with power."

The Transfiguration

2After six days Jesus took Peter, James and John with him and led them up a high mountain, where they were all alone. There he was transfigured before them. 3His clothes became dazzling white, whiter than anyone in the world could bleach them. 4And there appeared before them Elijah and Moses, who were talking with Jesus.

5Peter said to Jesus, "Rabbi, it is good for us to be here. Let us put up three shelters — one for you, one for Moses and one for Elijah." 6(He did not know what to say, they were so frightened.)

7Then a cloud appeared and enveloped them, and a voice came from the cloud: "This is my Son, whom I love. Listen to him!"

8Suddenly, when they looked around, they no longer saw anyone with them except Jesus.

9As they were coming down the mountain, Jesus gave them orders not to tell anyone what they had seen until the Son of Man had risen from the dead. 10They kept the matter to themselves, discussing what "rising from the dead" meant.

11And they asked him, "Why do the teachers of the law say that Elijah must come first?"

12Jesus replied, "To be sure, Elijah does come first, and restores all things. Why then is it written that the Son of Man must suffer much and be rejected? 13But I tell you, Elijah has come, and they have

---

a26 Some manuscripts *Don't go and tell anyone in the village* and "the Messiah" (Hebrew) both mean "the Anointed One." *soul*; also in verse 36.   *b29* Or *Messiah.* "The Christ" (Greek)   *c35* The Greek word means either *life* or

VERSE FOR THE DAY: AUTHOR: PASSAGE FOR THE DAY:
Mark 9:23   Mrs. Charles E. Cowman   Mark 9:14–32

Training in the Faith Life

THE "everything" in this verse does not always come simply for the asking. God is ever seeking to teach us the way of faith, and in our training in the faith life there must be room for the trial of faith, the discipline of faith, the patience of faith, the courage of faith, and often many stages are passed before we really realize what is the end of faith, namely, the victory of faith.

Real moral fiber is developed through discipline of faith. You have made your request of God, but the answer does not come. What are you to do?

Keep on believing God's Word; never be moved away from it by what you see or feel, and thus as you stand steady, enlarged power and experience is being developed. The fact of looking at the apparent contradiction as to God's Word and being unmoved from your position of faith make you stronger on every other line.

Often God delays purposely, and the delay is just as much an answer to your prayer as is the fulfillment when it comes.

In the lives of all the great Bible characters, God worked thus. Abraham, Moses and Elijah were not great in the beginning, but were made great through the discipline of their faith, and only thus were they fitted for the positions to which God had called them.

For example, in the case of Joseph whom the Lord was training for the throne of Egypt, it was not the prison life with its hard beds or poor food that tried him, but it was the word God had spoken into his heart in the early years concerning elevation and honor which were greater than his brethren were to receive; it was this which was ever before him, when every step in his career made it seem more and more impossible of fulfillment. These were hours that tried his soul, but hours of spiritual growth and development.

No amount of persecution tries like such experiences as these. When God has spoken of his purpose to do, and yet the days go on and he does not do it, that is truly hard; but it is a discipline of faith that will bring us into a knowledge of God which would otherwise be impossible.

Additional Scripture Readings:
James 5:10–11; 1 Peter 5:8–10

Go to page 60 for your next devotional reading.

done to him everything they wished, just as it is written about him."

The Healing of a Boy With an Evil Spirit

[14]When they came to the other disciples, they saw a large crowd around them and the teachers of the law arguing with them. [15]As soon as all the people saw Jesus, they were overwhelmed with wonder and ran to greet him.

[16]"What are you arguing with them about?" he asked.

[17]A man in the crowd answered, "Teacher, I brought you my son, who is possessed by a spirit that has robbed him of speech. [18]Whenever it seizes him, it throws him to the ground. He foams at the mouth, gnashes his teeth and becomes rigid. I asked your disciples to drive out the spirit, but they could not."

[19]"O unbelieving generation," Jesus replied, "how long shall I stay with you? How long shall I put up with you? Bring the boy to me."

[20]So they brought him. When the spirit saw Jesus, it immediately threw the boy into a convulsion. He fell to the ground and rolled around, foaming at the mouth.

[21]Jesus asked the boy's father, "How long has he been like this?"

"From childhood," he answered. [22]"It has often thrown him into fire or water to kill him. But if you can do anything, take pity on us and help us."

[23]" 'If you can'?" said Jesus. "Everything is possible for him who believes."

[24]Immediately the boy's father exclaimed, "I do believe; help me overcome my unbelief!"

[25]When Jesus saw that a crowd was running to the scene, he rebuked the evil[a] spirit. "You deaf and mute spirit," he said, "I command you, come out of him and never enter him again."

[26]The spirit shrieked, convulsed him violently and came out. The boy looked so much like a corpse that many said, "He's dead." [27]But Jesus took him by the hand and lifted him to his feet, and he stood up.

[28]After Jesus had gone indoors, his disciples asked him privately, "Why couldn't we drive it out?"

[29]He replied, "This kind can come out only by prayer.[b]

[30]They left that place and passed through Galilee. Jesus did not want anyone to know where they were, [31]because he was teaching his disciples. He said to them, "The Son of Man is going to be betrayed into the hands of men. They will kill him, and after three days he will rise." [32]But they did not understand what he meant and were afraid to ask him about it.

Who Is the Greatest?

[33]They came to Capernaum. When he was in the house, he asked them, "What were you arguing about on the road?" [34]But they kept quiet because on the way they had argued about who was the greatest.

[35]Sitting down, Jesus called the Twelve and said, "If anyone wants to be first, he must be the very last, and the servant of all."

[36]He took a little child and had him stand among them. Taking him in his arms, he said to them, [37]"Whoever welcomes one of these little children in my name welcomes me; and whoever welcomes me does not welcome me but the one who sent me."

Whoever Is Not Against Us Is for Us

[38]"Teacher," said John, "we saw a man driving out demons in your name and we told him to stop, because he was not one of us."

[39]"Do not stop him," Jesus said. "No one who does a miracle in my name can in the next moment say anything bad about me, [40]for whoever is not against us is for us. [41]I tell you the truth, anyone who gives you a cup of water in my name because you belong to Christ will certainly not lose his reward.

Causing to Sin

[42]"And if anyone causes one of these little ones who believe in me to sin, it would be better for him to be thrown into the sea with a large millstone tied around his neck. [43]If your hand causes you to sin, cut it off. It is better for you to enter life maimed than with two hands to go into hell, where the fire never goes out.[c] [45]And if your foot causes you to sin, cut it off. It is better for you to enter life crippled than to have two feet and be thrown

---

[a]25 Greek unclean   [b]29 Some manuscripts prayer and fasting   [c]43 Some manuscripts out, 44where / " 'their worm does not die, / and the fire is not quenched.'

WEEKENDING

REMEMBER

One morning I was reading the story of Jesus'
feeding of the five thousand. The disciples could
find only five loaves of bread and two fishes.
"Let me have them," said Jesus. He asked for
all. He took them, said the blessing, and broke
them before he gave them out. I remembered
what a chapel speaker, Ruth Stull of Peru, had
said: "If my life is broken when given to Jesus,
it is because pieces will feed a multitude, while
a loaf will satisfy only a little lad."

– Elisabeth Elliot

REVIVE

Saturday: Mark 6:30–44
Sunday: 2 Peter 1:5–11

Go to page 62 for your next devotional reading.

into hell. *a* 47And if your eye causes you to sin, pluck it out. It is better for you to enter the kingdom of God with one eye than to have two eyes and be thrown into hell, 48where

> " 'their worm does not die,
>   and the fire is not quenched.'*b*

49Everyone will be salted with fire.

50"Salt is good, but if it loses its saltiness, how can you make it salty again? Have salt in yourselves, and be at peace with each other."

Divorce

10 Jesus then left that place and went into the region of Judea and across the Jordan. Again crowds of people came to him, and as was his custom, he taught them.

2Some Pharisees came and tested him by asking, "Is it lawful for a man to divorce his wife?"

3"What did Moses command you?" he replied.

4They said, "Moses permitted a man to write a certificate of divorce and send her away."

5"It was because your hearts were hard that Moses wrote you this law," Jesus replied. 6"But at the beginning of creation God 'made them male and female.'*c* 7'For this reason a man will leave his father and mother and be united to his wife,*d* 8and the two will become one flesh.'*e* So they are no longer two, but one. 9Therefore what God has joined together, let man not separate."

10When they were in the house again, the disciples asked Jesus about this. 11He answered, "Anyone who divorces his wife and marries another woman commits adultery against her. 12And if she divorces her husband and marries another man, she commits adultery."

The Little Children and Jesus

13People were bringing little children to Jesus to have him touch them, but the disciples rebuked them. 14When Jesus saw this, he was indignant. He said to them, "Let the little children come to me, and do not hinder them, for the kingdom of God belongs to such as these. 15I tell you the truth, anyone who will not receive the kingdom of God like a little child will never enter it." 16And he took the children in his arms, put his hands on them and blessed them.

The Rich Young Man

17As Jesus started on his way, a man ran up to him and fell on his knees before him. "Good teacher," he asked, "what must I do to inherit eternal life?"

18"Why do you call me good?" Jesus answered. "No one is good—except God alone. 19You know the commandments: 'Do not murder, do not commit adultery, do not steal, do not give false testimony, do not defraud, honor your father and mother.'*f*"

20"Teacher," he declared, "all these I have kept since I was a boy."

21Jesus looked at him and loved him. "One thing you lack," he said. "Go, sell everything you have and give to the poor, and you will have treasure in heaven. Then come, follow me."

22At this the man's face fell. He went away sad, because he had great wealth.

23Jesus looked around and said to his disciples, "How hard it is for the rich to enter the kingdom of God!"

24The disciples were amazed at his words. But Jesus said again, "Children, how hard it is*g* to enter the kingdom of God! 25It is easier for a camel to go through the eye of a needle than for a rich man to enter the kingdom of God."

26The disciples were even more amazed, and said to each other, "Who then can be saved?"

27Jesus looked at them and said, "With man this is impossible, but not with God; all things are possible with God."

28Peter said to him, "We have left everything to follow you!"

29"I tell you the truth," Jesus replied, "no one who has left home or brothers or sisters or mother or father or children or fields for me and the gospel 30will fail to receive a hundred times as much in this present age (homes, brothers, sisters, mothers, children and fields—and with them, persecutions) and in the age to come, eternal life. 31But many who are first will be last, and the last first."

---

a45 Some manuscripts *hell,* 46*where* / " 'their worm does not die, / and the fire is not quenched.'
b48 Isaiah 66:24   *c6* Gen. 1:27   *d7* Some early manuscripts do not have *and be united to his wife.*
e8 Gen. 2:24   *f19* Exodus 20:12-16; Deut. 5:16-20   *g24* Some manuscripts *is for those who trust in riches*

VERSE FOR THE DAY:	AUTHOR:	PASSAGE FOR THE DAY:
Mark 10:14	Rosalind Rinker	Mark 10:13–16

Jesus and Little Children

AS you read Mark 10:13–16, picture yourself in the time of Christ, the sun warm on your hair and your sandals dusty as you watch Jesus surrounded by numerous people. In your imagination stand in one of the following roles:

> As a parent bringing your children to Jesus,
> As one of the crowd waiting to see Jesus,
> As a child yourself, needing Jesus.

Hear the indignation in Jesus' voice when the disciples tried to shield him. Hear the loving care and concern in his voice as he held out his arms inviting the children to come.

As a parent: Picture yourself bringing your child (or children). Watch other parents push a shy child forward, or an ailing child. The children love Jesus, and they touch him; one little girl lays her head on his shoulder. Jesus takes time for each one . . . blessing, touching, loving, and sending each back to his or her parents with joy. Who can ever be the same after having been touched by Jesus!

Are your children grown? Yet in your mind they are still your little ones, so bring those grown men or women to Jesus as the children you know them to be. Jesus will touch them and bless them. Do it now and do it often.

As a single person: There are children you love among your neighbors or relatives, whom you can bring to Jesus in your prayers as, in your imagination, you watch Jesus hold and bless them.

You, yourself: Right now be a child in the arms of Jesus, whatever your age. Let him hold you. No matter what age, deep in our hearts we are all children who desire to rest in those strong arms. My dear mother, at age eighty-three, reflected some of that when she said, "I am still a little girl of twelve running around my father's farm in Minnesota."

Close your eyes and see yourself as a child in the arms of Jesus. In reassuring words he speaks to you:

> "My child, I care about you. I love you unconditionally. Trust me. I love you."

Additional Scripture Readings:
Mark 9:36–37; Luke 7:11–15

Go to page 64 for your next devotional reading.

Jesus Again Predicts His Death

³²They were on their way up to Jerusalem, with Jesus leading the way, and the disciples were astonished, while those who followed were afraid. Again he took the Twelve aside and told them what was going to happen to him. ³³"We are going up to Jerusalem," he said, "and the Son of Man will be betrayed to the chief priests and teachers of the law. They will condemn him to death and will hand him over to the Gentiles, ³⁴who will mock him and spit on him, flog him and kill him. Three days later he will rise."

The Request of James and John

³⁵Then James and John, the sons of Zebedee, came to him. "Teacher," they said, "we want you to do for us whatever we ask."

³⁶"What do you want me to do for you?" he asked.

³⁷They replied, "Let one of us sit at your right and the other at your left in your glory."

³⁸"You don't know what you are asking," Jesus said. "Can you drink the cup I drink or be baptized with the baptism I am baptized with?"

³⁹"We can," they answered.

Jesus said to them, "You will drink the cup I drink and be baptized with the baptism I am baptized with, ⁴⁰but to sit at my right or left is not for me to grant. These places belong to those for whom they have been prepared."

⁴¹When the ten heard about this, they became indignant with James and John. ⁴²Jesus called them together and said, "You know that those who are regarded as rulers of the Gentiles lord it over them, and their high officials exercise authority over them. ⁴³Not so with you. Instead, whoever wants to become great among you must be your servant, ⁴⁴and whoever wants to be first must be slave of all. ⁴⁵For even the Son of Man did not come to be served, but to serve, and to give his life as a ransom for many."

Blind Bartimaeus Receives His Sight

⁴⁶Then they came to Jericho. As Jesus and his disciples, together with a large crowd, were leaving the city, a blind man, Bartimaeus (that is, the Son of Timaeus), was sitting by the roadside begging. ⁴⁷When he heard that it was Jesus of Naz-areth, he began to shout, "Jesus, Son of David, have mercy on me!"

⁴⁸Many rebuked him and told him to be quiet, but he shouted all the more, "Son of David, have mercy on me!"

⁴⁹Jesus stopped and said, "Call him."

So they called to the blind man, "Cheer up! On your feet! He's calling you." ⁵⁰Throwing his cloak aside, he jumped to his feet and came to Jesus.

⁵¹"What do you want me to do for you?" Jesus asked him.

The blind man said, "Rabbi, I want to see."

⁵²"Go," said Jesus, "your faith has healed you." Immediately he received his sight and followed Jesus along the road.

The Triumphal Entry

11 As they approached Jerusalem and came to Bethphage and Bethany at the Mount of Olives, Jesus sent two of his disciples, ²saying to them, "Go to the village ahead of you, and just as you enter it, you will find a colt tied there, which no one has ever ridden. Untie it and bring it here. ³If anyone asks you, 'Why are you doing this?' tell him, 'The Lord needs it and will send it back here shortly.' "

⁴They went and found a colt outside in the street, tied at a doorway. As they untied it, ⁵some people standing there asked, "What are you doing, untying that colt?" ⁶They answered as Jesus had told them to, and the people let them go. ⁷When they brought the colt to Jesus and threw their cloaks over it, he sat on it. ⁸Many people spread their cloaks on the road, while others spread branches they had cut in the fields. ⁹Those who went ahead and those who followed shouted,

"Hosanna!ᵃ"

"Blessed is he who comes in the name of the Lord!"ᵇ

¹⁰"Blessed is the coming kingdom of our father David!"

"Hosanna in the highest!"

¹¹Jesus entered Jerusalem and went to the temple. He looked around at everything, but since it was already late, he went out to Bethany with the Twelve.

Jesus Clears the Temple

¹²The next day as they were leaving

ᵃ9 A Hebrew expression meaning "Save!" which became an exclamation of praise; also in verse 10
ᵇ9 Psalm 118:25,26

Bethany, Jesus was hungry. ¹³Seeing in the distance a fig tree in leaf, he went to find out if it had any fruit. When he reached it, he found nothing but leaves, because it was not the season for figs. ¹⁴Then he said to the tree, "May no one ever eat fruit from you again." And his disciples heard him say it.

¹⁵On reaching Jerusalem, Jesus entered the temple area and began driving out those who were buying and selling there. He overturned the tables of the money changers and the benches of those selling doves, ¹⁶and would not allow anyone to carry merchandise through the temple courts. ¹⁷And as he taught them, he said, "Is it not written:

TUESDAY

VERSE FOR THE DAY: *AUTHOR:*   *PASSAGE FOR THE DAY:*
Mark 10:37   Ruth A. Tucker   *Mark 10:35–45*

The Sin of Self-Promotion

AS Americans, competition and rivalry seem to be in our blood. We are taught from early childhood that we must be better than others. We strive for recognition and prestige and tend to focus solely on ourselves. James and John would have fit well into our society. They sought the ultimate recognition—to sit at the right and left hand of Jesus in the kingdom.

Jesus had a pointed response for them that should give us all pause for reflection. While the rulers of the Gentiles lord it over those under them, such behavior is not befitting one who follows Christ. "Instead, whoever wants to become great among you must be your servant" (Mark 10:43).

That spirit of servanthood, which often is lacking in American culture, is much more visible among Africans—at least among African students at Moffat College of Bible in Kenya, where I have taught for several summers. Instead of the dog-eat-dog competition that is evident among my American students, I have noted a genuine concern for one another, especially in regard to grades at testing times. My African students appear most pleased, not when they alone perform well, but when the others perform well also. Indeed, if they were all to receive A's, there would be jubilation. Not so with my American students, whose real satisfaction comes only from being on top.

I have had to do some soul-searching myself on this issue. The competition for grades and the struggle for recognition in athletics that characterized my own student days have been subtly replaced by other forms of competition that are more befitting teachers and writers. But such a spirit is not becoming for a follower of Jesus. The Lord's words were direct, and he offered no excuses for those "handicapped" by their cultural heritage.

Additional Scripture Readings:
1 Samuel 24:1–13; Philippians 2:3–5

Go to page 66 for your next devotional reading.

" 'My house will be called
        a house of prayer for all nations'*a*?

But you have made it 'a den of robbers.'*b*"

[18]The chief priests and the teachers of the law heard this and began looking for a way to kill him, for they feared him, because the whole crowd was amazed at his teaching.

[19]When evening came, they*c* went out of the city.

The Withered Fig Tree

[20]In the morning, as they went along, they saw the fig tree withered from the roots. [21]Peter remembered and said to Jesus, "Rabbi, look! The fig tree you cursed has withered!"

[22]"Have*d* faith in God," Jesus answered. [23]"I tell you the truth, if anyone says to this mountain, 'Go, throw yourself into the sea,' and does not doubt in his heart but believes that what he says will happen, it will be done for him. [24]Therefore I tell you, whatever you ask for in prayer, believe that you have received it, and it will be yours. [25]And when you stand praying, if you hold anything against anyone, forgive him, so that your Father in heaven may forgive you your sins.*e* "

The Authority of Jesus Questioned

[27]They arrived again in Jerusalem, and while Jesus was walking in the temple courts, the chief priests, the teachers of the law and the elders came to him. [28]"By what authority are you doing these things?" they asked. "And who gave you authority to do this?"

[29]Jesus replied, "I will ask you one question. Answer me, and I will tell you by what authority I am doing these things. [30]John's baptism—was it from heaven, or from men? Tell me!"

[31]They discussed it among themselves and said, "If we say, 'From heaven,' he will ask, 'Then why didn't you believe him?' [32]But if we say, 'From men' . . . ." (They feared the people, for everyone held that John really was a prophet.)

[33]So they answered Jesus, "We don't know."

Jesus said, "Neither will I tell you by what authority I am doing these things."

The Parable of the Tenants

12 He then began to speak to them in parables: "A man planted a vineyard. He put a wall around it, dug a pit for the winepress and built a watchtower. Then he rented the vineyard to some farmers and went away on a journey. [2]At harvest time he sent a servant to the tenants to collect from them some of the fruit of the vineyard. [3]But they seized him, beat him and sent him away empty-handed. [4]Then he sent another servant to them; they struck this man on the head and treated him shamefully. [5]He sent still another, and that one they killed. He sent many others; some of them they beat, others they killed.

[6]"He had one left to send, a son, whom he loved. He sent him last of all, saying, 'They will respect my son.'

[7]"But the tenants said to one another, 'This is the heir. Come, let's kill him, and the inheritance will be ours.' [8]So they took him and killed him, and threw him out of the vineyard.

[9]"What then will the owner of the vineyard do? He will come and kill those tenants and give the vineyard to others. [10]Haven't you read this scripture:

" 'The stone the builders rejected
        has become the capstone*f*;
[11]the Lord has done this,
        and it is marvelous in our eyes'*g*?"

[12]Then they looked for a way to arrest him because they knew he had spoken the parable against them. But they were afraid of the crowd; so they left him and went away.

Paying Taxes to Caesar

[13]Later they sent some of the Pharisees and Herodians to Jesus to catch him in his words. [14]They came to him and said, "Teacher, we know you are a man of integrity. You aren't swayed by men, because you pay no attention to who they are; but you teach the way of God in accordance with the truth. Is it right to pay taxes to Caesar or not? [15]Should we pay or shouldn't we?"

But Jesus knew their hypocrisy. "Why are you trying to trap me?" he asked. "Bring me a denarius and let me look at it." [16]They brought the coin, and he asked

a17 Isaiah 56:7   *b17* Jer. 7:11   *c19* Some early manuscripts *he*   *d22* Some early manuscripts *If you have*   *e25* Some manuscripts *sins.* *26But if you do not forgive, neither will your Father who is in heaven forgive your sins.*   *f10* Or *cornerstone*   *g11* Psalm 118:22,23

VERSE FOR THE DAY:
Mark 11:24

AUTHOR:
Hope MacDonald

PASSAGE FOR THE DAY:
Mark 11:22–25

Our Great Helper

WHILE searching for a book I wanted to buy recently, I heard a pleasant voice ask, "May I help you?" Once I described the book, we soon found it. I left the store with my requested treasure happily tucked under my arm, and I thought, "I wonder how often God asks me this same question, but I'm too busy to hear?"

Maybe he's asking if there are any mountains in our lives that we need help in moving today—mountains of disappointment, heartache or fear. Sometimes these mountains can loom so large before us that we are no longer able to see Jesus. Yet it's here, while sitting in the shadow of our dark, cold mountain, that we can turn to Mark 11 and read what Jesus said. He gives us his pattern for prayer and sums up all we will ever need to know about it. The pattern is this: pray, ask, believe, forgive.

To pray is a supernatural way of getting to know a supernatural God. When we pray, God makes us his partners! He chooses us to become part of his ministry here on earth.

When Jesus inquires, "May I help you?" he wants us to respond in childlike trust. He wants us to ask. Sometimes he answers in a miraculous way, but most of the time he simply opens our spiritual eyes and shows us what *we* can do to bring about the answer. Then he gives us the ability to do it.

To believe is to give God the right to answer our prayer in the way he sees best. Remember, Jesus never gave a sermon on unanswered prayer because, from his viewpoint, all prayers are answered. When we learn to believe God, we find our attention is no longer on our mountain. It becomes focused instead on Jesus, who alone is worthy of our trust.

When we forgive, we open a channel to God. Jesus asks us to forgive others "so that your Father in heaven may forgive you your sins" (Mark 11:25).

God longs for us to live in the joy of walking by faith—praying, asking, believing, forgiving. When we do, we find we're no longer sitting alone in the shadow of the mountain.

Additional Scripture Readings:
Matthew 6:5–15; Philippians 4:6–7

Go to page 72 for your next devotional reading.

them, "Whose portrait is this? And whose inscription?"

"Caesar's," they replied.

[17]Then Jesus said to them, "Give to Caesar what is Caesar's and to God what is God's."

And they were amazed at him.

Marriage at the Resurrection

[18]Then the Sadducees, who say there is no resurrection, came to him with a question. [19]"Teacher," they said, "Moses wrote for us that if a man's brother dies and leaves a wife but no children, the man must marry the widow and have children for his brother. [20]Now there were seven brothers. The first one married and died without leaving any children. [21]The second one married the widow, but he also died, leaving no child. It was the same with the third. [22]In fact, none of the seven left any children. Last of all, the woman died too. [23]At the resurrection[a] whose wife will she be, since the seven were married to her?"

[24]Jesus replied, "Are you not in error because you do not know the Scriptures or the power of God? [25]When the dead rise, they will neither marry nor be given in marriage; they will be like the angels in heaven. [26]Now about the dead rising— have you not read in the book of Moses, in the account of the bush, how God said to him, 'I am the God of Abraham, the God of Isaac, and the God of Jacob'[b]? [27]He is not the God of the dead, but of the living. You are badly mistaken!"

The Greatest Commandment

[28]One of the teachers of the law came and heard them debating. Noticing that Jesus had given them a good answer, he asked him, "Of all the commandments, which is the most important?"

[29]"The most important one," answered Jesus, "is this: 'Hear, O Israel, the Lord our God, the Lord is one.[c] [30]Love the Lord your God with all your heart and with all your soul and with all your mind and with all your strength.'[d] [31]The second is this: 'Love your neighbor as yourself.'[e] There is no commandment greater than these."

[32]"Well said, teacher," the man replied. "You are right in saying that God is one and there is no other but him. [33]To love

him with all your heart, with all your understanding and with all your strength, and to love your neighbor as yourself is more important than all burnt offerings and sacrifices."

[34]When Jesus saw that he had answered wisely, he said to him, "You are not far from the kingdom of God." And from then on no one dared ask him any more questions.

Whose Son Is the Christ?

[35]While Jesus was teaching in the temple courts, he asked, "How is it that the teachers of the law say that the Christ[f] is the son of David? [36]David himself, speaking by the Holy Spirit, declared:

" 'The Lord said to my Lord:
    "Sit at my right hand
    until I put your enemies
        under your feet." '[g]

[37]David himself calls him 'Lord.' How then can he be his son?"

The large crowd listened to him with delight.

[38]As he taught, Jesus said, "Watch out for the teachers of the law. They like to walk around in flowing robes and be greeted in the marketplaces, [39]and have the most important seats in the synagogues and the places of honor at banquets. [40]They devour widows' houses and for a show make lengthy prayers. Such men will be punished most severely."

The Widow's Offering

[41]Jesus sat down opposite the place where the offerings were put and watched the crowd putting their money into the temple treasury. Many rich people threw in large amounts. [42]But a poor widow came and put in two very small copper coins,[h] worth only a fraction of a penny.[i]

[43]Calling his disciples to him, Jesus said, "I tell you the truth, this poor widow has put more into the treasury than all the others. [44]They all gave out of their wealth; but she, out of her poverty, put in everything—all she had to live on."

Signs of the End of the Age

13 As he was leaving the temple, one of his disciples said to him, "Look, Teacher! What massive stones! What magnificent buildings!"

---

[a]23 Some manuscripts *resurrection, when men rise from the dead,*   [b]26 Exodus 3:6   [c]29 Or *the Lord our God is one Lord*   [d]30 Deut. 6:4,5   [e]31 Lev. 19:18   [f]35 Or *Messiah*   [g]36 Psalm 110:1   [h]42 Greek *two lepta*   [i]42 Greek *kodrantes*

²"Do you see all these great buildings?" replied Jesus. "Not one stone here will be left on another; every one will be thrown down."

³As Jesus was sitting on the Mount of Olives opposite the temple, Peter, James, John and Andrew asked him privately, ⁴"Tell us, when will these things happen? And what will be the sign that they are all about to be fulfilled?"

⁵Jesus said to them: "Watch out that no one deceives you. ⁶Many will come in my name, claiming, 'I am he,' and will deceive many. ⁷When you hear of wars and rumors of wars, do not be alarmed. Such things must happen, but the end is still to come. ⁸Nation will rise against nation, and kingdom against kingdom. There will be earthquakes in various places, and famines. These are the beginning of birth pains.

⁹"You must be on your guard. You will be handed over to the local councils and flogged in the synagogues. On account of me you will stand before governors and kings as witnesses to them. ¹⁰And the gospel must first be preached to all nations. ¹¹Whenever you are arrested and brought to trial, do not worry beforehand about what to say. Just say whatever is given you at the time, for it is not you speaking, but the Holy Spirit.

¹²"Brother will betray brother to death, and a father his child. Children will rebel against their parents and have them put to death. ¹³All men will hate you because of me, but he who stands firm to the end will be saved.

¹⁴"When you see 'the abomination that causes desolation'ᵃ standing where itᵇ does not belong—let the reader understand—then let those who are in Judea flee to the mountains. ¹⁵Let no one on the roof of his house go down or enter the house to take anything out. ¹⁶Let no one in the field go back to get his cloak. ¹⁷How dreadful it will be in those days for pregnant women and nursing mothers! ¹⁸Pray that this will not take place in winter, ¹⁹because those will be days of distress unequaled from the beginning, when God created the world, until now—and never to be equaled again. ²⁰If the Lord had not cut short those days, no one would survive. But for the sake of the elect, whom he has chosen, he has shortened them. ²¹At that time if anyone says

to you, 'Look, here is the Christᶜ!' or, 'Look, there he is!' do not believe it. ²²For false Christs and false prophets will appear and perform signs and miracles to deceive the elect—if that were possible. ²³So be on your guard; I have told you everything ahead of time.

²⁴"But in those days, following that distress,

" 'the sun will be darkened,
    and the moon will not give its light;
²⁵the stars will fall from the sky,
    and the heavenly bodies will be
        shaken.'ᵈ

²⁶"At that time men will see the Son of Man coming in clouds with great power and glory. ²⁷And he will send his angels and gather his elect from the four winds, from the ends of the earth to the ends of the heavens.

²⁸"Now learn this lesson from the fig tree: As soon as its twigs get tender and its leaves come out, you know that summer is near. ²⁹Even so, when you see these things happening, you know that it is near, right at the door. ³⁰I tell you the truth, this generationᵉ will certainly not pass away until all these things have happened. ³¹Heaven and earth will pass away, but my words will never pass away.

The Day and Hour Unknown

³²"No one knows about that day or hour, not even the angels in heaven, nor the Son, but only the Father. ³³Be on guard! Be alert!ᶠ You do not know when that time will come. ³⁴It's like a man going away: He leaves his house and puts his servants in charge, each with his assigned task, and tells the one at the door to keep watch.

³⁵"Therefore keep watch because you do not know when the owner of the house will come back—whether in the evening, or at midnight, or when the rooster crows, or at dawn. ³⁶If he comes suddenly, do not let him find you sleeping. ³⁷What I say to you, I say to everyone: 'Watch!' "

Jesus Anointed at Bethany

14 Now the Passover and the Feast of Unleavened Bread were only two days away, and the chief priests and the teachers of the law were looking for some sly way to arrest Jesus and kill him. ²"But

---

ᵃ14 Daniel 9:27; 11:31; 12:11   ᵇ14 Or he; also in verse 29   ᶜ21 Or Messiah   ᵈ25 Isaiah 13:10; 34:4   ᵉ30 Or race   ᶠ33 Some manuscripts alert and pray not during the Feast," they said, "or the people may riot."

³While he was in Bethany, reclining at the table in the home of a man known as Simon the Leper, a woman came with an alabaster jar of very expensive perfume, made of pure nard. She broke the jar and poured the perfume on his head.

⁴Some of those present were saying indignantly to one another, "Why this waste of perfume? ⁵It could have been sold for more than a year's wages^a and the money given to the poor." And they rebuked her harshly.

⁶"Leave her alone," said Jesus. "Why are you bothering her? She has done a beautiful thing to me. ⁷The poor you will always have with you, and you can help them any time you want. But you will not always have me. ⁸She did what she could. She poured perfume on my body beforehand to prepare for my burial. ⁹I tell you the truth, wherever the gospel is preached throughout the world, what she has done will also be told, in memory of her."

¹⁰Then Judas Iscariot, one of the Twelve, went to the chief priests to betray Jesus to them. ¹¹They were delighted to hear this and promised to give him money. So he watched for an opportunity to hand him over.

The Lord's Supper

¹²On the first day of the Feast of Unleavened Bread, when it was customary to sacrifice the Passover lamb, Jesus' disciples asked him, "Where do you want us to go and make preparations for you to eat the Passover?"

¹³So he sent two of his disciples, telling them, "Go into the city, and a man carrying a jar of water will meet you. Follow him. ¹⁴Say to the owner of the house he enters, 'The Teacher asks: Where is my guest room, where I may eat the Passover with my disciples?' ¹⁵He will show you a large upper room, furnished and ready. Make preparations for us there."

¹⁶The disciples left, went into the city and found things just as Jesus had told them. So they prepared the Passover.

¹⁷When evening came, Jesus arrived with the Twelve. ¹⁸While they were reclining at the table eating, he said, "I tell you the truth, one of you will betray me—one who is eating with me."

¹⁹They were saddened, and one by one they said to him, "Surely not I?"

²⁰"It is one of the Twelve," he replied, "one who dips bread into the bowl with me. ²¹The Son of Man will go just as it is written about him. But woe to that man who betrays the Son of Man! It would be better for him if he had not been born."

²²While they were eating, Jesus took bread, gave thanks and broke it, and gave it to his disciples, saying, "Take it; this is my body."

²³Then he took the cup, gave thanks and offered it to them, and they all drank from it.

²⁴"This is my blood of the^b covenant, which is poured out for many," he said to them. ²⁵"I tell you the truth, I will not drink again of the fruit of the vine until that day when I drink it anew in the kingdom of God."

²⁶When they had sung a hymn, they went out to the Mount of Olives.

Jesus Predicts Peter's Denial

²⁷"You will all fall away," Jesus told them, "for it is written:

" 'I will strike the shepherd,
    and the sheep will be scattered.'^c

²⁸But after I have risen, I will go ahead of you into Galilee."

²⁹Peter declared, "Even if all fall away, I will not."

³⁰"I tell you the truth," Jesus answered, "today—yes, tonight—before the rooster crows twice^d you yourself will disown me three times."

³¹But Peter insisted emphatically, "Even if I have to die with you, I will never disown you." And all the others said the same.

Gethsemane

³²They went to a place called Gethsemane, and Jesus said to his disciples, "Sit here while I pray." ³³He took Peter, James and John along with him, and he began to be deeply distressed and troubled. ³⁴"My soul is overwhelmed with sorrow to the point of death," he said to them. "Stay here and keep watch."

³⁵Going a little farther, he fell to the ground and prayed that if possible the hour might pass from him. ³⁶"Abba,^e Father," he said, "everything is possible for

*a5 Greek than three hundred denarii   b24 Some manuscripts the new   c27 Zech. 13:7   d30 Some early manuscripts do not have twice.   e36 Aramaic for Father

you. Take this cup from me. Yet not what I will, but what you will."

37Then he returned to his disciples and found them sleeping. "Simon," he said to Peter, "are you asleep? Could you not keep watch for one hour? 38Watch and pray so that you will not fall into temptation. The spirit is willing, but the body is weak."

39Once more he went away and prayed the same thing. 40When he came back, he again found them sleeping, because their eyes were heavy. They did not know what to say to him.

41Returning the third time, he said to them, "Are you still sleeping and resting? Enough! The hour has come. Look, the Son of Man is betrayed into the hands of sinners. 42Rise! Let us go! Here comes my betrayer!"

Jesus Arrested

43Just as he was speaking, Judas, one of the Twelve, appeared. With him was a crowd armed with swords and clubs, sent from the chief priests, the teachers of the law, and the elders.

44Now the betrayer had arranged a signal with them: "The one I kiss is the man; arrest him and lead him away under guard." 45Going at once to Jesus, Judas said, "Rabbi!" and kissed him. 46The men seized Jesus and arrested him. 47Then one of those standing near drew his sword and struck the servant of the high priest, cutting off his ear.

48"Am I leading a rebellion," said Jesus, "that you have come out with swords and clubs to capture me? 49Every day I was with you, teaching in the temple courts, and you did not arrest me. But the Scriptures must be fulfilled." 50Then everyone deserted him and fled.

51A young man, wearing nothing but a linen garment, was following Jesus. When they seized him, 52he fled naked, leaving his garment behind.

Before the Sanhedrin

53They took Jesus to the high priest, and all the chief priests, elders and teachers of the law came together. 54Peter followed him at a distance, right into the courtyard of the high priest. There he sat with the guards and warmed himself at the fire.

55The chief priests and the whole San-

hedrin were looking for evidence against Jesus so that they could put him to death, but they did not find any. 56Many testified falsely against him, but their statements did not agree.

57Then some stood up and gave this false testimony against him: 58"We heard him say, 'I will destroy this man-made temple and in three days will build another, not made by man.' " 59Yet even then their testimony did not agree.

60Then the high priest stood up before them and asked Jesus, "Are you not going to answer? What is this testimony that these men are bringing against you?" 61But Jesus remained silent and gave no answer.

Again the high priest asked him, "Are you the Christ,a the Son of the Blessed One?"

62"I am," said Jesus. "And you will see the Son of Man sitting at the right hand of the Mighty One and coming on the clouds of heaven."

63The high priest tore his clothes. "Why do we need any more witnesses?" he asked. 64"You have heard the blasphemy. What do you think?"

They all condemned him as worthy of death. 65Then some began to spit at him; they blindfolded him, struck him with their fists, and said, "Prophesy!" And the guards took him and beat him.

Peter Disowns Jesus

66While Peter was below in the courtyard, one of the servant girls of the high priest came by. 67When she saw Peter warming himself, she looked closely at him.

"You also were with that Nazarene, Jesus," she said.

68But he denied it. "I don't know or understand what you're talking about," he said, and went out into the entryway.b

69When the servant girl saw him there, she said again to those standing around, "This fellow is one of them." 70Again he denied it.

After a little while, those standing near said to Peter, "Surely you are one of them, for you are a Galilean."

71He began to call down curses on himself, and he swore to them, "I don't know this man you're talking about."

72Immediately the rooster crowed the second time.c Then Peter remembered

---

a61 Or Messiah   b68 Some early manuscripts entryway and the rooster crowed   c72 Some early manuscripts do not have the second time.

the word Jesus had spoken to him: "Before the rooster crows twice [a] you will disown me three times." And he broke down and wept.

Jesus Before Pilate

15 Very early in the morning, the chief priests, with the elders, the teachers of the law and the whole Sanhedrin, reached a decision. They bound Jesus, led him away and handed him over to Pilate.

[2] "Are you the king of the Jews?" asked Pilate.

"Yes, it is as you say," Jesus replied.
[3] The chief priests accused him of many things. [4] So again Pilate asked him, "Aren't you going to answer? See how many things they are accusing you of."
[5] But Jesus still made no reply, and Pilate was amazed.

[6] Now it was the custom at the Feast to release a prisoner whom the people requested. [7] A man called Barabbas was in prison with the insurrectionists who had committed murder in the uprising. [8] The crowd came up and asked Pilate to do for them what he usually did.
[9] "Do you want me to release to you the king of the Jews?" asked Pilate, [10] knowing it was out of envy that the chief priests had handed Jesus over to him. [11] But the chief priests stirred up the crowd to have Pilate release Barabbas instead.

[12] "What shall I do, then, with the one you call the king of the Jews?" Pilate asked them.

[13] "Crucify him!" they shouted.

[14] "Why? What crime has he committed?" asked Pilate.

But they shouted all the louder, "Crucify him!"

[15] Wanting to satisfy the crowd, Pilate released Barabbas to them. He had Jesus flogged, and handed him over to be crucified.

The Soldiers Mock Jesus

[16] The soldiers led Jesus away into the palace (that is, the Praetorium) and called together the whole company of soldiers. [17] They put a purple robe on him, then twisted together a crown of thorns and set it on him. [18] And they began to call out to him, "Hail, king of the Jews!"

[19] Again and again they struck him on the head with a staff and spit on him. Falling on their knees, they paid homage to him. [20] And when they had mocked him, they took off the purple robe and put his own clothes on him. Then they led him out to crucify him.

The Crucifixion

[21] A certain man from Cyrene, Simon, the father of Alexander and Rufus, was passing by on his way in from the country, and they forced him to carry the cross. [22] They brought Jesus to the place called Golgotha (which means The Place of the Skull). [23] Then they offered him wine mixed with myrrh, but he did not take it. [24] And they crucified him. Dividing up his clothes, they cast lots to see what each would get.

[25] It was the third hour when they crucified him. [26] The written notice of the charge against him read: THE KING OF THE JEWS. [27] They crucified two robbers with him, one on his right and one on his left. [b] [29] Those who passed by hurled insults at him, shaking their heads and saying, "So! You who are going to destroy the temple and build it in three days, [30] come down from the cross and save yourself!"
[31] In the same way the chief priests and the teachers of the law mocked him among themselves. "He saved others," they said, "but he can't save himself! [32] Let this Christ, [c] this King of Israel, come down now from the cross, that we may see and believe." Those crucified with him also heaped insults on him.

The Death of Jesus

[33] At the sixth hour darkness came over the whole land until the ninth hour. [34] And at the ninth hour Jesus cried out in a loud voice, *"Eloi, Eloi, lama sabachthani?"* —which means, "My God, my God, why have you forsaken me?" [d]
[35] When some of those standing near heard this, they said, "Listen, he's calling Elijah."
[36] One man ran, filled a sponge with wine vinegar, put it on a stick, and offered it to Jesus to drink. "Now leave him alone. Let's see if Elijah comes to take him down," he said.
[37] With a loud cry, Jesus breathed his last.

---

a72 Some early manuscripts do not have twice.   *b27 Some manuscripts left, 28and the scripture was fulfilled which says, "He was counted with the lawless ones" (Isaiah 53:12)*   *c32 Or Messiah*   *d34 Psalm 22:1*

³⁸The curtain of the temple was torn in two from top to bottom. ³⁹And when the centurion, who stood there in front of Jesus, heard his cry and*a* saw how he died, he said, "Surely this man was the Son*b* of God!"

⁴⁰Some women were watching from a distance. Among them were Mary Magdalene, Mary the mother of James the younger and of Joses, and Salome. ⁴¹In Galilee these women had followed him and cared for his needs. Many other women who had come up with him to Jerusalem were also there.

The Burial of Jesus

⁴²It was Preparation Day (that is, the day before the Sabbath). So as evening approached, ⁴³Joseph of Arimathea, a prominent member of the Council, who was himself waiting for the kingdom of God, went boldly to Pilate and asked for Jesus' body. ⁴⁴Pilate was surprised to hear that he was already dead. Summoning the centurion, he asked him if Jesus had already died. ⁴⁵When he learned from the centurion that it was so, he gave the body to Joseph. ⁴⁶So Joseph bought some linen cloth, took down the body, wrapped it in the linen, and placed it in a tomb cut out of rock. Then he rolled a stone against the entrance of the tomb. ⁴⁷Mary Magdalene and Mary the mother of Joses saw where he was laid.

The Resurrection

16 When the Sabbath was over, Mary Magdalene, Mary the mother of James, and Salome bought spices so that they might go to anoint Jesus' body. ²Very early on the first day of the week, just after sunrise, they were on their way to the tomb ³and they asked each other,

a39 Some manuscripts do not have heard his cry and   *b39 Or a son*

┌──────────────────┤ T H U R S D A Y ├──────────────────┐

VERSE FOR THE DAY: *AUTHOR:*   *PASSAGE FOR THE DAY:*
Mark 15:18   *Anne Ortlund*   *Mark 15:16–37*

Ponderings of the Praetorium

O CHRIST, the crown of death was on Thy brow,
And in Thine eyes deep mystery and pain;
The Kingdom seemed forgotten then—but now,
Lord, take Thy crown and reign!

O Christ, with what derision did they bow
And mock Thee, stripped of robings and of
throne;
And hatred seemed to win the day—but now,
Lord, reign, and reign alone!

O Jesus, when I think of Peter's vow,
I wonder: might I curse Thee and depart?
Hold fast my consecration here and now;
Lord, reign within my heart!

Additional Scripture Readings: *Go to page 76 for your next*
Philippians 2:8–11; Hebrews 12:2–3   *devotional reading.*

"Who will roll the stone away from the entrance of the tomb?"

[4]But when they looked up, they saw that the stone, which was very large, had been rolled away. [5]As they entered the tomb, they saw a young man dressed in a white robe sitting on the right side, and they were alarmed.

[6]"Don't be alarmed," he said. "You are looking for Jesus the Nazarene, who was crucified. He has risen! He is not here. See the place where they laid him. [7]But go, tell his disciples and Peter, 'He is going ahead of you into Galilee. There you will see him, just as he told you.' "

[8]Trembling and bewildered, the women went out and fled from the tomb. They said nothing to anyone, because they were afraid.

[The earliest manuscripts and some other ancient witnesses do not have Mark 16:9–20.]

[9]When Jesus rose early on the first day of the week, he appeared first to Mary Magdalene, out of whom he had driven seven demons. [10]She went and told those who had been with him and who were mourning and weeping. [11]When they heard that Jesus was alive and that she had seen him, they did not believe it.

[12]Afterward Jesus appeared in a different form to two of them while they were walking in the country. [13]These returned and reported it to the rest; but they did not believe them either.

[14]Later Jesus appeared to the Eleven as they were eating; he rebuked them for their lack of faith and their stubborn refusal to believe those who had seen him after he had risen.

[15]He said to them, "Go into all the world and preach the good news to all creation. [16]Whoever believes and is baptized will be saved, but whoever does not believe will be condemned. [17]And these signs will accompany those who believe: In my name they will drive out demons; they will speak in new tongues; [18]they will pick up snakes with their hands; and when they drink deadly poison, it will not hurt them at all; they will place their hands on sick people, and they will get well."

[19]After the Lord Jesus had spoken to them, he was taken up into heaven and he sat at the right hand of God. [20]Then the disciples went out and preached everywhere, and the Lord worked with them and confirmed his word by the signs that accompanied it.

*L*UKE *writes this gospel to present Jesus as a Savior for the whole human race. The stories emphasize how kind and loving Jesus is to those despised by society (such as tax collectors, Samaritans, the poor, and women). He stresses the importance of prayer in Jesus' life. As you read this book, be sure that you have repented of your sins and have claimed Jesus as your own personal Savior. Ask yourself whether you show the same sort of compassion to others that Jesus showed.*

LUKE

Introduction

1 Many have undertaken to draw up an account of the things that have been fulfilled*a* among us, ²just as they were handed down to us by those who from the first were eyewitnesses and servants of the word. ³Therefore, since I myself have carefully investigated everything from the beginning, it seemed good also to me to write an orderly account for you, most excellent Theophilus, ⁴so that you may know the certainty of the things you have been taught.

The Birth of John the Baptist Foretold

⁵In the time of Herod king of Judea there was a priest named Zechariah, who belonged to the priestly division of Abijah; his wife Elizabeth was also a descendant of Aaron. ⁶Both of them were upright in the sight of God, observing all the Lord's commandments and regulations blamelessly. ⁷But they had no children, because Elizabeth was barren; and they were both well along in years.

⁸Once when Zechariah's division was

on duty and he was serving as priest before God, ⁹he was chosen by lot, according to the custom of the priesthood, to go into the temple of the Lord and burn incense. ¹⁰And when the time for the burning of incense came, all the assembled worshipers were praying outside.

¹¹Then an angel of the Lord appeared to him, standing at the right side of the altar of incense. ¹²When Zechariah saw him, he was startled and was gripped with fear. ¹³But the angel said to him: "Do not be afraid, Zechariah; your prayer has been heard. Your wife Elizabeth will bear you a son, and you are to give him the name John. ¹⁴He will be a joy and delight to you, and many will rejoice because of his birth, ¹⁵for he will be great in the sight of the Lord. He is never to take wine or other fermented drink, and he will be filled with the Holy Spirit even from birth.ᵃ ¹⁶Many of the people of Israel will he bring back to the Lord their God. ¹⁷And he will go on before the Lord, in the spirit and power of Elijah, to turn the hearts of the fathers to their children and the disobedient to the wisdom of the righteous —to make ready a people prepared for the Lord."

¹⁸Zechariah asked the angel, "How can I be sure of this? I am an old man and my wife is well along in years."

¹⁹The angel answered, "I am Gabriel. I stand in the presence of God, and I have been sent to speak to you and to tell you this good news. ²⁰And now you will be silent and not able to speak until the day this happens, because you did not believe my words, which will come true at their proper time."

²¹Meanwhile, the people were waiting for Zechariah and wondering why he stayed so long in the temple. ²²When he came out, he could not speak to them. They realized he had seen a vision in the temple, for he kept making signs to them but remained unable to speak.

²³When his time of service was completed, he returned home. ²⁴After this his wife Elizabeth became pregnant and for five months remained in seclusion. ²⁵"The Lord has done this for me," she said. "In these days he has shown his favor and taken away my disgrace among the people."

The Birth of Jesus Foretold

²⁶In the sixth month, God sent the angel Gabriel to Nazareth, a town in Galilee, ²⁷to a virgin pledged to be married to a man named Joseph, a descendant of David. The virgin's name was Mary. ²⁸The angel went to her and said, "Greetings, you who are highly favored! The Lord is with you."

²⁹Mary was greatly troubled at his words and wondered what kind of greeting this might be. ³⁰But the angel said to her, "Do not be afraid, Mary, you have found favor with God. ³¹You will be with child and give birth to a son, and you are to give him the name Jesus. ³²He will be great and will be called the Son of the Most High. The Lord God will give him the throne of his father David, ³³and he will reign over the house of Jacob forever; his kingdom will never end."

³⁴"How will this be," Mary asked the angel, "since I am a virgin?"

³⁵The angel answered, "The Holy Spirit will come upon you, and the power of the Most High will overshadow you. So the holy one to be born will be calledᵇ the Son of God. ³⁶Even Elizabeth your relative is going to have a child in her old age, and she who was said to be barren is in her sixth month. ³⁷For nothing is impossible with God."

³⁸"I am the Lord's servant," Mary answered. "May it be to me as you have said." Then the angel left her.

Mary Visits Elizabeth

³⁹At that time Mary got ready and hurried to a town in the hill country of Judea, ⁴⁰where she entered Zechariah's home and greeted Elizabeth. ⁴¹When Elizabeth heard Mary's greeting, the baby leaped in her womb, and Elizabeth was filled with the Holy Spirit. ⁴²In a loud voice she exclaimed: "Blessed are you among women, and blessed is the child you will bear! ⁴³But why am I so favored, that the mother of my Lord should come to me? ⁴⁴As soon as the sound of your greeting reached my ears, the baby in my womb leaped for joy. ⁴⁵Blessed is she who has believed that what the Lord has said to her will be accomplished!"

Mary's Song

⁴⁶And Mary said:

"My soul glorifies the Lord
⁴⁷   and my spirit rejoices in God my Savior,

ᵃ15 Or from his mother's womb   ᵇ35 Or So the child to be born will be called holy,

FRIDAY

VERSE FOR THE DAY:
Luke 1:46–47

AUTHOR:
Anne Ortlund

PASSAGE FOR THE DAY:
Luke 1:26–38

Incarnation

"THE Lord is in His holy house"—
Oh, grace beyond describing,
That Christ in me should please to dwell—
Immanuel residing!
"My soul doth magnify the Lord,"
I sing with lowly Mary,
That God should choose to enter in
This
    humble sanctuary!

Not now in little Bethlehem,
As in the tender story;
Not now upon a mercy seat,
The bright *Shekinah* glory,
But in the body of His saint
He maketh His residing,
Both He in me and I in Him
In
    fellowship abiding.

Within my heart a burning bush,
Within, a mountain smoking;
This flesh of mine a temple veil,
The wondrous Presence cloaking;
Within this broken earthenware
A high and holy treasure:
Oh, mystery of mysteries!
  Oh, grace
        beyond all measure!

"The Lord is in His Holy house"—
Mysterious habitation!
I feel His presence here within
And offer my oblation.
Keep burning, incense of my soul!
Keep cleansing me, O Laver!
I want to serve and praise my God
  Forever
        and forever!

Additional Scripture Readings:
John 14:23–27; 2 Corinthians 1:21–22

*Go to page 78 for your next
devotional reading.*

⁴⁸for he has been mindful
    of the humble state of his servant.
From now on all generations will call
    me blessed,
⁴⁹ for the Mighty One has done great
    things for me—
    holy is his name.
⁵⁰His mercy extends to those who fear
    him,
    from generation to generation.
⁵¹He has performed mighty deeds with
    his arm;
    he has scattered those who are
    proud in their inmost thoughts.
⁵²He has brought down rulers from
    their thrones
    but has lifted up the humble.
⁵³He has filled the hungry with good
    things
    but has sent the rich away empty.
⁵⁴He has helped his servant Israel,
    remembering to be merciful
⁵⁵to Abraham and his descendants
    forever,
    even as he said to our fathers."

⁵⁶Mary stayed with Elizabeth for about
three months and then returned home.

The Birth of John the Baptist

⁵⁷When it was time for Elizabeth to
have her baby, she gave birth to a son.
⁵⁸Her neighbors and relatives heard that
the Lord had shown her great mercy, and
they shared her joy.
⁵⁹On the eighth day they came to circumcise the child, and they were going to
name him after his father Zechariah,
⁶⁰but his mother spoke up and said, "No!
He is to be called John."
⁶¹They said to her, "There is no one
among your relatives who has that
name."
⁶²Then they made signs to his father, to
find out what he would like to name the
child. ⁶³He asked for a writing tablet, and
to everyone's astonishment he wrote,
"His name is John." ⁶⁴Immediately his
mouth was opened and his tongue was
loosed, and he began to speak, praising
God. ⁶⁵The neighbors were all filled with
awe, and throughout the hill country of
Judea people were talking about all these
things. ⁶⁶Everyone who heard this wondered about it, asking, "What then is this
child going to be?" For the Lord's hand
was with him.

Zechariah's Song

⁶⁷His father Zechariah was filled with
the Holy Spirit and prophesied:

⁶⁸"Praise be to the Lord, the God of
    Israel,
    because he has come and has
    redeemed his people.
⁶⁹He has raised up a horn*ᵃ* of salvation
    for us
    in the house of his servant David
⁷⁰(as he said through his holy prophets
    of long ago),
⁷¹salvation from our enemies
    and from the hand of all who hate
    us—
⁷²to show mercy to our fathers
    and to remember his holy covenant,
⁷³ the oath he swore to our father
    Abraham:
⁷⁴to rescue us from the hand of our
    enemies,
    and to enable us to serve him
    without fear
⁷⁵ in holiness and righteousness
    before him all our days.

⁷⁶And you, my child, will be called a
    prophet of the Most High;
    for you will go on before the Lord
    to prepare the way for him,
⁷⁷to give his people the knowledge of
    salvation
    through the forgiveness of their
    sins,
⁷⁸because of the tender mercy of our
    God,
    by which the rising sun will come
    to us from heaven
⁷⁹to shine on those living in darkness
    and in the shadow of death,
    to guide our feet into the path of
    peace."

⁸⁰And the child grew and became
strong in spirit; and he lived in the desert
until he appeared publicly to Israel.

The Birth of Jesus

2 In those days Caesar Augustus issued
a decree that a census should be tak-
en of the entire Roman world. ²(This was
the first census that took place while Qui-
rinius was governor of Syria.) ³And every
one went to his own town to register.

⁴So Joseph also went up from the town
of Nazareth in Galilee to Judea, to Bethlehem the town of David, because he be-

---

ᵃ69 Horn here symbolizes strength.

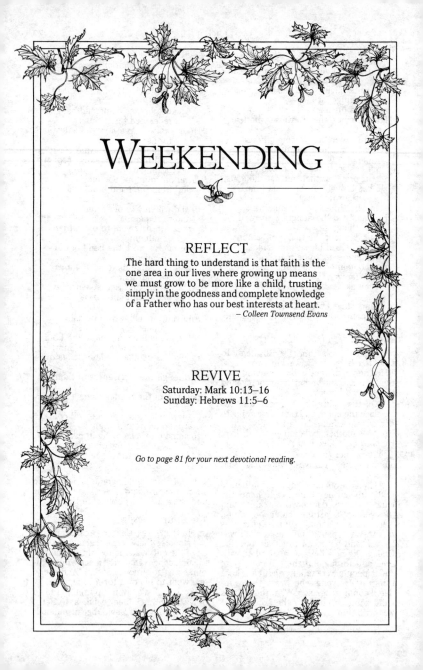

WEEKENDING

REFLECT

The hard thing to understand is that faith is the
one area in our lives where growing up means
we must grow to be more like a child, trusting
simply in the goodness and complete knowledge
of a Father who has our best interests at heart.

– Colleen Townsend Evans

REVIVE

Saturday: Mark 10:13–16
Sunday: Hebrews 11:5–6

Go to page 81 for your next devotional reading.

longed to the house and line of David. [5]He went there to register with Mary, who was pledged to be married to him and was expecting a child. [6]While they were there, the time came for the baby to be born, [7]and she gave birth to her firstborn, a son. She wrapped him in cloths and placed him in a manger, because there was no room for them in the inn.

The Shepherds and the Angels

[8]And there were shepherds living out in the fields nearby, keeping watch over their flocks at night. [9]An angel of the Lord appeared to them, and the glory of the Lord shone around them, and they were terrified. [10]But the angel said to them, "Do not be afraid. I bring you good news of great joy that will be for all the people. [11]Today in the town of David a Savior has been born to you; he is Christ[a] the Lord. [12]This will be a sign to you: You will find a baby wrapped in cloths and lying in a manger."

[13]Suddenly a great company of the heavenly host appeared with the angel, praising God and saying,

[14]"Glory to God in the highest,
    and on earth peace to men on
        whom his favor rests."

[15]When the angels had left them and gone into heaven, the shepherds said to one another, "Let's go to Bethlehem and see this thing that has happened, which the Lord has told us about." [16]So they hurried off and found Mary and Joseph, and the baby, who was lying in the manger. [17]When they had seen him, they spread the word concerning what had been told them about this child, [18]and all who heard it were amazed at what the shepherds said to them. [19]But Mary treasured up all these things and pondered them in her heart. [20]The shepherds returned, glorifying and praising God for all the things they had heard and seen, which were just as they had been told.

Jesus Presented in the Temple

[21]On the eighth day, when it was time to circumcise him, he was named Jesus, the name the angel had given him before he had been conceived.

[22]When the time of their purification according to the Law of Moses had been completed, Joseph and Mary took him to Jerusalem to present him to the Lord [23](as it is written in the Law of the Lord, "Every firstborn male is to be consecrated to the Lord"[b]), [24]and to offer a sacrifice in keeping with what is said in the Law of the Lord: "a pair of doves or two young pigeons."[c]

[25]Now there was a man in Jerusalem called Simeon, who was righteous and devout. He was waiting for the consolation of Israel, and the Holy Spirit was upon him. [26]It had been revealed to him by the Holy Spirit that he would not die before he had seen the Lord's Christ. [27]Moved by the Spirit, he went into the temple courts. When the parents brought in the child Jesus to do for him what the custom of the Law required, [28]Simeon took him in his arms and praised God, saying:

[29]"Sovereign Lord, as you have
        promised,
    you now dismiss[d] your servant in
        peace.
[30]For my eyes have seen your salvation,
[31]   which you have prepared in the
        sight of all people,
[32]a light for revelation to the Gentiles
    and for glory to your people Israel."

[33]The child's father and mother marveled at what was said about him. [34]Then Simeon blessed them and said to Mary, his mother: "This child is destined to cause the falling and rising of many in Israel, and to be a sign that will be spoken against, [35]so that the thoughts of many hearts will be revealed. And a sword will pierce your own soul too."

[36]There was also a prophetess, Anna, the daughter of Phanuel, of the tribe of Asher. She was very old; she had lived with her husband seven years after her marriage, [37]and then was a widow until she was eighty-four.[e] She never left the temple but worshiped night and day, fasting and praying. [38]Coming up to them at that very moment, she gave thanks to God and spoke about the child to all who were looking forward to the redemption of Jerusalem.

[39]When Joseph and Mary had done everything required by the Law of the Lord, they returned to Galilee to their own town of Nazareth. [40]And the child grew

---

[a]11 Or Messiah. "The Christ" (Greek) and "the Messiah" (Hebrew) both mean "the Anointed One"; also in verse 26.   [b]23 Exodus 13:2,12   [c]24 Lev. 12:8   [d]29 Or promised, / now dismiss   [e]37 Or widow for eighty-four years

and became strong; he was filled with wisdom, and the grace of God was upon him.

The Boy Jesus at the Temple

⁴¹Every year his parents went to Jerusalem for the Feast of the Passover. ⁴²When he was twelve years old, they went up to the Feast, according to the custom. ⁴³After the Feast was over, while his parents were returning home, the boy Jesus stayed behind in Jerusalem, but they were unaware of it. ⁴⁴Thinking he was in their company, they traveled on for a day. Then they began looking for him among their relatives and friends. ⁴⁵When they did not find him, they went back to Jerusalem to look for him. ⁴⁶After three days they found him in the temple courts, sitting among the teachers, listening to them and asking them questions. ⁴⁷Everyone who heard him was amazed at his understanding and his answers. ⁴⁸When his parents saw him, they were astonished. His mother said to him, "Son, why have you treated us like this? Your father and I have been anxiously searching for you."

⁴⁹"Why were you searching for me?" he asked. "Didn't you know I had to be in my Father's house?" ⁵⁰But they did not understand what he was saying to them.

⁵¹Then he went down to Nazareth with them and was obedient to them. But his mother treasured all these things in her heart. ⁵²And Jesus grew in wisdom and stature, and in favor with God and men.

John the Baptist Prepares the Way

3 In the fifteenth year of the reign of Tiberius Caesar—when Pontius Pilate was governor of Judea, Herod tetrarch of Galilee, his brother Philip tetrarch of Iturea and Traconitis, and Lysanias tetrarch of Abilene— ²during the high priesthood of Annas and Caiaphas, the word of God came to John son of Zechariah in the desert. ³He went into all the country around the Jordan, preaching a baptism of repentance for the forgiveness of sins. ⁴As is written in the book of the words of Isaiah the prophet:

"A voice of one calling in the desert,
'Prepare the way for the Lord,
    make straight paths for him.
⁵Every valley shall be filled in,
    every mountain and hill made low.

The crooked roads shall become
        straight,
    the rough ways smooth.
⁶And all mankind will see God's
        salvation.' "*a*

⁷John said to the crowds coming out to be baptized by him, "You brood of vipers! Who warned you to flee from the coming wrath? ⁸Produce fruit in keeping with repentance. And do not begin to say to yourselves, 'We have Abraham as our father.' For I tell you that out of these stones God can raise up children for Abraham. ⁹The ax is already at the root of the trees, and every tree that does not produce good fruit will be cut down and thrown into the fire."

¹⁰"What should we do then?" the crowd asked.

¹¹John answered, "The man with two tunics should share with him who has none, and the one who has food should do the same."

¹²Tax collectors also came to be baptized. "Teacher," they asked, "what should we do?"

¹³"Don't collect any more than you are required to," he told them.

¹⁴Then some soldiers asked him, "And what should we do?"

He replied, "Don't extort money and don't accuse people falsely—be content with your pay."

¹⁵The people were waiting expectantly and were all wondering in their hearts if John might possibly be the Christ.*b* ¹⁶John answered them all, "I baptize you with*c* water. But one more powerful than I will come, the thongs of whose sandals I am not worthy to untie. He will baptize you with the Holy Spirit and with fire. ¹⁷His winnowing fork is in his hand to clear his threshing floor and to gather the wheat into his barn, but he will burn up the chaff with unquenchable fire." ¹⁸And with many other words John exhorted the people and preached the good news to them.

¹⁹But when John rebuked Herod the tetrarch because of Herodias, his brother's wife, and all the other evil things he had done, ²⁰Herod added this to them all: He locked John up in prison.

The Baptism and Genealogy of Jesus

²¹When all the people were being baptized, Jesus was baptized too. And as he

---

a6 Isaiah 40:3-5   *b15* Or *Messiah*   *c16* Or *in*

VERSE FOR THE DAY:	AUTHOR:	PASSAGE FOR THE DAY:
Luke 2:52	Rosemary Jensen	Luke 2:41–52

Growing in Wisdom

IN Luke 2:52 we learn that "Jesus grew in wisdom and stature, and in favor with God and men." It is not difficult to understand how Jesus grew in stature—he just got taller! But how could the Son of God grow in wisdom? Did he not already have all wisdom? Did he lack anything? Was he not perfect? Yes, he was filled with wisdom—as much wisdom as a child without life experience can have.

It may help to remember that a few ounces of milk can fill an infant boy, but it would take a few quarts to fill a teenage boy. The difference is that the teenager has increased his capacity for milk. As Jesus grew physically, he also grew in his capacity for wisdom as he learned from his experiences. What is our individual capacity for wisdom? Could we increase that capacity?

Wisdom comes when we examine the experiences God gives us and discern what we have (or should have) learned from them. Nothing that has happened to us should be wasted (Romans 8:28). Because it is sometimes painful, often we do not take the time or effort to discover the reason for the "gift" of our personal experiences. When we do not learn as we should, we stop growing until we learn those same lessons through another experience tailor-made by God to make us mature (James 1:2–4). Most often we gain insight into our experiences only after earnest, persistent prayer. Psalm 43 is a wonderful model of persistent prayer; it opens up to us a person searching to know what God wants to reveal about a specific experience.

Perhaps we should try writing out what we have learned about God, ourselves and life during and then after an important experience. As we learn these lessons, I think we'll find that we will not need to learn them again in exactly the same way! This increases our individual capacity to learn greater lessons and gain deeper wisdom (Matthew 13:12).

Additional Scripture Readings:
1 Corinthians 13:11–12; James 1:22–25

Go to page 85 for your next devotional reading.

was praying, heaven was opened ²²and the Holy Spirit descended on him in bodily form like a dove. And a voice came from heaven: "You are my Son, whom I love; with you I am well pleased."

²³Now Jesus himself was about thirty years old when he began his ministry. He was the son, so it was thought, of Joseph,

the son of Heli, ²⁴the son of Matthat,
the son of Levi, the son of Melki,
the son of Jannai, the son of Joseph,
²⁵the son of Mattathias, the son of Amos,
the son of Nahum, the son of Esli,
the son of Naggai, ²⁶the son of Maath,
the son of Mattathias, the son of Semein,
the son of Josech, the son of Joda,
²⁷the son of Joanan, the son of Rhesa,
the son of Zerubbabel, the son of Shealtiel,
the son of Neri, ²⁸the son of Melki,
the son of Addi, the son of Cosam,
the son of Elmadam, the son of Er,
²⁹the son of Joshua, the son of Eliezer,
the son of Jorim, the son of Matthat,
the son of Levi, ³⁰the son of Simeon,
the son of Judah, the son of Joseph,
the son of Jonam, the son of Eliakim,
³¹the son of Melea, the son of Menna,
the son of Mattatha, the son of Nathan,
the son of David, ³²the son of Jesse,
the son of Obed, the son of Boaz,
the son of Salmon,ᵃ the son of Nahshon,
³³the son of Amminadab, the son of Ram,ᵇ
the son of Hezron, the son of Perez,
the son of Judah, ³⁴the son of Jacob,
the son of Isaac, the son of Abraham,
the son of Terah, the son of Nahor,
³⁵the son of Serug, the son of Reu,
the son of Peleg, the son of Eber,
the son of Shelah, ³⁶the son of Cainan,
the son of Arphaxad, the son of Shem,
the son of Noah, the son of Lamech,
³⁷the son of Methuselah, the son of Enoch,
the son of Jared, the son of Mahalalel,
the son of Kenan, ³⁸the son of Enosh,

the son of Seth, the son of Adam,
the son of God.

The Temptation of Jesus

4 Jesus, full of the Holy Spirit, returned from the Jordan and was led by the Spirit in the desert, ²where for forty days he was tempted by the devil. He ate nothing during those days, and at the end of them he was hungry.

³The devil said to him, "If you are the Son of God, tell this stone to become bread."

⁴Jesus answered, "It is written: 'Man does not live on bread alone.'ᶜ"

⁵The devil led him up to a high place and showed him in an instant all the kingdoms of the world. ⁶And he said to him, "I will give you all their authority and splendor, for it has been given to me, and I can give it to anyone I want to. ⁷So if you worship me, it will all be yours."

⁸Jesus answered, "It is written: 'Worship the Lord your God and serve him only.'ᵈ"

⁹The devil led him to Jerusalem and had him stand on the highest point of the temple. "If you are the Son of God," he said, "throw yourself down from here. ¹⁰For it is written:

" 'He will command his angels
        concerning you
    to guard you carefully;
¹¹they will lift you up in their hands,
    so that you will not strike your foot
        against a stone.'ᵉ"

¹²Jesus answered, "It says: 'Do not put the Lord your God to the test.'ᶠ"

¹³When the devil had finished all this tempting, he left him until an opportune time.

Jesus Rejected at Nazareth

¹⁴Jesus returned to Galilee in the power of the Spirit, and news about him spread through the whole countryside. ¹⁵He taught in their synagogues, and everyone praised him.

¹⁶He went to Nazareth, where he had been brought up, and on the Sabbath day he went into the synagogue, as was his custom. And he stood up to read. ¹⁷The scroll of the prophet Isaiah was handed to him. Unrolling it, he found the place where it is written:

¹⁸"The Spirit of the Lord is on me,

ᵃ32 Some early manuscripts *Sala*   ᵇ33 Some manuscripts *Amminadab, the son of Admin, the son of Arni*; other manuscripts vary widely.   ᶜ4 Deut. 8:3   ᵈ8 Deut. 6:13   ᵉ11 Psalm 91:11,12
ᶠ12 Deut. 6:16

because he has anointed me
to preach good news to the poor.
He has sent me to proclaim freedom
for the prisoners
and recovery of sight for the blind,
to release the oppressed,
¹⁹ to proclaim the year of the Lord's
favor."[a]

²⁰Then he rolled up the scroll, gave it back to the attendant and sat down. The eyes of everyone in the synagogue were fastened on him, ²¹and he began by saying to them, "Today this scripture is fulfilled in your hearing."

²²All spoke well of him and were amazed at the gracious words that came from his lips. "Isn't this Joseph's son?" they asked.

²³Jesus said to them, "Surely you will quote this proverb to me: 'Physician, heal yourself! Do here in your hometown what we have heard that you did in Capernaum.'"

²⁴"I tell you the truth," he continued, "no prophet is accepted in his hometown. ²⁵I assure you that there were many widows in Israel in Elijah's time, when the sky was shut for three and a half years and there was a severe famine throughout the land. ²⁶Yet Elijah was not sent to any of them, but to a widow in Zarephath in the region of Sidon. ²⁷And there were many in Israel with leprosy[b] in the time of Elisha the prophet, yet not one of them was cleansed—only Naaman the Syrian."

²⁸All the people in the synagogue were furious when they heard this. ²⁹They got up, drove him out of the town, and took him to the brow of the hill on which the town was built, in order to throw him down the cliff. ³⁰But he walked right through the crowd and went on his way.

Jesus Drives Out an Evil Spirit

³¹Then he went down to Capernaum, a town in Galilee, and on the Sabbath began to teach the people. ³²They were amazed at his teaching, because his message had authority.

³³In the synagogue there was a man possessed by a demon, an evil[c] spirit. He cried out at the top of his voice, ³⁴"Ha! What do you want with us, Jesus of Nazareth? Have you come to destroy us? I know who you are—the Holy One of God!"

³⁵"Be quiet!" Jesus said sternly. "Come out of him!" Then the demon threw the man down before them all and came out without injuring him.

³⁶All the people were amazed and said to each other, "What is this teaching? With authority and power he gives orders to evil spirits and they come out!" ³⁷And the news about him spread throughout the surrounding area.

Jesus Heals Many

³⁸Jesus left the synagogue and went to the home of Simon. Now Simon's mother-in-law was suffering from a high fever, and they asked Jesus to help her. ³⁹So he bent over her and rebuked the fever, and it left her. She got up at once and began to wait on them.

⁴⁰When the sun was setting, the people brought to Jesus all who had various kinds of sickness, and laying his hands on each one, he healed them. ⁴¹Moreover, demons came out of many people, shouting, "You are the Son of God!" But he rebuked them and would not allow them to speak, because they knew he was the Christ.[d]

⁴²At daybreak Jesus went out to a solitary place. The people were looking for him and when they came to where he was, they tried to keep him from leaving them. ⁴³But he said, "I must preach the good news of the kingdom of God to the other towns also, because that is why I was sent." ⁴⁴And he kept on preaching in the synagogues of Judea.[e]

The Calling of the First Disciples

5 One day as Jesus was standing by the Lake of Gennesaret,[f] with the people crowding around him and listening to the word of God, ²he saw at the water's edge two boats, left there by the fishermen, who were washing their nets. ³He got into one of the boats, the one belonging to Simon, and asked him to put out a little from shore. Then he sat down and taught the people from the boat.

⁴When he had finished speaking, he said to Simon, "Put out into deep water, and let down[g] the nets for a catch."

⁵Simon answered, "Master, we've worked hard all night and haven't caught anything. But because you say so, I will let down the nets."

---

[a]19 Isaiah 61:1,2   [b]27 The Greek word was used for various diseases affecting the skin—not necessarily leprosy.   [c]33 Greek unclean; also in verse 36   [d]41 Or Messiah   [e]44 Or the land of the Jews; some manuscripts Galilee   [f]1 That is, Sea of Galilee   [g]4 The Greek verb is plural.

⁶When they had done so, they caught such a large number of fish that their nets began to break. ⁷So they signaled their partners in the other boat to come and help them, and they came and filled both boats so full that they began to sink.

⁸When Simon Peter saw this, he fell at Jesus' knees and said, "Go away from me, Lord; I am a sinful man!" ⁹For he and all his companions were astonished at the catch of fish they had taken, ¹⁰and so were James and John, the sons of Zebedee, Simon's partners.

Then Jesus said to Simon, "Don't be afraid; from now on you will catch men." ¹¹So they pulled their boats up on shore, left everything and followed him.

The Man With Leprosy

¹²While Jesus was in one of the towns, a man came along who was covered with leprosy.[a] When he saw Jesus, he fell with his face to the ground and begged him, "Lord, if you are willing, you can make me clean."

¹³Jesus reached out his hand and touched the man. "I am willing," he said. "Be clean!" And immediately the leprosy left him.

¹⁴Then Jesus ordered him, "Don't tell anyone, but go, show yourself to the priest and offer the sacrifices that Moses commanded for your cleansing, as a testimony to them."

¹⁵Yet the news about him spread all the more, so that crowds of people came to hear him and to be healed of their sicknesses. ¹⁶But Jesus often withdrew to lonely places and prayed.

Jesus Heals a Paralytic

¹⁷One day as he was teaching, Pharisees and teachers of the law, who had come from every village of Galilee and from Judea and Jerusalem, were sitting there. And the power of the Lord was present for him to heal the sick. ¹⁸Some men came carrying a paralytic on a mat and tried to take him into the house to lay him before Jesus. ¹⁹When they could not find a way to do this because of the crowd, they went up on the roof and lowered him on his mat through the tiles into the middle of the crowd, right in front of Jesus.

²⁰When Jesus saw their faith, he said, "Friend, your sins are forgiven."

²¹The Pharisees and the teachers of the law began thinking to themselves, "Who is this fellow who speaks blasphemy? Who can forgive sins but God alone?"

²²Jesus knew what they were thinking and asked, "Why are you thinking these things in your hearts? ²³Which is easier: to say, 'Your sins are forgiven,' or to say, 'Get up and walk'? ²⁴But that you may know that the Son of Man has authority on earth to forgive sins. . . ." He said to the paralyzed man, "I tell you, get up, take your mat and go home." ²⁵Immediately he stood up in front of them, took what he had been lying on and went home praising God. ²⁶Everyone was amazed and gave praise to God. They were filled with awe and said, "We have seen remarkable things today."

The Calling of Levi

²⁷After this, Jesus went out and saw a tax collector by the name of Levi sitting at his tax booth. "Follow me," Jesus said to him, ²⁸and Levi got up, left everything and followed him.

²⁹Then Levi held a great banquet for Jesus at his house, and a large crowd of tax collectors and others were eating with them. ³⁰But the Pharisees and the teachers of the law who belonged to their sect complained to his disciples, "Why do you eat and drink with tax collectors and 'sinners'?"

³¹Jesus answered them, "It is not the healthy who need a doctor, but the sick. ³²I have not come to call the righteous, but sinners to repentance."

Jesus Questioned About Fasting

³³They said to him, "John's disciples often fast and pray, and so do the disciples of the Pharisees, but yours go on eating and drinking."

³⁴Jesus answered, "Can you make the guests of the bridegroom fast while he is with them? ³⁵But the time will come when the bridegroom will be taken from them; in those days they will fast."

³⁶He told them this parable: "No one tears a patch from a new garment and sews it on an old one. If he does, he will have torn the new garment, and the patch from the new will not match the old. ³⁷And no one pours new wine into old wineskins. If he does, the new wine will burst the skins, the wine will run out and the wineskins will be ruined. ³⁸No, new wine must be poured into new wineskins.

a12 The Greek word was used for various diseases affecting the skin—not necessarily leprosy.

VERSE FOR THE DAY:	AUTHOR:	PASSAGE FOR THE DAY:
Luke 5:16	Gini Andrews	Luke 5:12–16

Loneliness

LIKE fatigue, like hunger, loneliness is part of being human. Fatigue is cured by sleep and hunger by eating, but how do we handle loneliness? It's our very nature to seek an alter ego, a heart that responds to our human ache for understanding.

Our favorite women of the Bible were no strangers to periods of aloneness, which, interestingly, often presaged important events: Mary, during her pregnancy; Ruth, bereaved in Moab; Esther, in a pagan harem; Hannah, childless for years in a culture where barrenness was a disgrace.

In his crowded adult life, there were times when Jesus chose to be alone, deliberately making himself unavailable so that he might nourish his soul in communion with his Father. He experienced both isolation and alienation. His query to his disciples when the fawning crowds drifted off, "Will you also go away?" and his Gethsemane "Watch with me"—these are lonely words.

Yet even Jesus did not use his relationship with God as a substitute for human companionship. He found sustenance with his three closest disciples—Peter, James and John—and in the home of Mary, Martha and Lazarus.

But even the most congenial marriage, the closest friendship, the most satisfying child-parent relationship is both transient and unpredictable. Although some 1,500 years have passed since St. Augustine remarked that our hearts will never be at rest away from the One who made them, it's still true.

Just because he has created us as unique individuals, our Father knows the best way to fill each one's empty places. It is only God who can fill our deepest longings, who never has an appointment elsewhere, who never replaces us with someone he likes better, who promises never to leave us totally alone. He is the only one who wants to be and always can be the unfailing companion on our journey.

Additional Scripture Readings:
1 Kings 19:1–10; Psalm 27:7–10

Go to page 93 for your next devotional reading.

[39]And no one after drinking old wine wants the new, for he says, 'The old is better.' "

Lord of the Sabbath

6 One Sabbath Jesus was going through the grainfields, and his disciples began to pick some heads of grain, rub them in their hands and eat the kernels. [2]Some of the Pharisees asked, "Why are you doing what is unlawful on the Sabbath?"

[3]Jesus answered them, "Have you never read what David did when he and his companions were hungry? [4]He entered the house of God, and taking the consecrated bread, he ate what is lawful only for priests to eat. And he also gave some to his companions." [5]Then Jesus said to them, "The Son of Man is Lord of the Sabbath."

[6]On another Sabbath he went into the synagogue and was teaching, and a man was there whose right hand was shriveled. [7]The Pharisees and the teachers of the law were looking for a reason to accuse Jesus, so they watched him closely to see if he would heal on the Sabbath. [8]But Jesus knew what they were thinking and said to the man with the shriveled hand, "Get up and stand in front of everyone." So he got up and stood there.

[9]Then Jesus said to them, "I ask you, which is lawful on the Sabbath: to do good or to do evil, to save life or to destroy it?"

[10]He looked around at them all, and then said to the man, "Stretch out your hand." He did so, and his hand was completely restored. [11]But they were furious and began to discuss with one another what they might do to Jesus.

The Twelve Apostles

[12]One of those days Jesus went out to a mountainside to pray, and spent the night praying to God. [13]When morning came, he called his disciples to him and chose twelve of them, whom he also designated apostles: [14]Simon (whom he named Peter), his brother Andrew, James, John, Philip, Bartholomew, [15]Matthew, Thomas, James son of Alphaeus, Simon who was called the Zealot, [16]Judas son of James, and Judas Iscariot, who became a traitor.

Blessings and Woes

[17]He went down with them and stood on a level place. A large crowd of his disciples was there and a great number of people from all over Judea, from Jerusalem, and from the coast of Tyre and Sidon, [18]who had come to hear him and to be healed of their diseases. Those troubled by evil[a] spirits were cured, [19]and the people all tried to touch him, because power was coming from him and healing them all.

[20]Looking at his disciples, he said:

"Blessed are you who are poor,
for yours is the kingdom of God.
[21]Blessed are you who hunger now,
for you will be satisfied.
Blessed are you who weep now,
for you will laugh.
[22]Blessed are you when men hate you,
when they exclude you and insult you
and reject your name as evil,
because of the Son of Man.

[23]"Rejoice in that day and leap for joy, because great is your reward in heaven. For that is how their fathers treated the prophets.

[24]"But woe to you who are rich,
for you have already received your comfort.
[25]Woe to you who are well fed now,
for you will go hungry.
Woe to you who laugh now,
for you will mourn and weep.
[26]Woe to you when all men speak well of you,
for that is how their fathers treated the false prophets.

Love for Enemies

[27]"But I tell you who hear me: Love your enemies, do good to those who hate you, [28]bless those who curse you, pray for those who mistreat you. [29]If someone strikes you on one cheek, turn to him the other also. If someone takes your cloak, do not stop him from taking your tunic. [30]Give to everyone who asks you, and if anyone takes what belongs to you, do not demand it back. [31]Do to others as you would have them do to you.

[32]"If you love those who love you, what credit is that to you? Even 'sinners' love those who love them. [33]And if you do good to those who are good to you, what

---

a18 Greek *unclean*

credit is that to you? Even 'sinners' do that. [34]And if you lend to those from whom you expect repayment, what credit is that to you? Even 'sinners' lend to 'sinners,' expecting to be repaid in full. [35]But love your enemies, do good to them, and lend to them without expecting to get anything back. Then your reward will be great, and you will be sons of the Most High, because he is kind to the ungrateful and wicked. [36]Be merciful, just as your Father is merciful.

Judging Others

[37]"Do not judge, and you will not be judged. Do not condemn, and you will not be condemned. Forgive, and you will be forgiven. [38]Give, and it will be given to you. A good measure, pressed down, shaken together and running over, will be poured into your lap. For with the measure you use, it will be measured to you."

[39]He also told them this parable: "Can a blind man lead a blind man? Will they not both fall into a pit? [40]A student is not above his teacher, but everyone who is fully trained will be like his teacher.

[41]"Why do you look at the speck of sawdust in your brother's eye and pay no attention to the plank in your own eye? [42]How can you say to your brother, 'Brother, let me take the speck out of your eye,' when you yourself fail to see the plank in your own eye? You hypocrite, first take the plank out of your eye, and then you will see clearly to remove the speck from your brother's eye.

A Tree and Its Fruit

[43]"No good tree bears bad fruit, nor does a bad tree bear good fruit. [44]Each tree is recognized by its own fruit. People do not pick figs from thornbushes, or grapes from briers. [45]The good man brings good things out of the good stored up in his heart, and the evil man brings evil things out of the evil stored up in his heart. For out of the overflow of his heart his mouth speaks.

The Wise and Foolish Builders

[46]"Why do you call me, 'Lord, Lord,' and do not do what I say? [47]I will show you what he is like who comes to me and hears my words and puts them into practice. [48]He is like a man building a house, who dug down deep and laid the foundation on rock. When a flood came, the torrent struck that house but could not shake it, because it was well built. [49]But the one who hears my words and does not put them into practice is like a man who built a house on the ground without a foundation. The moment the torrent struck that house, it collapsed and its destruction was complete."

The Faith of the Centurion

7 When Jesus had finished saying all this in the hearing of the people, he entered Capernaum. [2]There a centurion's servant, whom his master valued highly, was sick and about to die. [3]The centurion heard of Jesus and sent some elders of the Jews to him, asking him to come and heal his servant. [4]When they came to Jesus, they pleaded earnestly with him, "This man deserves to have you do this, [5]because he loves our nation and has built our synagogue." [6]So Jesus went with them.

He was not far from the house when the centurion sent friends to say to him: "Lord, don't trouble yourself, for I do not deserve to have you come under my roof. [7]That is why I did not even consider myself worthy to come to you. But say the word, and my servant will be healed. [8]For I myself am a man under authority, with soldiers under me. I tell this one, 'Go,' and he goes; and that one, 'Come,' and he comes. I say to my servant, 'Do this,' and he does it."

[9]When Jesus heard this, he was amazed at him, and turning to the crowd following him, he said, "I tell you, I have not found such great faith even in Israel." [10]Then the men who had been sent returned to the house and found the servant well.

Jesus Raises a Widow's Son

[11]Soon afterward, Jesus went to a town called Nain, and his disciples and a large crowd went along with him. [12]As he approached the town gate, a dead person was being carried out—the only son of his mother, and she was a widow. And a large crowd from the town was with her. [13]When the Lord saw her, his heart went out to her and he said, "Don't cry."

[14]Then he went up and touched the coffin, and those carrying it stood still. He said, "Young man, I say to you, get up!" [15]The dead man sat up and began to talk, and Jesus gave him back to his mother.

[16]They were all filled with awe and praised God. "A great prophet has appeared among us," they said. "God has come to help his people." [17]This news

about Jesus spread throughout Judea*a*
and the surrounding country.

Jesus and John the Baptist

18John's disciples told him about all
these things. Calling two of them, 19he
sent them to the Lord to ask, "Are you the
one who was to come, or should we expect someone else?"

20When the men came to Jesus, they
said, "John the Baptist sent us to you to
ask, 'Are you the one who was to come, or
should we expect someone else?' "

21At that very time Jesus cured many
who had diseases, sicknesses and evil
spirits, and gave sight to many who were
blind. 22So he replied to the messengers,
"Go back and report to John what you
have seen and heard: The blind receive
sight, the lame walk, those who have leprosy*b* are cured, the deaf hear, the dead
are raised, and the good news is preached
to the poor. 23Blessed is the man who
does not fall away on account of me."

24After John's messengers left, Jesus
began to speak to the crowd about John:
"What did you go out into the desert to
see? A reed swayed by the wind? 25If not,
what did you go out to see? A man
dressed in fine clothes? No, those who
wear expensive clothes and indulge in
luxury are in palaces. 26But what did you
go out to see? A prophet? Yes, I tell you,
and more than a prophet. 27This is the
one about whom it is written:

" 'I will send my messenger ahead of
　　　you,
　　who will prepare your way before
　　　you.'*c*

28I tell you, among those born of women
there is no one greater than John; yet the
one who is least in the kingdom of God is
greater than he."

29(All the people, even the tax collectors, when they heard Jesus' words, acknowledged that God's way was right, because they had been baptized by John.
30But the Pharisees and experts in the law
rejected God's purpose for themselves,
because they had not been baptized by
John.)

31"To what, then, can I compare the
people of this generation? What are they
like? 32They are like children sitting in
the marketplace and calling out to each
other:

" 'We played the flute for you,
　　and you did not dance;
we sang a dirge,
　　and you did not cry.'

33For John the Baptist came neither eating bread nor drinking wine, and you say,
'He has a demon.' 34The Son of Man came
eating and drinking, and you say, 'Here is
a glutton and a drunkard, a friend of tax
collectors and "sinners." ' 35But wisdom
is proved right by all her children."

Jesus Anointed by a Sinful Woman

36Now one of the Pharisees invited
Jesus to have dinner with him, so he went
to the Pharisee's house and reclined at
the table. 37When a woman who had lived
a sinful life in that town learned that
Jesus was eating at the Pharisee's house,
she brought an alabaster jar of perfume,
38and as she stood behind him at his feet
weeping, she began to wet his feet with
her tears. Then she wiped them with her
hair, kissed them and poured perfume on
them.

39When the Pharisee who had invited
him saw this, he said to himself, "If this
man were a prophet, he would know who
is touching him and what kind of woman
she is—that she is a sinner."

40Jesus answered him, "Simon, I have
something to tell you."

"Tell me, teacher," he said.

41"Two men owed money to a certain
moneylender. One owed him five hundred denarii,*d* and the other fifty. 42Nei-
ther of them had the money to pay him
back, so he canceled the debts of both.
Now which of them will love him more?"

43Simon replied, "I suppose the one
who had the bigger debt canceled."

"You have judged correctly," Jesus
said.

44Then he turned toward the woman
and said to Simon, "Do you see this woman? I came into your house. You did not
give me any water for my feet, but she wet
my feet with her tears and wiped them
with her hair. 45You did not give me a
kiss, but this woman, from the time I entered, has not stopped kissing my feet.
46You did not put oil on my head, but she
has poured perfume on my feet. 47There-
fore, I tell you, her many sins have been
forgiven—for she loved much. But he
who has been forgiven little loves little."

*a*17 Or *the land of the Jews*　　*b*22 The Greek word was used for various diseases affecting the skin—not
necessarily leprosy.　　*c*27 Mal. 3:1　　*d*41 A denarius was a coin worth about a day's wages.

48Then Jesus said to her, "Your sins are forgiven."

49The other guests began to say among themselves, "Who is this who even forgives sins?"

50Jesus said to the woman, "Your faith has saved you; go in peace."

The Parable of the Sower

8 After this, Jesus traveled about from one town and village to another, proclaiming the good news of the kingdom of God. The Twelve were with him, 2and also some women who had been cured of evil spirits and diseases: Mary (called Magdalene) from whom seven demons had come out; 3Joanna the wife of Cuza, the manager of Herod's household; Susanna; and many others. These women were helping to support them out of their own means.

4While a large crowd was gathering and people were coming to Jesus from town after town, he told this parable: 5"A farmer went out to sow his seed. As he was scattering the seed, some fell along the path; it was trampled on, and the birds of the air ate it up. 6Some fell on rock, and when it came up, the plants withered because they had no moisture. 7Other seed fell among thorns, which grew up with it and choked the plants. 8Still other seed fell on good soil. It came up and yielded a crop, a hundred times more than was sown."

When he said this, he called out, "He who has ears to hear, let him hear."

9His disciples asked him what this parable meant. 10He said, "The knowledge of the secrets of the kingdom of God has been given to you, but to others I speak in parables, so that,

" 'though seeing, they may not see;
    though hearing, they may not
        understand.'*a*

11"This is the meaning of the parable: The seed is the word of God. 12Those along the path are the ones who hear, and then the devil comes and takes away the word from their hearts, so that they may not believe and be saved. 13Those on the rock are the ones who receive the word with joy when they hear it, but they have no root. They believe for a while, but in the time of testing they fall away. 14The seed that fell among thorns stands for those who hear, but as they go on their way they are choked by life's worries, riches and pleasures, and they do not mature. 15But the seed on good soil stands for those with a noble and good heart, who hear the word, retain it, and by persevering produce a crop.

A Lamp on a Stand

16"No one lights a lamp and hides it in a jar or puts it under a bed. Instead, he puts it on a stand, so that those who come in can see the light. 17For there is nothing hidden that will not be disclosed, and nothing concealed that will not be known or brought out into the open. 18Therefore consider carefully how you listen. Whoever has will be given more; whoever does not have, even what he thinks he has will be taken from him."

Jesus' Mother and Brothers

19Now Jesus' mother and brothers came to see him, but they were not able to get near him because of the crowd. 20Someone told him, "Your mother and brothers are standing outside, wanting to see you."

21He replied, "My mother and brothers are those who hear God's word and put it into practice."

Jesus Calms the Storm

22One day Jesus said to his disciples, "Let's go over to the other side of the lake." So they got into a boat and set out. 23As they sailed, he fell asleep. A squall came down on the lake, so that the boat was being swamped, and they were in great danger.

24The disciples went and woke him, saying, "Master, Master, we're going to drown!"

He got up and rebuked the wind and the raging waters; the storm subsided, and all was calm. 25"Where is your faith?" he asked his disciples.

In fear and amazement they asked one another, "Who is this? He commands even the winds and the water, and they obey him."

The Healing of a Demon-possessed Man

26They sailed to the region of the Gerasenes,*b* which is across the lake from Galilee. 27When Jesus stepped ashore, he was met by a demon-possessed man from the town. For a long time this man had

---

a10 Isaiah 6:9   *b26* Some manuscripts *Gadarenes*; other manuscripts *Gergesenes*; also in verse 37 not worn clothes or lived in a house, but had lived in the tombs. [28]When he saw Jesus, he cried out and fell at his feet, shouting at the top of his voice, "What do you want with me, Jesus, Son of the Most High God? I beg you, don't torture me!" [29]For Jesus had commanded the evil[a] spirit to come out of the man. Many times it had seized him, and though he was chained hand and foot and kept under guard, he had broken his chains and had been driven by the demon into solitary places.

[30]Jesus asked him, "What is your name?"

"Legion," he replied, because many demons had gone into him. [31]And they begged him repeatedly not to order them to go into the Abyss.

[32]A large herd of pigs was feeding there on the hillside. The demons begged Jesus to let them go into them, and he gave them permission. [33]When the demons came out of the man, they went into the pigs, and the herd rushed down the steep bank into the lake and was drowned.

[34]When those tending the pigs saw what had happened, they ran off and reported this in the town and countryside, [35]and the people went out to see what had happened. When they came to Jesus, they found the man from whom the demons had gone out, sitting at Jesus' feet, dressed and in his right mind; and they were afraid. [36]Those who had seen it told the people how the demon-possessed man had been cured. [37]Then all the people of the region of the Gerasenes asked Jesus to leave them, because they were overcome with fear. So he got into the boat and left.

[38]The man from whom the demons had gone out begged to go with him, but Jesus sent him away, saying, [39]"Return home and tell how much God has done for you." So the man went away and told all over town how much Jesus had done for him.

A Dead Girl and a Sick Woman

[40]Now when Jesus returned, a crowd welcomed him, for they were all expecting him. [41]Then a man named Jairus, a ruler of the synagogue, came and fell at Jesus' feet, pleading with him to come to his house [42]because his only daughter, a girl of about twelve, was dying.

As Jesus was on his way, the crowds almost crushed him. [43]And a woman was there who had been subject to bleeding for twelve years,[b] but no one could heal her. [44]She came up behind him and touched the edge of his cloak, and immediately her bleeding stopped.

[45]"Who touched me?" Jesus asked.

When they all denied it, Peter said, "Master, the people are crowding and pressing against you."

[46]But Jesus said, "Someone touched me; I know that power has gone out from me."

[47]Then the woman, seeing that she could not go unnoticed, came trembling and fell at his feet. In the presence of all the people, she told why she had touched him and how she had been instantly healed. [48]Then he said to her, "Daughter, your faith has healed you. Go in peace."

[49]While Jesus was still speaking, someone came from the house of Jairus, the synagogue ruler. "Your daughter is dead," he said. "Don't bother the teacher any more."

[50]Hearing this, Jesus said to Jairus, "Don't be afraid; just believe, and she will be healed."

[51]When he arrived at the house of Jairus, he did not let anyone go in with him except Peter, John and James, and the child's father and mother. [52]Meanwhile, all the people were wailing and mourning for her. "Stop wailing," Jesus said. "She is not dead but asleep."

[53]They laughed at him, knowing that she was dead. [54]But he took her by the hand and said, "My child, get up!" [55]Her spirit returned, and at once she stood up. Then Jesus told them to give her something to eat. [56]Her parents were astonished, but he ordered them not to tell anyone what had happened.

Jesus Sends Out the Twelve

9 When Jesus had called the Twelve together, he gave them power and authority to drive out all demons and to cure diseases, [2]and he sent them out to preach the kingdom of God and to heal the sick. [3]He told them: "Take nothing for the journey—no staff, no bag, no bread, no money, no extra tunic. [4]Whatever house you enter, stay there until you leave that town. [5]If people do not welcome you, shake the dust off your feet when you leave their town, as a testimony against them." [6]So they set out and went

---

[a]29 Greek *unclean*   [b]43 Many manuscripts *years, and she had spent all she had on doctors*

from village to village, preaching the gospel and healing people everywhere.

[7]Now Herod the tetrarch heard about all that was going on. And he was perplexed, because some were saying that John had been raised from the dead, [8]others that Elijah had appeared, and still others that one of the prophets of long ago had come back to life. [9]But Herod said, "I beheaded John. Who, then, is this I hear such things about?" And he tried to see him.

Jesus Feeds the Five Thousand

[10]When the apostles returned, they reported to Jesus what they had done. Then he took them with him and they withdrew by themselves to a town called Bethsaida, [11]but the crowds learned about it and followed him. He welcomed them and spoke to them about the kingdom of God, and healed those who needed healing.

[12]Late in the afternoon the Twelve came to him and said, "Send the crowd away so they can go to the surrounding villages and countryside and find food and lodging, because we are in a remote place here."

[13]He replied, "You give them something to eat."

They answered, "We have only five loaves of bread and two fish—unless we go and buy food for all this crowd." [14](About five thousand men were there.)

But he said to his disciples, "Have them sit down in groups of about fifty each." [15]The disciples did so, and everybody sat down. [16]Taking the five loaves and the two fish and looking up to heaven, he gave thanks and broke them. Then he gave them to the disciples to set before the people. [17]They all ate and were satisfied, and the disciples picked up twelve basketfuls of broken pieces that were left over.

Peter's Confession of Christ

[18]Once when Jesus was praying in private and his disciples were with him, he asked them, "Who do the crowds say I am?"

[19]They replied, "Some say John the Baptist; others say Elijah; and still others, that one of the prophets of long ago has come back to life."

[20]"But what about you?" he asked. "Who do you say I am?"

Peter answered, "The Christ[a] of God."

[21]Jesus strictly warned them not to tell this to anyone. [22]And he said, "The Son of Man must suffer many things and be rejected by the elders, chief priests and teachers of the law, and he must be killed and on the third day be raised to life."

[23]Then he said to them all: "If anyone would come after me, he must deny himself and take up his cross daily and follow me. [24]For whoever wants to save his life will lose it, but whoever loses his life for me will save it. [25]What good is it for a man to gain the whole world, and yet lose or forfeit his very self? [26]If anyone is ashamed of me and my words, the Son of Man will be ashamed of him when he comes in his glory and in the glory of the Father and of the holy angels. [27]I tell you the truth, some who are standing here will not taste death before they see the kingdom of God."

The Transfiguration

[28]About eight days after Jesus said this, he took Peter, John and James with him and went up onto a mountain to pray. [29]As he was praying, the appearance of his face changed, and his clothes became as bright as a flash of lightning. [30]Two men, Moses and Elijah, [31]appeared in glorious splendor, talking with Jesus. They spoke about his departure, which he was about to bring to fulfillment at Jerusalem. [32]Peter and his companions were very sleepy, but when they became fully awake, they saw his glory and the two men standing with him. [33]As the men were leaving Jesus, Peter said to him, "Master, it is good for us to be here. Let us put up three shelters—one for you, one for Moses and one for Elijah." (He did not know what he was saying.)

[34]While he was speaking, a cloud appeared and enveloped them, and they were afraid as they entered the cloud. [35]A voice came from the cloud, saying, "This is my Son, whom I have chosen; listen to him." [36]When the voice had spoken, they found that Jesus was alone. The disciples kept this to themselves, and told no one at that time what they had seen.

The Healing of a Boy With an Evil Spirit

[37]The next day, when they came down from the mountain, a large crowd met him. [38]A man in the crowd called out, "Teacher, I beg you to look at my son, for

[a]20 Or Messiah

he is my only child. [39]A spirit seizes him and he suddenly screams; it throws him into convulsions so that he foams at the mouth. It scarcely ever leaves him and is destroying him. [40]I begged your disciples to drive it out, but they could not."

[41]"O unbelieving and perverse generation," Jesus replied, "how long shall I stay with you and put up with you? Bring your son here."

[42]Even while the boy was coming, the demon threw him to the ground in a convulsion. But Jesus rebuked the evil[a] spirit, healed the boy and gave him back to his father. [43]And they were all amazed at the greatness of God.

While everyone was marveling at all that Jesus did, he said to his disciples, [44]"Listen carefully to what I am about to tell you: The Son of Man is going to be betrayed into the hands of men." [45]But they did not understand what this meant. It was hidden from them, so that they did not grasp it, and they were afraid to ask him about it.

Who Will Be the Greatest?

[46]An argument started among the disciples as to which of them would be the greatest. [47]Jesus, knowing their thoughts, took a little child and had him stand beside him. [48]Then he said to them, "Whoever welcomes this little child in my name welcomes me; and whoever welcomes me welcomes the one who sent me. For he who is least among you all — he is the greatest."

[49]"Master," said John, "we saw a man driving out demons in your name and we tried to stop him, because he is not one of us."

[50]"Do not stop him," Jesus said, "for whoever is not against you is for you."

Samaritan Opposition

[51]As the time approached for him to be taken up to heaven, Jesus resolutely set out for Jerusalem. [52]And he sent messengers on ahead, who went into a Samaritan village to get things ready for him; [53]but the people there did not welcome him, because he was heading for Jerusalem. [54]When the disciples James and John saw this, they asked, "Lord, do you want us to call fire down from heaven to destroy them[b]?" [55]But Jesus turned and rebuked

them, [56]and[c] they went to another village.

The Cost of Following Jesus

[57]As they were walking along the road, a man said to him, "I will follow you wherever you go."

[58]Jesus replied, "Foxes have holes and birds of the air have nests, but the Son of Man has no place to lay his head."

[59]He said to another man, "Follow me."

But the man replied, "Lord, first let me go and bury my father."

[60]Jesus said to him, "Let the dead bury their own dead, but you go and proclaim the kingdom of God."

[61]Still another said, "I will follow you, Lord; but first let me go back and say good-by to my family."

[62]Jesus replied, "No one who puts his hand to the plow and looks back is fit for service in the kingdom of God."

Jesus Sends Out the Seventy-two

10 After this the Lord appointed seventy-two[d] others and sent them two by two ahead of him to every town and place where he was about to go. [2]He told them, "The harvest is plentiful, but the workers are few. Ask the Lord of the harvest, therefore, to send out workers into his harvest field. [3]Go! I am sending you out like lambs among wolves. [4]Do not take a purse or bag or sandals; and do not greet anyone on the road.

[5]"When you enter a house, first say, 'Peace to this house.' [6]If a man of peace is there, your peace will rest on him; if not, it will return to you. [7]Stay in that house, eating and drinking whatever they give you, for the worker deserves his wages. Do not move around from house to house.

[8]"When you enter a town and are welcomed, eat what is set before you. [9]Heal the sick who are there and tell them, 'The kingdom of God is near you.' [10]But when you enter a town and are not welcomed, go into its streets and say, [11]'Even the dust of your town that sticks to our feet we wipe off against you. Yet be sure of this: The kingdom of God is near.' [12]I tell you, it will be more bearable on that day for Sodom than for that town.

[13]"Woe to you, Korazin! Woe to you,

---

[a]42 Greek *unclean*　　[b]54 Some manuscripts *them, even as Elijah did*　　[c]55,56 Some manuscripts *them. And he said, "You do not know what kind of spirit you are of, for the Son of Man did not come to destroy men's lives, but to save them." [56]And*　　[d]1 Some manuscripts *seventy*; also in verse 17

VERSE FOR THE DAY:	AUTHOR:	PASSAGE FOR THE DAY:
Luke 10:33	Alma Barkman	Luke 10:25–37

First Aid

ALTHOUGH not a registered professional, I do get my share of nursing experience, particularly while substituting for the school secretary. The minute I set foot inside the door, casualties start gravitating toward the office—scraped elbows, skinned knees, old wounds, fresh nosebleeds, raised toenails, broken blisters, upset stomachs.

I have learned that a school secretary opens a well-stocked first-aid kit long before sharpening any pencils. By midafternoon the office is apt to resemble a hospital ward.

Not only that, but old Florence Nightingale is not accorded any degree of privacy. The casualty victims from school are beginning to spill over into my house. Yesterday the doorbell rang, and a terrified young fellow hopping up and down on my doorstep tried to tell me that his pal was bleeding to death on the road—massive hemorrhage.

I ran to the site of the accident, where the victim was just untangling himself from the wreckage of his bicycle. Judging from his groans, I thought he had amputated his leg.

Somehow I managed to get him into my bathroom and wash off his wounds. An accurate diagnosis confirmed my suspicions: he had simply scraped the scab from a previous injury. I solemnly conjured up an impressive-looking bandage, and he was back on the road in no time at all, completely cured.

The therapeutic value of Band-Aids may well be disputed, but this is one "lady of the lamp" who keeps her medicine chest well stocked.

Whether it is a tiny sliver in a chubby finger, or cancer clawing at a ravaged frame, pain demands priority. Why then am I so hesitant in dispensing consolation? Do I wait until an emergency demands it before investing in a "first-aid" kit? Must I first suffer physically, mentally, emotionally, or spiritually before I learn the healing value of a soothing hand, a mutual tear, a sympathizing heart, an understanding word?

Surely I do well to keep my medicine chest well stocked with love and compassion as well as with bandages, for I never know when I will be called upon to deal with tragedy, or when tragedy may call to deal with me.

Additional Scripture Readings:
Acts 3:1–10; James 2:14–17

Go to page 95 for your next devotional reading.

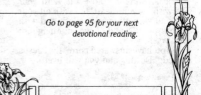

Bethsaida! For if the miracles that were performed in you had been performed in Tyre and Sidon, they would have repented long ago, sitting in sackcloth and ashes. [14]But it will be more bearable for Tyre and Sidon at the judgment than for you. [15]And you, Capernaum, will you be lifted up to the skies? No, you will go down to the depths. [a]

[16]"He who listens to you listens to me; he who rejects you rejects me; but he who rejects me rejects him who sent me."

[17]The seventy-two returned with joy and said, "Lord, even the demons submit to us in your name."

[18]He replied, "I saw Satan fall like lightning from heaven. [19]I have given you authority to trample on snakes and scorpions and to overcome all the power of the enemy; nothing will harm you. [20]However, do not rejoice that the spirits submit to you, but rejoice that your names are written in heaven."

[21]At that time Jesus, full of joy through the Holy Spirit, said, "I praise you, Father, Lord of heaven and earth, because you have hidden these things from the wise and learned, and revealed them to little children. Yes, Father, for this was your good pleasure.

[22]"All things have been committed to me by my Father. No one knows who the Son is except the Father, and no one knows who the Father is except the Son and those to whom the Son chooses to reveal him."

[23]Then he turned to his disciples and said privately, "Blessed are the eyes that see what you see. [24]For I tell you that many prophets and kings wanted to see what you see but did not see it, and to hear what you hear but did not hear it."

The Parable of the Good Samaritan

[25]On one occasion an expert in the law stood up to test Jesus. "Teacher," he asked, "what must I do to inherit eternal life?"

[26]"What is written in the Law?" he replied. "How do you read it?"

[27]He answered: " 'Love the Lord your God with all your heart and with all your soul and with all your strength and with all your mind'[b]; and, 'Love your neighbor as yourself.'[c]"

[28]"You have answered correctly," Jesus replied. "Do this and you will live."

[29]But he wanted to justify himself, so he asked Jesus, "And who is my neighbor?"

[30]In reply Jesus said: "A man was going down from Jerusalem to Jericho, when he fell into the hands of robbers. They stripped him of his clothes, beat him and went away, leaving him half dead. [31]A priest happened to be going down the same road, and when he saw the man, he passed by on the other side. [32]So too, a Levite, when he came to the place and saw him, passed by on the other side. [33]But a Samaritan, as he traveled, came where the man was; and when he saw him, he took pity on him. [34]He went to him and bandaged his wounds, pouring on oil and wine. Then he put the man on his own donkey, took him to an inn and took care of him. [35]The next day he took out two silver coins[d] and gave them to the innkeeper. 'Look after him,' he said, 'and when I return, I will reimburse you for any extra expense you may have.'

[36]"Which of these three do you think was a neighbor to the man who fell into the hands of robbers?"

[37]The expert in the law replied, "The one who had mercy on him."

Jesus told him, "Go and do likewise."

At the Home of Martha and Mary

[38]As Jesus and his disciples were on their way, he came to a village where a woman named Martha opened her home to him. [39]She had a sister called Mary, who sat at the Lord's feet listening to what he said. [40]But Martha was distracted by all the preparations that had to be made. She came to him and asked, "Lord, don't you care that my sister has left me to do the work by myself? Tell her to help me!"

[41]"Martha, Martha," the Lord answered, "you are worried and upset about many things, [42]but only one thing is needed.[e] Mary has chosen what is better, and it will not be taken away from her."

Jesus' Teaching on Prayer

11 One day Jesus was praying in a certain place. When he finished, one of his disciples said to him, "Lord, teach us to pray, just as John taught his disciples."

[2]He said to them, "When you pray, say:

---

[a]15 Greek Hades   [b]27 Deut. 6:5   [c]27 Lev. 19:18   [d]35 Greek two denarii   [e]42 Some manuscripts but few things are needed—or only one

" 'Father,[a]
hallowed be your name,
your kingdom come.[b]
[3]Give us each day our daily bread.
[4]Forgive us our sins,
　　for we also forgive everyone who
　　　sins against us.[c]
And lead us not into temptation.[d]' "

[5]Then he said to them, "Suppose one of you has a friend, and he goes to him at midnight and says, 'Friend, lend me three loaves of bread, [6]because a friend of mine on a journey has come to me, and I have nothing to set before him.'

[7]"Then the one inside answers, 'Don't bother me. The door is already locked, and my children are with me in bed. I can't get up and give you anything.' [8]I tell you, though he will not get up and give him the bread because he is his friend,

---

[a]2 Some manuscripts Our Father in heaven　　*[b]2 Some manuscripts come. May your will be done on earth as it is in heaven.*　　*[c]4 Greek everyone who is indebted to us*　　*[d]4 Some manuscripts temptation but deliver us from the evil one*

THURSDAY

VERSE FOR THE DAY:	AUTHOR:	PASSAGE FOR THE DAY:
Luke 10:40	Jill Briscoe	Luke 10:38–42

First Things First

I LOVE the way Jesus solved problems. He tackled them head on! He was a master at confronting people in such a way that it did not hinder his relationship with them afterward. Think of Martha, for instance. Jesus visited the home of Martha, Mary and Lazarus. Mary, Martha's sister, sat at Jesus' feet and listened to his words while Martha got mad about it! She got mad at Mary and she got mad at Jesus! There was a meal to prepare and nobody would help! I'm sure she got mad at Martha too, because you can't be happy with yourself when you're griping at other people!

It wasn't that Martha didn't know what it was to enjoy the Master's company, because we understand that Martha also sat at Jesus' feet. It was just a question of priorities. Martha was busy getting a banquet ready when soup and sandwiches would have been quite adequate. Jesus gently reminded her that she was worried and troubled about many "dishes" but Mary had chosen the best "dish"!

When Jesus saw women who were "distracted" by their serving—he did not fail to remind them that "man does not live on bread alone" (Matthew 4:4). First things need to come first! "First the Master, then the meat," he reminded Martha.

It isn't that the *doing* doesn't need doing, it's that the *being* must come first, and then we will find that the necessary part of the doing will get done! Later in Jesus' ministry we read that Martha served, and this time there was no complaining and no rebuke—first things *were* first (John 12:2).

Additional Scripture Readings:
Luke 9:57–62; John 12:1–3

Go to page 97 for your next devotional reading.

yet because of the man's boldness[a] he will get up and give him as much as he needs.

⁹"So I say to you: Ask and it will be given to you; seek and you will find; knock and the door will be opened to you. ¹⁰For everyone who asks receives; he who seeks finds; and to him who knocks, the door will be opened.

¹¹"Which of you fathers, if your son asks for[b] a fish, will give him a snake instead? ¹²Or if he asks for an egg, will give him a scorpion? ¹³If you then, though you are evil, know how to give good gifts to your children, how much more will your Father in heaven give the Holy Spirit to those who ask him!"

Jesus and Beelzebub

¹⁴Jesus was driving out a demon that was mute. When the demon left, the man who had been mute spoke, and the crowd was amazed. ¹⁵But some of them said, "By Beelzebub,[c] the prince of demons, he is driving out demons." ¹⁶Others tested him by asking for a sign from heaven.

¹⁷Jesus knew their thoughts and said to them: "Any kingdom divided against itself will be ruined, and a house divided against itself will fall. ¹⁸If Satan is divided against himself, how can his kingdom stand? I say this because you claim that I drive out demons by Beelzebub. ¹⁹Now if I drive out demons by Beelzebub, by whom do your followers drive them out? So then, they will be your judges. ²⁰But if I drive out demons by the finger of God, then the kingdom of God has come to you.

²¹"When a strong man, fully armed, guards his own house, his possessions are safe. ²²But when someone stronger attacks and overpowers him, he takes away the armor in which the man trusted and divides up the spoils.

²³"He who is not with me is against me, and he who does not gather with me, scatters.

²⁴"When an evil[d] spirit comes out of a man, it goes through arid places seeking rest and does not find it. Then it says, 'I will return to the house I left.' ²⁵When it arrives, it finds the house swept clean and put in order. ²⁶Then it goes and takes seven other spirits more wicked than itself, and they go in and live there. And the final condition of that man is worse than the first."

²⁷As Jesus was saying these things, a woman in the crowd called out, "Blessed is the mother who gave you birth and nursed you."

²⁸He replied, "Blessed rather are those who hear the word of God and obey it."

The Sign of Jonah

²⁹As the crowds increased, Jesus said, "This is a wicked generation. It asks for a miraculous sign, but none will be given it except the sign of Jonah. ³⁰For as Jonah was a sign to the Ninevites, so also will the Son of Man be to this generation. ³¹The Queen of the South will rise at the judgment with the men of this generation and condemn them; for she came from the ends of the earth to listen to Solomon's wisdom, and now one[e] greater than Solomon is here. ³²The men of Nineveh will stand up at the judgment with this generation and condemn it; for they repented at the preaching of Jonah, and now one greater than Jonah is here.

The Lamp of the Body

³³"No one lights a lamp and puts it in a place where it will be hidden, or under a bowl. Instead he puts it on its stand, so that those who come in may see the light. ³⁴Your eye is the lamp of your body. When your eyes are good, your whole body also is full of light. But when they are bad, your body also is full of darkness. ³⁵See to it, then, that the light within you is not darkness. ³⁶Therefore, if your whole body is full of light, and no part of it dark, it will be completely lighted, as when the light of a lamp shines on you."

Six Woes

³⁷When Jesus had finished speaking, a Pharisee invited him to eat with him; so he went in and reclined at the table. ³⁸But the Pharisee, noticing that Jesus did not first wash before the meal, was surprised.

³⁹Then the Lord said to him, "Now then, you Pharisees clean the outside of the cup and dish, but inside you are full of greed and wickedness. ⁴⁰You foolish people! Did not the one who made the outside make the inside also? ⁴¹But give what is inside ‚the dish,[f] to the poor, and everything will be clean for you.

---

[a]8 Or *persistence*   [b]11 Some manuscripts *for bread, will give him a stone; or if he asks for*   [c]15 Greek *Beezeboul* or *Beelzeboul*; also in verses 18 and 19   [d]24 Greek *unclean*   [e]31 Or *something*; also in verse 32   [f]41 Or *what you have*

VERSE FOR THE DAY:
Luke 11:33

AUTHOR:
June Masters Bacher

PASSAGE FOR THE DAY:
Luke 11:33–36

Where Are the Lamps?

IN a certain mountain village in Europe several centuries ago (so the story goes), a nobleman wondered what legacy to leave his townspeople. At last he decided to build them a church.

Nobody saw the complete plans until the church was finished. When the people gathered, they marveled at its beauty. But one noticed an incompleteness. "Where are the lamps?" he asked. "How will the church be lighted?"

The nobleman smiled. Then he gave each family a lamp. "Each time you are here, the area in which you sit will be lighted. But when you are not here, some part of God's house will be dark."

Today we live in a world of darkness, a darkness in which even our secular problem-solvers are beginning to stumble. In spite of our "social conscience," all around us is evidence of ignorance, illiteracy, and dark imaginings. Romans 2:19 tells us that we, as Christians, are "a light for those who are in the dark."

But the world is so big. And our lamp is so small. Yes, but we can light some small part each day. Look to the star-struck heavens. How small each star looks in the distance. Yet, put together, those tiny jewels can light the darkest night. Not one of those little lamps of heaven is ever missing—else the heavens would be less bright. Each of us is a star (or a lamp, if you will). And yes, we can make this world a brighter place. It all begins with the desire expressed in Michelangelo's prayer: "God, grant me the desire always to desire to be more that I can ever accomplish."

To think and pray about: Light your lamps. Let God send you in a new direction today. Meet someone at the crossroads of his or her life. Put on a bright face whether you feel like it or not. Gladness will come.

Additional Scripture Readings:
Matthew 5:14–16; 1 John 1:5–7

Go to page 100 for your next devotional reading.

42"Woe to you Pharisees, because you give God a tenth of your mint, rue and all other kinds of garden herbs, but you neglect justice and the love of God. You should have practiced the latter without leaving the former undone.

43"Woe to you Pharisees, because you love the most important seats in the synagogues and greetings in the marketplaces.

44"Woe to you, because you are like unmarked graves, which men walk over without knowing it."

45One of the experts in the law answered him, "Teacher, when you say these things, you insult us also."

46Jesus replied, "And you experts in the law, woe to you, because you load people down with burdens they can hardly carry, and you yourselves will not lift one finger to help them.

47"Woe to you, because you build tombs for the prophets, and it was your forefathers who killed them. 48So you testify that you approve of what your forefathers did; they killed the prophets, and you build their tombs. 49Because of this, God in his wisdom said, 'I will send them prophets and apostles, some of whom they will kill and others they will persecute.' 50Therefore this generation will be held responsible for the blood of all the prophets that has been shed since the beginning of the world, 51from the blood of Abel to the blood of Zechariah, who was killed between the altar and the sanctuary. Yes, I tell you, this generation will be held responsible for it all.

52"Woe to you experts in the law, because you have taken away the key to knowledge. You yourselves have not entered, and you have hindered those who were entering."

53When Jesus left there, the Pharisees and the teachers of the law began to oppose him fiercely and to besiege him with questions, 54waiting to catch him in something he might say.

Warnings and Encouragements

12 Meanwhile, when a crowd of many thousands had gathered, so that they were trampling on one another, Jesus began to speak first to his disciples, saying: "Be on your guard against the yeast of the Pharisees, which is hypocrisy. 2There is nothing concealed that will not be disclosed, or hidden that will not be

made known. 3What you have said in the dark will be heard in the daylight, and what you have whispered in the ear in the inner rooms will be proclaimed from the roofs.

4"I tell you, my friends, do not be afraid of those who kill the body and after that can do no more. 5But I will show you whom you should fear: Fear him who, after the killing of the body, has power to throw you into hell. Yes, I tell you, fear him. 6Are not five sparrows sold for two pennies^a? Yet not one of them is forgotten by God. 7Indeed, the very hairs of your head are all numbered. Don't be afraid; you are worth more than many sparrows.

8"I tell you, whoever acknowledges me before men, the Son of Man will also acknowledge him before the angels of God. 9But he who disowns me before men will be disowned before the angels of God. 10And everyone who speaks a word against the Son of Man will be forgiven, but anyone who blasphemes against the Holy Spirit will not be forgiven.

11"When you are brought before synagogues, rulers and authorities, do not worry about how you will defend yourselves or what you will say, 12for the Holy Spirit will teach you at that time what you should say."

The Parable of the Rich Fool

13Someone in the crowd said to him, "Teacher, tell my brother to divide the inheritance with me."

14Jesus replied, "Man, who appointed me a judge or an arbiter between you?" 15Then he said to them, "Watch out! Be on your guard against all kinds of greed; a man's life does not consist in the abundance of his possessions."

16And he told them this parable: "The ground of a certain rich man produced a good crop. 17He thought to himself, 'What shall I do? I have no place to store my crops.'

18"Then he said, 'This is what I'll do. I will tear down my barns and build bigger ones, and there I will store all my grain and my goods. 19And I'll say to myself, "You have plenty of good things laid up for many years. Take life easy; eat, drink and be merry." '

20"But God said to him, 'You fool! This very night your life will be demanded from you. Then who will get what you have prepared for yourself?'

^a6 Greek two assaria

[21]"This is how it will be with anyone who stores up things for himself but is not rich toward God."

Do Not Worry

[22]Then Jesus said to his disciples: "Therefore I tell you, do not worry about your life, what you will eat; or about your body, what you will wear. [23]Life is more than food, and the body more than clothes. [24]Consider the ravens: They do not sow or reap, they have no storeroom or barn; yet God feeds them. And how much more valuable you are than birds! [25]Who of you by worrying can add a single hour to his life[a]? [26]Since you cannot do this very little thing, why do you worry about the rest?

[27]"Consider how the lilies grow. They do not labor or spin. Yet I tell you, not even Solomon in all his splendor was dressed like one of these. [28]If that is how God clothes the grass of the field, which is here today, and tomorrow is thrown into the fire, how much more will he clothe you, O you of little faith! [29]And do not set your heart on what you will eat or drink; do not worry about it. [30]For the pagan world runs after all such things, and your Father knows that you need them. [31]But seek his kingdom, and these things will be given to you as well.

[32]"Do not be afraid, little flock, for your Father has been pleased to give you the kingdom. [33]Sell your possessions and give to the poor. Provide purses for yourselves that will not wear out, a treasure in heaven that will not be exhausted, where no thief comes near and no moth destroys. [34]For where your treasure is, there your heart will be also.

Watchfulness

[35]"Be dressed ready for service and keep your lamps burning, [36]like men waiting for their master to return from a wedding banquet, so that when he comes and knocks they can immediately open the door for him. [37]It will be good for those servants whose master finds them watching when he comes. I tell you the truth, he will dress himself to serve, will have them recline at the table and will come and wait on them. [38]It will be good for those servants whose master finds them ready, even if he comes in the second or third watch of the night. [39]But understand this: If the owner of the house

had known at what hour the thief was coming, he would not have let his house be broken into. [40]You also must be ready, because the Son of Man will come at an hour when you do not expect him."

[41]Peter asked, "Lord, are you telling this parable to us, or to everyone?"

[42]The Lord answered, "Who then is the faithful and wise manager, whom the master puts in charge of his servants to give them their food allowance at the proper time? [43]It will be good for that servant whom the master finds doing so when he returns. [44]I tell you the truth, he will put him in charge of all his possessions. [45]But suppose the servant says to himself, 'My master is taking a long time in coming,' and he then begins to beat the menservants and maidservants and to eat and drink and get drunk. [46]The master of that servant will come on a day when he does not expect him and at an hour he is not aware of. He will cut him to pieces and assign him a place with the unbelievers.

[47]"That servant who knows his master's will and does not get ready or does not do what his master wants will be beaten with many blows. [48]But the one who does not know and does things deserving punishment will be beaten with few blows. From everyone who has been given much, much will be demanded; and from the one who has been entrusted with much, much more will be asked.

Not Peace but Division

[49]"I have come to bring fire on the earth, and how I wish it were already kindled! [50]But I have a baptism to undergo, and how distressed I am until it is completed! [51]Do you think I came to bring peace on earth? No, I tell you, but division. [52]From now on there will be five in one family divided against each other, three against two and two against three. [53]They will be divided, father against son and son against father, mother against daughter and daughter against mother, mother-in-law against daughter-in-law and daughter-in-law against mother-in-law."

Interpreting the Times

[54]He said to the crowd: "When you see a cloud rising in the west, immediately you say, 'It's going to rain,' and it does. [55]And when the south wind blows, you

---

[a]25 Or single cubit to his height

WEEKENDING

REVIEW

For even the Son of Man did not come to be served, but to serve, and to give his life as a ransom for many (Mark 10:45).

RECAP

Those words were spoken by the Son of God on a day when his disciples needed a proper perspective on servanthood (Mark 10:36) and when a blind man cried out for mercy (Mark 10:51).

The son of God, surrounded by endless requests and wearied by miles of walking, looked *need* squarely in the face and asked, "What do you want me to do for you?" (Mark 10:51). He saw the burden another carried and offered to help with the load.

In a day when *servanthood* is dying for lack of examples and we get all tied up in theological knots over even the meaning of the word, we might do well to start where Jesus did—with a simple question, "What can I do for you?" Who knows? Those words might revolutionize our marriages as well as our relationships with our children and friends.

— Ruth Senter

REVIVE

Saturday: Mark 10:32–45
Sunday: Mark 10:46–52

Go to page 102 for your next devotional reading.

say, 'It's going to be hot,' and it is. 56Hypocrites! You know how to interpret the appearance of the earth and the sky. How is it that you don't know how to interpret this present time?

57"Why don't you judge for yourselves what is right? 58As you are going with your adversary to the magistrate, try hard to be reconciled to him on the way, or he may drag you off to the judge, and the judge turn you over to the officer, and the officer throw you into prison. 59I tell you, you will not get out until you have paid the last penny.a "

Repent or Perish

13 Now there were some present at that time who told Jesus about the Galileans whose blood Pilate had mixed with their sacrifices. 2Jesus answered, "Do you think that these Galileans were worse sinners than all the other Galileans because they suffered this way? 3I tell you, no! But unless you repent, you too will all perish. 4Or those eighteen who died when the tower in Siloam fell on them—do you think they were more guilty than all the others living in Jerusalem? 5I tell you, no! But unless you repent, you too will all perish."

6Then he told this parable: "A man had a fig tree, planted in his vineyard, and he went to look for fruit on it, but did not find any. 7So he said to the man who took care of the vineyard, 'For three years now I've been coming to look for fruit on this fig tree and haven't found any. Cut it down! Why should it use up the soil?'

8" 'Sir,' the man replied, 'leave it alone for one more year, and I'll dig around it and fertilize it. 9If it bears fruit next year, fine! If not, then cut it down.' "

A Crippled Woman Healed on the Sabbath

10On a Sabbath Jesus was teaching in one of the synagogues, 11and a woman was there who had been crippled by a spirit for eighteen years. She was bent over and could not straighten up at all. 12When Jesus saw her, he called her forward and said to her, "Woman, you are set free from your infirmity." 13Then he put his hands on her, and immediately she straightened up and praised God.

14Indignant because Jesus had healed on the Sabbath, the synagogue ruler said to the people, "There are six days for work. So come and be healed on those days, not on the Sabbath."

15The Lord answered him, "You hypocrites! Doesn't each of you on the Sabbath untie his ox or donkey from the stall and lead it out to give it water? 16Then should not this woman, a daughter of Abraham, whom Satan has kept bound for eighteen long years, be set free on the Sabbath day from what bound her?"

17When he said this, all his opponents were humiliated, but the people were delighted with all the wonderful things he was doing.

The Parables of the Mustard Seed and the Yeast

18Then Jesus asked, "What is the kingdom of God like? What shall I compare it to? 19It is like a mustard seed, which a man took and planted in his garden. It grew and became a tree, and the birds of the air perched in its branches."

20Again he asked, "What shall I compare the kingdom of God to? 21It is like yeast that a woman took and mixed into a large amountb of flour until it worked all through the dough."

The Narrow Door

22Then Jesus went through the towns and villages, teaching as he made his way to Jerusalem. 23Someone asked him, "Lord, are only a few people going to be saved?"

He said to them, 24"Make every effort to enter through the narrow door, because many, I tell you, will try to enter and will not be able to. 25Once the owner of the house gets up and closes the door, you will stand outside knocking and pleading, 'Sir, open the door for us.'

"But he will answer, 'I don't know you or where you come from.'

26"Then you will say, 'We ate and drank with you, and you taught in our streets.'

27"But he will reply, 'I don't know you or where you come from. Away from me, all you evildoers!'

28"There will be weeping there, and gnashing of teeth, when you see Abraham, Isaac and Jacob and all the prophets in the kingdom of God, but you yourselves thrown out. 29People will come from east and west and north and south, and will take their places at the feast in

a59 Greek lepton   b21 Greek three satas (probably about 1/2 bushel or 22 liters) the kingdom of God. [30]Indeed there are those who are last who will be first, and first who will be last."

Jesus' Sorrow for Jerusalem

[31]At that time some Pharisees came to Jesus and said to him, "Leave this place and go somewhere else. Herod wants to kill you."

[32]He replied, "Go tell that fox, 'I will drive out demons and heal people today and tomorrow, and on the third day I will reach my goal.' [33]In any case, I must keep going today and tomorrow and the next day—for surely no prophet can die outside Jerusalem!

[34]"O Jerusalem, Jerusalem, you who kill the prophets and stone those sent to you, how often I have longed to gather your children together, as a hen gathers her chicks under her wings, but you were not willing! [35]Look, your house is left to you desolate. I tell you, you will not see me again until you say, 'Blessed is he who comes in the name of the Lord.'[a]"

[a]35 Psalm 118:26

| VERSE FOR THE DAY: | AUTHOR: | PASSAGE FOR THE DAY: |
| Luke 13:16 | Jill Briscoe | Luke 13:10–17 |

The Language of Love

JESUS understood us. Yes, he did! You can tell it by his language. It was the language of love. Paul says that love has good manners (1 Corinthians 13:5), and if you care to read the way the Lord Jesus addressed the women he met, you can actually hear love talking. He said "daughter," "little girl," and even "daughter of Abraham," as in this passage. What courtesy and comfort, for women in Jesus' day were treated like dirt. When the priggish Pharisees dragged a woman in front of him who was "caught in adultery," Jesus saved her from possible stoning and then dealt firmly with her (John 8:3–11). He was not rude or rough, but polite while firm.

It's awfully important how you talk to people. Jesus always seemed to say the right thing the right way! When I was a young youth worker I was given a lot of responsibility suddenly. It went to my head. Being a strong sort of character, it was not long before I was busy bossing everyone about. "Jill," my fellow worker sweetly said to me one day, "I would like to be asked—not told." I needed that! Jesus didn't boss women around. He understood us; he knew we liked to be asked, not told. He used the language of love, and so must we if we would follow in his steps and if we would see anything accomplished. Let's try a few good manners. It's amazing how many people will respond. Try saying "please" and "thank you" and "do you mind"—this is the language of love.

Additional Scripture Readings:
John 4:7–27; Colossians 4:6

Go to page 104 for your next devotional reading.

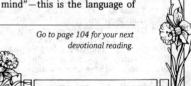

Jesus at a Pharisee's House

14 One Sabbath, when Jesus went to eat in the house of a prominent Pharisee, he was being carefully watched. [2]There in front of him was a man suffering from dropsy. [3]Jesus asked the Pharisees and experts in the law, "Is it lawful to heal on the Sabbath or not?" [4]But they remained silent. So taking hold of the man, he healed him and sent him away.

[5]Then he asked them, "If one of you has a son[a] or an ox that falls into a well on the Sabbath day, will you not immediately pull him out?" [6]And they had nothing to say.

[7]When he noticed how the guests picked the places of honor at the table, he told them this parable: [8]"When someone invites you to a wedding feast, do not take the place of honor, for a person more distinguished than you may have been invited. [9]If so, the host who invited both of you will come and say to you, 'Give this man your seat.' Then, humiliated, you will have to take the least important place. [10]But when you are invited, take the lowest place, so that when your host comes, he will say to you, 'Friend, move up to a better place.' Then you will be honored in the presence of all your fellow guests. [11]For everyone who exalts himself will be humbled, and he who humbles himself will be exalted."

[12]Then Jesus said to his host, "When you give a luncheon or dinner, do not invite your friends, your brothers or relatives, or your rich neighbors; if you do, they may invite you back and so you will be repaid. [13]But when you give a banquet, invite the poor, the crippled, the lame, the blind, [14]and you will be blessed. Although they cannot repay you, you will be repaid at the resurrection of the righteous."

The Parable of the Great Banquet

[15]When one of those at the table with him heard this, he said to Jesus, "Blessed is the man who will eat at the feast in the kingdom of God."

[16]Jesus replied: "A certain man was preparing a great banquet and invited many guests. [17]At the time of the banquet he sent his servant to tell those who had been invited, 'Come, for everything is now ready.'

[18]"But they all alike began to make excuses. The first said, 'I have just bought a field, and I must go and see it. Please excuse me.'

[19]"Another said, 'I have just bought five yoke of oxen, and I'm on my way to try them out. Please excuse me.'

[20]"Still another said, 'I just got married, so I can't come.'

[21]"The servant came back and reported this to his master. Then the owner of the house became angry and ordered his servant, 'Go out quickly into the streets and alleys of the town and bring in the poor, the crippled, the blind and the lame.'

[22]"'Sir,' the servant said, 'what you ordered has been done, but there is still room.'

[23]"Then the master told his servant, 'Go out to the roads and country lanes and make them come in, so that my house will be full. [24]I tell you, not one of those men who were invited will get a taste of my banquet.'"

The Cost of Being a Disciple

[25]Large crowds were traveling with Jesus, and turning to them he said: [26]"If anyone comes to me and does not hate his father and mother, his wife and children, his brothers and sisters—yes, even his own life—he cannot be my disciple. [27]And anyone who does not carry his cross and follow me cannot be my disciple.

[28]"Suppose one of you wants to build a tower. Will he not first sit down and estimate the cost to see if he has enough money to complete it? [29]For if he lays the foundation and is not able to finish it, everyone who sees it will ridicule him, [30]saying, 'This fellow began to build and was not able to finish.'

[31]"Or suppose a king is about to go to war against another king. Will he not first sit down and consider whether he is able with ten thousand men to oppose the one coming against him with twenty thousand? [32]If he is not able, he will send a delegation while the other is still a long way off and will ask for terms of peace. [33]In the same way, any of you who does not give up everything he has cannot be my disciple.

[34]"Salt is good, but if it loses its saltiness, how can it be made salty again? [35]It is fit neither for the soil nor for the manure pile; it is thrown out.

[a]5 Some manuscripts *donkey*

VERSE FOR THE DAY:	AUTHOR:	PASSAGE FOR THE DAY:
Luke 14:12	Joni Eareckson Tada	Luke 14:1–35

Changing the Subject

IMAGINE the scene in Luke 14:1–24. Jesus was invited to dinner at a Pharisee's home in the rich suburbs of Jerusalem. He noticed the wealthy people grabbing the best seats around the table. At that point, Jesus launched into a story about the sorts of dinner parties people ought to give—feasts for the forgotten, the homeless, the poor and the disabled.

The Lord added that although these poor people would not be able to repay them, the hosts would, nevertheless, be repaid at the resurrection (Luke 14:14).

You can imagine what happened next. Jesus probably sat down, put his napkin on his lap, and quietly picked up an hors d'oeuvre. Dead silence hung over the table as the wealthy people shot nervous glances at each other. Jesus had put a damper on the party spirit.

Finally, one of the dinner guests cleared his throat and spoke up. "Blessed is the man who will eat at the feast in the kingdom of God" (Luke 14:15). What an odd thing to say! It's as if he was thinking:

> *Jesus, I can't say that I follow your strange ideas about dining with cripples, but I do agree with what you said about heaven—it's so comforting to know that everything will turn out perfectly in the end.* *

The man, in other words, was trying his best to change the spiritual subject.

Sound familiar? I can't tell you how many times I have either consciously or unconsciously tried to change the spiritual subject with God when I sensed he was laying heavy, convicting things on my heart. But just as the Lord did not allow those dinner guests to change the subject (read Luke 14:15–24), we will find it just as difficult to divert God's attention from those issues that need to be addressed in our lives.

Additional Scripture Readings:
Luke 11:27–28; James 2:1–7

Go to page 106 for your next devotional reading.

*Robert Farrar Capon, *The Parables of Grace* (Grand Rapids: William B. Eerdmans Publishing Company. 1988), 130-131.

"He who has ears to hear, let him hear."

The Parable of the Lost Sheep

15 Now the tax collectors and "sinners" were all gathering around to hear him. [2]But the Pharisees and the teachers of the law muttered, "This man welcomes sinners and eats with them."

[3]Then Jesus told them this parable: [4]"Suppose one of you has a hundred sheep and loses one of them. Does he not leave the ninety-nine in the open country and go after the lost sheep until he finds it? [5]And when he finds it, he joyfully puts it on his shoulders [6]and goes home. Then he calls his friends and neighbors together and says, 'Rejoice with me; I have found my lost sheep.' [7]I tell you that in the same way there will be more rejoicing in heaven over one sinner who repents than over ninety-nine righteous persons who do not need to repent.

The Parable of the Lost Coin

[8]"Or suppose a woman has ten silver coins[a] and loses one. Does she not light a lamp, sweep the house and search carefully until she finds it? [9]And when she finds it, she calls her friends and neighbors together and says, 'Rejoice with me; I have found my lost coin.' [10]In the same way, I tell you, there is rejoicing in the presence of the angels of God over one sinner who repents."

The Parable of the Lost Son

[11]Jesus continued: "There was a man who had two sons. [12]The younger one said to his father, 'Father, give me my share of the estate.' So he divided his property between them.

[13]"Not long after that, the younger son got together all he had, set off for a distant country and there squandered his wealth in wild living. [14]After he had spent everything, there was a severe famine in that whole country, and he began to be in need. [15]So he went and hired himself out to a citizen of that country, who sent him to his fields to feed pigs. [16]He longed to fill his stomach with the pods that the pigs were eating, but no one gave him anything.

[17]"When he came to his senses, he said, 'How many of my father's hired men have food to spare, and here I am starving to death! [18]I will set out and go back to my father and say to him: Father, I have sinned against heaven and against you. [19]I am no longer worthy to be called your son; make me like one of your hired men.' [20]So he got up and went to his father.

"But while he was still a long way off, his father saw him and was filled with compassion for him; he ran to his son, threw his arms around him and kissed him.

[21]"The son said to him, 'Father, I have sinned against heaven and against you. I am no longer worthy to be called your son.[b]'

[22]"But the father said to his servants, 'Quick! Bring the best robe and put it on him. Put a ring on his finger and sandals on his feet. [23]Bring the fattened calf and kill it. Let's have a feast and celebrate. [24]For this son of mine was dead and is alive again; he was lost and is found.' So they began to celebrate.

[25]"Meanwhile, the older son was in the field. When he came near the house, he heard music and dancing. [26]So he called one of the servants and asked him what was going on. [27]'Your brother has come,' he replied, 'and your father has killed the fattened calf because he has him back safe and sound.'

[28]"The older brother became angry and refused to go in. So his father went out and pleaded with him. [29]But he answered his father, 'Look! All these years I've been slaving for you and never disobeyed your orders. Yet you never gave me even a young goat so I could celebrate with my friends. [30]But when this son of yours who has squandered your property with prostitutes comes home, you kill the fattened calf for him!'

[31]"'My son,' the father said, 'you are always with me, and everything I have is yours. [32]But we had to celebrate and be glad, because this brother of yours was dead and is alive again; he was lost and is found.'"

The Parable of the Shrewd Manager

16 Jesus told his disciples: "There was a rich man whose manager was accused of wasting his possessions. [2]So he called him in and asked him, 'What is this I hear about you? Give an account of your management, because you cannot be manager any longer.'

---

[a]8 Greek *ten drachmas,* each worth about a day's wages   [b]21 Some early manuscripts *son. Make me like one of your hired men.*

VERSE FOR THE DAY:
Luke 15:6

AUTHOR:
Rosalind Rinker

PASSAGE FOR THE DAY:
Luke 15:1–7

The Parable of the Lost Sheep

JESUS told the parable of the lost sheep to self-righteous leaders who criticized him because he welcomed sinners and even ate with them. His love and mercy are still reaching out to us today, for we are his sheep who have (with or without our consent) wandered into forbidden paths that seemed very innocent. We often shrink from calling anything "sin," but we do admit that sometimes we find ourselves alone, lost, and away from our Shepherd.

For a few moments, imagine you are that little lost one. How did you get lost?

* * * *

There you are, with the rest of the flock, on a hilltop chosen for its tender green grass. Suddenly something tastes better than grass. You don't know that it is tender young thistles but you do know you want more. Searching here and there, you are unaware that you are going downhill to find that delicious stuff. Then, your tummy full, you tuck your legs under your belly and fall right to sleep.

In the meantime, your Good Shepherd takes his flock back to the shelter. Only ninety-nine! Where is that missing little one? Leaving his faithful dog to guard the flock, he retraces his steps to the hilltop, searching, calling, praying.

And what about you? After a good nap you awaken, and . . . oh-oh . . . where are you? It is pitch-dark. Where are the other sheep? Where is your Shepherd? Strange noises frighten you and you say to yourself, "How did I ever get into this mess? How can I ever get out of it?"

With all your strength you cry out, "Maaa . . . maaa . . . Jesus, here I am!" The Good Shepherd hears that cry, and soon you are in his arms. His strong, tender hands are holding you. Feeling the beating of your little heart, he reassures you of his love, and your fears quiet down as you nestle in his arms.

> "My little one, you belong to me. I know what led
> you astray, but I found you. I'll always be there
> when you need me. My love is unconditional and
> eternal."

Additional Scripture Readings:
Psalm 23:1–4; John 10:11–16

*Go to page 110 for your next
devotional reading.*

³"The manager said to himself, 'What shall I do now? My master is taking away my job. I'm not strong enough to dig, and I'm ashamed to beg— ⁴I know what I'll do so that, when I lose my job here, people will welcome me into their houses.'

⁵"So he called in each one of his master's debtors. He asked the first, 'How much do you owe my master?'

⁶" 'Eight hundred gallons^a of olive oil,' he replied.

"The manager told him, 'Take your bill, sit down quickly, and make it four hundred.'

⁷"Then he asked the second, 'And how much do you owe?'

" 'A thousand bushels^b of wheat,' he replied.

"He told him, 'Take your bill and make it eight hundred.'

⁸"The master commended the dishonest manager because he had acted shrewdly. For the people of this world are more shrewd in dealing with their own kind than are the people of the light. ⁹I tell you, use worldly wealth to gain friends for yourselves, so that when it is gone, you will be welcomed into eternal dwellings.

¹⁰"Whoever can be trusted with very little can also be trusted with much, and whoever is dishonest with very little will also be dishonest with much. ¹¹So if you have not been trustworthy in handling worldly wealth, who will trust you with true riches? ¹²And if you have not been trustworthy with someone else's property, who will give you property of your own?

¹³"No servant can serve two masters. Either he will hate the one and love the other, or he will be devoted to the one and despise the other. You cannot serve both God and Money."

¹⁴The Pharisees, who loved money, heard all this and were sneering at Jesus. ¹⁵He said to them, "You are the ones who justify yourselves in the eyes of men, but God knows your hearts. What is highly valued among men is detestable in God's sight.

Additional Teachings

¹⁶"The Law and the Prophets were proclaimed until John. Since that time, the good news of the kingdom of God is being preached, and everyone is forcing his way into it. ¹⁷It is easier for heaven and earth to disappear than for the least stroke of a pen to drop out of the Law.

¹⁸"Anyone who divorces his wife and marries another woman commits adultery, and the man who marries a divorced woman commits adultery.

The Rich Man and Lazarus

¹⁹"There was a rich man who was dressed in purple and fine linen and lived in luxury every day. ²⁰At his gate was laid a beggar named Lazarus, covered with sores ²¹and longing to eat what fell from the rich man's table. Even the dogs came and licked his sores.

²²"The time came when the beggar died and the angels carried him to Abraham's side. The rich man also died and was buried. ²³In hell,^c where he was in torment, he looked up and saw Abraham far away, with Lazarus by his side. ²⁴So he called to him, 'Father Abraham, have pity on me and send Lazarus to dip the tip of his finger in water and cool my tongue, because I am in agony in this fire.'

²⁵"But Abraham replied, 'Son, remember that in your lifetime you received your good things, while Lazarus received bad things, but now he is comforted here and you are in agony. ²⁶And besides all this, between us and you a great chasm has been fixed, so that those who want to go from here to you cannot, nor can anyone cross over from there to us.'

²⁷"He answered, 'Then I beg you, father, send Lazarus to my father's house, ²⁸for I have five brothers. Let him warn them, so that they will not also come to this place of torment.'

²⁹"Abraham replied, 'They have Moses and the Prophets; let them listen to them.'

³⁰" 'No, father Abraham,' he said, 'but if someone from the dead goes to them, they will repent.'

³¹"He said to him, 'If they do not listen to Moses and the Prophets, they will not be convinced even if someone rises from the dead.' "

Sin, Faith, Duty

17 Jesus said to his disciples: "Things that cause people to sin are bound to come, but woe to that person through whom they come. ²It would be better for him to be thrown into the sea with a mill-

---

^a6 Greek *one hundred batous* (probably about 3 kiloliters)   ^b7 Greek *one hundred korous* (probably about 35 kiloliters)   ^c23 Greek *Hades*

stone tied around his neck than for him to cause one of these little ones to sin. ⁵So watch yourselves.

"If your brother sins, rebuke him, and if he repents, forgive him. ⁴If he sins against you seven times in a day, and seven times comes back to you and says, 'I repent,' forgive him."

⁵The apostles said to the Lord, "Increase our faith!"

⁶He replied, "If you have faith as small as a mustard seed, you can say to this mulberry tree, 'Be uprooted and planted in the sea,' and it will obey you.

⁷"Suppose one of you had a servant plowing or looking after the sheep. Would he say to the servant when he comes in from the field, 'Come along now and sit down to eat'? ⁸Would he not rather say, 'Prepare my supper, get yourself ready and wait on me while I eat and drink; after that you may eat and drink'? ⁹Would he thank the servant because he did what he was told to do? ¹⁰So you also, when you have done everything you were told to do, should say, 'We are unworthy servants; we have only done our duty.' "

Ten Healed of Leprosy

¹¹Now on his way to Jerusalem, Jesus traveled along the border between Samaria and Galilee. ¹²As he was going into a village, ten men who had leprosy[a] met him. They stood at a distance ¹³and called out in a loud voice, "Jesus, Master, have pity on us!"

¹⁴When he saw them, he said, "Go, show yourselves to the priests." And as they went, they were cleansed.

¹⁵One of them, when he saw he was healed, came back, praising God in a loud voice. ¹⁶He threw himself at Jesus' feet and thanked him—and he was a Samaritan.

¹⁷Jesus asked, "Were not all ten cleansed? Where are the other nine? ¹⁸Was no one found to return and give praise to God except this foreigner?" ¹⁹Then he said to him, "Rise and go; your faith has made you well."

The Coming of the Kingdom of God

²⁰Once, having been asked by the Pharisees when the kingdom of God would come, Jesus replied, "The kingdom of God does not come with your careful ob-

servation, ²¹nor will people say, 'Here it is,' or 'There it is,' because the kingdom of God is within[b] you."

²²Then he said to his disciples, "The time is coming when you will long to see one of the days of the Son of Man, but you will not see it. ²³Men will tell you, 'There he is!' or 'Here he is!' Do not go running off after them. ²⁴For the Son of Man in his day[c] will be like the lightning, which flashes and lights up the sky from one end to the other. ²⁵But first he must suffer many things and be rejected by this generation.

²⁶"Just as it was in the days of Noah, so also will it be in the days of the Son of Man. ²⁷People were eating, drinking, marrying and being given in marriage up to the day Noah entered the ark. Then the flood came and destroyed them all.

²⁸"It was the same in the days of Lot. People were eating and drinking, buying and selling, planting and building. ²⁹But the day Lot left Sodom, fire and sulfur rained down from heaven and destroyed them all.

³⁰"It will be just like this on the day the Son of Man is revealed. ³¹On that day no one who is on the roof of his house, with his goods inside, should go down to get them. Likewise, no one in the field should go back for anything. ³²Remember Lot's wife! ³³Whoever tries to keep his life will lose it, and whoever loses his life will preserve it. ³⁴I tell you, on that night two people will be in one bed; one will be taken and the other left. ³⁵Two women will be grinding grain together; one will be taken and the other left.[d] "

³⁷"Where, Lord?" they asked.

He replied, "Where there is a dead body, there the vultures will gather."

The Parable of the Persistent Widow

18 Then Jesus told his disciples a parable to show them that they should always pray and not give up. ²He said: "In a certain town there was a judge who neither feared God nor cared about men. ³And there was a widow in that town who kept coming to him with the plea, 'Grant me justice against my adversary.'

⁴"For some time he refused. But finally he said to himself, 'Even though I don't fear God or care about men, ⁵yet because this widow keeps bothering me, I will see

---

a12 The Greek word was used for various diseases affecting the skin—not necessarily leprosy.   *b21* Or *among*   *c24* Some manuscripts do not have *in his day.*   *d35* Some manuscripts *left.* ³⁶*Two men will be in the field; one will be taken and the other left.*

that she gets justice, so that she won't eventually wear me out with her coming!' "

[6]And the Lord said, "Listen to what the unjust judge says. [7]And will not God bring about justice for his chosen ones, who cry out to him day and night? Will he keep putting them off? [8]I tell you, he will see that they get justice, and quickly. However, when the Son of Man comes, will he find faith on the earth?"

The Parable of the Pharisee and the Tax Collector

[9]To some who were confident of their own righteousness and looked down on everybody else, Jesus told this parable: [10]"Two men went up to the temple to pray, one a Pharisee and the other a tax collector. [11]The Pharisee stood up and prayed about[a] himself: 'God, I thank you that I am not like other men—robbers, evildoers, adulterers—or even like this tax collector. [12]I fast twice a week and give a tenth of all I get.'

[13]"But the tax collector stood at a distance. He would not even look up to heaven, but beat his breast and said, 'God, have mercy on me, a sinner.'

[14]"I tell you that this man, rather than the other, went home justified before God. For everyone who exalts himself will be humbled, and he who humbles himself will be exalted."

The Little Children and Jesus

[15]People were also bringing babies to Jesus to have him touch them. When the disciples saw this, they rebuked them. [16]But Jesus called the children to him and said, "Let the little children come to me, and do not hinder them, for the kingdom of God belongs to such as these. [17]I tell you the truth, anyone who will not receive the kingdom of God like a little child will never enter it."

The Rich Ruler

[18]A certain ruler asked him, "Good teacher, what must I do to inherit eternal life?"

[19]"Why do you call me good?" Jesus answered. "No one is good—except God alone. [20]You know the commandments: 'Do not commit adultery, do not murder, do not steal, do not give false testimony, honor your father and mother.'[b]"

[21]"All these I have kept since I was a boy," he said.

[22]When Jesus heard this, he said to him, "You still lack one thing. Sell everything you have and give to the poor, and you will have treasure in heaven. Then come, follow me."

[23]When he heard this, he became very sad, because he was a man of great wealth. [24]Jesus looked at him and said, "How hard it is for the rich to enter the kingdom of God! [25]Indeed, it is easier for a camel to go through the eye of a needle than for a rich man to enter the kingdom of God."

[26]Those who heard this asked, "Who then can be saved?"

[27]Jesus replied, "What is impossible with men is possible with God."

[28]Peter said to him, "We have left all we had to follow you!"

[29]"I tell you the truth," Jesus said to them, "no one who has left home or wife or brothers or parents or children for the sake of the kingdom of God [30]will fail to receive many times as much in this age and, in the age to come, eternal life."

Jesus Again Predicts His Death

[31]Jesus took the Twelve aside and told them, "We are going up to Jerusalem, and everything that is written by the prophets about the Son of Man will be fulfilled. [32]He will be handed over to the Gentiles. They will mock him, insult him, spit on him, flog him and kill him. [33]On the third day he will rise again."

[34]The disciples did not understand any of this. Its meaning was hidden from them, and they did not know what he was talking about.

A Blind Beggar Receives His Sight

[35]As Jesus approached Jericho, a blind man was sitting by the roadside begging. [36]When he heard the crowd going by, he asked what was happening. [37]They told him, "Jesus of Nazareth is passing by."

[38]He called out, "Jesus, Son of David, have mercy on me!"

[39]Those who led the way rebuked him and told him to be quiet, but he shouted all the more, "Son of David, have mercy on me!"

[40]Jesus stopped and ordered the man to be brought to him. When he came near, Jesus asked him, [41]"What do you want me to do for you?"

---

[a]11 Or to   [b]20 Exodus 20:12-16; Deut. 5:16-20

"Lord, I want to see," he replied.

⁴²Jesus said to him, "Receive your sight; your faith has healed you." ⁴³Immediately he received his sight and followed Jesus, praising God. When all the people saw it, they also praised God.

Zacchaeus the Tax Collector

19 Jesus entered Jericho and was passing through. ²A man was there by the name of Zacchaeus; he was a chief tax collector and was wealthy. ³He wanted to see who Jesus was, but being a short man he could not, because of the crowd. ⁴So he ran ahead and climbed a sycamore-fig tree to see him, since Jesus was coming that way.

⁵When Jesus reached the spot, he looked up and said to him, "Zacchaeus, come down immediately. I must stay at your house today." ⁶So he came down at once and welcomed him gladly.

⁷All the people saw this and began to mutter, "He has gone to be the guest of a 'sinner.' "

⁸But Zacchaeus stood up and said to the Lord, "Look, Lord! Here and now I give half of my possessions to the poor, and if I have cheated anybody out of anything, I will pay back four times the amount."

⁹Jesus said to him, "Today salvation has come to this house, because this man, too, is a son of Abraham. ¹⁰For the Son of Man came to seek and to save what was lost."

The Parable of the Ten Minas

¹¹While they were listening to this, he went on to tell them a parable, because he was near Jerusalem and the people

THURSDAY

VERSE FOR THE DAY: AUTHOR: PASSAGE FOR THE DAY:
Luke 18:29–30   Corrie ten Boom   Luke 18:18–30

Sisters

BETSIE'S sleeping place beside me in prison was empty. She had just died. I motioned to a newly arrived Russian prisoner who was looking for a place to sleep, and she gratefully joined me.

We were sharing the same pillow, and with our faces so close, I wanted to speak. But I did not know her language.

"Jezus Christus?" I asked softly.

"Oh!" she exclaimed. Quickly making the sign of the cross, she threw her arms around me.

She who had been my sister for fifty-two years had left me. A Russian woman now claimed my love. And there would be others, too, who would be my sisters and brothers in Christ all around the world.

> "I tell you the truth," Jesus said to them, "no one who has left home or wife or brothers or parents or children for the sake of the kingdom of God will fail to receive many times as much in this age and, in the age to come, eternal life" (Luke 18:29–30).

Additional Scripture Readings: *Go to page 113 for your next*
Galatians 6:9–10; Philemon 10–16   *devotional reading.*

thought that the kingdom of God was going to appear at once. [12]He said: "A man of noble birth went to a distant country to have himself appointed king and then to return. [13]So he called ten of his servants and gave them ten minas.[a] 'Put this money to work,' he said, 'until I come back.'

[14]"But his subjects hated him and sent a delegation after him to say, 'We don't want this man to be our king.'

[15]"He was made king, however, and returned home. Then he sent for the servants to whom he had given the money, in order to find out what they had gained with it.

[16]"The first one came and said, 'Sir, your mina has earned ten more.'

[17]" 'Well done, my good servant!' his master replied. 'Because you have been trustworthy in a very small matter, take charge of ten cities.'

[18]"The second came and said, 'Sir, your mina has earned five more.'

[19]"His master answered, 'You take charge of five cities.'

[20]"Then another servant came and said, 'Sir, here is your mina; I have kept it laid away in a piece of cloth. [21]I was afraid of you, because you are a hard man. You take out what you did not put in and reap what you did not sow.'

[22]"His master replied, 'I will judge you by your own words, you wicked servant! You knew, did you, that I am a hard man, taking out what I did not put in, and reaping what I did not sow? [23]Why then didn't you put my money on deposit, so that when I came back, I could have collected it with interest?'

[24]"Then he said to those standing by, 'Take his mina away from him and give it to the one who has ten minas.'

[25]" 'Sir,' they said, 'he already has ten!'

[26]"He replied, 'I tell you that to everyone who has, more will be given, but as for the one who has nothing, even what he has will be taken away. [27]But those enemies of mine who did not want me to be king over them—bring them here and kill them in front of me.' "

The Triumphal Entry

[28]After Jesus had said this, he went on ahead, going up to Jerusalem. [29]As he approached Bethphage and Bethany at the hill called the Mount of Olives, he sent two of his disciples, saying to them, [30]"Go to the village ahead of you, and as you enter it, you will find a colt tied there, which no one has ever ridden. Untie it and bring it here. [31]If anyone asks you, 'Why are you untying it?' tell him, 'The Lord needs it.' "

[32]Those who were sent ahead went and found it just as he had told them. [33]As they were untying the colt, its owners asked them, "Why are you untying the colt?"

[34]They replied, "The Lord needs it."

[35]They brought it to Jesus, threw their cloaks on the colt and put Jesus on it. [36]As he went along, people spread their cloaks on the road.

[37]When he came near the place where the road goes down the Mount of Olives, the whole crowd of disciples began joyfully to praise God in loud voices for all the miracles they had seen:

[38]"Blessed is the king who comes in the name of the Lord!"[b]

"Peace in heaven and glory in the highest!"

[39]Some of the Pharisees in the crowd said to Jesus, "Teacher, rebuke your disciples!"

[40]"I tell you," he replied, "if they keep quiet, the stones will cry out."

[41]As he approached Jerusalem and saw the city, he wept over it [42]and said, "If you, even you, had only known on this day what would bring you peace—but now it is hidden from your eyes. [43]The days will come upon you when your enemies will build an embankment against you and encircle you and hem you in on every side. [44]They will dash you to the ground, you and the children within your walls. They will not leave one stone on another, because you did not recognize the time of God's coming to you."

Jesus at the Temple

[45]Then he entered the temple area and began driving out those who were selling. [46]"It is written," he said to them, " 'My house will be a house of prayer'[c]; but you have made it 'a den of robbers.'[d] "

[47]Every day he was teaching at the temple. But the chief priests, the teachers of the law and the leaders among the people were trying to kill him. [48]Yet they could not find any way to do it, because all the people hung on his words.

[a]13 A mina was about three months' wages.   [b]38 Psalm 118:26   [c]46 Isaiah 56:7   [d]46 Jer. 7:11

The Authority of Jesus Questioned

20 One day as he was teaching the people in the temple courts and preaching the gospel, the chief priests and the teachers of the law, together with the elders, came up to him. ²"Tell us by what authority you are doing these things," they said. "Who gave you this authority?"

³He replied, "I will also ask you a question. Tell me, ⁴John's baptism—was it from heaven, or from men?"

⁵They discussed it among themselves and said, "If we say, 'From heaven,' he will ask, 'Why didn't you believe him?' ⁶But if we say, 'From men,' all the people will stone us, because they are persuaded that John was a prophet."

⁷So they answered, "We don't know where it was from."

⁸Jesus said, "Neither will I tell you by what authority I am doing these things."

The Parable of the Tenants

⁹He went on to tell the people this parable: "A man planted a vineyard, rented it to some farmers and went away for a long time. ¹⁰At harvest time he sent a servant to the tenants so they would give him some of the fruit of the vineyard. But the tenants beat him and sent him away empty-handed. ¹¹He sent another servant, but that one also they beat and treated shamefully and sent away empty-handed. ¹²He sent still a third, and they wounded him and threw him out.

¹³"Then the owner of the vineyard said, 'What shall I do? I will send my son, whom I love; perhaps they will respect him.'

¹⁴"But when the tenants saw him, they talked the matter over. 'This is the heir,' they said. 'Let's kill him, and the inheritance will be ours.' ¹⁵So they threw him out of the vineyard and killed him.

"What then will the owner of the vineyard do to them? ¹⁶He will come and kill those tenants and give the vineyard to others."

When the people heard this, they said, "May this never be!"

¹⁷Jesus looked directly at them and asked, "Then what is the meaning of that which is written:

  " 'The stone the builders rejected
    has become the capstone*ᵃ'ᵇ*?

¹⁸Everyone who falls on that stone will be broken to pieces, but he on whom it falls will be crushed."

¹⁹The teachers of the law and the chief priests looked for a way to arrest him immediately, because they knew he had spoken this parable against them. But they were afraid of the people.

Paying Taxes to Caesar

²⁰Keeping a close watch on him, they sent spies, who pretended to be honest. They hoped to catch Jesus in something he said so that they might hand him over to the power and authority of the governor. ²¹So the spies questioned him: "Teacher, we know that you speak and teach what is right, and that you do not show partiality but teach the way of God in accordance with the truth. ²²Is it right for us to pay taxes to Caesar or not?"

²³He saw through their duplicity and said to them, ²⁴"Show me a denarius. Whose portrait and inscription are on it?"

²⁵"Caesar's," they replied.

He said to them, "Then give to Caesar what is Caesar's, and to God what is God's."

²⁶They were unable to trap him in what he had said there in public. And astonished by his answer, they became silent.

The Resurrection and Marriage

²⁷Some of the Sadducees, who say there is no resurrection, came to Jesus with a question. ²⁸"Teacher," they said, "Moses wrote for us that if a man's brother dies and leaves a wife but no children, the man must marry the widow and have children for his brother. ²⁹Now there were seven brothers. The first one married a woman and died childless. ³⁰The second ³¹and then the third married her, and in the same way the seven died, leaving no children. ³²Finally, the woman died too. ³³Now then, at the resurrection whose wife will she be, since the seven were married to her?"

³⁴Jesus replied, "The people of this age marry and are given in marriage. ³⁵But those who are considered worthy of taking part in that age and in the resurrection from the dead will neither marry nor be given in marriage, ³⁶and they can no longer die; for they are like the angels. They are God's children, since they are children of the resurrection. ³⁷But in the account of the bush, even Moses showed

ᵃ17 Or cornerstone   ᵇ17 Psalm 118:22

that the dead rise, for he calls the Lord 'the God of Abraham, and the God of Isaac, and the God of Jacob.'[a] [38]He is not the God of the dead, but of the living, for to him all are alive."

[39]Some of the teachers of the law responded, "Well said, teacher!" [40]And no one dared to ask him any more questions.

Whose Son Is the Christ?

[41]Then Jesus said to them, "How is it that they say the Christ[b] is the Son of David? [42]David himself declares in the Book of Psalms:

" 'The Lord said to my Lord:
"Sit at my right hand
[43]until I make your enemies
a footstool for your feet." '[c]

[44]David calls him 'Lord.' How then can he be his son?"

[45]While all the people were listening, Jesus said to his disciples, [46]"Beware of the teachers of the law. They like to walk around in flowing robes and love to be greeted in the marketplaces and have the most important seats in the synagogues and the places of honor at banquets.

a37 Exodus 3:6   *b41* Or *Messiah*   *c43* Psalm 110:1

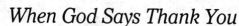

FRIDAY

VERSE FOR THE DAY:	*AUTHOR:*	*PASSAGE FOR THE DAY:*
Luke 21:2	*Jill Briscoe*	*Luke 21:1–4*

When God Says Thank You

JESUS always notices women who throw everything they've got into the Lord's work! Sitting near the treasury at the temple, Jesus drew his disciples' attention to a poor widow. She was, I'm sure, unaware that Jesus was watching. She didn't have to be watched as she gave God everything she had. Her two small copper coins would have bought her a morsel of bread or five sparrows to eat (Luke 12:6–7), but she decided to go hungry and give her money to God instead. Two small coins weren't much. They weren't noticed, they weren't appreciated by other people until Jesus came along and saw what she did and made sure the twelve apostles saw it. He made sure that Luke and Mark recorded it and that the whole world read about it! Solomon's temple would stand without the help of the widow's coins, but Jesus knew that that sort of giving was the stuff of which the kingdom was made.

Jesus always notices the small offerings. Even if the widow herself didn't think her offering was worth the notice, Jesus disagreed and affirmed her in her service. Have you cast in all you can? Are you married to a man who will not allow you to serve God as you wish? Does financial strain limit you to giving little when you desire to give much? If you've indeed cast in all you possibly can of your money, time and service, God understands. He affirms you in it. He says thank you.

Additional Scripture Readings:
Acts 10:1–4; 2 Corinthians 9:6–7

Go to page 116 for your next devotional reading.

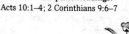

[47]They devour widows' houses and for a show make lengthy prayers. Such men will be punished most severely."

The Widow's Offering

21 As he looked up, Jesus saw the rich putting their gifts into the temple treasury. [2]He also saw a poor widow put in two very small copper coins.[a] [3]"I tell you the truth," he said, "this poor widow has put in more than all the others. [4]All these people gave their gifts out of their wealth; but she out of her poverty put in all she had to live on."

Signs of the End of the Age

[5]Some of his disciples were remarking about how the temple was adorned with beautiful stones and with gifts dedicated to God. But Jesus said, [6]"As for what you see here, the time will come when not one stone will be left on another; every one of them will be thrown down."

[7]"Teacher," they asked, "when will these things happen? And what will be the sign that they are about to take place?"

[8]He replied: "Watch out that you are not deceived. For many will come in my name, claiming, 'I am he,' and, 'The time is near.' Do not follow them. [9]When you hear of wars and revolutions, do not be frightened. These things must happen first, but the end will not come right away."

[10]Then he said to them: "Nation will rise against nation, and kingdom against kingdom. [11]There will be great earthquakes, famines and pestilences in various places, and fearful events and great signs from heaven.

[12]"But before all this, they will lay hands on you and persecute you. They will deliver you to synagogues and prisons, and you will be brought before kings and governors, and all on account of my name. [13]This will result in your being witnesses to them. [14]But make up your mind not to worry beforehand how you will defend yourselves. [15]For I will give you words and wisdom that none of your adversaries will be able to resist or contradict. [16]You will be betrayed even by parents, brothers, relatives and friends, and they will put some of you to death. [17]All men will hate you because of me. [18]But

not a hair of your head will perish. [19]By standing firm you will gain life.

[20]"When you see Jerusalem being surrounded by armies, you will know that its desolation is near. [21]Then let those who are in Judea flee to the mountains, let those in the city get out, and let those in the country not enter the city. [22]For this is the time of punishment in fulfillment of all that has been written. [23]How dreadful it will be in those days for pregnant women and nursing mothers! There will be great distress in the land and wrath against this people. [24]They will fall by the sword and will be taken as prisoners to all the nations. Jerusalem will be trampled on by the Gentiles until the times of the Gentiles are fulfilled.

[25]"There will be signs in the sun, moon and stars. On the earth, nations will be in anguish and perplexity at the roaring and tossing of the sea. [26]Men will faint from terror, apprehensive of what is coming on the world, for the heavenly bodies will be shaken. [27]At that time they will see the Son of Man coming in a cloud with power and great glory. [28]When these things begin to take place, stand up and lift up your heads, because your redemption is drawing near."

[29]He told them this parable: "Look at the fig tree and all the trees. [30]When they sprout leaves, you can see for yourselves and know that summer is near. [31]Even so, when you see these things happening, you know that the kingdom of God is near.

[32]"I tell you the truth, this generation[b] will certainly not pass away until all these things have happened. [33]Heaven and earth will pass away, but my words will never pass away.

[34]"Be careful, or your hearts will be weighed down with dissipation, drunkenness and the anxieties of life, and that day will close on you unexpectedly like a trap. [35]For it will come upon all those who live on the face of the whole earth. [36]Be always on the watch, and pray that you may be able to escape all that is about to happen, and that you may be able to stand before the Son of Man."

[37]Each day Jesus was teaching at the temple, and each evening he went out to spend the night on the hill called the Mount of Olives, [38]and all the people came early in the morning to hear him at the temple.

a2 Greek two lepta   b32 Or race

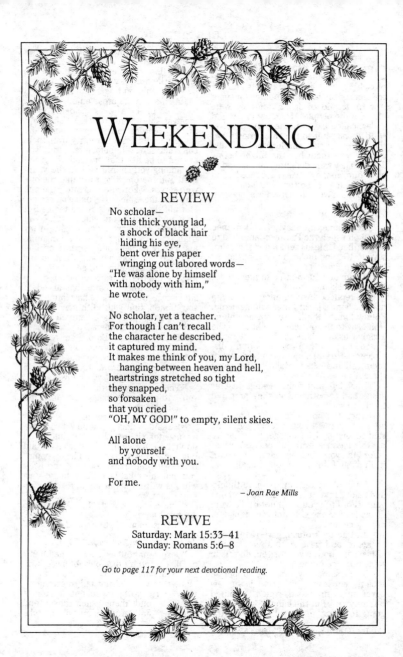

WEEKENDING

REVIEW

No scholar—
  this thick young lad,
  a shock of black hair
  hiding his eye,
  bent over his paper
  wringing out labored words—
"He was alone by himself
with nobody with him,"
he wrote.

No scholar, yet a teacher.
For though I can't recall
the character he described,
it captured my mind.
It makes me think of you, my Lord,
  hanging between heaven and hell,
heartstrings stretched so tight
they snapped,
so forsaken
that you cried
"OH, MY GOD!" to empty, silent skies.

All alone
  by yourself
and nobody with you.

For me.

— *Joan Rae Mills*

REVIVE
Saturday: Mark 15:33–41
Sunday: Romans 5:6–8

Go to page 117 for your next devotional reading.

Judas Agrees to Betray Jesus

22 Now the Feast of Unleavened Bread, called the Passover, was approaching, ²and the chief priests and the teachers of the law were looking for some way to get rid of Jesus, for they were afraid of the people. ³Then Satan entered Judas, called Iscariot, one of the Twelve. ⁴And Judas went to the chief priests and the officers of the temple guard and discussed with them how he might betray Jesus. ⁵They were delighted and agreed to give him money. ⁶He consented, and watched for an opportunity to hand Jesus over to them when no crowd was present.

The Last Supper

⁷Then came the day of Unleavened Bread on which the Passover lamb had to be sacrificed. ⁸Jesus sent Peter and John, saying, "Go and make preparations for us to eat the Passover."

⁹"Where do you want us to prepare for it?" they asked.

¹⁰He replied, "As you enter the city, a man carrying a jar of water will meet you. Follow him to the house that he enters, ¹¹and say to the owner of the house, 'The Teacher asks: Where is the guest room, where I may eat the Passover with my disciples?' ¹²He will show you a large upper room, all furnished. Make preparations there."

¹³They left and found things just as Jesus had told them. So they prepared the Passover.

¹⁴When the hour came, Jesus and his apostles reclined at the table. ¹⁵And he said to them, "I have eagerly desired to eat this Passover with you before I suffer. ¹⁶For I tell you, I will not eat it again until it finds fulfillment in the kingdom of God."

¹⁷After taking the cup, he gave thanks and said, "Take this and divide it among you. ¹⁸For I tell you I will not drink again of the fruit of the vine until the kingdom of God comes."

¹⁹And he took bread, gave thanks and broke it, and gave it to them, saying, "This is my body given for you; do this in remembrance of me."

²⁰In the same way, after the supper he took the cup, saying, "This cup is the new covenant in my blood, which is poured out for you. ²¹But the hand of him who is going to betray me is with mine on the table. ²²The Son of Man will go as it has been decreed, but woe to that man who betrays him." ²³They began to question among themselves which of them it might be who would do this.

²⁴Also a dispute arose among them as to which of them was considered to be greatest. ²⁵Jesus said to them, "The kings of the Gentiles lord it over them; and those who exercise authority over them call themselves Benefactors. ²⁶But you are not to be like that. Instead, the greatest among you should be like the youngest, and the one who rules like the one who serves. ²⁷For who is greater, the one who is at the table or the one who serves? Is it not the one who is at the table? But I am among you as one who serves. ²⁸You are those who have stood by me in my trials. ²⁹And I confer on you a kingdom, just as my Father conferred one on me, ³⁰so that you may eat and drink at my table in my kingdom and sit on thrones, judging the twelve tribes of Israel.

³¹"Simon, Simon, Satan has asked to sift you*ᵃ* as wheat. ³²But I have prayed for you, Simon, that your faith may not fail. And when you have turned back, strengthen your brothers."

³³But he replied, "Lord, I am ready to go with you to prison and to death."

³⁴Jesus answered, "I tell you, Peter, before the rooster crows today, you will deny three times that you know me."

³⁵Then Jesus asked them, "When I sent you without purse, bag or sandals, did you lack anything?"

"Nothing," they answered.

³⁶He said to them, "But now if you have a purse, take it, and also a bag; and if you don't have a sword, sell your cloak and buy one. ³⁷It is written: 'And he was numbered with the transgressors'*ᵇ*; and I tell you that this must be fulfilled in me. Yes, what is written about me is reaching its fulfillment."

³⁸The disciples said, "See, Lord, here are two swords."

"That is enough," he replied.

Jesus Prays on the Mount of Olives

³⁹Jesus went out as usual to the Mount of Olives, and his disciples followed him. ⁴⁰On reaching the place, he said to them, "Pray that you will not fall into temptation." ⁴¹He withdrew about a stone's throw beyond them, knelt down and prayed, ⁴²"Father, if you are willing, take

---

ᵃ31 The Greek is plural.   *ᵇ37* Isaiah 53:12

this cup from me; yet not my will, but yours be done." [43]An angel from heaven appeared to him and strengthened him. [44]And being in anguish, he prayed more earnestly, and his sweat was like drops of blood falling to the ground.[a]

[45]When he rose from prayer and went back to the disciples, he found them asleep, exhausted from sorrow. [46]"Why are you sleeping?" he asked them. "Get up and pray so that you will not fall into temptation."

Jesus Arrested

[47]While he was still speaking a crowd came up, and the man who was called Judas, one of the Twelve, was leading them. He approached Jesus to kiss him, [48]but Jesus asked him, "Judas, are you betraying the Son of Man with a kiss?"

[49]When Jesus' followers saw what was going to happen, they said, "Lord, should we strike with our swords?" [50]And one of them struck the servant of the high priest, cutting off his right ear.

[51]But Jesus answered, "No more of this!" And he touched the man's ear and healed him.

[52]Then Jesus said to the chief priests, the officers of the temple guard, and the elders, who had come for him, "Am I leading a rebellion, that you have come with swords and clubs? [53]Every day I was with you in the temple courts, and you did not lay a hand on me. But this is your hour—when darkness reigns."

Peter Disowns Jesus

[54]Then seizing him, they led him away and took him into the house of the high

[a]44 Some early manuscripts do not have verses 43 and 44.

MONDAY

VERSE FOR THE DAY:
Luke 22:27

AUTHOR:
Karen Burton Mains

PASSAGE FOR THE DAY:
Luke 22:24–30

Servanting

BEING a servant is one of the most important lessons for Christians to learn; but unfortunately, we often have to work through gross misconceptions. We have fears about entrusting ourselves to any boss, but we must learn in our spiritual journey that this Master is unlike any other. He will not abuse us or misuse us. He has our greatest interest at heart. He encourages us through our servanting to be all that we can be and then gives us his own Holy Spirit to empower us to become so. This Master is one who even laid down his life for those who were his servants.

He is a Master unlike any other. Not to be feared, he is worthy of our service.

Many of us think servanting means losing ourselves in such a way that we become people without personality, people without original thinking ability, people without giftedness. But when one serves this Master, the opposite is true: He makes us full, complete human beings filled with his own image, with his own amazing mentality. Paradoxically, while teaching us to be more like him, we become more of whom he created us to be.

Additional Scripture Readings:
John 13:12–17; 1 Peter 4:8–11

Go to page 119 for your next devotional reading.

priest. Peter followed at a distance. ⁵⁵But when they had kindled a fire in the middle of the courtyard and had sat down together, Peter sat down with them. ⁵⁶A servant girl saw him seated there in the firelight. She looked closely at him and said, "This man was with him."

⁵⁷But he denied it. "Woman, I don't know him," he said.

⁵⁸A little later someone else saw him and said, "You also are one of them."

"Man, I am not!" Peter replied.

⁵⁹About an hour later another asserted, "Certainly this fellow was with him, for he is a Galilean."

⁶⁰Peter replied, "Man, I don't know what you're talking about!" Just as he was speaking, the rooster crowed. ⁶¹The Lord turned and looked straight at Peter. Then Peter remembered the word the Lord had spoken to him: "Before the rooster crows today, you will disown me three times." ⁶²And he went outside and wept bitterly.

The Guards Mock Jesus

⁶³The men who were guarding Jesus began mocking and beating him. ⁶⁴They blindfolded him and demanded, "Prophesy! Who hit you?" ⁶⁵And they said many other insulting things to him.

Jesus Before Pilate and Herod

⁶⁶At daybreak the council of the elders of the people, both the chief priests and teachers of the law, met together, and Jesus was led before them. ⁶⁷"If you are the Christ,ᵃ" they said, "tell us."

Jesus answered, "If I tell you, you will not believe me, ⁶⁸and if I asked you, you would not answer. ⁶⁹But from now on, the Son of Man will be seated at the right hand of the mighty God."

⁷⁰They all asked, "Are you then the Son of God?"

He replied, "You are right in saying I am."

⁷¹Then they said, "Why do we need any more testimony? We have heard it from his own lips."

23 Then the whole assembly rose and led him off to Pilate. ²And they began to accuse him, saying, "We have found this man subverting our nation. He opposes payment of taxes to Caesar and claims to be Christ,ᵇ a king."

³So Pilate asked Jesus, "Are you the king of the Jews?"

"Yes, it is as you say," Jesus replied.

⁴Then Pilate announced to the chief priests and the crowd, "I find no basis for a charge against this man."

⁵But they insisted, "He stirs up the people all over Judeaᶜ by his teaching. He started in Galilee and has come all the way here."

⁶On hearing this, Pilate asked if the man was a Galilean. ⁷When he learned that Jesus was under Herod's jurisdiction, he sent him to Herod, who was also in Jerusalem at that time.

⁸When Herod saw Jesus, he was greatly pleased, because for a long time he had been wanting to see him. From what he had heard about him, he hoped to see him perform some miracle. ⁹He plied him with many questions, but Jesus gave him no answer. ¹⁰The chief priests and the teachers of the law were standing there, vehemently accusing him. ¹¹Then Herod and his soldiers ridiculed and mocked him. Dressing him in an elegant robe, they sent him back to Pilate. ¹²That day Herod and Pilate became friends—before this they had been enemies.

¹³Pilate called together the chief priests, the rulers and the people, ¹⁴and said to them, "You brought me this man as one who was inciting the people to rebellion. I have examined him in your presence and have found no basis for your charges against him. ¹⁵Neither has Herod, for he sent him back to us; as you can see, he has done nothing to deserve death. ¹⁶Therefore, I will punish him and then release him.ᵈ"

¹⁸With one voice they cried out, "Away with this man! Release Barabbas to us!" ¹⁹(Barabbas had been thrown into prison for an insurrection in the city, and for murder.)

²⁰Wanting to release Jesus, Pilate appealed to them again. ²¹But they kept shouting, "Crucify him! Crucify him!"

²²For the third time he spoke to them: "Why? What crime has this man committed? I have found in him no grounds for the death penalty. Therefore I will have him punished and then release him."

²³But with loud shouts they insistently demanded that he be crucified, and their shouts prevailed. ²⁴So Pilate decided to grant their demand. ²⁵He released the man who had been thrown into prison for insurrection and murder,

---

ᵃ67 Or *Messiah*   ᵇ2 Or *Messiah*; also in verses 35 and 39   ᶜ5 Or *over the land of the Jews*
ᵈ16 Some manuscripts *him." ¹⁷Now he was obliged to release one man to them at the Feast.*

the one they asked for, and surrendered Jesus to their will.

The Crucifixion

26As they led him away, they seized Simon from Cyrene, who was on his way in from the country, and put the cross on him and made him carry it behind Jesus. 27A large number of people followed him, including women who mourned and wailed for him. 28Jesus turned and said to them, "Daughters of Jerusalem, do not weep for me; weep for yourselves and for your children. 29For the time will come when you will say, 'Blessed are the barren women, the wombs that never bore and the breasts that never nursed!' 30Then

" 'they will say to the mountains,
    "Fall on us!"
and to the hills, "Cover us!" ' a

31For if men do these things when the tree is green, what will happen when it is dry?"

32Two other men, both criminals, were also led out with him to be executed. 33When they came to the place called the Skull, there they crucified him, along with the criminals—one on his right, the other on his left. 34Jesus said, "Father, forgive them, for they do not know what they are doing." b And they divided up his clothes by casting lots.

35The people stood watching, and the rulers even sneered at him. They said,

a30 Hosea 10:8   b34 Some early manuscripts do not have this sentence.

| TUESDAY |

VERSE FOR THE DAY: AUTHOR: PASSAGE FOR THE DAY:
Luke 23:34   Eugenia Price   Luke 23:26–43

Redemptive Love

FOR three days they thought they had made it. His quiet, unbroken strength (almighty meekness) fanned their fury as they stood watching the heavy nails pierce his hands and feet, when the Roman soldiers secured him to his cross. He was taking into his heart the very sin that motivated this. Their hearts and minds were blinded by that sin. The same dark, inner drive which prodded the first man and woman toward the forbidden tree to satisfy their desire to know as much as God knew. In the heart of each man who plotted his death, there twisted the tormentor whom God hated. He did not hate these murderers, he hated the disease that had made them murderers. As the God-Man hung above them, praying for them, he loved them with the kind of love that could have healed them on the spot!

"Father, forgive them, for they do not know what they are doing" (Luke 23:34).

Down from his cross poured redemptive love in quantity enough for the whole human race. Enough for you. Enough for me. Far from decreasing because of our behavior against him, it seemed rather to increase. The same situation still exists today and will exist as long as the earth stands.

Additional Scripture Readings: *Go to page 124 for your next*
Matthew 23:37; Romans 5:8–11   *devotional reading.*

"He saved others; let him save himself if he is the Christ of God, the Chosen One."

[36]The soldiers also came up and mocked him. They offered him wine vinegar [37]and said, "If you are the king of the Jews, save yourself."

[38]There was a written notice above him, which read: THIS IS THE KING OF THE JEWS.

[39]One of the criminals who hung there hurled insults at him: "Aren't you the Christ? Save yourself and us!"

[40]But the other criminal rebuked him. "Don't you fear God," he said, "since you are under the same sentence? [41]We are punished justly, for we are getting what our deeds deserve. But this man has done nothing wrong."

[42]Then he said, "Jesus, remember me when you come into your kingdom.[a]"

[43]Jesus answered him, "I tell you the truth, today you will be with me in paradise."

Jesus' Death

[44]It was now about the sixth hour, and darkness came over the whole land until the ninth hour, [45]for the sun stopped shining. And the curtain of the temple was torn in two. [46]Jesus called out with a loud voice, "Father, into your hands I commit my spirit." When he had said this, he breathed his last.

[47]The centurion, seeing what had happened, praised God and said, "Surely this was a righteous man." [48]When all the people who had gathered to witness this sight saw what took place, they beat their breasts and went away. [49]But all those who knew him, including the women who had followed him from Galilee, stood at a distance, watching these things.

Jesus' Burial

[50]Now there was a man named Joseph, a member of the Council, a good and upright man, [51]who had not consented to their decision and action. He came from the Judean town of Arimathea and he was waiting for the kingdom of God. [52]Going to Pilate, he asked for Jesus' body. [53]Then he took it down, wrapped it in linen cloth and placed it in a tomb cut in the rock, one in which no one had yet been laid. [54]It was Preparation Day, and the Sabbath was about to begin.

[55]The women who had come with Jesus from Galilee followed Joseph and saw the tomb and how his body was laid in it. [56]Then they went home and prepared spices and perfumes. But they rested on the Sabbath in obedience to the commandment.

The Resurrection

24 On the first day of the week, very early in the morning, the women took the spices they had prepared and went to the tomb. [2]They found the stone rolled away from the tomb, [3]but when they entered, they did not find the body of the Lord Jesus. [4]While they were wondering about this, suddenly two men in clothes that gleamed like lightning stood beside them. [5]In their fright the women bowed down with their faces to the ground, but the men said to them, "Why do you look for the living among the dead? [6]He is not here; he has risen! Remember how he told you, while he was still with you in Galilee: [7]'The Son of Man must be delivered into the hands of sinful men, be crucified and on the third day be raised again.' " [8]Then they remembered his words.

[9]When they came back from the tomb, they told all these things to the Eleven and to all the others. [10]It was Mary Magdalene, Joanna, Mary the mother of James, and the others with them who told this to the apostles. [11]But they did not believe the women, because their words seemed to them like nonsense. [12]Peter, however, got up and ran to the tomb. Bending over, he saw the strips of linen lying by themselves, and he went away, wondering to himself what had happened.

On the Road to Emmaus

[13]Now that same day two of them were going to a village called Emmaus, about seven miles[b] from Jerusalem. [14]They were talking with each other about everything that had happened. [15]As they talked and discussed these things with each other, Jesus himself came up and walked along with them; [16]but they were kept from recognizing him.

[17]He asked them, "What are you discussing together as you walk along?"

They stood still, their faces downcast. [18]One of them, named Cleopas, asked him, "Are you only a visitor to Jerusalem and do not know the things that have happened there in these days?"

---

[a]42 Some manuscripts *come with your kingly power*   [b]13 Greek *sixty stadia* (about 11 kilometers)

¹⁹"What things?" he asked.

"About Jesus of Nazareth," they replied. "He was a prophet, powerful in word and deed before God and all the people. ²⁰The chief priests and our rulers handed him over to be sentenced to death, and they crucified him; ²¹but we had hoped that he was the one who was going to redeem Israel. And what is more, it is the third day since all this took place. ²²In addition, some of our women amazed us. They went to the tomb early this morning ²³but didn't find his body. They came and told us that they had seen a vision of angels, who said he was alive. ²⁴Then some of our companions went to the tomb and found it just as the women had said, but him they did not see."

²⁵He said to them, "How foolish you are, and how slow of heart to believe all that the prophets have spoken! ²⁶Did not the Christ*a* have to suffer these things and then enter his glory?" ²⁷And beginning with Moses and all the Prophets, he explained to them what was said in all the Scriptures concerning himself.

²⁸As they approached the village to which they were going, Jesus acted as if he were going farther. ²⁹But they urged him strongly, "Stay with us, for it is nearly evening; the day is almost over." So he went in to stay with them.

³⁰When he was at the table with them, he took bread, gave thanks, broke it and began to give it to them. ³¹Then their eyes were opened and they recognized him, and he disappeared from their sight. ³²They asked each other, "Were not our hearts burning within us while he talked with us on the road and opened the Scriptures to us?"

³³They got up and returned at once to Jerusalem. There they found the Eleven and those with them, assembled together ³⁴and saying, "It is true! The Lord has risen and has appeared to Simon." ³⁵Then the two told what had happened on the way, and how Jesus was recognized by them when he broke the bread.

Jesus Appears to the Disciples

³⁶While they were still talking about this, Jesus himself stood among them and said to them, "Peace be with you."

³⁷They were startled and frightened, thinking they saw a ghost. ³⁸He said to them, "Why are you troubled, and why do doubts rise in your minds? ³⁹Look at my hands and my feet. It is I myself! Touch me and see; a ghost does not have flesh and bones, as you see I have."

⁴⁰When he had said this, he showed them his hands and feet. ⁴¹And while they still did not believe it because of joy and amazement, he asked them, "Do you have anything here to eat?" ⁴²They gave him a piece of broiled fish, ⁴³and he took it and ate it in their presence.

⁴⁴He said to them, "This is what I told you while I was still with you: Everything must be fulfilled that is written about me in the Law of Moses, the Prophets and the Psalms."

⁴⁵Then he opened their minds so they could understand the Scriptures. ⁴⁶He told them, "This is what is written: The Christ will suffer and rise from the dead on the third day, ⁴⁷and repentance and forgiveness of sins will be preached in his name to all nations, beginning at Jerusalem. ⁴⁸You are witnesses of these things. ⁴⁹I am going to send you what my Father has promised; but stay in the city until you have been clothed with power from on high."

The Ascension

⁵⁰When he had led them out to the vicinity of Bethany, he lifted up his hands and blessed them. ⁵¹While he was blessing them, he left them and was taken up into heaven. ⁵²Then they worshiped him and returned to Jerusalem with great joy. ⁵³And they stayed continually at the temple, praising God.

a26 Or *Messiah*; also in verse 46

*J*OHN *writes this gospel to present Jesus, the powerful Son of God, who comes in human flesh, gives his life on the cross, and then returns to the Father—all with a view that we may believe in him and receive eternal life. His coming shows us how much the Father and the Son love us, and his parting command is that we should show the same sacrificial love to one another. As you read this book, be sure that you believe that Jesus is the Christ, the Son of God, and promise him that you will love others as he loves you.*

JOHN

The Word Became Flesh

1 In the beginning was the Word, and the Word was with God, and the Word was God. ²He was with God in the beginning.

³Through him all things were made; without him nothing was made that has been made. ⁴In him was life, and that life was the light of men. ⁵The light shines in the darkness, but the darkness has not understood*ᵃ* it.

⁶There came a man who was sent from God; his name was John. ⁷He came as a witness to testify concerning that light, so that through him all men might believe. ⁸He himself was not the light; he came only as a witness to the light. ⁹The true light that gives light to every man was coming into the world.*ᵇ*

¹⁰He was in the world, and though the world was made through him, the world did not recognize him. ¹¹He came to that which was his own, but his own did not

---

ᵃ5 Or *darkness, and the darkness has not overcome every man who comes into the world*

ᵇ9 Or *This was the true light that gives light to*

receive him. [12]Yet to all who received him, to those who believed in his name, he gave the right to become children of God— [13]children born not of natural descent,[a] nor of human decision or a husband's will, but born of God.

[14]The Word became flesh and made his dwelling among us. We have seen his glory, the glory of the One and Only,[b] who came from the Father, full of grace and truth.

[15]John testifies concerning him. He cries out, saying, "This was he of whom I said, 'He who comes after me has surpassed me because he was before me.' " [16]From the fullness of his grace we have all received one blessing after another. [17]For the law was given through Moses; grace and truth came through Jesus Christ. [18]No one has ever seen God, but God the One and Only,[b, c] who is at the Father's side, has made him known.

John the Baptist Denies Being the Christ

[19]Now this was John's testimony when the Jews of Jerusalem sent priests and Levites to ask him who he was. [20]He did not fail to confess, but confessed freely, "I am not the Christ.[d]"

[21]They asked him, "Then who are you? Are you Elijah?"

He said, "I am not."

"Are you the Prophet?"

He answered, "No."

[22]Finally they said, "Who are you? Give us an answer to take back to those who sent us. What do you say about yourself?"

[23]John replied in the words of Isaiah the prophet, "I am the voice of one calling in the desert, 'Make straight the way for the Lord.' "[e]

[24]Now some Pharisees who had been sent [25]questioned him, "Why then do you baptize if you are not the Christ, nor Elijah, nor the Prophet?"

[26]"I baptize with[f] water," John replied, "but among you stands one you do not know. [27]He is the one who comes after me, the thongs of whose sandals I am not worthy to untie."

[28]This all happened at Bethany on the other side of the Jordan, where John was baptizing.

Jesus the Lamb of God

[29]The next day John saw Jesus coming toward him and said, "Look, the Lamb of God, who takes away the sin of the world! [30]This is the one I meant when I said, 'A man who comes after me has surpassed me because he was before me.' [31]I myself did not know him, but the reason I came baptizing with water was that he might be revealed to Israel."

[32]Then John gave this testimony: "I saw the Spirit come down from heaven as a dove and remain on him. [33]I would not have known him, except that the one who sent me to baptize with water told me, 'The man on whom you see the Spirit come down and remain is he who will baptize with the Holy Spirit.' [34]I have seen and I testify that this is the Son of God."

Jesus' First Disciples

[35]The next day John was there again with two of his disciples. [36]When he saw Jesus passing by, he said, "Look, the Lamb of God!"

[37]When the two disciples heard him say this, they followed Jesus. [38]Turning around, Jesus saw them following and asked, "What do you want?"

They said, "Rabbi" (which means Teacher), "where are you staying?"

[39]"Come," he replied, "and you will see."

So they went and saw where he was staying, and spent that day with him. It was about the tenth hour.

[40]Andrew, Simon Peter's brother, was one of the two who heard what John had said and who had followed Jesus. [41]The first thing Andrew did was to find his brother Simon and tell him, "We have found the Messiah" (that is, the Christ). [42]And he brought him to Jesus.

Jesus looked at him and said, "You are Simon son of John. You will be called Cephas" (which, when translated, is Peter[g]).

Jesus Calls Philip and Nathanael

[43]The next day Jesus decided to leave for Galilee. Finding Philip, he said to him, "Follow me."

[44]Philip, like Andrew and Peter, was from the town of Bethsaida. [45]Philip

---

[a]13 Greek *of bloods*   [b]14,18 Or *the Only Begotten begotten*) *Son*   [d]20 Or *Messiah.* "The Christ" (Greek) and "the Messiah" (Hebrew) both mean "the Anointed One"; also in verse 25.   [e]23 Isaiah 40:3   [f]26 Or *in*; also in verses 31 and 33   [g]42 Both *Cephas* (Aramaic) and *Peter* (Greek) mean *rock*.   [c]18 Some manuscripts *but the only* (or *only*

The Word Became Flesh

THAT the Word, Jesus Christ, became a man is the wonder of wonders expressed simply in the phrase, "The Word became flesh" (John 1:14). Jesus had a human body just like you and I have. The *extraordinary* embraced the *ordinary* and produced a living person, fully God and fully human. The Holy Spirit extraordinarily impregnated an egg within the ordinary body of a woman. How could it happen? This is a mystery too profound to understand, but the written Word clearly says it is true.

And the Word "made his dwelling among us." He lived, breathed, ate, drank, slept, worked, laughed and spoke among us. He was real to the eye, real to the touch, real to the ear. He was here—in human flesh—living with men and women and little children.

You have probably wished that Jesus lived today in human flesh and that his house was in your neighborhood. Have you ever thought how wonderful it would be to knock on his door and say, "Jesus, would you show me what the Father is like?" Or, "Jesus, could you give me a hand building a desk for my child?" Or, "Jesus, I'm miserable, please tell me what I should do to patch it up with my husband."

As children of God we have the privilege of "fleshing out" Jesus Christ to others who also would like him as a neighbor. We, as Christians, have received the written Word into our hearts as a seed, miraculously affecting our whole person so that the very life of Christ is produced in us. We each live next door to people who can knock on our doors and say, "Will you please show me what God the Father is like?" And you and I can show them, because we have become somewhat like him as we have studied, worshiped and obeyed him. When someone says, "Could you please help me?" we can lend a helping hand because we have given our bodies over to be used in service to others. When a friend says, "Please help me with a broken relationship," we can give loving counsel because we have contemplated the Lord Jesus Christ in his Word and are able to tackle the problems that the people around us face.

As Christ became flesh and made his dwelling in us, will we become Christ in flesh to our neighbors?

Additional Scripture Readings:
John 14:11–14; Hebrews 2:14–18

Go to page 127 for your next devotional reading.

found Nathanael and told him, "We have found the one Moses wrote about in the Law, and about whom the prophets also wrote—Jesus of Nazareth, the son of Joseph."

[46]"Nazareth! Can anything good come from there?" Nathanael asked.

"Come and see," said Philip.

[47]When Jesus saw Nathanael approaching, he said of him, "Here is a true Israelite, in whom there is nothing false."

[48]"How do you know me?" Nathanael asked.

Jesus answered, "I saw you while you were still under the fig tree before Philip called you."

[49]Then Nathanael declared, "Rabbi, you are the Son of God; you are the King of Israel."

[50]Jesus said, "You believe[a] because I told you I saw you under the fig tree. You shall see greater things than that." [51]He then added, "I tell you[b] the truth, you[b] shall see heaven open, and the angels of God ascending and descending on the Son of Man."

Jesus Changes Water to Wine

2 On the third day a wedding took place at Cana in Galilee. Jesus' mother was there, [2]and Jesus and his disciples had also been invited to the wedding. [3]When the wine was gone, Jesus' mother said to him, "They have no more wine."

[4]"Dear woman, why do you involve me?" Jesus replied. "My time has not yet come."

[5]His mother said to the servants, "Do whatever he tells you."

[6]Nearby stood six stone water jars, the kind used by the Jews for ceremonial washing, each holding from twenty to thirty gallons.[c]

[7]Jesus said to the servants, "Fill the jars with water"; so they filled them to the brim.

[8]Then he told them, "Now draw some out and take it to the master of the banquet."

They did so, [9]and the master of the banquet tasted the water that had been turned into wine. He did not realize where it had come from, though the servants who had drawn the water knew. Then he called the bridegroom aside [10]and said, "Everyone brings out the choice wine first and then the cheaper wine after the guests have had too much to drink; but you have saved the best till now."

[11]This, the first of his miraculous signs, Jesus performed at Cana in Galilee. He thus revealed his glory, and his disciples put their faith in him.

Jesus Clears the Temple

[12]After this he went down to Capernaum with his mother and brothers and his disciples. There they stayed for a few days.

[13]When it was almost time for the Jewish Passover, Jesus went up to Jerusalem. [14]In the temple courts he found men selling cattle, sheep and doves, and others sitting at tables exchanging money. [15]So he made a whip out of cords, and drove all from the temple area, both sheep and cattle; he scattered the coins of the money changers and overturned their tables. [16]To those who sold doves he said, "Get these out of here! How dare you turn my Father's house into a market!"

[17]His disciples remembered that it is written: "Zeal for your house will consume me."[d]

[18]Then the Jews demanded of him, "What miraculous sign can you show us to prove your authority to do all this?"

[19]Jesus answered them, "Destroy this temple, and I will raise it again in three days."

[20]The Jews replied, "It has taken forty-six years to build this temple, and you are going to raise it in three days?" [21]But the temple he had spoken of was his body. [22]After he was raised from the dead, his disciples recalled what he had said. Then they believed the Scripture and the words that Jesus had spoken.

[23]Now while he was in Jerusalem at the Passover Feast, many people saw the miraculous signs he was doing and believed in his name.[e] [24]But Jesus would not entrust himself to them, for he knew all men. [25]He did not need man's testimony about man, for he knew what was in a man.

Jesus Teaches Nicodemus

3 Now there was a man of the Pharisees named Nicodemus, a member of the Jewish ruling council. [2]He came to Jesus at night and said, "Rabbi, we know you are a teacher who has come from God.

[a]50 Or Do you believe ... ?   [b]51 The Greek is plural.   [c]6 Greek two to three metretes (probably about 75 to 115 liters)   [d]17 Psalm 69:9   [e]23 Or and believed in him

For no one could perform the miraculous signs you are doing if God were not with him."

[3]In reply Jesus declared, "I tell you the truth, no one can see the kingdom of God unless he is born again.[a]"

[4]"How can a man be born when he is old?" Nicodemus asked. "Surely he cannot enter a second time into his mother's womb to be born!"

[5]Jesus answered, "I tell you the truth, no one can enter the kingdom of God unless he is born of water and the Spirit. [6]Flesh gives birth to flesh, but the Spirit[b] gives birth to spirit. [7]You should not be surprised at my saying, 'You[c] must be born again.' [8]The wind blows wherever it pleases. You hear its sound, but you cannot tell where it comes from or where it is going. So it is with everyone born of the Spirit."

[9]"How can this be?" Nicodemus asked.

[10]"You are Israel's teacher," said Jesus, "and do you not understand these things? [11]I tell you the truth, we speak of what we know, and we testify to what we have seen, but still you people do not accept our testimony. [12]I have spoken to you of earthly things and you do not believe; how then will you believe if I speak of heavenly things? [13]No one has ever gone into heaven except the one who came from heaven—the Son of Man.[d] [14]Just as Moses lifted up the snake in the desert, so the Son of Man must be lifted up, [15]that everyone who believes in him may have eternal life.[e]

[16]"For God so loved the world that he gave his one and only Son,[f] that whoever believes in him shall not perish but have eternal life. [17]For God did not send his Son into the world to condemn the world, but to save the world through him. [18]Whoever believes in him is not condemned, but whoever does not believe stands condemned already because he has not believed in the name of God's one and only Son.[g] [19]This is the verdict: Light has come into the world, but men loved darkness instead of light because their deeds were evil. [20]Everyone who does evil hates the light, and will not come into the light for fear that his deeds will be exposed. [21]But whoever lives by the truth comes into the light, so that it may be seen plainly that what he has done has been done through God."[h]

John the Baptist's Testimony About Jesus

[22]After this, Jesus and his disciples went out into the Judean countryside, where he spent some time with them, and baptized. [23]Now John also was baptizing at Aenon near Salim, because there was plenty of water, and people were constantly coming to be baptized. [24](This was before John was put in prison.) [25]An argument developed between some of John's disciples and a certain Jew[i] over the matter of ceremonial washing. [26]They came to John and said to him, "Rabbi, that man who was with you on the other side of the Jordan—the one you testified about—well, he is baptizing, and everyone is going to him."

[27]To this John replied, "A man can receive only what is given him from heaven. [28]You yourselves can testify that I said, 'I am not the Christ[j] but am sent ahead of him.' [29]The bride belongs to the bridegroom. The friend who attends the bridegroom waits and listens for him, and is full of joy when he hears the bridegroom's voice. That joy is mine, and it is now complete. [30]He must become greater; I must become less.

[31]"The one who comes from above is above all; the one who is from the earth belongs to the earth, and speaks as one from the earth. The one who comes from heaven is above all. [32]He testifies to what he has seen and heard, but no one accepts his testimony. [33]The man who has accepted it has certified that God is truthful. [34]For the one whom God has sent speaks the words of God, for God[k] gives the Spirit without limit. [35]The Father loves the Son and has placed everything in his hands. [36]Whoever believes in the Son has eternal life, but whoever rejects the Son will not see life, for God's wrath remains on him."[l]

Jesus Talks With a Samaritan Woman

4 The Pharisees heard that Jesus was gaining and baptizing more disciples

---

[a]3 Or born from above; also in verse 7   [b]6 Or but spirit   [c]7 The Greek is plural.   [d]13 Some manuscripts Man, who is in heaven   [e]15 Or believes may have eternal life in him   [f]16 Or his only begotten Son   [g]18 Or God's only begotten Son   [h]21 Some interpreters end the quotation after verse 15.   [i]25 Some manuscripts and certain Jews   [j]28 Or Messiah   [k]34 Greek he   [l]36 Some interpreters end the quotation after verse 30.

than John, [2]although in fact it was not Jesus who baptized, but his disciples. [3]When the Lord learned of this, he left Judea and went back once more to Galilee.

[4]Now he had to go through Samaria. [5]So he came to a town in Samaria called Sychar, near the plot of ground Jacob had given to his son Joseph. [6]Jacob's well was there, and Jesus, tired as he was from the journey, sat down by the well. It was about the sixth hour.

[7]When a Samaritan woman came to draw water, Jesus said to her, "Will you give me a drink?" [8](His disciples had gone into the town to buy food.)

[9]The Samaritan woman said to him,

"You are a Jew and I am a Samaritan woman. How can you ask me for a drink?" (For Jews do not associate with Samaritans. [a])

[10]Jesus answered her, "If you knew the gift of God and who it is that asks you for a drink, you would have asked him and he would have given you living water."

[11]"Sir," the woman said, "you have nothing to draw with and the well is deep. Where can you get this living water? [12]Are you greater than our father Jacob, who gave us the well and drank from it himself, as did also his sons and his flocks and herds?"

[13]Jesus answered, "Everyone who drinks this water will be thirsty again,

[a]9 Or *do not use dishes Samaritans have used*

THURSDAY

VERSE FOR THE DAY:
John 3:16

AUTHOR:
Kathryn Hillen

PASSAGE FOR THE DAY:
John 3:1–21

Chosen

IT was the day before Mother's Day, and our daughter Linda wanted to go shopping even though she was so little that her head was hardly visible over the store counter. Asking me to stay at the front, she headed for the back of Woolworth's, clutching her dollar bill. As I watched, she chose a relish dish and stood by the cash register, where she was overlooked by the busy clerks. She waited, dish in hand, jostled by other customers and ignored by the salespeople but firm in her resolve to buy a gift of her own choosing for her mother. She finally returned to me with her package and a smile of triumph.

That inexpensive dish is one of my most prized possessions, for it cost someone I love all that she had. It was bought with real sacrifice by one who went alone with no other aim than to please me. I cherish it, display it with my crystal and china, and use it proudly.

God's beloved Son, Jesus, came to the dime store of earth and chose to sacrifice his all for our redemption. As the Father watched, his love for his Son must have deepened. And how does God feel about those he purchased through death on the cross? Does God love us even more because of what his Son did for us? After all, that's what gives us worth.

Additional Scripture Readings:
2 Thessalonians 2:13–14; 1 Peter 2:9–10

Go to page 129 for your next devotional reading.

¹⁴but whoever drinks the water I give him will never thirst. Indeed, the water I give him will become in him a spring of water welling up to eternal life."

¹⁵The woman said to him, "Sir, give me this water so that I won't get thirsty and have to keep coming here to draw water."

¹⁶He told her, "Go, call your husband and come back."

¹⁷"I have no husband," she replied.

Jesus said to her, "You are right when you say you have no husband. ¹⁸The fact is, you have had five husbands, and the man you now have is not your husband. What you have just said is quite true."

¹⁹"Sir," the woman said, "I can see that you are a prophet. ²⁰Our fathers worshiped on this mountain, but you Jews claim that the place where we must worship is in Jerusalem."

²¹Jesus declared, "Believe me, woman, a time is coming when you will worship the Father neither on this mountain nor in Jerusalem. ²²You Samaritans worship what you do not know; we worship what we do know, for salvation is from the Jews. ²³Yet a time is coming and has now come when the true worshipers will worship the Father in spirit and truth, for they are the kind of worshipers the Father seeks. ²⁴God is spirit, and his worshipers must worship in spirit and in truth."

²⁵The woman said, "I know that Messiah" (called Christ) "is coming. When he comes, he will explain everything to us."

²⁶Then Jesus declared, "I who speak to you am he."

The Disciples Rejoin Jesus

²⁷Just then his disciples returned and were surprised to find him talking with a woman. But no one asked, "What do you want?" or "Why are you talking with her?"

²⁸Then, leaving her water jar, the woman went back to the town and said to the people, ²⁹"Come, see a man who told me everything I ever did. Could this be the Christ*a*?" ³⁰They came out of the town and made their way toward him.

³¹Meanwhile his disciples urged him, "Rabbi, eat something."

³²But he said to them, "I have food to eat that you know nothing about."

³³Then his disciples said to each other, "Could someone have brought him food?"

³⁴"My food," said Jesus, "is to do the will of him who sent me and to finish his work. ³⁵Do you not say, 'Four months more and then the harvest'? I tell you, open your eyes and look at the fields! They are ripe for harvest. ³⁶Even now the reaper draws his wages, even now he harvests the crop for eternal life, so that the sower and the reaper may be glad together. ³⁷Thus the saying 'One sows and another reaps' is true. ³⁸I sent you to reap what you have not worked for. Others have done the hard work, and you have reaped the benefits of their labor."

Many Samaritans Believe

³⁹Many of the Samaritans from that town believed in him because of the woman's testimony, "He told me everything I ever did." ⁴⁰So when the Samaritans came to him, they urged him to stay with them, and he stayed two days. ⁴¹And because of his words many more became believers.

⁴²They said to the woman, "We no longer believe just because of what you said; now we have heard for ourselves, and we know that this man really is the Savior of the world."

Jesus Heals the Official's Son

⁴³After the two days he left for Galilee. ⁴⁴(Now Jesus himself had pointed out that a prophet has no honor in his own country.) ⁴⁵When he arrived in Galilee, the Galileans welcomed him. They had seen all that he had done in Jerusalem at the Passover Feast, for they also had been there.

⁴⁶Once more he visited Cana in Galilee, where he had turned the water into wine. And there was a certain royal official whose son lay sick at Capernaum. ⁴⁷When this man heard that Jesus had arrived in Galilee from Judea, he went to him and begged him to come and heal his son, who was close to death.

⁴⁸"Unless you people see miraculous signs and wonders," Jesus told him, "you will never believe."

⁴⁹The royal official said, "Sir, come down before my child dies."

⁵⁰Jesus replied, "You may go. Your son will live."

The man took Jesus at his word and departed. ⁵¹While he was still on the way, his servants met him with the news that

a29 Or *Messiah*

his boy was living. [52]When he inquired as to the time when his son got better, they said to him, "The fever left him yesterday at the seventh hour."

[53]Then the father realized that this was the exact time at which Jesus had said to him, "Your son will live." So he and all his household believed.

[54]This was the second miraculous sign that Jesus performed, having come from Judea to Galilee.

The Healing at the Pool

5 Some time later, Jesus went up to Jerusalem for a feast of the Jews. [2]Now there is in Jerusalem near the Sheep Gate a pool, which in Aramaic is called Bethesda[a] and which is surrounded by five covered colonnades. [3]Here a great number of disabled people used to lie—the blind, the lame, the paralyzed.[b] [5]One who was there had been an invalid for thirty-eight

---

[a]2 Some manuscripts *Bethzatha*; other manuscripts *Bethsaida*   [b]3 Some less important manuscripts *paralyzed—and they waited for the moving of the waters. [4]From time to time an angel of the Lord would come down and stir up the waters. The first one into the pool after each such disturbance would be cured of whatever disease he had.*

FRIDAY

VERSE FOR THE DAY:
John 4:34

AUTHOR:
Jill Briscoe

PASSAGE FOR THE DAY:
John 4:27–38

More Important Than Lunch

JESUS had a heart for God. He had a sense of urgency that meant that some things were even more important than his lunch. I suspect some of us would rather die before we missed our lunch in order to do something for God! Jesus had a sense of purpose. He knew what he was supposed to be doing. He was on earth to talk to men and women about himself. That was why he took time out—even when he was tired and hungry—to explain the things of God to a rather disreputable lady. By the time the disciples came back after buying food, they found Jesus sitting by the well where they had left him; he was tired but triumphant. There is nothing that lifts the spirits as much as seeing someone respond to the gospel. As he watched the woman bringing back the men of her village to "see a man who told me everything I ever did," Jesus was satisfied!

There is nothing quite so fulfilling as completing an assignment for God. You said what was needed, you prayed with a child, you organized the study, you cooked for the homeless, and you finished it! You stuck to it till the job was done. The joy comes, of course, when you are doing *his* work. I will lose heart if I consider the work mine. Stuart caught me talking about "my women in my Bible study" one day, and he rightly rebuked me. They were not "my" women at all—they were Jesus' women! When I have a heart for God he will give me a heart for women, and ministry with them will always be more important than my lunch!

Additional Scripture Readings:
Mark 3:20; Hebrews 6:10–12

Go to page 131 for your next devotional reading.

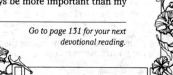

years. ⁶When Jesus saw him lying there and learned that he had been in this condition for a long time, he asked him, "Do you want to get well?"

⁷"Sir," the invalid replied, "I have no one to help me into the pool when the water is stirred. While I am trying to get in, someone else goes down ahead of me."

⁸Then Jesus said to him, "Get up! Pick up your mat and walk." ⁹At once the man was cured; he picked up his mat and walked.

The day on which this took place was a Sabbath, ¹⁰and so the Jews said to the man who had been healed, "It is the Sabbath; the law forbids you to carry your mat."

¹¹But he replied, "The man who made me well said to me, 'Pick up your mat and walk.' "

¹²So they asked him, "Who is this fellow who told you to pick it up and walk?"

¹³The man who was healed had no idea who it was, for Jesus had slipped away into the crowd that was there.

¹⁴Later Jesus found him at the temple and said to him, "See, you are well again. Stop sinning or something worse may happen to you." ¹⁵The man went away and told the Jews that it was Jesus who had made him well.

Life Through the Son

¹⁶So, because Jesus was doing these things on the Sabbath, the Jews persecuted him. ¹⁷Jesus said to them, "My Father is always at his work to this very day, and I, too, am working." ¹⁸For this reason the Jews tried all the harder to kill him; not only was he breaking the Sabbath, but he was even calling God his own Father, making himself equal with God.

¹⁹Jesus gave them this answer: "I tell you the truth, the Son can do nothing by himself; he can do only what he sees his Father doing, because whatever the Father does the Son also does. ²⁰For the Father loves the Son and shows him all he does. Yes, to your amazement he will show him even greater things than these. ²¹For just as the Father raises the dead and gives them life, even so the Son gives life to whom he is pleased to give it. ²²Moreover, the Father judges no one, but has entrusted all judgment to the Son, ²³that all may honor the Son just as they honor the Father. He who does not honor

the Son does not honor the Father, who sent him.

²⁴"I tell you the truth, whoever hears my word and believes him who sent me has eternal life and will not be condemned; he has crossed over from death to life. ²⁵I tell you the truth, a time is coming and has now come when the dead will hear the voice of the Son of God and those who hear will live. ²⁶For as the Father has life in himself, so he has granted the Son to have life in himself. ²⁷And he has given him authority to judge because he is the Son of Man.

²⁸"Do not be amazed at this, for a time is coming when all who are in their graves will hear his voice ²⁹and come out—those who have done good will rise to live, and those who have done evil will rise to be condemned. ³⁰By myself I can do nothing; I judge only as I hear, and my judgment is just, for I seek not to please myself but him who sent me.

Testimonies About Jesus

³¹"If I testify about myself, my testimony is not valid. ³²There is another who testifies in my favor, and I know that his testimony about me is valid.

³³"You have sent to John and he has testified to the truth. ³⁴Not that I accept human testimony; but I mention it that you may be saved. ³⁵John was a lamp that burned and gave light, and you chose for a time to enjoy his light.

³⁶"I have testimony weightier than that of John. For the very work that the Father has given me to finish, and which I am doing, testifies that the Father has sent me. ³⁷And the Father who sent me has himself testified concerning me. You have never heard his voice nor seen his form, ³⁸nor does his word dwell in you, for you do not believe the one he sent. ³⁹You diligently study*a* the Scriptures because you think that by them you possess eternal life. These are the Scriptures that testify about me, ⁴⁰yet you refuse to come to me to have life.

⁴¹"I do not accept praise from men, ⁴²but I know you. I know that you do not have the love of God in your hearts. ⁴³I have come in my Father's name, and you do not accept me; but if someone else comes in his own name, you will accept him. ⁴⁴How can you believe if you accept praise from one another, yet make no ef-

a39 Or Study diligently (the imperative)

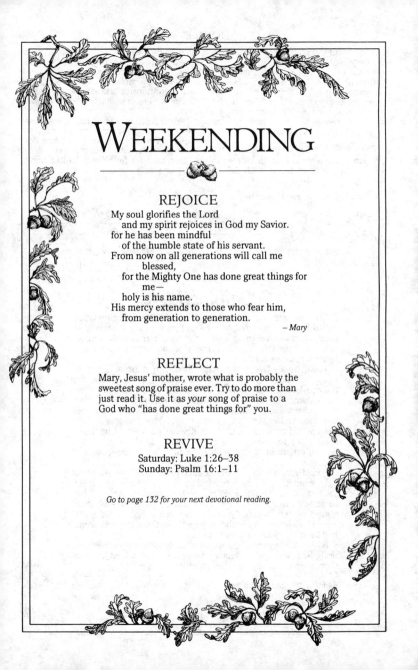

WEEKENDING

REJOICE

My soul glorifies the Lord
    and my spirit rejoices in God my Savior.
for he has been mindful
    of the humble state of his servant.
From now on all generations will call me
        blessed,
    for the Mighty One has done great things for
        me—
    holy is his name.
His mercy extends to those who fear him,
    from generation to generation.

— Mary

REFLECT

Mary, Jesus' mother, wrote what is probably the
sweetest song of praise ever. Try to do more than
just read it. Use it as *your* song of praise to a
God who "has done great things for" you.

REVIVE

Saturday: Luke 1:26–38
Sunday: Psalm 16:1–11

Go to page 132 for your next devotional reading.

fort to obtain the praise that comes from the only God[a]?

45"But do not think I will accuse you before the Father. Your accuser is Moses, on whom your hopes are set. 46If you believed Moses, you would believe me, for he wrote about me. 47But since you do not believe what he wrote, how are you going to believe what I say?"

Jesus Feeds the Five Thousand

6 Some time after this, Jesus crossed to the far shore of the Sea of Galilee (that is, the Sea of Tiberias), 2and a great crowd of people followed him because they saw the miraculous signs he had performed on the sick. 3Then Jesus went up on a mountainside and sat down with his disciples. 4The Jewish Passover Feast was near.

5When Jesus looked up and saw a great crowd coming toward him, he said to Philip, "Where shall we buy bread for these people to eat?" 6He asked this only to test him, for he already had in mind what he was going to do.

---

[a]44 Some early manuscripts *the Only One*

MONDAY

| VERSE FOR THE DAY:
John 5:35 | AUTHOR:
Millie Stamm | PASSAGE FOR THE DAY:
John 5:31–47 |

A Shining Light

JESUS, in speaking of John the Baptist in this Scripture verse, called him "a lamp that burned and gave light." Wherever he went, John was a shining light, pointing others to Jesus Christ.

Throughout the centuries, many people have been shining lights for Jesus Christ.

Today we are living in a world filled with spiritual darkness. People all about us are groping for something to bring light into their darkened lives. God has entrusted to us the ministry of being a shining light for Jesus Christ, the light of the world. Paul wrote that we are "children of God without fault in a crooked and depraved generation, in which you shine like stars in the universe" (Philippians 2:15). He doesn't place all of us in the same place to shine. Some may be called to shine in faraway places; others in their families, neighborhoods and places of business.

Sometimes we are in such a dark place we think our small light cannot be seen. I remember the first time we visited Carlsbad Caverns. When we reached the deepest section, they turned off all the lights. We experienced a darkness that could almost be felt. Suddenly in the distance a light came on. It seemed so small, yet it shone brightly in the large area which had been dark just a moment before.

So Jesus, the light of the world, shining through our lives, can bring light into the darkness wherever he has placed us, even though we think our light very small.

Additional Scripture Readings:
Isaiah 49:5–6; 2 Corinthians 4:4–6

Go to page 135 for your next devotional reading.

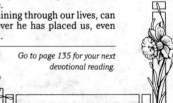

7Philip answered him, "Eight months' wages[a] would not buy enough bread for each one to have a bite!"

8Another of his disciples, Andrew, Simon Peter's brother, spoke up, 9"Here is a boy with five small barley loaves and two small fish, but how far will they go among so many?"

10Jesus said, "Have the people sit down." There was plenty of grass in that place, and the men sat down, about five thousand of them. 11Jesus then took the loaves, gave thanks, and distributed to those who were seated as much as they wanted. He did the same with the fish.

12When they had all had enough to eat, he said to his disciples, "Gather the pieces that are left over. Let nothing be wasted." 13So they gathered them and filled twelve baskets with the pieces of the five barley loaves left over by those who had eaten.

14After the people saw the miraculous sign that Jesus did, they began to say, "Surely this is the Prophet who is to come into the world." 15Jesus, knowing that they intended to come and make him king by force, withdrew again to a mountain by himself.

Jesus Walks on the Water

16When evening came, his disciples went down to the lake, 17where they got into a boat and set off across the lake for Capernaum. By now it was dark, and Jesus had not yet joined them. 18A strong wind was blowing and the waters grew rough. 19When they had rowed three or three and a half miles,[b] they saw Jesus approaching the boat, walking on the water; and they were terrified. 20But he said to them, "It is I; don't be afraid." 21Then they were willing to take him into the boat, and immediately the boat reached the shore where they were heading.

22The next day the crowd that had stayed on the opposite shore of the lake realized that only one boat had been there, and that Jesus had not entered it with his disciples, but that they had gone away alone. 23Then some boats from Tiberias landed near the place where the people had eaten the bread after the Lord had given thanks. 24Once the crowd realized that neither Jesus nor his disciples were there, they got into the boats and went to Capernaum in search of Jesus.

Jesus the Bread of Life

25When they found him on the other side of the lake, they asked him, "Rabbi, when did you get here?"

26Jesus answered, "I tell you the truth, you are looking for me, not because you saw miraculous signs but because you ate the loaves and had your fill. 27Do not work for food that spoils, but for food that endures to eternal life, which the Son of Man will give you. On him God the Father has placed his seal of approval."

28Then they asked him, "What must we do to do the works God requires?"

29Jesus answered, "The work of God is this: to believe in the one he has sent."

30So they asked him, "What miraculous sign then will you give that we may see it and believe you? What will you do? 31Our forefathers ate the manna in the desert; as it is written: 'He gave them bread from heaven to eat.'[c]"

32Jesus said to them, "I tell you the truth, it is not Moses who has given you the bread from heaven, but it is my Father who gives you the true bread from heaven. 33For the bread of God is he who comes down from heaven and gives life to the world."

34"Sir," they said, "from now on give us this bread."

35Then Jesus declared, "I am the bread of life. He who comes to me will never go hungry, and he who believes in me will never be thirsty. 36But as I told you, you have seen me and still you do not believe. 37All that the Father gives me will come to me, and whoever comes to me I will never drive away. 38For I have come down from heaven not to do my will but to do the will of him who sent me. 39And this is the will of him who sent me, that I shall lose none of all that he has given me, but raise them up at the last day. 40For my Father's will is that everyone who looks to the Son and believes in him shall have eternal life, and I will raise him up at the last day."

41At this the Jews began to grumble about him because he said, "I am the bread that came down from heaven." 42They said, "Is this not Jesus, the son of Joseph, whose father and mother we know? How can he now say, 'I came down from heaven'?"

43"Stop grumbling among yourselves," Jesus answered. 44"No one can come to

a7 Greek two hundred denarii   b19 Greek rowed twenty-five or thirty stadia (about 5 or 6 kilometers)
c31 Exodus 16:4; Neh. 9:15; Psalm 78:24,25

me unless the Father who sent me draws him, and I will raise him up at the last day. ⁴⁵It is written in the Prophets: 'They will all be taught by God.'ᵃ Everyone who listens to the Father and learns from him comes to me. ⁴⁶No one has seen the Father except the one who is from God; only he has seen the Father. ⁴⁷I tell you the truth, he who believes has everlasting life. ⁴⁸I am the bread of life. ⁴⁹Your forefathers ate the manna in the desert, yet they died. ⁵⁰But here is the bread that comes down from heaven, which a man may eat and not die. ⁵¹I am the living bread that came down from heaven. If anyone eats of this bread, he will live forever. This bread is my flesh, which I will give for the life of the world."

⁵²Then the Jews began to argue sharply among themselves, "How can this man give us his flesh to eat?"

⁵³Jesus said to them, "I tell you the truth, unless you eat the flesh of the Son of Man and drink his blood, you have no life in you. ⁵⁴Whoever eats my flesh and drinks my blood has eternal life, and I will raise him up at the last day. ⁵⁵For my flesh is real food and my blood is real drink. ⁵⁶Whoever eats my flesh and drinks my blood remains in me, and I in him. ⁵⁷Just as the living Father sent me and I live because of the Father, so the one who feeds on me will live because of me. ⁵⁸This is the bread that came down from heaven. Your forefathers ate manna and died, but he who feeds on this bread will live forever." ⁵⁹He said this while teaching in the synagogue in Capernaum.

Many Disciples Desert Jesus

⁶⁰On hearing it, many of his disciples said, "This is a hard teaching. Who can accept it?"

⁶¹Aware that his disciples were grumbling about this, Jesus said to them, "Does this offend you? ⁶²What if you see the Son of Man ascend to where he was before! ⁶³The Spirit gives life; the flesh counts for nothing. The words I have spoken to you are spiritᵇ and they are life. ⁶⁴Yet there are some of you who do not believe." For Jesus had known from the beginning which of them did not believe and who would betray him. ⁶⁵He went on to say, "This is why I told you that no one can come to me unless the Father has enabled him."

⁶⁶From this time many of his disciples turned back and no longer followed him.

⁶⁷"You do not want to leave too, do you?" Jesus asked the Twelve.

⁶⁸Simon Peter answered him, "Lord, to whom shall we go? You have the words of eternal life. ⁶⁹We believe and know that you are the Holy One of God."

⁷⁰Then Jesus replied, "Have I not chosen you, the Twelve? Yet one of you is a devil!" ⁷¹(He meant Judas, the son of Simon Iscariot, who, though one of the Twelve, was later to betray him.)

Jesus Goes to the Feast of Tabernacles

7 After this, Jesus went around in Galilee, purposely staying away from Judea because the Jews there were waiting to take his life. ²But when the Jewish Feast of Tabernacles was near, ³Jesus' brothers said to him, "You ought to leave here and go to Judea, so that your disciples may see the miracles you do. ⁴No one who wants to become a public figure acts in secret. Since you are doing these things, show yourself to the world." ⁵For even his own brothers did not believe in him.

⁶Therefore Jesus told them, "The right time for me has not yet come; for you any time is right. ⁷The world cannot hate you, but it hates me because I testify that what it does is evil. ⁸You go to the Feast. I am not yetᶜ going up to this Feast, because for me the right time has not yet come." ⁹Having said this, he stayed in Galilee.

¹⁰However, after his brothers had left for the Feast, he went also, not publicly, but in secret. ¹¹Now at the Feast the Jews were watching for him and asking, "Where is that man?"

¹²Among the crowds there was widespread whispering about him. Some said, "He is a good man."

Others replied, "No, he deceives the people." ¹³But no one would say anything publicly about him for fear of the Jews.

Jesus Teaches at the Feast

¹⁴Not until halfway through the Feast did Jesus go up to the temple courts and begin to teach. ¹⁵The Jews were amazed and asked, "How did this man get such learning without having studied?"

¹⁶Jesus answered, "My teaching is not my own. It comes from him who sent me.

ᵃ45 Isaiah 54:13   ᵇ63 Or Spirit   ᶜ8 Some early manuscripts do not have yet.

VERSE FOR THE DAY:
John 6:35

AUTHOR:
Rosalind Rinker

PASSAGE FOR THE DAY:
John 6:1–71

I Am the Living Bread

JOHN 6 is another miracle chapter. Here we see one more instance when Jesus taught spiritual truth through everyday things, as he had with water, seeds, a candle, a lamp, and a pearl.

This time, Jesus fed more than five thousand people when he broke five small barley loaves and distributed two small fish. Bread and water can sustain physical life indefinitely, yet Jesus said, "Man does not live on bread alone, but on every word that comes from the mouth of God" (Matthew 4:4).

Bread must be given, broken, and taken before it sustains life. The little boy gave his lunch, but Jesus gave his life. This relates directly to the central truth of the John 6 miracle because it concerns the person of our Lord. "I am the living bread that came down from heaven. If anyone eats of this bread, he will live forever. This bread is my flesh, which I will give for the life of the world" (John 6:51). Much as the barley loaves were broken, so too was Christ's *body* broken so that we could be takers of "living bread."

Jesus is capable of being the living bread because he is the Son of God. Just by observing Jesus in John 6 we can see how he deals with the crowd from an other-worldly perspective: 1. He knew what he was going to do (John 6:6). 2. He knew the superficial curiosity of the crowd (John 6:2). 3. He had compassion because of their physical and spiritual hunger (John 6:5,36–37). 4. He wanted cooperation (the boy, the disciples) before he would feed the crowd (John 6:8–9). 5. He had a sense of order and frugality (John 6:10,12–13). 6. He had a deep sense of mission, and the courage to tell of it in a language the crowd could understand and remember (John 6:35–40). 7. He predicted the Eucharist (Holy Communion) (John 6:56–57). 8. He was able to make a little count for a lot (John 6:10–11).

Dear ones, let us be takers and feed on the words of Jesus, the Son of God, our living bread. His words lead us directly back to him, the Redeemer and Savior of the world.

> I am the bread of life. He who comes to me will
> never go hungry, and he who believes in me will
> never be thirsty (John 6:35).

Additional Scripture Readings:
Psalm 119:103–104; Matthew 26:26

*Go to page 145 for your next
devotional reading.*

¹⁷If anyone chooses to do God's will, he will find out whether my teaching comes from God or whether I speak on my own. ¹⁸He who speaks on his own does so to gain honor for himself, but he who works for the honor of the one who sent him is a man of truth; there is nothing false about him. ¹⁹Has not Moses given you the law? Yet not one of you keeps the law. Why are you trying to kill me?"

²⁰"You are demon-possessed," the crowd answered. "Who is trying to kill you?"

²¹Jesus said to them, "I did one miracle, and you are all astonished. ²²Yet, because Moses gave you circumcision (though actually it did not come from Moses, but from the patriarchs), you circumcise a child on the Sabbath. ²³Now if a child can be circumcised on the Sabbath so that the law of Moses may not be broken, why are you angry with me for healing the whole man on the Sabbath? ²⁴Stop judging by mere appearances, and make a right judgment."

Is Jesus the Christ?

²⁵At that point some of the people of Jerusalem began to ask, "Isn't this the man they are trying to kill? ²⁶Here he is, speaking publicly, and they are not saying a word to him. Have the authorities really concluded that he is the Christ^a? ²⁷But we know where this man is from; when the Christ comes, no one will know where he is from."

²⁸Then Jesus, still teaching in the temple courts, cried out, "Yes, you know me, and you know where I am from. I am not here on my own, but he who sent me is true. You do not know him, ²⁹but I know him because I am from him and he sent me."

³⁰At this they tried to seize him, but no one laid a hand on him, because his time had not yet come. ³¹Still, many in the crowd put their faith in him. They said, "When the Christ comes, will he do more miraculous signs than this man?"

³²The Pharisees heard the crowd whispering such things about him. Then the chief priests and the Pharisees sent temple guards to arrest him.

³³Jesus said, "I am with you for only a short time, and then I go to the one who sent me. ³⁴You will look for me, but you will not find me; and where I am, you cannot come."

³⁵The Jews said to one another, "Where does this man intend to go that we cannot find him? Will he go where our people live scattered among the Greeks, and teach the Greeks? ³⁶What did he mean when he said, 'You will look for me, but you will not find me,' and 'Where I am, you cannot come'?"

³⁷On the last and greatest day of the Feast, Jesus stood and said in a loud voice, "If anyone is thirsty, let him come to me and drink. ³⁸Whoever believes in me, as^b the Scripture has said, streams of living water will flow from within him." ³⁹By this he meant the Spirit, whom those who believed in him were later to receive. Up to that time the Spirit had not been given, since Jesus had not yet been glorified.

⁴⁰On hearing his words, some of the people said, "Surely this man is the Prophet."

⁴¹Others said, "He is the Christ."

Still others asked, "How can the Christ come from Galilee? ⁴²Does not the Scripture say that the Christ will come from David's family^c and from Bethlehem, the town where David lived?" ⁴³Thus the people were divided because of Jesus. ⁴⁴Some wanted to seize him, but no one laid a hand on him.

Unbelief of the Jewish Leaders

⁴⁵Finally the temple guards went back to the chief priests and Pharisees, who asked them, "Why didn't you bring him in?"

⁴⁶"No one ever spoke the way this man does," the guards declared.

⁴⁷"You mean he has deceived you also?" the Pharisees retorted. ⁴⁸"Has any of the rulers or of the Pharisees believed in him? ⁴⁹No! But this mob that knows nothing of the law—there is a curse on them."

⁵⁰Nicodemus, who had gone to Jesus earlier and who was one of their own number, asked, ⁵¹"Does our law condemn anyone without first hearing him to find out what he is doing?"

⁵²They replied, "Are you from Galilee, too? Look into it, and you will find that a prophet^d does not come out of Galilee."

---

^a26 Or *Messiah*; also in verses 27, 31, 41 and 42   ^b37,38 Or / *If anyone is thirsty, let him come to me. / And let him drink,* ³⁸*who believes in me. / As*   ^c42 Greek *seed*   ^d52 Two early manuscripts *the Prophet*

[The earliest manuscripts and many other ancient witnesses do not have John 7:53–8:11.]

⁵³Then each went to his own home. ⁸But Jesus went to the Mount of Olives. ²At dawn he appeared again in the temple courts, where all the people gathered around him, and he sat down to teach them. ³The teachers of the law and the Pharisees brought in a woman caught in adultery. They made her stand before the group ⁴and said to Jesus, "Teacher, this woman was caught in the act of adultery. ⁵In the Law Moses commanded us to stone such women. Now what do you say?" ⁶They were using this question as a trap, in order to have a basis for accusing him.

But Jesus bent down and started to write on the ground with his finger. ⁷When they kept on questioning him, he straightened up and said to them, "If any one of you is without sin, let him be the first to throw a stone at her." ⁸Again he stooped down and wrote on the ground.

⁹At this, those who heard began to go away one at a time, the older ones first, until only Jesus was left, with the woman still standing there. ¹⁰Jesus straightened up and asked her, "Woman, where are they? Has no one condemned you?"

¹¹"No one, sir," she said.

"Then neither do I condemn you," Jesus declared. "Go now and leave your life of sin."

The Validity of Jesus' Testimony

¹²When Jesus spoke again to the people, he said, "I am the light of the world. Whoever follows me will never walk in darkness, but will have the light of life." ¹³The Pharisees challenged him, "Here you are, appearing as your own witness; your testimony is not valid."

¹⁴Jesus answered, "Even if I testify on my own behalf, my testimony is valid, for I know where I came from and where I am going. But you have no idea where I come from or where I am going. ¹⁵You judge by human standards; I pass judgment on no one. ¹⁶But if I do judge, my decisions are right, because I am not alone. I stand with the Father, who sent me. ¹⁷In your own Law it is written that the testimony of two

men is valid. ¹⁸I am one who testifies for myself; my other witness is the Father, who sent me."

¹⁹Then they asked him, "Where is your father?"

"You do not know me or my Father," Jesus replied. "If you knew me, you would know my Father also." ²⁰He spoke these words while teaching in the temple area near the place where the offerings were put. Yet no one seized him, because his time had not yet come.

²¹Once more Jesus said to them, "I am going away, and you will look for me, and you will die in your sin. Where I go, you cannot come."

²²This made the Jews ask, "Will he kill himself? Is that why he says, 'Where I go, you cannot come'?"

²³But he continued, "You are from below; I am from above. You are of this world; I am not of this world. ²⁴I told you that you would die in your sins; if you do not believe that I am the one I claim to be,[a] you will indeed die in your sins."

²⁵"Who are you?" they asked.

"Just what I have been claiming all along," Jesus replied. ²⁶"I have much to say in judgment of you. But he who sent me is reliable, and what I have heard from him I tell the world."

²⁷They did not understand that he was telling them about his Father. ²⁸So Jesus said, "When you have lifted up the Son of Man, then you will know that I am the one I claim to be, and that I do nothing on my own but speak just what the Father has taught me. ²⁹The one who sent me is with me; he has not left me alone, for I always do what pleases him." ³⁰Even as he spoke, many put their faith in him.

The Children of Abraham

³¹To the Jews who had believed him, Jesus said, "If you hold to my teaching, you are really my disciples. ³²Then you will know the truth, and the truth will set you free."

³³They answered him, "We are Abraham's descendants[b] and have never been slaves of anyone. How can you say that we shall be set free?"

³⁴Jesus replied, "I tell you the truth, everyone who sins is a slave to sin. ³⁵Now a slave has no permanent place in the family, but a son belongs to it forever. ³⁶So if the Son sets you free, you will be free indeed. ³⁷I know you are Abraham's

---

[a]24 Or I am he; also in verse 28　　　[b]33 Greek seed; also in verse 37

descendants. Yet you are ready to kill me, because you have no room for my word. [38]I am telling you what I have seen in the Father's presence, and you do what you have heard from your father.[a]"

[39]"Abraham is our father," they answered.

"If you were Abraham's children," said Jesus, "then you would[b] do the things Abraham did. [40]As it is, you are determined to kill me, a man who has told you the truth that I heard from God. Abraham did not do such things. [41]You are doing the things your own father does."

"We are not illegitimate children," they protested. "The only Father we have is God himself."

The Children of the Devil

[42]Jesus said to them, "If God were your Father, you would love me, for I came from God and now am here. I have not come on my own; but he sent me. [43]Why is my language not clear to you? Because you are unable to hear what I say. [44]You belong to your father, the devil, and you want to carry out your father's desire. He was a murderer from the beginning, not holding to the truth, for there is no truth in him. When he lies, he speaks his native language, for he is a liar and the father of lies. [45]Yet because I tell the truth, you do not believe me! [46]Can any of you prove me guilty of sin? If I am telling the truth, why don't you believe me? [47]He who belongs to God hears what God says. The reason you do not hear is that you do not belong to God."

The Claims of Jesus About Himself

[48]The Jews answered him, "Aren't we right in saying that you are a Samaritan and demon-possessed?"

[49]"I am not possessed by a demon," said Jesus, "but I honor my Father and you dishonor me. [50]I am not seeking glory for myself; but there is one who seeks it, and he is the judge. [51]I tell you the truth, if anyone keeps my word, he will never see death."

[52]At this the Jews exclaimed, "Now we know that you are demon-possessed! Abraham died and so did the prophets, yet you say that if anyone keeps your word, he will never taste death. [53]Are you greater than our father Abraham? He died, and so did the prophets. Who do you think you are?"

[54]Jesus replied, "If I glorify myself, my glory means nothing. My Father, whom you claim as your God, is the one who glorifies me. [55]Though you do not know him, I know him. If I said I did not, I would be a liar like you, but I do know him and keep his word. [56]Your father Abraham rejoiced at the thought of seeing my day; he saw it and was glad."

[57]"You are not yet fifty years old," the Jews said to him, "and you have seen Abraham!"

[58]"I tell you the truth," Jesus answered, "before Abraham was born, I am!" [59]At this, they picked up stones to stone him, but Jesus hid himself, slipping away from the temple grounds.

Jesus Heals a Man Born Blind

9 As he went along, he saw a man blind from birth. [2]His disciples asked him, "Rabbi, who sinned, this man or his parents, that he was born blind?"

[3]"Neither this man nor his parents sinned," said Jesus, "but this happened so that the work of God might be displayed in his life. [4]As long as it is day, we must do the work of him who sent me. Night is coming, when no one can work. [5]While I am in the world, I am the light of the world."

[6]Having said this, he spit on the ground, made some mud with the saliva, and put it on the man's eyes. [7]"Go," he told him, "wash in the Pool of Siloam" (this word means Sent). So the man went and washed, and came home seeing.

[8]His neighbors and those who had formerly seen him begging asked, "Isn't this the same man who used to sit and beg?" [9]Some claimed that he was.

Others said, "No, he only looks like him."

But he himself insisted, "I am the man."

[10]"How then were your eyes opened?" they demanded.

[11]He replied, "The man they call Jesus made some mud and put it on my eyes. He told me to go to Siloam and wash. So I went and washed, and then I could see."

[12]"Where is this man?" they asked him.

"I don't know," he said.

---

[a]38 Or presence. Therefore do what you have heard from the Father.   [b]39 Some early manuscripts "If you are Abraham's children," said Jesus, "then

The Pharisees Investigate the Healing

[13]They brought to the Pharisees the man who had been blind. [14]Now the day on which Jesus had made the mud and opened the man's eyes was a Sabbath. [15]Therefore the Pharisees also asked him how he had received his sight. "He put mud on my eyes," the man replied, "and I washed, and now I see."

[16]Some of the Pharisees said, "This man is not from God, for he does not keep the Sabbath."

But others asked, "How can a sinner do such miraculous signs?" So they were divided.

[17]Finally they turned again to the blind man, "What have you to say about him? It was your eyes he opened."

The man replied, "He is a prophet."

[18]The Jews still did not believe that he had been blind and had received his sight until they sent for the man's parents. [19]"Is this your son?" they asked. "Is this the one you say was born blind? How is it that now he can see?"

[20]"We know he is our son," the parents answered, "and we know he was born blind. [21]But how he can see now, or who opened his eyes, we don't know. Ask him. He is of age; he will speak for himself." [22]His parents said this because they were afraid of the Jews, for already the Jews had decided that anyone who acknowledged that Jesus was the Christ[a] would be put out of the synagogue. [23]That was why his parents said, "He is of age; ask him."

[24]A second time they summoned the man who had been blind. "Give glory to God,[b]" they said. "We know this man is a sinner."

[25]He replied, "Whether he is a sinner or not, I don't know. One thing I do know. I was blind but now I see!"

[26]Then they asked him, "What did he do to you? How did he open your eyes?"

[27]He answered, "I have told you already and you did not listen. Why do you want to hear it again? Do you want to become his disciples, too?"

[28]Then they hurled insults at him and said, "You are this fellow's disciple! We are disciples of Moses! [29]We know that God spoke to Moses, but as for this fellow, we don't even know where he comes from."

[30]The man answered, "Now that is remarkable! You don't know where he comes from, yet he opened my eyes. [31]We know that God does not listen to sinners. He listens to the godly man who does his will. [32]Nobody has ever heard of opening the eyes of a man born blind. [33]If this man were not from God, he could do nothing."

[34]To this they replied, "You were steeped in sin at birth; how dare you lecture us!" And they threw him out.

Spiritual Blindness

[35]Jesus heard that they had thrown him out, and when he found him, he said, "Do you believe in the Son of Man?"

[36]"Who is he, sir?" the man asked. "Tell me so that I may believe in him."

[37]Jesus said, "You have now seen him; in fact, he is the one speaking with you."

[38]Then the man said, "Lord, I believe," and he worshiped him.

[39]Jesus said, "For judgment I have come into this world, so that the blind will see and those who see will become blind."

[40]Some Pharisees who were with him heard him say this and asked, "What? Are we blind too?"

[41]Jesus said, "If you were blind, you would not be guilty of sin; but now that you claim you can see, your guilt remains.

The Shepherd and His Flock

10 "I tell you the truth, the man who does not enter the sheep pen by the gate, but climbs in by some other way, is a thief and a robber. [2]The man who enters by the gate is the shepherd of his sheep. [3]The watchman opens the gate for him, and the sheep listen to his voice. He calls his own sheep by name and leads them out. [4]When he has brought out all his own, he goes on ahead of them, and his sheep follow him because they know his voice. [5]But they will never follow a stranger; in fact, they will run away from him because they do not recognize a stranger's voice." [6]Jesus used this figure of speech, but they did not understand what he was telling them.

[7]Therefore Jesus said again, "I tell you the truth, I am the gate for the sheep. [8]All who ever came before me were thieves and robbers, but the sheep did not listen to them. [9]I am the gate; whoever enters through me will be saved.[c] He will come in and go out, and find pasture. [10]The

thief comes only to steal and kill and destroy; I have come that they may have life, and have it to the full.

[11]"I am the good shepherd. The good shepherd lays down his life for the sheep. [12]The hired hand is not the shepherd who owns the sheep. So when he sees the wolf coming, he abandons the sheep and runs away. Then the wolf attacks the flock and scatters it. [13]The man runs away because he is a hired hand and cares nothing for the sheep.

[14]"I am the good shepherd; I know my sheep and my sheep know me— [15]just as the Father knows me and I know the Father—and I lay down my life for the sheep. [16]I have other sheep that are not of this sheep pen. I must bring them also. They too will listen to my voice, and there shall be one flock and one shepherd. [17]The reason my Father loves me is that I lay down my life—only to take it up again. [18]No one takes it from me, but I lay it down of my own accord. I have authority to lay it down and authority to take it up again. This command I received from my Father."

[19]At these words the Jews were again divided. [20]Many of them said, "He is demon-possessed and raving mad. Why listen to him?"

[21]But others said, "These are not the sayings of a man possessed by a demon. Can a demon open the eyes of the blind?"

The Unbelief of the Jews

[22]Then came the Feast of Dedication[a] at Jerusalem. It was winter, [23]and Jesus was in the temple area walking in Solomon's Colonnade. [24]The Jews gathered around him, saying, "How long will you keep us in suspense? If you are the Christ,[b] tell us plainly."

[25]Jesus answered, "I did tell you, but you do not believe. The miracles I do in my Father's name speak for me, [26]but you do not believe because you are not my sheep. [27]My sheep listen to my voice; I know them, and they follow me. [28]I give them eternal life, and they shall never perish; no one can snatch them out of my hand. [29]My Father, who has given them to me, is greater than all[c]; no one can snatch them out of my Father's hand. [30]I and the Father are one."

[31]Again the Jews picked up stones to stone him, [32]but Jesus said to them, "I

have shown you many great miracles from the Father. For which of these do you stone me?"

[33]"We are not stoning you for any of these," replied the Jews, "but for blasphemy, because you, a mere man, claim to be God."

[34]Jesus answered them, "Is it not written in your Law, 'I have said you are gods'[d]? [35]If he called them 'gods,' to whom the word of God came—and the Scripture cannot be broken— [36]what about the one whom the Father set apart as his very own and sent into the world? Why then do you accuse me of blasphemy because I said, 'I am God's Son'? [37]Do not believe me unless I do what my Father does. [38]But if I do it, even though you do not believe me, believe the miracles, that you may know and understand that the Father is in me, and I in the Father." [39]Again they tried to seize him, but he escaped their grasp.

[40]Then Jesus went back across the Jordan to the place where John had been baptizing in the early days. Here he stayed [41]and many people came to him. They said, "Though John never performed a miraculous sign, all that John said about this man was true." [42]And in that place many believed in Jesus.

The Death of Lazarus

11 Now a man named Lazarus was sick. He was from Bethany, the village of Mary and her sister Martha. [2]This Mary, whose brother Lazarus now lay sick, was the same one who poured perfume on the Lord and wiped his feet with her hair. [3]So the sisters sent word to Jesus, "Lord, the one you love is sick."

[4]When he heard this, Jesus said, "This sickness will not end in death. No, it is for God's glory so that God's Son may be glorified through it." [5]Jesus loved Martha and her sister and Lazarus. [6]Yet when he heard that Lazarus was sick, he stayed where he was two more days.

[7]Then he said to his disciples, "Let us go back to Judea."

[8]"But Rabbi," they said, "a short while ago the Jews tried to stone you, and yet you are going back there?"

[9]Jesus answered, "Are there not twelve hours of daylight? A man who walks by day will not stumble, for he sees by this world's light. [10]It is when he walks by

---

[a]22 That is, Hanukkah   [b]24 Or Messiah   [c]29 Many early manuscripts What my Father has given me is greater than all   [d]34 Psalm 82:6

night that he stumbles, for he has no light."

[11]After he had said this, he went on to tell them, "Our friend Lazarus has fallen asleep; but I am going there to wake him up."

[12]His disciples replied, "Lord, if he sleeps, he will get better." [13]Jesus had been speaking of his death, but his disciples thought he meant natural sleep.

[14]So then he told them plainly, "Lazarus is dead, [15]and for your sake I am glad I was not there, so that you may believe. But let us go to him."

[16]Then Thomas (called Didymus) said to the rest of the disciples, "Let us also go, that we may die with him."

Jesus Comforts the Sisters

[17]On his arrival, Jesus found that Lazarus had already been in the tomb for four days. [18]Bethany was less than two miles[a] from Jerusalem, [19]and many Jews had come to Martha and Mary to comfort them in the loss of their brother. [20]When Martha heard that Jesus was coming, she went out to meet him, but Mary stayed at home.

[21]"Lord," Martha said to Jesus, "if you had been here, my brother would not have died. [22]But I know that even now God will give you whatever you ask."

[23]Jesus said to her, "Your brother will rise again."

[24]Martha answered, "I know he will rise again in the resurrection at the last day."

[25]Jesus said to her, "I am the resurrection and the life. He who believes in me will live, even though he dies; [26]and whoever lives and believes in me will never die. Do you believe this?"

[27]"Yes, Lord," she told him, "I believe that you are the Christ,[b] the Son of God, who was to come into the world."

[28]And after she had said this, she went back and called her sister Mary aside. "The Teacher is here," she said, "and is asking for you." [29]When Mary heard this, she got up quickly and went to him. [30]Now Jesus had not yet entered the village, but was still at the place where Martha had met him. [31]When the Jews who had been with Mary in the house, comforting her, noticed how quickly she got up and went out, they followed her, supposing she was going to the tomb to mourn there.

[32]When Mary reached the place where Jesus was and saw him, she fell at his feet and said, "Lord, if you had been here, my brother would not have died."

[33]When Jesus saw her weeping, and the Jews who had come along with her also weeping, he was deeply moved in spirit and troubled. [34]"Where have you laid him?" he asked.

"Come and see, Lord," they replied.

[35]Jesus wept.

[36]Then the Jews said, "See how he loved him!"

[37]But some of them said, "Could not he who opened the eyes of the blind man have kept this man from dying?"

Jesus Raises Lazarus From the Dead

[38]Jesus, once more deeply moved, came to the tomb. It was a cave with a stone laid across the entrance. [39]"Take away the stone," he said.

"But, Lord," said Martha, the sister of the dead man, "by this time there is a bad odor, for he has been there four days."

[40]Then Jesus said, "Did I not tell you that if you believed, you would see the glory of God?"

[41]So they took away the stone. Then Jesus looked up and said, "Father, I thank you that you have heard me. [42]I knew that you always hear me, but I said this for the benefit of the people standing here, that they may believe that you sent me."

[43]When he had said this, Jesus called in a loud voice, "Lazarus, come out!" [44]The dead man came out, his hands and feet wrapped with strips of linen, and a cloth around his face.

Jesus said to them, "Take off the grave clothes and let him go."

The Plot to Kill Jesus

[45]Therefore many of the Jews who had come to visit Mary, and had seen what Jesus did, put their faith in him. [46]But some of them went to the Pharisees and told them what Jesus had done. [47]Then the chief priests and the Pharisees called a meeting of the Sanhedrin.

"What are we accomplishing?" they asked. "Here is this man performing many miraculous signs. [48]If we let him go on like this, everyone will believe in him, and then the Romans will come and take away both our place[c] and our nation."

[49]Then one of them, named Caiaphas, who was high priest that year, spoke up,

---

[a]18 Greek *fifteen stadia* (about 3 kilometers)   [b]27 Or *Messiah*   [c]48 Or *temple*

"You know nothing at all! ⁵⁰You do not realize that it is better for you that one man die for the people than that the whole nation perish."

⁵¹He did not say this on his own, but as high priest that year he prophesied that Jesus would die for the Jewish nation, ⁵²and not only for that nation but also for the scattered children of God, to bring them together and make them one. ⁵³So from that day on they plotted to take his life.

⁵⁴Therefore Jesus no longer moved about publicly among the Jews. Instead he withdrew to a region near the desert, to a village called Ephraim, where he stayed with his disciples.

⁵⁵When it was almost time for the Jewish Passover, many went up from the country to Jerusalem for their ceremonial cleansing before the Passover. ⁵⁶They kept looking for Jesus, and as they stood in the temple area they asked one another, "What do you think? Isn't he coming to the Feast at all?" ⁵⁷But the chief priests and Pharisees had given orders that if anyone found out where Jesus was, he should report it so that they might arrest him.

Jesus Anointed at Bethany

12 Six days before the Passover, Jesus arrived at Bethany, where Lazarus lived, whom Jesus had raised from the dead. ²Here a dinner was given in Jesus' honor. Martha served, while Lazarus was among those reclining at the table with him. ³Then Mary took about a pint*a* of pure nard, an expensive perfume; she poured it on Jesus' feet and wiped his feet with her hair. And the house was filled with the fragrance of the perfume.

⁴But one of his disciples, Judas Iscariot, who was later to betray him, objected, ⁵"Why wasn't this perfume sold and the money given to the poor? It was worth a year's wages.*b* " ⁶He did not say this because he cared about the poor but because he was a thief; as keeper of the money bag, he used to help himself to what was put into it.

⁷"Leave her alone," Jesus replied. ".It was intended, that she should save this perfume for the day of my burial. ⁸You will always have the poor among you, but you will not always have me."

⁹Meanwhile a large crowd of Jews found out that Jesus was there and came, not only because of him but also to see Lazarus, whom he had raised from the dead. ¹⁰So the chief priests made plans to kill Lazarus as well, ¹¹for on account of him many of the Jews were going over to Jesus and putting their faith in him.

The Triumphal Entry

¹²The next day the great crowd that had come for the Feast heard that Jesus was on his way to Jerusalem. ¹³They took palm branches and went out to meet him, shouting,

"Hosanna!*c*"

"Blessed is he who comes in the
        name of the Lord!"*d*

"Blessed is the King of Israel!"

¹⁴Jesus found a young donkey and sat upon it, as it is written,

¹⁵"Do not be afraid, O Daughter of
        Zion;
    see, your king is coming,
    seated on a donkey's colt."*e*

¹⁶At first his disciples did not understand all this. Only after Jesus was glorified did they realize that these things had been written about him and that they had done these things to him.

¹⁷Now the crowd that was with him when he called Lazarus from the tomb and raised him from the dead continued to spread the word. ¹⁸Many people, because they had heard that he had given this miraculous sign, went out to meet him. ¹⁹So the Pharisees said to one another, "See, this is getting us nowhere. Look how the whole world has gone after him!"

Jesus Predicts His Death

²⁰Now there were some Greeks among those who went up to worship at the Feast. ²¹They came to Philip, who was from Bethsaida in Galilee, with a request. "Sir," they said, "we would like to see Jesus." ²²Philip went to tell Andrew; Andrew and Philip in turn told Jesus.

²³Jesus replied, "The hour has come for the Son of Man to be glorified. ²⁴I tell you the truth, unless a kernel of wheat falls to the ground and dies, it remains only a single seed. But if it dies, it produces many

---

a3 Greek *a litra* (probably about 0.5 liter)   *b5* Greek *three hundred denarii*   *c13* A Hebrew expression meaning "Save!" which became an exclamation of praise   *d13* Psalm 118:25, 26   *e15* Zech. 9:9

seeds. ²⁵The man who loves his life will lose it, while the man who hates his life in this world will keep it for eternal life. ²⁶Whoever serves me must follow me; and where I am, my servant also will be. My Father will honor the one who serves me.

²⁷"Now my heart is troubled, and what shall I say? 'Father, save me from this hour'? No, it was for this very reason I came to this hour. ²⁸Father, glorify your name!"

Then a voice came from heaven, "I have glorified it, and will glorify it again." ²⁹The crowd that was there and heard it said it had thundered; others said an angel had spoken to him.

³⁰Jesus said, "This voice was for your benefit, not mine. ³¹Now is the time for judgment on this world; now the prince of this world will be driven out. ³²But I, when I am lifted up from the earth, will draw all men to myself." ³³He said this to show the kind of death he was going to die.

³⁴The crowd spoke up, "We have heard from the Law that the Christ*a* will remain forever, so how can you say, 'The Son of Man must be lifted up'? Who is this 'Son of Man'?"

³⁵Then Jesus told them, "You are going to have the light just a little while longer. Walk while you have the light, before darkness overtakes you. The man who walks in the dark does not know where he is going. ³⁶Put your trust in the light while you have it, so that you may become sons of light." When he had finished speaking, Jesus left and hid himself from them.

The Jews Continue in Their Unbelief

³⁷Even after Jesus had done all these miraculous signs in their presence, they still would not believe in him. ³⁸This was to fulfill the word of Isaiah the prophet:

> "Lord, who has believed our message
> and to whom has the arm of the
> Lord been revealed?"*b*

³⁹For this reason they could not believe, because, as Isaiah says elsewhere:

⁴⁰"He has blinded their eyes
and deadened their hearts,
so they can neither see with their
eyes,
nor understand with their hearts,
nor turn—and I would heal
them."*c*

⁴¹Isaiah said this because he saw Jesus' glory and spoke about him.

⁴²Yet at the same time many even among the leaders believed in him. But because of the Pharisees they would not confess their faith for fear they would be put out of the synagogue; ⁴³for they loved praise from men more than praise from God.

⁴⁴Then Jesus cried out, "When a man believes in me, he does not believe in me only, but in the one who sent me. ⁴⁵When he looks at me, he sees the one who sent me. ⁴⁶I have come into the world as a light, so that no one who believes in me should stay in darkness.

⁴⁷"As for the person who hears my words but does not keep them, I do not judge him. For I did not come to judge the world, but to save it. ⁴⁸There is a judge for the one who rejects me and does not accept my words; that very word which I spoke will condemn him at the last day. ⁴⁹For I did not speak of my own accord, but the Father who sent me commanded me what to say and how to say it. ⁵⁰I know that his command leads to eternal life. So whatever I say is just what the Father has told me to say."

Jesus Washes His Disciples' Feet

13 It was just before the Passover Feast. Jesus knew that the time had come for him to leave this world and go to the Father. Having loved his own who were in the world, he now showed them the full extent of his love.*d*

²The evening meal was being served, and the devil had already prompted Judas Iscariot, son of Simon, to betray Jesus. ³Jesus knew that the Father had put all things under his power, and that he had come from God and was returning to God; ⁴so he got up from the meal, took off his outer clothing, and wrapped a towel around his waist. ⁵After that, he poured water into a basin and began to wash his disciples' feet, drying them with the towel that was wrapped around him.

⁶He came to Simon Peter, who said to him, "Lord, are you going to wash my feet?"

⁷Jesus replied, "You do not realize now what I am doing, but later you will understand."

⁸"No," said Peter, "you shall never wash my feet."

---

a34 Or *Messiah*　　*b38* Isaiah 53:1　　*c40* Isaiah 6:10　　*d1* Or *he loved them to the last*

JOHN 13

Jesus answered, "Unless I wash you, you have no part with me."

9"Then, Lord," Simon Peter replied, "not just my feet but my hands and my head as well!"

10Jesus answered, "A person who has had a bath needs only to wash his feet; his whole body is clean. And you are clean, though not every one of you." 11For he knew who was going to betray him, and that was why he said not every one was clean.

12When he had finished washing their feet, he put on his clothes and returned to his place. "Do you understand what I have done for you?" he asked them. 13"You call me 'Teacher' and 'Lord,' and rightly so, for that is what I am. 14Now that I, your Lord and Teacher, have washed your feet, you also should wash one another's feet. 15I have set you an example that you should do as I have done for you. 16I tell you the truth, no servant is greater than his master, nor is a messenger greater than the one who sent him. 17Now that you know these things, you will be blessed if you do them.

Jesus Predicts His Betrayal

18"I am not referring to all of you; I know those I have chosen. But this is to fulfill the scripture: 'He who shares my bread has lifted up his heel against me.'*a*

19"I am telling you now before it happens, so that when it does happen you will believe that I am He. 20I tell you the truth, whoever accepts anyone I send accepts me; and whoever accepts me accepts the one who sent me."

21After he had said this, Jesus was troubled in spirit and testified, "I tell you the truth, one of you is going to betray me."

22His disciples stared at one another, at a loss to know which of them he meant. 23One of them, the disciple whom Jesus loved, was reclining next to him. 24Simon Peter motioned to this disciple and said, "Ask him which one he means."

25Leaning back against Jesus, he asked him, "Lord, who is it?"

26Jesus answered, "It is the one to whom I will give this piece of bread when I have dipped it in the dish." Then, dipping the piece of bread, he gave it to Judas Iscariot, son of Simon. 27As soon as Judas took the bread, Satan entered into him.

"What you are about to do, do quickly," Jesus told him, 28but no one at the meal understood why Jesus said this to him. 29Since Judas had charge of the money, some thought Jesus was telling him to buy what was needed for the Feast, or to give something to the poor. 30As soon as Judas had taken the bread, he went out. And it was night.

Jesus Predicts Peter's Denial

31When he was gone, Jesus said, "Now is the Son of Man glorified and God is glorified in him. 32If God is glorified in him,*b* God will glorify the Son in himself, and will glorify him at once.

33"My children, I will be with you only a little longer. You will look for me, and just as I told the Jews, so I tell you now: Where I am going, you cannot come.

34"A new command I give you: Love one another. As I have loved you, so you must love one another. 35By this all men will know that you are my disciples, if you love one another."

36Simon Peter asked him, "Lord, where are you going?"

Jesus replied, "Where I am going, you cannot follow now, but you will follow later."

37Peter asked, "Lord, why can't I follow you now? I will lay down my life for you."

38Then Jesus answered, "Will you really lay down your life for me? I tell you the truth, before the rooster crows, you will disown me three times!

Jesus Comforts His Disciples

14 "Do not let your hearts be troubled. Trust in God*c*; trust also in me. 2In my Father's house are many rooms; if it were not so, I would have told you. I am going there to prepare a place for you. 3And if I go and prepare a place for you, I will come back and take you to be with me that you also may be where I am. 4You know the way to the place where I am going."

Jesus the Way to the Father

5Thomas said to him, "Lord, we don't know where you are going, so how can we know the way?"

6Jesus answered, "I am the way and the truth and the life. No one comes to the Father except through me. 7If you really knew me, you would know*d* my Father as

a18 Psalm 41:9   *b32* Many early manuscripts do not have *If God is glorified in him.*   *c1* Or *You trust in God*   *d7* Some early manuscripts *If you really have known me, you will know*

WEDNESDAY

VERSE FOR THE DAY:
John 14:1

AUTHOR:
Gloria Gaither

PASSAGE FOR THE DAY:
John 13:1–14:31

On Saying Good-by

TRAVELING has been a part of our lives from the very early days of our marriage. When our children were little, our singing took us away nearly every weekend and occasionally for longer periods of time. Although leaving was common, it was never easy. Suzanne said to us when she was three, "I know you have to go, but don't go without saying good-by." She knew that the leave-taking was very important to everyone's security and sense of purpose.

Even when the children were young, before we left they always insisted on knowing the answers to five very important questions: Where are you going? How long will you be gone? Can we come with you? Who will stay with us? When will you be back?

Over and over we would answer those questions with specific information. Then we would give advice like, "Don't argue. Take care of the dogs, and always love each other. Remember that whatever you do or wherever you go, you represent our family."

When Jesus was leaving his disciples to return to his Father, he, too, knew that leave-taking was very important. He didn't leave them without saying good-by. And the questions his children asked were the same ones our children used to ask. With specific clarity Jesus gave them answers, although they could not fully comprehend the dimensions of what he was telling them.

"I go to my Father," he said. "You can't come with me yet, but don't worry, I won't leave you alone. The Holy Spirit will be your constant companion, and I must go so that he can come. While I'm gone he will teach you everything you need to know. I will be gone, by my time, only a little while, though it may seem long to you. When I come again, it will be to take you where I have been all this time fixing up a special place for all of us to be together . . . forever. After that, we won't have to say good-by again."

Then Jesus gave some special parental instructions. "Love and take care of each other. The way you treat each other will tell the world about our family, so remember whose child you are. Some problems may come up, but whatever you need, you can ask for it using my name. All I have is at your disposal, and the Holy Spirit will see that you have it. When you feel lonely or afraid, rely on my promise that I have insulated you in prayer, and you belong to me."

Additional Scripture Readings:
Acts 1:6–11; 20:17–38

*Go to page 147 for your next
devotional reading.*

well. From now on, you do know him and have seen him."

[8]Philip said, "Lord, show us the Father and that will be enough for us."

[9]Jesus answered: "Don't you know me, Philip, even after I have been among you such a long time? Anyone who has seen me has seen the Father. How can you say, 'Show us the Father'? [10]Don't you believe that I am in the Father, and that the Father is in me? The words I say to you are not just my own. Rather, it is the Father, living in me, who is doing his work. [11]Believe me when I say that I am in the Father and the Father is in me; or at least believe on the evidence of the miracles themselves. [12]I tell you the truth, anyone who has faith in me will do what I have been doing. He will do even greater things than these, because I am going to the Father. [13]And I will do whatever you ask in my name, so that the Son may bring glory to the Father. [14]You may ask me for anything in my name, and I will do it.

Jesus Promises the Holy Spirit

[15]"If you love me, you will obey what I command. [16]And I will ask the Father, and he will give you another Counselor to be with you forever— [17]the Spirit of truth. The world cannot accept him, because it neither sees him nor knows him. But you know him, for he lives with you and will be[a] in you. [18]I will not leave you as orphans; I will come to you. [19]Before long, the world will not see me anymore, but you will see me. Because I live, you also will live. [20]On that day you will realize that I am in my Father, and you are in me, and I am in you. [21]Whoever has my commands and obeys them, he is the one who loves me. He who loves me will be loved by my Father, and I too will love him and show myself to him."

[22]Then Judas (not Judas Iscariot) said, "But, Lord, why do you intend to show yourself to us and not to the world?"

[23]Jesus replied, "If anyone loves me, he will obey my teaching. My Father will love him, and we will come to him and make our home with him. [24]He who does not love me will not obey my teaching. These words you hear are not my own; they belong to the Father who sent me.

[25]"All this I have spoken while still with you. [26]But the Counselor, the Holy Spirit, whom the Father will send in my name, will teach you all things and will remind you of everything I have said to you. [27]Peace I leave with you; my peace I give you. I do not give to you as the world gives. Do not let your hearts be troubled and do not be afraid.

[28]"You heard me say, 'I am going away and I am coming back to you.' If you loved me, you would be glad that I am going to the Father, for the Father is greater than I. [29]I have told you now before it happens, so that when it does happen you will believe. [30]I will not speak with you much longer, for the prince of this world is coming. He has no hold on me, [31]but the world must learn that I love the Father and that I do exactly what my Father has commanded me.

"Come now; let us leave.

The Vine and the Branches

15 "I am the true vine, and my Father is the gardener. [2]He cuts off every branch in me that bears no fruit, while every branch that does bear fruit he prunes[b] so that it will be even more fruitful. [3]You are already clean because of the word I have spoken to you. [4]Remain in me, and I will remain in you. No branch can bear fruit by itself; it must remain in the vine. Neither can you bear fruit unless you remain in me.

[5]"I am the vine; you are the branches. If a man remains in me and I in him, he will bear much fruit; apart from me you can do nothing. [6]If anyone does not remain in me, he is like a branch that is thrown away and withers; such branches are picked up, thrown into the fire and burned. [7]If you remain in me and my words remain in you, ask whatever you wish, and it will be given you. [8]This is to my Father's glory, that you bear much fruit, showing yourselves to be my disciples.

[9]"As the Father has loved me, so have I loved you. Now remain in my love. [10]If you obey my commands, you will remain in my love, just as I have obeyed my Father's commands and remain in his love. [11]I have told you this so that my joy may be in you and that your joy may be complete. [12]My command is this: Love each other as I have loved you. [13]Greater love has no one than this, that he lay down his life for his friends. [14]You are my friends if you do what I command. [15]I no longer call you servants, because a servant does not know his master's business. Instead, I

---

[a]17 Some early manuscripts *and is*   [b]2 The Greek for *prunes* also means *cleans*.

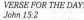

VERSE FOR THE DAY:
John 15:2

AUTHOR:
Carol L. Baldwin

PASSAGE FOR THE DAY:
John 15:1–6

Divine Pruning

WHAT would you think if your best friend told you that she thought you needed to endure a long, intense and difficult trial so that God could prune away some of the sin in your life? You would probably think she was crazy! What if she persisted and said that you would perform your job as a mother, wife, teacher or saleswoman better after your trial was over? Which of us would willingly submit to those pruning shears, and which of us would turn, run and hide?

Jesus himself is the one who says that we need pruning:

> "I am the true vine, and my Father is the gardener. He cuts off every branch in me that bears no fruit, while every branch that does bear fruit he prunes so that it will be even more fruitful. . . . Neither can you bear fruit unless you remain in me" (John 15:1–2,4).

Here Jesus has issued warnings to all who profess to be believers. Unfruitful branches are those who confess Christ but never bear fruit because they don't genuinely remain in him—they will be cut away. Fruitful branches, those who truly remain in Christ, will be pruned in order to bear more fruit for his glory.

When was the last time you felt "pruned"? Perhaps it was when your invalid mother came to live with you and suddenly your responsibilities and work load at home increased dramatically. Or maybe it was when your employer passed you over for a promotion because he thought you weren't working hard enough.

Pruning is painful but profitable. James tells us that trials are occasions for joy because they will test our faith and develop in us perseverance and maturity (James 1:2–4).

We need God's help even to *desire* to yield ourselves to his pruning. May God bring people and events into our lives that will sanctify us so that we might bear true spiritual fruit for his glory and his kingdom's sake.

Additional Scripture Readings:
Matthew 7:16–20; Luke 13:6–9

Go to page 148 for your next devotional reading.

have called you friends, for everything that I learned from my Father I have made known to you. 16You did not choose me, but I chose you and appointed you to go and bear fruit—fruit that will last. Then the Father will give you whatever you ask in my name. 17This is my command: Love each other.

The World Hates the Disciples

18"If the world hates you, keep in mind that it hated me first. 19If you belonged to the world, it would love you as its own. As it is, you do not belong to the world, but I have chosen you out of the world. That is why the world hates you. 20Remember the words I spoke to you: 'No servant is greater than his master.'[a] If they persecuted me, they will persecute you also. If they obeyed my teaching, they will obey yours also. 21They will treat you this way because of my name, for they do not know the One who sent me. 22If I had not come and spoken to them, they would not be guilty of sin. Now, however, they have no excuse for their sin. 23He who hates me hates my Father as well. 24If I had not done among them what no one else did, they would not be guilty of sin. But now they have seen these miracles, and yet they have hated both me and my Father. 25But this is to fulfill what is written in their Law: 'They hated me without reason.'[b]

26"When the Counselor comes, whom I will send to you from the Father, the Spirit of truth who goes out from the Father, he will testify about me. 27And you also must testify, for you have been with me from the beginning.

16 "All this I have told you so that you will not go astray. 2They will put

a20 John 13:16   b25 Psalms 35:19; 69:4

FRIDAY

VERSE FOR THE DAY:
John 15:12–13

AUTHOR:
Kathy Narramore
Alice Hill

PASSAGE FOR THE DAY:
John 15:9–17

Velvet and Sandpaper

WE all have known family or friends who bring out the worst in us instead of the best, rubbing us at just the wrong spots, uncovering our weaknesses rather than our strengths. They're like sandpaper. It is good to remember that Jesus encountered these sandpaper experiences at times even from within his inner circle. It is also good to remember that one of his close friends was one he knew would never understand him and would even betray him. He was a constant sandpaper to Jesus, yet Jesus loved him daily as he did the others. Even in this way he was laying down his life. Since we are also loved sacrificially we are to lay down our lives for each other (1 John 3:16).

But the Lord gives us others who are like velvet, whose words are comforting and supportive, and who really understand us. They are the soft cushions we need when we are scraped with the "sandpapers" and can listen to us as we explore the weaknesses and needs they bring out in us. They tangibly reveal God's perspective—just when we most need it.

Additional Scripture Readings:
John 13:18–30; Acts 9:23–28; 11:22–26

Go to page 149 for your next devotional reading.

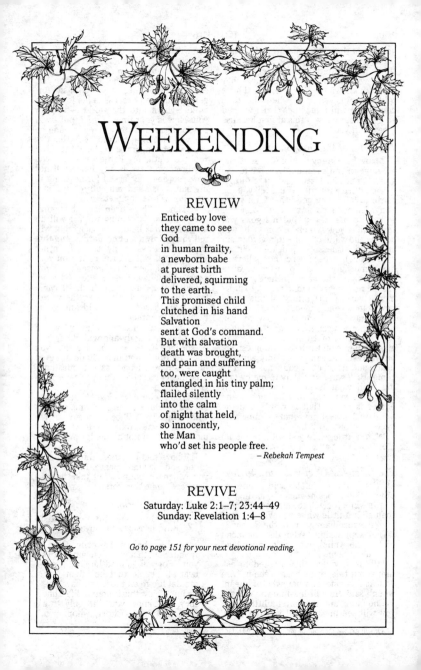

WEEKENDING

REVIEW

Enticed by love
they came to see
God
in human frailty,
a newborn babe
at purest birth
delivered, squirming
to the earth.
This promised child
clutched in his hand
Salvation
sent at God's command.
But with salvation
death was brought,
and pain and suffering
too, were caught
entangled in his tiny palm;
flailed silently
into the calm
of night that held,
so innocently,
the Man
who'd set his people free.

– Rebekah Tempest

REVIVE

Saturday: Luke 2:1–7; 23:44–49
Sunday: Revelation 1:4–8

Go to page 151 for your next devotional reading.

you out of the synagogue; in fact, a time is coming when anyone who kills you will think he is offering a service to God. [3]They will do such things because they have not known the Father or me. [4]I have told you this, so that when the time comes you will remember that I warned you. I did not tell you this at first because I was with you.

The Work of the Holy Spirit

[5]"Now I am going to him who sent me, yet none of you asks me, 'Where are you going?' [6]Because I have said these things, you are filled with grief. [7]But I tell you the truth: It is for your good that I am going away. Unless I go away, the Counselor will not come to you; but if I go, I will send him to you. [8]When he comes, he will convict the world of guilt[a] in regard to sin and righteousness and judgment: [9]in regard to sin, because men do not believe in me; [10]in regard to righteousness, because I am going to the Father, where you can see me no longer; [11]and in regard to judgment, because the prince of this world now stands condemned.

[12]"I have much more to say to you, more than you can now bear. [13]But when he, the Spirit of truth, comes, he will guide you into all truth. He will not speak on his own; he will speak only what he hears, and he will tell you what is yet to come. [14]He will bring glory to me by taking from what is mine and making it known to you. [15]All that belongs to the Father is mine. That is why I said the Spirit will take from what is mine and make it known to you.

[16]"In a little while you will see me no more, and then after a little while you will see me."

The Disciples' Grief Will Turn to Joy

[17]Some of his disciples said to one another, "What does he mean by saying, 'In a little while you will see me no more, and then after a little while you will see me,' and 'Because I am going to the Father'?" [18]They kept asking, "What does he mean by 'a little while'? We don't understand what he is saying."

[19]Jesus saw that they wanted to ask him about this, so he said to them, "Are you asking one another what I meant when I said, 'In a little while you will see me no more, and then after a little while you will see me'? [20]I tell you the truth,

you will weep and mourn while the world rejoices. You will grieve, but your grief will turn to joy. [21]A woman giving birth to a child has pain because her time has come; but when her baby is born she forgets the anguish because of her joy that a child is born into the world. [22]So with you: Now is your time of grief, but I will see you again and you will rejoice, and no one will take away your joy. [23]In that day you will no longer ask me anything. I tell you the truth, my Father will give you whatever you ask in my name. [24]Until now you have not asked for anything in my name. Ask and you will receive, and your joy will be complete.

[25]"Though I have been speaking figuratively, a time is coming when I will no longer use this kind of language but will tell you plainly about my Father. [26]In that day you will ask in my name. I am not saying that I will ask the Father on your behalf. [27]No, the Father himself loves you because you have loved me and have believed that I came from God. [28]I came from the Father and entered the world; now I am leaving the world and going back to the Father."

[29]Then Jesus' disciples said, "Now you are speaking clearly and without figures of speech. [30]Now we can see that you know all things and that you do not even need to have anyone ask you questions. This makes us believe that you came from God."

[31]"You believe at last!"[b] Jesus answered. [32]"But a time is coming, and has come, when you will be scattered, each to his own home. You will leave me all alone. Yet I am not alone, for my Father is with me.

[33]"I have told you these things, so that in me you may have peace. In this world you will have trouble. But take heart! I have overcome the world."

Jesus Prays for Himself

17 After Jesus said this, he looked toward heaven and prayed:

"Father, the time has come. Glorify your Son, that your Son may glorify you. [2]For you granted him authority over all people that he might give eternal life to all those you have given him. [3]Now this is eternal life: that they may know you, the only true God, and Jesus Christ, whom you

---

[a]8 Or will expose the guilt of the world   [b]31 Or "Do you now believe?"

VERSE FOR THE DAY:
John 16:20,22

AUTHOR:
Sue Richards

PASSAGE FOR THE DAY:
John 16:17–24

Coming Joy

AS much as two years after becoming single, I frequently found myself in tears at suppertime. My toddlers seemed to be tired by then, scrapping with each other, whining, hanging on me, and incessantly tattling on the crimes they committed against each other.

This is when Daddy is supposed to appear at the door, and both children run to their hero. Dad's arrival gives Mom a few minutes of peace while she prepares the evening meal, and later she has someone to share and commiserate with.

But no one comes while I'm preparing supper. And all I have to look forward to in the hours that lie ahead is refereeing my young wrecking crew, doing dishes, giving baths, reading stories, ending the nightly bedtime battle, and then my own lonely bed.

The thought that I'll always be a single parent is enough to start me sobbing at suppertime.

After a year of grieving for the loss of mate, companion, and father of my children, I knew I had to do something to survive the suppertime slump. I remembered some promises about joy that I'd cut out and stuck in a drawer years before. Though yellowed, wrinkled, and stained with an ancient cake batter, my promises were more precious than gold!

"Restore to me the joy of your salvation" (Psalm 51:12).

"You will grieve, but your grief will turn to joy . . . . and no one will take away your joy" (John 16:20,22).

> "He who goes out weeping,
>   carrying seed to sow,
> will return with songs of joy,
>   carrying sheaves with him" (Psalm 126:6).

Those words don't always start me dancing around the house. But they give me the courage to continue.

Thank you, Father, that joy will follow my sorrows.

Additional Scripture Readings:
Psalm 51:11–12; Isaiah 35:3–10

Go to page 153 for your next devotional reading.

have sent. ⁴I have brought you glory on earth by completing the work you gave me to do. ⁵And now, Father, glorify me in your presence with the glory I had with you before the world began.

Jesus Prays for His Disciples

⁶"I have revealed you*ᵃ* to those whom you gave me out of the world. They were yours; you gave them to me and they have obeyed your word. ⁷Now they know that everything you have given me comes from you. ⁸For I gave them the words you gave me and they accepted them. They knew with certainty that I came from you, and they believed that you sent me. ⁹I pray for them. I am not praying for the world, but for those you have given me, for they are yours. ¹⁰All I have is yours, and all you have is mine. And glory has come to me through them. ¹¹I will remain in the world no longer, but they are still in the world, and I am coming to you. Holy Father, protect them by the power of your name—the name you gave me—so that they may be one as we are one. ¹²While I was with them, I protected them and kept them safe by that name you gave me. None has been lost except the one doomed to destruction so that Scripture would be fulfilled.

¹³"I am coming to you now, but I say these things while I am still in the world, so that they may have the full measure of my joy within them. ¹⁴I have given them your word and the world has hated them, for they are not of the world any more than I am of the world. ¹⁵My prayer is not that you take them out of the world but that you protect them from the evil one. ¹⁶They are not of the world, even as I am not of it. ¹⁷Sanctify*ᵇ* them by the truth; your word is truth. ¹⁸As you sent me into the world, I have sent them into the world. ¹⁹For them I sanctify myself, that they too may be truly sanctified.

Jesus Prays for All Believers

²⁰"My prayer is not for them alone. I pray also for those who will believe in me through their message, ²¹that

all of them may be one, Father, just as you are in me and I am in you. May they also be in us so that the world may believe that you have sent me. ²²I have given them the glory that you gave me, that they may be one as we are one: ²³I in them and you in me. May they be brought to complete unity to let the world know that you sent me and have loved them even as you have loved me.

²⁴"Father, I want those you have given me to be with me where I am, and to see my glory, the glory you have given me because you loved me before the creation of the world. ²⁵"Righteous Father, though the world does not know you, I know you, and they know that you have sent me. ²⁶I have made you known to them, and will continue to make you known in order that the love you have for me may be in them and that I myself may be in them."

Jesus Arrested

18 When he had finished praying, Jesus left with his disciples and crossed the Kidron Valley. On the other side there was an olive grove, and he and his disciples went into it.

²Now Judas, who betrayed him, knew the place, because Jesus had often met there with his disciples. ³So Judas came to the grove, guiding a detachment of soldiers and some officials from the chief priests and Pharisees. They were carrying torches, lanterns and weapons.

⁴Jesus, knowing all that was going to happen to him, went out and asked them, "Who is it you want?"

⁵"Jesus of Nazareth," they replied.

"I am he," Jesus said. (And Judas the traitor was standing there with them.) ⁶When Jesus said, "I am he," they drew back and fell to the ground.

⁷Again he asked them, "Who is it you want?"

And they said, "Jesus of Nazareth."

⁸"I told you that I am he," Jesus answered. "If you are looking for me, then let these men go." ⁹This happened so that the words he had spoken would be fulfilled: "I have not lost one of those you gave me."*ᶜ*

¹⁰Then Simon Peter, who had a sword, drew it and struck the high priest's ser-

---

ᵃ6 Greek *your name*; also in verse 26   *ᵇ17* Greek *hagiazo (set apart for sacred use* or *make holy)*; also in verse 19   *ᶜ9* John 6:39

VERSE FOR THE DAY:
John 17:26

AUTHOR:
Anne Ortlund

PASSAGE FOR THE DAY:
John 17:1–26

Holy Ground

IT'S time to take off your shoes. You're about to move onto holy ground.

In all the literature written by human beings on this planet, John 17 is the only lengthy conversation ever recorded between God and God! You have quickies: "Let us make man in our image" (Genesis 1:26). "I praise you, Father . . . because you have hidden these things from the wise and learned, and revealed them to little children" (Matthew 11:25).

But here's a long discussion by God the Son with God the Father. (How self-revealing God is!) And when God talks with God, what are his godly, all-encompassing concerns? There are basically three:

1. John 17:1–5: the glory of the Father and the glory of the Son.

2. John 17:6–19: the well-being of believers—their protection, their unity, their joy, their sanctification . . . How he loves us!

3. John 17:20–26: the salvation of the world—that others will believe, that they will know. God yearns for them!

Do you want to move into the heart of God? Do you want to be "in sync" with him, sharing his own priorities? In John 15, just before Jesus went to the cross, he communicated these same three priorities among his final commands to his eleven disciples. And they're for you and me as well:

1. Make your chief concern the glory of the Father and the glory of the Son, through the power of the Spirit. Be zealous above all to put him first, first, first! Move away from all competition with his firstness; settle into him. As he said, "Remain in me" (John 15:1–11). That's your first priority.

2. Share his concern for the well-being of your fellow believers—their protection, their unity, their joy, their sanctification. Give your time, your gifts, yourself! As Jesus said, "Love each other" (John 15:12–17). That's your second priority.

3. Share his concern for this needy world; reach out! As he said, "You also must testify, for you have been with me from the beginning" (John 15:18–27). That's your third priority, your third area of concern.

So, here in John 17, take off your shoes. You're on holy ground. Sit at Jesus' feet. Learn his thinking. And give all you are to share his concerns, love his loves, accomplish his purposes.

Additional Scripture Readings:
Exodus 3:1–10; Mark 4:13–20

Go to page 157 for your next devotional reading.

vant, cutting off his right ear. (The servant's name was Malchus.)

[11]Jesus commanded Peter, "Put your sword away! Shall I not drink the cup the Father has given me?"

Jesus Taken to Annas

[12]Then the detachment of soldiers with its commander and the Jewish officials arrested Jesus. They bound him [13]and brought him first to Annas, who was the father-in-law of Caiaphas, the high priest that year. [14]Caiaphas was the one who had advised the Jews that it would be good if one man died for the people.

Peter's First Denial

[15]Simon Peter and another disciple were following Jesus. Because this disciple was known to the high priest, he went with Jesus into the high priest's courtyard, [16]but Peter had to wait outside at the door. The other disciple, who was known to the high priest, came back, spoke to the girl on duty there and brought Peter in.

[17]"You are not one of his disciples, are you?" the girl at the door asked Peter.

He replied, "I am not."

[18]It was cold, and the servants and officials stood around a fire they had made to keep warm. Peter also was standing with them, warming himself.

The High Priest Questions Jesus

[19]Meanwhile, the high priest questioned Jesus about his disciples and his teaching.

[20]"I have spoken openly to the world," Jesus replied. "I always taught in synagogues or at the temple, where all the Jews come together. I said nothing in secret. [21]Why question me? Ask those who heard me. Surely they know what I said."

[22]When Jesus said this, one of the officials nearby struck him in the face. "Is this the way you answer the high priest?" he demanded.

[23]"If I said something wrong," Jesus replied, "testify as to what is wrong. But if I spoke the truth, why did you strike me?" [24]Then Annas sent him, still bound, to Caiaphas the high priest.[a]

Peter's Second and Third Denials

[25]As Simon Peter stood warming himself, he was asked, "You are not one of his disciples, are you?"

He denied it, saying, "I am not."

[26]One of the high priest's servants, a relative of the man whose ear Peter had cut off, challenged him, "Didn't I see you with him in the olive grove?" [27]Again Peter denied it, and at that moment a rooster began to crow.

Jesus Before Pilate

[28]Then the Jews led Jesus from Caiaphas to the palace of the Roman governor. By now it was early morning, and to avoid ceremonial uncleanness the Jews did not enter the palace; they wanted to be able to eat the Passover. [29]So Pilate came out to them and asked, "What charges are you bringing against this man?"

[30]"If he were not a criminal," they replied, "we would not have handed him over to you."

[31]Pilate said, "Take him yourselves and judge him by your own law."

"But we have no right to execute anyone," the Jews objected. [32]This happened so that the words Jesus had spoken indicating the kind of death he was going to die would be fulfilled.

[33]Pilate then went back inside the palace, summoned Jesus and asked him, "Are you the king of the Jews?"

[34]"Is that your own idea," Jesus asked, "or did others talk to you about me?"

[35]"Am I a Jew?" Pilate replied. "It was your people and your chief priests who handed you over to me. What is it you have done?"

[36]Jesus said, "My kingdom is not of this world. If it were, my servants would fight to prevent my arrest by the Jews. But now my kingdom is from another place."

[37]"You are a king, then!" said Pilate.

Jesus answered, "You are right in saying I am a king. In fact, for this reason I was born, and for this I came into the world, to testify to the truth. Everyone on the side of truth listens to me."

[38]"What is truth?" Pilate asked. With this he went out again to the Jews and said, "I find no basis for a charge against him. [39]But it is your custom for me to release to you one prisoner at the time of the Passover. Do you want me to release 'the king of the Jews'?"

[40]They shouted back, "No, not him! Give us Barabbas!" Now Barabbas had taken part in a rebellion.

[a]24 Or (Now Annas had sent him, still bound, to Caiaphas the high priest.)

Jesus Sentenced to be Crucified

19 Then Pilate took Jesus and had him flogged. [2]The soldiers twisted together a crown of thorns and put it on his head. They clothed him in a purple robe [3]and went up to him again and again, saying, "Hail, king of the Jews!" And they struck him in the face.

[4]Once more Pilate came out and said to the Jews, "Look, I am bringing him out to you to let you know that I find no basis for a charge against him." [5]When Jesus came out wearing the crown of thorns and the purple robe, Pilate said to them, "Here is the man!"

[6]As soon as the chief priests and their officials saw him, they shouted, "Crucify! Crucify!"

But Pilate answered, "You take him and crucify him. As for me, I find no basis for a charge against him."

[7]The Jews insisted, "We have a law, and according to that law he must die, because he claimed to be the Son of God."

[8]When Pilate heard this, he was even more afraid, [9]and he went back inside the palace. "Where do you come from?" he asked Jesus, but Jesus gave him no answer. [10]"Do you refuse to speak to me?" Pilate said. "Don't you realize I have power either to free you or to crucify you?"

[11]Jesus answered, "You would have no power over me if it were not given to you from above. Therefore the one who handed me over to you is guilty of a greater sin."

[12]From then on, Pilate tried to set Jesus free, but the Jews kept shouting, "If you let this man go, you are no friend of Caesar. Anyone who claims to be a king opposes Caesar."

[13]When Pilate heard this, he brought Jesus out and sat down on the judge's seat at a place known as the Stone Pavement (which in Aramaic is Gabbatha). [14]It was the day of Preparation of Passover Week, about the sixth hour.

"Here is your king," Pilate said to the Jews.

[15]But they shouted, "Take him away! Take him away! Crucify him!"

"Shall I crucify your king?" Pilate asked.

"We have no king but Caesar," the chief priests answered.

[16]Finally Pilate handed him over to them to be crucified.

The Crucifixion

So the soldiers took charge of Jesus. [17]Carrying his own cross, he went out to the place of the Skull (which in Aramaic is called Golgotha). [18]Here they crucified him, and with him two others—one on each side and Jesus in the middle.

[19]Pilate had a notice prepared and fastened to the cross. It read: JESUS OF NAZARETH, THE KING OF THE JEWS. [20]Many of the Jews read this sign, for the place where Jesus was crucified was near the city, and the sign was written in Aramaic, Latin and Greek. [21]The chief priests of the Jews protested to Pilate, "Do not write 'The King of the Jews,' but that this man claimed to be king of the Jews."

[22]Pilate answered, "What I have written, I have written."

[23]When the soldiers crucified Jesus, they took his clothes, dividing them into four shares, one for each of them, with the undergarment remaining. This garment was seamless, woven in one piece from top to bottom.

[24]"Let's not tear it," they said to one another. "Let's decide by lot who will get it."

This happened that the scripture might be fulfilled which said,

"They divided my garments among them
    and cast lots for my clothing."[a]

So this is what the soldiers did.

[25]Near the cross of Jesus stood his mother, his mother's sister, Mary the wife of Clopas, and Mary Magdalene. [26]When Jesus saw his mother there, and the disciple whom he loved standing nearby, he said to his mother, "Dear woman, here is your son," [27]and to the disciple, "Here is your mother." From that time on, this disciple took her into his home.

The Death of Jesus

[28]Later, knowing that all was now completed, and so that the Scripture would be fulfilled, Jesus said, "I am thirsty." [29]A jar of wine vinegar was there, so they soaked a sponge in it, put the sponge on a stalk of the hyssop plant, and lifted it to Jesus' lips. [30]When he had received the drink, Jesus said, "It is finished." With that, he bowed his head and gave up his spirit.

a24 Psalm 22:18

³¹Now it was the day of Preparation, and the next day was to be a special Sabbath. Because the Jews did not want the bodies left on the crosses during the Sabbath, they asked Pilate to have the legs broken and the bodies taken down. ³²The soldiers therefore came and broke the legs of the first man who had been crucified with Jesus, and then those of the other. ³³But when they came to Jesus and found that he was already dead, they did not break his legs. ³⁴Instead, one of the soldiers pierced Jesus' side with a spear, bringing a sudden flow of blood and water. ³⁵The man who saw it has given testimony, and his testimony is true. He knows that he tells the truth, and he testifies so that you also may believe. ³⁶These things happened so that the scripture would be fulfilled: "Not one of his bones will be broken,"[a] ³⁷and, as another scripture says, "They will look on the one they have pierced."[b]

The Burial of Jesus

³⁸Later, Joseph of Arimathea asked Pilate for the body of Jesus. Now Joseph was a disciple of Jesus, but secretly because he feared the Jews. With Pilate's permission, he came and took the body away. ³⁹He was accompanied by Nicodemus, the man who earlier had visited Jesus at night. Nicodemus brought a mixture of myrrh and aloes, about seventy-five pounds.[c] ⁴⁰Taking Jesus' body, the two of them wrapped it, with the spices, in strips of linen. This was in accordance with Jewish burial customs. ⁴¹At the place where Jesus was crucified, there was a garden, and in the garden a new tomb, in which no one had ever been laid. ⁴²Because it was the Jewish day of Preparation and since the tomb was nearby, they laid Jesus there.

The Empty Tomb

20 Early on the first day of the week, while it was still dark, Mary Magdalene went to the tomb and saw that the stone had been removed from the entrance. ²So she came running to Simon Peter and the other disciple, the one Jesus loved, and said, "They have taken the Lord out of the tomb, and we don't know where they have put him!"

³So Peter and the other disciple started for the tomb. ⁴Both were running, but the other disciple outran Peter and reached the tomb first. ⁵He bent over and looked in at the strips of linen lying there but did not go in. ⁶Then Simon Peter, who was behind him, arrived and went into the tomb. He saw the strips of linen lying there, ⁷as well as the burial cloth that had been around Jesus' head. The cloth was folded up by itself, separate from the linen. ⁸Finally the other disciple, who had reached the tomb first, also went inside. He saw and believed. ⁹(They still did not understand from Scripture that Jesus had to rise from the dead.)

Jesus Appears to Mary Magdalene

¹⁰Then the disciples went back to their homes, ¹¹but Mary stood outside the tomb crying. As she wept, she bent over to look into the tomb ¹²and saw two angels in white, seated where Jesus' body had been, one at the head and the other at the foot.

¹³They asked her, "Woman, why are you crying?"

"They have taken my Lord away," she said, "and I don't know where they have put him." ¹⁴At this, she turned around and saw Jesus standing there, but she did not realize that it was Jesus.

¹⁵"Woman," he said, "why are you crying? Who is it you are looking for?"

Thinking he was the gardener, she said, "Sir, if you have carried him away, tell me where you have put him, and I will get him."

¹⁶Jesus said to her, "Mary."

She turned toward him and cried out in Aramaic, "Rabboni!" (which means Teacher).

¹⁷Jesus said, "Do not hold on to me, for I have not yet returned to the Father. Go instead to my brothers and tell them, 'I am returning to my Father and your Father, to my God and your God.' "

¹⁸Mary Magdalene went to the disciples with the news: "I have seen the Lord!" And she told them that he had said these things to her.

Jesus Appears to His Disciples

¹⁹On the evening of that first day of the week, when the disciples were together, with the doors locked for fear of the Jews, Jesus came and stood among them and said, "Peace be with you!" ²⁰After he said this, he showed them his hands and side.

---

a36 Exodus 12:46; Num. 9:12; Psalm 34:20   *b37* Zech. 12:10   *c39* Greek *a hundred litrai* (about 34 kilograms)

VERSE FOR THE DAY:
John 20:25

AUTHOR:
Ruth A. Tucker

PASSAGE FOR THE DAY:
John 20:24–31

Doubting Believers

IT is not the faithful women (who told the doubting disciples of their risen Lord) with whom I identify most in the cast of characters who surround Jesus in the days before and after his death and resurrection. No, as I examine myself and my struggle with faith *and* doubt, I find that it is Thomas with whom I most identify.

Thomas was more than simply one doubting disciple who held out for proof of the resurrection—a skeptic who will be remembered forever for his lack of faith. No, Thomas stood in for all the rest of the followers of Jesus who, through the ages, have been afflicted with a disposition toward doubt. Like him, we are disciples, but disciples who are cynical at times, who often need more time to assimilate and test the facts.

Thomas merits no praise for his unbelieving mindset. But he and the other disciples, who initially doubted, offer skeptics through the ages assurance because they did not take for granted anything involving the Easter events. Indeed, the most powerful evidence for the resurrection of Jesus is the very fact that the disciples doubted. They were not like some people who are ready to latch on to any rumor or report that comes along—particularly if it bolsters their position. No, they demanded proof, and in doing so benefited the Christian church for all time.

For Jesus, however, the disciples' lack of faith was a deep disappointment, and I know that my own lack of faith at times surely must grieve the heart of my Lord. Yet, I know he understands my struggle, and I know he understands my prayer that reiterates the plea of another who struggled with unbelief when he cried out, "I do believe; help me overcome my unbelief!" (Mark 9:24).

Additional Scripture Readings:
Matthew 14:28–31; 1 John 1:1–3

Go to page 161 for your next devotional reading.

The disciples were overjoyed when they saw the Lord.

²¹Again Jesus said, "Peace be with you! As the Father has sent me, I am sending you." ²²And with that he breathed on them and said, "Receive the Holy Spirit. ²³If you forgive anyone his sins, they are forgiven; if you do not forgive them, they are not forgiven."

Jesus Appears to Thomas

²⁴Now Thomas (called Didymus), one of the Twelve, was not with the disciples when Jesus came. ²⁵So the other disciples told him, "We have seen the Lord!"

But he said to them, "Unless I see the nail marks in his hands and put my finger where the nails were, and put my hand into his side, I will not believe it."

²⁶A week later his disciples were in the house again, and Thomas was with them. Though the doors were locked, Jesus came and stood among them and said, "Peace be with you!" ²⁷Then he said to Thomas, "Put your finger here; see my hands. Reach out your hand and put it into my side. Stop doubting and believe."

²⁸Thomas said to him, "My Lord and my God!"

²⁹Then Jesus told him, "Because you have seen me, you have believed; blessed are those who have not seen and yet have believed."

³⁰Jesus did many other miraculous signs in the presence of his disciples, which are not recorded in this book. ³¹But these are written that you may*a* believe that Jesus is the Christ, the Son of God, and that by believing you may have life in his name.

Jesus and the Miraculous Catch of Fish

21 Afterward Jesus appeared again to his disciples, by the Sea of Tiberias.*b* It happened this way: ²Simon Peter, Thomas (called Didymus), Nathanael from Cana in Galilee, the sons of Zebedee, and two other disciples were together. ³"I'm going out to fish," Simon Peter told them, and they said, "We'll go with you." So they went out and got into the boat, but that night they caught nothing.

⁴Early in the morning, Jesus stood on the shore, but the disciples did not realize that it was Jesus.

⁵He called out to them, "Friends, haven't you any fish?"

"No," they answered.

⁶He said, "Throw your net on the right side of the boat and you will find some." When they did, they were unable to haul the net in because of the large number of fish.

⁷Then the disciple whom Jesus loved said to Peter, "It is the Lord!" As soon as Simon Peter heard him say, "It is the Lord," he wrapped his outer garment around him (for he had taken it off) and jumped into the water. ⁸The other disciples followed in the boat, towing the net full of fish, for they were not far from shore, about a hundred yards.*c* ⁹When they landed, they saw a fire of burning coals there with fish on it, and some bread.

¹⁰Jesus said to them, "Bring some of the fish you have just caught."

¹¹Simon Peter climbed aboard and dragged the net ashore. It was full of large fish, 153, but even with so many the net was not torn. ¹²Jesus said to them, "Come and have breakfast." None of the disciples dared ask him, "Who are you?" They knew it was the Lord. ¹³Jesus came, took the bread and gave it to them, and did the same with the fish. ¹⁴This was now the third time Jesus appeared to his disciples after he was raised from the dead.

Jesus Reinstates Peter

¹⁵When they had finished eating, Jesus said to Simon Peter, "Simon son of John, do you truly love me more than these?"

"Yes, Lord," he said, "you know that I love you."

Jesus said, "Feed my lambs."

¹⁶Again Jesus said, "Simon son of John, do you truly love me?"

He answered, "Yes, Lord, you know that I love you."

Jesus said, "Take care of my sheep."

¹⁷The third time he said to him, "Simon son of John, do you love me?"

Peter was hurt because Jesus asked him the third time, "Do you love me?" He said, "Lord, you know all things; you know that I love you."

Jesus said, "Feed my sheep. ¹⁸I tell you the truth, when you were younger you dressed yourself and went where you wanted; but when you are old you will stretch out your hands, and someone else

---

a31 Some manuscripts *may continue to cubits* (about 90 meters)   *b1* That is, Sea of Galilee   *c8* Greek *about two hundred* will dress you and lead you where you do not want to go." [19]Jesus said this to indicate the kind of death by which Peter would glorify God. Then he said to him, "Follow me!"

[20]Peter turned and saw that the disciple whom Jesus loved was following them. (This was the one who had leaned back against Jesus at the supper and had said, "Lord, who is going to betray you?") [21]When Peter saw him, he asked, "Lord, what about him?"

[22]Jesus answered, "If I want him to remain alive until I return, what is that to you? You must follow me." [23]Because of this, the rumor spread among the brothers that this disciple would not die. But Jesus did not say that he would not die; he only said, "If I want him to remain alive until I return, what is that to you?"

[24]This is the disciple who testifies to these things and who wrote them down. We know that his testimony is true.

[25]Jesus did many other things as well. If every one of them were written down, I suppose that even the whole world would not have room for the books that would be written.

*L*UKE begins the second volume of his history of Christianity (Acts 1:1–3) by telling how Jesus pours out the Holy Spirit on the apostles. The Spirit in turn inspires them to spread the message of salvation from Jerusalem to Rome. In his story Luke stresses how unity and love prevail in the church and how God protects the missionaries from their enemies. As you read this book, think about how powerful the Holy Spirit still is in the church and in your own life and how God protects you against the forces of evil.

ACTS

Jesus Taken Up Into Heaven

1 In my former book, Theophilus, I wrote about all that Jesus began to do and to teach ²until the day he was taken up to heaven, after giving instructions through the Holy Spirit to the apostles he had chosen. ³After his suffering, he showed himself to these men and gave many convincing proofs that he was alive. He appeared to them over a period of forty days and spoke about the kingdom of God. ⁴On one occasion, while he was eating with them, he gave them this command: "Do not leave Jerusalem, but wait for the gift my Father promised, which you have heard me speak about. ⁵For John baptized with*ᵃ* water, but in a few days you will be baptized with the Holy Spirit."

⁶So when they met together, they asked him, "Lord, are you at this time going to restore the kingdom to Israel?"

⁷He said to them: "It is not for you to know the times or dates the Father has

---

set by his own authority. [8]But you will receive power when the Holy Spirit comes on you; and you will be my witnesses in Jerusalem, and in all Judea and Samaria, and to the ends of the earth."

[9]After he said this, he was taken up before their very eyes, and a cloud hid him from their sight.

[10]They were looking intently up into the sky as he was going, when suddenly two men dressed in white stood beside them. [11]"Men of Galilee," they said, "why do you stand here looking into the sky? This same Jesus, who has been taken from you into heaven, will come back in the same way you have seen him go into heaven."

Matthias Chosen to Replace Judas

[12]Then they returned to Jerusalem from the hill called the Mount of Olives, a Sabbath day's walk[a] from the city.

---

[a]12 That is, about 3/4 mile (about 1,100 meters)

| THURSDAY |

| VERSE FOR THE DAY: | AUTHOR: | PASSAGE FOR THE DAY: |
| Acts 1:8 | Rebecca Manley Pippert | Acts 1:1–11 |

Jesus the Evangelist

JESUS told us that as the Father sent him into the world, so he is sending us (John 17:18; Acts 1:8). How then did the Father send him? Essentially he became one of us. "The Word became flesh" (John 1:14). God didn't send a telegram or shower evangelistic Bible study books from heaven or drop a million bumper stickers from the sky saying, "Smile, Jesus loves you." He sent a man, his Son, to communicate the message. His strategy hasn't changed. He still sends men and women—before he sends tracts and techniques—to change the world. You may think his strategy is risky, but that is God's problem, not yours.

In Jesus, then, we have our model for how to relate to the world, and it is a model of openness and identification. Jesus was a remarkably open man. He didn't think it was unspiritual for him (fully realizing he was the Son of God) to share his physical needs (John 4:7). He didn't fear losing his testimony by revealing to his disciples the depths of his emotional stress in the Garden of Gethsemane (Mark 14:32–52). Here is our model for genuine godliness. We see him asking for support and desiring others to minister to him. We must learn then to relate transparently and genuinely to others because that is God's style of relating to us. Jesus commands us to go and then preach, not to preach and then leave. We are not to shout the gospel from a safe and respectable distance, and remain detached. We must open our lives enough to let people see that we too laugh and hurt and cry. If Jesus left all of heaven and glory to become one of us, shouldn't we at least be willing to leave our dorm room or Bible study circle to reach out to a friend?

Additional Scripture Readings:
John 11:33–44; 1 Corinthians 2:1–5

Go to page 165 for your next devotional reading.

[13] When they arrived, they went upstairs to the room where they were staying. Those present were Peter, John, James and Andrew; Philip and Thomas, Bartholomew and Matthew; James son of Alphaeus and Simon the Zealot, and Judas son of James. [14] They all joined together constantly in prayer, along with the women and Mary the mother of Jesus, and with his brothers.

[15] In those days Peter stood up among the believers[a] (a group numbering about a hundred and twenty) [16] and said, "Brothers, the Scripture had to be fulfilled which the Holy Spirit spoke long ago through the mouth of David concerning Judas, who served as guide for those who arrested Jesus— [17] he was one of our number and shared in this ministry."

[18] (With the reward he got for his wickedness, Judas bought a field; there he fell headlong, his body burst open and all his intestines spilled out. [19] Everyone in Jerusalem heard about this, so they called that field in their language Akeldama, that is, Field of Blood.)

[20] "For," said Peter, "it is written in the book of Psalms,

" 'May his place be deserted;
    let there be no one to dwell in it,'[b]

and,

" 'May another take his place of
    leadership.'[c]

[21] Therefore it is necessary to choose one of the men who have been with us the whole time the Lord Jesus went in and out among us, [22] beginning from John's baptism to the time when Jesus was taken up from us. For one of these must become a witness with us of his resurrection."

[23] So they proposed two men: Joseph called Barsabbas (also known as Justus) and Matthias. [24] Then they prayed, "Lord, you know everyone's heart. Show us which of these two you have chosen [25] to take over this apostolic ministry, which Judas left to go where he belongs." [26] Then they cast lots, and the lot fell to Matthias; so he was added to the eleven apostles.

The Holy Spirit Comes at Pentecost

2 When the day of Pentecost came, they were all together in one place. [2] Suddenly a sound like the blowing of a violent wind came from heaven and filled the whole house where they were sitting. [3] They saw what seemed to be tongues of fire that separated and came to rest on each of them. [4] All of them were filled with the Holy Spirit and began to speak in other tongues[d] as the Spirit enabled them.

[5] Now there were staying in Jerusalem God-fearing Jews from every nation under heaven. [6] When they heard this sound, a crowd came together in bewilderment, because each one heard them speaking in his own language. [7] Utterly amazed, they asked: "Are not all these men who are speaking Galileans? [8] Then how is it that each of us hears them in his own native language? [9] Parthians, Medes and Elamites; residents of Mesopotamia, Judea and Cappadocia, Pontus and Asia, [10] Phrygia and Pamphylia, Egypt and the parts of Libya near Cyrene; visitors from Rome [11] (both Jews and converts to Judaism); Cretans and Arabs—we hear them declaring the wonders of God in our own tongues!" [12] Amazed and perplexed, they asked one another, "What does this mean?"

[13] Some, however, made fun of them and said, "They have had too much wine.[e]"

Peter Addresses the Crowd

[14] Then Peter stood up with the Eleven, raised his voice and addressed the crowd: "Fellow Jews and all of you who live in Jerusalem, let me explain this to you; listen carefully to what I say. [15] These men are not drunk, as you suppose. It's only nine in the morning! [16] No, this is what was spoken by the prophet Joel:

[17] " 'In the last days, God says,
    I will pour out my Spirit on all
        people.
Your sons and daughters will
        prophesy,
    your young men will see visions,
    your old men will dream dreams.
[18] Even on my servants, both men and
        women,
    I will pour out my Spirit in those
        days,
    and they will prophesy.
[19] I will show wonders in the heaven
        above

---

[a]15 Greek *brothers*   [b]20 Psalm 69:25   [c]20 Psalm 109:8   [d]4 Or *languages*; also in verse 11
[e]13 Or *sweet wine*

and signs on the earth below,
blood and fire and billows of
smoke.
20The sun will be turned to darkness
and the moon to blood
before the coming of the great and
glorious day of the Lord.
21And everyone who calls
on the name of the Lord will be
saved.'*a*

22"Men of Israel, listen to this: Jesus of Nazareth was a man accredited by God to you by miracles, wonders and signs, which God did among you through him, as you yourselves know. 23This man was handed over to you by God's set purpose and foreknowledge; and you, with the help of wicked men,*b* put him to death by nailing him to the cross. 24But God raised him from the dead, freeing him from the agony of death, because it was impossible for death to keep its hold on him. 25David said about him:

" 'I saw the Lord always before me.
Because he is at my right hand,
I will not be shaken.
26Therefore my heart is glad and my
tongue rejoices;
my body also will live in hope,
27because you will not abandon me to
the grave,
nor will you let your Holy One see
decay.
28You have made known to me the
paths of life;
you will fill me with joy in your
presence.'*c*

29"Brothers, I can tell you confidently that the patriarch David died and was buried, and his tomb is here to this day. 30But he was a prophet and knew that God had promised him on oath that he would place one of his descendants on his throne. 31Seeing what was ahead, he spoke of the resurrection of the Christ,*d* that he was not abandoned to the grave, nor did his body see decay. 32God has raised this Jesus to life, and we are all witnesses of the fact. 33Exalted to the right hand of God, he has received from the Father the promised Holy Spirit and has poured out what you now see and hear. 34For David did not ascend to heaven, and yet he said,

" 'The Lord said to my Lord:
"Sit at my right hand
35until I make your enemies
a footstool for your feet." '*e*

36"Therefore let all Israel be assured of this: God has made this Jesus, whom you crucified, both Lord and Christ."

37When the people heard this, they were cut to the heart and said to Peter and the other apostles, "Brothers, what shall we do?"

38Peter replied, "Repent and be baptized, every one of you, in the name of Jesus Christ for the forgiveness of your sins. And you will receive the gift of the Holy Spirit. 39The promise is for you and your children and for all who are far off—for all whom the Lord our God will call."

40With many other words he warned them; and he pleaded with them, "Save yourselves from this corrupt generation." 41Those who accepted his message were baptized, and about three thousand were added to their number that day.

The Fellowship of the Believers

42They devoted themselves to the apostles' teaching and to the fellowship, to the breaking of bread and to prayer. 43Everyone was filled with awe, and many wonders and miraculous signs were done by the apostles. 44All the believers were together and had everything in common. 45Selling their possessions and goods, they gave to anyone as he had need. 46Every day they continued to meet together in the temple courts. They broke bread in their homes and ate together with glad and sincere hearts, 47praising God and enjoying the favor of all the people. And the Lord added to their number daily those who were being saved.

Peter Heals the Crippled Beggar

3 One day Peter and John were going up to the temple at the time of prayer —at three in the afternoon. 2Now a man crippled from birth was being carried to the temple gate called Beautiful, where he was put every day to beg from those going into the temple courts. 3When he saw Peter and John about to enter, he asked them for money. 4Peter looked straight at him, as did John. Then Peter said, "Look at us!" 5So the man gave them

a21 Joel 2:28-32   *b23* Or *of those not having the law* (that is, Gentiles)   *c28* Psalm 16:8-11
d31 Or *Messiah.* "The Christ" (Greek) and "the Messiah" (Hebrew) both mean "the Anointed One"; also in verse 36.   *e35* Psalm 110:1

his attention, expecting to get something from them.

⁶Then Peter said, "Silver or gold I do not have, but what I have I give you. In the name of Jesus Christ of Nazareth, walk." ⁷Taking him by the right hand, he helped him up, and instantly the man's feet and ankles became strong. ⁸He jumped to his feet and began to walk. Then he went with them into the temple courts, walking and jumping, and praising God. ⁹When all the people saw him walking and praising God, ¹⁰they recognized him as the same man who used to sit begging at the temple gate called Beautiful, and they were filled with wonder and amazement at what had happened to him.

Peter Speaks to the Onlookers

¹¹While the beggar held on to Peter and John, all the people were astonished and came running to them in the place called Solomon's Colonnade. ¹²When Peter saw this, he said to them: "Men of Israel, why does this surprise you? Why do you stare at us as if by our own power or godliness we had made this man walk? ¹³The God of Abraham, Isaac and Jacob, the God of our fathers, has glorified his servant Jesus. You handed him over to be killed, and you disowned him before Pilate, though he had decided to let him go. ¹⁴You disowned the Holy and Righteous One and asked that a murderer be released to you. ¹⁵You killed the author of life, but God raised him from the dead. We are witnesses of this. ¹⁶By faith in the name of Jesus, this man whom you see and know was made strong. It is Jesus' name and the faith that comes through him that has given this complete healing to him, as you can all see.

¹⁷"Now, brothers, I know that you acted in ignorance, as did your leaders. ¹⁸But this is how God fulfilled what he had foretold through all the prophets, saying that his Christ[a] would suffer. ¹⁹Repent, then, and turn to God, so that your sins may be wiped out, that times of refreshing may come from the Lord, ²⁰and that he may send the Christ, who has been appointed for you—even Jesus. ²¹He must remain in heaven until the time comes for God to restore everything, as he promised long ago through his holy prophets. ²²For Moses said, 'The Lord your God will raise up for you a prophet like me from among

your own people; you must listen to everything he tells you. ²³Anyone who does not listen to him will be completely cut off from among his people.'[b]

²⁴"Indeed, all the prophets from Samuel on, as many as have spoken, have foretold these days. ²⁵And you are heirs of the prophets and of the covenant God made with your fathers. He said to Abraham, 'Through your offspring all peoples on earth will be blessed.'[c] ²⁶When God raised up his servant, he sent him first to you to bless you by turning each of you from your wicked ways."

Peter and John Before the Sanhedrin

4 The priests and the captain of the temple guard and the Sadducees came up to Peter and John while they were speaking to the people. ²They were greatly disturbed because the apostles were teaching the people and proclaiming in Jesus the resurrection of the dead. ³They seized Peter and John, and because it was evening, they put them in jail until the next day. ⁴But many who heard the message believed, and the number of men grew to about five thousand.

⁵The next day the rulers, elders and teachers of the law met in Jerusalem. ⁶Annas the high priest was there, and so were Caiaphas, John, Alexander and the other men of the high priest's family. ⁷They had Peter and John brought before them and began to question them: "By what power or what name did you do this?"

⁸Then Peter, filled with the Holy Spirit, said to them: "Rulers and elders of the people! ⁹If we are being called to account today for an act of kindness shown to a cripple and are asked how he was healed, ¹⁰then know this, you and all the people of Israel: It is by the name of Jesus Christ of Nazareth, whom you crucified but whom God raised from the dead, that this man stands before you healed. ¹¹He is

" 'the stone you builders rejected,
    which has become the capstone.[d][e]

¹²Salvation is found in no one else, for there is no other name under heaven given to men by which we must be saved."

¹³When they saw the courage of Peter and John and realized that they were unschooled, ordinary men, they were astonished and they took note that these men

---

a18 Or *Messiah;* also in verse 20   *b23* Deut. 18:15,18,19   *c25* Gen. 22:18; 26:4   *d11* Or *cornerstone*   *e11* Psalm 118:22

had been with Jesus. ¹⁴But since they could see the man who had been healed standing there with them, there was nothing they could say. ¹⁵So they ordered them to withdraw from the Sanhedrin and then conferred together. ¹⁶"What are we going to do with these men?" they asked. "Everybody living in Jerusalem knows they have done an outstanding miracle, and we cannot deny it. ¹⁷But to stop this thing from spreading any further among the people, we must warn these men to speak no longer to anyone in this name."

¹⁸Then they called them in again and commanded them not to speak or teach at all in the name of Jesus. ¹⁹But Peter and John replied, "Judge for yourselves whether it is right in God's sight to obey you rather than God. ²⁰For we cannot help speaking about what we have seen and heard."

²¹After further threats they let them go. They could not decide how to punish

FRIDAY

VERSE FOR THE DAY:
Acts 4:32

AUTHOR:
Linda Ching Sledge

PASSAGE FOR THE DAY:
Acts 4:23–35

No East or West

MY hometown church is on a winding street on the outskirts of old Honolulu. It was built in the 1880s by Boston missionaries who served the earliest Christian immigrants to Hawaii from Canton, China. After a century, the descendants of those first Cantonese Christians still worship there. It's a proud heritage. But for a youngster growing up in that church, it was sometimes confusing.

There were two sermons, one in English and one in Cantonese for the "old folks" who couldn't speak the language of their adopted homeland. As a child, I found the Chinese sermon long and boring. I could understand only a few words of Chinese so the words made no sense. Oh, how the long minutes dragged by!

Then one Sunday, at the closing hymn, I heard strange sounds from the pew behind me. It was an old Chinese grandfather singing at the top of his lungs . . . in Chinese!

It was so funny to hear two sets of words sung to the same tune at the same time. I couldn't resist peeking. The old man's head was thrown back, his eyes closed, and he was singing as if the words were pulled from his heart.

And suddenly, though I didn't know his words, I understood their meaning. And I began to sing too, straight from the heart:

> In Christ there is no East or West,
> In Him no South or North;
> But one great fellowship of love
> Throughout the whole wide earth.

Additional Scripture Readings:
Ephesians 2:12–20; Revelation 7:9–10

Go to page 167 for your next devotional reading.

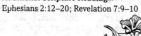

them, because all the people were praising God for what had happened. ²²For the man who was miraculously healed was over forty years old.

The Believers' Prayer

²³On their release, Peter and John went back to their own people and reported all that the chief priests and elders had said to them. ²⁴When they heard this, they raised their voices together in prayer to God. "Sovereign Lord," they said, "you made the heaven and the earth and the sea, and everything in them. ²⁵You spoke by the Holy Spirit through the mouth of your servant, our father David:

" 'Why do the nations rage
    and the peoples plot in vain?
²⁶The kings of the earth take their stand
    and the rulers gather together
  against the Lord
    and against his Anointed One.ᵃ'ᵇ

²⁷Indeed Herod and Pontius Pilate met together with the Gentiles and the peopleᶜ of Israel in this city to conspire against your holy servant Jesus, whom you anointed. ²⁸They did what your power and will had decided beforehand should happen. ²⁹Now, Lord, consider their threats and enable your servants to speak your word with great boldness. ³⁰Stretch out your hand to heal and perform miraculous signs and wonders through the name of your holy servant Jesus."

³¹After they prayed, the place where they were meeting was shaken. And they were all filled with the Holy Spirit and spoke the word of God boldly.

The Believers Share Their Possessions

³²All the believers were one in heart and mind. No one claimed that any of his possessions was his own, but they shared everything they had. ³³With great power the apostles continued to testify to the resurrection of the Lord Jesus, and much grace was upon them all. ³⁴There were no needy persons among them. For from time to time those who owned lands or houses sold them, brought the money from the sales ³⁵and put it at the apostles' feet, and it was distributed to anyone as he had need.

³⁶Joseph, a Levite from Cyprus, whom the apostles called Barnabas (which means Son of Encouragement), ³⁷sold a field he owned and brought the money and put it at the apostles' feet.

Ananias and Sapphira

5 Now a man named Ananias, together with his wife Sapphira, also sold a piece of property. ²With his wife's full knowledge he kept back part of the money for himself, but brought the rest and put it at the apostles' feet.

³Then Peter said, "Ananias, how is it that Satan has so filled your heart that you have lied to the Holy Spirit and have kept for yourself some of the money you received for the land? ⁴Didn't it belong to you before it was sold? And after it was sold, wasn't the money at your disposal? What made you think of doing such a thing? You have not lied to men but to God."

⁵When Ananias heard this, he fell down and died. And great fear seized all who heard what had happened. ⁶Then the young men came forward, wrapped up his body, and carried him out and buried him.

⁷About three hours later his wife came in, not knowing what had happened. ⁸Peter asked her, "Tell me, is this the price you and Ananias got for the land?"

"Yes," she said, "that is the price."

⁹Peter said to her, "How could you agree to test the Spirit of the Lord? Look! The feet of the men who buried your husband are at the door, and they will carry you out also."

¹⁰At that moment she fell down at his feet and died. Then the young men came in and, finding her dead, carried her out and buried her beside her husband. ¹¹Great fear seized the whole church and all who heard about these events.

The Apostles Heal Many

¹²The apostles performed many miraculous signs and wonders among the people. And all the believers used to meet together in Solomon's Colonnade. ¹³No one else dared join them, even though they were highly regarded by the people. ¹⁴Nevertheless, more and more men and women believed in the Lord and were added to their number. ¹⁵As a result, people brought the sick into the streets and laid them on beds and mats so that at least Peter's shadow might fall on some of them as he passed by. ¹⁶Crowds gathered

ᵃ26 That is, Christ or Messiah   ᵇ26 Psalm 2:1,2   ᶜ27 The Greek is plural.

WEEKENDING

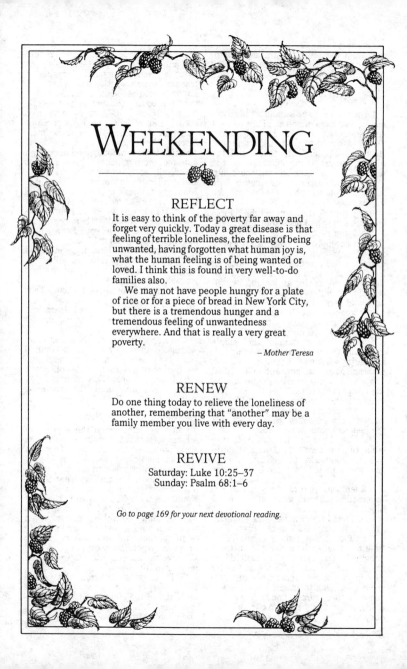

REFLECT

It is easy to think of the poverty far away and forget very quickly. Today a great disease is that feeling of terrible loneliness, the feeling of being unwanted, having forgotten what human joy is, what the human feeling is of being wanted or loved. I think this is found in very well-to-do families also.

We may not have people hungry for a plate of rice or for a piece of bread in New York City, but there is a tremendous hunger and a tremendous feeling of unwantedness everywhere. And that is really a very great poverty.

– Mother Teresa

RENEW

Do one thing today to relieve the loneliness of another, remembering that "another" may be a family member you live with every day.

REVIVE

Saturday: Luke 10:25–37
Sunday: Psalm 68:1–6

Go to page 169 for your next devotional reading.

also from the towns around Jerusalem, bringing their sick and those tormented by evil[a] spirits, and all of them were healed.

The Apostles Persecuted

17Then the high priest and all his associates, who were members of the party of the Sadducees, were filled with jealousy. 18They arrested the apostles and put them in the public jail. 19But during the night an angel of the Lord opened the doors of the jail and brought them out. 20"Go, stand in the temple courts," he said, "and tell the people the full message of this new life."

21At daybreak they entered the temple courts, as they had been told, and began to teach the people.

When the high priest and his associates arrived, they called together the Sanhedrin—the full assembly of the elders of Israel—and sent to the jail for the apostles. 22But on arriving at the jail, the officers did not find them there. So they went back and reported, 23"We found the jail securely locked, with the guards standing at the doors; but when we opened them, we found no one inside." 24On hearing this report, the captain of the temple guard and the chief priests were puzzled, wondering what would come of this.

25Then someone came and said, "Look! The men you put in jail are standing in the temple courts teaching the people." 26At that, the captain went with his officers and brought the apostles. They did not use force, because they feared that the people would stone them.

27Having brought the apostles, they made them appear before the Sanhedrin to be questioned by the high priest. 28"We gave you strict orders not to teach in this name," he said. "Yet you have filled Jerusalem with your teaching and are determined to make us guilty of this man's blood."

29Peter and the other apostles replied: "We must obey God rather than men! 30The God of our fathers raised Jesus from the dead—whom you had killed by hanging him on a tree. 31God exalted him to his own right hand as Prince and Savior that he might give repentance and forgiveness of sins to Israel. 32We are witnesses of these things, and so is the Holy Spirit, whom God has given to those who obey him."

33When they heard this, they were furious and wanted to put them to death. 34But a Pharisee named Gamaliel, a teacher of the law, who was honored by all the people, stood up in the Sanhedrin and ordered that the men be put outside for a little while. 35Then he addressed them: "Men of Israel, consider carefully what you intend to do to these men. 36Some time ago Theudas appeared, claiming to be somebody, and about four hundred men rallied to him. He was killed, all his followers were dispersed, and it all came to nothing. 37After him, Judas the Galilean appeared in the days of the census and led a band of people in revolt. He too was killed, and all his followers were scattered. 38Therefore, in the present case I advise you: Leave these men alone! Let them go! For if their purpose or activity is of human origin, it will fail. 39But if it is from God, you will not be able to stop these men; you will only find yourselves fighting against God."

40His speech persuaded them. They called the apostles in and had them flogged. Then they ordered them not to speak in the name of Jesus, and let them go.

41The apostles left the Sanhedrin, rejoicing because they had been counted worthy of suffering disgrace for the Name. 42Day after day, in the temple courts and from house to house, they never stopped teaching and proclaiming the good news that Jesus is the Christ.[b]

The Choosing of the Seven

6 In those days when the number of disciples was increasing, the Grecian Jews among them complained against the Hebraic Jews because their widows were being overlooked in the daily distribution of food. 2So the Twelve gathered all the disciples together and said, "It would not be right for us to neglect the ministry of the word of God in order to wait on tables. 3Brothers, choose seven men from among you who are known to be full of the Spirit and wisdom. We will turn this responsibility over to them 4and will give our attention to prayer and the ministry of the word."

5This proposal pleased the whole group. They chose Stephen, a man full of faith and of the Holy Spirit; also Philip, Procorus, Nicanor, Timon, Parmenas, and Nicolas from Antioch, a convert to

a16 Greek unclean   b42 Or Messiah

VERSE FOR THE DAY:
Acts 5:9

AUTHOR:
June Gunden

PASSAGE FOR THE DAY:
Acts 5:1–11

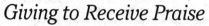

Giving to Receive Praise

GIVING generously to the needy is one sure way of impressing other Christians. If it becomes known that a certain family has given a lot of money or service to the church, other people respect and admire them for it.

This must have been especially true in a day when "from time to time those who owned lands or houses sold them, brought the money from the sales and put it at the apostles' feet, and it was distributed to anyone as he had need" (Acts 4:34–35). When someone sold property it would have been common knowledge what it was worth, and therefore other people would know how much had been given to the apostles.

In light of such widespread generosity, people of that day may have felt a little chagrined for it to be known that they had sold some property but had not shared the profits. Their "spiritual" reputation may have become tarnished, and they may never have been as highly thought of as those who were willing to give it all.

Accordingly, Ananias and Sapphira probably convinced themselves that by keeping some of the money for themselves they wouldn't be hurting anyone else (and they wouldn't be hurting their own reputation either). They opted to let others think they had given more than they really had. This hypocrisy, and the love of money and praise that motivated it, cost them their lives.

Jesus taught very clearly that giving to the needy must not be done for praise (Matthew 6:1–4). "When you give to the needy," he said, give "in secret" and "your Father . . . will reward you."

What if no one ever finds out that I've made a large contribution to the church? Does it matter? What if no one notices the hours I've spent helping someone else? Do I care? What if my efforts for the kingdom are largely unappreciated? Do I become discouraged?

If I am happy to serve when no one is there to give me credit, I am truly working for the Lord.

Additional Scripture Readings:
Matthew 23:5–12; Ephesians 6:7–8

Go to page 174 for your next devotional reading.

Judaism. [6]They presented these men to the apostles, who prayed and laid their hands on them.

[7]So the word of God spread. The number of disciples in Jerusalem increased rapidly, and a large number of priests became obedient to the faith.

Stephen Seized

[8]Now Stephen, a man full of God's grace and power, did great wonders and miraculous signs among the people. [9]Opposition arose, however, from members of the Synagogue of the Freedmen (as it was called)—Jews of Cyrene and Alexandria as well as the provinces of Cilicia and Asia. These men began to argue with Stephen, [10]but they could not stand up against his wisdom or the Spirit by whom he spoke.

[11]Then they secretly persuaded some men to say, "We have heard Stephen speak words of blasphemy against Moses and against God."

[12]So they stirred up the people and the elders and the teachers of the law. They seized Stephen and brought him before the Sanhedrin. [13]They produced false witnesses, who testified, "This fellow never stops speaking against this holy place and against the law. [14]For we have heard him say that this Jesus of Nazareth will destroy this place and change the customs Moses handed down to us."

[15]All who were sitting in the Sanhedrin looked intently at Stephen, and they saw that his face was like the face of an angel.

Stephen's Speech to the Sanhedrin

7 Then the high priest asked him, "Are these charges true?"

[2]To this he replied: "Brothers and fathers, listen to me! The God of glory appeared to our father Abraham while he was still in Mesopotamia, before he lived in Haran. [3]'Leave your country and your people,' God said, 'and go to the land I will show you.'[a]

[4]"So he left the land of the Chaldeans and settled in Haran. After the death of his father, God sent him to this land where you are now living. [5]He gave him no inheritance here, not even a foot of ground. But God promised him that he and his descendants after him would possess the land, even though at that time Abraham had no child. [6]God spoke to him in this way: 'Your descendants will be strangers in a country not their own, and they will be enslaved and mistreated four hundred years. [7]But I will punish the nation they serve as slaves,' God said, 'and afterward they will come out of that country and worship me in this place.'[b] [8]Then he gave Abraham the covenant of circumcision. And Abraham became the father of Isaac and circumcised him eight days after his birth. Later Isaac became the father of Jacob, and Jacob became the father of the twelve patriarchs.

[9]"Because the patriarchs were jealous of Joseph, they sold him as a slave into Egypt. But God was with him [10]and rescued him from all his troubles. He gave Joseph wisdom and enabled him to gain the goodwill of Pharaoh king of Egypt; so he made him ruler over Egypt and all his palace.

[11]"Then a famine struck all Egypt and Canaan, bringing great suffering, and our fathers could not find food. [12]When Jacob heard that there was grain in Egypt, he sent our fathers on their first visit. [13]On their second visit, Joseph told his brothers who he was, and Pharaoh learned about Joseph's family. [14]After this, Joseph sent for his father Jacob and his whole family, seventy-five in all. [15]Then Jacob went down to Egypt, where he and our fathers died. [16]Their bodies were brought back to Shechem and placed in the tomb that Abraham had bought from the sons of Hamor at Shechem for a certain sum of money.

[17]"As the time drew near for God to fulfill his promise to Abraham, the number of our people in Egypt greatly increased. [18]Then another king, who knew nothing about Joseph, became ruler of Egypt. [19]He dealt treacherously with our people and oppressed our forefathers by forcing them to throw out their newborn babies so that they would die.

[20]"At that time Moses was born, and he was no ordinary child.[c] For three months he was cared for in his father's house. [21]When he was placed outside, Pharaoh's daughter took him and brought him up as her own son. [22]Moses was educated in all the wisdom of the Egyptians and was powerful in speech and action.

[23]"When Moses was forty years old, he decided to visit his fellow Israelites. [24]He saw one of them being mistreated by an Egyptian, so he went to his defense and avenged him by killing the Egyptian.

[a]3 Gen. 12:1   [b]7 Gen. 15:13,14   [c]20 Or *was fair in the sight of God*

25Moses thought that his own people would realize that God was using him to rescue them, but they did not. 26The next day Moses came upon two Israelites who were fighting. He tried to reconcile them by saying, 'Men, you are brothers; why do you want to hurt each other?'

27"But the man who was mistreating the other pushed Moses aside and said, 'Who made you ruler and judge over us? 28Do you want to kill me as you killed the Egyptian yesterday?'a 29When Moses heard this, he fled to Midian, where he settled as a foreigner and had two sons.

30"After forty years had passed, an angel appeared to Moses in the flames of a burning bush in the desert near Mount Sinai. 31When he saw this, he was amazed at the sight. As he went over to look more closely, he heard the Lord's voice: 32'I am the God of your fathers, the God of Abraham, Isaac and Jacob.'b Moses trembled with fear and did not dare to look.

33"Then the Lord said to him, 'Take off your sandals; the place where you are standing is holy ground. 34I have indeed seen the oppression of my people in Egypt. I have heard their groaning and have come down to set them free. Now come, I will send you back to Egypt.'c

35"This is the same Moses whom they had rejected with the words, 'Who made you ruler and judge?' He was sent to be their ruler and deliverer by God himself, through the angel who appeared to him in the bush. 36He led them out of Egypt and did wonders and miraculous signs in Egypt, at the Red Sead and for forty years in the desert.

37"This is that Moses who told the Israelites, 'God will send you a prophet like me from your own people.'e 38He was in the assembly in the desert, with the angel who spoke to him on Mount Sinai, and with our fathers; and he received living words to pass on to us.

39"But our fathers refused to obey him. Instead, they rejected him and in their hearts turned back to Egypt. 40They told Aaron, 'Make us gods who will go before us. As for this fellow Moses who led us out of Egypt—we don't know what has happened to him!'f 41That was the time they made an idol in the form of a calf. They brought sacrifices to it and held a celebration in honor of what their hands had made. 42But God turned away and gave them over to the worship of the heavenly bodies. This agrees with what is written in the book of the prophets:

" 'Did you bring me sacrifices and offerings
    forty years in the desert, O house of Israel?
43You have lifted up the shrine of Molech
    and the star of your god Rephan,
    the idols you made to worship.
Therefore I will send you into exile'g beyond Babylon.

44"Our forefathers had the tabernacle of the Testimony with them in the desert. It had been made as God directed Moses, according to the pattern he had seen. 45Having received the tabernacle, our fathers under Joshua brought it with them when they took the land from the nations God drove out before them. It remained in the land until the time of David, 46who enjoyed God's favor and asked that he might provide a dwelling place for the God of Jacob.h 47But it was Solomon who built the house for him.

48"However, the Most High does not live in houses made by men. As the prophet says:

49" 'Heaven is my throne,
    and the earth is my footstool.
What kind of house will you build for me?
                                    says the Lord.
Or where will my resting place be?
50Has not my hand made all these things?'i

51"You stiff-necked people, with uncircumcised hearts and ears! You are just like your fathers: You always resist the Holy Spirit! 52Was there ever a prophet your fathers did not persecute? They even killed those who predicted the coming of the Righteous One. And now you have betrayed and murdered him— 53you who have received the law that was put into effect through angels but have not obeyed it."

The Stoning of Stephen

54When they heard this, they were furious and gnashed their teeth at him. 55But

a28 Exodus 2:14   b32 Exodus 3:6   c34 Exodus 3:5,7,8,10   d36 That is, Sea of Reeds
e37 Deut. 18:15   f40 Exodus 32:1   g43 Amos 5:25-27   h46 Some early manuscripts the house of
Jacob   i50 Isaiah 66:1,2

Stephen, full of the Holy Spirit, looked up to heaven and saw the glory of God, and Jesus standing at the right hand of God. 56"Look," he said, "I see heaven open and the Son of Man standing at the right hand of God."

57At this they covered their ears and, yelling at the top of their voices, they all rushed at him, 58dragged him out of the city and began to stone him. Meanwhile, the witnesses laid their clothes at the feet of a young man named Saul.

59While they were stoning him, Stephen prayed, "Lord Jesus, receive my spirit." 60Then he fell on his knees and cried out, "Lord, do not hold this sin against them." When he had said this, he fell asleep.

8 And Saul was there, giving approval to his death.

The Church Persecuted and Scattered

On that day a great persecution broke out against the church at Jerusalem, and all except the apostles were scattered throughout Judea and Samaria. 2Godly men buried Stephen and mourned deeply for him. 3But Saul began to destroy the church. Going from house to house, he dragged off men and women and put them in prison.

Philip in Samaria

4Those who had been scattered preached the word wherever they went. 5Philip went down to a city in Samaria and proclaimed the Christ*a* there. 6When the crowds heard Philip and saw the miraculous signs he did, they all paid close attention to what he said. 7With shrieks, evil*b* spirits came out of many, and many paralytics and cripples were healed. 8So there was great joy in that city.

Simon the Sorcerer

9Now for some time a man named Simon had practiced sorcery in the city and amazed all the people of Samaria. He boasted that he was someone great, 10and all the people, both high and low, gave him their attention and exclaimed, "This man is the divine power known as the Great Power." 11They followed him because he had amazed them for a long time with his magic. 12But when they be-

lieved Philip as he preached the good news of the kingdom of God and the name of Jesus Christ, they were baptized, both men and women. 13Simon himself believed and was baptized. And he followed Philip everywhere, astonished by the great signs and miracles he saw.

14When the apostles in Jerusalem heard that Samaria had accepted the word of God, they sent Peter and John to them. 15When they arrived, they prayed for them that they might receive the Holy Spirit, 16because the Holy Spirit had not yet come upon any of them; they had simply been baptized into*c* the name of the Lord Jesus. 17Then Peter and John placed their hands on them, and they received the Holy Spirit.

18When Simon saw that the Spirit was given at the laying on of the apostles' hands, he offered them money 19and said, "Give me also this ability so that everyone on whom I lay my hands may receive the Holy Spirit."

20Peter answered: "May your money perish with you, because you thought you could buy the gift of God with money! 21You have no part or share in this ministry, because your heart is not right before God. 22Repent of this wickedness and pray to the Lord. Perhaps he will forgive you for having such a thought in your heart. 23For I see that you are full of bitterness and captive to sin."

24Then Simon answered, "Pray to the Lord for me so that nothing you have said may happen to me."

25When they had testified and proclaimed the word of the Lord, Peter and John returned to Jerusalem, preaching the gospel in many Samaritan villages.

Philip and the Ethiopian

26Now an angel of the Lord said to Philip, "Go south to the road—the desert road—that goes down from Jerusalem to Gaza." 27So he started out, and on his way he met an Ethiopian*d* eunuch, an important official in charge of all the treasury of Candace, queen of the Ethiopians. This man had gone to Jerusalem to worship, 28and on his way home was sitting in his chariot reading the book of Isaiah the prophet. 29The Spirit told Philip, "Go to that chariot and stay near it."

30Then Philip ran up to the chariot and heard the man reading Isaiah the pro-

---

a5 Or *Messiah*   *b7* Greek *unclean*   *c16* Or *in*   *d27* That is, from the upper Nile region phet. "Do you understand what you are reading?" Philip asked.

³¹"How can I," he said, "unless someone explains it to me?" So he invited Philip to come up and sit with him.

³²The eunuch was reading this passage of Scripture:

"He was led like a sheep to the
        slaughter,
    and as a lamb before the shearer is
        silent,
    so he did not open his mouth.
³³In his humiliation he was deprived of
        justice.
    Who can speak of his descendants?
    For his life was taken from the
        earth."ᵃ

³⁴The eunuch asked Philip, "Tell me, please, who is the prophet talking about, himself or someone else?" ³⁵Then Philip began with that very passage of Scripture and told him the good news about Jesus.

³⁶As they traveled along the road, they came to some water and the eunuch said, "Look, here is water. Why shouldn't I be baptized?"ᵇ ³⁸And he gave orders to stop the chariot. Then both Philip and the eunuch went down into the water and Philip baptized him. ³⁹When they came up out of the water, the Spirit of the Lord suddenly took Philip away, and the eunuch did not see him again, but went on his way rejoicing. ⁴⁰Philip, however, appeared at Azotus and traveled about, preaching the gospel in all the towns until he reached Caesarea.

Saul's Conversion

9 Meanwhile, Saul was still breathing out murderous threats against the Lord's disciples. He went to the high priest ²and asked him for letters to the synagogues in Damascus, so that if he found any there who belonged to the Way, whether men or women, he might take them as prisoners to Jerusalem. ³As he neared Damascus on his journey, suddenly a light from heaven flashed around him. ⁴He fell to the ground and heard a voice say to him, "Saul, Saul, why do you persecute me?"

⁵"Who are you, Lord?" Saul asked.

"I am Jesus, whom you are persecuting," he replied. ⁶"Now get up and go into the city, and you will be told what you must do."

⁷The men traveling with Saul stood there speechless; they heard the sound but did not see anyone. ⁸Saul got up from the ground, but when he opened his eyes he could see nothing. So they led him by the hand into Damascus. ⁹For three days he was blind, and did not eat or drink anything.

¹⁰In Damascus there was a disciple named Ananias. The Lord called to him in a vision, "Ananias!"

"Yes, Lord," he answered.

¹¹The Lord told him, "Go to the house of Judas on Straight Street and ask for a man from Tarsus named Saul, for he is praying. ¹²In a vision he has seen a man named Ananias come and place his hands on him to restore his sight."

¹³"Lord," Ananias answered, "I have heard many reports about this man and all the harm he has done to your saints in Jerusalem. ¹⁴And he has come here with authority from the chief priests to arrest all who call on your name."

¹⁵But the Lord said to Ananias, "Go! This man is my chosen instrument to carry my name before the Gentiles and their kings and before the people of Israel. ¹⁶I will show him how much he must suffer for my name."

¹⁷Then Ananias went to the house and entered it. Placing his hands on Saul, he said, "Brother Saul, the Lord—Jesus, who appeared to you on the road as you were coming here—has sent me so that you may see again and be filled with the Holy Spirit." ¹⁸Immediately, something like scales fell from Saul's eyes, and he could see again. He got up and was baptized, ¹⁹and after taking some food, he regained his strength.

Saul in Damascus and Jerusalem

Saul spent several days with the disciples in Damascus. ²⁰At once he began to preach in the synagogues that Jesus is the Son of God. ²¹All those who heard him were astonished and asked, "Isn't he the man who raised havoc in Jerusalem among those who call on this name? And hasn't he come here to take them as prisoners to the chief priests?" ²²Yet Saul grew more and more powerful and baffled the Jews living in Damascus by proving that Jesus is the Christ.ᶜ

²³After many days had gone by, the Jews conspired to kill him, ²⁴but Saul

ᵃ33 Isaiah 53:7,8   ᵇ36 Some late manuscripts baptized?" ³⁷Philip said, "If you believe with all your heart, you may." The eunuch answered, "I believe that Jesus Christ is the Son of God."   ᶜ22 Or Messiah

TUESDAY

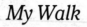

VERSE FOR THE DAY:
Acts 9:3–4

AUTHOR:
Jean Syswerda

PASSAGE FOR THE DAY:
Acts 9:1–19

My Walk

SAUL was about as opposed to Christ and Christianity as one could get. He stood at Stephen's stoning, "giving approval to his death" (Acts 8:1). He was the one who was "breathing out murderous threats against the Lord's disciples" (Acts 9:1). Doesn't sound like someone I'd like to know on a personal basis.

Then, Christ appeared to Saul. A flashy conversion experience, with Christ speaking from the heaven to which he had returned. And Saul became Paul, the most effective Christian missionary the world has ever known.

It's hard for me to relate to that sort of experience. You see, I can't recall a time when I didn't love the Lord and want to serve him. I don't say that to sound pious or self-righteous . . . it's just the truth. I rebelled as a teenager against parental strictures and traditional structures, but I never rebelled against God.

There have been times when I thought I was lacking something because I had no dazzling experience to relate. But over the years I've come to realize the value of my quiet sort of experience.

And even though there haven't been blinding visions or bright lights, there have been times of definite comfort and guidance from God. Like when he spoke to me from Isaiah as a teenager, reassuring me that I wasn't a nobody:

> Fear not, for I have redeemed you;
> I have summoned you by name; you are mine
> (Isaiah 43:1).

Or when, as a young single adult, he promised to always stay with the project of making me all I should be in him: "Being confident of this, that he who began a good work in you will carry it on to completion until the day of Christ Jesus" (Philippians 1:6).

Your walk with God may not resemble Saul's (or Connie's or Mary's or Cheryl's), but it's *your* walk with a God who loves you and relates to you where you are.

Additional Scripture Readings:
Romans 8:30–39; 2 Peter 1:3–11

Go to page 177 for your next devotional reading.

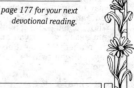

learned of their plan. Day and night they kept close watch on the city gates in order to kill him. ²⁵But his followers took him by night and lowered him in a basket through an opening in the wall.

²⁶When he came to Jerusalem, he tried to join the disciples, but they were all afraid of him, not believing that he really was a disciple. ²⁷But Barnabas took him and brought him to the apostles. He told them how Saul on his journey had seen the Lord and that the Lord had spoken to him, and how in Damascus he had preached fearlessly in the name of Jesus. ²⁸So Saul stayed with them and moved about freely in Jerusalem, speaking boldly in the name of the Lord. ²⁹He talked and debated with the Grecian Jews, but they tried to kill him. ³⁰When the brothers learned of this, they took him down to Caesarea and sent him off to Tarsus.

³¹Then the church throughout Judea, Galilee and Samaria enjoyed a time of peace. It was strengthened; and encouraged by the Holy Spirit, it grew in numbers, living in the fear of the Lord.

Aeneas and Dorcas

³²As Peter traveled about the country, he went to visit the saints in Lydda. ³³There he found a man named Aeneas, a paralytic who had been bedridden for eight years. ³⁴"Aeneas," Peter said to him, "Jesus Christ heals you. Get up and take care of your mat." Immediately Aeneas got up. ³⁵All those who lived in Lydda and Sharon saw him and turned to the Lord.

³⁶In Joppa there was a disciple named Tabitha (which, when translated, is Dorcas*a*), who was always doing good and helping the poor. ³⁷About that time she became sick and died, and her body was washed and placed in an upstairs room. ³⁸Lydda was near Joppa; so when the disciples heard that Peter was in Lydda, they sent two men to him and urged him, "Please come at once!"

³⁹Peter went with them, and when he arrived he was taken upstairs to the room. All the widows stood around him, crying and showing him the robes and other clothing that Dorcas had made while she was still with them. ⁴⁰Peter sent them all out of the room; then he got down on his knees and prayed. Turning toward the dead woman, he said, "Tabitha, get up." She opened her eyes, and seeing Peter she sat up.

⁴¹He took her by the hand and helped her to her feet. Then he called the believers and the widows and presented her to them alive. ⁴²This became known all over Joppa, and many people believed in the Lord. ⁴³Peter stayed in Joppa for some time with a tanner named Simon.

Cornelius Calls for Peter

10 At Caesarea there was a man named Cornelius, a centurion in what was known as the Italian Regiment. ²He and all his family were devout and God-fearing; he gave generously to those in need and prayed to God regularly. ³One day at about three in the afternoon he had a vision. He distinctly saw an angel of God, who came to him and said, "Cornelius!"

⁴Cornelius stared at him in fear. "What is it, Lord?" he asked.

The angel answered, "Your prayers and gifts to the poor have come up as a memorial offering before God. ⁵Now send men to Joppa to bring back a man named Simon who is called Peter. ⁶He is staying with Simon the tanner, whose house is by the sea."

⁷When the angel who spoke to him had gone, Cornelius called two of his servants and a devout soldier who was one of his attendants. ⁸He told them everything that had happened and sent them to Joppa.

Peter's Vision

⁹About noon the following day as they were on their journey and approaching the city, Peter went up on the roof to pray. ¹⁰He became hungry and wanted something to eat, and while the meal was being prepared, he fell into a trance. ¹¹He saw heaven opened and something like a large sheet being let down to earth by its four corners. ¹²It contained all kinds of four-footed animals, as well as reptiles of the earth and birds of the air. ¹³Then a voice told him, "Get up, Peter. Kill and eat."

¹⁴"Surely not, Lord!" Peter replied. "I have never eaten anything impure or unclean."

¹⁵The voice spoke to him a second time, "Do not call anything impure that God has made clean."

¹⁶This happened three times, and immediately the sheet was taken back to heaven.

¹⁷While Peter was wondering about the

---

a36 Both *Tabitha* (Aramaic) and *Dorcas* (Greek) mean *gazelle.*

meaning of the vision, the men sent by Cornelius found out where Simon's house was and stopped at the gate. ¹⁸They called out, asking if Simon who was known as Peter was staying there.

¹⁹While Peter was still thinking about the vision, the Spirit said to him, "Simon, three*a* men are looking for you. ²⁰So get up and go downstairs. Do not hesitate to go with them, for I have sent them."

²¹Peter went down and said to the men, "I'm the one you're looking for. Why have you come?"

²²The men replied, "We have come from Cornelius the centurion. He is a righteous and God-fearing man, who is respected by all the Jewish people. A holy angel told him to have you come to his house so that he could hear what you have to say." ²³Then Peter invited the men into the house to be his guests.

Peter at Cornelius' House

The next day Peter started out with them, and some of the brothers from Joppa went along. ²⁴The following day he arrived in Caesarea. Cornelius was expecting them and had called together his relatives and close friends. ²⁵As Peter entered the house, Cornelius met him and fell at his feet in reverence. ²⁶But Peter made him get up. "Stand up," he said, "I am only a man myself."

²⁷Talking with him, Peter went inside and found a large gathering of people. ²⁸He said to them: "You are well aware that it is against our law for a Jew to associate with a Gentile or visit him. But God has shown me that I should not call any man impure or unclean. ²⁹So when I was sent for, I came without raising any objection. May I ask why you sent for me?"

³⁰Cornelius answered: "Four days ago I was in my house praying at this hour, at three in the afternoon. Suddenly a man in shining clothes stood before me ³¹and said, 'Cornelius, God has heard your prayer and remembered your gifts to the poor. ³²Send to Joppa for Simon who is called Peter. He is a guest in the home of Simon the tanner, who lives by the sea.' ³³So I sent for you immediately, and it was good of you to come. Now we are all here in the presence of God to listen to everything the Lord has commanded you to tell us."

³⁴Then Peter began to speak: "I now realize how true it is that God does not show favoritism ³⁵but accepts men from every nation who fear him and do what is right. ³⁶You know the message God sent to the people of Israel, telling the good news of peace through Jesus Christ, who is Lord of all. ³⁷You know what has happened throughout Judea, beginning in Galilee after the baptism that John preached— ³⁸how God anointed Jesus of Nazareth with the Holy Spirit and power, and how he went around doing good and healing all who were under the power of the devil, because God was with him.

³⁹"We are witnesses of everything he did in the country of the Jews and in Jerusalem. They killed him by hanging him on a tree, ⁴⁰but God raised him from the dead on the third day and caused him to be seen. ⁴¹He was not seen by all the people, but by witnesses whom God had already chosen—by us who ate and drank with him after he rose from the dead. ⁴²He commanded us to preach to the people and to testify that he is the one whom God appointed as judge of the living and the dead. ⁴³All the prophets testify about him that everyone who believes in him receives forgiveness of sins through his name."

⁴⁴While Peter was still speaking these words, the Holy Spirit came on all who heard the message. ⁴⁵The circumcised believers who had come with Peter were astonished that the gift of the Holy Spirit had been poured out even on the Gentiles. ⁴⁶For they heard them speaking in tongues*b* and praising God.

Then Peter said, ⁴⁷"Can anyone keep these people from being baptized with water? They have received the Holy Spirit just as we have." ⁴⁸So he ordered that they be baptized in the name of Jesus Christ. Then they asked Peter to stay with them for a few days.

Peter Explains His Actions

11 The apostles and the brothers throughout Judea heard that the Gentiles also had received the word of God. ²So when Peter went up to Jerusalem, the circumcised believers criticized him ³and said, "You went into the house of uncircumcised men and ate with them."

⁴Peter began and explained everything to them precisely as it had happened: ⁵"I was in the city of Joppa praying, and in a trance I saw a vision. I saw something like

VERSE FOR THE DAY:
Acts 10:34

AUTHOR:
Mary Beckwith

PASSAGE FOR THE DAY:
Acts 10:34–38

When Did Prejudice Creep In?

"IT must be a gentlemanbug," I thought I heard my little boy say.

"What did you say?" I asked him.

He said it again. "It must be a gentlemanbug."

Rob, then Robbie, gently pushed the ladybug onto his pudgy little hand. He had been playing with it for at least ten minutes. I was impressed that, at four years old, he knew the opposite for lady was gentleman and was able to label his new little friend accordingly.

But then I asked, "Why do you think it's a gentlemanbug?"

"Because he's smart!" was his ready reply.

Needless to say, I was in shock for a moment. Where had he gotten the idea that, in order to be smart, you had to be a man? And at the age of four, at that!

I quickly tried to recall if, in the last few days, I had said something that would have implied men were smarter than women. I couldn't remember anything. Maybe his father had made that implication somehow. I'd have to ask him.

I do recall at times when the kids asked me questions I didn't have the answers to I'd say, "We'll ask Daddy when he gets home." Maybe I'd done it enough to give the impression that dads are smarter than moms.

Anyway, this little episode made me question, How do prejudice and bias enter our lives? What causes us to judge others because of gender or color or whatever? It also taught me that when we show partiality and prejudice, we are setting examples for our children.

I am so thankful we have a heavenly Father who is no respecter of persons. He loves each one of us the same. And he desires that we in turn love one another with the same kind of love.

When I'm reminded of his unconditional, steadfast love, it helps me fight against the prejudice that tries to creep in, distort my conception of others, and tempts me to look at myself more highly than I should.

Additional Scripture Readings:
Romans 12:3–5; Galatians 3:26–28

Go to page 182 for your next devotional reading.

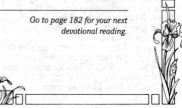

a large sheet being let down from heaven by its four corners, and it came down to where I was. 6I looked into it and saw four-footed animals of the earth, wild beasts, reptiles, and birds of the air. 7Then I heard a voice telling me, 'Get up, Peter. Kill and eat.'

8"I replied, 'Surely not, Lord! Nothing impure or unclean has ever entered my mouth.'

9"The voice spoke from heaven a second time, 'Do not call anything impure that God has made clean.' 10This happened three times, and then it was all pulled up to heaven again.

11"Right then three men who had been sent to me from Caesarea stopped at the house where I was staying. 12The Spirit told me to have no hesitation about going with them. These six brothers also went with me, and we entered the man's house. 13He told us how he had seen an angel appear in his house and say, 'Send to Joppa for Simon who is called Peter. 14He will bring you a message through which you and all your household will be saved.'

15"As I began to speak, the Holy Spirit came on them as he had come on us at the beginning. 16Then I remembered what the Lord had said: 'John baptized with*a* water, but you will be baptized with the Holy Spirit.' 17So if God gave them the same gift as he gave us, who believed in the Lord Jesus Christ, who was I to think that I could oppose God?"

18When they heard this, they had no further objections and praised God, saying, "So then, God has granted even the Gentiles repentance unto life."

The Church in Antioch

19Now those who had been scattered by the persecution in connection with Stephen traveled as far as Phoenicia, Cyprus and Antioch, telling the message only to Jews. 20Some of them, however, men from Cyprus and Cyrene, went to Antioch and began to speak to Greeks also, telling them the good news about the Lord Jesus. 21The Lord's hand was with them, and a great number of people believed and turned to the Lord.

22News of this reached the ears of the church at Jerusalem, and they sent Barnabas to Antioch. 23When he arrived and saw the evidence of the grace of God, he was glad and encouraged them all to re-

main true to the Lord with all their hearts. 24He was a good man, full of the Holy Spirit and faith, and a great number of people were brought to the Lord.

25Then Barnabas went to Tarsus to look for Saul, 26and when he found him, he brought him to Antioch. So for a whole year Barnabas and Saul met with the church and taught great numbers of people. The disciples were called Christians first at Antioch.

27During this time some prophets came down from Jerusalem to Antioch. 28One of them, named Agabus, stood up and through the Spirit predicted that a severe famine would spread over the entire Roman world. (This happened during the reign of Claudius.) 29The disciples, each according to his ability, decided to provide help for the brothers living in Judea. 30This they did, sending their gift to the elders by Barnabas and Saul.

Peter's Miraculous Escape From Prison

12 It was about this time that King Herod arrested some who belonged to the church, intending to persecute them. 2He had James, the brother of John, put to death with the sword. 3When he saw that this pleased the Jews, he proceeded to seize Peter also. This happened during the Feast of Unleavened Bread. 4After arresting him, he put him in prison, handing him over to be guarded by four squads of four soldiers each. Herod intended to bring him out for public trial after the Passover.

5So Peter was kept in prison, but the church was earnestly praying to God for him.

6The night before Herod was to bring him to trial, Peter was sleeping between two soldiers, bound with two chains, and sentries stood guard at the entrance. 7Suddenly an angel of the Lord appeared and a light shone in the cell. He struck Peter on the side and woke him up. "Quick, get up!" he said, and the chains fell off Peter's wrists.

8Then the angel said to him, "Put on your clothes and sandals." And Peter did so. "Wrap your cloak around you and follow me," the angel told him. 9Peter followed him out of the prison, but he had no idea that what the angel was doing was really happening; he thought he was seeing a vision. 10They passed the first and

*a*16 Or *in*

second guards and came to the iron gate leading to the city. It opened for them by itself, and they went through it. When they had walked the length of one street, suddenly the angel left him.

[11]Then Peter came to himself and said, "Now I know without a doubt that the Lord sent his angel and rescued me from Herod's clutches and from everything the Jewish people were anticipating."

[12]When this had dawned on him, he went to the house of Mary the mother of John, also called Mark, where many people had gathered and were praying. [13]Peter knocked at the outer entrance, and a servant girl named Rhoda came to answer the door. [14]When she recognized Peter's voice, she was so overjoyed she ran back without opening it and exclaimed, "Peter is at the door!"

[15]"You're out of your mind," they told her. When she kept insisting that it was so, they said, "It must be his angel."

[16]But Peter kept on knocking, and when they opened the door and saw him, they were astonished. [17]Peter motioned with his hand for them to be quiet and described how the Lord had brought him out of prison. "Tell James and the brothers about this," he said, and then he left for another place.

[18]In the morning, there was no small commotion among the soldiers as to what had become of Peter. [19]After Herod had a thorough search made for him and did not find him, he cross-examined the guards and ordered that they be executed.

Herod's Death

Then Herod went from Judea to Caesarea and stayed there a while. [20]He had been quarreling with the people of Tyre and Sidon; they now joined together and sought an audience with him. Having secured the support of Blastus, a trusted personal servant of the king, they asked for peace, because they depended on the king's country for their food supply.

[21]On the appointed day Herod, wearing his royal robes, sat on his throne and delivered a public address to the people. [22]They shouted, "This is the voice of a god, not of a man." [23]Immediately, because Herod did not give praise to God, an angel of the Lord struck him down, and he was eaten by worms and died.

[24]But the word of God continued to increase and spread.

[25]When Barnabas and Saul had finished their mission, they returned from[a] Jerusalem, taking with them John, also called Mark.

Barnabas and Saul Sent Off

13 In the church at Antioch there were prophets and teachers: Barnabas, Simeon called Niger, Lucius of Cyrene, Manaen (who had been brought up with Herod the tetrarch) and Saul. [2]While they were worshiping the Lord and fasting, the Holy Spirit said, "Set apart for me Barnabas and Saul for the work to which I have called them." [3]So after they had fasted and prayed, they placed their hands on them and sent them off.

On Cyprus

[4]The two of them, sent on their way by the Holy Spirit, went down to Seleucia and sailed from there to Cyprus. [5]When they arrived at Salamis, they proclaimed the word of God in the Jewish synagogues. John was with them as their helper.

[6]They traveled through the whole island until they came to Paphos. There they met a Jewish sorcerer and false prophet named Bar-Jesus, [7]who was an attendant of the proconsul, Sergius Paulus. The proconsul, an intelligent man, sent for Barnabas and Saul because he wanted to hear the word of God. [8]But Elymas the sorcerer (for that is what his name means) opposed them and tried to turn the proconsul from the faith. [9]Then Saul, who was also called Paul, filled with the Holy Spirit, looked straight at Elymas and said, [10]"You are a child of the devil and an enemy of everything that is right! You are full of all kinds of deceit and trickery. Will you never stop perverting the right ways of the Lord? [11]Now the hand of the Lord is against you. You are going to be blind, and for a time you will be unable to see the light of the sun."

Immediately mist and darkness came over him, and he groped about, seeking someone to lead him by the hand. [12]When the proconsul saw what had happened, he believed, for he was amazed at the teaching about the Lord.

In Pisidian Antioch

[13]From Paphos, Paul and his compan-

ions sailed to Perga in Pamphylia, where John left them to return to Jerusalem. ¹⁴From Perga they went on to Pisidian Antioch. On the Sabbath they entered the synagogue and sat down. ¹⁵After the reading from the Law and the Prophets, the synagogue rulers sent word to them, saying, "Brothers, if you have a message of encouragement for the people, please speak."

¹⁶Standing up, Paul motioned with his hand and said: "Men of Israel and you Gentiles who worship God, listen to me! ¹⁷The God of the people of Israel chose our fathers; he made the people prosper during their stay in Egypt, with mighty power he led them out of that country, ¹⁸he endured their conduct*a* for about forty years in the desert, ¹⁹he overthrew seven nations in Canaan and gave their land to his people as their inheritance. ²⁰All this took about 450 years.

"After this, God gave them judges until the time of Samuel the prophet. ²¹Then the people asked for a king, and he gave them Saul son of Kish, of the tribe of Benjamin, who ruled forty years. ²²After removing Saul, he made David their king. He testified concerning him: 'I have found David son of Jesse a man after my own heart; he will do everything I want him to do.'

²³"From this man's descendants God has brought to Israel the Savior Jesus, as he promised. ²⁴Before the coming of Jesus, John preached repentance and baptism to all the people of Israel. ²⁵As John was completing his work, he said: 'Who do you think I am? I am not that one. No, but he is coming after me, whose sandals I am not worthy to untie.'

²⁶"Brothers, children of Abraham, and you God-fearing Gentiles, it is to us that this message of salvation has been sent. ²⁷The people of Jerusalem and their rulers did not recognize Jesus, yet in condemning him they fulfilled the words of the prophets that are read every Sabbath. ²⁸Though they found no proper ground for a death sentence, they asked Pilate to have him executed. ²⁹When they had carried out all that was written about him, they took him down from the tree and laid him in a tomb. ³⁰But God raised him from the dead, ³¹and for many days he was seen by those who had traveled with

him from Galilee to Jerusalem. They are now his witnesses to our people.

³²"We tell you the good news: What God promised our fathers ³³he has fulfilled for us, their children, by raising up Jesus. As it is written in the second Psalm:

" 'You are my Son;
today I have become your
Father.*b*'*c*

³⁴The fact that God raised him from the dead, never to decay, is stated in these words:

" 'I will give you the holy and sure
blessings promised to David.'*d*

³⁵So it is stated elsewhere:

" 'You will not let your Holy One see
decay.'*e*

³⁶"For when David had served God's purpose in his own generation, he fell asleep; he was buried with his fathers and his body decayed. ³⁷But the one whom God raised from the dead did not see decay.

³⁸"Therefore, my brothers, I want you to know that through Jesus the forgiveness of sins is proclaimed to you. ³⁹Through him everyone who believes is justified from everything you could not be justified from by the law of Moses. ⁴⁰Take care that what the prophets have said does not happen to you:

⁴¹" 'Look, you scoffers,
wonder and perish,
for I am going to do something in
your days
that you would never believe,
even if someone told you.'*f*"

⁴²As Paul and Barnabas were leaving the synagogue, the people invited them to speak further about these things on the next Sabbath. ⁴³When the congregation was dismissed, many of the Jews and devout converts to Judaism followed Paul and Barnabas, who talked with them and urged them to continue in the grace of God.

⁴⁴On the next Sabbath almost the whole city gathered to hear the word of the Lord. ⁴⁵When the Jews saw the crowds, they were filled with jealousy and talked abusively against what Paul was saying.

---

a18 Some manuscripts *and cared for them*   *b33* Or *have begotten you*   *c33* Psalm 2:7   *d34* Isaiah 55:3   *e35* Psalm 16:10   *f41* Hab. 1:5

⁴⁶Then Paul and Barnabas answered them boldly: "We had to speak the word of God to you first. Since you reject it and do not consider yourselves worthy of eternal life, we now turn to the Gentiles. ⁴⁷For this is what the Lord has commanded us:

"'I have made you*ᵃ* a light for the Gentiles,
    that you*ᵃ* may bring salvation to
    the ends of the earth.'*ᵇ*"

⁴⁸When the Gentiles heard this, they were glad and honored the word of the Lord; and all who were appointed for eternal life believed.

⁴⁹The word of the Lord spread through the whole region. ⁵⁰But the Jews incited the God-fearing women of high standing and the leading men of the city. They stirred up persecution against Paul and Barnabas, and expelled them from their region. ⁵¹So they shook the dust from their feet in protest against them and went to Iconium. ⁵²And the disciples were filled with joy and with the Holy Spirit.

In Iconium

14 At Iconium Paul and Barnabas went as usual into the Jewish synagogue. There they spoke so effectively that a great number of Jews and Gentiles believed. ²But the Jews who refused to believe stirred up the Gentiles and poisoned their minds against the brothers. ³So Paul and Barnabas spent considerable time there, speaking boldly for the Lord, who confirmed the message of his grace by enabling them to do miraculous signs and wonders. ⁴The people of the city were divided; some sided with the Jews, others with the apostles. ⁵There was a plot afoot among the Gentiles and Jews, together with their leaders, to mistreat them and stone them. ⁶But they found out about it and fled to the Lycaonian cities of Lystra and Derbe and to the surrounding country, ⁷where they continued to preach the good news.

In Lystra and Derbe

⁸In Lystra there sat a man crippled in his feet, who was lame from birth and had never walked. ⁹He listened to Paul as he was speaking. Paul looked directly at him, saw that he had faith to be healed ¹⁰and called out, "Stand up on your feet!"

At that, the man jumped up and began to walk.

¹¹When the crowd saw what Paul had done, they shouted in the Lycaonian language, "The gods have come down to us in human form!" ¹²Barnabas they called Zeus, and Paul they called Hermes because he was the chief speaker. ¹³The priest of Zeus, whose temple was just outside the city, brought bulls and wreaths to the city gates because he and the crowd wanted to offer sacrifices to them.

¹⁴But when the apostles Barnabas and Paul heard of this, they tore their clothes and rushed out into the crowd, shouting: ¹⁵"Men, why are you doing this? We too are only men, human like you. We are bringing you good news, telling you to turn from these worthless things to the living God, who made heaven and earth and sea and everything in them. ¹⁶In the past, he let all nations go their own way. ¹⁷Yet he has not left himself without testimony: He has shown kindness by giving you rain from heaven and crops in their seasons; he provides you with plenty of food and fills your hearts with joy." ¹⁸Even with these words, they had difficulty keeping the crowd from sacrificing to them.

¹⁹Then some Jews came from Antioch and Iconium and won the crowd over. They stoned Paul and dragged him outside the city, thinking he was dead. ²⁰But after the disciples had gathered around him, he got up and went back into the city. The next day he and Barnabas left for Derbe.

The Return to Antioch in Syria

²¹They preached the good news in that city and won a large number of disciples. Then they returned to Lystra, Iconium and Antioch, ²²strengthening the disciples and encouraging them to remain true to the faith. "We must go through many hardships to enter the kingdom of God," they said. ²³Paul and Barnabas appointed elders*ᶜ* for them in each church and, with prayer and fasting, committed them to the Lord, in whom they had put their trust. ²⁴After going through Pisidia, they came into Pamphylia, ²⁵and when they had preached the word in Perga, they went down to Attalia. ²⁶From Attalia they sailed back to Antioch, where they had been committed to

---

ᵃ47 The Greek is singular.   *ᵇ47* Isaiah 49:6   *ᶜ23* Or *Barnabas ordained elders;* or *Barnabas had elders elected*

VERSE FOR THE DAY: AUTHOR: PASSAGE FOR THE DAY:
Acts 14:17   June Masters Bacher   Acts 14:14–18

After the Storm

I WONDER how agnostics or atheists deal with mornings like this. But then, I (a believer!) had had trouble dealing with yesterday.

Following days of drenching rain, killer floods and general chaos, there came a freak downpour. Without warning, a black curtain of rain simply swallowed our city. I waded a lake that came to the hem of my skirt trying to find my car in the teachers' parking lot. Paperwork for the day was a total loss. My freshly done hair was soaked. I dripped in the front door to hear three children screaming like banshees (one mine, two somebody else's); a cold-nosed dog demanding dinner; and a husband who announced cheerfully that the roof was leaking in five places and the septic tank was overflowing.

"Let me in the door, *please!*" So began our evening. When my husband and I crept into bed, exhausted (at midnight), the boys were still giggling. The roof was still leaking (into pans and buckets). The rain was still raining. And the septic tank would have to be dealt with tomorrow.

I awoke with a start, wondering if once again the power had failed and our electric clock had stopped. It was full daylight, surely seven o'clock on a March day, and far too late to hope to get everybody off on a weekday morning. The clock appeared to be working, but how could it be so light at 4:30 A.M.?

I ran barefoot to the window and there hung the most breath-taking moon I've ever seen, suspended in a sky so clear that it appeared blue even in the pre-dawn. I watched in prayerful wonder until it was time to get the day on its feet. Only God could create such a day from yesterday's chaos—and put my heart back together!

To think and pray about: Do you think this kind of beauty follows chaos by accident? In what other ways does God, through nature, cleanse the world, the spirit? We walk through storms that strip us bare or cleanse us so we can grow again—according to our faith. God assures us that he's in charge. We can cope through prayer.

Additional Scripture Readings:
Genesis 9:12–16; Jonah 2:3–3:3

Go to page 185 for your next devotional reading.

the grace of God for the work they had now completed. [27]On arriving there, they gathered the church together and reported all that God had done through them and how he had opened the door of faith to the Gentiles. [28]And they stayed there a long time with the disciples.

The Council at Jerusalem

15 Some men came down from Judea to Antioch and were teaching the brothers: "Unless you are circumcised, according to the custom taught by Moses, you cannot be saved." [2]This brought Paul and Barnabas into sharp dispute and debate with them. So Paul and Barnabas were appointed, along with some other believers, to go up to Jerusalem to see the apostles and elders about this question. [3]The church sent them on their way, and as they traveled through Phoenicia and Samaria, they told how the Gentiles had been converted. This news made all the brothers very glad. [4]When they came to Jerusalem, they were welcomed by the church and the apostles and elders, to whom they reported everything God had done through them.

[5]Then some of the believers who belonged to the party of the Pharisees stood up and said, "The Gentiles must be circumcised and required to obey the law of Moses."

[6]The apostles and elders met to consider this question. [7]After much discussion, Peter got up and addressed them: "Brothers, you know that some time ago God made a choice among you that the Gentiles might hear from my lips the message of the gospel and believe. [8]God, who knows the heart, showed that he accepted them by giving the Holy Spirit to them, just as he did to us. [9]He made no distinction between us and them, for he purified their hearts by faith. [10]Now then, why do you try to test God by putting on the necks of the disciples a yoke that neither we nor our fathers have been able to bear? [11]No! We believe it is through the grace of our Lord Jesus that we are saved, just as they are."

[12]The whole assembly became silent as they listened to Barnabas and Paul telling about the miraculous signs and wonders God had done among the Gentiles through them. [13]When they finished, James spoke up: "Brothers, listen to me.

[14]Simon[a] has described to us how God at first showed his concern by taking from the Gentiles a people for himself. [15]The words of the prophets are in agreement with this, as it is written:

[16]" 'After this I will return
     and rebuild David's fallen tent.
   Its ruins I will rebuild,
     and I will restore it,
[17]that the remnant of men may seek
       the Lord,
     and all the Gentiles who bear my
       name,
   says the Lord, who does these
       things'[b]
[18] that have been known for ages.[c]

[19]"It is my judgment, therefore, that we should not make it difficult for the Gentiles who are turning to God. [20]Instead we should write to them, telling them to abstain from food polluted by idols, from sexual immorality, from the meat of strangled animals and from blood. [21]For Moses has been preached in every city from the earliest times and is read in the synagogues on every Sabbath."

The Council's Letter to Gentile Believers

[22]Then the apostles and elders, with the whole church, decided to choose some of their own men and send them to Antioch with Paul and Barnabas. They chose Judas (called Barsabbas) and Silas, two men who were leaders among the brothers. [23]With them they sent the following letter:

The apostles and elders, your brothers,

To the Gentile believers in Antioch, Syria and Cilicia:

Greetings.

[24]We have heard that some went out from us without our authorization and disturbed you, troubling your minds by what they said. [25]So we all agreed to choose some men and send them to you with our dear friends Barnabas and Paul — [26]men who have risked their lives for the name of our Lord Jesus Christ. [27]Therefore we are sending Judas and Silas to confirm by word of

---

[a]14 Greek *Simeon*, a variant of *Simon*; that is, Peter   [b]17 Amos 9:11,12   [c]17,18 Some manuscripts *things'— / [18]known to the Lord for ages is his work*

mouth what we are writing. [28]It seemed good to the Holy Spirit and to us not to burden you with anything beyond the following requirements: [29]You are to abstain from food sacrificed to idols, from blood, from the meat of strangled animals and from sexual immorality. You will do well to avoid these things.

Farewell.

[30]The men were sent off and went down to Antioch, where they gathered the church together and delivered the letter. [31]The people read it and were glad for its encouraging message. [32]Judas and Silas, who themselves were prophets, said much to encourage and strengthen the brothers. [33]After spending some time there, they were sent off by the brothers with the blessing of peace to return to those who had sent them.[a] [35]But Paul and Barnabas remained in Antioch, where they and many others taught and preached the word of the Lord.

Disagreement Between Paul and Barnabas

[36]Some time later Paul said to Barnabas, "Let us go back and visit the brothers in all the towns where we preached the word of the Lord and see how they are doing." [37]Barnabas wanted to take John, also called Mark, with them, [38]but Paul did not think it wise to take him, because he had deserted them in Pamphylia and had not continued with them in the work. [39]They had such a sharp disagreement that they parted company. Barnabas took Mark and sailed for Cyprus, [40]but Paul chose Silas and left, commended by the brothers to the grace of the Lord. [41]He went through Syria and Cilicia, strengthening the churches.

Timothy Joins Paul and Silas

16 He came to Derbe and then to Lystra, where a disciple named Timothy lived, whose mother was a Jewess and a believer, but whose father was a Greek. [2]The brothers at Lystra and Iconium spoke well of him. [3]Paul wanted to take him along on the journey, so he circumcised him because of the Jews who lived in that area, for they all knew that his father was a Greek. [4]As they traveled from town to town, they delivered the decisions reached by the apostles and el-

ders in Jerusalem for the people to obey. [5]So the churches were strengthened in the faith and grew daily in numbers.

Paul's Vision of the Man of Macedonia

[6]Paul and his companions traveled throughout the region of Phrygia and Galatia, having been kept by the Holy Spirit from preaching the word in the province of Asia. [7]When they came to the border of Mysia, they tried to enter Bithynia, but the Spirit of Jesus would not allow them to. [8]So they passed by Mysia and went down to Troas. [9]During the night Paul had a vision of a man of Macedonia standing and begging him, "Come over to Macedonia and help us." [10]After Paul had seen the vision, we got ready at once to leave for Macedonia, concluding that God had called us to preach the gospel to them.

Lydia's Conversion in Philippi

[11]From Troas we put out to sea and sailed straight for Samothrace, and the next day on to Neapolis. [12]From there we traveled to Philippi, a Roman colony and the leading city of that district of Macedonia. And we stayed there several days.

[13]On the Sabbath we went outside the city gate to the river, where we expected to find a place of prayer. We sat down and began to speak to the women who had gathered there. [14]One of those listening was a woman named Lydia, a dealer in purple cloth from the city of Thyatira, who was a worshiper of God. The Lord opened her heart to respond to Paul's message. [15]When she and the members of her household were baptized, she invited us to her home. "If you consider me a believer in the Lord," she said, "come and stay at my house." And she persuaded us.

Paul and Silas in Prison

[16]Once when we were going to the place of prayer, we were met by a slave girl who had a spirit by which she predicted the future. She earned a great deal of money for her owners by fortune-telling. [17]This girl followed Paul and the rest of us, shouting, "These men are servants of the Most High God, who are telling you the way to be saved." [18]She kept this up for many days. Finally Paul became so troubled that he turned around and said to the spirit, "In the name of Jesus Christ

[a]33 Some manuscripts *them,* [34]*but Silas decided to remain there*

I command you to come out of her!" At that moment the spirit left her.

¹⁹When the owners of the slave girl realized that their hope of making money was gone, they seized Paul and Silas and dragged them into the marketplace to face the authorities. ²⁰They brought them before the magistrates and said, "These men are Jews, and are throwing our city into an uproar ²¹by advocating customs unlawful for us Romans to accept or practice."

²²The crowd joined in the attack against Paul and Silas, and the magis-trates ordered them to be stripped and beaten. ²³After they had been severely flogged, they were thrown into prison, and the jailer was commanded to guard them carefully. ²⁴Upon receiving such orders, he put them in the inner cell and fastened their feet in the stocks.

²⁵About midnight Paul and Silas were praying and singing hymns to God, and the other prisoners were listening to them. ²⁶Suddenly there was such a violent earthquake that the foundations of the prison were shaken. At once all the prison doors flew open, and everybody's

FRIDAY

VERSE FOR THE DAY:
Act 16:30

AUTHOR:
June Masters Bacher

PASSAGE FOR THE DAY:
Acts 16:25–40

What Can I Do?

"WHAT must I do to be saved?" asked the Philippian jailer. "Believe in the Lord Jesus " was the apostle Paul's answer. This single question and answer neatly summarize the teachings of the New Testament.

"What can I do?" ask our ministers and our doctors. "What can I do?" ask men caught in financial straits. Parents ask the question of teachers regarding their children's behavior or academic problems. A survey might show that this is one of the most common questions around. It became such a common rainy-day question in our home, I made a list of activities for our son to engage in so that he began looking forward to a storm! I made a list of stories, collected craft ideas, added suggestions for poems and Scripture passages to memorize and ended with "Look for a rainbow." The result was a happy day.

Jesus tells us that he came to earth that we might have life and have it more abundantly. How do we achieve an abundant Christian life? First, we believe with a faith so strong that the storms of life can threaten, but they cannot destroy. The abundant life begins for us here on earth and leads in natural transition into eternity. A wonderful thing, faith; a positive thing.

The positive attitude of Christian living communicates to those around us. "I am convinced," said my retiring principal after having spent over forty years in education (and an equal number of years teaching church school class), "that most folks are just about as happy as they set out to be!" He had the happiest faculty I have ever worked with.

Additional Scripture Readings:
John 10:9–10; Philippians 4:11–13

Go to page 186 for your next
devotional reading.

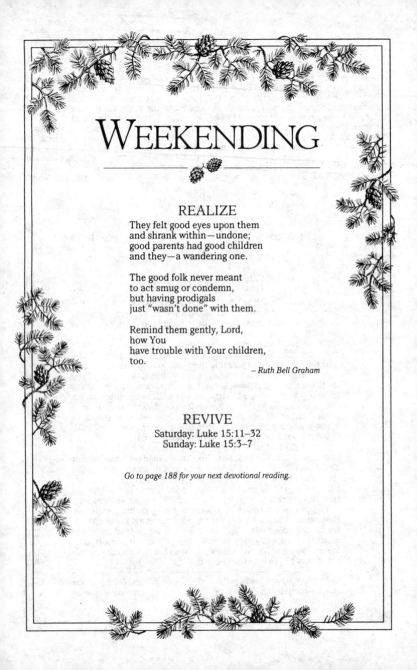

WEEKENDING

REALIZE

They felt good eyes upon them
and shrank within—undone;
good parents had good children
and they—a wandering one.

The good folk never meant
to act smug or condemn,
but having prodigals
just "wasn't done" with them.

Remind them gently, Lord,
how You
have trouble with Your children,
too.

— *Ruth Bell Graham*

REVIVE

Saturday: Luke 15:11–32
Sunday: Luke 15:3–7

Go to page 188 for your next devotional reading.

chains came loose. [27]The jailer woke up, and when he saw the prison doors open, he drew his sword and was about to kill himself because he thought the prisoners had escaped. [28]But Paul shouted, "Don't harm yourself! We are all here!"

[29]The jailer called for lights, rushed in and fell trembling before Paul and Silas. [30]He then brought them out and asked, "Sirs, what must I do to be saved?"

[31]They replied, "Believe in the Lord Jesus, and you will be saved—you and your household." [32]Then they spoke the word of the Lord to him and to all the others in his house. [33]At that hour of the night the jailer took them and washed their wounds; then immediately he and all his family were baptized. [34]The jailer brought them into his house and set a meal before them; he was filled with joy because he had come to believe in God— he and his whole family.

[35]When it was daylight, the magistrates sent their officers to the jailer with the order: "Release those men." [36]The jailer told Paul, "The magistrates have ordered that you and Silas be released. Now you can leave. Go in peace."

[37]But Paul said to the officers: "They beat us publicly without a trial, even though we are Roman citizens, and threw us into prison. And now do they want to get rid of us quietly? No! Let them come themselves and escort us out."

[38]The officers reported this to the magistrates, and when they heard that Paul and Silas were Roman citizens, they were alarmed. [39]They came to appease them and escorted them from the prison, requesting them to leave the city. [40]After Paul and Silas came out of the prison, they went to Lydia's house, where they met with the brothers and encouraged them. Then they left.

In Thessalonica

17 When they had passed through Amphipolis and Apollonia, they came to Thessalonica, where there was a Jewish synagogue. [2]As his custom was, Paul went into the synagogue, and on three Sabbath days he reasoned with them from the Scriptures, [3]explaining and proving that the Christ[a] had to suffer and rise from the dead. "This Jesus I am proclaiming to you is the Christ,[a]" he said. [4]Some of the Jews were persuaded and joined Paul and Silas, as did a large

number of God-fearing Greeks and not a few prominent women.

[5]But the Jews were jealous; so they rounded up some bad characters from the marketplace, formed a mob and started a riot in the city. They rushed to Jason's house in search of Paul and Silas in order to bring them out to the crowd.[b] [6]But when they did not find them, they dragged Jason and some other brothers before the city officials, shouting: "These men who have caused trouble all over the world have now come here, [7]and Jason has welcomed them into his house. They are all defying Caesar's decrees, saying that there is another king, one called Jesus." [8]When they heard this, the crowd and the city officials were thrown into turmoil. [9]Then they made Jason and the others post bond and let them go.

In Berea

[10]As soon as it was night, the brothers sent Paul and Silas away to Berea. On arriving there, they went to the Jewish synagogue. [11]Now the Bereans were of more noble character than the Thessalonians, for they received the message with great eagerness and examined the Scriptures every day to see if what Paul said was true. [12]Many of the Jews believed, as did also a number of prominent Greek women and many Greek men.

[13]When the Jews in Thessalonica learned that Paul was preaching the word of God at Berea, they went there too, agitating the crowds and stirring them up. [14]The brothers immediately sent Paul to the coast, but Silas and Timothy stayed at Berea. [15]The men who escorted Paul brought him to Athens and then left with instructions for Silas and Timothy to join him as soon as possible.

In Athens

[16]While Paul was waiting for them in Athens, he was greatly distressed to see that the city was full of idols. [17]So he reasoned in the synagogue with the Jews and the God-fearing Greeks, as well as in the marketplace day by day with those who happened to be there. [18]A group of Epicurean and Stoic philosophers began to dispute with him. Some of them asked, "What is this babbler trying to say?" Others remarked, "He seems to be advocating foreign gods." They said this because

a3 Or Messiah   b5 Or the assembly of the people

VERSE FOR THE DAY:	AUTHOR:	PASSAGE FOR THE DAY:
Acts 17:11	Elizabeth Larson	Acts 17:10–15

Counting the Cost

WE have many Bibles in our home, but one in particular is my sentimental favorite. It belonged to my husband before I adopted it, which makes it all the more dear to me. It has all his favorite passages underlined, his many little notes in the margins (I've read each one), and innumerable creases, smudges and torn spots, which are inevitable when a book is subjected to prolonged, loving abuse.

I must confess, I have added some features of my own: a few scribbles, various folds to mark my spot when I stop reading, the footprints of my preschooler who trampled the poor old book when I threw it behind the front seat of my car. But, worst of all, the cover is now threatening to fall off, due to the fact that I literally drop everything when my attention is caught by something else.

My favorite Bible. Its worth to me is great, but it wasn't until a few months ago that I realized the true cost of that book—a cost paid by others that I might freely possess my beloved book.

I was studying a history book when I came across a paragraph noting the words of a fifteenth-century bishop of England who wrote scornfully of certain women "which make themselves so wise by the Bible." It was the opinion of this bishop that women should have no right to study the Word of God. As I continued to read, I learned that some of the women so ridiculed by this bishop were wives and mothers who eventually died at the stake for refusing to accept any beliefs as God's truth "save what they can find expressly in the Bible."

I turned to my old favorite then, seeing it afresh. This book, which I handle with such careless, casual ease and freedom, would not be mine if it were not for those women (and men) who boldly claimed their right to have the Word of God—a right they paid for with their own blood.

Additional Scripture Readings:
Psalm 119:129–131; 2 Peter 1:15–21

Go to page 193 for your next devotional reading.

Paul was preaching the good news about Jesus and the resurrection. ¹⁹Then they took him and brought him to a meeting of the Areopagus, where they said to him, "May we know what this new teaching is that you are presenting? ²⁰You are bringing some strange ideas to our ears, and we want to know what they mean." ²¹(All the Athenians and the foreigners who lived there spent their time doing nothing but talking about and listening to the latest ideas.)

²²Paul then stood up in the meeting of the Areopagus and said: "Men of Athens! I see that in every way you are very religious. ²³For as I walked around and looked carefully at your objects of worship, I even found an altar with this inscription: TO AN UNKNOWN GOD. Now what you worship as something unknown I am going to proclaim to you.

²⁴"The God who made the world and everything in it is the Lord of heaven and earth and does not live in temples built by hands. ²⁵And he is not served by human hands, as if he needed anything, because he himself gives all men life and breath and everything else. ²⁶From one man he made every nation of men, that they should inhabit the whole earth; and he determined the times set for them and the exact places where they should live. ²⁷God did this so that men would seek him and perhaps reach out for him and find him, though he is not far from each one of us. ²⁸'For in him we live and move and have our being.' As some of your own poets have said, 'We are his offspring.'

²⁹"Therefore since we are God's offspring, we should not think that the divine being is like gold or silver or stone— an image made by man's design and skill. ³⁰In the past God overlooked such ignorance, but now he commands all people everywhere to repent. ³¹For he has set a day when he will judge the world with justice by the man he has appointed. He has given proof of this to all men by raising him from the dead."

³²When they heard about the resurrection of the dead, some of them sneered, but others said, "We want to hear you again on this subject." ³³At that, Paul left the Council. ³⁴A few men became followers of Paul and believed. Among them was Dionysius, a member of the Areopagus, also a woman named Damaris, and a number of others.

In Corinth

18 After this, Paul left Athens and went to Corinth. ²There he met a Jew named Aquila, a native of Pontus, who had recently come from Italy with his wife Priscilla, because Claudius had ordered all the Jews to leave Rome. Paul went to see them, ³and because he was a tentmaker as they were, he stayed and worked with them. ⁴Every Sabbath he reasoned in the synagogue, trying to persuade Jews and Greeks.

⁵When Silas and Timothy came from Macedonia, Paul devoted himself exclusively to preaching, testifying to the Jews that Jesus was the Christ.ᵃ ⁶But when the Jews opposed Paul and became abusive, he shook out his clothes in protest and said to them, "Your blood be on your own heads! I am clear of my responsibility. From now on I will go to the Gentiles."

⁷Then Paul left the synagogue and went next door to the house of Titius Justus, a worshiper of God. ⁸Crispus, the synagogue ruler, and his entire household believed in the Lord; and many of the Corinthians who heard him believed and were baptized.

⁹One night the Lord spoke to Paul in a vision: "Do not be afraid; keep on speaking, do not be silent. ¹⁰For I am with you, and no one is going to attack and harm you, because I have many people in this city." ¹¹So Paul stayed for a year and a half, teaching them the word of God.

¹²While Gallio was proconsul of Achaia, the Jews made a united attack on Paul and brought him into court. ¹³"This man," they charged, "is persuading the people to worship God in ways contrary to the law."

¹⁴Just as Paul was about to speak, Gallio said to the Jews, "If you Jews were making a complaint about some misdemeanor or serious crime, it would be reasonable for me to listen to you. ¹⁵But since it involves questions about words and names and your own law—settle the matter yourselves. I will not be a judge of such things." ¹⁶So he had them ejected from the court. ¹⁷Then they all turned on Sosthenes the synagogue ruler and beat him in front of the court. But Gallio showed no concern whatever.

Priscilla, Aquila and Apollos

¹⁸Paul stayed on in Corinth for some

ᵃ5 Or *Messiah;* also in verse 28

time. Then he left the brothers and sailed for Syria, accompanied by Priscilla and Aquila. Before he sailed, he had his hair cut off at Cenchrea because of a vow he had taken. [19]They arrived at Ephesus, where Paul left Priscilla and Aquila. He himself went into the synagogue and reasoned with the Jews. [20]When they asked him to spend more time with them, he declined. [21]But as he left, he promised, "I will come back if it is God's will." Then he set sail from Ephesus. [22]When he landed at Caesarea, he went up and greeted the church and then went down to Antioch.

[23]After spending some time in Antioch, Paul set out from there and traveled from place to place throughout the region of Galatia and Phrygia, strengthening all the disciples.

[24]Meanwhile a Jew named Apollos, a native of Alexandria, came to Ephesus. He was a learned man, with a thorough knowledge of the Scriptures. [25]He had been instructed in the way of the Lord, and he spoke with great fervor[a] and taught about Jesus accurately, though he knew only the baptism of John. [26]He began to speak boldly in the synagogue. When Priscilla and Aquila heard him, they invited him to their home and explained to him the way of God more adequately.

[27]When Apollos wanted to go to Achaia, the brothers encouraged him and wrote to the disciples there to welcome him. On arriving, he was a great help to those who by grace had believed. [28]For he vigorously refuted the Jews in public debate, proving from the Scriptures that Jesus was the Christ.

Paul in Ephesus

19 While Apollos was at Corinth, Paul took the road through the interior and arrived at Ephesus. There he found some disciples [2]and asked them, "Did you receive the Holy Spirit when[b] you believed?"

They answered, "No, we have not even heard that there is a Holy Spirit."

[3]So Paul asked, "Then what baptism did you receive?"

"John's baptism," they replied.

[4]Paul said, "John's baptism was a baptism of repentance. He told the people to believe in the one coming after him, that is, in Jesus." [5]On hearing this, they were baptized into[c] the name of the Lord Jesus. [6]When Paul placed his hands on them, the Holy Spirit came on them, and they spoke in tongues[d] and prophesied. [7]There were about twelve men in all.

[8]Paul entered the synagogue and spoke boldly there for three months, arguing persuasively about the kingdom of God. [9]But some of them became obstinate; they refused to believe and publicly maligned the Way. So Paul left them. He took the disciples with him and had discussions daily in the lecture hall of Tyrannus. [10]This went on for two years, so that all the Jews and Greeks who lived in the province of Asia heard the word of the Lord.

[11]God did extraordinary miracles through Paul, [12]so that even handkerchiefs and aprons that had touched him were taken to the sick, and their illnesses were cured and the evil spirits left them.

[13]Some Jews who went around driving out evil spirits tried to invoke the name of the Lord Jesus over those who were demon-possessed. They would say, "In the name of Jesus, whom Paul preaches, I command you to come out." [14]Seven sons of Sceva, a Jewish chief priest, were doing this. [15]One day, the evil spirit answered them, "Jesus I know, and I know about Paul, but who are you?" [16]Then the man who had the evil spirit jumped on them and overpowered them all. He gave them such a beating that they ran out of the house naked and bleeding.

[17]When this became known to the Jews and Greeks living in Ephesus, they were all seized with fear, and the name of the Lord Jesus was held in high honor. [18]Many of those who believed now came and openly confessed their evil deeds. [19]A number who had practiced sorcery brought their scrolls together and burned them publicly. When they calculated the value of the scrolls, the total came to fifty thousand drachmas.[e] [20]In this way the word of the Lord spread widely and grew in power.

[21]After all this had happened, Paul decided to go to Jerusalem, passing through Macedonia and Achaia. "After I have been there," he said, "I must visit Rome also." [22]He sent two of his helpers, Timothy and Erastus, to Macedonia, while

---

a25 Or *with fervor in the Spirit*   *b2* Or *after*   *c5* Or *in*   *d6* Or *other languages*   *e19* A drachma was a silver coin worth about a day's wages.

he stayed in the province of Asia a little longer.

The Riot in Ephesus

23About that time there arose a great disturbance about the Way. 24A silversmith named Demetrius, who made silver shrines of Artemis, brought in no little business for the craftsmen. 25He called them together, along with the workmen in related trades, and said: "Men, you know we receive a good income from this business. 26And you see and hear how this fellow Paul has convinced and led astray large numbers of people here in Ephesus and in practically the whole province of Asia. He says that man-made gods are no gods at all. 27There is danger not only that our trade will lose its good name, but also that the temple of the great goddess Artemis will be discredited, and the goddess herself, who is worshiped throughout the province of Asia and the world, will be robbed of her divine majesty."

28When they heard this, they were furious and began shouting: "Great is Artemis of the Ephesians!" 29Soon the whole city was in an uproar. The people seized Gaius and Aristarchus, Paul's traveling companions from Macedonia, and rushed as one man into the theater. 30Paul wanted to appear before the crowd, but the disciples would not let him. 31Even some of the officials of the province, friends of Paul, sent him a message begging him not to venture into the theater.

32The assembly was in confusion: Some were shouting one thing, some another. Most of the people did not even know why they were there. 33The Jews pushed Alexander to the front, and some of the crowd shouted instructions to him. He motioned for silence in order to make a defense before the people. 34But when they realized he was a Jew, they all shouted in unison for about two hours: "Great is Artemis of the Ephesians!"

35The city clerk quieted the crowd and said: "Men of Ephesus, doesn't all the world know that the city of Ephesus is the guardian of the temple of the great Artemis and of her image, which fell from heaven? 36Therefore, since these facts are undeniable, you ought to be quiet and not do anything rash. 37You have brought these men here, though they have neither robbed temples nor blasphemed our goddess. 38If, then, Demetrius and his fellow craftsmen have a grievance against any-

body, the courts are open and there are proconsuls. They can press charges. 39If there is anything further you want to bring up, it must be settled in a legal assembly. 40As it is, we are in danger of being charged with rioting because of today's events. In that case we would not be able to account for this commotion, since there is no reason for it." 41After he had said this, he dismissed the assembly.

Through Macedonia and Greece

20 When the uproar had ended, Paul sent for the disciples and, after encouraging them, said good-by and set out for Macedonia. 2He traveled through that area, speaking many words of encouragement to the people, and finally arrived in Greece, 3where he stayed three months. Because the Jews made a plot against him just as he was about to sail for Syria, he decided to go back through Macedonia. 4He was accompanied by Sopater son of Pyrrhus from Berea, Aristarchus and Secundus from Thessalonica, Gaius from Derbe, Timothy also, and Tychicus and Trophimus from the province of Asia. 5These men went on ahead and waited for us at Troas. 6But we sailed from Philippi after the Feast of Unleavened Bread, and five days later joined the others at Troas, where we stayed seven days.

Eutychus Raised From the Dead at Troas

7On the first day of the week we came together to break bread. Paul spoke to the people and, because he intended to leave the next day, kept on talking until midnight. 8There were many lamps in the upstairs room where we were meeting. 9Seated in a window was a young man named Eutychus, who was sinking into a deep sleep as Paul talked on and on. When he was sound asleep, he fell to the ground from the third story and was picked up dead. 10Paul went down, threw himself on the young man and put his arms around him. "Don't be alarmed," he said. "He's alive!" 11Then he went upstairs again and broke bread and ate. After talking until daylight, he left. 12The people took the young man home alive and were greatly comforted.

Paul's Farewell to the Ephesian Elders

13We went on ahead to the ship and sailed for Assos, where we were going to take Paul aboard. He had made this arrangement because he was going there on foot. ¹⁴When he met us at Assos, we took him aboard and went on to Mitylene. ¹⁵The next day we set sail from there and arrived off Kios. The day after that we crossed over to Samos, and on the following day arrived at Miletus. ¹⁶Paul had decided to sail past Ephesus to avoid spending time in the province of Asia, for he was in a hurry to reach Jerusalem, if possible, by the day of Pentecost.

¹⁷From Miletus, Paul sent to Ephesus for the elders of the church. ¹⁸When they arrived, he said to them: "You know how I lived the whole time I was with you, from the first day I came into the province of Asia. ¹⁹I served the Lord with great humility and with tears, although I was severely tested by the plots of the Jews. ²⁰You know that I have not hesitated to preach anything that would be helpful to you but have taught you publicly and from house to house. ²¹I have declared to both Jews and Greeks that they must turn to God in repentance and have faith in our Lord Jesus.

²²"And now, compelled by the Spirit, I am going to Jerusalem, not knowing what will happen to me there. ²³I only know that in every city the Holy Spirit warns me that prison and hardships are facing me. ²⁴However, I consider my life worth nothing to me, if only I may finish the race and complete the task the Lord Jesus has given me—the task of testifying to the gospel of God's grace.

²⁵"Now I know that none of you among whom I have gone about preaching the kingdom will ever see me again. ²⁶Therefore, I declare to you today that I am innocent of the blood of all men. ²⁷For I have not hesitated to proclaim to you the whole will of God. ²⁸Keep watch over yourselves and all the flock of which the Holy Spirit has made you overseers.ᵃ Be shepherds of the church of God,ᵇ which he bought with his own blood. ²⁹I know that after I leave, savage wolves will come in among you and will not spare the flock. ³⁰Even from your own number men will arise and distort the truth in order to draw away disciples after them. ³¹So be on your guard! Remember that for three years I never stopped warning each of you night and day with tears.

³²"Now I commit you to God and to the word of his grace, which can build you up

and give you an inheritance among all those who are sanctified. ³³I have not coveted anyone's silver or gold or clothing. ³⁴You yourselves know that these hands of mine have supplied my own needs and the needs of my companions. ³⁵In everything I did, I showed you that by this kind of hard work we must help the weak, remembering the words the Lord Jesus himself said: 'It is more blessed to give than to receive.' "

³⁶When he had said this, he knelt down with all of them and prayed. ³⁷They all wept as they embraced him and kissed him. ³⁸What grieved them most was his statement that they would never see his face again. Then they accompanied him to the ship.

On to Jerusalem

21 After we had torn ourselves away from them, we put out to sea and sailed straight to Cos. The next day we went to Rhodes and from there to Patara. ²We found a ship crossing over to Phoenicia, went on board and set sail. ³After sighting Cyprus and passing to the south of it, we sailed on to Syria. We landed at Tyre, where our ship was to unload its cargo. ⁴Finding the disciples there, we stayed with them seven days. Through the Spirit they urged Paul not to go on to Jerusalem. ⁵But when our time was up, we left and continued on our way. All the disciples and their wives and children accompanied us out of the city, and there on the beach we knelt to pray. ⁶After saying good-by to each other, we went aboard the ship, and they returned home.

⁷We continued our voyage from Tyre and landed at Ptolemais, where we greeted the brothers and stayed with them for a day. ⁸Leaving the next day, we reached Caesarea and stayed at the house of Philip the evangelist, one of the Seven. ⁹He had four unmarried daughters who prophesied.

¹⁰After we had been there a number of days, a prophet named Agabus came down from Judea. ¹¹Coming over to us, he took Paul's belt, tied his own hands and feet with it and said, "The Holy Spirit says, 'In this way the Jews of Jerusalem will bind the owner of this belt and will hand him over to the Gentiles.' "

¹²When we heard this, we and the people there pleaded with Paul not to go up to Jerusalem. ¹³Then Paul answered,

ᵃ28 Traditionally *bishops*   ᵇ28 Many manuscripts *of the Lord*

"Why are you weeping and breaking my heart? I am ready not only to be bound, but also to die in Jerusalem for the name of the Lord Jesus." [14]When he would not be dissuaded, we gave up and said, "The Lord's will be done."

[15]After this, we got ready and went up to Jerusalem. [16]Some of the disciples from Caesarea accompanied us and brought us to the home of Mnason, where we were to stay. He was a man from Cyprus and one of the early disciples.

Paul's Arrival at Jerusalem

[17]When we arrived at Jerusalem, the brothers received us warmly. [18]The next day Paul and the rest of us went to see James, and all the elders were present. [19]Paul greeted them and reported in detail what God had done among the Gentiles through his ministry.

[20]When they heard this, they praised God. Then they said to Paul: "You see, brother, how many thousands of Jews have believed, and all of them are zealous for the law. [21]They have been informed that you teach all the Jews who live among the Gentiles to turn away from Moses, telling them not to circumcise their children or live according to our customs. [22]What shall we do? They will certainly hear that you have come, [23]so do

TUESDAY

VERSE FOR THE DAY:	AUTHOR:	PASSAGE FOR THE DAY:
Acts 20:35	Sue Monk Kidd	Acts 20:13–38

On Giving

I have always been fascinated with Brother Roger of Taize, France, the founder of a Christian community where persons from twenty different countries and many Christian denominations live, work and pray together. One of the remarkable things about Taize is that so many young people have flocked there.

In an interview Brother Roger was asked why the young were so attracted to Taize. He responded by telling a story about his life. When he was young, children were made to keep their distance from their elders, he said. More that anything he longed for someone to give him an ear, to listen and understand what was in his heart of hearts. But it never happened. Finally Brother Roger made the resolution that became the motivation of his entire life. He determined to give to others the very thing he yearned for himself. He committed himself to listen to and understand every human being, especially the young. So at Taize he sat and listened to the young, asking himself: What are they suffering? What lies beneath their hearts? What are their gifts?

By attempting to give the very understanding he was seeking, Brother Roger found it in even greater measure. This principle never fails. If you seek to be understood, then dedicate your life to understanding others. If you seek to be comforted, then dedicate yourself to giving comfort. If you seek a greater faith, then commit yourself to planting it in others.

Additional Scripture Readings:
Luke 6:32–38; 1 John 4:10–12

Go to page 204 for your next devotional reading.

what we tell you. There are four men with us who have made a vow. ²⁴Take these men, join in their purification rites and pay their expenses, so that they can have their heads shaved. Then everybody will know there is no truth in these reports about you, but that you yourself are living in obedience to the law. ²⁵As for the Gentile believers, we have written to them our decision that they should abstain from food sacrificed to idols, from blood, from the meat of strangled animals and from sexual immorality."

²⁶The next day Paul took the men and purified himself along with them. Then he went to the temple to give notice of the date when the days of purification would end and the offering would be made for each of them.

Paul Arrested

²⁷When the seven days were nearly over, some Jews from the province of Asia saw Paul at the temple. They stirred up the whole crowd and seized him, ²⁸shouting, "Men of Israel, help us! This is the man who teaches all men everywhere against our people and our law and this place. And besides, he has brought Greeks into the temple area and defiled this holy place." ²⁹(They had previously seen Trophimus the Ephesian in the city with Paul and assumed that Paul had brought him into the temple area.)

³⁰The whole city was aroused, and the people came running from all directions. Seizing Paul, they dragged him from the temple, and immediately the gates were shut. ³¹While they were trying to kill him, news reached the commander of the Roman troops that the whole city of Jerusalem was in an uproar. ³²He at once took some officers and soldiers and ran down to the crowd. When the rioters saw the commander and his soldiers, they stopped beating Paul.

³³The commander came up and arrested him and ordered him to be bound with two chains. Then he asked who he was and what he had done. ³⁴Some in the crowd shouted one thing and some another, and since the commander could not get at the truth because of the uproar, he ordered that Paul be taken into the barracks. ³⁵When Paul reached the steps, the violence of the mob was so great he had to be carried by the soldiers. ³⁶The crowd that followed kept shouting, "Away with him!"

Paul Speaks to the Crowd

³⁷As the soldiers were about to take Paul into the barracks, he asked the commander, "May I say something to you?"

"Do you speak Greek?" he replied. ³⁸"Aren't you the Egyptian who started a revolt and led four thousand terrorists out into the desert some time ago?"

³⁹Paul answered, "I am a Jew, from Tarsus in Cilicia, a citizen of no ordinary city. Please let me speak to the people."

⁴⁰Having received the commander's permission, Paul stood on the steps and motioned to the crowd. When they were all silent, he said to them in Aramaicᵃ:

22 ¹"Brothers and fathers, listen now to my defense."

²When they heard him speak to them in Aramaic, they became very quiet.

Then Paul said: ³"I am a Jew, born in Tarsus of Cilicia, but brought up in this city. Under Gamaliel I was thoroughly trained in the law of our fathers and was just as zealous for God as any of you are today. ⁴I persecuted the followers of this Way to their death, arresting both men and women and throwing them into prison, ⁵as also the high priest and all the Council can testify. I even obtained letters from them to their brothers in Damascus, and went there to bring these people as prisoners to Jerusalem to be punished.

⁶"About noon as I came near Damascus, suddenly a bright light from heaven flashed around me. ⁷I fell to the ground and heard a voice say to me, 'Saul! Saul! Why do you persecute me?'

⁸"'Who are you, Lord?' I asked.

"'I am Jesus of Nazareth, whom you are persecuting,' he replied. ⁹My companions saw the light, but they did not understand the voice of him who was speaking to me.

¹⁰"'What shall I do, Lord?' I asked.

"'Get up,' the Lord said, 'and go into Damascus. There you will be told all that you have been assigned to do.' ¹¹My companions led me by the hand into Damascus, because the brilliance of the light had blinded me.

¹²"A man named Ananias came to see me. He was a devout observer of the law and highly respected by all the Jews living there. ¹³He stood beside me and said,

ᵃ40 Or possibly *Hebrew*; also in 22:2

'Brother Saul, receive your sight!' And at that very moment I was able to see him.

[14] "Then he said: 'The God of our fathers has chosen you to know his will and to see the Righteous One and to hear words from his mouth. [15] You will be his witness to all men of what you have seen and heard. [16] And now what are you waiting for? Get up, be baptized and wash your sins away, calling on his name.'

[17] "When I returned to Jerusalem and was praying at the temple, I fell into a trance [18] and saw the Lord speaking. 'Quick!' he said to me. 'Leave Jerusalem immediately, because they will not accept your testimony about me.'

[19] " 'Lord,' I replied, 'these men know that I went from one synagogue to another to imprison and beat those who believe in you. [20] And when the blood of your martyr[a] Stephen was shed, I stood there giving my approval and guarding the clothes of those who were killing him.'

[21] "Then the Lord said to me, 'Go; I will send you far away to the Gentiles.' "

Paul the Roman Citizen

[22] The crowd listened to Paul until he said this. Then they raised their voices and shouted, "Rid the earth of him! He's not fit to live!"

[23] As they were shouting and throwing off their cloaks and flinging dust into the air, [24] the commander ordered Paul to be taken into the barracks. He directed that he be flogged and questioned in order to find out why the people were shouting at him like this. [25] As they stretched him out to flog him, Paul said to the centurion standing there, "Is it legal for you to flog a Roman citizen who hasn't even been found guilty?"

[26] When the centurion heard this, he went to the commander and reported it. "What are you going to do?" he asked. "This man is a Roman citizen."

[27] The commander went to Paul and asked, "Tell me, are you a Roman citizen?"

"Yes, I am," he answered.

[28] Then the commander said, "I had to pay a big price for my citizenship."

"But I was born a citizen," Paul replied.

[29] Those who were about to question him withdrew immediately. The commander himself was alarmed when he realized that he had put Paul, a Roman citizen, in chains.

Before the Sanhedrin

[30] The next day, since the commander wanted to find out exactly why Paul was being accused by the Jews, he released him and ordered the chief priests and all the Sanhedrin to assemble. Then he brought Paul and had him stand before them.

23 Paul looked straight at the Sanhedrin and said, "My brothers, I have fulfilled my duty to God in all good conscience to this day." [2] At this the high priest Ananias ordered those standing near Paul to strike him on the mouth. [3] Then Paul said to him, "God will strike you, you whitewashed wall! You sit there to judge me according to the law, yet you yourself violate the law by commanding that I be struck!"

[4] Those who were standing near Paul said, "You dare to insult God's high priest?"

[5] Paul replied, "Brothers, I did not realize that he was the high priest; for it is written: 'Do not speak evil about the ruler of your people.'[b] "

[6] Then Paul, knowing that some of them were Sadducees and the others Pharisees, called out in the Sanhedrin, "My brothers, I am a Pharisee, the son of a Pharisee. I stand on trial because of my hope in the resurrection of the dead." [7] When he said this, a dispute broke out between the Pharisees and the Sadducees, and the assembly was divided. [8] (The Sadducees say that there is no resurrection, and that there are neither angels nor spirits, but the Pharisees acknowledge them all.)

[9] There was a great uproar, and some of the teachers of the law who were Pharisees stood up and argued vigorously. "We find nothing wrong with this man," they said. "What if a spirit or an angel has spoken to him?" [10] The dispute became so violent that the commander was afraid Paul would be torn to pieces by them. He ordered the troops to go down and take him away from them by force and bring him into the barracks.

[11] The following night the Lord stood near Paul and said, "Take courage! As you have testified about me in Jerusalem, so you must also testify in Rome."

The Plot to Kill Paul

[12] The next morning the Jews formed a

conspiracy and bound themselves with an oath not to eat or drink until they had killed Paul. [13]More than forty men were involved in this plot. [14]They went to the chief priests and elders and said, "We have taken a solemn oath not to eat anything until we have killed Paul. [15]Now then, you and the Sanhedrin petition the commander to bring him before you on the pretext of wanting more accurate information about his case. We are ready to kill him before he gets here."

[16]But when the son of Paul's sister heard of this plot, he went into the barracks and told Paul.

[17]Then Paul called one of the centurions and said, "Take this young man to the commander; he has something to tell him." [18]So he took him to the commander.

The centurion said, "Paul, the prisoner, sent for me and asked me to bring this young man to you because he has something to tell you."

[19]The commander took the young man by the hand, drew him aside and asked, "What is it you want to tell me?"

[20]He said: "The Jews have agreed to ask you to bring Paul before the Sanhedrin tomorrow on the pretext of wanting more accurate information about him. [21]Don't give in to them, because more than forty of them are waiting in ambush for him. They have taken an oath not to eat or drink until they have killed him. They are ready now, waiting for your consent to their request."

[22]The commander dismissed the young man and cautioned him, "Don't tell anyone that you have reported this to me."

Paul Transferred to Caesarea

[23]Then he called two of his centurions and ordered them, "Get ready a detachment of two hundred soldiers, seventy horsemen and two hundred spearmen[a] to go to Caesarea at nine tonight. [24]Provide mounts for Paul so that he may be taken safely to Governor Felix."

[25]He wrote a letter as follows:

[26]Claudius Lysias,

To His Excellency, Governor Felix:

Greetings.

[27]This man was seized by the Jews and they were about to kill him, but I came with my troops and rescued him, for I had learned that he is a Roman citizen. [28]I wanted to know why they were accusing him, so I brought him to their Sanhedrin. [29]I found that the accusation had to do with questions about their law, but there was no charge against him that deserved death or imprisonment. [30]When I was informed of a plot to be carried out against the man, I sent him to you at once. I also ordered his accusers to present to you their case against him.

[31]So the soldiers, carrying out their orders, took Paul with them during the night and brought him as far as Antipatris. [32]The next day they let the cavalry go on with him, while they returned to the barracks. [33]When the cavalry arrived in Caesarea, they delivered the letter to the governor and handed Paul over to him. [34]The governor read the letter and asked what province he was from. Learning that he was from Cilicia, [35]he said, "I will hear your case when your accusers get here." Then he ordered that Paul be kept under guard in Herod's palace.

The Trial Before Felix

24 Five days later the high priest Ananias went down to Caesarea with some of the elders and a lawyer named Tertullus, and they brought their charges against Paul before the governor. [2]When Paul was called in, Tertullus presented his case before Felix: "We have enjoyed a long period of peace under you, and your foresight has brought about reforms in this nation. [3]Everywhere and in every way, most excellent Felix, we acknowledge this with profound gratitude. [4]But in order not to weary you further, I would request that you be kind enough to hear us briefly.

[5]"We have found this man to be a troublemaker, stirring up riots among the Jews all over the world. He is a ringleader of the Nazarene sect [6]and even tried to desecrate the temple; so we seized him. [8]By[b] examining him yourself you will be able to learn the truth about all these charges we are bringing against him."

---

[a]23 The meaning of the Greek for this word is uncertain.   [b]6-8 Some manuscripts *him and wanted to judge him according to our law. [7]But the commander, Lysias, came and with the use of much force snatched him from our hands [8]and ordered his accusers to come before you. By*

⁹The Jews joined in the accusation, asserting that these things were true.

¹⁰When the governor motioned for him to speak, Paul replied: "I know that for a number of years you have been a judge over this nation; so I gladly make my defense. ¹¹You can easily verify that no more than twelve days ago I went up to Jerusalem to worship. ¹²My accusers did not find me arguing with anyone at the temple, or stirring up a crowd in the synagogues or anywhere else in the city. ¹³And they cannot prove to you the charges they are now making against me. ¹⁴However, I admit that I worship the God of our fathers as a follower of the Way, which they call a sect. I believe everything that agrees with the Law and that is written in the Prophets, ¹⁵and I have the same hope in God as these men, that there will be a resurrection of both the righteous and the wicked. ¹⁶So I strive always to keep my conscience clear before God and man.

¹⁷"After an absence of several years, I came to Jerusalem to bring my people gifts for the poor and to present offerings. ¹⁸I was ceremonially clean when they found me in the temple courts doing this. There was no crowd with me, nor was I involved in any disturbance. ¹⁹But there are some Jews from the province of Asia, who ought to be here before you and bring charges if they have anything against me. ²⁰Or these who are here should state what crime they found in me when I stood before the Sanhedrin— ²¹unless it was this one thing I shouted as I stood in their presence: 'It is concerning the resurrection of the dead that I am on trial before you today.' "

²²Then Felix, who was well acquainted with the Way, adjourned the proceedings. "When Lysias the commander comes," he said, "I will decide your case." ²³He ordered the centurion to keep Paul under guard but to give him some freedom and permit his friends to take care of his needs.

²⁴Several days later Felix came with his wife Drusilla, who was a Jewess. He sent for Paul and listened to him as he spoke about faith in Christ Jesus. ²⁵As Paul discoursed on righteousness, self-control and the judgment to come, Felix was afraid and said, "That's enough for now! You may leave. When I find it convenient, I will send for you." ²⁶At the same time he was hoping that Paul would offer him a bribe, so he sent for him frequently and talked with him.

²⁷When two years had passed, Felix was succeeded by Porcius Festus, but because Felix wanted to grant a favor to the Jews, he left Paul in prison.

The Trial Before Festus

25 Three days after arriving in the province, Festus went up from Caesarea to Jerusalem, ²where the chief priests and Jewish leaders appeared before him and presented the charges against Paul. ³They urgently requested Festus, as a favor to them, to have Paul transferred to Jerusalem, for they were preparing an ambush to kill him along the way. ⁴Festus answered, "Paul is being held at Caesarea, and I myself am going there soon. ⁵Let some of your leaders come with me and press charges against the man there, if he has done anything wrong."

⁶After spending eight or ten days with them, he went down to Caesarea, and the next day he convened the court and ordered that Paul be brought before him. ⁷When Paul appeared, the Jews who had come down from Jerusalem stood around him, bringing many serious charges against him, which they could not prove.

⁸Then Paul made his defense: "I have done nothing wrong against the law of the Jews or against the temple or against Caesar."

⁹Festus, wishing to do the Jews a favor, said to Paul, "Are you willing to go up to Jerusalem and stand trial before me there on these charges?"

¹⁰Paul answered: "I am now standing before Caesar's court, where I ought to be tried. I have not done any wrong to the Jews, as you yourself know very well. ¹¹If, however, I am guilty of doing anything deserving death, I do not refuse to die. But if the charges brought against me by these Jews are not true, no one has the right to hand me over to them. I appeal to Caesar!"

¹²After Festus had conferred with his council, he declared: "You have appealed to Caesar. To Caesar you will go!"

Festus Consults King Agrippa

¹³A few days later King Agrippa and Bernice arrived at Caesarea to pay their respects to Festus. ¹⁴Since they were spending many days there, Festus discussed Paul's case with the king. He said: "There is a man here whom Felix left as a prisoner. ¹⁵When I went to Jerusalem, the chief priests and elders of the Jews

brought charges against him and asked that he be condemned.

[16]"I told them that it is not the Roman custom to hand over any man before he has faced his accusers and has had an opportunity to defend himself against their charges. [17]When they came here with me, I did not delay the case, but convened the court the next day and ordered the man to be brought in. [18]When his accusers got up to speak, they did not charge him with any of the crimes I had expected. [19]Instead, they had some points of dispute with him about their own religion and about a dead man named Jesus who Paul claimed was alive. [20]I was at a loss how to investigate such matters; so I asked if he would be willing to go to Jerusalem and stand trial there on these charges. [21]When Paul made his appeal to be held over for the Emperor's decision, I ordered him held until I could send him to Caesar."

[22]Then Agrippa said to Festus, "I would like to hear this man myself."

He replied, "Tomorrow you will hear him."

Paul Before Agrippa

[23]The next day Agrippa and Bernice came with great pomp and entered the audience room with the high ranking officers and the leading men of the city. At the command of Festus, Paul was brought in. [24]Festus said: "King Agrippa, and all who are present with us, you see this man! The whole Jewish community has petitioned me about him in Jerusalem and here in Caesarea, shouting that he ought not to live any longer. [25]I found he had done nothing deserving of death, but because he made his appeal to the Emperor I decided to send him to Rome. [26]But I have nothing definite to write to His Majesty about him. Therefore I have brought him before all of you, and especially before you, King Agrippa, so that as a result of this investigation I may have something to write. [27]For I think it is unreasonable to send on a prisoner without specifying the charges against him."

26 Then Agrippa said to Paul, "You have permission to speak for yourself."

So Paul motioned with his hand and began his defense: [2]"King Agrippa, I consider myself fortunate to stand before you today as I make my defense against all

the accusations of the Jews, [3]and especially so because you are well acquainted with all the Jewish customs and controversies. Therefore, I beg you to listen to me patiently.

[4]"The Jews all know the way I have lived ever since I was a child, from the beginning of my life in my own country, and also in Jerusalem. [5]They have known me for a long time and can testify, if they are willing, that according to the strictest sect of our religion, I lived as a Pharisee. [6]And now it is because of my hope in what God has promised our fathers that I am on trial today. [7]This is the promise our twelve tribes are hoping to see fulfilled as they earnestly serve God day and night. O king, it is because of this hope that the Jews are accusing me. [8]Why should any of you consider it incredible that God raises the dead?

[9]"I too was convinced that I ought to do all that was possible to oppose the name of Jesus of Nazareth. [10]And that is just what I did in Jerusalem. On the authority of the chief priests I put many of the saints in prison, and when they were put to death, I cast my vote against them. [11]Many a time I went from one synagogue to another to have them punished, and I tried to force them to blaspheme. In my obsession against them, I even went to foreign cities to persecute them.

[12]"On one of these journeys I was going to Damascus with the authority and commission of the chief priests. [13]About noon, O king, as I was on the road, I saw a light from heaven, brighter than the sun, blazing around me and my companions. [14]We all fell to the ground, and I heard a voice saying to me in Aramaic,[a] 'Saul, Saul, why do you persecute me? It is hard for you to kick against the goads.'

[15]"Then I asked, 'Who are you, Lord?'

" 'I am Jesus, whom you are persecuting,' the Lord replied. [16]'Now get up and stand on your feet. I have appeared to you to appoint you as a servant and as a witness of what you have seen of me and what I will show you. [17]I will rescue you from your own people and from the Gentiles. I am sending you to them [18]to open their eyes and turn them from darkness to light, and from the power of Satan to God, so that they may receive forgiveness of sins and a place among those who are sanctified by faith in me.'

[19]"So then, King Agrippa, I was not

[a]14 Or Hebrew

disobedient to the vision from heaven. [20]First to those in Damascus, then to those in Jerusalem and in all Judea, and to the Gentiles also, I preached that they should repent and turn to God and prove their repentance by their deeds. [21]That is why the Jews seized me in the temple courts and tried to kill me. [22]But I have had God's help to this very day, and so I stand here and testify to small and great alike. I am saying nothing beyond what the prophets and Moses said would happen— [23]that the Christ[a] would suffer and, as the first to rise from the dead, would proclaim light to his own people and to the Gentiles."

[24]At this point Festus interrupted Paul's defense. "You are out of your mind, Paul!" he shouted. "Your great learning is driving you insane."

[25]"I am not insane, most excellent Festus," Paul replied. "What I am saying is true and reasonable. [26]The king is familiar with these things, and I can speak freely to him. I am convinced that none of this has escaped his notice, because it was not done in a corner. [27]King Agrippa, do you believe the prophets? I know you do."

[28]Then Agrippa said to Paul, "Do you think that in such a short time you can persuade me to be a Christian?"

[29]Paul replied, "Short time or long—I pray God that not only you but all who are listening to me today may become what I am, except for these chains."

[30]The king rose, and with him the governor and Bernice and those sitting with them. [31]They left the room, and while talking with one another, they said, "This man is not doing anything that deserves death or imprisonment."

[32]Agrippa said to Festus, "This man could have been set free if he had not appealed to Caesar."

Paul Sails for Rome

27 When it was decided that we would sail for Italy, Paul and some other prisoners were handed over to a centurion named Julius, who belonged to the Imperial Regiment. [2]We boarded a ship from Adramyttium about to sail for ports along the coast of the province of Asia, and we put out to sea. Aristarchus, a Macedonian from Thessalonica, was with us.

[3]The next day we landed at Sidon; and Julius, in kindness to Paul, allowed him to go to his friends so they might provide for his needs. [4]From there we put out to sea again and passed to the lee of Cyprus because the winds were against us. [5]When we had sailed across the open sea off the coast of Cilicia and Pamphylia, we landed at Myra in Lycia. [6]There the centurion found an Alexandrian ship sailing for Italy and put us on board. [7]We made slow headway for many days and had difficulty arriving off Cnidus. When the wind did not allow us to hold our course, we sailed to the lee of Crete, opposite Salmone. [8]We moved along the coast with difficulty and came to a place called Fair Havens, near the town of Lasea.

[9]Much time had been lost, and sailing had already become dangerous because by now it was after the Fast.[b] So Paul warned them, [10]"Men, I can see that our voyage is going to be disastrous and bring great loss to ship and cargo, and to our own lives also." [11]But the centurion, instead of listening to what Paul said, followed the advice of the pilot and the owner of the ship. [12]Since the harbor was unsuitable to winter in, the majority decided that we should sail on, hoping to reach Phoenix and winter there. This was a harbor in Crete, facing both southwest and northwest.

The Storm

[13]When a gentle south wind began to blow, they thought they had obtained what they wanted; so they weighed anchor and sailed along the shore of Crete. [14]Before very long, a wind of hurricane force, called the "northeaster," swept down from the island. [15]The ship was caught by the storm and could not head into the wind; so we gave way to it and were driven along. [16]As we passed to the lee of a small island called Cauda, we were hardly able to make the lifeboat secure. [17]When the men had hoisted it aboard, they passed ropes under the ship itself to hold it together. Fearing that they would run aground on the sandbars of Syrtis, they lowered the sea anchor and let the ship be driven along. [18]We took such a violent battering from the storm that the next day they began to throw the cargo overboard. [19]On the third day, they threw the ship's tackle overboard with their own hands. [20]When neither sun nor stars appeared for many days and the

---

[a]23 Or *Messiah*   [b]9 That is, the Day of Atonement (Yom Kippur)

storm continued raging, we finally gave up all hope of being saved.

²¹After the men had gone a long time without food, Paul stood up before them and said: "Men, you should have taken my advice not to sail from Crete; then you would have spared yourselves this damage and loss. ²²But now I urge you to keep up your courage, because not one of you will be lost; only the ship will be destroyed. ²³Last night an angel of the God whose I am and whom I serve stood beside me ²⁴and said, 'Do not be afraid, Paul. You must stand trial before Caesar; and God has graciously given you the lives of all who sail with you.' ²⁵So keep up your courage, men, for I have faith in God that it will happen just as he told me. ²⁶Nevertheless, we must run aground on some island."

The Shipwreck

²⁷On the fourteenth night we were still being driven across the Adriatic*ᵃ* Sea, when about midnight the sailors sensed they were approaching land. ²⁸They took soundings and found that the water was a hundred and twenty feet*ᵇ* deep. A short time later they took soundings again and found it was ninety feet*ᶜ* deep. ²⁹Fearing that we would be dashed against the rocks, they dropped four anchors from the stern and prayed for daylight. ³⁰In an attempt to escape from the ship, the sailors let the lifeboat down into the sea, pretending they were going to lower some anchors from the bow. ³¹Then Paul said to the centurion and the soldiers, "Unless these men stay with the ship, you cannot be saved." ³²So the soldiers cut the ropes that held the lifeboat and let it fall away.

³³Just before dawn Paul urged them all to eat. "For the last fourteen days," he said, "you have been in constant suspense and have gone without food—you haven't eaten anything. ³⁴Now I urge you to take some food. You need it to survive. Not one of you will lose a single hair from his head." ³⁵After he said this, he took some bread and gave thanks to God in front of them all. Then he broke it and began to eat. ³⁶They were all encouraged and ate some food themselves. ³⁷Altogether there were 276 of us on board. ³⁸When they had eaten as much as they wanted, they lightened the ship by throwing the grain into the sea.

³⁹When daylight came, they did not recognize the land, but they saw a bay with a sandy beach, where they decided to run the ship aground if they could. ⁴⁰Cutting loose the anchors, they left them in the sea and at the same time untied the ropes that held the rudders. Then they hoisted the foresail to the wind and made for the beach. ⁴¹But the ship struck a sandbar and ran aground. The bow stuck fast and would not move, and the stern was broken to pieces by the pounding of the surf.

⁴²The soldiers planned to kill the prisoners to prevent any of them from swimming away and escaping. ⁴³But the centurion wanted to spare Paul's life and kept them from carrying out their plan. He ordered those who could swim to jump overboard first and get to land. ⁴⁴The rest were to get there on planks or on pieces of the ship. In this way everyone reached land in safety.

Ashore on Malta

28 Once safely on shore, we found out that the island was called Malta. ²The islanders showed us unusual kindness. They built a fire and welcomed us all because it was raining and cold. ³Paul gathered a pile of brushwood and, as he put it on the fire, a viper, driven out by the heat, fastened itself on his hand. ⁴When the islanders saw the snake hanging from his hand, they said to each other, "This man must be a murderer; for though he escaped from the sea, Justice has not allowed him to live." ⁵But Paul shook the snake off into the fire and suffered no ill effects. ⁶The people expected him to swell up or suddenly fall dead, but after waiting a long time and seeing nothing unusual happen to him, they changed their minds and said he was a god.

⁷There was an estate nearby that belonged to Publius, the chief official of the island. He welcomed us to his home and for three days entertained us hospitably. ⁸His father was sick in bed, suffering from fever and dysentery. Paul went in to see him and, after prayer, placed his hands on him and healed him. ⁹When this had happened, the rest of the sick on the island came and were cured. ¹⁰They honored us in many ways and when we were ready to sail, they furnished us with the supplies we needed.

ᵃ27 In ancient times the name referred to an area extending well south of Italy.   *ᵇ28* Greek *twenty orguias* (about 37 meters)   *ᶜ28* Greek *fifteen orguias* (about 27 meters)

Arrival at Rome

[11]After three months we put out to sea in a ship that had wintered in the island. It was an Alexandrian ship with the figurehead of the twin gods Castor and Pollux. [12]We put in at Syracuse and stayed there three days. [13]From there we set sail and arrived at Rhegium. The next day the south wind came up, and on the following day we reached Puteoli. [14]There we found some brothers who invited us to spend a week with them. And so we came to Rome. [15]The brothers there had heard that we were coming, and they traveled as far as the Forum of Appius and the Three Taverns to meet us. At the sight of these men Paul thanked God and was encouraged. [16]When we got to Rome, Paul was allowed to live by himself, with a soldier to guard him.

Paul Preaches at Rome Under Guard

[17]Three days later he called together the leaders of the Jews. When they had assembled, Paul said to them: "My brothers, although I have done nothing against our people or against the customs of our ancestors, I was arrested in Jerusalem and handed over to the Romans. [18]They examined me and wanted to release me, because I was not guilty of any crime deserving death. [19]But when the Jews objected, I was compelled to appeal to Caesar—not that I had any charge to bring against my own people. [20]For this reason I have asked to see you and talk with you. It is because of the hope of Israel that I am bound with this chain."

[21]They replied, "We have not received any letters from Judea concerning you, and none of the brothers who have come from there has reported or said anything bad about you. [22]But we want to hear what your views are, for we know that people everywhere are talking against this sect."

[23]They arranged to meet Paul on a certain day, and came in even larger numbers to the place where he was staying. From morning till evening he explained and declared to them the kingdom of God and tried to convince them about Jesus from the Law of Moses and from the Prophets. [24]Some were convinced by what he said, but others would not believe. [25]They disagreed among themselves and began to leave after Paul had made this final statement: "The Holy Spirit spoke the truth to your forefathers when he said through Isaiah the prophet:

[26]" 'Go to this people and say,
   "You will be ever hearing but never
        understanding;
      you will be ever seeing but never
        perceiving."
[27]For this people's heart has become
        calloused;
      they hardly hear with their ears,
      and they have closed their eyes.
   Otherwise they might see with their
        eyes,
      hear with their ears,
      understand with their hearts
   and turn, and I would heal them.'[a]

[28]"Therefore I want you to know that God's salvation has been sent to the Gentiles, and they will listen!"[b]

[30]For two whole years Paul stayed there in his own rented house and welcomed all who came to see him. [31]Boldly and without hindrance he preached the kingdom of God and taught about the Lord Jesus Christ.

---

[a]27 Isaiah 6:9,10   [b]28 Some manuscripts listen!" [29]After he said this, the Jews left, arguing vigorously among themselves.

*P*AUL, *planning a mission trip to Spain (Romans 15:23–29), writes this letter to introduce himself to the church at Rome. In it he summarizes what he has been preaching about sin, Christ, and the way of salvation. Everything you need to know about God's great plan for redemption lies in these sixteen chapters. As you read the book, think about how much God loves you in sending his Son Jesus and how you can say thank you to him by the life you live.*

ROMANS

1 Paul, a servant of Christ Jesus, called to be an apostle and set apart for the gospel of God— ²the gospel he promised beforehand through his prophets in the Holy Scriptures ³regarding his Son, who as to his human nature was a descendant of David, ⁴and who through the Spirit*ᵃ* of holiness was declared with power to be the Son of God*ᵇ* by his resurrection from the dead: Jesus Christ our Lord. ⁵Through him and for his name's sake, we received grace and apostleship to call people from among all the Gentiles to the obedience that comes from faith. ⁶And you also are among those who are called to belong to Jesus Christ.

⁷To all in Rome who are loved by God and called to be saints:

Grace and peace to you from God our Father and from the Lord Jesus Christ.

Paul's Longing to Visit Rome

⁸First, I thank my God through Jesus Christ for all of you, because your faith is being reported all over the world. ⁹God, whom I serve with my whole heart in preaching the gospel of his Son, is my witness how constantly I remember you ¹⁰in my prayers at all times; and I pray that

ᵃ4 Or *who as to his spirit*   *ᵇ4* Or *was appointed to be the Son of God with power* now at last by God's will the way may be opened for me to come to you.

[11]I long to see you so that I may impart to you some spiritual gift to make you strong— [12]that is, that you and I may be mutually encouraged by each other's faith. [13]I do not want you to be unaware, brothers, that I planned many times to come to you (but have been prevented from doing so until now) in order that I might have a harvest among you, just as I have had among the other Gentiles.

[14]I am obligated both to Greeks and non-Greeks, both to the wise and the foolish. [15]That is why I am so eager to preach the gospel also to you who are at Rome.

[16]I am not ashamed of the gospel, because it is the power of God for the salvation of everyone who believes: first for the Jew, then for the Gentile. [17]For in the gospel a righteousness from God is revealed, a righteousness that is by faith from first to last,[a] just as it is written: "The righteous will live by faith."[b]

God's Wrath Against Mankind

[18]The wrath of God is being revealed from heaven against all the godlessness and wickedness of men who suppress the truth by their wickedness, [19]since what may be known about God is plain to them, because God has made it plain to them. [20]For since the creation of the world God's invisible qualities—his eternal power and divine nature—have been clearly seen, being understood from what has been made, so that men are without excuse.

[21]For although they knew God, they neither glorified him as God nor gave thanks to him, but their thinking became futile and their foolish hearts were darkened. [22]Although they claimed to be wise, they became fools [23]and exchanged the glory of the immortal God for images made to look like mortal man and birds and animals and reptiles.

[24]Therefore God gave them over in the sinful desires of their hearts to sexual impurity for the degrading of their bodies with one another. [25]They exchanged the truth of God for a lie, and worshiped and served created things rather than the Creator—who is forever praised. Amen.

[26]Because of this, God gave them over to shameful lusts. Even their women ex-

changed natural relations for unnatural ones. [27]In the same way the men also abandoned natural relations with women and were inflamed with lust for one another. Men committed indecent acts with other men, and received in themselves the due penalty for their perversion.

[28]Furthermore, since they did not think it worthwhile to retain the knowledge of God, he gave them over to a depraved mind, to do what ought not to be done. [29]They have become filled with every kind of wickedness, evil, greed and depravity. They are full of envy, murder, strife, deceit and malice. They are gossips, [30]slanderers, God-haters, insolent, arrogant and boastful; they invent ways of doing evil; they disobey their parents; [31]they are senseless, faithless, heartless, ruthless. [32]Although they know God's righteous decree that those who do such things deserve death, they not only continue to do these very things but also approve of those who practice them.

God's Righteous Judgment

2 You, therefore, have no excuse, you who pass judgment on someone else, for at whatever point you judge the other, you are condemning yourself, because you who pass judgment do the same things. [2]Now we know that God's judgment against those who do such things is based on truth. [3]So when you, a mere man, pass judgment on them and yet do the same things, do you think you will escape God's judgment? [4]Or do you show contempt for the riches of his kindness, tolerance and patience, not realizing that God's kindness leads you toward repentance?

[5]But because of your stubbornness and your unrepentant heart, you are storing up wrath against yourself for the day of God's wrath, when his righteous judgment will be revealed. [6]God "will give to each person according to what he has done."[c] [7]To those who by persistence in doing good seek glory, honor and immortality, he will give eternal life. [8]But for those who are self-seeking and who reject the truth and follow evil, there will be wrath and anger. [9]There will be trouble and distress for every human being who does evil: first for the Jew, then for the Gentile; [10]but glory, honor and peace for

VERSE FOR THE DAY:
Romans 1:25

AUTHOR:
Carol L. Baldwin

PASSAGE FOR THE DAY:
Romans 1:18–25

From the Created to the Creator

WHICH one of us hasn't looked on a newborn baby with amazement and wondered at the exquisite delicacy of each limb, facial feature, fingernail or eyelash? Especially if that baby is our own, there is always the temptation to think this child is the perfect example of human conception—in spite of the fact that he or she may have no hair, be bright red or be shaped like a little potato!

Even the psalmist agrees that every baby has been "fearfully and wonderfully made" (Psalm 139:14).

From the first moment of awe when we gaze at our newborn children, and then during the hours, days and years that go into caring for them, it is tempting for us to allow these children to become the center of our lives—almost to become objects of our *worship*.

How can we keep ourselves from revolving our whole lives around these precious gifts from the Lord?

The answer is to look up from the intricacy and delicacy of these *creations* to see the one behind the magnificent way they have been knit together—their *Creator*.

Isn't this a part of Paul's warning to us in Romans 1:25? We must avoid the sin of the unbeliever, who sees God's eternal power and divine nature in all of creation, but neither glorifies him nor gives thanks to him (Romans 1:20–21). Unlike unbelievers, we Christians have been given by God new hearts and minds, enabling us to look at the product and praise the Master Craftsman.

It is our responsibility and joy to look at those babies and delight in their perfectly formed tiny hands and feet—and then worship the one who created those parts with infinite wisdom, care and direction.

Additional Scripture Readings:
Psalm 104:24–31; Acts 17:24–27

Go to page 207 for your next devotional reading.

everyone who does good: first for the Jew, then for the Gentile. [11]For God does not show favoritism.

[12]All who sin apart from the law will also perish apart from the law, and all who sin under the law will be judged by the law. [13]For it is not those who hear the law who are righteous in God's sight, but it is those who obey the law who will be declared righteous. [14](Indeed, when Gentiles, who do not have the law, do by nature things required by the law, they are a law for themselves, even though they do not have the law, [15]since they show that the requirements of the law are written on their hearts, their consciences also bearing witness, and their thoughts now accusing, now even defending them.) [16]This will take place on the day when God will judge men's secrets through Jesus Christ, as my gospel declares.

The Jews and the Law

[17]Now you, if you call yourself a Jew; if you rely on the law and brag about your relationship to God; [18]if you know his will and approve of what is superior because you are instructed by the law; [19]if you are convinced that you are a guide for the blind, a light for those who are in the dark, [20]an instructor of the foolish, a teacher of infants, because you have in the law the embodiment of knowledge and truth— [21]you, then, who teach others, do you not teach yourself? You who preach against stealing, do you steal? [22]You who say that people should not commit adultery, do you commit adultery? You who abhor idols, do you rob temples? [23]You who brag about the law, do you dishonor God by breaking the law? [24]As it is written: "God's name is blasphemed among the Gentiles because of you."[a]

[25]Circumcision has value if you observe the law, but if you break the law, you have become as though you had not been circumcised. [26]If those who are not circumcised keep the law's requirements, will they not be regarded as though they were circumcised? [27]The one who is not circumcised physically and yet obeys the law will condemn you who, even though you have the[b] written code and circumcision, are a lawbreaker.

[28]A man is not a Jew if he is only one outwardly, nor is circumcision merely outward and physical. [29]No, a man is a Jew if he is one inwardly; and circumcision is circumcision of the heart, by the Spirit, not by the written code. Such a man's praise is not from men, but from God.

God's Faithfulness

3 What advantage, then, is there in being a Jew, or what value is there in circumcision? [2]Much in every way! First of all, they have been entrusted with the very words of God.

[3]What if some did not have faith? Will their lack of faith nullify God's faithfulness? [4]Not at all! Let God be true, and every man a liar. As it is written:

"So that you may be proved right
　　when you speak
and prevail when you judge."[c]

[5]But if our unrighteousness brings out God's righteousness more clearly, what shall we say? That God is unjust in bringing his wrath on us? (I am using a human argument.) [6]Certainly not! If that were so, how could God judge the world? [7]Someone might argue, "If my falsehood enhances God's truthfulness and so increases his glory, why am I still condemned as a sinner?" [8]Why not say—as we are being slanderously reported as saying and as some claim that we say— "Let us do evil that good may result"? Their condemnation is deserved.

No One Is Righteous

[9]What shall we conclude then? Are we any better[d]? Not at all! We have already made the charge that Jews and Gentiles alike are all under sin. [10]As it is written:

"There is no one righteous, not even
　　one;
[11]　there is no one who understands,
　　no one who seeks God.
[12]All have turned away,
　　they have together become
　　　　worthless;
there is no one who does good,
　　not even one."[e]
[13]"Their throats are open graves;
　　their tongues practice deceit."[f]
"The poison of vipers is on their
　　lips."[g]
[14]　"Their mouths are full of cursing
　　and bitterness."[h]

---

[a]24 Isaiah 52:5; Ezek. 36:22　　[b]27 Or who, by means of a　　[c]4 Psalm 51:4　　[d]9 Or worse
[e]12 Psalms 14:1-3; 53:1-3; Eccles. 7:20　　[f]13 Psalm 5:9　　[g]13 Psalm 140:3　　[h]14 Psalm 10:7

[15]"Their feet are swift to shed blood;
[16]   ruin and misery mark their ways,
[17]and the way of peace they do not
         know."[a]
[18]   "There is no fear of God before
         their eyes."[b]

[19]Now we know that whatever the law
says, it says to those who are under the
law, so that every mouth may be silenced
and the whole world held accountable to
God. [20]Therefore no one will be declared
righteous in his sight by observing the
law; rather, through the law we become
conscious of sin.

Righteousness Through Faith

[21]But now a righteousness from God,
apart from law, has been made known, to
which the Law and the Prophets testify.
[22]This righteousness from God comes
through faith in Jesus Christ to all who
believe. There is no difference, [23]for all
have sinned and fall short of the glory of
God, [24]and are justified freely by his grace
through the redemption that came by
Christ Jesus. [25]God presented him as a
sacrifice of atonement,[c] through faith in
his blood. He did this to demonstrate his
justice, because in his forbearance he had
left the sins committed beforehand unpunished— [26]he did it to demonstrate his
justice at the present time, so as to be
just and the one who justifies those who
have faith in Jesus.

[27]Where, then, is boasting? It is excluded. On what principle? On that of observing the law? No, but on that of faith. [28]For
we maintain that a man is justified by
faith apart from observing the law. [29]Is
God the God of Jews only? Is he not the
God of Gentiles too? Yes, of Gentiles too,
[30]since there is only one God, who will
justify the circumcised by faith and the
uncircumcised through that same faith.
[31]Do we, then, nullify the law by this
faith? Not at all! Rather, we uphold the
law.

Abraham Justified by Faith

4 What then shall we say that Abraham,
   our forefather, discovered in this matter? [2]If, in fact, Abraham was justified by
works, he had something to boast about
—but not before God. [3]What does the

Scripture say? "Abraham believed God,
and it was credited to him as righteousness."[d]

[4]Now when a man works, his wages are
not credited to him as a gift, but as an
obligation. [5]However, to the man who
does not work but trusts God who justifies the wicked, his faith is credited as
righteousness. [6]David says the same thing
when he speaks of the blessedness of the
man to whom God credits righteousness
apart from works:

[7]"Blessed are they
      whose transgressions are forgiven,
      whose sins are covered.
[8]Blessed is the man
      whose sin the Lord will never count
         against him."[e]

[9]Is this blessedness only for the circumcised, or also for the uncircumcised?
We have been saying that Abraham's faith
was credited to him as righteousness.
[10]Under what circumstances was it credited? Was it after he was circumcised, or
before? It was not after, but before! [11]And
he received the sign of circumcision, a
seal of the righteousness that he had by
faith while he was still uncircumcised. So
then, he is the father of all who believe
but have not been circumcised, in order
that righteousness might be credited to
them. [12]And he is also the father of the
circumcised who not only are circumcised but who also walk in the footsteps
of the faith that our father Abraham had
before he was circumcised.

[13]It was not through law that Abraham
and his offspring received the promise
that he would be heir of the world, but
through the righteousness that comes by
faith. [14]For if those who live by law are
heirs, faith has no value and the promise
is worthless, [15]because law brings wrath.
And where there is no law there is no
transgression.

[16]Therefore, the promise comes by
faith, so that it may be by grace and may
be guaranteed to all Abraham's offspring
—not only to those who are of the law but
also to those who are of the faith of
Abraham. He is the father of us all. [17]As
it is written: "I have made you a father of
many nations."[f] He is our father in the
sight of God, in whom he believed—the
God who gives life to the dead and calls

---

a17 Isaiah 59:7,8   b18 Psalm 36:1   c25 Or as the one who would turn aside his wrath, taking away
sin   d3 Gen. 15:6; also in verse 22   e8 Psalm 32:1,2   f17 Gen. 17:5

VERSE FOR THE DAY:
Romans 3:22

AUTHOR:
Gladys M. Hunt

PASSAGE FOR THE DAY:
Romans 3:9–27

Changed to Fit the Standard

THESE verses tell it like it is. No one is good enough for God. You can't pile up Brownie points and hope they make you acceptable in his sight. The only people who think they can make it on their own are people who have cut God down to their size. The problem is that God is *who he is* and he is perfect holiness. That's the bad news and it's the good news.

How can people like you or me be made right with God? Where do we get the righteousness we need? The good news is that God's kind of righteousness has been made available to us (Romans 3:21) as a free gift (Romans 3:24). It's for anyone who has faith in Jesus Christ (Romans 3:22), which simply means you don't get the gift unless you take it.

God can't pretend sin doesn't exist. He doesn't look at us and make excuses for us. He had to do something about sin to break its power over us. So he sent Jesus and we have been rescued—redeemed—by him (Romans 3:24). Jesus died as a sacrifice to pay sin's penalty (Romans 3:25), and to those who believe and receive his offer, he does a wonderful thing: he justifies us (Romans 3:24).

If you need to be justified, it means something is wrong. You don't match the standard. In justifying us, God takes care of our sin—and then does something even greater—he gives us the righteousness of Jesus Christ. It's like receiving new clothes that fit us and are appropriate for going into the presence of the king. What do we lack? Righteousness. What does Jesus give us? His righteousness. He doesn't change his standard in order to include us. He changes us to fit the standard.

We must take a good look at ourselves. Do we deserve this? No, it is God's grace (Romans 3:24) that brings about this marvelous change in our lives. How should a person respond to such a gift? Receive it thankfully. Remember who you are and whose clothes you are wearing. Remember how you came to belong to Jesus Christ. Share the Good News.

Additional Scripture Readings:
Matthew 22:8–13; Titus 3:3–7

*Go to page 209 for your next
devotional reading.*

things that are not as though they were. [18]Against all hope, Abraham in hope believed and so became the father of many nations, just as it had been said to him, "So shall your offspring be."[a] [19]Without weakening in his faith, he faced the fact that his body was as good as dead—since he was about a hundred years old—and that Sarah's womb was also dead. [20]Yet he did not waver through unbelief regarding the promise of God, but was strengthened in his faith and gave glory to God, [21]being fully persuaded that God had power to do what he had promised. [22]This is why "it was credited to him as righteousness." [23]The words "it was credited to him" were written not for him alone, [24]but also for us, to whom God will credit righteousness—for us who believe in him who raised Jesus our Lord from the dead. [25]He was delivered over to death for our sins and was raised to life for our justification.

Peace and Joy

5 Therefore, since we have been justified through faith, we[b] have peace with God through our Lord Jesus Christ, [2]through whom we have gained access by faith into this grace in which we now stand. And we[b] rejoice in the hope of the glory of God. [3]Not only so, but we[b] also rejoice in our sufferings, because we know that suffering produces perseverance; [4]perseverance, character; and character, hope. [5]And hope does not disappoint us, because God has poured out his love into our hearts by the Holy Spirit, whom he has given us.

[6]You see, at just the right time, when we were still powerless, Christ died for the ungodly. [7]Very rarely will anyone die for a righteous man, though for a good man someone might possibly dare to die. [8]But God demonstrates his own love for us in this: While we were still sinners, Christ died for us.

[9]Since we have now been justified by his blood, how much more shall we be saved from God's wrath through him! [10]For if, when we were God's enemies, we were reconciled to him through the death of his Son, how much more, having been reconciled, shall we be saved through his life! [11]Not only is this so, but we also rejoice in God through our Lord Jesus Christ, through whom we have now received reconciliation.

Death Through Adam, Life Through Christ

[12]Therefore, just as sin entered the world through one man, and death through sin, and in this way death came to all men, because all sinned— [13]for before the law was given, sin was in the world. But sin is not taken into account when there is no law. [14]Nevertheless, death reigned from the time of Adam to the time of Moses, even over those who did not sin by breaking a command, as did Adam, who was a pattern of the one to come.

[15]But the gift is not like the trespass. For if the many died by the trespass of the one man, how much more did God's grace and the gift that came by the grace of the one man, Jesus Christ, overflow to the many! [16]Again, the gift of God is not like the result of the one man's sin: The judgment followed one sin and brought condemnation, but the gift followed many trespasses and brought justification. [17]For if, by the trespass of the one man, death reigned through that one man, how much more will those who receive God's abundant provision of grace and of the gift of righteousness reign in life through the one man, Jesus Christ.

[18]Consequently, just as the result of one trespass was condemnation for all men, so also the result of one act of righteousness was justification that brings life for all men. [19]For just as through the disobedience of the one man the many were made sinners, so also through the obedience of the one man the many will be made righteous.

[20]The law was added so that the trespass might increase. But where sin increased, grace increased all the more, [21]so that, just as sin reigned in death, so also grace might reign through righteousness to bring eternal life through Jesus Christ our Lord.

Dead to Sin, Alive in Christ

6 What shall we say, then? Shall we go on sinning so that grace may increase? [2]By no means! We died to sin; how can we live in it any longer? [3]Or don't you know that all of us who were baptized into Christ Jesus were baptized into his death? [4]We were therefore buried with him through baptism into death in order that, just as Christ was raised from the

---

[a]18 Gen. 15:5   [b]1,2,3 Or let us

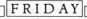

VERSE FOR THE DAY:
Romans 5:1

AUTHOR:
Gladys M. Hunt

PASSAGE FOR THE DAY:
Romans 5:1–5

Access to God

BECOMING a Christian has enormous consequences. Relationships are changed; we are given privileges; we look at life differently; our resources are inexhaustible. How do we receive all of this? Paul makes it clear: *through our Lord Jesus Christ* (Romans 5:1).

Our relationships are changed: we have peace *with* God (Romans 5:1). When we are at odds with God, inner peace eludes us. Becoming a Christian necessitates being made right with God, and what a difference it makes! *Peace with God* is enough to sing about.

We are given privileges: we have access by faith into God's very presence (Romans 5:2). Once we knew only hostility; now we are invited into the King's presence. Once we were outside; now we are welcome inside. Access. What are you doing with the privilege of coming into God's presence?

We look at life differently: we can be joyful even when facing the hard things that come into our lives (Romans 5:3). We know life isn't purposeless. God is taking the stuff of our lives and making something good out of it. We are on our way somewhere. God wants to get us ready for heaven. Our joy is real because we know we will one day share the glory of God.

Our resources are inexhaustible: God keeps pouring his love into our hearts (Romans 5:5). He not only makes us feel very loved, but he is so generous in his supply that we have an overflow of love for other people. He gives us the Holy Spirit, who not only transforms our thinking, but makes God's love real to us.

Our trouble begins when we forget these great realities and concentrate on our inadequacies, our fears, and all the other manifestations of our smallness. The proof of God's love is that Jesus Christ died for us. We are no longer shivering outside in the cold with no credentials to come before the King. Jesus has invited us into his very presence and has given us all we need and more besides. This passage in Romans 5 is a renewed invitation to take advantage of your privileges as a daughter of the King.

Additional Scripture Readings:
John 14:6–14; Hebrews 4:14–16

Go to page 211 for your next devotional reading.

dead through the glory of the Father, we too may live a new life.

[5]If we have been united with him like this in his death, we will certainly also be united with him in his resurrection. [6]For we know that our old self was crucified with him so that the body of sin might be done away with,[a] that we should no longer be slaves to sin— [7]because anyone who has died has been freed from sin.

[8]Now if we died with Christ, we believe that we will also live with him. [9]For we know that since Christ was raised from the dead, he cannot die again; death no longer has mastery over him. [10]The death he died, he died to sin once for all; but the life he lives, he lives to God.

[11]In the same way, count yourselves dead to sin but alive to God in Christ Jesus. [12]Therefore do not let sin reign in your mortal body so that you obey its evil desires. [13]Do not offer the parts of your body to sin, as instruments of wickedness, but rather offer yourselves to God, as those who have been brought from death to life; and offer the parts of your body to him as instruments of righteousness. [14]For sin shall not be your master, because you are not under law, but under grace.

Slaves to Righteousness

[15]What then? Shall we sin because we are not under law but under grace? By no means! [16]Don't you know that when you offer yourselves to someone to obey him as slaves, you are slaves to the one whom you obey—whether you are slaves to sin, which leads to death, or to obedience, which leads to righteousness? [17]But thanks be to God that, though you used to be slaves to sin, you wholeheartedly obeyed the form of teaching to which you were entrusted. [18]You have been set free from sin and have become slaves to righteousness.

[19]I put this in human terms because you are weak in your natural selves. Just as you used to offer the parts of your body in slavery to impurity and to ever-increasing wickedness, so now offer them in slavery to righteousness leading to holiness. [20]When you were slaves to sin, you were free from the control of righteousness. [21]What benefit did you reap at that time from the things you are now ashamed of? Those things result in death! [22]But now

that you have been set free from sin and have become slaves to God, the benefit you reap leads to holiness, and the result is eternal life. [23]For the wages of sin is death, but the gift of God is eternal life in[b] Christ Jesus our Lord.

An Illustration From Marriage

7 Do you not know, brothers—for I am speaking to men who know the law— that the law has authority over a man only as long as he lives? [2]For example, by law a married woman is bound to her husband as long as he is alive, but if her husband dies, she is released from the law of marriage. [3]So then, if she marries another man while her husband is still alive, she is called an adulteress. But if her husband dies, she is released from that law and is not an adulteress, even though she marries another man.

[4]So, my brothers, you also died to the law through the body of Christ, that you might belong to another, to him who was raised from the dead, in order that we might bear fruit to God. [5]For when we were controlled by the sinful nature,[c] the sinful passions aroused by the law were at work in our bodies, so that we bore fruit for death. [6]But now, by dying to what once bound us, we have been released from the law so that we serve in the new way of the Spirit, and not in the old way of the written code.

Struggling With Sin

[7]What shall we say, then? Is the law sin? Certainly not! Indeed I would not have known what sin was except through the law. For I would not have known what coveting really was if the law had not said, "Do not covet."[d] [8]But sin, seizing the opportunity afforded by the commandment, produced in me every kind of covetous desire. For apart from law, sin is dead. [9]Once I was alive apart from law; but when the commandment came, sin sprang to life and I died. [10]I found that the very commandment that was intended to bring life actually brought death. [11]For sin, seizing the opportunity afforded by the commandment, deceived me, and through the commandment put me to death. [12]So then, the law is holy, and the commandment is holy, righteous and good.

---

[a]6 Or be rendered powerless   [b]23 Or through   [c]5 Or the flesh; also in verse 25   [d]7 Exodus 20:17; Deut. 5:21

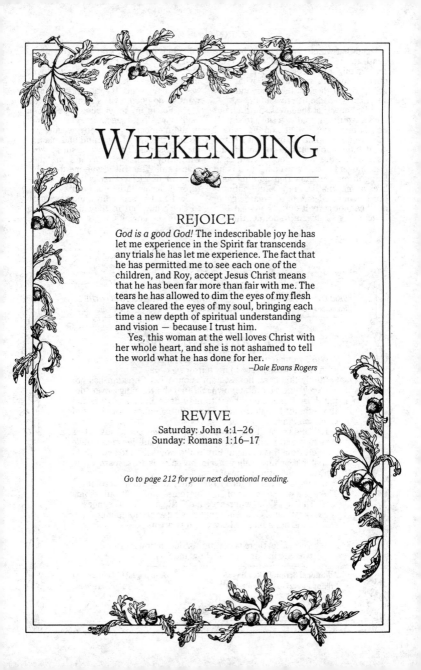

WEEKENDING

REJOICE

God is a good God! The indescribable joy he has let me experience in the Spirit far transcends any trials he has let me experience. The fact that he has permitted me to see each one of the children, and Roy, accept Jesus Christ means that he has been far more than fair with me. The tears he has allowed to dim the eyes of my flesh have cleared the eyes of my soul, bringing each time a new depth of spiritual understanding and vision — because I trust him.

Yes, this woman at the well loves Christ with her whole heart, and she is not ashamed to tell the world what he has done for her.

–Dale Evans Rogers

REVIVE
Saturday: John 4:1–26
Sunday: Romans 1:16–17

Go to page 212 for your next devotional reading.

13Did that which is good, then, become death to me? By no means! But in order that sin might be recognized as sin, it produced death in me through what was good, so that through the commandment sin might become utterly sinful.

14We know that the law is spiritual; but I am unspiritual, sold as a slave to sin. 15I do not understand what I do. For what I want to do I do not do, but what I hate I do. 16And if I do what I do not want to do, I agree that the law is good. 17As it is, it is no longer I myself who do it, but it is sin living in me. 18I know that nothing good lives in me, that is, in my sinful nature.ᵃ For I have the desire to do what is good, but I cannot carry it out. 19For what I do is not the good I want to do; no, the evil

I do not want to do—this I keep on doing. 20Now if I do what I do not want to do, it is no longer I who do it, but it is sin living in me that does it.

21So I find this law at work: When I want to do good, evil is right there with me. 22For in my inner being I delight in God's law; 23but I see another law at work in the members of my body, waging war against the law of my mind and making me a prisoner of the law of sin at work within my members. 24What a wretched man I am! Who will rescue me from this body of death? 25Thanks be to God— through Jesus Christ our Lord!

So then, I myself in my mind am a slave to God's law, but in the sinful nature a slave to the law of sin.

ᵃ18 Or *my flesh*

MONDAY

VERSE FOR THE DAY:
Romans 7:15

AUTHOR:
Jeanette Lockerbie

PASSAGE FOR THE DAY:
Romans 7:14–21

Troublesome Me

A WISE woman once said, "The person I have the most trouble with is the person I see in my mirror every day."

Surely this is an honest admission. What Christian has not sincerely grieved over her own spiritual shortcomings: over "doing those things I ought not to have done and leaving undone those things I ought to have done" (to paraphrase the Book of Common Prayer).

No follower of Christ was ever more acutely conscious of this very trait and tendency than the apostle Paul. We might take comfort from this thought. But to allow ourselves to be trapped in Satan's snare—wallowing in despair—is to disparage the limitless, liberating grace of God.

Let us then not linger in this valley of spiritual desolation. There is a way to get rid of "troublesome you," or "troublesome me." The cry, "Who will rescue me?" (Romans 7:24) echoes to the very throne of God. The reply, ringing with triumphant deliverance and assurance, echoes to our very ears.

Therefore, there is now no condemnation for those who are in Christ Jesus (Romans 8:1).

Additional Scripture Readings:
Philippians 3:7–11; Hebrews 12:1–2

Go to page 214 for your next devotional reading.

Life Through the Spirit

8 Therefore, there is now no condemnation for those who are in Christ Jesus,[a] [2]because through Christ Jesus the law of the Spirit of life set me free from the law of sin and death. [3]For what the law was powerless to do in that it was weakened by the sinful nature,[b] God did by sending his own Son in the likeness of sinful man to be a sin offering.[c] And so he condemned sin in sinful man,[d] [4]in order that the righteous requirements of the law might be fully met in us, who do not live according to the sinful nature but according to the Spirit.

[5]Those who live according to the sinful nature have their minds set on what that nature desires; but those who live in accordance with the Spirit have their minds set on what the Spirit desires. [6]The mind of sinful man[e] is death, but the mind controlled by the Spirit is life and peace; [7]the sinful mind[f] is hostile to God. It does not submit to God's law, nor can it do so. [8]Those controlled by the sinful nature cannot please God.

[9]You, however, are controlled not by the sinful nature but by the Spirit, if the Spirit of God lives in you. And if anyone does not have the Spirit of Christ, he does not belong to Christ. [10]But if Christ is in you, your body is dead because of sin, yet your spirit is alive because of righteousness. [11]And if the Spirit of him who raised Jesus from the dead is living in you, he who raised Christ from the dead will also give life to your mortal bodies through his Spirit, who lives in you.

[12]Therefore, brothers, we have an obligation—but it is not to the sinful nature, to live according to it. [13]For if you live according to the sinful nature, you will die; but if by the Spirit you put to death the misdeeds of the body, you will live, [14]because those who are led by the Spirit of God are sons of God. [15]For you did not receive a spirit that makes you a slave again to fear, but you received a spirit of sonship.[g] And by him we cry, *"Abba,*[h] *Father."* [16]The Spirit himself testifies with our spirit that we are God's children. [17]Now if we are children, then we are heirs—heirs of God and co-heirs with Christ, if indeed we share in his sufferings in order that we may also share in his glory.

Future Glory

[18]I consider that our present sufferings are not worth comparing with the glory that will be revealed in us. [19]The creation waits in eager expectation for the sons of God to be revealed. [20]For the creation was subjected to frustration, not by its own choice, but by the will of the one who subjected it, in hope [21]that[i] the creation itself will be liberated from its bondage to decay and brought into the glorious freedom of the children of God.

[22]We know that the whole creation has been groaning as in the pains of childbirth right up to the present time. [23]Not only so, but we ourselves, who have the firstfruits of the Spirit, groan inwardly as we wait eagerly for our adoption as sons, the redemption of our bodies. [24]For in this hope we were saved. But hope that is seen is no hope at all. Who hopes for what he already has? [25]But if we hope for what we do not yet have, we wait for it patiently.

[26]In the same way, the Spirit helps us in our weakness. We do not know what we ought to pray for, but the Spirit himself intercedes for us with groans that words cannot express. [27]And he who searches our hearts knows the mind of the Spirit, because the Spirit intercedes for the saints in accordance with God's will.

More Than Conquerors

[28]And we know that in all things God works for the good of those who love him,[j] who[k] have been called according to his purpose. [29]For those God foreknew he also predestined to be conformed to the likeness of his Son, that he might be the firstborn among many brothers. [30]And those he predestined, he also called; those he called, he also justified; those he justified, he also glorified.

[31]What, then, shall we say in response to this? If God is for us, who can be against us? [32]He who did not spare his own Son, but gave him up for us all—how will he not also, along with him, graciously give us all things? [33]Who will bring any

---

[a]1 Some later manuscripts *Jesus, who do not live according to the sinful nature but according to the Spirit,*
[b]3 Or *the flesh;* also in verses 4, 5, 8, 9, 12 and 13   [c]3 Or *man, for sin*   [d]3 Or *in the flesh*   [e]6 Or *mind set on the flesh*   [f]7 Or *the mind set on the flesh*   [g]15 Or *adoption*   [h]15 Aramaic for *Father*
[i]20,21 Or *subjected it in hope.* 21For   [j]28 Some manuscripts *And we know that all things work together for good to those who love God*   [k]28 Or *works together with those who love him to bring about what is good—with those who*

TUESDAY

VERSE FOR THE DAY:
Romans 8:26–27

AUTHOR:
Sue Richards

PASSAGE FOR THE DAY:
Romans 8:18–27

When It Hurts So Much . . .

THERE are times in the lives of all God's children when we are called on to suffer. We read in Romans 5:3–4 that "suffering produces perseverance; perseverance, character; and character, hope." For me suffering has also produced times of physical and emotional weakness. After the death of my first child, as I lay near death myself, I tried to pray, but I was in shock and heavily medicated. No words would come into my mind or to my lips. I wish I had known Romans 8:26–27 then. Yet, although I could not speak, I felt in close communication with the Lord. I just didn't understand how this was possible.

While believers are sustained in their suffering by hope, we also are sustained in our weakness in the most special way of all:

> The Spirit helps us in our weakness. We do not know what we ought to pray for, but the Spirit himself intercedes for us with groans that words cannot express. And he who searches our hearts knows the mind of the Spirit, because the Spirit intercedes for the saints in accordance with God's will (Romans 8:26–27).

God himself, who dwells within us in the person of the Holy Spirit, intercedes for us in our weakness. Not with flowery or powerful words, but with groans that words cannot express. How empowering in our weakest moments, when we don't know how to express our own overwhelming needs, to cling to the words of God.

"The Spirit himself intercedes for us with groans that words cannot express." And all of this intercession on our behalf is done "in accordance with God's will" for us personally. When Christ gave us the Holy Spirit, he left us much more than an inner spiritual discernment. Our triune God lives within and intercedes for each of us when we are in our weakest moments.

Abba, Father, your love and concern for me when I am at my most vulnerable times in life is beyond my understanding. I thank you for the gracious gift of your Holy Spirit. Amen.

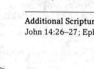

Additional Scripture Readings:
John 14:26–27; Ephesians 6:17–18

Go to page 216 for your next devotional reading.

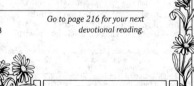

charge against those whom God has chosen? It is God who justifies. [34]Who is he that condemns? Christ Jesus, who died— more than that, who was raised to life—is at the right hand of God and is also interceding for us. [35]Who shall separate us from the love of Christ? Shall trouble or hardship or persecution or famine or nakedness or danger or sword? [36]As it is written:

> "For your sake we face death all day long;
> we are considered as sheep to be slaughtered."[a]

[37]No, in all these things we are more than conquerors through him who loved us. [38]For I am convinced that neither death nor life, neither angels nor demons,[b] neither the present nor the future, nor any powers, [39]neither height nor depth, nor anything else in all creation, will be able to separate us from the love of God that is in Christ Jesus our Lord.

God's Sovereign Choice

9 I speak the truth in Christ—I am not lying, my conscience confirms it in the Holy Spirit— [2]I have great sorrow and unceasing anguish in my heart. [3]For I could wish that I myself were cursed and cut off from Christ for the sake of my brothers, those of my own race, [4]the people of Israel. Theirs is the adoption as sons; theirs the divine glory, the covenants, the receiving of the law, the temple worship and the promises. [5]Theirs are the patriarchs, and from them is traced the human ancestry of Christ, who is God over all, forever praised![c] Amen.

[6]It is not as though God's word had failed. For not all who are descended from Israel are Israel. [7]Nor because they are his descendants are they all Abraham's children. On the contrary, "It is through Isaac that your offspring will be reckoned."[d] [8]In other words, it is not the natural children who are God's children, but it is the children of the promise who are regarded as Abraham's offspring. [9]For this is how the promise was stated: "At the appointed time I will return, and Sarah will have a son."[e]

[10]Not only that, but Rebekah's children had one and the same father, our father Isaac. [11]Yet, before the twins were born or had done anything good or bad—in order that God's purpose in election might stand: [12]not by works but by him who calls—she was told, "The older will serve the younger."[f] [13]Just as it is written: "Jacob I loved, but Esau I hated."[g]

[14]What then shall we say? Is God unjust? Not at all! [15]For he says to Moses,

> "I will have mercy on whom I have mercy,
> and I will have compassion on whom I have compassion."[h]

[16]It does not, therefore, depend on man's desire or effort, but on God's mercy. [17]For the Scripture says to Pharaoh: "I raised you up for this very purpose, that I might display my power in you and that my name might be proclaimed in all the earth."[i] [18]Therefore God has mercy on whom he wants to have mercy, and he hardens whom he wants to harden.

[19]One of you will say to me: "Then why does God still blame us? For who resists his will?" [20]But who are you, O man, to talk back to God? "Shall what is formed say to him who formed it, 'Why did you make me like this?' "[j] [21]Does not the potter have the right to make out of the same lump of clay some pottery for noble purposes and some for common use?

[22]What if God, choosing to show his wrath and make his power known, bore with great patience the objects of his wrath—prepared for destruction? [23]What if he did this to make the riches of his glory known to the objects of his mercy, whom he prepared in advance for glory— [24]even us, whom he also called, not only from the Jews but also from the Gentiles? [25]As he says in Hosea:

> "I will call them 'my people' who are not my people;
> and I will call her 'my loved one' who is not my loved one,"[k]

[26]and,

> "It will happen that in the very place where it was said to them,
> 'You are not my people,'
> they will be called 'sons of the living God.' "[l]

[27]Isaiah cries out concerning Israel:

---

[a]36 Psalm 44:22   [b]38 Or nor heavenly rulers Or Christ. God who is over all be forever praised!   [c]5 Or Christ, who is over all. God be forever praised! Or Christ. God who is over all forever praised!   [d]7 Gen. 21:12   [e]9 Gen. 18:10,14   [f]12 Gen. 25:23   [g]13 Mal. 1:2,3   [h]15 Exodus 33:19   [i]17 Exodus 9:16   [j]20 Isaiah 29:16; 45:9   [k]25 Hosea 2:23   [l]26 Hosea 1:10

"Though the number of the Israelites
    be like the sand by the sea,
    only the remnant will be saved.
[28]For the Lord will carry out
    his sentence on earth with speed
    and finality."[a]

[29]It is just as Isaiah said previously:

"Unless the Lord Almighty
    had left us descendants,

we would have become like Sodom,
    we would have been like
    Gomorrah."[b]

Israel's Unbelief

[30]What then shall we say? That the
Gentiles, who did not pursue righteousness, have obtained it, a righteousness
that is by faith; [31]but Israel, who pursued
a law of righteousness, has not attained

a28 Isaiah 10:22,23   *b29* Isaiah 1:9

WEDNESDAY

VERSE FOR THE DAY: AUTHOR: PASSAGE FOR THE DAY:
Romans 8:28   *ann kiemel anderson*   *Romans 8:28–39*

all things . . .

ROMANS 8:28 is engraved in my wedding band. it was the
theme at my house as a child. my father, a preacher, clung to
these words because they were a PROMISE from a Sovereign
God with a PERFECT track record.

"in ALL things God works for the good" (caps mine). the rejection in one's childhood. alcoholic parents. the birth of a
handicapped child. a husband leaving home for another
woman. illness. no matter what life may have in store . . . absolutely ANYTHING . . . will turn into blessing if we love God.

i was 35 and will 38 when we married. both for the first time.
we decided to try for a baby our first year. but i found i had a tendency to miscarry. to work with singleminded concentration to
get pregnant and then be disappointed over and over. without
romans 8:28 becoming my best friend, i would have been
sucked under. i had been taught to UTTERLY trust God's Word.
this verse had been stamped across my forehead and my heart.

it means God never takes away except to give us back something better. it means we must be brave enough and determined
enough to wait . . . because it often takes God time to turn a
painful situation to good. it means we can embrace our pain and
not resent it because a blessing is coming!

today will and i stand in awe over four little boys . . . age four
and under . . . God gave us through adoption. and we would be
so shallow and careless with our love had we not traveled that
black, seemingly hopeless, journey.

i love you. i run this glorious, hard race beside you. because of
Jesus, everything . . . anything . . . will work for good as you love
God.

Additional Scripture Readings: *Go to page 219 for your next*
Proverbs 19:21; Isaiah 55:8–11   *devotional reading.*

Go to page 219 for your next devotional reading.

it. [32]Why not? Because they pursued it not by faith but as if it were by works. They stumbled over the "stumbling stone." [33]As it is written:

"See, I lay in Zion a stone that causes
　　men to stumble
and a rock that makes them fall,
and the one who trusts in him will
　　never be put to shame." [a]

10 Brothers, my heart's desire and prayer to God for the Israelites is that they may be saved. [2]For I can testify about them that they are zealous for God, but their zeal is not based on knowledge. [3]Since they did not know the righteousness that comes from God and sought to establish their own, they did not submit to God's righteousness. [4]Christ is the end of the law so that there may be righteousness for everyone who believes.

[5]Moses describes in this way the righteousness that is by the law: "The man who does these things will live by them." [b] [6]But the righteousness that is by faith says: "Do not say in your heart, 'Who will ascend into heaven?' [c]" (that is, to bring Christ down) [7]"or 'Who will descend into the deep?' [d]" (that is, to bring Christ up from the dead). [8]But what does it say? "The word is near you; it is in your mouth and in your heart," [e] that is, the word of faith we are proclaiming: [9]That if you confess with your mouth, "Jesus is Lord," and believe in your heart that God raised him from the dead, you will be saved. [10]For it is with your heart that you believe and are justified, and it is with your mouth that you confess and are saved. [11]As the Scripture says, "Anyone who trusts in him will never be put to shame." [f] [12]For there is no difference between Jew and Gentile—the same Lord is Lord of all and richly blesses all who call on him, [13]for, "Everyone who calls on the name of the Lord will be saved." [g]

[14]How, then, can they call on the one they have not believed in? And how can they believe in the one of whom they have not heard? And how can they hear without someone preaching to them? [15]And how can they preach unless they are sent? As it is written, "How beautiful are the feet of those who bring good news!" [h]

[16]But not all the Israelites accepted the good news. For Isaiah says, "Lord, who has believed our message?" [i] [17]Consequently, faith comes from hearing the message, and the message is heard through the word of Christ. [18]But I ask: Did they not hear? Of course they did:

"Their voice has gone out into all the
　　earth,
　　their words to the ends of the
　　world." [j]

[19]Again I ask: Did Israel not understand? First, Moses says,

"I will make you envious by those
　　who are not a nation;
I will make you angry by a nation
　　that has no understanding." [k]

[20]And Isaiah boldly says,

"I was found by those who did not
　　seek me;
I revealed myself to those who did
　　not ask for me." [l]

[21]But concerning Israel he says,

"All day long I have held out my
　　hands
to a disobedient and obstinate
　　people." [m]

The Remnant of Israel

11 I ask then: Did God reject his people? By no means! I am an Israelite myself, a descendant of Abraham, from the tribe of Benjamin. [2]God did not reject his people, whom he foreknew. Don't you know what the Scripture says in the passage about Elijah—how he appealed to God against Israel: [3]"Lord, they have killed your prophets and torn down your altars; I am the only one left, and they are trying to kill me" [n]? [4]And what was God's answer to him? "I have reserved for myself seven thousand who have not bowed the knee to Baal." [o] [5]So too, at the present time there is a remnant chosen by grace. [6]And if by grace, then it is no longer by works; if it were, grace would no longer be grace. [p]

[7]What then? What Israel sought so earnestly it did not obtain, but the elect did. The others were hardened, [8]as it is written:

---

[a]33 Isaiah 8:14; 28:16　　[b]5 Lev. 18:5　　[c]6 Deut. 30:12　　[d]7 Deut. 30:13　　[e]8 Deut. 30:14
[f]11 Isaiah 28:16　　[g]13 Joel 2:32　　[h]15 Isaiah 52:7　　[i]16 Isaiah 53:1　　[j]18 Psalm 19:4
[k]19 Deut. 32:21　　[l]20 Isaiah 65:1　　[m]21 Isaiah 65:2　　[n]3 1 Kings 19:10,14　　[o]4 1 Kings 19:18
[p]6 Some manuscripts *by grace. But if by works, then it is no longer grace; if it were, work would no longer be work.*

"God gave them a spirit of stupor,
  eyes so that they could not see
  and ears so that they could not
    hear,
to this very day."[a]

[9]And David says:

"May their table become a snare and
    a trap,
  a stumbling block and a retribution
    for them.
[10]May their eyes be darkened so they
    cannot see,
  and their backs be bent forever."[b]

Ingrafted Branches

[11]Again I ask: Did they stumble so as to fall beyond recovery? Not at all! Rather, because of their transgression, salvation has come to the Gentiles to make Israel envious. [12]But if their transgression means riches for the world, and their loss means riches for the Gentiles, how much greater riches will their fullness bring!

[13]I am talking to you Gentiles. Inasmuch as I am the apostle to the Gentiles, I make much of my ministry [14]in the hope that I may somehow arouse my own people to envy and save some of them. [15]For if their rejection is the reconciliation of the world, what will their acceptance be but life from the dead? [16]If the part of the dough offered as firstfruits is holy, then the whole batch is holy; if the root is holy, so are the branches.

[17]If some of the branches have been broken off, and you, though a wild olive shoot, have been grafted in among the others and now share in the nourishing sap from the olive root, [18]do not boast over those branches. If you do, consider this: You do not support the root, but the root supports you. [19]You will say then, "Branches were broken off so that I could be grafted in." [20]Granted. But they were broken off because of unbelief, and you stand by faith. Do not be arrogant, but be afraid. [21]For if God did not spare the natural branches, he will not spare you either.

[22]Consider therefore the kindness and sternness of God: sternness to those who fell, but kindness to you, provided that you continue in his kindness. Otherwise, you also will be cut off. [23]And if they do not persist in unbelief, they will be graft-

ed in, for God is able to graft them in again. [24]After all, if you were cut out of an olive tree that is wild by nature, and contrary to nature were grafted into a cultivated olive tree, how much more readily will these, the natural branches, be grafted into their own olive tree!

All Israel Will Be Saved

[25]I do not want you to be ignorant of this mystery, brothers, so that you may not be conceited: Israel has experienced a hardening in part until the full number of the Gentiles has come in. [26]And so all Israel will be saved, as it is written:

"The deliverer will come from Zion;
  he will turn godlessness away from
    Jacob.
[27]And this is[c] my covenant with them
  when I take away their sins."[d]

[28]As far as the gospel is concerned, they are enemies on your account; but as far as election is concerned, they are loved on account of the patriarchs, [29]for God's gifts and his call are irrevocable. [30]Just as you who were at one time disobedient to God have now received mercy as a result of their disobedience, [31]so they too have now become disobedient in order that they too may now[e] receive mercy as a result of God's mercy to you. [32]For God has bound all men over to disobedience so that he may have mercy on them all.

Doxology

[33]Oh, the depth of the riches of the
      wisdom and[f] knowledge of
      God!
  How unsearchable his judgments,
    and his paths beyond tracing out!
[34]"Who has known the mind of the
      Lord?
  Or who has been his counselor?"[g]
[35]"Who has ever given to God,
    that God should repay him?"[h]
[36]For from him and through him and to
      him are all things.
  To him be the glory forever! Amen.

Living Sacrifices

12 Therefore, I urge you, brothers, in view of God's mercy, to offer your bodies as living sacrifices, holy and pleasing to God—this is your spiritual[i] act of worship. [2]Do not conform any longer to

---

[a]8 Deut. 29:4; Isaiah 29:10   [b]10 Psalm 69:22,23   [c]27 Or will be   [d]27 Isaiah 59:20,21; 27:9;
Jer. 31:33,34   [e]31 Some manuscripts do not have now.   [f]33 Or riches and the wisdom and the
[g]34 Isaiah 40:13   [h]35 Job 41:11   [i]1 Or reasonable

VERSE FOR THE DAY:
Romans 12:1–2

AUTHOR:
Marie Chapian

PASSAGE FOR THE DAY:
Romans 12:1–8

Living Sacrifices

IT is a challenge to live our lives as sacrifices to God. When we do, we aren't the masters of our bodies and minds—God is. All that we do or think must conform to the Word of God. Such a high calling is impossible without the Holy Spirit's guidance and help. We cannot make spiritual progress without the Holy Spirit, and that is why in Romans 12:1 the Lord tells us to offer our bodies to him as living sacrifices. If we try to grow and change spiritually without the supernatural empowering of the Holy Spirit, we are conforming to the pattern of the world. The Lord tells us to avoid this by becoming transformed by the renewing of our minds (Romans 12:1–2).

As a sacrificial act of worship, God expects us to be holy and pleasing to him. When I was sharing Romans 12 with a group of young people, one fifteen-year-old girl asked, "Does that mean that everything I do every day—at school, at home, in sports, in art and with friends—all these should be an act of worship to God?"

Another student replied, "How can I stay on my knees that long?"

We chuckled, knowing that we worship not only on our knees but also as we live our lives. Our everyday lives are important to God, important enough that he sent his Son to die on the cross so that Jesus could live in us through each day—including the ordinary ones.

We can now say: "I'm going to school to worship God." "I'm going to paint a picture to worship God." "I'm going to clean the kitchen to worship God." "I'm going to my job to worship God," as well as "I'm going to church to worship God."

When we conform to the world's patterns and methods, we do not please God, no matter how good we feel about ourselves or how much other people approve of us. But we do please God when our minds are renewed. Then we are able to test and approve God's perfect will (Romans 12:2).

Additional Scripture Readings:
Ephesians 4:22–24; 1 Peter 1:13–16

Go to page 221 for your next devotional reading.

the pattern of this world, but be transformed by the renewing of your mind. Then you will be able to test and approve what God's will is—his good, pleasing and perfect will.

³For by the grace given me I say to every one of you: Do not think of yourself more highly than you ought, but rather think of yourself with sober judgment, in accordance with the measure of faith God has given you. ⁴Just as each of us has one body with many members, and these members do not all have the same function, ⁵so in Christ we who are many form one body, and each member belongs to all the others. ⁶We have different gifts, according to the grace given us. If a man's gift is prophesying, let him use it in proportion to his[a] faith. ⁷If it is serving, let him serve; if it is teaching, let him teach; ⁸if it is encouraging, let him encourage; if it is contributing to the needs of others, let him give generously; if it is leadership, let him govern diligently; if it is showing mercy, let him do it cheerfully.

Love

⁹Love must be sincere. Hate what is evil; cling to what is good. ¹⁰Be devoted to one another in brotherly love. Honor one another above yourselves. ¹¹Never be lacking in zeal, but keep your spiritual fervor, serving the Lord. ¹²Be joyful in hope, patient in affliction, faithful in prayer. ¹³Share with God's people who are in need. Practice hospitality.

¹⁴Bless those who persecute you; bless and do not curse. ¹⁵Rejoice with those who rejoice; mourn with those who mourn. ¹⁶Live in harmony with one another. Do not be proud, but be willing to associate with people of low position.[b] Do not be conceited.

¹⁷Do not repay anyone evil for evil. Be careful to do what is right in the eyes of everybody. ¹⁸If it is possible, as far as it depends on you, live at peace with everyone. ¹⁹Do not take revenge, my friends, but leave room for God's wrath, for it is written: "It is mine to avenge; I will repay,"[c] says the Lord. ²⁰On the contrary:

"If your enemy is hungry, feed him;
　if he is thirsty, give him something
　　to drink.
In doing this, you will heap burning
　coals on his head."[d]

²¹Do not be overcome by evil, but overcome evil with good.

Submission to the Authorities

13 Everyone must submit himself to the governing authorities, for there is no authority except that which God has established. The authorities that exist have been established by God. ²Consequently, he who rebels against the authority is rebelling against what God has instituted, and those who do so will bring judgment on themselves. ³For rulers hold no terror for those who do right, but for those who do wrong. Do you want to be free from fear of the one in authority? Then do what is right and he will commend you. ⁴For he is God's servant to do you good. But if you do wrong, be afraid, for he does not bear the sword for nothing. He is God's servant, an agent of wrath to bring punishment on the wrongdoer. ⁵Therefore, it is necessary to submit to the authorities, not only because of possible punishment but also because of conscience.

⁶This is also why you pay taxes, for the authorities are God's servants, who give their full time to governing. ⁷Give everyone what you owe him: If you owe taxes, pay taxes; if revenue, then revenue; if respect, then respect; if honor, then honor.

Love, for the Day Is Near

⁸Let no debt remain outstanding, except the continuing debt to love one another, for he who loves his fellowman has fulfilled the law. ⁹The commandments, "Do not commit adultery," "Do not murder," "Do not steal," "Do not covet,"[e] and whatever other commandment there may be, are summed up in this one rule: "Love your neighbor as yourself."[f] ¹⁰Love does no harm to its neighbor. Therefore love is the fulfillment of the law.

¹¹And do this, understanding the present time. The hour has come for you to wake up from your slumber, because our salvation is nearer now than when we first believed. ¹²The night is nearly over; the day is almost here. So let us put aside the deeds of darkness and put on the armor of light. ¹³Let us behave decently, as in the daytime, not in orgies and drunkenness, not in sexual immorality and debauchery, not in dissension and jealousy. ¹⁴Rather,

---

a6 Or *in agreement with the*   b16 Or *willing to do menial work*   c19 Deut. 32:35   d20 Prov. 25:21,22   e9 Exodus 20:13-15,17; Deut. 5:17-19,21   f9 Lev. 19:18

VERSE FOR THE DAY:	AUTHOR:	PASSAGE FOR THE DAY:
Romans 12:11,16	Gigi Graham Tchividjian	Romans 12:9–21

Even This?

THOUGH early morning is not my best time of day, after a couple of cups of coffee, I managed to fix breakfast, wash the dishes, and usher six children out the door to school before heading for the laundry room.

I stopped abruptly at the door and stood gazing in disbelief at the mountain of dirty clothes. Hadn't I just washed three loads yesterday? Sudden tears of frustration stung my eyes. I quickly brushed them away, a bit ashamed of myself, and put the first load in the washer.

Then I continued to tidy up, picking up the morning newspaper and various cups and glasses left from snacks the night before. Soon I found myself in my son's bathroom, scrubbing the tub. Once again the tears insisted on imposing themselves against my will. This time they found little resistance. I was frustrated and discouraged, and my self-esteem was about as low as it could get.

It was still morning, but I was tired—tired of the same mess day after day—of washing clothes that only yesterday I had folded and returned to their proper places; of doing the dishes, only to get them out a short time later to reset the table. I was sick of spending hours cooking a meal that was consumed in minutes.

Sitting in the middle of the bathroom floor, sponge and cleanser in hand and tears streaming down my cheeks, I found myself fussing, crying and praying all at the same time.

God in his loving-kindness came to meet me: "I tell you the truth, whatever you did for one of the least of these brothers of mine, you did for me" (Matthew 25:40).

"Lord, even this?" I asked.

"Especially this," he replied. "Who else is going to do it for me? In all these small ways, you are serving me."

Lovingly reassured and encouraged, I dried my tears and continued to scrub the tub.

Additional Scripture Readings:
Matthew 11:28–30; Philippians 2:1–8

Go to page 223 for your next devotional reading.

clothe yourselves with the Lord Jesus Christ, and do not think about how to gratify the desires of the sinful nature.[a]

The Weak and the Strong

14 Accept him whose faith is weak, without passing judgment on disputable matters. [2]One man's faith allows him to eat everything, but another man, whose faith is weak, eats only vegetables. [3]The man who eats everything must not look down on him who does not, and the man who does not eat everything must not condemn the man who does, for God has accepted him. [4]Who are you to judge someone else's servant? To his own master he stands or falls. And he will stand, for the Lord is able to make him stand.

[5]One man considers one day more sacred than another; another man considers every day alike. Each one should be fully convinced in his own mind. [6]He who regards one day as special, does so to the Lord. He who eats meat, eats to the Lord, for he gives thanks to God; and he who abstains, does so to the Lord and gives thanks to God. [7]For none of us lives to himself alone and none of us dies to himself alone. [8]If we live, we live to the Lord; and if we die, we die to the Lord. So, whether we live or die, we belong to the Lord.

[9]For this very reason, Christ died and returned to life so that he might be the Lord of both the dead and the living. [10]You, then, why do you judge your brother? Or why do you look down on your brother? For we will all stand before God's judgment seat. [11]It is written:

" 'As surely as I live,' says the Lord,
'every knee will bow before me;
　every tongue will confess to
　　God.' "[b]

[12]So then, each of us will give an account of himself to God.

[13]Therefore let us stop passing judgment on one another. Instead, make up your mind not to put any stumbling block or obstacle in your brother's way. [14]As one who is in the Lord Jesus, I am fully convinced that no food[c] is unclean in itself. But if anyone regards something as unclean, then for him it is unclean. [15]If your brother is distressed because of what you eat, you are no longer acting in love. Do not by your eating destroy your brother for whom Christ died. [16]Do not allow what you consider good to be spoken of as evil. [17]For the kingdom of God is not a matter of eating and drinking, but of righteousness, peace and joy in the Holy Spirit, [18]because anyone who serves Christ in this way is pleasing to God and approved by men.

[19]Let us therefore make every effort to do what leads to peace and to mutual edification. [20]Do not destroy the work of God for the sake of food. All food is clean, but it is wrong for a man to eat anything that causes someone else to stumble. [21]It is better not to eat meat or drink wine or to do anything else that will cause your brother to fall.

[22]So whatever you believe about these things keep between yourself and God. Blessed is the man who does not condemn himself by what he approves. [23]But the man who has doubts is condemned if he eats, because his eating is not from faith; and everything that does not come from faith is sin.

15 We who are strong ought to bear with the failings of the weak and not to please ourselves. [2]Each of us should please his neighbor for his good, to build him up. [3]For even Christ did not please himself but, as it is written: "The insults of those who insult you have fallen on me."[d] [4]For everything that was written in the past was written to teach us, so that through endurance and the encouragement of the Scriptures we might have hope.

[5]May the God who gives endurance and encouragement give you a spirit of unity among yourselves as you follow Christ Jesus, [6]so that with one heart and mouth you may glorify the God and Father of our Lord Jesus Christ.

[7]Accept one another, then, just as Christ accepted you, in order to bring praise to God. [8]For I tell you that Christ has become a servant of the Jews[e] on behalf of God's truth, to confirm the promises made to the patriarchs [9]so that the Gentiles may glorify God for his mercy, as it is written:

"Therefore I will praise you among
　　the Gentiles;
　I will sing hymns to your name."[f]

[10]Again, it says,

---

[a]14 Or the flesh　　[b]11 Isaiah 45:23　　[c]14 Or that nothing　　[d]3 Psalm 69:9　　[e]8 Greek circumcision　　[f]9 2 Samuel 22:50; Psalm 18:49

WEEKENDING

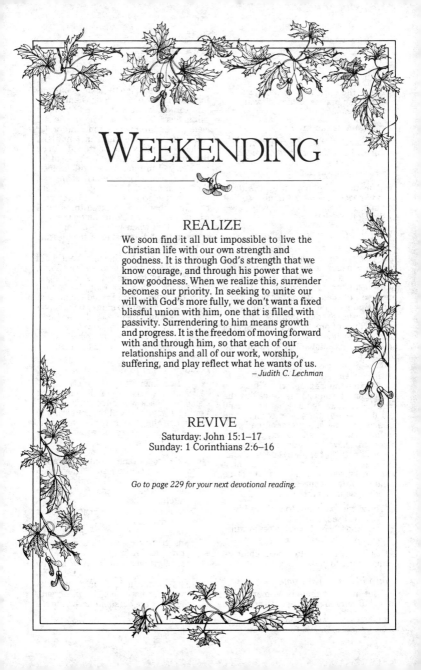

REALIZE

We soon find it all but impossible to live the
Christian life with our own strength and
goodness. It is through God's strength that we
know courage, and through his power that we
know goodness. When we realize this, surrender
becomes our priority. In seeking to unite our
will with God's more fully, we don't want a fixed
blissful union with him, one that is filled with
passivity. Surrendering to him means growth
and progress. It is the freedom of moving forward
with and through him, so that each of our
relationships and all of our work, worship,
suffering, and play reflect what he wants of us.

– Judith C. Lechman

REVIVE

Saturday: John 15:1–17
Sunday: 1 Corinthians 2:6–16

Go to page 229 for your next devotional reading.

"Rejoice, O Gentiles, with his
    people."[a]

[11]And again,

"Praise the Lord, all you Gentiles,
    and sing praises to him, all you
    peoples."[b]

[12]And again, Isaiah says,

"The Root of Jesse will spring up,
    one who will arise to rule over the
        nations;
the Gentiles will hope in him."[c]

[13]May the God of hope fill you with all
joy and peace as you trust in him, so that
you may overflow with hope by the power
of the Holy Spirit.

Paul the Minister to the Gentiles

[14]I myself am convinced, my brothers,
that you yourselves are full of goodness,
complete in knowledge and competent to
instruct one another. [15]I have written you
quite boldly on some points, as if to remind you of them again, because of the
grace God gave me [16]to be a minister of
Christ Jesus to the Gentiles with the
priestly duty of proclaiming the gospel of
God, so that the Gentiles might become
an offering acceptable to God, sanctified
by the Holy Spirit.

[17]Therefore I glory in Christ Jesus in my
service to God. [18]I will not venture to
speak of anything except what Christ has
accomplished through me in leading the
Gentiles to obey God by what I have said
and done— [19]by the power of signs and
miracles, through the power of the Spirit.
So from Jerusalem all the way around to
Illyricum, I have fully proclaimed the gospel of Christ. [20]It has always been my ambition to preach the gospel where Christ
was not known, so that I would not be
building on someone else's foundation.
[21]Rather, as it is written:

"Those who were not told about him
    will see,
and those who have not heard will
    understand."[d]

[22]This is why I have often been hindered
from coming to you.

Paul's Plan to Visit Rome

[23]But now that there is no more place
for me to work in these regions, and since

I have been longing for many years to see
you, [24]I plan to do so when I go to Spain.
I hope to visit you while passing through
and to have you assist me on my journey
there, after I have enjoyed your company
for a while. [25]Now, however, I am on my
way to Jerusalem in the service of the
saints there. [26]For Macedonia and Achaia
were pleased to make a contribution for
the poor among the saints in Jerusalem.
[27]They were pleased to do it, and indeed
they owe it to them. For if the Gentiles
have shared in the Jews' spiritual blessings, they owe it to the Jews to share with
them their material blessings. [28]So after I
have completed this task and have made
sure that they have received this fruit, I
will go to Spain and visit you on the way.
[29]I know that when I come to you, I will
come in the full measure of the blessing
of Christ.

[30]I urge you, brothers, by our Lord
Jesus Christ and by the love of the Spirit,
to join me in my struggle by praying to
God for me. [31]Pray that I may be rescued
from the unbelievers in Judea and that
my service in Jerusalem may be acceptable to the saints there, [32]so that by God's
will I may come to you with joy and
together with you be refreshed. [33]The
God of peace be with you all. Amen.

Personal Greetings

16 I commend to you our sister Pho-
ebe, a servant[e] of the church in
Cenchrea. [2]I ask you to receive her in the
Lord in a way worthy of the saints and to
give her any help she may need from you,
for she has been a great help to many people, including me.

[3]Greet Priscilla[f] and Aquila, my fellow
    workers in Christ Jesus. [4]They risked
    their lives for me. Not only I but all
    the churches of the Gentiles are
    grateful to them.

[5]Greet also the church that meets at
    their house.

Greet my dear friend Epenetus, who
    was the first convert to Christ in the
    province of Asia.

[6]Greet Mary, who worked very hard for
    you.

[7]Greet Andronicus and Junias, my rela-
    tives who have been in prison with
    me. They are outstanding among the

---

[a]10 Deut. 32:43   [b]11 Psalm 117:1   [c]12 Isaiah 11:10   [d]21 Isaiah 52:15   [e]1 Or deaconess
[f]3 Greek Prisca, a variant of Priscilla

apostles, and they were in Christ before I was. [8]Greet Ampliatus, whom I love in the Lord. [9]Greet Urbanus, our fellow worker in Christ, and my dear friend Stachys. [10]Greet Apelles, tested and approved in Christ.

Greet those who belong to the household of Aristobulus. [11]Greet Herodion, my relative.

Greet those in the household of Narcissus who are in the Lord. [12]Greet Tryphena and Tryphosa, those women who work hard in the Lord.

Greet my dear friend Persis, another woman who has worked very hard in the Lord. [13]Greet Rufus, chosen in the Lord, and his mother, who has been a mother to me, too. [14]Greet Asyncritus, Phlegon, Hermes, Patrobas, Hermas and the brothers with them. [15]Greet Philologus, Julia, Nereus and his sister, and Olympas and all the saints with them.

[16]Greet one another with a holy kiss.

All the churches of Christ send greetings.

[17]I urge you, brothers, to watch out for those who cause divisions and put obstacles in your way that are contrary to the teaching you have learned. Keep away from them. [18]For such people are not serving our Lord Christ, but their own appetites. By smooth talk and flattery they deceive the minds of naive people. [19]Everyone has heard about your obedience, so I am full of joy over you; but I want you to be wise about what is good, and innocent about what is evil.

[20]The God of peace will soon crush Satan under your feet.

The grace of our Lord Jesus be with you.

[21]Timothy, my fellow worker, sends his greetings to you, as do Lucius, Jason and Sosipater, my relatives.

[22]I, Tertius, who wrote down this letter, greet you in the Lord.

[23]Gaius, whose hospitality I and the whole church here enjoy, sends you his greetings.

Erastus, who is the city's director of public works, and our brother Quartus send you their greetings. [a]

[25]Now to him who is able to establish you by my gospel and the proclamation of Jesus Christ, according to the revelation of the mystery hidden for long ages past, [26]but now revealed and made known through the prophetic writings by the command of the eternal God, so that all nations might believe and obey him— [27]to the only wise God be glory forever through Jesus Christ! Amen.

---

[a]23 Some manuscripts *their greetings.* [24]*May the grace of our Lord Jesus Christ be with all of you. Amen.*

*PAUL, while staying in Ephesus
(Acts 19), writes this letter to the
church he started in Corinth (Acts
18:1–17). He addresses various problems he has heard about and answers
questions they have asked of him in a
letter (see 1 Corinthians 7:1). He
places a high priority on being obedient
to Christ and on striving for unity, humility and love in the church. As you
read this book, make a decision to seek
the Lord's will in everything you do and
to work hard to be humble, to love others, and to become one in spirit with
your fellow believers.*

1 CORINTHIANS

1 Paul, called to be an apostle of Christ Jesus by the will of God, and our brother Sosthenes,

²To the church of God in Corinth, to those sanctified in Christ Jesus and called to be holy, together with all those everywhere who call on the name of our Lord Jesus Christ—their Lord and ours:

³Grace and peace to you from God our Father and the Lord Jesus Christ.

Thanksgiving

⁴I always thank God for you because of his grace given you in Christ Jesus. ⁵For in him you have been enriched in every way—in all your speaking and in all your knowledge— ⁶because our testimony about Christ was confirmed in you. ⁷Therefore you do not lack any spiritual gift as you eagerly wait for our Lord Jesus Christ to be revealed. ⁸He will keep you strong to the end, so that you will be blameless on the day of our Lord Jesus

Christ. [9]God, who has called you into fellowship with his Son Jesus Christ our Lord, is faithful.

Divisions in the Church

[10]I appeal to you, brothers, in the name of our Lord Jesus Christ, that all of you agree with one another so that there may be no divisions among you and that you may be perfectly united in mind and thought. [11]My brothers, some from Chloe's household have informed me that there are quarrels among you. [12]What I mean is this: One of you says, "I follow Paul"; another, "I follow Apollos"; another, "I follow Cephas[a]"; still another, "I follow Christ."

[13]Is Christ divided? Was Paul crucified for you? Were you baptized into[b] the name of Paul? [14]I am thankful that I did not baptize any of you except Crispus and Gaius, [15]so no one can say that you were baptized into my name. [16](Yes, I also baptized the household of Stephanas; beyond that, I don't remember if I baptized anyone else.) [17]For Christ did not send me to baptize, but to preach the gospel—not with words of human wisdom, lest the cross of Christ be emptied of its power.

Christ the Wisdom and Power of God

[18]For the message of the cross is foolishness to those who are perishing, but to us who are being saved it is the power of God. [19]For it is written:

"I will destroy the wisdom of the
    wise;
the intelligence of the intelligent I
    will frustrate."[c]

[20]Where is the wise man? Where is the scholar? Where is the philosopher of this age? Has not God made foolish the wisdom of the world? [21]For since in the wisdom of God the world through its wisdom did not know him, God was pleased through the foolishness of what was preached to save those who believe. [22]Jews demand miraculous signs and Greeks look for wisdom, [23]but we preach Christ crucified: a stumbling block to Jews and foolishness to Gentiles, [24]but to those whom God has called, both Jews and Greeks, Christ the power of God and the wisdom of God. [25]For the foolishness of God is wiser than man's wisdom, and

the weakness of God is stronger than man's strength.

[26]Brothers, think of what you were when you were called. Not many of you were wise by human standards; not many were influential; not many were of noble birth. [27]But God chose the foolish things of the world to shame the wise; God chose the weak things of the world to shame the strong. [28]He chose the lowly things of this world and the despised things—and the things that are not—to nullify the things that are, [29]so that no one may boast before him. [30]It is because of him that you are in Christ Jesus, who has become for us wisdom from God—that is, our righteousness, holiness and redemption. [31]Therefore, as it is written: "Let him who boasts boast in the Lord."[d]

2 When I came to you, brothers, I did not come with eloquence or superior wisdom as I proclaimed to you the testimony about God.[e] [2]For I resolved to know nothing while I was with you except Jesus Christ and him crucified. [3]I came to you in weakness and fear, and with much trembling. [4]My message and my preaching were not with wise and persuasive words, but with a demonstration of the Spirit's power, [5]so that your faith might not rest on men's wisdom, but on God's power.

Wisdom From the Spirit

[6]We do, however, speak a message of wisdom among the mature, but not the wisdom of this age or of the rulers of this age, who are coming to nothing. [7]No, we speak of God's secret wisdom, a wisdom that has been hidden and that God destined for our glory before time began. [8]None of the rulers of this age understood it, for if they had, they would not have crucified the Lord of glory. [9]However, as it is written:

"No eye has seen,
    no ear has heard,
no mind has conceived
    what God has prepared for those
    who love him"[f]—

[10]but God has revealed it to us by his Spirit.

The Spirit searches all things, even the deep things of God. [11]For who among men knows the thoughts of a man except the man's spirit within him? In the same

---

[a]12 That is, Peter   [b]13 Or in; also in verse 15 manuscripts as I proclaimed to you God's mystery   [c]19 Isaiah 29:14   [d]31 Jer. 9:24   [e]1 Some   [f]9 Isaiah 64:4

way no one knows the thoughts of God except the Spirit of God. [12]We have not received the spirit of the world but the Spirit who is from God, that we may understand what God has freely given us. [13]This is what we speak, not in words taught us by human wisdom but in words taught by the Spirit, expressing spiritual truths in spiritual words.[a] [14]The man without the Spirit does not accept the things that come from the Spirit of God, for they are foolishness to him, and he cannot understand them, because they are spiritually discerned. [15]The spiritual man makes judgments about all things, but he himself is not subject to any man's judgment:

[16]"For who has known the mind of the
  Lord
    that he may instruct him?"[b]

But we have the mind of Christ.

On Divisions in the Church

3 Brothers, I could not address you as spiritual but as worldly—mere infants in Christ. [2]I gave you milk, not solid food, for you were not yet ready for it. Indeed, you are still not ready. [3]You are still worldly. For since there is jealousy and quarreling among you, are you not worldly? Are you not acting like mere men? [4]For when one says, "I follow Paul," and another, "I follow Apollos," are you not mere men?

[5]What, after all, is Apollos? And what is Paul? Only servants, through whom you came to believe—as the Lord has assigned to each his task. [6]I planted the seed, Apollos watered it, but God made it grow. [7]So neither he who plants nor he who waters is anything, but only God, who makes things grow. [8]The man who plants and the man who waters have one purpose, and each will be rewarded according to his own labor. [9]For we are God's fellow workers; you are God's field, God's building.

[10]By the grace God has given me, I laid a foundation as an expert builder, and someone else is building on it. But each one should be careful how he builds. [11]For no one can lay any foundation other than the one already laid, which is Jesus Christ. [12]If any man builds on this foundation using gold, silver, costly stones, wood, hay or straw, [13]his work will be

shown for what it is, because the Day will bring it to light. It will be revealed with fire, and the fire will test the quality of each man's work. [14]If what he has built survives, he will receive his reward. [15]If it is burned up, he will suffer loss; he himself will be saved, but only as one escaping through the flames.

[16]Don't you know that you yourselves are God's temple and that God's Spirit lives in you? [17]If anyone destroys God's temple, God will destroy him; for God's temple is sacred, and you are that temple.

[18]Do not deceive yourselves. If any one of you thinks he is wise by the standards of this age, he should become a "fool" so that he may become wise. [19]For the wisdom of this world is foolishness in God's sight. As it is written: "He catches the wise in their craftiness"[c]; [20]and again, "The Lord knows that the thoughts of the wise are futile."[d] [21]So then, no more boasting about men! All things are yours, [22]whether Paul or Apollos or Cephas[e] or the world or life or death or the present or the future—all are yours, [23]and you are of Christ, and Christ is of God.

Apostles of Christ

4 So then, men ought to regard us as servants of Christ and as those entrusted with the secret things of God. [2]Now it is required that those who have been given a trust must prove faithful. [3]I care very little if I am judged by you or by any human court; indeed, I do not even judge myself. [4]My conscience is clear, but that does not make me innocent. It is the Lord who judges me. [5]Therefore judge nothing before the appointed time; wait till the Lord comes. He will bring to light what is hidden in darkness and will expose the motives of men's hearts. At that time each will receive his praise from God.

[6]Now, brothers, I have applied these things to myself and Apollos for your benefit, so that you may learn from us the meaning of the saying, "Do not go beyond what is written." Then you will not take pride in one man over against another. [7]For who makes you different from anyone else? What do you have that you did not receive? And if you did receive it, why do you boast as though you did not?

[8]Already you have all you want! Already you have become rich! You have become

---

[a]13 Or *Spirit, interpreting spiritual truths to spiritual men*   [b]16 Isaiah 40:13   [c]19 Job 5:13
[d]20 Psalm 94:11   [e]22 That is, Peter

VERSE FOR THE DAY:
1 Corinthians 2:12

AUTHOR:
June Hunt

PASSAGE FOR THE DAY:
1 Corinthians 2:11–16

The Holy Spirit

THE blackout took my neighborhood by surprise. Suddenly in total darkness, I inched my way to the bedside table and fumbled for the flashlight. What frustration . . . it didn't work. How useless—a flashlight that didn't function.

Just as useless is the person unable to function according to God's divine plan. Why? Because God originally designed the human spirit to contain the Holy Spirit. In the garden, Adam and Eve had perfect oneness with God. The Holy Spirit lived in their human spirits and enlightened every aspect of their lives. Once they pronounced their "declaration of independence" from God, however, sin came in and the Spirit went out. The pair were like a flashlight without batteries; with no power on the inside, there was no light on the outside. They spiraled downward into spiritual darkness.

Yet God did not give up on all those who were to be born into that same darkness. "The lamp of the LORD searches the spirit of a man" (Proverbs 20:27). God desired to reunite the Holy Spirit with the human spirit so that they could again be one.

When you feel the frustration of wandering in the dark, know that the Lord has already provided the perfect guide for your life. For "when he, the Spirit of truth, comes, he will guide you into all truth" (John 16:13). Your own personal Counselor, Conscience, Convictor and Comforter fills your soul—your mind, will and emotions—with perfect truth. He teaches your mind, directs your will and guides your emotions. As a result, those who are joined to the Spirit better understand spiritual things (1 Corinthians 2:14).

Like the flashlight, you were designed to shine; but you can never shine with your own power. The Holy Spirit provides the power to produce the light. And once you shine as you were intended to shine, you will never be useless!

Additional Scripture Readings:
Ephesians 5:8–14; 2 Timothy 1:8–14

Go to page 231 for your next devotional reading.

kings—and that without us! How I wish that you really had become kings so that we might be kings with you! 9For it seems to me that God has put us apostles on display at the end of the procession, like men condemned to die in the arena. We have been made a spectacle to the whole universe, to angels as well as to men. 10We are fools for Christ, but you are so wise in Christ! We are weak, but you are strong! You are honored, we are dishonored! 11To this very hour we go hungry and thirsty, we are in rags, we are brutally treated, we are homeless. 12We work hard with our own hands. When we are cursed, we bless; when we are persecuted, we endure it; 13when we are slandered, we answer kindly. Up to this moment we have become the scum of the earth, the refuse of the world.

14I am not writing this to shame you, but to warn you, as my dear children. 15Even though you have ten thousand guardians in Christ, you do not have many fathers, for in Christ Jesus I became your father through the gospel. 16Therefore I urge you to imitate me. 17For this reason I am sending to you Timothy, my son whom I love, who is faithful in the Lord. He will remind you of my way of life in Christ Jesus, which agrees with what I teach everywhere in every church.

18Some of you have become arrogant, as if I were not coming to you. 19But I will come to you very soon, if the Lord is willing, and then I will find out not only how these arrogant people are talking, but what power they have. 20For the kingdom of God is not a matter of talk but of power. 21What do you prefer? Shall I come to you with a whip, or in love and with a gentle spirit?

Expel the Immoral Brother!

5 It is actually reported that there is sexual immorality among you, and of a kind that does not occur even among pagans: A man has his father's wife. 2And you are proud! Shouldn't you rather have been filled with grief and have put out of your fellowship the man who did this? 3Even though I am not physically present, I am with you in spirit. And I have already passed judgment on the one who did this, just as if I were present. 4When you are assembled in the name of our Lord Jesus and I am with you in spirit, and the power

of our Lord Jesus is present, 5hand this man over to Satan, so that the sinful nature[a] may be destroyed and his spirit saved on the day of the Lord.

6Your boasting is not good. Don't you know that a little yeast works through the whole batch of dough? 7Get rid of the old yeast that you may be a new batch without yeast—as you really are. For Christ, our Passover lamb, has been sacrificed. 8Therefore let us keep the Festival, not with the old yeast, the yeast of malice and wickedness, but with bread without yeast, the bread of sincerity and truth.

9I have written you in my letter not to associate with sexually immoral people— 10not at all meaning the people of this world who are immoral, or the greedy and swindlers, or idolaters. In that case you would have to leave this world. 11But now I am writing you that you must not associate with anyone who calls himself a brother but is sexually immoral or greedy, an idolater or a slanderer, a drunkard or a swindler. With such a man do not even eat.

12What business is it of mine to judge those outside the church? Are you not to judge those inside? 13God will judge those outside. "Expel the wicked man from among you."[b]

Lawsuits Among Believers

6 If any of you has a dispute with another, dare he take it before the ungodly for judgment instead of before the saints? 2Do you not know that the saints will judge the world? And if you are to judge the world, are you not competent to judge trivial cases? 3Do you not know that we will judge angels? How much more the things of this life! 4Therefore, if you have disputes about such matters, appoint as judges even men of little account in the church![c] 5I say this to shame you. Is it possible that there is nobody among you wise enough to judge a dispute between believers? 6But instead, one brother goes to law against another— and this in front of unbelievers!

7The very fact that you have lawsuits among you means you have been completely defeated already. Why not rather be wronged? Why not rather be cheated? 8Instead, you yourselves cheat and do wrong, and you do this to your brothers. 9Do you not know that the wicked will

a5 Or that his body; or that the flesh   b13 Deut. 17:7; 19:19; 21:21; 22:21,24; 24:7   c4 Or matters, do you appoint as judges men of little account in the church?

VERSE FOR THE DAY:	AUTHOR:	PASSAGE FOR THE DAY:
1 Corinthians 4:21	Rebecca Manley Pippert	1 Corinthians 4:14–21

With Love and Gentleness

WHEN I first came to Portland, Oregon, I met a student on one of the campuses where I worked. He was brilliant and looked like he was always pondering the esoteric. His hair was always mussy, and in the entire time I knew him, I never once saw him wear a pair of shoes. Rain, sleet or snow, Bill was always barefoot. While he was attending college he had become a Christian. At this time a well-dressed, middle-class church across the street from the campus wanted to develop more of a ministry to the students. They were not sure how to go about it, but they tried to make them feel welcome. One day Bill decided to worship there. He walked into this church, wearing his blue jeans, tee shirt and of course no shoes. People looked a bit uncomfortable, but no one said anything. So Bill began walking down the aisle looking for a seat. The church was quite crowded that Sunday, so as he got down to the front pew and realized that there were no seats, he just squatted on the carpet—perfectly acceptable behavior at a college fellowship, but perhaps unnerving for a church.

Suddenly an elderly man began walking down the aisle toward the boy. Was he going to scold Bill? My friends who saw him approaching said they thought, "You can't blame him. He'd never guess Bill is a Christian. And his world is too distant from Bill's to understand. You can't blame him for what he's going to do."

As the man kept walking slowly down the aisle, the church became utterly silent, all eyes were focused on him, you could not hear anyone breathe. When the man reached Bill, with some difficulty he lowered himself and sat down next to him on the carpet. He and Bill worshiped together on the floor that Sunday. I was told there was not a dry eye in the congregation.

The irony is that probably the only one who failed to see how great the giving had been that Sunday was Bill. But grace is always that way. It gives without the receiver realizing how great the gift really is. As this man walked alongside his brother and loved him with all that he had received from Christ's love, so must we.

Additional Scripture Readings:
1 Samuel 16:7; James 2:1–5

Go to page 232 for your next devotional reading.

not inherit the kingdom of God? Do not be deceived: Neither the sexually immoral nor idolaters nor adulterers nor male prostitutes nor homosexual offenders [10]nor thieves nor the greedy nor drunkards nor slanderers nor swindlers will inherit the kingdom of God. [11]And that is what some of you were. But you were washed, you were sanctified, you were justified in the name of the Lord Jesus Christ and by the Spirit of our God.

Sexual Immorality

[12]"Everything is permissible for me"—but not everything is beneficial. "Everything is permissible for me"—but I will not be mastered by anything. [13]"Food for the stomach and the stomach for food"—but God will destroy them both. The body is not meant for sexual immorality, but for the Lord, and the Lord for the body. [14]By his power God raised the Lord from the dead, and he will raise us also. [15]Do you not know that your bodies are members of Christ himself? Shall I then take the members of Christ and unite them with a prostitute? Never! [16]Do you not know that he who unites himself with a prostitute is one with her in body? For it is said, "The two will become one

WEDNESDAY

VERSE FOR THE DAY: AUTHOR: PASSAGE FOR THE DAY:
1 Corinthians 5:3   Susan L. Lenzkes   1 Corinthians 5:1–5

Saying Good-by

ONE of the most heartrending moments of life comes when close friends say good-by, knowing that many miles will separate them from their countless shared experiences. Distance takes on the menacing look of an enemy when it dares to stand between such friends!

Soon they will find themselves building protective shields around the ache of separation. They will feel themselves both courting and resisting the urge to clip those threads that bind their hearts in love. And they will argue repeatedly with a voice that warns, "Don't build new friendships—life has a demolition crew around every corner!"

But discovery lies ahead. Real friendship is resilient. The very cords that make it strong—commitment, creativity, caring and sharing—are elastic, and friends can remain committed and even more creative in their long-distance sharing.

Now cards and letters—stackable memories to be relived over a cup of coffee—will communicate love in indelible ink. Now calls—where the value of every word, enhanced by the coming bill—will set precious priorities and release sentiment from the soul. Anticipated visits will be far richer for their infrequency. Thoughts and feelings long saved and protected will be unlocked and shared.

Best of all, a discovery will be made that hearts in harmony can just as easily carry a tune long-distance.

Additional Scripture Readings: *Go to page 236 for your next*
1 Samuel 20:41–42; Philippians 2:25–30   *devotional reading.*

flesh."ᵃ ¹⁷But he who unites himself with the Lord is one with him in spirit.

¹⁸Flee from sexual immorality. All other sins a man commits are outside his body, but he who sins sexually sins against his own body. ¹⁹Do you not know that your body is a temple of the Holy Spirit, who is in you, whom you have received from God? You are not your own; ²⁰you were bought at a price. Therefore honor God with your body.

Marriage

7 Now for the matters you wrote about: It is good for a man not to marry.ᵇ ²But since there is so much immorality, each man should have his own wife, and each woman her own husband. ³The husband should fulfill his marital duty to his wife, and likewise the wife to her husband. ⁴The wife's body does not belong to her alone but also to her husband. In the same way, the husband's body does not belong to him alone but also to his wife. ⁵Do not deprive each other except by mutual consent and for a time, so that you may devote yourselves to prayer. Then come together again so that Satan will not tempt you because of your lack of self-control. ⁶I say this as a concession, not as a command. ⁷I wish that all men were as I am. But each man has his own gift from God; one has this gift, another has that.

⁸Now to the unmarried and the widows I say: It is good for them to stay unmarried, as I am. ⁹But if they cannot control themselves, they should marry, for it is better to marry than to burn with passion.

¹⁰To the married I give this command (not I, but the Lord): A wife must not separate from her husband. ¹¹But if she does, she must remain unmarried or else be reconciled to her husband. And a husband must not divorce his wife.

¹²To the rest I say this (I, not the Lord): If any brother has a wife who is not a believer and she is willing to live with him, he must not divorce her. ¹³And if a woman has a husband who is not a believer and he is willing to live with her, she must not divorce him. ¹⁴For the unbelieving husband has been sanctified through his wife, and the unbelieving wife has been sanctified through her believing husband. Otherwise your children would be unclean, but as it is, they are holy.

¹⁵But if the unbeliever leaves, let him do so. A believing man or woman is not bound in such circumstances; God has called us to live in peace. ¹⁶How do you know, wife, whether you will save your husband? Or, how do you know, husband, whether you will save your wife?

¹⁷Nevertheless, each one should retain the place in life that the Lord assigned to him and to which God has called him. This is the rule I lay down in all the churches. ¹⁸Was a man already circumcised when he was called? He should not become uncircumcised. Was a man uncircumcised when he was called? He should not be circumcised. ¹⁹Circumcision is nothing and uncircumcision is nothing. Keeping God's commands is what counts. ²⁰Each one should remain in the situation which he was in when God called him. ²¹Were you a slave when you were called? Don't let it trouble you—although if you can gain your freedom, do so. ²²For he who was a slave when he was called by the Lord is the Lord's freedman; similarly, he who was a free man when he was called is Christ's slave. ²³You were bought at a price; do not become slaves of men. ²⁴Brothers, each man, as responsible to God, should remain in the situation God called him to.

²⁵Now about virgins: I have no command from the Lord, but I give a judgment as one who by the Lord's mercy is trustworthy. ²⁶Because of the present crisis, I think that it is good for you to remain as you are. ²⁷Are you married? Do not seek a divorce. Are you unmarried? Do not look for a wife. ²⁸But if you do marry, you have not sinned; and if a virgin marries, she has not sinned. But those who marry will face many troubles in this life, and I want to spare you this.

²⁹What I mean, brothers, is that the time is short. From now on those who have wives should live as if they had none; ³⁰those who mourn, as if they did not; those who are happy, as if they were not; those who buy something, as if it were not theirs to keep; ³¹those who use the things of the world, as if not engrossed in them. For this world in its present form is passing away.

³²I would like you to be free from concern. An unmarried man is concerned about the Lord's affairs—how he can please the Lord. ³³But a married man is concerned about the affairs of this world—how he can please his wife— ³⁴and his

ᵃ16 Gen. 2:24   ᵇ1 Or "It is good for a man not to have sexual relations with a woman."

interests are divided. An unmarried woman or virgin is concerned about the Lord's affairs: Her aim is to be devoted to the Lord in both body and spirit. But a married woman is concerned about the affairs of this world—how she can please her husband. [35]I am saying this for your own good, not to restrict you, but that you may live in a right way in undivided devotion to the Lord.

[36]If anyone thinks he is acting improperly toward the virgin he is engaged to, and if she is getting along in years and he feels he ought to marry, he should do as he wants. He is not sinning. They should get married. [37]But the man who has settled the matter in his own mind, who is under no compulsion but has control over his own will, and who has made up his mind not to marry the virgin—this man also does the right thing. [38]So then, he who marries the virgin does right, but he who does not marry her does even better.[a]

[39]A woman is bound to her husband as long as he lives. But if her husband dies, she is free to marry anyone she wishes, but he must belong to the Lord. [40]In my judgment, she is happier if she stays as she is—and I think that I too have the Spirit of God.

Food Sacrificed to Idols

8 Now about food sacrificed to idols: We know that we all possess knowledge.[b] Knowledge puffs up, but love builds up. [2]The man who thinks he knows something does not yet know as he ought to know. [3]But the man who loves God is known by God.

[4]So then, about eating food sacrificed to idols: We know that an idol is nothing at all in the world and that there is no God but one. [5]For even if there are so-called gods, whether in heaven or on earth (as indeed there are many "gods" and many "lords"), [6]yet for us there is but one God, the Father, from whom all things came and for whom we live; and there is but one Lord, Jesus Christ, through whom all things came and through whom we live.

[7]But not everyone knows this. Some people are still so accustomed to idols that when they eat such food they think of it as having been sacrificed to an idol, and since their conscience is weak, it is defiled. [8]But food does not bring us near to God; we are no worse if we do not eat, and no better if we do.

[9]Be careful, however, that the exercise of your freedom does not become a stumbling block to the weak. [10]For if anyone with a weak conscience sees you who have this knowledge eating in an idol's temple, won't he be emboldened to eat what has been sacrificed to idols? [11]So this weak brother, for whom Christ died, is destroyed by your knowledge. [12]When you sin against your brothers in this way and wound their weak conscience, you sin against Christ. [13]Therefore, if what I eat causes my brother to fall into sin, I will never eat meat again, so that I will not cause him to fall.

The Rights of an Apostle

9 Am I not free? Am I not an apostle? Have I not seen Jesus our Lord? Are you not the result of my work in the Lord? [2]Even though I may not be an apostle to others, surely I am to you! For you are the seal of my apostleship in the Lord.

[3]This is my defense to those who sit in judgment on me. [4]Don't we have the right to food and drink? [5]Don't we have the right to take a believing wife along with us, as do the other apostles and the Lord's brothers and Cephas[c]? [6]Or is it only I and Barnabas who must work for a living?

[7]Who serves as a soldier at his own expense? Who plants a vineyard and does not eat of its grapes? Who tends a flock and does not drink of the milk? [8]Do I say this merely from a human point of view? Doesn't the Law say the same thing? [9]For it is written in the Law of Moses: "Do not muzzle an ox while it is treading out the grain."[d] Is it about oxen that God is concerned? [10]Surely he says this for us, doesn't he? Yes, this was written for us, because when the plowman plows and the thresher threshes, they ought to do so in the hope of sharing in the harvest. [11]If we have sown spiritual seed among you, is it

---

[a]36-38 Or [36]If anyone thinks he is not treating his daughter properly, and if she is getting along in years, and he feels she ought to marry, he should do as he wants. He is not sinning. He should let her get married. [37]But the man who has settled the matter in his own mind, who is under no compulsion but has control over his own will, and who has made up his mind to keep the virgin unmarried—this man also does the right thing. [38]So then, he who gives his virgin in marriage does right, but he who does not give her in marriage does even better.   [b]1 Or "We all possess knowledge," as you say   [c]5 That is, Peter   [d]9 Deut. 25:4

too much if we reap a material harvest from you? [12]If others have this right of support from you, shouldn't we have it all the more?

But we did not use this right. On the contrary, we put up with anything rather than hinder the gospel of Christ. [13]Don't you know that those who work in the temple get their food from the temple, and those who serve at the altar share in what is offered on the altar? [14]In the same way, the Lord has commanded that those who preach the gospel should receive their living from the gospel.

[15]But I have not used any of these rights. And I am not writing this in the hope that you will do such things for me. I would rather die than have anyone deprive me of this boast. [16]Yet when I preach the gospel, I cannot boast, for I am compelled to preach. Woe to me if I do not preach the gospel! [17]If I preach voluntarily, I have a reward; if not voluntarily, I am simply discharging the trust committed to me. [18]What then is my reward? Just this: that in preaching the gospel I may offer it free of charge, and so not make use of my rights in preaching it.

[19]Though I am free and belong to no man, I make myself a slave to everyone, to win as many as possible. [20]To the Jews I became like a Jew, to win the Jews. To those under the law I became like one under the law (though I myself am not under the law), so as to win those under the law. [21]To those not having the law I became like one not having the law (though I am not free from God's law but am under Christ's law), so as to win those not having the law. [22]To the weak I became weak, to win the weak. I have become all things to all men so that by all possible means I might save some. [23]I do all this for the sake of the gospel, that I may share in its blessings.

[24]Do you not know that in a race all the runners run, but only one gets the prize? Run in such a way as to get the prize. [25]Everyone who competes in the games goes into strict training. They do it to get a crown that will not last; but we do it to get a crown that will last forever. [26]Therefore I do not run like a man running aimlessly; I do not fight like a man beating the air. [27]No, I beat my body and make it my slave so that after I have preached to others, I myself will not be disqualified for the prize.

Warnings From Israel's History

10 For I do not want you to be ignorant of the fact, brothers, that our forefathers were all under the cloud and that they all passed through the sea. [2]They were all baptized into Moses in the cloud and in the sea. [3]They all ate the same spiritual food [4]and drank the same spiritual drink; for they drank from the spiritual rock that accompanied them, and that rock was Christ. [5]Nevertheless, God was not pleased with most of them; their bodies were scattered over the desert.

[6]Now these things occurred as examples[a] to keep us from setting our hearts on evil things as they did. [7]Do not be idolaters, as some of them were; as it is written: "The people sat down to eat and drink and got up to indulge in pagan revelry."[b] [8]We should not commit sexual immorality, as some of them did—and in one day twenty-three thousand of them died. [9]We should not test the Lord, as some of them did—and were killed by snakes. [10]And do not grumble, as some of them did—and were killed by the destroying angel.

[11]These things happened to them as examples and were written down as warnings for us, on whom the fulfillment of the ages has come. [12]So, if you think you are standing firm, be careful that you don't fall! [13]No temptation has seized you except what is common to man. And God is faithful; he will not let you be tempted beyond what you can bear. But when you are tempted, he will also provide a way out so that you can stand up under it.

Idol Feasts and the Lord's Supper

[14]Therefore, my dear friends, flee from idolatry. [15]I speak to sensible people; judge for yourselves what I say. [16]Is not the cup of thanksgiving for which we give thanks a participation in the blood of Christ? And is not the bread that we break a participation in the body of Christ? [17]Because there is one loaf, we, who are many, are one body, for we all partake of the one loaf.

[18]Consider the people of Israel: Do not those who eat the sacrifices participate in the altar? [19]Do I mean then that a sacrifice offered to an idol is anything, or that an idol is anything? [20]No, but the sacrifices of pagans are offered to demons, not

a6 Or types; also in verse 11   b7 Exodus 32:6

VERSE FOR THE DAY:
1 Corinthians 10:13

AUTHOR:
June Hunt

PASSAGE FOR THE DAY:
1 Corinthians 10:1–13

God Gives Me Strength

FOR thousands of years a popular club has been offering memberships throughout the world. It's a prolific club. It's the "I Can't" club.

Under the bylaws, club members are required to make "I can't" statements with conviction: "I can't help but hate after what he's done to me." "I can't quit this sin." "I can't forgive again!" Because of the fervor of these statements, it sounds as if each is an unchangeable, universal law.

Everyone is subject to one law of science, the law of gravity—the force that pulls every object to the center of the earth. In a similar way, members of the "I Can't" club are prisoners to the downward pull of defeat—they are not only ground-bound, but sin-bound.

Do you feel bound to a specific sin? Does quitting the "I Can't" club seem impossible? The Father refuses to let "can't" be the universal password of his children. At your salvation he gave you the Spirit of God so that you would have the *strength* of God. He made it possible for you to overcome any sin. How? By replacing one law with another:

> The law of the Spirit of life set me free from the law
> of sin and death (Romans 8:2).

Let's think about the law of gravity again. Can you imagine a 190-ton mass of metal rising against gravity's pull? Impossible? It can't be done! Oh, yes it can . . . by using a "higher law." When you, in faith, give yourself over to the principle of aerodynamics, you can enter an airplane with full confidence that it will fly you from one city to another. You are no longer ground-bound.

Similarly, when you, in faith, give yourself over to the Spirit's control, the "I can't" statements will no longer bind you. When God fills your spirit with his Spirit and infuses you with his strength, you are no longer captive to any temptation. Every *can't* becomes a *can*.

Additional Scripture Readings:
2 Corinthians 12:7–10; 1 Peter 5:6–11

*Go to page 238 for your next
devotional reading.*

to God, and I do not want you to be participants with demons. [21]You cannot drink the cup of the Lord and the cup of demons too; you cannot have a part in both the Lord's table and the table of demons. [22]Are we trying to arouse the Lord's jealousy? Are we stronger than he?

The Believer's Freedom

[23]"Everything is permissible"—but not everything is beneficial. "Everything is permissible"—but not everything is constructive. [24]Nobody should seek his own good, but the good of others.

[25]Eat anything sold in the meat market without raising questions of conscience, [26]for, "The earth is the Lord's, and everything in it."[a]

[27]If some unbeliever invites you to a meal and you want to go, eat whatever is put before you without raising questions of conscience. [28]But if anyone says to you, "This has been offered in sacrifice," then do not eat it, both for the sake of the man who told you and for conscience' sake[b]— [29]the other man's conscience, I mean, not yours. For why should my freedom be judged by another's conscience? [30]If I take part in the meal with thankfulness, why am I denounced because of something I thank God for?

[31]So whether you eat or drink or whatever you do, do it all for the glory of God. [32]Do not cause anyone to stumble, whether Jews, Greeks or the church of God— [33]even as I try to please everybody in every way. For I am not seeking my own good but the good of many, so that they may be saved. [1]Follow my example, as I follow the example of Christ.

Propriety in Worship

[2]I praise you for remembering me in everything and for holding to the teachings,[c] just as I passed them on to you.

[3]Now I want you to realize that the head of every man is Christ, and the head of the woman is man, and the head of Christ is God. [4]Every man who prays or prophesies with his head covered dishonors his head. [5]And every woman who

prays or prophesies with her head uncovered dishonors her head—it is just as though her head were shaved. [6]If a woman does not cover her head, she should have her hair cut off; and if it is a disgrace for a woman to have her hair cut or shaved off, she should cover her head. [7]A man ought not to cover his head,[d] since he is the image and glory of God; but the woman is the glory of man. [8]For man did not come from woman, but woman from man; [9]neither was man created for woman, but woman for man. [10]For this reason, and because of the angels, the woman ought to have a sign of authority on her head.

[11]In the Lord, however, woman is not independent of man, nor is man independent of woman. [12]For as woman came from man, so also man is born of woman. But everything comes from God. [13]Judge for yourselves: Is it proper for a woman to pray to God with her head uncovered? [14]Does not the very nature of things teach you that if a man has long hair, it is a disgrace to him, [15]but that if a woman has long hair, it is her glory? For long hair is given to her as a covering. [16]If anyone wants to be contentious about this, we have no other practice—nor do the churches of God.

The Lord's Supper

[17]In the following directives I have no praise for you, for your meetings do more harm than good. [18]In the first place, I hear that when you come together as a church, there are divisions among you, and to some extent I believe it. [19]No doubt there have to be differences among you to show which of you have God's approval. [20]When you come together, it is not the Lord's Supper you eat, [21]for as you eat, each of you goes ahead without waiting for anybody else. One remains hungry, another gets drunk. [22]Don't you have homes to eat and drink in? Or do you despise the church of God and humiliate those who have nothing? What shall I say to you? Shall I praise you for this? Certainly not!

[23]For I received from the Lord what I also passed on to you: The Lord Jesus, on

---

[a]26 Psalm 24:1   [b]28 Some manuscripts conscience' sake, for "the earth is the Lord's and everything in it"   [c]2 Or traditions   [d]4-7 Or [4]Every man who prays or prophesies with long hair dishonors his [5]Head. And every woman who prays or prophesies with no covering ,of hair, on her head dishonors her head— she is just like one of the "shorn women." [6]If a woman has no covering, let her be for now with short hair, but since it is a disgrace for a woman to have her hair shorn or shaved, she should grow it again. [7]A man ought not to have long hair

VERSE FOR THE DAY:
1 Corinthians 11:2

AUTHOR:
Alma Barkman

PASSAGE FOR THE DAY:
1 Corinthians 11:2–16

Pass It On

BACK in the days of our courtship, friend Hubby suggested I get the recipe for Jam Gem cookies from his mother. I duly inquired as to the ingredients, mixed up a batch and proudly served them to him the next time he came to call.

"They are quite good," he remarked as he reached for seconds.

"Quite good" was not good enough. I tried again. And again. I could never solicit the kind of praise I hoped to hear.

It wasn't until long after we were married that he very sheepishly divulged the reason for his reserved comments. "Those cookies have to be a certain shape to taste best."

"And what shape is that, pray tell?"

"Oval and about so big."

I went on a wild goose chase the likes of which uncovered every conceivable cookie cutter ever invented, but not one was "oval and about so big."

Months later I decided to confide in his mother. "Do you know," I whispered, "that your son insists that a genuine Jam Gem cookie has to be oval and about so big?"

She chuckled. "I suppose that's because I always made them that shape. Would you like my cookie cutter?"

I literally pounced on the offer. Wiping her hands on her apron, she pulled open a drawer and produced the elusive cookie cutter. It was the lid of a talcum powder can.

I have it still. Most people would consider it just another piece of junk, but my teenage daughter already has claimed it as an heirloom.

I suppose every family has little traditions that are handed down from one generation to the next. The family of God is no exception. Those spiritual values that have shaped our lives are cherished and retained for the benefit of our children. Sometimes, like Grandma's cookie cutter, they are temporarily forgotten, tossed aside in the clutter of daily living.

But eventually a growing emptiness creates a hunger for the Christian principles that once guided us, the fellowship that church involvement provided us, the family devotions that once united us. I believe the Holy Spirit uses our childhood memories to whet our appetite for the things of God. As we obediently search out his will and obey it, we in turn are establishing a Christian tradition for our children.

Additional Scripture Readings:
Psalm 78:4–7; 2 Timothy 3:14–15

Go to page 240 for your next devotional reading.

the night he was betrayed, took bread, 24and when he had given thanks, he broke it and said, "This is my body, which is for you; do this in remembrance of me." 25In the same way, after supper he took the cup, saying, "This cup is the new covenant in my blood; do this, whenever you drink it, in remembrance of me." 26For whenever you eat this bread and drink this cup, you proclaim the Lord's death until he comes.

27Therefore, whoever eats the bread or drinks the cup of the Lord in an unworthy manner will be guilty of sinning against the body and blood of the Lord. 28A man ought to examine himself before he eats of the bread and drinks of the cup. 29For anyone who eats and drinks without recognizing the body of the Lord eats and drinks judgment on himself. 30That is why many among you are weak and sick, and a number of you have fallen asleep. 31But if we judged ourselves, we would not come under judgment. 32When we are judged by the Lord, we are being disciplined so that we will not be condemned with the world.

33So then, my brothers, when you come together to eat, wait for each other. 34If anyone is hungry, he should eat at home, so that when you meet together it may not result in judgment.

And when I come I will give further directions.

Spiritual Gifts

12 Now about spiritual gifts, brothers, I do not want you to be ignorant. 2You know that when you were pagans, somehow or other you were influenced and led astray to mute idols. 3Therefore I tell you that no one who is speaking by the Spirit of God says, "Jesus be cursed," and no one can say, "Jesus is Lord," except by the Holy Spirit.

4There are different kinds of gifts, but the same Spirit. 5There are different kinds of service, but the same Lord. 6There are different kinds of working, but the same God works all of them in all men.

7Now to each one the manifestation of the Spirit is given for the common good. 8To one there is given through the Spirit the message of wisdom, to another the message of knowledge by means of the same Spirit, 9to another faith by the same

Spirit, to another gifts of healing by that one Spirit, 10to another miraculous powers, to another prophecy, to another distinguishing between spirits, to another speaking in different kinds of tongues,a and to still another the interpretation of tongues.a 11All these are the work of one and the same Spirit, and he gives them to each one, just as he determines.

One Body, Many Parts

12The body is a unit, though it is made up of many parts; and though all its parts are many, they form one body. So it is with Christ. 13For we were all baptized byb one Spirit into one body—whether Jews or Greeks, slave or free—and we were all given the one Spirit to drink.

14Now the body is not made up of one part but of many. 15If the foot should say, "Because I am not a hand, I do not belong to the body," it would not for that reason cease to be part of the body. 16And if the ear should say, "Because I am not an eye, I do not belong to the body," it would not for that reason cease to be part of the body. 17If the whole body were an eye, where would the sense of hearing be? If the whole body were an ear, where would the sense of smell be? 18But in fact God has arranged the parts in the body, every one of them, just as he wanted them to be. 19If they were all one part, where would the body be? 20As it is, there are many parts, but one body.

21The eye cannot say to the hand, "I don't need you!" And the head cannot say to the feet, "I don't need you!" 22On the contrary, those parts of the body that seem to be weaker are indispensable, 23and the parts that we think are less honorable we treat with special honor. And the parts that are unpresentable are treated with special modesty, 24while our presentable parts need no special treatment. But God has combined the members of the body and has given greater honor to the parts that lacked it, 25so that there should be no division in the body, but that its parts should have equal concern for each other. 26If one part suffers, every part suffers with it; if one part is honored, every part rejoices with it.

27Now you are the body of Christ, and each one of you is a part of it. 28And in the church God has appointed first of all apostles, second prophets, third teachers,

---

a10 Or *languages*; also in verse 28   b13 Or *with*; or *in*

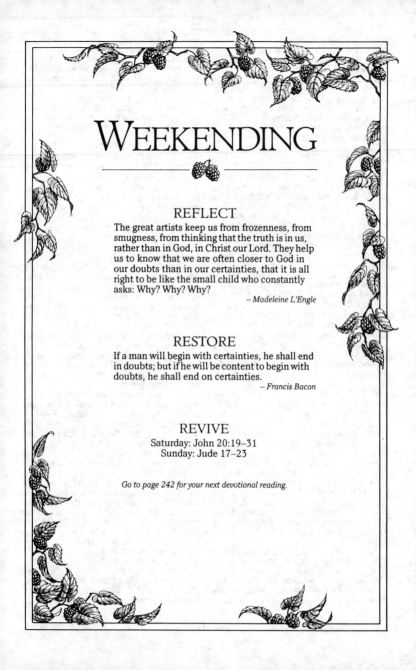

WEEKENDING

REFLECT

The great artists keep us from frozenness, from
smugness, from thinking that the truth is in us,
rather than in God, in Christ our Lord. They help
us to know that we are often closer to God in
our doubts than our certainties, that it is all
right to be like the small child who constantly
asks: Why? Why? Why?

– Madeleine L'Engle

RESTORE

If a man will begin with certainties, he shall end
in doubts; but if he will be content to begin with
doubts, he shall end on certainties.

– Francis Bacon

REVIVE

Saturday: John 20:19–31
Sunday: Jude 17–23

Go to page 242 for your next devotional reading.

then workers of miracles, also those having gifts of healing, those able to help others, those with gifts of administration, and those speaking in different kinds of tongues. ²⁹Are all apostles? Are all prophets? Are all teachers? Do all work miracles? ³⁰Do all have gifts of healing? Do all speak in tongues*a*? Do all interpret? ³¹But eagerly desire*b* the greater gifts.

Love

And now I will show you the most excellent way.

13 If I speak in the tongues*c* of men and of angels, but have not love, I am only a resounding gong or a clanging cymbal. ²If I have the gift of prophecy and can fathom all mysteries and all knowledge, and if I have a faith that can move mountains, but have not love, I am nothing. ³If I give all I possess to the poor and surrender my body to the flames,*d* but have not love, I gain nothing.

⁴Love is patient, love is kind. It does not envy, it does not boast, it is not proud. ⁵It is not rude, it is not self-seeking, it is not easily angered, it keeps no record of wrongs. ⁶Love does not delight in evil but rejoices with the truth. ⁷It always protects, always trusts, always hopes, always perseveres.

⁸Love never fails. But where there are prophecies, they will cease; where there are tongues, they will be stilled; where there is knowledge, it will pass away. ⁹For we know in part and we prophesy in part, ¹⁰but when perfection comes, the imperfect disappears. ¹¹When I was a child, I talked like a child, I thought like a child, I reasoned like a child. When I became a man, I put childish ways behind me. ¹²Now we see but a poor reflection as in a mirror; then we shall see face to face. Now I know in part; then I shall know fully, even as I am fully known.

¹³And now these three remain: faith, hope and love. But the greatest of these is love.

Gifts of Prophecy and Tongues

14 Follow the way of love and eagerly desire spiritual gifts, especially the gift of prophecy. ²For anyone who speaks in a tongue*e* does not speak to men but to God. Indeed, no one understands him; he utters mysteries with his spirit.*f* ³But everyone who prophesies speaks to men for their strengthening, encouragement and comfort. ⁴He who speaks in a tongue edifies himself, but he who prophesies edifies the church. ⁵I would like every one of you to speak in tongues,*g* but I would rather have you prophesy. He who prophesies is greater than one who speaks in tongues,*g* unless he interprets, so that the church may be edified.

⁶Now, brothers, if I come to you and speak in tongues, what good will I be to you, unless I bring you some revelation or knowledge or prophecy or word of instruction? ⁷Even in the case of lifeless things that make sounds, such as the flute or harp, how will anyone know what tune is being played unless there is a distinction in the notes? ⁸Again, if the trumpet does not sound a clear call, who will get ready for battle? ⁹So it is with you. Unless you speak intelligible words with your tongue, how will anyone know what you are saying? You will just be speaking into the air. ¹⁰Undoubtedly there are all sorts of languages in the world, yet none of them is without meaning. ¹¹If then I do not grasp the meaning of what someone is saying, I am a foreigner to the speaker, and he is a foreigner to me. ¹²So it is with you. Since you are eager to have spiritual gifts, try to excel in gifts that build up the church.

¹³For this reason anyone who speaks in a tongue should pray that he may interpret what he says. ¹⁴For if I pray in a tongue, my spirit prays, but my mind is unfruitful. ¹⁵So what shall I do? I will pray with my spirit, but I will also pray with my mind; I will sing with my spirit, but I will also sing with my mind. ¹⁶If you are praising God with your spirit, how can one who finds himself among those who do not understand*h* say "Amen" to your thanksgiving, since he does not know what you are saying? ¹⁷You may be giving thanks well enough, but the other man is not edified.

¹⁸I thank God that I speak in tongues more than all of you. ¹⁹But in the church

---

*a*30 Or *other languages*   *b*31 Or *But you are eagerly desiring*   *c*1 Or *languages*   *d*3 Some early manuscripts *body that I may boast*   *e*2 Or *another language*; also in verses 4, 13, 14, 19, 26 and 27   *f*2 Or *by the Spirit*   *g*5 Or *other languages*; also in verses 6, 18, 22, 23 and 39   *h*16 Or *among the inquirers*

I would rather speak five intelligible words to instruct others than ten thousand words in a tongue.

²⁰Brothers, stop thinking like children. In regard to evil be infants, but in your thinking be adults. ²¹In the Law it is written:

"Through men of strange tongues
    and through the lips of foreigners
I will speak to this people,
    but even then they will not listen
        to me,"^a
says the Lord.

²²Tongues, then, are a sign, not for believers but for unbelievers; prophecy, however, is for believers, not for unbelievers. ²³So if the whole church comes together and everyone speaks in tongues, and some who do not understand^b or some unbelievers come in, will they not say that you are out of your mind? ²⁴But if an unbeliever or someone who does not understand^c comes in while everybody is prophesying, he will be convinced by all that he is a sinner and will be judged by all, ²⁵and the secrets of his heart will be laid bare. So he will fall down and worship God, exclaiming, "God is really among you!"

Orderly Worship

²⁶What then shall we say, brothers? When you come together, everyone has a hymn, or a word of instruction, a revelation, a tongue or an interpretation. All of these must be done for the strengthening of the church. ²⁷If anyone speaks in a

^a21 Isaiah 28:11,12   ^b23 Or *some inquirers*   ^c24 Or *or some inquirer*

MONDAY

VERSE FOR THE DAY:	AUTHOR:	PASSAGE FOR THE DAY:
1 Corinthians 13:5	Shirley Pope Waite	1 Corinthians 13:1–13

Love Is Not "Rudeness"

WE have a Japanese "daughter," whom we first met when we hosted her and a classmate during a student exchange program. Later we were able to visit Sayuri and her family in Kamakura, Japan.

Our guidebook had told us that the Japanese are a very correct, proper people and offense is easily taken. So we were a little surprised when the family said good-by with such emotion. Sayuri shed tears and pointed to her watch, which she kept set at Walla Walla time.

Our surprise continued when we received the next letter from Sayuri. She ended with these words, "Can I write 'love'! Is it rudeness? But, I love you."

Yes, Sayuri, you may write love any time you want. Love is never rudeness. In fact 1 Corinthians 13 states, "Love . . . is not rude." Love transcends all cultures, races, nationalities and social status.

We love you too, dear Sayuri, our Japanese "daughter"!

Additional Scripture Readings:
John 13:34–35; 1 John 4:19–21

Go to page 243 for your next
devotional reading.

tongue, two—or at the most three—should speak, one at a time, and someone must interpret. [28]If there is no interpreter, the speaker should keep quiet in the church and speak to himself and God.

[29]Two or three prophets should speak, and the others should weigh carefully what is said. [30]And if a revelation comes to someone who is sitting down, the first speaker should stop. [31]For you can all prophesy in turn so that everyone may be instructed and encouraged. [32]The spirits of prophets are subject to the control of prophets. [33]For God is not a God of disorder but of peace.

As in all the congregations of the saints, [34]women should remain silent in the churches. They are not allowed to speak, but must be in submission, as the Law says. [35]If they want to inquire about something, they should ask their own husbands at home; for it is disgraceful for a woman to speak in the church.

[36]Did the word of God originate with you? Or are you the only people it has reached? [37]If anybody thinks he is a prophet or spiritually gifted, let him acknowledge that what I am writing to you is the Lord's command. [38]If he ignores this, he himself will be ignored.[a]

[39]Therefore, my brothers, be eager to prophesy, and do not forbid speaking in tongues. [40]But everything should be done in a fitting and orderly way.

---

[a]38 Some manuscripts *If he is ignorant of this, let him be ignorant*

TUESDAY

VERSE FOR THE DAY:
1 Corinthians 14:7–8

AUTHOR:
Delores Taylor

PASSAGE FOR THE DAY:
1 Corinthians 14:6–12

Sounds of Distinction

PAUL says that it is better to speak five words that people can understand than to speak volumes that they cannot comprehend. What good is a flute, harp or trumpet unless they play the notes written on the score? But when each player plays the notes written for her instrument, the result is beautiful harmony.

Paul adds that if the trumpet does not give a clear sound, men will not know to prepare for battle. How interesting that Paul mentions both types of instruments. The flute and harp are soft, melodic instruments. Some people are like that—so gentle, kind, comforting and calming. But there is also a need in God's musical ensemble for a trumpeter to warn us of his approach.

When the "notes" are sounding clear, the unbeliever who comes into our Christian gatherings will be convicted of his sin, and his heart will be laid open to the Word of God. Another lost one will have joined God's family.

May he help us to live according to the notes in the "Book."

Additional Scripture Readings:
Judges 7:17–22; Ezekiel 33:1–9

Go to page 248 for your next devotional reading.

The Resurrection of Christ

15 Now, brothers, I want to remind you of the gospel I preached to you, which you received and on which you have taken your stand. ²By this gospel you are saved, if you hold firmly to the word I preached to you. Otherwise, you have believed in vain.

³For what I received I passed on to you as of first importance*ᵃ*: that Christ died for our sins according to the Scriptures, ⁴that he was buried, that he was raised on the third day according to the Scriptures, ⁵and that he appeared to Peter,*ᵇ* and then to the Twelve. ⁶After that, he appeared to more than five hundred of the brothers at the same time, most of whom are still living, though some have fallen asleep. ⁷Then he appeared to James, then to all the apostles, ⁸and last of all he appeared to me also, as to one abnormally born.

⁹For I am the least of the apostles and do not even deserve to be called an apostle, because I persecuted the church of God. ¹⁰But by the grace of God I am what I am, and his grace to me was not without effect. No, I worked harder than all of them—yet not I, but the grace of God that was with me. ¹¹Whether, then, it was I or they, this is what we preach, and this is what you believed.

The Resurrection of the Dead

¹²But if it is preached that Christ has been raised from the dead, how can some of you say that there is no resurrection of the dead? ¹³If there is no resurrection of the dead, then not even Christ has been raised. ¹⁴And if Christ has not been raised, our preaching is useless and so is your faith. ¹⁵More than that, we are then found to be false witnesses about God, for we have testified about God that he raised Christ from the dead. But he did not raise him if in fact the dead are not raised. ¹⁶For if the dead are not raised, then Christ has not been raised either. ¹⁷And if Christ has not been raised, your faith is futile; you are still in your sins. ¹⁸Then those also who have fallen asleep in Christ are lost. ¹⁹If only for this life we have hope in Christ, we are to be pitied more than all men.

²⁰But Christ has indeed been raised from the dead, the firstfruits of those who have fallen asleep. ²¹For since death came through a man, the resurrection of the dead comes also through a man. ²²For as in Adam all die, so in Christ all will be made alive. ²³But each in his own turn: Christ, the firstfruits; then, when he comes, those who belong to him. ²⁴Then the end will come, when he hands over the kingdom to God the Father after he has destroyed all dominion, authority and power. ²⁵For he must reign until he has put all his enemies under his feet. ²⁶The last enemy to be destroyed is death. ²⁷For he "has put everything under his feet."*ᶜ* Now when it says that "everything" has been put under him, it is clear that this does not include God himself, who put everything under Christ. ²⁸When he has done this, then the Son himself will be made subject to him who put everything under him, so that God may be all in all.

²⁹Now if there is no resurrection, what will those do who are baptized for the dead? If the dead are not raised at all, why are people baptized for them? ³⁰And as for us, why do we endanger ourselves every hour? ³¹I die every day—I mean that, brothers—just as surely as I glory over you in Christ Jesus our Lord. ³²If I fought wild beasts in Ephesus for merely human reasons, what have I gained? If the dead are not raised,

"Let us eat and drink,
    for tomorrow we die."*ᵈ*

³³Do not be misled: "Bad company corrupts good character." ³⁴Come back to your senses as you ought, and stop sinning; for there are some who are ignorant of God—I say this to your shame.

The Resurrection Body

³⁵But someone may ask, "How are the dead raised? With what kind of body will they come?" ³⁶How foolish! What you sow does not come to life unless it dies. ³⁷When you sow, you do not plant the body that will be, but just a seed, perhaps of wheat or of something else. ³⁸But God gives it a body as he has determined, and to each kind of seed he gives its own body. ³⁹All flesh is not the same: Men have one kind of flesh, animals have another, birds another and fish another. ⁴⁰There are also heavenly bodies and

*ᵃ*3 Or *you at the first*   *ᵇ*5 Greek *Cephas*   *ᶜ*27 Psalm 8:6   *ᵈ*32 Isaiah 22:13

there are earthly bodies; but the splendor of the heavenly bodies is one kind, and the splendor of the earthly bodies is another. [41]The sun has one kind of splendor, the moon another and the stars another; and star differs from star in splendor.

[42]So will it be with the resurrection of the dead. The body that is sown is perishable, it is raised imperishable; [43]it is sown in dishonor, it is raised in glory; it is sown in weakness, it is raised in power; [44]it is sown a natural body, it is raised a spiritual body.

If there is a natural body, there is also a spiritual body. [45]So it is written: "The first man Adam became a living being"[a]; the last Adam, a life-giving spirit. [46]The spiritual did not come first, but the natural, and after that the spiritual. [47]The first man was of the dust of the earth, the second man from heaven. [48]As was the earthly man, so are those who are of the earth; and as is the man from heaven, so also are those who are of heaven. [49]And just as we have borne the likeness of the earthly man, so shall we[b] bear the likeness of the man from heaven.

[50]I declare to you, brothers, that flesh and blood cannot inherit the kingdom of God, nor does the perishable inherit the imperishable. [51]Listen, I tell you a mystery: We will not all sleep, but we will all be changed— [52]in a flash, in the twinkling of an eye, at the last trumpet. For the trumpet will sound, the dead will be raised imperishable, and we will be changed. [53]For the perishable must clothe itself with the imperishable, and the mortal with immortality. [54]When the perishable has been clothed with the imperishable, and the mortal with immortality, then the saying that is written will come true: "Death has been swallowed up in victory."[c]

[55]"Where, O death, is your victory?
    Where, O death, is your sting?"[d]

[56]The sting of death is sin, and the power of sin is the law. [57]But thanks be to God! He gives us the victory through our Lord Jesus Christ.

[58]Therefore, my dear brothers, stand firm. Let nothing move you. Always give yourselves fully to the work of the Lord, because you know that your labor in the Lord is not in vain.

The Collection for God's People

16 Now about the collection for God's people: Do what I told the Galatian churches to do. [2]On the first day of every week, each one of you should set aside a sum of money in keeping with his income, saving it up, so that when I come no collections will have to be made. [3]Then, when I arrive, I will give letters of introduction to the men you approve and send them with your gift to Jerusalem. [4]If it seems advisable for me to go also, they will accompany me.

Personal Requests

[5]After I go through Macedonia, I will come to you—for I will be going through Macedonia. [6]Perhaps I will stay with you awhile, or even spend the winter, so that you can help me on my journey, wherever I go. [7]I do not want to see you now and make only a passing visit; I hope to spend some time with you, if the Lord permits. [8]But I will stay on at Ephesus until Pentecost, [9]because a great door for effective work has opened to me, and there are many who oppose me.

[10]If Timothy comes, see to it that he has nothing to fear while he is with you, for he is carrying on the work of the Lord, just as I am. [11]No one, then, should refuse to accept him. Send him on his way in peace so that he may return to me. I am expecting him along with the brothers.

[12]Now about our brother Apollos: I strongly urged him to go to you with the brothers. He was quite unwilling to go now, but he will go when he has the opportunity.

[13]Be on your guard; stand firm in the faith; be men of courage; be strong. [14]Do everything in love.

[15]You know that the household of Stephanas were the first converts in Achaia, and they have devoted themselves to the service of the saints. I urge you, brothers, [16]to submit to such as these and to everyone who joins in the work, and labors at it. [17]I was glad when Stephanas, Fortunatus and Achaicus arrived, because they have supplied what was lacking from you. [18]For they refreshed my spirit and yours also. Such men deserve recognition.

---

[a]45 Gen. 2:7   [b]49 Some early manuscripts *so let us*   [c]54 Isaiah 25:8   [d]55 Hosea 13:14

Final Greetings

¹⁹The churches in the province of Asia send you greetings. Aquila and Priscilla*a* greet you warmly in the Lord, and so does the church that meets at their house. ²⁰All the brothers here send you greetings. Greet one another with a holy kiss.

²¹I, Paul, write this greeting in my own hand.

²²If anyone does not love the Lord—a curse be on him. Come, O Lord*b*!

²³The grace of the Lord Jesus be with you.

²⁴My love to all of you in Christ Jesus. Amen.*c*

---

a19 Greek *Prisca*, a variant of *Priscilla*   *b22* In Aramaic the expression *Come, O Lord* is *Marana tha.*
c24 Some manuscripts do not have *Amen.*

*P*AUL *writes this second letter to the church in Corinth from Macedonia (Acts 20:1; 2 Corinthians 7:5), while on his way to Corinth (2 Corinthians 13:1). As the most personal of all his letters, he expresses both how exciting and how painful his life as a mission-ary has been. He also finds it necessary to defend himself against those who are criticizing him. As you read this letter, think about how exciting it can be to serve the Lord, but realize too that be-ing a Christian can sometimes lead to pain and suffering.*

2 CORINTHIANS

1 Paul, an apostle of Christ Jesus by the will of God, and Timothy our brother,

To the church of God in Corinth, together with all the saints throughout Achaia:

[2]Grace and peace to you from God our Father and the Lord Jesus Christ.

The God of All Comfort

[3]Praise be to the God and Father of our Lord Jesus Christ, the Father of compas-sion and the God of all comfort, [4]who comforts us in all our troubles, so that we can comfort those in any trouble with the comfort we ourselves have received from God. [5]For just as the sufferings of Christ flow over into our lives, so also through Christ our comfort overflows. [6]If we are distressed, it is for your comfort and sal-vation; if we are comforted, it is for your comfort, which produces in you patient endurance of the same sufferings we suf-fer. [7]And our hope for you is firm, because we know that just as you share in our suf-ferings, so also you share in our comfort.

⁸We do not want you to be uninformed, brothers, about the hardships we suffered in the province of Asia. We were under great pressure, far beyond our ability to endure, so that we despaired even of life. ⁹Indeed, in our hearts we felt the sentence of death. But this happened that we might not rely on ourselves but on God, who raises the dead. ¹⁰He has delivered us from such a deadly peril, and he will deliver us. On him we have set our hope that he will continue to deliver us, ¹¹as you help us by your prayers. Then many will give thanks on our*a* behalf for the gracious favor granted us in answer to the prayers of many.

a11 Many manuscripts your

Paul's Change of Plans

¹²Now this is our boast: Our conscience testifies that we have conducted ourselves in the world, and especially in our relations with you, in the holiness and sincerity that are from God. We have done so not according to worldly wisdom but according to God's grace. ¹³For we do not write you anything you cannot read or understand. And I hope that, ¹⁴as you have understood us in part, you will come to understand fully that you can boast of us just as we will boast of you in the day of the Lord Jesus.

¹⁵Because I was confident of this, I planned to visit you first so that you

WEDNESDAY

VERSE FOR THE DAY:	AUTHOR:	PASSAGE FOR THE DAY:
2 Corinthians 1:6	Barbara Bush	2 Corinthians 1:3–11

Contented Heart, Patient Heart

IT is common to hear women bemoaning their lack of patience as if it were the most difficult gift to pry from God's hand. In fact impatience stems almost solely from our exaggerated notions of what is due us. If we could but lower our estimation of the importance of *our* time, *our* plans and *our* feelings, we would find ourselves almost automatically more patient.

If we are impatient about the same things that anger God—repeated sin, inattention to his Word, social injustice—we cannot really be called impatient (as long as our opinions are expressed in love). Neither can we expect a woman to remain totally unperturbed if someone smashes into her new car. Certainly "learning patience" is not an acceptable reason for failure to discipline a rebellious child. Patience is not the same thing as resignation or the cynical attitude that always expects the worst possible outcome.

Patience is a more positive trait. It is the ability to bear affliction, delay and interruption with calmness, perseverance and confidence in the goodness of God (Colossians 1:11–12). It is inward peace as well as outward control. It is the submission of our schedules, our viewpoints, our dreams to the greater plan of God, with the conviction that he has a good reason for every delay he allows to come our way.

Additional Scripture Readings:
Romans 2:1–8; Colossians 1:10–12

Go to page 250 for your next devotional reading.

might benefit twice. [16]I planned to visit you on my way to Macedonia and to come back to you from Macedonia, and then to have you send me on my way to Judea. [17]When I planned this, did I do it lightly? Or do I make my plans in a worldly manner so that in the same breath I say, "Yes, yes" and "No, no"?

[18]But as surely as God is faithful, our message to you is not "Yes" and "No." [19]For the Son of God, Jesus Christ, who was preached among you by me and Silas[a] and Timothy, was not "Yes" and "No," but in him it has always been "Yes." [20]For no matter how many promises God has made, they are "Yes" in Christ. And so through him the "Amen" is spoken by us to the glory of God. [21]Now it is God who makes both us and you stand firm in Christ. He anointed us, [22]set his seal of ownership on us, and put his Spirit in our hearts as a deposit, guaranteeing what is to come.

[23]I call God as my witness that it was in order to spare you that I did not return to Corinth. [24]Not that we lord it over your faith, but we work with you for your joy, because it is by faith you stand firm.

2 [1]So I made up my mind that I would not make another painful visit to you. [2]For if I grieve you, who is left to make me glad but you whom I have grieved? [3]I wrote as I did so that when I came I should not be distressed by those who ought to make me rejoice. I had confidence in all of you, that you would all share my joy. [4]For I wrote you out of great distress and anguish of heart and with many tears, not to grieve you but to let you know the depth of my love for you.

Forgiveness for the Sinner

[5]If anyone has caused grief, he has not so much grieved me as he has grieved all of you, to some extent—not to put it too severely. [6]The punishment inflicted on him by the majority is sufficient for him. [7]Now instead, you ought to forgive and comfort him, so that he will not be overwhelmed by excessive sorrow. [8]I urge you, therefore, to reaffirm your love for him. [9]The reason I wrote you was to see if you would stand the test and be obedient in everything. [10]If you forgive anyone, I also forgive him. And what I have forgiven—if there was anything to forgive—I have forgiven in the sight of Christ for your sake,

[11]in order that Satan might not outwit us. For we are not unaware of his schemes.

Ministers of the New Covenant

[12]Now when I went to Troas to preach the gospel of Christ and found that the Lord had opened a door for me, [13]I still had no peace of mind, because I did not find my brother Titus there. So I said good-by to them and went on to Macedonia.

[14]But thanks be to God, who always leads us in triumphal procession in Christ and through us spreads everywhere the fragrance of the knowledge of him. [15]For we are to God the aroma of Christ among those who are being saved and those who are perishing. [16]To the one we are the smell of death; to the other, the fragrance of life. And who is equal to such a task? [17]Unlike so many, we do not peddle the word of God for profit. On the contrary, in Christ we speak before God with sincerity, like men sent from God.

3 Are we beginning to commend ourselves again? Or do we need, like some people, letters of recommendation to you or from you? [2]You yourselves are our letter, written on our hearts, known and read by everybody. [3]You show that you are a letter from Christ, the result of our ministry, written not with ink but with the Spirit of the living God, not on tablets of stone but on tablets of human hearts.

[4]Such confidence as this is ours through Christ before God. [5]Not that we are competent in ourselves to claim anything for ourselves, but our competence comes from God. [6]He has made us competent as ministers of a new covenant—not of the letter but of the Spirit; for the letter kills, but the Spirit gives life.

The Glory of the New Covenant

[7]Now if the ministry that brought death, which was engraved in letters on stone, came with glory, so that the Israelites could not look steadily at the face of Moses because of its glory, fading though it was, [8]will not the ministry of the Spirit be even more glorious? [9]If the ministry that condemns men is glorious, how much more glorious is the ministry that brings righteousness! [10]For what was glorious has no glory now in comparison with the surpassing glory. [11]And if what

---

[a]19 Greek *Silvanus*, a variant of *Silas*

| VERSE FOR THE DAY: | AUTHOR: | PASSAGE FOR THE DAY: |
| 2 Corinthians 3:3 | Beth Donigan Seversen | 2 Corinthians 3:3–5 |

A Lost Letter

The Screwtape Letters, by C. S. Lewis, is a fictitious diary of scolding letters from a mature demon (Screwtape) to his young nephew (Wormwood). It is Wormwood's job to keep a recent convert to Christianity from being productive for Christ (the Enemy). Screwtape's letters point out where Wormwood has failed or missed an opportunity. I have often mused that there must be a missing appendix to these letters somewhere that reads like this . . .

My dear Wormwood,

The following instructions shall help you proceed in handicapping your convert's effectiveness in the Enemy's kingdom. One of our great allies at present is her perception of herself. It is your task, therefore, to feed her poor self-esteem. Already she wastes time primping in front of the mirror and worrying about her looks.

You must continue to encourage her to compare herself with so-called "spiritual giants" whom she admires. This will eventually immobilize her. When she feels inadequate she will no longer attempt anything for the Enemy's kingdom because of her fear of failure. Her warped self-image will lead to unhealthy relationships and hinder her ability to love others. The more often she tells herself that she is a bad person—that she's not competent—the more easily she will feel threatened by others. This will turn others off to the Enemy and his loathsome Christianity.

Ultimately, her relationship with the Enemy himself will be adversely affected. Since she is not satisfied with how the Enemy has created her, her intimacy with him will be destroyed and she will find it difficult to trust the Enemy, pray to him or read that detestable Book.

Finally, emphasize her weaknesses so repeatedly that she begins to believe that she is unimportant to the Enemy. This will push her to compulsive striving to please him through her own accomplishments. Her works will no longer be motivated by faith, but by a dislike for herself. Confuse her so that she never feels forgiven. If you successfully convince her that the Enemy is never pleased with her, she will grow weary and give up altogether. But, more of this in my next letter.

Your affectionate uncle,
Screwtape

Additional Scripture Readings:
Jeremiah 17:7–8; Galatians 6:2–10

*Go to page 252 for your next
devotional reading.*

was fading away came with glory, how much greater is the glory of that which lasts!

[12]Therefore, since we have such a hope, we are very bold. [13]We are not like Moses, who would put a veil over his face to keep the Israelites from gazing at it while the radiance was fading away. [14]But their minds were made dull, for to this day the same veil remains when the old covenant is read. It has not been removed, because only in Christ is it taken away. [15]Even to this day when Moses is read, a veil covers their hearts. [16]But whenever anyone turns to the Lord, the veil is taken away. [17]Now the Lord is the Spirit, and where the Spirit of the Lord is, there is freedom. [18]And we, who with unveiled faces all reflect[a] the Lord's glory, are being transformed into his likeness with ever-increasing glory, which comes from the Lord, who is the Spirit.

Treasures in Jars of Clay

4 Therefore, since through God's mercy we have this ministry, we do not lose heart. [2]Rather, we have renounced secret and shameful ways; we do not use deception, nor do we distort the word of God. On the contrary, by setting forth the truth plainly we commend ourselves to every man's conscience in the sight of God. [3]And even if our gospel is veiled, it is veiled to those who are perishing. [4]The god of this age has blinded the minds of unbelievers, so that they cannot see the light of the gospel of the glory of Christ, who is the image of God. [5]For we do not preach ourselves, but Jesus Christ as Lord, and ourselves as your servants for Jesus' sake. [6]For God, who said, "Let light shine out of darkness,"[b] made his light shine in our hearts to give us the light of the knowledge of the glory of God in the face of Christ.

[7]But we have this treasure in jars of clay to show that this all-surpassing power is from God and not from us. [8]We are hard pressed on every side, but not crushed; perplexed, but not in despair; [9]persecuted, but not abandoned; struck down, but not destroyed. [10]We always carry around in our body the death of Jesus, so that the life of Jesus may also be revealed in our body. [11]For we who are alive are always being given over to death for Jesus' sake, so that his life may be revealed in our mortal body. [12]So then,

death is at work in us, but life is at work in you.

[13]It is written: "I believed; therefore I have spoken."[c] With that same spirit of faith we also believe and therefore speak, [14]because we know that the one who raised the Lord Jesus from the dead will also raise us with Jesus and present us with you in his presence. [15]All this is for your benefit, so that the grace that is reaching more and more people may cause thanksgiving to overflow to the glory of God.

[16]Therefore we do not lose heart. Though outwardly we are wasting away, yet inwardly we are being renewed day by day. [17]For our light and momentary troubles are achieving for us an eternal glory that far outweighs them all. [18]So we fix our eyes not on what is seen, but on what is unseen. For what is seen is temporary, but what is unseen is eternal.

Our Heavenly Dwelling

5 Now we know that if the earthly tent we live in is destroyed, we have a building from God, an eternal house in heaven, not built by human hands. [2]Meanwhile we groan, longing to be clothed with our heavenly dwelling, [3]because when we are clothed, we will not be found naked. [4]For while we are in this tent, we groan and are burdened, because we do not wish to be unclothed but to be clothed with our heavenly dwelling, so that what is mortal may be swallowed up by life. [5]Now it is God who has made us for this very purpose and has given us the Spirit as a deposit, guaranteeing what is to come.

[6]Therefore we are always confident and know that as long as we are at home in the body we are away from the Lord. [7]We live by faith, not by sight. [8]We are confident, I say, and would prefer to be away from the body and at home with the Lord. [9]So we make it our goal to please him, whether we are at home in the body or away from it. [10]For we must all appear before the judgment seat of Christ, that each one may receive what is due him for the things done while in the body, whether good or bad.

The Ministry of Reconciliation

[11]Since, then, we know what it is to fear the Lord, we try to persuade men. What we are is plain to God, and I hope it is also

---

a18 Or *contemplate*   *b6* Gen. 1:3   *c13* Psalm 116:10

VERSE FOR THE DAY:
2 Corinthians 4:16

AUTHOR:
Karen Burton Mains

PASSAGE FOR THE DAY:
2 Corinthians 4:1–18

Keepin' Talkin'

FOR years, February days when I was housebound with small children were the hardest times of all. I longed for the sun to shine two days in a row. I yearned for spring, knowing all too well that madding March with its melted layers of accreted winter's filth barred my isolated heart from the rioting green blooms of April. It was during these shadowy days, dragging with plodding prisoner's feet, that I learned how important it is to "keepin' talkin' " (a phrase coined by my son David when he was two) with God.

A major part of the mature Christian journey is learning how to handle those times when the heavens locked, when our lives are weighted with the winter garments of despair, pain, worry and loss. We try desperately to convince ourselves that we don't serve a God who has absented himself from the listening post, who has hung up a "Shop's Closed" sign and taken off to vacation somewhere in the balmy south.

The Psalms are a prayer journal, an ongoing record of one man's conversations with God. Many of these poem-songs are about times when David hit a roadblock to intimate dialogue with God:

> O LORD, how many are my foes!
>   How many rise up against me!
> Many are saying of me,
>   "God will not deliver him" (Psalm 3:1).

> Give ear to my words, O LORD,
>   consider my sighing.
> Listen to my cry for help,
>   my King and my God (Psalm 5:1–2).

> O LORD, do not rebuke me in your anger
>   or discipline me in your wrath.
> Be merciful to me, LORD, for I am faint;
>   O LORD, heal me, for my bones are in agony
>   (Psalm 6:1–2).

David's words reiterate the old truth I began to learn while sitting at the dining table, tutored by my own small child: When your soul feels like a gray February day, and all seems to be rain, fog and chill drizzle, the overcast can be lifted if you will learn to just "keepin' talkin' " with God.

Additional Scripture Readings:
1 Samuel 1:9–18; 1 Kings 19:3–18

Go to page 254 for your next devotional reading.

plain to your conscience. [12]We are not trying to commend ourselves to you again, but are giving you an opportunity to take pride in us, so that you can answer those who take pride in what is seen rather than in what is in the heart. [13]If we are out of our mind, it is for the sake of God; if we are in our right mind, it is for you. [14]For Christ's love compels us, because we are convinced that one died for all, and therefore all died. [15]And he died for all, that those who live should no longer live for themselves but for him who died for them and was raised again.

[16]So from now on we regard no one from a worldly point of view. Though we once regarded Christ in this way, we do so no longer. [17]Therefore, if anyone is in Christ, he is a new creation; the old has gone, the new has come! [18]All this is from God, who reconciled us to himself through Christ and gave us the ministry of reconciliation: [19]that God was reconciling the world to himself in Christ, not counting men's sins against them. And he has committed to us the message of reconciliation. [20]We are therefore Christ's ambassadors, as though God were making his appeal through us. We implore you on Christ's behalf: Be reconciled to God. [21]God made him who had no sin to be sin[a] for us, so that in him we might become the righteousness of God.

6 As God's fellow workers we urge you not to receive God's grace in vain. [2]For he says,

"In the time of my favor I heard you, and in the day of salvation I helped you."[b]

I tell you, now is the time of God's favor, now is the day of salvation.

Paul's Hardships

[3]We put no stumbling block in anyone's path, so that our ministry will not be discredited. [4]Rather, as servants of God we commend ourselves in every way: in great endurance; in troubles, hardships and distresses; [5]in beatings, imprisonments and riots; in hard work, sleepless nights and hunger; [6]in purity, understanding, patience and kindness; in the Holy Spirit and in sincere love; [7]in truthful speech and in the power of God; with weapons of righteousness in the right hand and in the left; [8]through glory and

dishonor, bad report and good report; genuine, yet regarded as impostors; [9]known, yet regarded as unknown; dying, and yet we live on; beaten, and yet not killed; [10]sorrowful, yet always rejoicing; poor, yet making many rich; having nothing, and yet possessing everything.

[11]We have spoken freely to you, Corinthians, and opened wide our hearts to you. [12]We are not withholding our affection from you, but you are withholding yours from us. [13]As a fair exchange—I speak as to my children—open wide your hearts also.

Do Not Be Yoked With Unbelievers

[14]Do not be yoked together with unbelievers. For what do righteousness and wickedness have in common? Or what fellowship can light have with darkness? [15]What harmony is there between Christ and Belial[c]? What does a believer have in common with an unbeliever? [16]What agreement is there between the temple of God and idols? For we are the temple of the living God. As God has said: "I will live with them and walk among them, and I will be their God, and they will be my people."[d]

[17]"Therefore come out from them
    and be separate,
                            says the Lord.
Touch no unclean thing,
    and I will receive you."[e]
[18]"I will be a Father to you,
    and you will be my sons and
        daughters,
                    says the Lord Almighty."[f]

7 Since we have these promises, dear friends, let us purify ourselves from everything that contaminates body and spirit, perfecting holiness out of reverence for God.

Paul's Joy

[2]Make room for us in your hearts. We have wronged no one, we have corrupted no one, we have exploited no one. [3]I do not say this to condemn you; I have said before that you have such a place in our hearts that we would live or die with you. [4]I have great confidence in you; I take great pride in you. I am greatly encouraged; in all our troubles my joy knows no bounds.

[5]For when we came into Macedonia,

---

a21 Or *be a sin offering*   *b2* Isaiah 49:8   *c15* Greek *Beliar,* a variant of *Belial*   *d16* Lev. 26:12;
Jer. 32:38; Ezek. 37:27   *e17* Isaiah 52:11; Ezek. 20:34,41   *f18* 2 Samuel 7:14; 7:8

WEEKENDING

RECORD

The most important part of our task will be to
tell everyone who will listen that Jesus is the
only answer to the problems that are disturbing
the hearts of men and nations.
   We shall have the right to speak because we
can tell from our experience that his light is
more powerful than the deepest darkness . . .
How wonderful that the reality of his presence is
greater than the reality of the hell about us.
— Betsie ten Boom

RECAP

Betsie ten Boom, sister of author and speaker
Corrie ten Boom, died in a Nazi concentration
camp during World War II.

REVIVE

Saturday: Romans 8:28–39
Sunday: Psalm 146:1–10

Go to page 257 for your next devotional reading.

this body of ours had no rest, but we were harassed at every turn—conflicts on the outside, fears within. [6]But God, who comforts the downcast, comforted us by the coming of Titus, [7]and not only by his coming but also by the comfort you had given him. He told us about your longing for me, your deep sorrow, your ardent concern for me, so that my joy was greater than ever.

[8]Even if I caused you sorrow by my letter, I do not regret it. Though I did regret it—I see that my letter hurt you, but only for a little while— [9]yet now I am happy, not because you were made sorry, but because your sorrow led you to repentance. For you became sorrowful as God intended and so were not harmed in any way by us. [10]Godly sorrow brings repentance that leads to salvation and leaves no regret, but worldly sorrow brings death. [11]See what this godly sorrow has produced in you: what earnestness, what eagerness to clear yourselves, what indignation, what alarm, what longing, what concern, what readiness to see justice done. At every point you have proved yourselves to be innocent in this matter. [12]So even though I wrote to you, it was not on account of the one who did the wrong or of the injured party, but rather that before God you could see for yourselves how devoted to us you are. [13]By all this we are encouraged.

In addition to our own encouragement, we were especially delighted to see how happy Titus was, because his spirit has been refreshed by all of you. [14]I had boasted to him about you, and you have not embarrassed me. But just as everything we said to you was true, so our boasting about you to Titus has proved to be true as well. [15]And his affection for you is all the greater when he remembers that you were all obedient, receiving him with fear and trembling. [16]I am glad I can have complete confidence in you.

Generosity Encouraged

8 And now, brothers, we want you to know about the grace that God has given the Macedonian churches. [2]Out of the most severe trial, their overflowing joy and their extreme poverty welled up in rich generosity. [3]For I testify that they gave as much as they were able, and even beyond their ability. Entirely on their own, [4]they urgently pleaded with us for

the privilege of sharing in this service to the saints. [5]And they did not do as we expected, but they gave themselves first to the Lord and then to us in keeping with God's will. [6]So we urged Titus, since he had earlier made a beginning, to bring also to completion this act of grace on your part. [7]But just as you excel in everything—in faith, in speech, in knowledge, in complete earnestness and in your love for us[a]—see that you also excel in this grace of giving.

[8]I am not commanding you, but I want to test the sincerity of your love by comparing it with the earnestness of others. [9]For you know the grace of our Lord Jesus Christ, that though he was rich, yet for your sakes he became poor, so that you through his poverty might become rich.

[10]And here is my advice about what is best for you in this matter: Last year you were the first not only to give but also to have the desire to do so. [11]Now finish the work, so that your eager willingness to do it may be matched by your completion of it, according to your means. [12]For if the willingness is there, the gift is acceptable according to what one has, not according to what he does not have.

[13]Our desire is not that others might be relieved while you are hard pressed, but that there might be equality. [14]At the present time your plenty will supply what they need, so that in turn their plenty will supply what you need. Then there will be equality, [15]as it is written: "He who gathered much did not have too much, and he who gathered little did not have too little."[b]

Titus Sent to Corinth

[16]I thank God, who put into the heart of Titus the same concern I have for you. [17]For Titus not only welcomed our appeal, but he is coming to you with much enthusiasm and on his own initiative. [18]And we are sending along with him the brother who is praised by all the churches for his service to the gospel. [19]What is more, he was chosen by the churches to accompany us as we carry the offering, which we administer in order to honor the Lord himself and to show our eagerness to help. [20]We want to avoid any criticism of the way we administer this liberal gift. [21]For we are taking pains to do what is right, not only in the eyes of the Lord but also in the eyes of men.

[a]7 Some manuscripts *in our love for you*   [b]15 Exodus 16:18

²²In addition, we are sending with them our brother who has often proved to us in many ways that he is zealous, and now even more so because of his great confidence in you. ²³As for Titus, he is my partner and fellow worker among you; as for our brothers, they are representatives of the churches and an honor to Christ. ²⁴Therefore show these men the proof of your love and the reason for our pride in you, so that the churches can see it.

9 There is no need for me to write to you about this service to the saints. ²For I know your eagerness to help, and I have been boasting about it to the Macedonians, telling them that since last year you in Achaia were ready to give; and your enthusiasm has stirred most of them to action. ³But I am sending the brothers in order that our boasting about you in this matter should not prove hollow, but that you may be ready, as I said you would be. ⁴For if any Macedonians come with me and find you unprepared, we—not to say anything about you—would be ashamed of having been so confident. ⁵So I thought it necessary to urge the brothers to visit you in advance and finish the arrangements for the generous gift you had promised. Then it will be ready as a generous gift, not as one grudgingly given.

Sowing Generously

⁶Remember this: Whoever sows sparingly will also reap sparingly, and whoever sows generously will also reap generously. ⁷Each man should give what he has decided in his heart to give, not reluctantly or under compulsion, for God loves a cheerful giver. ⁸And God is able to make all grace abound to you, so that in all things at all times, having all that you need, you will abound in every good work. ⁹As it is written:

"He has scattered abroad his gifts to
    the poor;
  his righteousness endures forever."ᵃ

¹⁰Now he who supplies seed to the sower and bread for food will also supply and increase your store of seed and will enlarge the harvest of your righteousness. ¹¹You will be made rich in every way so that you can be generous on every occasion, and through us your generosity will result in thanksgiving to God.

¹²This service that you perform is not only supplying the needs of God's people but is also overflowing in many expressions of thanks to God. ¹³Because of the service by which you have proved yourselves, men will praise God for the obedience that accompanies your confession of the gospel of Christ, and for your generosity in sharing with them and with everyone else. ¹⁴And in their prayers for you their hearts will go out to you, because of the surpassing grace God has given you. ¹⁵Thanks be to God for his indescribable gift!

Paul's Defense of His Ministry

10 By the meekness and gentleness of Christ, I appeal to you—I, Paul, who am "timid" when face to face with you, but "bold" when away! ²I beg you that when I come I may not have to be as bold as I expect to be toward some people who think that we live by the standards of this world. ³For though we live in the world, we do not wage war as the world does. ⁴The weapons we fight with are not the weapons of the world. On the contrary, they have divine power to demolish strongholds. ⁵We demolish arguments and every pretension that sets itself up against the knowledge of God, and we take captive every thought to make it obedient to Christ. ⁶And we will be ready to punish every act of disobedience, once your obedience is complete.

⁷You are looking only on the surface of things.ᵇ If anyone is confident that he belongs to Christ, he should consider again that we belong to Christ just as much as he. ⁸For even if I boast somewhat freely about the authority the Lord gave us for building you up rather than pulling you down, I will not be ashamed of it. ⁹I do not want to seem to be trying to frighten you with my letters. ¹⁰For some say, "His letters are weighty and forceful, but in person he is unimpressive and his speaking amounts to nothing." ¹¹Such people should realize that what we are in our letters when we are absent, we will be in our actions when we are present.

¹²We do not dare to classify or compare ourselves with some who commend themselves. When they measure themselves by themselves and compare themselves with themselves, they are not wise. ¹³We, however, will not boast beyond

---

ᵃ9 Psalm 112:9   ᵇ7 Or *Look at the obvious facts*

proper limits, but will confine our boasting to the field God has assigned to us, a field that reaches even to you. ¹⁴We are not going too far in our boasting, as would be the case if we had not come to you, for we did get as far as you with the gospel of Christ. ¹⁵Neither do we go beyond our limits by boasting of work done by others. *a* Our hope is that, as your faith continues to grow, our area of activity among you will greatly expand, ¹⁶so that we can preach the gospel in the regions beyond you. For we do not want to boast about work already done in another man's territory. ¹⁷But, "Let him who boasts boast in the Lord." *b* ¹⁸For it is not the one who commends himself who is approved, but the one whom the Lord commends.

a13-15 Or *¹³We, however, will not boast about things that cannot be measured, but we will boast according to the standard of measurement that the God of measure has assigned us—a measurement that relates even to you. 14 . . . . ¹⁵Neither do we boast about things that cannot be measured in regard to the work done by others.*   *b17* Jer. 9:24

MONDAY

VERSE FOR THE DAY: AUTHOR: PASSAGE FOR THE DAY:
2 Corinthians 9:8   *Wanda K. Jones*   *2 Corinthians 9:6–11*

God Is Able

I NEEDED assurance from God that he would be with me when I was about to graduate from college, get married six weeks later and then leave with my minister husband to work in Harlem, New York. He gave me that assurance in 2 Corinthians 9:8.

The Lord proved to me over and over that his grace and favor are plentiful. He gave me wisdom and love as I sought to help young people handle the problems of daily living in the midst of poverty. As a result, many found that God is able to help them "abound in every good work." I found that God was able to give our family strength and courage during the time my husband was caught in a coup d'etat just as his evangelistic meetings had ended in Ghana. And God was able to bring my husband back to us.

I found that God was able to quiet fear when I visited one of my retarded students who was very ill in the hospital. She was apprehensive because she was not able to be at home or at school with the rest of her friends. But I prayed with her and said softly when I left, "Mary, don't be afraid. Jesus is in this very room. He is able to keep you from being afraid. He is here even though you can't see him." With that assurance of God's ability to care for her, Mary quietly smiled.

Perhaps as you read the "all's" of God in 2 Corinthians 9:8, you might think of some circumstances in your life that seem insurmountable. It's true that sometimes simple, everyday things can loom so large that you feel caught up in a maze with no exit.

In times like these, remember: God is able!

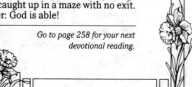

Additional Scripture Readings:
Ephesians 1:18–21; Jude 20–25

Go to page 258 for your next devotional reading.

Paul and the False Apostles

11 I hope you will put up with a little of my foolishness; but you are already doing that. ²I am jealous for you with a godly jealousy. I promised you to one husband, to Christ, so that I might present you as a pure virgin to him. ³But I am afraid that just as Eve was deceived by the serpent's cunning, your minds may somehow be led astray from your sincere and pure devotion to Christ. ⁴For if someone comes to you and preaches a Jesus other than the Jesus we preached, or if you receive a different spirit from the one you received, or a different gospel from the one you accepted, you put up with it easily enough. ⁵But I do not think I am in the least inferior to those "super-apostles." ⁶I may not be a trained speaker, but I do have knowledge. We have made this perfectly clear to you in every way.

⁷Was it a sin for me to lower myself in order to elevate you by preaching the gospel of God to you free of charge? ⁸I robbed other churches by receiving support from them so as to serve you. ⁹And when I was with you and needed something, I was

TUESDAY

VERSE FOR THE DAY:
2 Corinthians 10:14

AUTHOR:
Linda Ching Sledge

PASSAGE FOR THE DAY:
2 Corinthians 10:12–18

Just Right!

"HEY, it fits good!" said five-year-old Geoffrey from inside the floppy tent of his older brother's sweatshirt.

When he heard me laugh, Geoffrey poked his head out like a turtle and said, "I'm NOT too little!" Then he stormed upstairs and slammed his door.

Later, I peeked in to find both boys sprawled on the bed.

"You're big enough," Tim was saying. "Bigger than the babies next door. You're just right for five years old."

I was struck by Tim's answer: You're just right . . . . For the last year, I had tried to model myself after a woman I admired: a well-known Christian churchwoman, mother and wife. How did she integrate God so effortlessly into her busy life? With a simple phrase, she turned ordinary events into unforgettable celebrations of God's love. I, on the other hand, was always scrambling to pull together a church school lesson a half hour before church.

It took me some time to see it, but gradually it dawned on me that growing spiritually is not climbing to perfection; it's doing what you do with genuine devotion. Looking back, I hadn't even come close to emulating the woman I admired. I wasn't her size! Nevertheless I had grown in simple and essential areas: reading the Bible regularly, enjoying teaching at church, praying often and walking closer to him.

Sometimes the desire to grow makes us feel "too little," when in reality we are just the right size for now—and always good enough in God's eyes.

Additional Scripture Readings:
Ephesians 2:8–10; 2 Thessalonians 1:3–4

Go to page 260 for your next devotional reading.

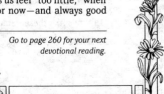

not a burden to anyone, for the brothers who came from Macedonia supplied what I needed. I have kept myself from being a burden to you in any way, and will continue to do so. [10]As surely as the truth of Christ is in me, nobody in the regions of Achaia will stop this boasting of mine. [11]Why? Because I do not love you? God knows I do! [12]And I will keep on doing what I am doing in order to cut the ground from under those who want an opportunity to be considered equal with us in the things they boast about.

[13]For such men are false apostles, deceitful workmen, masquerading as apostles of Christ. [14]And no wonder, for Satan himself masquerades as an angel of light. [15]It is not surprising, then, if his servants masquerade as servants of righteousness. Their end will be what their actions deserve.

Paul Boasts About His Sufferings

[16]I repeat: Let no one take me for a fool. But if you do, then receive me just as you would a fool, so that I may do a little boasting. [17]In this self-confident boasting I am not talking as the Lord would, but as a fool. [18]Since many are boasting in the way the world does, I too will boast. [19]You gladly put up with fools since you are so wise! [20]In fact, you even put up with anyone who enslaves you or exploits you or takes advantage of you or pushes himself forward or slaps you in the face. [21]To my shame I admit that we were too weak for that!

What anyone else dares to boast about — I am speaking as a fool — I also dare to boast about. [22]Are they Hebrews? So am I. Are they Israelites? So am I. Are they Abraham's descendants? So am I. [23]Are they servants of Christ? (I am out of my mind to talk like this.) I am more. I have worked much harder, been in prison more frequently, been flogged more severely, and been exposed to death again and again. [24]Five times I received from the Jews the forty lashes minus one. [25]Three times I was beaten with rods, once I was stoned, three times I was shipwrecked, I spent a night and a day in the open sea. [26]I have been constantly on the move. I have been in danger from rivers, in danger from bandits, in danger from my own countrymen, in danger from Gentiles; in danger in the city, in danger in the country, in danger at sea; and in danger from false brothers. [27]I have labored and toiled and have often gone without sleep; I have

known hunger and thirst and have often gone without food; I have been cold and naked. [28]Besides everything else, I face daily the pressure of my concern for all the churches. [29]Who is weak, and I do not feel weak? Who is led into sin, and I do not inwardly burn?

[30]If I must boast, I will boast of the things that show my weakness. [31]The God and Father of the Lord Jesus, who is to be praised forever, knows that I am not lying. [32]In Damascus the governor under King Aretas had the city of the Damascenes guarded in order to arrest me. [33]But I was lowered in a basket from a window in the wall and slipped through his hands.

Paul's Vision and His Thorn

12 I must go on boasting. Although there is nothing to be gained, I will go on to visions and revelations from the Lord. [2]I know a man in Christ who fourteen years ago was caught up to the third heaven. Whether it was in the body or out of the body I do not know — God knows. [3]And I know that this man — whether in the body or apart from the body I do not know, but God knows — [4]was caught up to paradise. He heard inexpressible things, things that man is not permitted to tell. [5]I will boast about a man like that, but I will not boast about myself, except about my weaknesses. [6]Even if I should choose to boast, I would not be a fool, because I would be speaking the truth. But I refrain, so no one will think more of me than is warranted by what I do or say.

[7]To keep me from becoming conceited because of these surpassingly great revelations, there was given me a thorn in my flesh, a messenger of Satan, to torment me. [8]Three times I pleaded with the Lord to take it away from me. [9]But he said to me, "My grace is sufficient for you, for my power is made perfect in weakness." Therefore I will boast all the more gladly about my weaknesses, so that Christ's power may rest on me. [10]That is why, for Christ's sake, I delight in weaknesses, in insults, in hardships, in persecutions, in difficulties. For when I am weak, then I am strong.

Paul's Concern for the Corinthians

[11]I have made a fool of myself, but you drove me to it. I ought to have been commended by you, for I am not in the least inferior to the "super-apostles," even though I am nothing. [12]The things that mark an apostle — signs, wonders and

VERSE FOR THE DAY:	AUTHOR:	PASSAGE FOR THE DAY:
2 Corinthians 12:9	Marie Chapian	2 Corinthians 12:1–10

His Power Made Perfect

WHILE in Europe researching my book *Of Whom the World Was Not Worthy* (Bethany House, 1979), I traveled through Yugoslavia from Slovenia to Macedonia. I interviewed factory workers, peasants, gypsies, doctors and laborers, as well as former Communist party officials. I wanted to know how Christians sustained their faith through the devastation of two world wars. I heard story after story of courage in the face of seemingly insurmountable obstacles.

I talked to those who had been imprisoned and whose future seemed hopeless; people who had been sick and wasted physically; frail women who fought in the Partisan army against the Fascists with only sticks for weapons; people who were starving, who ate scraps out of garbage cans. These were brave people—weak, defenseless people—but those for whom the grace of the Lord was sufficient. In their weakness, his power was made perfect.

I looked at my own life and asked myself if my weaknesses were an opportunity for God's power to be made perfect in me. Did I really accept his grace as sufficient in every situation? The apostle Paul suffered a thorn in the flesh that he begged the Lord to remove. The Lord responded not by removing the agonizing source of pain but by giving the apostle the strength to bear it (2 Corinthians 12:7–9). This is how God often works. He does not spare us from suffering but enables us to conquer it.

I've seen shy people become great leaders, and I've seen physically ill people become charged with spiritual energy and touch other lives with the power of the gospel of Christ. I've seen suffering people become shining examples of strength and power. And through this I've learned that nothing can break or destroy us when we allow our weaknesses to make us strong.

There is sublime joy in holy boasting of the power of God in a life that is totally dependent on him. There is sublime peace in accepting the sufficiency of God's grace by allowing him to be strong in us where we are weak.

Additional Scripture Readings:
Romans 8:26–27; 1 Corinthians 1:25–31

Go to page 263 for your next devotional reading.

miracles—were done among you with great perseverance. [13]How were you inferior to the other churches, except that I was never a burden to you? Forgive me this wrong!

[14]Now I am ready to visit you for the third time, and I will not be a burden to you, because what I want is not your possessions but you. After all, children should not have to save up for their parents, but parents for their children. [15]So I will very gladly spend for you everything I have and expend myself as well. If I love you more, will you love me less? [16]Be that as it may, I have not been a burden to you. Yet, crafty fellow that I am, I caught you by trickery! [17]Did I exploit you through any of the men I sent you? [18]I urged Titus to go to you and I sent our brother with him. Titus did not exploit you, did he? Did we not act in the same spirit and follow the same course?

[19]Have you been thinking all along that we have been defending ourselves to you? We have been speaking in the sight of God as those in Christ; and everything we do, dear friends, is for your strengthening. [20]For I am afraid that when I come I may not find you as I want you to be, and you may not find me as you want me to be. I fear that there may be quarreling, jealousy, outbursts of anger, factions, slander, gossip, arrogance and disorder. [21]I am afraid that when I come again my God will humble me before you, and I will be grieved over many who have sinned earlier and have not repented of the impurity, sexual sin and debauchery in which they have indulged.

Final Warnings

13 This will be my third visit to you. "Every matter must be established by the testimony of two or three witnesses."[a] [2]I already gave you a warning when I was with you the second time. I now repeat it while absent: On my return I will not spare those who sinned earlier or any of the others, [3]since you are demanding proof that Christ is speaking through me. He is not weak in dealing with you, but is powerful among you. [4]For to be sure, he was crucified in weakness, yet he lives by God's power. Likewise, we are weak in him, yet by God's power we will live with him to serve you.

[5]Examine yourselves to see whether you are in the faith; test yourselves. Do you not realize that Christ Jesus is in you—unless, of course, you fail the test? [6]And I trust that you will discover that we have not failed the test. [7]Now we pray to God that you will not do anything wrong. Not that people will see that we have stood the test but that you will do what is right even though we may seem to have failed. [8]For we cannot do anything against the truth, but only for the truth. [9]We are glad whenever we are weak but you are strong; and our prayer is for your perfection. [10]This is why I write these things when I am absent, that when I come I may not have to be harsh in my use of authority—the authority the Lord gave me for building you up, not for tearing you down.

Final Greetings

[11]Finally, brothers, good-by. Aim for perfection, listen to my appeal, be of one mind, live in peace. And the God of love and peace will be with you.

[12]Greet one another with a holy kiss. [13]All the saints send their greetings.

[14]May the grace of the Lord Jesus Christ, and the love of God, and the fellowship of the Holy Spirit be with you all.

a1 Deut. 19:15

*P*AUL *writes this letter to the churches he founded in Galatia (Acts 13:13–14:28), warning them against certain false teachers. He reminds them of the simple message of salvation by faith alone, which he and other church leaders teach, and concludes with advice on how to live a Spirit-filled life. As you read this book, be sure that you are saved by a personal faith in Jesus, and ask God's Spirit to help you walk in Christian love and peace.*

GALATIANS

1 Paul, an apostle—sent not from men nor by man, but by Jesus Christ and God the Father, who raised him from the dead— ²and all the brothers with me,

To the churches in Galatia:

³Grace and peace to you from God our Father and the Lord Jesus Christ, ⁴who gave himself for our sins to rescue us from the present evil age, according to the will of our God and Father, ⁵to whom be glory for ever and ever. Amen.

No Other Gospel

⁶I am astonished that you are so quickly deserting the one who called you by the grace of Christ and are turning to a different gospel— ⁷which is really no gospel at all. Evidently some people are throwing you into confusion and are trying to pervert the gospel of Christ. ⁸But even if we or an angel from heaven should preach a gospel other than the one we preached to you, let him be eternally condemned! ⁹As we have already said, so now I say again: If anybody is preaching to you a gospel other than what you accepted, let him be eternally condemned!

¹⁰Am I now trying to win the approval of men, or of God? Or am I trying to please men? If I were still trying to please men, I would not be a servant of Christ.

Paul Called by God

[11]I want you to know, brothers, that the gospel I preached is not something that man made up. [12]I did not receive it from any man, nor was I taught it; rather, I received it by revelation from Jesus Christ.

[13]For you have heard of my previous way of life in Judaism, how intensely I persecuted the church of God and tried to destroy it. [14]I was advancing in Judaism beyond many Jews of my own age and was extremely zealous for the traditions of my fathers. [15]But when God, who set me apart from birth[a] and called me by his grace, was pleased [16]to reveal his Son in me so that I might preach him among the Gentiles, I did not consult any man, [17]nor did I go up to Jerusalem to see those who were apostles before I was, but I went immediately into Arabia and later returned to Damascus.

[18]Then after three years, I went up to Jerusalem to get acquainted with Peter[b]

---

[a]15 Or *from my mother's womb*   [b]18 Greek *Cephas*

THURSDAY

VERSE FOR THE DAY:	AUTHOR:	PASSAGE FOR THE DAY:
Galatians 2:20	Rebecca Manley Pippert	Galatians 2:15–21

More Myself

CHRISTIANITY isn't a narcotic that dulls you into obedience. It involves battle—it's excruciating to give up control. But that is why we must not feel despair if we are struggling. To struggle does not mean we are incorrigible. It means we are *alive!*

A disciple says, "I hear you, Lord. It's the nuttiest thing I ever heard of. It's risky. I'll look like a fool, but I'll do it. Because my life is no longer committed to doing my thing but your thing." Heaven will not be filled with innocent people, running around saying, "Oh, was there another way? I guess I never noticed." Rather they will say, "You bet there were other options that begged to control me. By God's grace and my struggle, Jesus is my Lord."

Is Jesus' desire to be the Lord of our lives some little fetish of his? Why is it so important to him? Why should we want him to have control of our lives? Besides the fact that he deserves it because of who he is, he knows he is the only one in the universe who can control us without destroying us. No one will ever love you like Jesus. No one will ever know you better, care more for your wholeness. The last breath Jesus breathed on this planet was for you. Jesus will meet you wherever you are and he will help you. He is not intimidated by past failures, broken promises or wounds. He will make sense out of your brokenness. But he can only begin to be the Lord of your life today, not next Monday or next month, but now.

And the great and joyful paradox is that while he totally transforms us he makes us more ourselves than ever before.

Additional Scripture Readings:
Luke 9:23–25; Philippians 3:20–21

Go to page 265 for your next devotional reading.

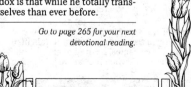

and stayed with him fifteen days. [19]I saw none of the other apostles—only James, the Lord's brother. [20]I assure you before God that what I am writing you is no lie. [21]Later I went to Syria and Cilicia. [22]I was personally unknown to the churches of Judea that are in Christ. [23]They only heard the report: "The man who formerly persecuted us is now preaching the faith he once tried to destroy." [24]And they praised God because of me.

Paul Accepted by the Apostles

2 Fourteen years later I went up again to Jerusalem, this time with Barnabas. I took Titus along also. [2]I went in response to a revelation and set before them the gospel that I preach among the Gentiles. But I did this privately to those who seemed to be leaders, for fear that I was running or had run my race in vain. [3]Yet not even Titus, who was with me, was compelled to be circumcised, even though he was a Greek. [4]This matter arose, because some false brothers had infiltrated our ranks to spy on the freedom we have in Christ Jesus and to make us slaves. [5]We did not give in to them for a moment, so that the truth of the gospel might remain with you.

[6]As for those who seemed to be important—whatever they were makes no difference to me; God does not judge by external appearance—those men added nothing to my message. [7]On the contrary, they saw that I had been entrusted with the task of preaching the gospel to the Gentiles,[a] just as Peter had been to the Jews.[b] [8]For God, who was at work in the ministry of Peter as an apostle to the Jews, was also at work in my ministry as an apostle to the Gentiles. [9]James, Peter[c] and John, those reputed to be pillars, gave me and Barnabas the right hand of fellowship when they recognized the grace given to me. They agreed that we should go to the Gentiles, and they to the Jews. [10]All they asked was that we should continue to remember the poor, the very thing I was eager to do.

Paul Opposes Peter

[11]When Peter came to Antioch, I opposed him to his face, because he was clearly in the wrong. [12]Before certain men came from James, he used to eat with the Gentiles. But when they arrived, he began to draw back and separate himself from the Gentiles because he was afraid of those who belonged to the circumcision group. [13]The other Jews joined him in his hypocrisy, so that by their hypocrisy even Barnabas was led astray.

[14]When I saw that they were not acting in line with the truth of the gospel, I said to Peter in front of them all, "You are a Jew, yet you live like a Gentile and not like a Jew. How is it, then, that you force Gentiles to follow Jewish customs?

[15]"We who are Jews by birth and not 'Gentile sinners' [16]know that a man is not justified by observing the law, but by faith in Jesus Christ. So we, too, have put our faith in Christ Jesus that we may be justified by faith in Christ and not by observing the law, because by observing the law no one will be justified.

[17]"If, while we seek to be justified in Christ, it becomes evident that we ourselves are sinners, does that mean that Christ promotes sin? Absolutely not! [18]If I rebuild what I destroyed, I prove that I am a lawbreaker. [19]For through the law I died to the law so that I might live for God. [20]I have been crucified with Christ and I no longer live, but Christ lives in me. The life I live in the body, I live by faith in the Son of God, who loved me and gave himself for me. [21]I do not set aside the grace of God, for if righteousness could be gained through the law, Christ died for nothing!"[d]

Faith or Observance of the Law

3 You foolish Galatians! Who has bewitched you? Before your very eyes Jesus Christ was clearly portrayed as crucified. [2]I would like to learn just one thing from you: Did you receive the Spirit by observing the law, or by believing what you heard? [3]Are you so foolish? After beginning with the Spirit, are you now trying to attain your goal by human effort? [4]Have you suffered so much for nothing—if it really was for nothing? [5]Does God give you his Spirit and work miracles among you because you observe the law, or because you believe what you heard?

[6]Consider Abraham: "He believed God, and it was credited to him as righteousness."[e] [7]Understand, then, that those who believe are children of Abraham. [8]The Scripture foresaw that God would justify the Gentiles by faith, and an-

---

[a]7 Greek *uncircumcised*   [b]7 Greek *circumcised*; also in verses 8 and 9   [c]9 Greek *Cephas*; also in verses 11 and 14   [d]21 Some interpreters end the quotation after verse 14.   [e]6 Gen. 15:6

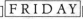

VERSE FOR THE DAY:
Galatians 3:6,11,27

AUTHOR:
June Hunt

PASSAGE FOR THE DAY:
Galatians 3:1–29

Righteousness and Authority

YOU'RE at the beach . . . you're famished . . . you find a restaurant . . . you rush in . . . you spot a sign:

> No Shirt
> No Shoes
> No Service

This message is clear. To be accepted, you must be clothed according to the restaurant's standard.

God also has a standard. But he makes it possible for you to be acceptable to him at all times when he gives you "righteousness as [your] clothing" (Job 29:14). The word *righteous*, in its simplest form, means "right" and "just." The word also means "acquitted, vindicated." Your faith in Christ enables God to regard you as righteous. He doesn't see your sin any longer, but he sees you as clothed with the righteousness of Christ. As such you are acceptable and properly dressed to "come and dine."

If you have struggled with feeling too unworthy to be called "the righteousness of God" (2 Corinthians 5:21), realize that this "clothing" you are given is like a uniform that, because it represents righteousness, also carries authority.

Have you ever seen a gigantic eighteen-wheel semitrailer truck groaning to a stop just because a police officer walks in front of the traffic and holds up his or her hand? What gives this person the right to command such respect? Certainly not parentage, social status, education, personality or even church affiliation. The officer stands confidently in front of this awesome "king of the road" because of the *right clothing*—the uniform has undeniable authority.

At the moment of conversion you were issued a righteous uniform. The Lord not only covered your past but also gave you authority over your future. With the "breastplate of righteousness" (Ephesians 6:14), God gave you power over sin.

As a child of God, you have the righteousness of God. You have the power that backs the badge.

Additional Scripture Readings:
Isaiah 61:10; Revelation 3:4–5

Go to page 266 for your next devotional reading.

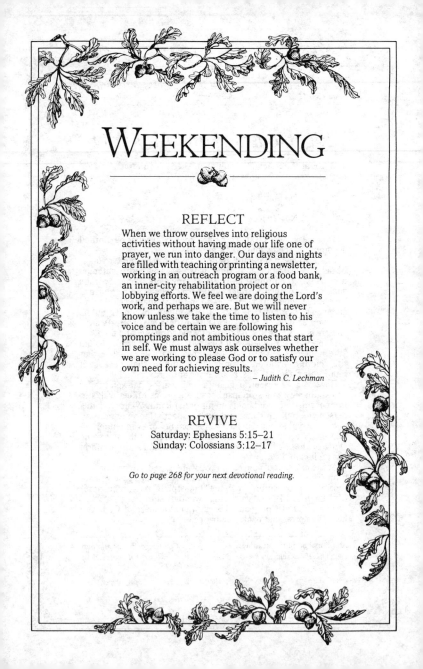

WEEKENDING

REFLECT

When we throw ourselves into religious
activities without having made our life one of
prayer, we run into danger. Our days and nights
are filled with teaching or printing a newsletter,
working in an outreach program or a food bank,
an inner-city rehabilitation project or on
lobbying efforts. We feel we are doing the Lord's
work, and perhaps we are. But we will never
know unless we take the time to listen to his
voice and be certain we are following his
promptings and not ambitious ones that start
in self. We must always ask ourselves whether
we are working to please God or to satisfy our
own need for achieving results.

– *Judith C. Lechman*

REVIVE

Saturday: Ephesians 5:15–21
Sunday: Colossians 3:12–17

Go to page 268 for your next devotional reading.

nounced the gospel in advance to Abraham: "All nations will be blessed through you."*a* 9So those who have faith are blessed along with Abraham, the man of faith.

10All who rely on observing the law are under a curse, for it is written: "Cursed is everyone who does not continue to do everything written in the Book of the Law."*b* 11Clearly no one is justified before God by the law, because, "The righteous will live by faith."*c* 12The law is not based on faith; on the contrary, "The man who does these things will live by them."*d* 13Christ redeemed us from the curse of the law by becoming a curse for us, for it is written: "Cursed is everyone who is hung on a tree."*e* 14He redeemed us in order that the blessing given to Abraham might come to the Gentiles through Christ Jesus, so that by faith we might receive the promise of the Spirit.

The Law and the Promise

15Brothers, let me take an example from everyday life. Just as no one can set aside or add to a human covenant that has been duly established, so it is in this case. 16The promises were spoken to Abraham and to his seed. The Scripture does not say "and to seeds," meaning many people, but "and to your seed,"*f* meaning one person, who is Christ. 17What I mean is this: The law, introduced 430 years later, does not set aside the covenant previously established by God and thus do away with the promise. 18For if the inheritance depends on the law, then it no longer depends on a promise; but God in his grace gave it to Abraham through a promise.

19What, then, was the purpose of the law? It was added because of transgressions until the Seed to whom the promise referred had come. The law was put into effect through angels by a mediator. 20A mediator, however, does not represent just one party; but God is one.

21Is the law, therefore, opposed to the promises of God? Absolutely not! For if a law had been given that could impart life, then righteousness would certainly have come by the law. 22But the Scripture declares that the whole world is a prisoner of sin, so that what was promised, being given through faith in Jesus Christ, might be given to those who believe.

23Before this faith came, we were held prisoners by the law, locked up until faith should be revealed. 24So the law was put in charge to lead us to Christ*g* that we might be justified by faith. 25Now that faith has come, we are no longer under the supervision of the law.

Sons of God

26You are all sons of God through faith in Christ Jesus, 27for all of you who were baptized into Christ have clothed yourselves with Christ. 28There is neither Jew nor Greek, slave nor free, male nor female, for you are all one in Christ Jesus. 29If you belong to Christ, then you are Abraham's seed, and heirs according to the promise.

4 What I am saying is that as long as the heir is a child, he is no different from a slave, although he owns the whole estate. 2He is subject to guardians and trustees until the time set by his father. 3So also, when we were children, we were in slavery under the basic principles of the world. 4But when the time had fully come, God sent his Son, born of a woman, born under law, 5to redeem those under law, that we might receive the full rights of sons. 6Because you are sons, God sent the Spirit of his Son into our hearts, the Spirit who calls out, *"Abba,*h* Father."* 7So you are no longer a slave, but a son; and since you are a son, God has made you also an heir.

Paul's Concern for the Galatians

8Formerly, when you did not know God, you were slaves to those who by nature are not gods. 9But now that you know God—or rather are known by God—how is it that you are turning back to those weak and miserable principles? Do you wish to be enslaved by them all over again? 10You are observing special days and months and seasons and years! 11I fear for you, that somehow I have wasted my efforts on you.

12I plead with you, brothers, become like me, for I became like you. You have done me no wrong. 13As you know, it was because of an illness that I first preached the gospel to you. 14Even though my illness was a trial to you, you did not treat me with contempt or scorn. Instead, you welcomed me as if I were an angel of God, as if I were Christ Jesus himself. 15What

---

a8 Gen. 12:3; 18:18; 22:18   *b10* Deut. 27:26   *c11* Hab. 2:4   *d12* Lev. 18:5   *e13* Deut. 21:23
f16 Gen. 12:7; 13:15; 24:7   *g24* Or *charge until Christ came*   *h6* Aramaic for *Father*

VERSE FOR THE DAY:
Galatians 5:13

AUTHOR:
Kathy Narramore
Alice Hill

PASSAGE FOR THE DAY:
Galatians 5:13–15

Serving as a Friend

AS friends we need to be two people discovering Christ together, standing at eye level equally in need of the Lord's redemption and grace, seeing each other as both gifted and needy. This Biblical perspective of each other creates a safe emotional climate in which we "serve one another" (Galatians 5:13) and "submit to one another" (Ephesians 5:21).

Serving each other is another way of expressing God's love. It means freely undertaking any task or commitment necessary or helpful to another's spiritual, emotional or physical welfare. It may even be menial such as Jesus offered when he bathed the sore and dirty feet of his followers, or it may be offering empathy, bearing a burden, comforting. But however we do serve in his spirit, we make his love tangible.

We also make his love real to each other as we submit to each other. We are to be adaptable to each other in working out decisions, solutions to problems, and in accepting instruction. Keep in mind that this is quite different from obedience, which is something that can be demanded or coerced. Submission in this Biblical sense must be freely and voluntarily given. It is self-imposed out of humility and desire to serve. The motives to be submissive can only be healthy when the choice is coming from a strong sense of worth and identity in Christ. Then it will not be submission out of fear and a slavish desire to please. It will reflect that characteristic of Christ so contrary to human nature, "Who, being in very nature God, did not consider equality with God something to be grasped, but made himself nothing, taking the very nature of a servant, being made in human likeness" (Philippians 2:6–7).

You may not encounter any of the barriers we have faced as friends, but you can be sure Satan will put some roadblocks in the path of godly friendships. He would love to have you limp along as a Christian lone ranger or as a person with many nice acquaintances but no one who really knows you well.

Additional Scripture Readings:
Ephesians 4:22–32; Philippians 2:1–4

Go to page 270 for your next devotional reading.

has happened to all your joy? I can testify that, if you could have done so, you would have torn out your eyes and given them to me. [16]Have I now become your enemy by telling you the truth?

[17]Those people are zealous to win you over, but for no good. What they want is to alienate you ,from us,, so that you may be zealous for them. [18]It is fine to be zealous, provided the purpose is good, and to be so always and not just when I am with you. [19]My dear children, for whom I am again in the pains of childbirth until Christ is formed in you, [20]how I wish I could be with you now and change my tone, because I am perplexed about you!

Hagar and Sarah

[21]Tell me, you who want to be under the law, are you not aware of what the law says? [22]For it is written that Abraham had two sons, one by the slave woman and the other by the free woman. [23]His son by the slave woman was born in the ordinary way; but his son by the free woman was born as the result of a promise.

[24]These things may be taken figuratively, for the women represent two covenants. One covenant is from Mount Sinai and bears children who are to be slaves: This is Hagar. [25]Now Hagar stands for Mount Sinai in Arabia and corresponds to the present city of Jerusalem, because she is in slavery with her children. [26]But the Jerusalem that is above is free, and she is our mother. [27]For it is written:

"Be glad, O barren woman,
  who bears no children;
break forth and cry aloud,
  you who have no labor pains;
because more are the children of the
  desolate woman
    than of her who has a husband." [a]

[28]Now you, brothers, like Isaac, are children of promise. [29]At that time the son born in the ordinary way persecuted the son born by the power of the Spirit. It is the same now. [30]But what does the Scripture say? "Get rid of the slave woman and her son, for the slave woman's son will never share in the inheritance with the free woman's son." [b] [31]Therefore, brothers, we are not children of the slave woman, but of the free woman.

Freedom in Christ

5 It is for freedom that Christ has set us free. Stand firm, then, and do not let yourselves be burdened again by a yoke of slavery.

[2]Mark my words! I, Paul, tell you that if you let yourselves be circumcised, Christ will be of no value to you at all. [3]Again I declare to every man who lets himself be circumcised that he is obligated to obey the whole law. [4]You who are trying to be justified by law have been alienated from Christ; you have fallen away from grace. [5]But by faith we eagerly await through the Spirit the righteousness for which we hope. [6]For in Christ Jesus neither circumcision nor uncircumcision has any value. The only thing that counts is faith expressing itself through love.

[7]You were running a good race. Who cut in on you and kept you from obeying the truth? [8]That kind of persuasion does not come from the one who calls you. [9]"A little yeast works through the whole batch of dough." [10]I am confident in the Lord that you will take no other view. The one who is throwing you into confusion will pay the penalty, whoever he may be. [11]Brothers, if I am still preaching circumcision, why am I still being persecuted? In that case the offense of the cross has been abolished. [12]As for those agitators, I wish they would go the whole way and emasculate themselves!

[13]You, my brothers, were called to be free. But do not use your freedom to indulge the sinful nature[c]; rather, serve one another in love. [14]The entire law is summed up in a single command: "Love your neighbor as yourself." [d] [15]If you keep on biting and devouring each other, watch out or you will be destroyed by each other.

Life by the Spirit

[16]So I say, live by the Spirit, and you will not gratify the desires of the sinful nature. [17]For the sinful nature desires what is contrary to the Spirit, and the Spirit what is contrary to the sinful nature. They are in conflict with each other, so that you do not do what you want. [18]But if you are led by the Spirit, you are not under law.

[19]The acts of the sinful nature are obvious: sexual immorality, impurity and debauchery; [20]idolatry and witchcraft; ha-

a27 Isaiah 54:1   *b30* Gen. 21:10   *c13* Or *the flesh*; also in verses 16, 17, 19 and 24   *d14* Lev. 19:18

tred, discord, jealousy, fits of rage, selfish ambition, dissensions, factions ²¹and envy; drunkenness, orgies, and the like. I warn you, as I did before, that those who live like this will not inherit the kingdom of God.

²²But the fruit of the Spirit is love, joy, peace, patience, kindness, goodness, faithfulness, ²³gentleness and self-control. Against such things there is no law. ²⁴Those who belong to Christ Jesus have crucified the sinful nature with its pas-

TUESDAY

VERSE FOR THE DAY:
Galatians 6:4

AUTHOR:
June Masters Bacher

PASSAGE FOR THE DAY:
Galatians 6:1–10

Starting Anew at 65

MY mother's friend had a thing about birthdays. She overcame it at 65.

It rained on Jo's birthday. "That figures," she said. "Gray month. Gray hair. Gray mood." She inspected herself from all angles looking for a bigger bulge or a new liver spot. Always bad, this one was the worst of all—a time (she said) when husbands became interesting "older men" and wives became dull "elderly women."

"Wanting to punish myself," she remembers, "I looked in my scrapbook at the list of advantages of being 21. A glorious day!"

She could vote, date, marry, seek a career, choose her own clothes, travel, live where she wished, read what she chose, forget school routine for a time and *enjoy her freedom!* So?

"That one did it," Jo admitted. "When had I ever been as free as *now?*" And that was when the dear lady began her list of advantages of turning 65.

Ah yes, she could draw Social Security, ride the city bus free, visit city parks without paying for admission, take adult ed courses free, collect Medicare, serve as the sage whose ideas were considered wise and whose services were valuable. There was nothing, in fact, in the first list Jo was unable to do or had not done already. There were countless things she could do now but not then. "Why, I'm a liberated woman!" she cried in discovery.

To think and pray about: It is good to pause and count our blessings at every birthday. They pile up with the years. God is changeless. He has work for us here and each milestone shows that he chose to have us remain to give him a hand. Resolve this year to enjoy your new freedom. Ask God how you can make it count.

Additional Scripture Readings:
Genesis 12:1–4; Hebrews 6:9–12

Go to page 273 for your next devotional reading.

sions and desires. 25Since we live by the Spirit, let us keep in step with the Spirit. 26Let us not become conceited, provoking and envying each other.

Doing Good to All

6 Brothers, if someone is caught in a sin, you who are spiritual should restore him gently. But watch yourself, or you also may be tempted. 2Carry each other's burdens, and in this way you will fulfill the law of Christ. 3If anyone thinks he is something when he is nothing, he deceives himself. 4Each one should test his own actions. Then he can take pride in himself, without comparing himself to somebody else, 5for each one should carry his own load.

6Anyone who receives instruction in the word must share all good things with his instructor.

7Do not be deceived: God cannot be mocked. A man reaps what he sows. 8The one who sows to please his sinful nature, from that natureª will reap destruction; the one who sows to please the Spirit, from the Spirit will reap eternal life. 9Let us not become weary in doing good, for at the proper time we will reap a harvest if

we do not give up. 10Therefore, as we have opportunity, let us do good to all people, especially to those who belong to the family of believers.

Not Circumcision but a New Creation

11See what large letters I use as I write to you with my own hand!

12Those who want to make a good impression outwardly are trying to compel you to be circumcised. The only reason they do this is to avoid being persecuted for the cross of Christ. 13Not even those who are circumcised obey the law, yet they want you to be circumcised that they may boast about your flesh. 14May I never boast except in the cross of our Lord Jesus Christ, through whichᵇ the world has been crucified to me, and I to the world. 15Neither circumcision nor uncircumcision means anything; what counts is a new creation. 16Peace and mercy to all who follow this rule, even to the Israel of God.

17Finally, let no one cause me trouble, for I bear on my body the marks of Jesus.

18The grace of our Lord Jesus Christ be with your spirit, brothers. Amen.

ª8 Or his flesh, from the flesh   ᵇ14 Or whom

*PAUL writes this letter from prison
(Ephesians 4:1; probably in Rome, see
Acts 28:30–31) to the church he
started in Ephesus (Acts 19). In the
first half he explains God's great plan
to redeem the world through Christ,
showing what this means for individual
Christians and for the whole church. In
the second half he gives practical advice on how to live the Christian life. As
you read this book, first examine yourself to be sure that you are saved. Then
move on to fight against Satan and
show your love to your family, your
church and your community.*

EPHESIANS

1 Paul, an apostle of Christ Jesus by the will of God,

To the saints in Ephesus,[a] the faithful[b] in Christ Jesus:

[2] Grace and peace to you from God our Father and the Lord Jesus Christ.

Spiritual Blessings in Christ

[3] Praise be to the God and Father of our Lord Jesus Christ, who has blessed us in the heavenly realms with every spiritual blessing in Christ. [4] For he chose us in him before the creation of the world to be holy and blameless in his sight. In love [5] he[c] predestined us to be adopted as his sons through Jesus Christ, in accordance with his pleasure and will — [6] to the praise of his glorious grace, which he has freely given us in the One he loves. [7] In him we

---

a1 Some early manuscripts do not have in Ephesus.
in love. *5He*   *b1 Or* believers who are   *c4,5 Or* sight

VERSE FOR THE DAY:	AUTHOR:	PASSAGE FOR THE DAY:
Ephesians 1:17–23	Debby Boone	Ephesians 1:3–23

Resurrection Power

JAMES talks about the prayer of a righteous man being "power-ful and effective" (James 5:16). I think Paul's prayer for the people of Ephesus here in Ephesians 1:17–23 is a model for one of the most essential and important prayers we could ever pray for ourselves or one another. This prayer has taken hold of my heart so firmly that I have committed it to memory (quite a feat in itself) and pray it for family members, friends who are struggling, and for the body of Christ in general. Frequently, I pray it aloud over the people at my concerts.

Of course, there are other ways one should pray for people's needs, but this one prayer seems to cover the most basic and fundamental needs of every believer. It addresses our core desire that God will enlighten our hearts with the truth about himself and the hope to which he has called each of us.

The way we see God—the positive or negative way we view him as a father and provider—will shape the way we live our lives as believers in a dark and weary world. All of us, to some extent, no matter how long or fervently we have walked with the Lord, have shades and colorations of falseness about what God is like or how we are to relate to him. Only as he reveals himself in truth can we be set free to walk with an understanding of the hope of the riches of the inheritance he has set before us.

The question that naturally evolves from this is: "Yes, that would be great, but can God really do that for me? I am so weak." That's exactly why Paul spends the rest of Ephesians 1 talking about the greatness of God's power and the strength of his might . . . the same power he used when he raised Jesus from the dead. That's the power that God has committed to use while working in my life. Resurrection power! And the areas of my life that I feel are barren . . . useless . . . dead . . . burnt-out . . . those are the areas that he will fill with nothing less than himself so that I too can be "the fullness of him who fills everything in every way" (Ephesians 1:23). Hallelujah!

Additional Scripture Readings:
Romans 6:8–14; 1 Corinthians 15:56–58

Go to page 275 for your next devotional reading.

have redemption through his blood, the forgiveness of sins, in accordance with the riches of God's grace ⁸that he lavished on us with all wisdom and understanding. ⁹And he*ᵃ* made known to us the mystery of his will according to his good pleasure, which he purposed in Christ, ¹⁰to be put into effect when the times will have reached their fulfillment—to bring all things in heaven and on earth together under one head, even Christ.

¹¹In him we were also chosen,*ᵇ* having been predestined according to the plan of him who works out everything in conformity with the purpose of his will, ¹²in order that we, who were the first to hope in Christ, might be for the praise of his glory. ¹³And you also were included in Christ when you heard the word of truth, the gospel of your salvation. Having believed, you were marked in him with a seal, the promised Holy Spirit, ¹⁴who is a deposit guaranteeing our inheritance until the redemption of those who are God's possession—to the praise of his glory.

Thanksgiving and Prayer

¹⁵For this reason, ever since I heard about your faith in the Lord Jesus and your love for all the saints, ¹⁶I have not stopped giving thanks for you, remembering you in my prayers. ¹⁷I keep asking that the God of our Lord Jesus Christ, the glorious Father, may give you the Spirit*ᶜ* of wisdom and revelation, so that you may know him better. ¹⁸I pray also that the eyes of your heart may be enlightened in order that you may know the hope to which he has called you, the riches of his glorious inheritance in the saints, ¹⁹and his incomparably great power for us who believe. That power is like the working of his mighty strength, ²⁰which he exerted in Christ when he raised him from the dead and seated him at his right hand in the heavenly realms, ²¹far above all rule and authority, power and dominion, and every title that can be given, not only in the present age but also in the one to come. ²²And God placed all things under his feet and appointed him to be head over everything for the church, ²³which is his body, the fullness of him who fills everything in every way.

Made Alive in Christ

2 As for you, you were dead in your transgressions and sins, ²in which you used to live when you followed the ways of this world and of the ruler of the kingdom of the air, the spirit who is now at work in those who are disobedient. ³All of us also lived among them at one time, gratifying the cravings of our sinful nature*ᵈ* and following its desires and thoughts. Like the rest, we were by nature objects of wrath. ⁴But because of his great love for us, God, who is rich in mercy, ⁵made us alive with Christ even when we were dead in transgressions—it is by grace you have been saved. ⁶And God raised us up with Christ and seated us with him in the heavenly realms in Christ Jesus, ⁷in order that in the coming ages he might show the incomparable riches of his grace, expressed in his kindness to us in Christ Jesus. ⁸For it is by grace you have been saved, through faith—and this not from yourselves, it is the gift of God— ⁹not by works, so that no one can boast. ¹⁰For we are God's workmanship, created in Christ Jesus to do good works, which God prepared in advance for us to do.

One in Christ

¹¹Therefore, remember that formerly you who are Gentiles by birth and called "uncircumcised" by those who call themselves "the circumcision" (that done in the body by the hands of men)— ¹²remember that at that time you were separate from Christ, excluded from citizenship in Israel and foreigners to the covenants of the promise, without hope and without God in the world. ¹³But now in Christ Jesus you who once were far away have been brought near through the blood of Christ.

¹⁴For he himself is our peace, who has made the two one and has destroyed the barrier, the dividing wall of hostility, ¹⁵by abolishing in his flesh the law with its commandments and regulations. His purpose was to create in himself one new man out of the two, thus making peace, ¹⁶and in this one body to reconcile both of them to God through the cross, by which he put to death their hostility. ¹⁷He came and preached peace to you who were far away and peace to those who were near. ¹⁸For through him we both

ᵃ8,9 Or *us. With all wisdom and understanding,* ⁹*he*   *ᵇ11* Or *were made heirs*   *ᶜ17* Or *a spirit*
ᵈ3 Or *our flesh*

have access to the Father by one Spirit. ¹⁹Consequently, you are no longer foreigners and aliens, but fellow citizens with God's people and members of God's household, ²⁰built on the foundation of the apostles and prophets, with Christ Jesus himself as the chief cornerstone. ²¹In him the whole building is joined together and rises to become a holy temple in the Lord. ²²And in him you too are being built together to become a dwelling in which God lives by his Spirit.

Paul the Preacher to the Gentiles

3 For this reason I, Paul, the prisoner of Christ Jesus for the sake of you Gentiles—

²Surely you have heard about the administration of God's grace that was given to me for you, ³that is, the mystery made known to me by revelation, as I have already written briefly. ⁴In reading this, then, you will be able to understand my insight into the mystery of Christ, ⁵which was not made known to men in

THURSDAY

VERSE FOR THE DAY:
Ephesians 3:16

AUTHOR:
Gloria Gaither

PASSAGE FOR THE DAY:
Ephesians 3:16–20

I Wish You

IT was Suzanne's college graduation party. Family friends and relatives, schoolmates and former teachers all sipped punch and ate raspberry cake under the willow trees beside the gazebo at the creek. She had played there as a child, fishing for catfish and catching turtles and garter snakes. Memories raced across the green hillside and peeped out from behind the apple tree in the orchard.

I listened as our friends wished her success as a writer, fame as a lyricist, fortune in her chosen work, and honor in grad school. What would we wish her, Bill and I later asked ourselves, as we sat in the yard swing apart from the others. It wouldn't be wealth, we decided, or notability. And success would be hard to define. What we would wish her would be some sunshine and some rain. We would wish her growth . . . and vision . . . and the ability to feel what those who are hurt or left out or lonely feel.

As we had done very often before, we found ourselves drawn that night to the passage of Scripture that had been read probably more often in our home than any other, for it stated very well what we wished then for Suzanne and for all our children as they faced life's shifts and changes . . . "that out of his glorious riches he may strengthen you with power through his Spirit in your inner being, so that Christ may dwell in your hearts through faith. And I pray that you, being rooted and established in love, may have power, together with all the saints, to grasp how wide and long and high and deep is the love of Christ, and to know this love that surpasses knowledge—that you may be filled to the measure of all the fullness of God" (Ephesians 3:16–19).

Additional Scripture Readings:
Philippians 1:9–11; Colossians 2:2–7

Go to page 276 for your next devotional reading.

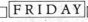
VERSE FOR THE DAY:
Ephesians 5:8

AUTHOR:
Luci Swindoll

PASSAGE FOR THE DAY:
Ephesians 5:8–10

We Are Light

A FRIEND of mine was caught in an elevator in New York City during a power failure. He just happened to have a tiny flashlight in his pocket . . . the type of guy who always was prepared for emergencies. There were seven people, all strangers, on the elevator; and at first, in that pitch-black darkness, there was momentary panic as everybody talked at once. When he remembered the flashlight in his pocket and turned it on, the fear dissipated. During the forty-five minutes they were stuck shoulder-to-shoulder in that small space, they became pretty good friends, laughing, telling jokes, and even singing. The way he presented the story to me, it sounded more fun than fearsome.

Ephesians 5:8 says we are that flashlight. Note, it doesn't say we are *like* light, it says we *are* light. Just as the flashlight draws power from its batteries, we draw power from the Son of God. As light, we dissipate fear, bring relief and lift spirits. We don't even have to be big to be effective. We just have to be "on."

The last two lines of T.S. Eliot's poem, "The Rock," read:

> And we thank Thee that the darkness reminds us
>   of light.
> O Light Invisible, we give Thee Thanks for Thy
>   great glory!

As we grope in darkness, what do we want most? Light! We want direction, illumination. Darkness reminds us of our oppressive, burdensome need. It "feels" heavy even though it's intangible. Only light, which also is intangible, pushes that feeling away. It provides relief.

Today, let's pursue that which is good, right and truthful by shining through darkened circumstances. Don't keep the switch off or hold back as though our batteries have run down. Our source is the glorious "Light Invisible." Being switched on pleases the Lord. Stay on. Stay bright.

Additional Scripture Readings:
Proverbs 4:18–19; Matthew 6:14–16

*Go to page 278 for your next
devotional reading.*

other generations as it has now been revealed by the Spirit to God's holy apostles and prophets. [6]This mystery is that through the gospel the Gentiles are heirs together with Israel, members together of one body, and sharers together in the promise in Christ Jesus.

[7]I became a servant of this gospel by the gift of God's grace given me through the working of his power. [8]Although I am less than the least of all God's people, this grace was given me: to preach to the Gentiles the unsearchable riches of Christ, [9]and to make plain to everyone the administration of this mystery, which for ages past was kept hidden in God, who created all things. [10]His intent was that now, through the church, the manifold wisdom of God should be made known to the rulers and authorities in the heavenly realms, [11]according to his eternal purpose which he accomplished in Christ Jesus our Lord. [12]In him and through faith in him we may approach God with freedom and confidence. [13]I ask you, therefore, not to be discouraged because of my sufferings for you, which are your glory.

A Prayer for the Ephesians

[14]For this reason I kneel before the Father, [15]from whom his whole family[a] in heaven and on earth derives its name. [16]I pray that out of his glorious riches he may strengthen you with power through his Spirit in your inner being, [17]so that Christ may dwell in your hearts through faith. And I pray that you, being rooted and established in love, [18]may have power, together with all the saints, to grasp how wide and long and high and deep is the love of Christ, [19]and to know this love that surpasses knowledge—that you may be filled to the measure of all the fullness of God.

[20]Now to him who is able to do immeasurably more than all we ask or imagine, according to his power that is at work within us, [21]to him be glory in the church and in Christ Jesus throughout all generations, for ever and ever! Amen.

Unity in the Body of Christ

4 As a prisoner for the Lord, then, I urge you to live a life worthy of the calling you have received. [2]Be completely humble and gentle; be patient, bearing with one another in love. [3]Make every effort to keep the unity of the Spirit through the

bond of peace. [4]There is one body and one Spirit— just as you were called to one hope when you were called— [5]one Lord, one faith, one baptism; [6]one God and Father of all, who is over all and through all and in all.

[7]But to each one of us grace has been given as Christ apportioned it. [8]This is why it[b] says:

"When he ascended on high,
    he led captives in his train
    and gave gifts to men."[c]

[9](What does "he ascended" mean except that he also descended to the lower, earthly regions[d]? [10]He who descended is the very one who ascended higher than all the heavens, in order to fill the whole universe.) [11]It was he who gave some to be apostles, some to be prophets, some to be evangelists, and some to be pastors and teachers, [12]to prepare God's people for works of service, so that the body of Christ may be built up [13]until we all reach unity in the faith and in the knowledge of the Son of God and become mature, attaining to the whole measure of the fullness of Christ.

[14]Then we will no longer be infants, tossed back and forth by the waves, and blown here and there by every wind of teaching and by the cunning and craftiness of men in their deceitful scheming. [15]Instead, speaking the truth in love, we will in all things grow up into him who is the Head, that is, Christ. [16]From him the whole body, joined and held together by every supporting ligament, grows and builds itself up in love, as each part does its work.

Living as Children of Light

[17]So I tell you this, and insist on it in the Lord, that you must no longer live as the Gentiles do, in the futility of their thinking. [18]They are darkened in their understanding and separated from the life of God because of the ignorance that is in them due to the hardening of their hearts. [19]Having lost all sensitivity, they have given themselves over to sensuality so as to indulge in every kind of impurity, with a continual lust for more.

[20]You, however, did not come to know Christ that way. [21]Surely you heard of him and were taught in him in accordance with the truth that is in Jesus. [22]You were taught, with regard to your former way of

---

[a]15 Or whom all fatherhood   [b]8 Or God   [c]8 Psalm 68:18   [d]9 Or the depths of the earth

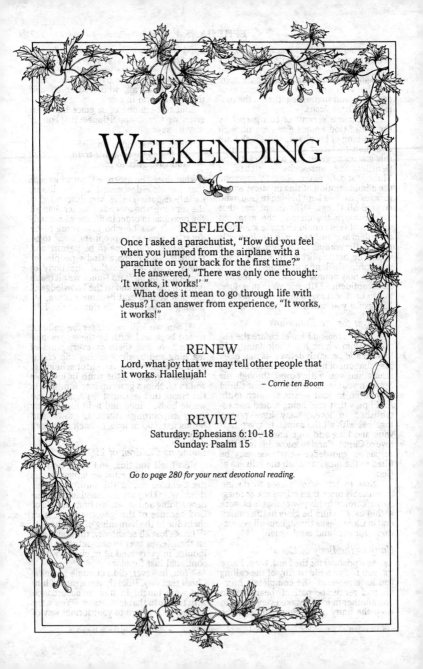

WEEKENDING

REFLECT

Once I asked a parachutist, "How did you feel
when you jumped from the airplane with a
parachute on your back for the first time?"

He answered, "There was only one thought:
'It works, it works!'"

What does it mean to go through life with
Jesus? I can answer from experience, "It works,
it works!"

RENEW

Lord, what joy that we may tell other people that
it works. Hallelujah!

– Corrie ten Boom

REVIVE

Saturday: Ephesians 6:10–18
Sunday: Psalm 15

Go to page 280 for your next devotional reading.

life, to put off your old self, which is being corrupted by its deceitful desires; [23]to be made new in the attitude of your minds; [24]and to put on the new self, created to be like God in true righteousness and holiness.

[25]Therefore each of you must put off falsehood and speak truthfully to his neighbor, for we are all members of one body. [26]"In your anger do not sin"[a]: Do not let the sun go down while you are still angry, [27]and do not give the devil a foothold. [28]He who has been stealing must steal no longer, but must work, doing something useful with his own hands, that he may have something to share with those in need.

[29]Do not let any unwholesome talk come out of your mouths, but only what is helpful for building others up according to their needs, that it may benefit those who listen. [30]And do not grieve the Holy Spirit of God, with whom you were sealed for the day of redemption. [31]Get rid of all bitterness, rage and anger, brawling and slander, along with every form of malice. [32]Be kind and compassionate to one another, forgiving each other, just as in Christ God forgave you.

5 Be imitators of God, therefore, as dearly loved children [2]and live a life of love, just as Christ loved us and gave himself up for us as a fragrant offering and sacrifice to God.

[3]But among you there must not be even a hint of sexual immorality, or of any kind of impurity, or of greed, because these are improper for God's holy people. [4]Nor should there be obscenity, foolish talk or coarse joking, which are out of place, but rather thanksgiving. [5]For of this you can be sure: No immoral, impure or greedy person—such a man is an idolater—has any inheritance in the kingdom of Christ and of God.[b] [6]Let no one deceive you with empty words, for because of such things God's wrath comes on those who are disobedient. [7]Therefore do not be partners with them.

[8]For you were once darkness, but now you are light in the Lord. Live as children of light [9](for the fruit of the light consists in all goodness, righteousness and truth) [10]and find out what pleases the Lord. [11]Have nothing to do with the fruitless deeds of darkness, but rather expose them. [12]For it is shameful even to mention what the disobedient do in secret.

[13]But everything exposed by the light becomes visible, [14]for it is light that makes everything visible. This is why it is said:

"Wake up, O sleeper,
    rise from the dead,
and Christ will shine on you."

[15]Be very careful, then, how you live—not as unwise but as wise, [16]making the most of every opportunity, because the days are evil. [17]Therefore do not be foolish, but understand what the Lord's will is. [18]Do not get drunk on wine, which leads to debauchery. Instead, be filled with the Spirit. [19]Speak to one another with psalms, hymns and spiritual songs. Sing and make music in your heart to the Lord, [20]always giving thanks to God the Father for everything, in the name of our Lord Jesus Christ.

[21]Submit to one another out of reverence for Christ.

Wives and Husbands

[22]Wives, submit to your husbands as to the Lord. [23]For the husband is the head of the wife as Christ is the head of the church, his body, of which he is the Savior. [24]Now as the church submits to Christ, so also wives should submit to their husbands in everything.

[25]Husbands, love your wives, just as Christ loved the church and gave himself up for her [26]to make her holy, cleansing[c] her by the washing with water through the word, [27]and to present her to himself as a radiant church, without stain or wrinkle or any other blemish, but holy and blameless. [28]In this same way, husbands ought to love their wives as their own bodies. He who loves his wife loves himself. [29]After all, no one ever hated his own body, but he feeds and cares for it, just as Christ does the church— [30]for we are members of his body. [31]"For this reason a man will leave his father and mother and be united to his wife, and the two will become one flesh."[d] [32]This is a profound mystery—but I am talking about Christ and the church. [33]However, each one of you also must love his wife as he loves himself, and the wife must respect her husband.

Children and Parents

6 Children, obey your parents in the Lord, for this is right. [2]"Honor your father and mother"—which is the first

---

[a]26 Psalm 4:4   [b]5 Or kingdom of the Christ and God   [c]26 Or having cleansed   [d]31 Gen. 2:24

VERSE FOR THE DAY:
Ephesians 6:13

AUTHOR:
Beverly LaHaye

PASSAGE FOR THE DAY:
Ephesians 6:10–18

Worth Defending in Battle

WHEN you read Ephesians 6:10–18, you begin to realize that these verses prepare us for warfare. One of those battles is to fight against those things that keep us from having strong marriages and families. The last half of chapter five discusses husband-wife relationships within marriage. The first half of chapter six teaches children to obey, and then discusses the responsibilities of the father. Then verse ten says, "Finally, be strong in the Lord. . . ." These instructions help us clearly see that there *is* a way to keep marriages and families strong.

In this time when the divorce rate has skyrocketed, marriages *can* be strong in the Lord. Even now when family life is rapidly deteriorating, families *can* be strong.

The promises of Ephesians are an encouragement to young couples who wonder if they should marry in light of the high divorce rate. Other couples question if they should have children because the world is such an evil place in which to raise them. Ephesians 6:11 and 13 encourage us to know that we can stand against the schemes of the devil and that we can withstand in the evil day by taking the whole armor of God as our defense—the armor made up of truth, righteousness, the gospel of peace, faith, salvation, and the sword of the Spirit. A lasting marriage is of great value, but you have to be prepared for warfare to preserve it. The same is true with the family. It will be necessary to stand against the schemes of the devil to keep a family strong.

These verses have been a source of great strength to us in raising our family. There were times when all would have been lost were it not for the wisdom and strength we derived from the Word of God.

My husband and I have been teaching Family Life Seminars for many years. Most of the books we have written are based on some phase of family life. We have come across almost every problem possible in marriage and family relationships, and we still believe that it is possible to have a strong family life and marriage relationship if the Word of God is used as the armor to withstand every trial. We must use the Word of God as our basis for sorting out right from wrong, the basis for making decisions or resolving conflicts.

Marriage and the family are institutions founded by God. They are considered his highest priority for individuals next to personal salvation. They are worth defending in battle.

Additional Scripture Readings:
Malachi 2:13–16; Matthew 19:3–14

Go to page 283 for your next devotional reading.

commandment with a promise— [3]"that it may go well with you and that you may enjoy long life on the earth."[a]

[4]Fathers, do not exasperate your children; instead, bring them up in the training and instruction of the Lord.

Slaves and Masters

[5]Slaves, obey your earthly masters with respect and fear, and with sincerity of heart, just as you would obey Christ. [6]Obey them not only to win their favor when their eye is on you, but like slaves of Christ, doing the will of God from your heart. [7]Serve wholeheartedly, as if you were serving the Lord, not men, [8]because you know that the Lord will reward everyone for whatever good he does, whether he is slave or free.

[9]And masters, treat your slaves in the same way. Do not threaten them, since you know that he who is both their Master and yours is in heaven, and there is no favoritism with him.

The Armor of God

[10]Finally, be strong in the Lord and in his mighty power. [11]Put on the full armor of God so that you can take your stand against the devil's schemes. [12]For our struggle is not against flesh and blood, but against the rulers, against the authorities, against the powers of this dark world and against the spiritual forces of evil in the heavenly realms. [13]Therefore put on the full armor of God, so that when the day of evil comes, you may be able to stand your ground, and after you have done everything, to stand. [14]Stand firm then, with the belt of truth buckled around your waist, with the breastplate of righteousness in place, [15]and with your feet fitted with the readiness that comes from the gospel of peace. [16]In addition to all this, take up the shield of faith, with which you can extinguish all the flaming arrows of the evil one. [17]Take the helmet of salvation and the sword of the Spirit, which is the word of God. [18]And pray in the Spirit on all occasions with all kinds of prayers and requests. With this in mind, be alert and always keep on praying for all the saints.

[19]Pray also for me, that whenever I open my mouth, words may be given me so that I will fearlessly make known the mystery of the gospel, [20]for which I am an ambassador in chains. Pray that I may declare it fearlessly, as I should.

Final Greetings

[21]Tychicus, the dear brother and faithful servant in the Lord, will tell you everything, so that you also may know how I am and what I am doing. [22]I am sending him to you for this very purpose, that you may know how we are, and that he may encourage you.

[23]Peace to the brothers, and love with faith from God the Father and the Lord Jesus Christ. [24]Grace to all who love our Lord Jesus Christ with an undying love.

[a]3 Deut. 5:16

*P*AUL *writes this letter to the church
he started in Philippi (Acts
16:11–40). Even though he is in
prison, he feels happy when he thinks of
what Christ means to him and of what
the Philippians are doing for him. He
gives some very practical advice on how
to live the Christian life. As you read
this book, remember always to rejoice in
the Lord and to be content, whatever
the circumstances.*

PHILIPPIANS

1 Paul and Timothy, servants of Christ Jesus,

To all the saints in Christ Jesus at Philippi, together with the overseers*a* and deacons:

²Grace and peace to you from God our Father and the Lord Jesus Christ.

Thanksgiving and Prayer

³I thank my God every time I remember you. ⁴In all my prayers for all of you, I always pray with joy ⁵because of your partnership in the gospel from the first day until now, ⁶being confident of this, that he who began a good work in you will carry it on to completion until the day of Christ Jesus.

⁷It is right for me to feel this way about all of you, since I have you in my heart; for whether I am in chains or defending and confirming the gospel, all of you share in God's grace with me. ⁸God can testify how I long for all of you with the affection of Christ Jesus.

⁹And this is my prayer: that your love may abound more and more in knowledge and depth of insight, ¹⁰so that you may be able to discern what is best and may be pure and blameless until the day of Christ, ¹¹filled with the fruit of righteousness that comes through Jesus Christ—to the glory and praise of God.

a1 Traditionally *bishops*

VERSE FOR THE DAY:	AUTHOR:	PASSAGE FOR THE DAY:
Philippians 2:5	Gigi Graham Tchividjian	Philippians 2:1–5

The Problem

I STOOD in the upstairs hallway, looking down over the bannister and waiting for the younger children to come in for their baths. My oldest daughter, taking a piano lesson, was in the living room directly below, and the repetitive melody she was playing echoed through my mind.

Suddenly the little ones bounded through the door. They bounced up to their rooms, cheeks flushed and eyes bright from their play.

I noticed, however, that one of my young sons was trudging slowly up the stairs, his head bowed, grubby hands covering his small, dirt-streaked face. When he reached the top, I asked him what was wrong.

"Aw, nothing," he replied.

"Then why are you holding your face in your hands?" I persisted.

"Oh, I was just praying."

Quite curious now, I asked what he was praying about.

"I can't tell you," he insisted, "because if I do, you'll be mad."

After much persuasion I convinced him that he could confide in me and that, whatever he told me, I would not get mad. So he explained that he was praying about a problem he had with his mind.

"A problem with your mind?" I asked, now more curious than ever, wondering what kind of problem a child of six could have with his mind. "What kind of problem?"

"Well," he said, "You see, every time I pass by the living room, I see my piano teacher, and my tongue sticks out."

Needless to say, it was hard to keep a straight face, but I took his problem seriously and assured him that God could, indeed, help him with it.

Later, on my knees beside the bathtub as I bathed this little fellow, I thought how I still struggle with the problem of controlling my mind and my tongue. That afternoon as I knelt to scrub that sturdy little body, the tub became my altar; the bathroom, my temple. I bowed my head, covered my face, and acknowledged that I, like my son, had a problem with my mind and tongue. I asked the Lord to forgive me and to give me more and more the mind and heart and attitude of Christ.

Additional Scripture Readings:
Psalm 39:1–2; James 1:26; 3:3–8

Go to page 285 for your next devotional reading.

Paul's Chains Advance the Gospel

[12]Now I want you to know, brothers, that what has happened to me has really served to advance the gospel. [13]As a result, it has become clear throughout the whole palace guard[a] and to everyone else that I am in chains for Christ. [14]Because of my chains, most of the brothers in the Lord have been encouraged to speak the word of God more courageously and fearlessly.

[15]It is true that some preach Christ out of envy and rivalry, but others out of goodwill. [16]The latter do so in love, knowing that I am put here for the defense of the gospel. [17]The former preach Christ out of selfish ambition, not sincerely, supposing that they can stir up trouble for me while I am in chains.[b] [18]But what does it matter? The important thing is that in every way, whether from false motives or true, Christ is preached. And because of this I rejoice.

Yes, and I will continue to rejoice, [19]for I know that through your prayers and the help given by the Spirit of Jesus Christ, what has happened to me will turn out for my deliverance.[c] [20]I eagerly expect and hope that I will in no way be ashamed, but will have sufficient courage so that now as always Christ will be exalted in my body, whether by life or by death. [21]For to me, to live is Christ and to die is gain. [22]If I am to go on living in the body, this will mean fruitful labor for me. Yet what shall I choose? I do not know! [23]I am torn between the two: I desire to depart and be with Christ, which is better by far; [24]but it is more necessary for you that I remain in the body. [25]Convinced of this, I know that I will remain, and I will continue with all of you for your progress and joy in the faith, [26]so that through my being with you again your joy in Christ Jesus will overflow on account of me.

[27]Whatever happens, conduct yourselves in a manner worthy of the gospel of Christ. Then, whether I come and see you or only hear about you in my absence, I will know that you stand firm in one spirit, contending as one man for the faith of the gospel [28]without being frightened in any way by those who oppose you. This is a sign to them that they will be destroyed, but that you will be saved—and that by God. [29]For it has been granted to you on behalf of Christ not only to believe on

him, but also to suffer for him, [30]since you are going through the same struggle you saw I had, and now hear that I still have.

Imitating Christ's Humility

2 If you have any encouragement from being united with Christ, if any comfort from his love, if any fellowship with the Spirit, if any tenderness and compassion, [2]then make my joy complete by being like-minded, having the same love, being one in spirit and purpose. [3]Do nothing out of selfish ambition or vain conceit, but in humility consider others better than yourselves. [4]Each of you should look not only to your own interests, but also to the interests of others.

[5]Your attitude should be the same as that of Christ Jesus:

[6]Who, being in very nature[d] God,
      did not consider equality with God
            something to be grasped,
[7]but made himself nothing,
      taking the very nature[e] of a
            servant,
      being made in human likeness.
[8]And being found in appearance as a
            man,
      he humbled himself
      and became obedient to death—
            even death on a cross!
[9]Therefore God exalted him to the
            highest place
      and gave him the name that is
            above every name,
[10]that at the name of Jesus every knee
            should bow,
      in heaven and on earth and under
            the earth,
[11]and every tongue confess that Jesus
            Christ is Lord,
      to the glory of God the Father.

Shining as Stars

[12]Therefore, my dear friends, as you have always obeyed—not only in my presence, but now much more in my absence—continue to work out your salvation with fear and trembling, [13]for it is God who works in you to will and to act according to his good purpose.

[14]Do everything without complaining or arguing, [15]so that you may become blameless and pure, children of God without fault in a crooked and depraved

VERSE FOR THE DAY:
Philippians 3:13

AUTHOR:
Anne Ortlund

PASSAGE FOR THE DAY:
Philippians 3:12–14

"One-Thing" People

"NOT that I've already arrived!" says the apostle Paul as he begins these comments. Well, whew! That makes us all identify with him!

Then we'd better pay attention to the rest of what he says—that even with all his imperfections and weaknesses Paul has in mind only *one thing:*

> Forgetting what is behind and straining toward what is ahead, I press on toward the goal to win the prize for which God has called me heavenward in Christ Jesus (Philippians 3:13–14).

"Forgetting what is behind"! We're little amateur psychologists these days, trying to remember all our pasts—bringing up why our mothers did this and our fathers did that—to explain all our idiosyncrasies and quirks.

The Bible doesn't so deal with us. It pronounces us sinners and then says to *get on with it,* to look up and forward! All the great people of faith in Hebrews 11 *looked forward* (Hebrews 11:10,14–16,20–22,26,39–40). So did Jesus: he endured the cross "for the joy set before him" (Hebrews 12:2).

Then, with Paul, we must strain toward what's ahead and fix our attention on that: all God's promises, all our inheritance, and the goal, the prize—Jesus himself!

"One thing I do," says Paul. It's "one-thing" believers who shed the clutter and baggage and *get there.* They "eliminate and concentrate," and they *make it.*

Take David, for instance:

> *One thing* I ask of the LORD,
>   this is what I seek:
> that I may dwell in the house of the LORD
>   all the days of my life,
> to gaze upon the beauty of the LORD
>   and to seek him in his temple (Psalm 27:4,
>   italics mine).

Or take Mary. She sat at the feet of Jesus. And he said to her bustling sister Martha, "Only *one thing* is needed. Mary has chosen what is better, and it will not be take away from her" (Luke 10:42, italics mine).

Be a "one-thing" Christian! Focus! Concentrate! Press on —and up!

Additional Scripture Readings:
Colossians 3:1–2; Hebrews 12:1–2

*Go to page 287 for your next
devotional reading.*

generation, in which you shine like stars in the universe [16]as you hold out[a] the word of life—in order that I may boast on the day of Christ that I did not run or labor for nothing. [17]But even if I am being poured out like a drink offering on the sacrifice and service coming from your faith, I am glad and rejoice with all of you. [18]So you too should be glad and rejoice with me.

Timothy and Epaphroditus

[19]I hope in the Lord Jesus to send Timothy to you soon, that I also may be cheered when I receive news about you. [20]I have no one else like him, who takes a genuine interest in your welfare. [21]For everyone looks out for his own interests, not those of Jesus Christ. [22]But you know that Timothy has proved himself, because as a son with his father he has served with me in the work of the gospel. [23]I hope, therefore, to send him as soon as I see how things go with me. [24]And I am confident in the Lord that I myself will come soon.

[25]But I think it is necessary to send back to you Epaphroditus, my brother, fellow worker and fellow soldier, who is also your messenger, whom you sent to take care of my needs. [26]For he longs for all of you and is distressed because you heard he was ill. [27]Indeed he was ill, and almost died. But God had mercy on him, and not on him only but also on me, to spare me sorrow upon sorrow. [28]Therefore I am all the more eager to send him, so that when you see him again you may be glad and I may have less anxiety. [29]Welcome him in the Lord with great joy, and honor men like him, [30]because he almost died for the work of Christ, risking his life to make up for the help you could not give me.

No Confidence in the Flesh

3 Finally, my brothers, rejoice in the Lord! It is no trouble for me to write the same things to you again, and it is a safeguard for you.

[2]Watch out for those dogs, those men who do evil, those mutilators of the flesh. [3]For it is we who are the circumcision, who worship by the Spirit of God, who glory in Christ Jesus, and who put no confidence in the flesh— [4]though I myself have reasons for such confidence.

If anyone else thinks he has reasons to put confidence in the flesh, I have more: [5]circumcised on the eighth day, of the people of Israel, of the tribe of Benjamin, a Hebrew of Hebrews; in regard to the law, a Pharisee; [6]as for zeal, persecuting the church; as for legalistic righteousness, faultless.

[7]But whatever was to my profit I now consider loss for the sake of Christ. [8]What is more, I consider everything a loss compared to the surpassing greatness of knowing Christ Jesus my Lord, for whose sake I have lost all things. I consider them rubbish, that I may gain Christ [9]and be found in him, not having a righteousness of my own that comes from the law, but that which is through faith in Christ—the righteousness that comes from God and is by faith. [10]I want to know Christ and the power of his resurrection and the fellowship of sharing in his sufferings, becoming like him in his death, [11]and so, somehow, to attain to the resurrection from the dead.

Pressing on Toward the Goal

[12]Not that I have already obtained all this, or have already been made perfect, but I press on to take hold of that for which Christ Jesus took hold of me. [13]Brothers, I do not consider myself yet to have taken hold of it. But one thing I do: Forgetting what is behind and straining toward what is ahead, [14]I press on toward the goal to win the prize for which God has called me heavenward in Christ Jesus.

[15]All of us who are mature should take such a view of things. And if on some point you think differently, that too God will make clear to you. [16]Only let us live up to what we have already attained.

[17]Join with others in following my example, brothers, and take note of those who live according to the pattern we gave you. [18]For, as I have often told you before and now say again even with tears, many live as enemies of the cross of Christ. [19]Their destiny is destruction, their god is their stomach, and their glory is in their shame. Their mind is on earthly things. [20]But our citizenship is in heaven. And we eagerly await a Savior from there, the Lord Jesus Christ, [21]who, by the power that enables him to bring everything under his control, will transform our lowly bodies so that they will be like his glorious body.

a16 Or hold on to

VERSE FOR THE DAY:
Philippians 4:6

AUTHOR:
Hope MacDonald

PASSAGE FOR THE DAY:
Philippians 4:4–9

The Lord Is Near

THIS passage was very significant to me today. My life seemed filled with worries and anxieties. It was the kind of day when I just wanted to pull the covers back over my head and forget everything. Have you ever felt that way?

While reading these verses, I was reminded of the profound truth that prayer isn't something I *had* to do, rather, prayer is something I *get* to do. I *get* to bring to God every worry and concern that is on my heart today. In fact, I discovered when worry and anxiety knock on the door of life, if the door is opened by prayer, no one is there! God's cure for worry is always the same—prayer—not pulling the covers back over my head. His way is always action. That action begins with making everything known to him.

Why do we get to pray this way? Because "the Lord is near" (Philippians 4:5). This is the key to this entire magnificent passage. Because he is near, we need not be anxious for anything. Because he is near, we have peace within. A deep, abiding peace that passes all understanding. Because the Lord is near, a wellspring of joy fills every part of our lives. And because the Lord is near, our hearts and minds are renewed and restored in Christ Jesus. With this restoration we become, once again, fresh, vibrant and alive Christians.

Then we can understand the importance of taking our eyes off ourselves and thinking instead about whatever is true and noble, right, pure, admirable and lovely. We can see clearly again that a great deal that surrounds us is excellent and praiseworthy (Philippians 4:8). This doesn't come naturally to us, does it? But then, God never called us to a natural lifestyle.

This is the encouragement and comfort I received this morning as I set out to face another day under the care and direction of the Holy Spirit.

"Thank you, Jesus, for your power in every part of my life today—renewing me physically, mentally and spiritually."

Additional Scripture Readings:
Psalm 73:23–26; 2 Corinthians 4:16–18

Go to page 290 for your next devotional reading.

4 Therefore, my brothers, you whom I love and long for, my joy and crown, that is how you should stand firm in the Lord, dear friends!

Exhortations

²I plead with Euodia and I plead with Syntyche to agree with each other in the Lord. ³Yes, and I ask you, loyal yokefellow,ᵃ help these women who have contended at my side in the cause of the gospel, along with Clement and the rest of my fellow workers, whose names are in the book of life.

⁴Rejoice in the Lord always. I will say it again: Rejoice! ⁵Let your gentleness be evident to all. The Lord is near. ⁶Do not be anxious about anything, but in everything, by prayer and petition, with thanksgiving, present your requests to God. ⁷And the peace of God, which transcends all understanding, will guard your hearts and your minds in Christ Jesus.

⁸Finally, brothers, whatever is true, whatever is noble, whatever is right, whatever is pure, whatever is lovely, whatever is admirable—if anything is excellent or praiseworthy—think about such things. ⁹Whatever you have learned or received or heard from me, or seen in me—put it into practice. And the God of peace will be with you.

Thanks for Their Gifts

¹⁰I rejoice greatly in the Lord that at last you have renewed your concern for me. Indeed, you have been concerned, but you had no opportunity to show it. ¹¹I am not saying this because I am in need, for I have learned to be content whatever the circumstances. ¹²I know what it is to be in need, and I know what it is to have plenty. I have learned the secret of being content in any and every situation, whether well fed or hungry, whether living in plenty or in want. ¹³I can do everything through him who gives me strength.

¹⁴Yet it was good of you to share in my troubles. ¹⁵Moreover, as you Philippians know, in the early days of your acquaintance with the gospel, when I set out from Macedonia, not one church shared with me in the matter of giving and receiving, except you only; ¹⁶for even when I was in Thessalonica, you sent me aid again and again when I was in need. ¹⁷Not that I am looking for a gift, but I am looking for what may be credited to your account. ¹⁸I have received full payment and even more; I am amply supplied, now that I have received from Epaphroditus the gifts you sent. They are a fragrant offering, an acceptable sacrifice, pleasing to God. ¹⁹And my God will meet all your needs according to his glorious riches in Christ Jesus.

²⁰To our God and Father be glory for ever and ever. Amen.

Final Greetings

²¹Greet all the saints in Christ Jesus. The brothers who are with me send greetings. ²²All the saints send you greetings, especially those who belong to Caesar's household.

²³The grace of the Lord Jesus Christ be with your spirit. Amen.ᵇ

ᵃ3 Or loyal Syzygus   ᵇ23 Some manuscripts do not have Amen.

*P*AUL *writes this letter to the church in Colosse at about the same time as he writes Ephesians. False teachers are deceiving some of those to whom he writes (Colossians 2:4). Therefore, Paul stresses the power and glory of Christ and instructs his readers on how to live as Christians. As you read this book, put your faith in this glorious Savior who died for you, and promise him that you will show Christian love and compassion to others.*

COLOSSIANS

1 Paul, an apostle of Christ Jesus by the will of God, and Timothy our brother,

[2]To the holy and faithful[a] brothers in Christ at Colosse:

Grace and peace to you from God our Father.[b]

Thanksgiving and Prayer

[3]We always thank God, the Father of our Lord Jesus Christ, when we pray for you, [4]because we have heard of your faith in Christ Jesus and of the love you have for all the saints — [5]the faith and love that spring from the hope that is stored up for you in heaven and that you have already heard about in the word of truth, the gospel [6]that has come to you. All over the world this gospel is bearing fruit and growing, just as it has been doing among you since the day you heard it and understood God's grace in all its truth. [7]You learned it from Epaphras, our dear fellow servant, who is a faithful minister of Christ on our[c] behalf, [8]and who also told us of your love in the Spirit.

[9]For this reason, since the day we heard about you, we have not stopped praying for you and asking God to fill you with the knowledge of his will through

---

[a]2 Or *believing*   [b]2 Some manuscripts *Father and the Lord Jesus Christ*   [c]7 Some manuscripts *your*

all spiritual wisdom and understanding. [10]And we pray this in order that you may live a life worthy of the Lord and may please him in every way: bearing fruit in every good work, growing in the knowledge of God, [11]being strengthened with all power according to his glorious might so that you may have great endurance and patience, and joyfully [12]giving thanks to the Father, who has qualified you[a] to share in the inheritance of the saints in the kingdom of light. [13]For he has rescued us from the dominion of darkness and brought us into the kingdom of the Son he loves, [14]in whom we have redemption,[b] the forgiveness of sins.

The Supremacy of Christ

[15]He is the image of the invisible God, the firstborn over all creation. [16]For by

---

[a]12 Some manuscripts *us*   [b]14 A few late manuscripts *redemption through his blood*

FRIDAY

VERSE FOR THE DAY:
Colossians 1:9

AUTHOR:
Debbie Smith

PASSAGE FOR THE DAY:
Colossians 1:3–14

Friends Forever

TIME has a way of defining true friends. I have discovered that passing years and growing distance are ineffective obstacles to the mutual love between my friends and me. Perhaps it is because of our common walk with the Lord that we can just pick up where we left off whenever we are together. And these are the dear ones I will spend eternity loving!

Of course, prayer is an important part of continuing that bond. Colossians 1:3–14 is an eloquent description of a Christian's prayer for her friends. Even though Paul had not even visited the Christians at Colosse (Colossians 1:7), his love for them through Christ was strong and ardent.

One Sunday afternoon soon after our wedding, Michael and I were getting ready for the weekly Bible study that would meet in our living room that night. It would be the final study led by Bill Jackson before he moved away. On a sudden whim, we decided to write a song for Bill. Michael went to take a shower; I sat down with the Bible and a pen. In less than an hour Michael had found a melody on the piano for the lyrics to "friends." We were happy to have something special for Bill, though it never occurred to us that anyone else would find this simple song meaningful.

God had different plans! He has used "Friends" for graduations, funerals, weddings and gatherings of all kinds. Michael and I continue to be blessed by letters from people who identify with this song and find comfort in its message. Both the Colossians passage and the song are a call to prayer for those we love—and a reminder that God's love unites people as friends forever!

Additional Scripture Readings:
Ephesians 3:14–19; Philemon 4–7

*Go to page 291 for your next
devotional reading.*

WEEKENDING

RECOMMIT

I thought that prattling boys and girls
  Would fill this empty room;
That my rich heart would gather flowers
  From childhood's opening bloom:
One child and two green graves are mine,
  This is God's gift to me;
A bleeding, fainting, broken heart,
  This is my gift to Thee.

RELATE

This touching poem was written by Mrs. Prentiss
after the loss of two young children. During this
same time, while thinking on how God met
Jacob during his times of deep need, she wrote
the familiar hymn "More Love to Thee":
  Let sorrow do its work,
  Send grief and pain;
  Sweet are Thy messengers,
  Sweet their refrain,
  When they can sing with me,

  More love, O Christ, to Thee,
  More love to Thee,
  More love to Thee!

  – Elizabeth P. Prentiss

REVIVE

Saturday: Philippians 1:9–11
Sunday: 1 John 4:7–21

Go to page 293 for your next devotional reading.

him all things were created: things in heaven and on earth, visible and invisible, whether thrones or powers or rulers or authorities; all things were created by him and for him. [17]He is before all things, and in him all things hold together. [18]And he is the head of the body, the church; he is the beginning and the firstborn from among the dead, so that in everything he might have the supremacy. [19]For God was pleased to have all his fullness dwell in him, [20]and through him to reconcile to himself all things, whether things on earth or things in heaven, by making peace through his blood, shed on the cross.

[21]Once you were alienated from God and were enemies in your minds because of[a] your evil behavior. [22]But now he has reconciled you by Christ's physical body through death to present you holy in his sight, without blemish and free from accusation— [23]if you continue in your faith, established and firm, not moved from the hope held out in the gospel. This is the gospel that you heard and that has been proclaimed to every creature under heaven, and of which I, Paul, have become a servant.

Paul's Labor for the Church

[24]Now I rejoice in what was suffered for you, and I fill up in my flesh what is still lacking in regard to Christ's afflictions, for the sake of his body, which is the church. [25]I have become its servant by the commission God gave me to present to you the word of God in its fullness— [26]the mystery that has been kept hidden for ages and generations, but is now disclosed to the saints. [27]To them God has chosen to make known among the Gentiles the glorious riches of this mystery, which is Christ in you, the hope of glory. [28]We proclaim him, admonishing and teaching everyone with all wisdom, so that we may present everyone perfect in Christ. [29]To this end I labor, struggling with all his energy, which so powerfully works in me.

2 I want you to know how much I am struggling for you and for those at Laodicea, and for all who have not met me personally. [2]My purpose is that they may be encouraged in heart and united in love, so that they may have the full riches of complete understanding, in order that

they may know the mystery of God, namely, Christ, [3]in whom are hidden all the treasures of wisdom and knowledge. [4]I tell you this so that no one may deceive you by fine-sounding arguments. [5]For though I am absent from you in body, I am present with you in spirit and delight to see how orderly you are and how firm your faith in Christ is.

Freedom From Human Regulations Through Life With Christ

[6]So then, just as you received Christ Jesus as Lord, continue to live in him, [7]rooted and built up in him, strengthened in the faith as you were taught, and overflowing with thankfulness.

[8]See to it that no one takes you captive through hollow and deceptive philosophy, which depends on human tradition and the basic principles of this world rather than on Christ.

[9]For in Christ all the fullness of the Deity lives in bodily form, [10]and you have been given fullness in Christ, who is the head over every power and authority. [11]In him you were also circumcised, in the putting off of the sinful nature,[b] not with a circumcision done by the hands of men but with the circumcision done by Christ, [12]having been buried with him in baptism and raised with him through your faith in the power of God, who raised him from the dead. [13]When you were dead in your sins and in the uncircumcision of your sinful nature,[c] God made you[d] alive with Christ. He forgave us all our sins, [14]having canceled the written code, with its regulations, that was against us and that stood opposed to us; he took it away, nailing it to the cross. [15]And having disarmed the powers and authorities, he made a public spectacle of them, triumphing over them by the cross.[e]

[16]Therefore do not let anyone judge you by what you eat or drink, or with regard to a religious festival, a New Moon celebration or a Sabbath day. [17]These are a shadow of the things that were to come; the reality, however, is found in Christ. [18]Do not let anyone who delights in false humility and the worship of angels disqualify you for the prize. Such a person goes into great detail about what he has seen, and his unspiritual mind puffs him up with idle notions. [19]He has lost con-

---

[a]21 Or minds, as shown by   [b]11 Or the flesh   [c]13 Or your flesh   [d]13 Some manuscripts us
[e]15 Or them in him

VERSE FOR THE DAY:
Colossians 2:10

AUTHOR:
Marie Chapian

PASSAGE FOR THE DAY:
Colossians 2:6–12

Fullness in Christ

EVERY time somebody asks me what my astrological sign is, I tell them, "Jesus is my sign. I'm a Christian." Often the person will continue, "Yes, but what month were you born in?" Still I persist, "I'm a Christian. I'm born again."

For centuries people have believed that their destiny is controlled by the month of their birth. They are slaves to the stars. Thank goodness that for those who believe in Jesus Christ there is freedom from such bondage.

Colossians 2:10 tells us we are complete in Christ—not in anything else. He is the head over every power in the universe. We need never be threatened by the forces of darkness that may surround us. Christ reigns above those forces. The stars can't control our destinies—Jesus created the stars! He is our authority.

It is a wonderful thing to be made whole and full. This means we can stop searching for identity and self-worth in the elemental and base philosophies of the world. Our future is sure in Christ because no longer are we incomplete creatures, helpless in the face of an unseen destiny.

Nonetheless, we must guard against seductive philosophies and false religions, just as we must look inward at our own personal, unbridled needs. I have counseled countless people who are insecure, fearful, moody, and desperately dependent on the approval of other people. These things can imprison us just as miserably as the deceptive philosophy of astrology.

Jesus Christ is the head over every power and authority, and he is more powerful than sorrow, gloom, fear, insecurity and the need for approval. It is important that we tell ourselves daily, "I find my personhood in the Lord Jesus and not in other people, not in success, relationships, ideal circumstances or the stars." Then tell the Lord triumphantly, "Thank you for giving me fullness in you."

Additional Scripture Readings:
Isaiah 47:8–15; Ephesians 6:11–18

*Go to page 295 for your next
devotional reading.*

nection with the Head, from whom the whole body, supported and held together by its ligaments and sinews, grows as God causes it to grow.

²⁰Since you died with Christ to the basic principles of this world, why, as though you still belonged to it, do you submit to its rules: ²¹"Do not handle! Do not taste! Do not touch!"? ²²These are all destined to perish with use, because they are based on human commands and teachings. ²³Such regulations indeed have an appearance of wisdom, with their self-imposed worship, their false humility and their harsh treatment of the body, but they lack any value in restraining sensual indulgence.

Rules for Holy Living

3 Since, then, you have been raised with Christ, set your hearts on things above, where Christ is seated at the right hand of God. ²Set your minds on things above, not on earthly things. ³For you died, and your life is now hidden with Christ in God. ⁴When Christ, who is your*ª* life, appears, then you also will appear with him in glory.

⁵Put to death, therefore, whatever belongs to your earthly nature: sexual immorality, impurity, lust, evil desires and greed, which is idolatry. ⁶Because of these, the wrath of God is coming.*ᵇ* ⁷You used to walk in these ways, in the life you once lived. ⁸But now you must rid yourselves of all such things as these: anger, rage, malice, slander, and filthy language from your lips. ⁹Do not lie to each other, since you have taken off your old self with its practices ¹⁰and have put on the new self, which is being renewed in knowledge in the image of its Creator. ¹¹Here there is no Greek or Jew, circumcised or uncircumcised, barbarian, Scythian, slave or free, but Christ is all, and is in all.

¹²Therefore, as God's chosen people, holy and dearly loved, clothe yourselves with compassion, kindness, humility, gentleness and patience. ¹³Bear with each other and forgive whatever grievances you may have against one another. Forgive as the Lord forgave you. ¹⁴And over all these virtues put on love, which binds them all together in perfect unity. ¹⁵Let the peace of Christ rule in your hearts, since as members of one body you were called to peace. And be thankful.

¹⁶Let the word of Christ dwell in you richly as you teach and admonish one another with all wisdom, and as you sing psalms, hymns and spiritual songs with gratitude in your hearts to God. ¹⁷And whatever you do, whether in word or deed, do it all in the name of the Lord Jesus, giving thanks to God the Father through him.

Rules for Christian Households

¹⁸Wives, submit to your husbands, as is fitting in the Lord.

¹⁹Husbands, love your wives and do not be harsh with them.

²⁰Children, obey your parents in everything, for this pleases the Lord.

²¹Fathers, do not embitter your children, or they will become discouraged.

²²Slaves, obey your earthly masters in everything; and do it, not only when their eye is on you and to win their favor, but with sincerity of heart and reverence for the Lord. ²³Whatever you do, work at it with all your heart, as working for the Lord, not for men, ²⁴since you know that you will receive an inheritance from the Lord as a reward. It is the Lord Christ you are serving. ²⁵Anyone who does wrong will be repaid for his wrong, and there is no favoritism.

4 Masters, provide your slaves with what is right and fair, because you know that you also have a Master in heaven.

Further Instructions

²Devote yourselves to prayer, being watchful and thankful. ³And pray for us, too, that God may open a door for our message, so that we may proclaim the mystery of Christ, for which I am in chains. ⁴Pray that I may proclaim it clearly, as I should. ⁵Be wise in the way you act toward outsiders; make the most of every opportunity. ⁶Let your conversation be always full of grace, seasoned with salt, so that you may know how to answer everyone.

Final Greetings

⁷Tychicus will tell you all the news about me. He is a dear brother, a faithful minister and fellow servant in the Lord. ⁸I am sending him to you for the express purpose that you may know about our*ᶜ* circumstances and that he may encour-

---

ª4 Some manuscripts *our*   *ᵇ6* Some early manuscripts *coming on those who are disobedient*
ᶜ8 Some manuscripts *that he may know about your*

VERSE FOR THE DAY:
Colossians 3:15–17

AUTHOR:
Martha Manikas-Foster

PASSAGE FOR THE DAY:
Colossians 3:1–17

The Peace of Christ

IT was a working holiday for my husband. It turned into two weeks of baby-tending isolation for me. The chill of the northern Michigan spring was too much for my three-month-old daughter. So we spent much of our time in the small bedroom of a cottage bordering Lake Huron.

I was held captive. I was trapped only a few feet from my favorite piece of wilderness. I had spent times very close to God here, skiing among these trees and walking within range of the sound of the waves. But that was before.

This visit, I resigned myself to spending two weeks in closed quarters, and I unpacked the pens and editing supplies from my briefcase. I determined not to yearn for the birch trees, the sandy cove and the bay outside my window.

Several days into our stay, Connie's nap extended beyond its usual, frustratingly short fifteen-minute duration. I seized the opportunity and, grabbing the portable baby monitor, dashed out the door. I wanted to appreciate God's spellbinding creation. But my electronic tether kept me close to the cabin.

With the zeal of an eager girl scout, I began cutting tall grass and reed from along the bay and laying the bundles on a picnic table in the sun. I watched the sea gulls, sang favorite hymns, and from the pile on the table began to weave the still-damp materials into something of a basket. It wasn't much of a basket, but my efforts were sincere and my spirit exuberant.

I was at peace. It shouldn't have surprised me that enjoying God as revealed through his creation would bring peace. But it did. And once peaceful, it was easier to see my circumstances as opportunities to worship God through all I did. Thus, when my daughter woke up and called me to return, I went with renewed compassion and patience.

Since that time, when I have felt confined or frustrated, I have reached again to touch a part of God's creation. God's character is revealed, in part, through his excellent work in the details—his attention to the minuscule fibers of each tulip, each pine needle, each crab apple blossom. It is only by focusing on the One whose creation surrounds us and brings us peace that we can do "all in the name of the Lord Jesus, giving thanks to God the Father through him" (Colossians 3:17).

Additional Scripture Readings:
Psalm 104:24–34; Isaiah 55:12–13

Go to page 299 for your next devotional reading.

age your hearts. [9]He is coming with Onesimus, our faithful and dear brother, who is one of you. They will tell you everything that is happening here.

[10]My fellow prisoner Aristarchus sends you his greetings, as does Mark, the cousin of Barnabas. (You have received instructions about him; if he comes to you, welcome him.) [11]Jesus, who is called Justus, also sends greetings. These are the only Jews among my fellow workers for the kingdom of God, and they have proved a comfort to me. [12]Epaphras, who is one of you and a servant of Christ Jesus, sends greetings. He is always wrestling in prayer for you, that you may stand firm in all the will of God, mature and fully assured. [13]I vouch for him that he is working hard for you and for those at Laodicea and Hierapolis. [14]Our dear friend Luke, the doctor, and Demas send greetings. [15]Give my greetings to the brothers at Laodicea, and to Nympha and the church in her house.

[16]After this letter has been read to you, see that it is also read in the church of the Laodiceans and that you in turn read the letter from Laodicea.

[17]Tell Archippus: "See to it that you complete the work you have received in the Lord."

[18]I, Paul, write this greeting in my own hand. Remember my chains. Grace be with you.

PAUL writes this letter to the church he began in Thessalonica (Acts 17:1–9), shortly after leaving them and being unable to return (1 Thessalonians 2:17–18). He is excited about their Christian faith, reminds them of his intense love for them, and answers questions about what death means for a Christian. As you read this book, find comfort as a believer that when you die you will still be under God's care and will "be with the Lord forever" (1 Thessalonians 4:17).

1 THESSALONIANS

1 Paul, Silas*a* and Timothy,

To the church of the Thessalonians in God the Father and the Lord Jesus Christ:

Grace and peace to you.*b*

Thanksgiving for the Thessalonians' Faith

[2] We always thank God for all of you, mentioning you in our prayers. [3] We continually remember before our God and Father your work produced by faith, your labor prompted by love, and your endurance inspired by hope in our Lord Jesus Christ.

[4] For we know, brothers loved by God, that he has chosen you, [5] because our gospel came to you not simply with words, but also with power, with the Holy Spirit and with deep conviction. You know how we lived among you for your sake. [6] You became imitators of us and of the Lord; in spite of severe suffering, you welcomed the message with the joy given by the Holy Spirit. [7] And so you became a model to all the believers in Macedonia and

---

a1 Greek *Silvanus*, a variant of *Silas*   *b1* Some early manuscripts *you from God our Father and the Lord Jesus Christ*

Achaia. [8]The Lord's message rang out from you not only in Macedonia and Achaia—your faith in God has become known everywhere. Therefore we do not need to say anything about it, [9]for they themselves report what kind of reception you gave us. They tell how you turned to God from idols to serve the living and true God, [10]and to wait for his Son from heaven, whom he raised from the dead—Jesus, who rescues us from the coming wrath.

Paul's Ministry in Thessalonica

2 You know, brothers, that our visit to you was not a failure. [2]We had previously suffered and been insulted in Philippi, as you know, but with the help of our God we dared to tell you his gospel in spite of strong opposition. [3]For the appeal we make does not spring from error or impure motives, nor are we trying to trick you. [4]On the contrary, we speak as men approved by God to be entrusted with the gospel. We are not trying to please men but God, who tests our hearts. [5]You know we never used flattery, nor did we put on a mask to cover up greed—God is our witness. [6]We were not looking for praise from men, not from you or anyone else.

As apostles of Christ we could have been a burden to you, [7]but we were gentle among you, like a mother caring for her little children. [8]We loved you so much that we were delighted to share with you not only the gospel of God but our lives as well, because you had become so dear to us. [9]Surely you remember, brothers, our toil and hardship; we worked night and day in order not to be a burden to anyone while we preached the gospel of God to you.

[10]You are witnesses, and so is God, of how holy, righteous and blameless we were among you who believed. [11]For you know that we dealt with each of you as a father deals with his own children, [12]encouraging, comforting and urging you to live lives worthy of God, who calls you into his kingdom and glory.

[13]And we also thank God continually because, when you received the word of God, which you heard from us, you accepted it not as the word of men, but as it actually is, the word of God, which is at work in you who believe. [14]For you, broth-ers, became imitators of God's churches in Judea, which are in Christ Jesus: You suffered from your own countrymen the same things those churches suffered from the Jews, [15]who killed the Lord Jesus and the prophets and also drove us out. They displease God and are hostile to all men [16]in their effort to keep us from speaking to the Gentiles so that they may be saved. In this way they always heap up their sins to the limit. The wrath of God has come upon them at last.[a]

Paul's Longing to See the Thessalonians

[17]But, brothers, when we were torn away from you for a short time (in person, not in thought), out of our intense longing we made every effort to see you. [18]For we wanted to come to you—certainly I, Paul, did, again and again—but Satan stopped us. [19]For what is our hope, our joy, or the crown in which we will glory in the presence of our Lord Jesus when he comes? Is it not you? [20]Indeed, you are our glory and joy.

3 So when we could stand it no longer, we thought it best to be left by ourselves in Athens. [2]We sent Timothy, who is our brother and God's fellow worker[b] in spreading the gospel of Christ, to strengthen and encourage you in your faith, [3]so that no one would be unsettled by these trials. You know quite well that we were destined for them. [4]In fact, when we were with you, we kept telling you that we would be persecuted. And it turned out that way, as you well know. [5]For this reason, when I could stand it no longer, I sent to find out about your faith. I was afraid that in some way the tempter might have tempted you and our efforts might have been useless.

Timothy's Encouraging Report

[6]But Timothy has just now come to us from you and has brought good news about your faith and love. He has told us that you always have pleasant memories of us and that you long to see us, just as we also long to see you. [7]Therefore, brothers, in all our distress and persecution we were encouraged about you because of your faith. [8]For now we really live, since you are standing firm in the Lord. [9]How can we thank God enough for you in return for all the joy we have in the

---

[a]16 Or them fully   [b]2 Some manuscripts brother and fellow worker; other manuscripts brother and God's servant

VERSE FOR THE DAY:	AUTHOR:	PASSAGE FOR THE DAY:
1 Thessalonians 4:14	Martha Manikas-Foster	1 Thessalonians 4:13–15

Because of the Resurrection

WHEN I was in high school, a Campus Life leader commented that before our group graduated, quite likely one of our classmates would die. Death is that near, he said. Even young people die.

His prediction was wrong. None of my high school classmates died. But a few years later, on one day, in the instant it takes for a car and truck to collide, six college classmates died.

These weren't anonymous men and women; I knew each of them. When they died I was hundreds of miles away taking classes at another university. After the phone call, I was overwhelmed by my powerlessness. Alone, I had no one to share my grief, to hold me when I sobbed. To grieve for one would have been torture enough. Grieving for six tore me apart.

Loving sets us up for sorrow, that's true. But it also encourages us to hope. Although I didn't understand it immediately, I grew to realize that the affection I had for these classmates had grown from a foundation of common faith. On such a foundation my hope began to flourish. What we had most in common was the very thing that assured me of their well-being. Because of the resurrection, the horror of death melted away. I would see them again because:

> We believe that Jesus died and rose again and so we believe that God will bring with Jesus those who have fallen asleep in him. According to the Lord's own word, we tell you that we who are still alive, who are left till the coming of the Lord, will certainly not precede those who have fallen asleep. . . . And so we will be with the Lord forever. Therefore encourage each other with these words (1 Thessalonians 4:14–15,17–18).

I can't help but grow sad when I look at some of the photographs in my college yearbooks. But I have hope because I know that "death has been swallowed up in victory" (1 Corinthians 15:54). Jesus Christ is the victor! He "has destroyed death and has brought life and immortality to light through the gospel" (2 Timothy 1:10).

Additional Scripture Readings:
John 11:21–27; 1 Corinthians 15:20–23

Go to page 301 for your next devotional reading.

presence of our God because of you? [10]Night and day we pray most earnestly that we may see you again and supply what is lacking in your faith.

[11]Now may our God and Father himself and our Lord Jesus clear the way for us to come to you. [12]May the Lord make your love increase and overflow for each other and for everyone else, just as ours does for you. [13]May he strengthen your hearts so that you will be blameless and holy in the presence of our God and Father when our Lord Jesus comes with all his holy ones.

Living to Please God

4 Finally, brothers, we instructed you how to live in order to please God, as in fact you are living. Now we ask you and urge you in the Lord Jesus to do this more and more. [2]For you know what instructions we gave you by the authority of the Lord Jesus.

[3]It is God's will that you should be sanctified: that you should avoid sexual immorality; [4]that each of you should learn to control his own body[a] in a way that is holy and honorable, [5]not in passionate lust like the heathen, who do not know God; [6]and that in this matter no one should wrong his brother or take advantage of him. The Lord will punish men for all such sins, as we have already told you and warned you. [7]For God did not call us to be impure, but to live a holy life. [8]Therefore, he who rejects this instruction does not reject man but God, who gives you his Holy Spirit.

[9]Now about brotherly love we do not need to write to you, for you yourselves have been taught by God to love each other. [10]And in fact, you do love all the brothers throughout Macedonia. Yet we urge you, brothers, to do so more and more. [11]Make it your ambition to lead a quiet life, to mind your own business and to work with your hands, just as we told you, [12]so that your daily life may win the respect of outsiders and so that you will not be dependent on anybody.

The Coming of the Lord

[13]Brothers, we do not want you to be ignorant about those who fall asleep, or to grieve like the rest of men, who have no hope. [14]We believe that Jesus died and rose again and so we believe that God will bring with Jesus those who have fallen asleep in him. [15]According to the Lord's own word, we tell you that we who are still alive, who are left till the coming of the Lord, will certainly not precede those who have fallen asleep. [16]For the Lord himself will come down from heaven, with a loud command, with the voice of the archangel and with the trumpet call of God, and the dead in Christ will rise first. [17]After that, we who are still alive and are left will be caught up together with them in the clouds to meet the Lord in the air. And so we will be with the Lord forever. [18]Therefore encourage each other with these words.

5 Now, brothers, about times and dates we do not need to write to you, [2]for you know very well that the day of the Lord will come like a thief in the night. [3]While people are saying, "Peace and safety," destruction will come on them suddenly, as labor pains on a pregnant woman, and they will not escape.

[4]But you, brothers, are not in darkness so that this day should surprise you like a thief. [5]You are all sons of the light and sons of the day. We do not belong to the night or to the darkness. [6]So then, let us not be like others, who are asleep, but let us be alert and self-controlled. [7]For those who sleep, sleep at night, and those who get drunk, get drunk at night. [8]But since we belong to the day, let us be self-controlled, putting on faith and love as a breastplate, and the hope of salvation as a helmet. [9]For God did not appoint us to suffer wrath but to receive salvation through our Lord Jesus Christ. [10]He died for us so that, whether we are awake or asleep, we may live together with him. [11]Therefore encourage one another and build each other up, just as in fact you are doing.

Final Instructions

[12]Now we ask you, brothers, to respect those who work hard among you, who are over you in the Lord and who admonish you. [13]Hold them in the highest regard in love because of their work. Live in peace with each other. [14]And we urge you, brothers, warn those who are idle, encourage the timid, help the weak, be patient with everyone. [15]Make sure that nobody pays back wrong for wrong, but always try to be kind to each other and to everyone else.

[16]Be joyful always; [17]pray continually; [18]give thanks in all circumstances, for

VERSE FOR THE DAY:
1 Thessalonians 5:18

AUTHOR:
Carol L. Baldwin

PASSAGE FOR THE DAY:
1 Thessalonians 5:16–22

Thanksgiving for All Things

"LORD, how can I thank you when I am single and want to be married?"

"Dear God, how can I ever be happy in this dead-end job?"

"God, how can I thank you for broken plumbing in our bathroom when we don't have the money to make repairs?"

How can we have thankful, contented hearts when the circumstances in our lives are not what we had planned and when they lie outside our control or our power to change?

Let's look at our alternatives. If we are not thankful, we become bitter and angry with God: he is not providing what we "rightfully" deserve. If we are not content, we become rebellious and complaining: after all, he gives our friends everything they pray for—why does he refuse us?

Underlying these complaints and questions lie two errors in our thinking: that God is not trustworthy and that he does not desire our good. When we compare these conclusions with Scripture, we discover how wrong we are! God's Word instructs us that God is sovereignly in control, providing for and working out *all* the circumstances in the lives of those who love him and whom he has called (Romans 8:28; 1 Corinthians 10:13a; Philippians 4:6–7). He is intimately involved with us; he works out his purposes through the events in our lives so that we may be conformed to the image of his Son.

We have further reason to praise him. The same God who formed the world in six days knows every hair on our heads. The same God who chose a people for himself before we were born sent his Son to die on the cross to redeem us from our sins.

God's love for his people is not determined by the circumstances in our lives. His love is steadfast. Our marital status, career or finances might fluctuate or totally break apart. In spite of that, however, we can and must give him thanks for his love toward us. We must serve him with unhesitating hearts.

Additional Scripture Readings:
Philippians 1:12–19; Colossians 2:6–7

Go to page 305 for your next devotional reading.

this is God's will for you in Christ Jesus.

19Do not put out the Spirit's fire; 20do not treat prophecies with contempt. 21Test everything. Hold on to the good. 22Avoid every kind of evil.

23May God himself, the God of peace, sanctify you through and through. May your whole spirit, soul and body be kept blameless at the coming of our Lord Jesus Christ. 24The one who calls you is faithful and he will do it.

25Brothers, pray for us. 26Greet all the brothers with a holy kiss. 27I charge you before the Lord to have this letter read to all the brothers.

28The grace of our Lord Jesus Christ be with you.

*PAUL writes this letter shortly after
1 Thessalonians to clarify some things
that the church failed to understand in
his first letter. He tells them that the
antichrist is coming, but they must continue with their regular schedules until
Jesus returns. As you read this book,
remember that God wants you to look
forward to Christ's return as well as to
continue doing your daily work.*

2 THESSALONIANS

1 Paul, Silas*a* and Timothy,

To the church of the Thessalonians in
God our Father and the Lord Jesus Christ:

²Grace and peace to you from God the
Father and the Lord Jesus Christ.

Thanksgiving and Prayer

³We ought always to thank God for you,
brothers, and rightly so, because your
faith is growing more and more, and the
love every one of you has for each other is
increasing. ⁴Therefore, among God's
churches we boast about your perseverance and faith in all the persecutions and
trials you are enduring.

⁵All this is evidence that God's judgment is right, and as a result you will be
counted worthy of the kingdom of God,
for which you are suffering. ⁶God is just:
He will pay back trouble to those who
trouble you ⁷and give relief to you who are
troubled, and to us as well. This will happen when the Lord Jesus is revealed from
heaven in blazing fire with his powerful
angels. ⁸He will punish those who do not
know God and do not obey the gospel of
our Lord Jesus. ⁹They will be punished
with everlasting destruction and shut out
from the presence of the Lord and from
the majesty of his power ¹⁰on the day he
comes to be glorified in his holy people
and to be marveled at among all those
who have believed. This includes you, because you believed our testimony to you.

¹¹With this in mind, we constantly pray
for you, that our God may count you
worthy of his calling, and that by his pow-

a1 Greek *Silvanus*, a variant of *Silas*

er he may fulfill every good purpose of yours and every act prompted by your faith. [12]We pray this so that the name of our Lord Jesus may be glorified in you, and you in him, according to the grace of our God and the Lord Jesus Christ. [a]

The Man of Lawlessness

2 Concerning the coming of our Lord Jesus Christ and our being gathered to him, we ask you, brothers, [2]not to become easily unsettled or alarmed by some prophecy, report or letter supposed to have come from us, saying that the day of the Lord has already come. [3]Don't let anyone deceive you in any way, for that day will not come, until the rebellion occurs and the man of lawlessness[b] is revealed, the man doomed to destruction. [4]He will oppose and will exalt himself over everything that is called God or is worshiped, so that he sets himself up in God's temple, proclaiming himself to be God.

[5]Don't you remember that when I was with you I used to tell you these things? [6]And now you know what is holding him back, so that he may be revealed at the proper time. [7]For the secret power of lawlessness is already at work; but the one who now holds it back will continue to do so till he is taken out of the way. [8]And then the lawless one will be revealed, whom the Lord Jesus will overthrow with the breath of his mouth and destroy by the splendor of his coming. [9]The coming of the lawless one will be in accordance with the work of Satan displayed in all kinds of counterfeit miracles, signs and wonders, [10]and in every sort of evil that deceives those who are perishing. They perish because they refused to love the truth and so be saved. [11]For this reason God sends them a powerful delusion so that they will believe the lie [12]and so that all will be condemned who have not believed the truth but have delighted in wickedness.

Stand Firm

[13]But we ought always to thank God for you, brothers loved by the Lord, because from the beginning God chose you[c] to be saved through the sanctifying work of the Spirit and through belief in the truth.

[14]He called you to this through our gospel, that you might share in the glory of our Lord Jesus Christ. [15]So then, brothers, stand firm and hold to the teachings[d] we passed on to you, whether by word of mouth or by letter.

[16]May our Lord Jesus Christ himself and God our Father, who loved us and by his grace gave us eternal encouragement and good hope, [17]encourage your hearts and strengthen you in every good deed and word.

Request for Prayer

3 Finally, brothers, pray for us that the message of the Lord may spread rapidly and be honored, just as it was with you. [2]And pray that we may be delivered from wicked and evil men, for not everyone has faith. [3]But the Lord is faithful, and he will strengthen and protect you from the evil one. [4]We have confidence in the Lord that you are doing and will continue to do the things we command. [5]May the Lord direct your hearts into God's love and Christ's perseverance.

Warning Against Idleness

[6]In the name of the Lord Jesus Christ, we command you, brothers, to keep away from every brother who is idle and does not live according to the teaching[e] you received from us. [7]For you yourselves know how you ought to follow our example. We were not idle when we were with you, [8]nor did we eat anyone's food without paying for it. On the contrary, we worked night and day, laboring and toiling so that we would not be a burden to any of you. [9]We did this, not because we do not have the right to such help, but in order to make ourselves a model for you to follow. [10]For even when we were with you, we gave you this rule: "If a man will not work, he shall not eat."

[11]We hear that some among you are idle. They are not busy; they are busybodies. [12]Such people we command and urge in the Lord Jesus Christ to settle down and earn the bread they eat. [13]And as for you, brothers, never tire of doing what is right.

[14]If anyone does not obey our instruction in this letter, take special note of him. Do not associate with him, in order

---

[a]12 Or *God and Lord, Jesus Christ*   [b]3 Some manuscripts *sin*   [c]13 Some manuscripts *because God chose you as his firstfruits*   [d]15 Or *traditions*   [e]6 Or *tradition*

VERSE FOR THE DAY:
2 Thessalonians 3:5,16

AUTHOR:
Gien Karssen

PASSAGE FOR THE DAY:
2 Thessalonians 3:1–18

Practicing Peace

EACH of Paul's letters begins with a greeting of peace. Some, like this one to the Christians in the Greek city of Thessalonica, end the same way. These words were full of meaning. Paul was reminding the Thessalonians that the Lord, the author of peace, would give his peace always, in every way and under all circumstances. The Thessalonians needed this encouragement badly. They were people who suffered from oppression and persecution, who were confronted with the problem of immorality, who were full of sorrow because of loved ones who had died, who lived among difficult and pagan people, and who were confronted by false religious teachers and people with warped minds.

Paul's words referred back to the reality of the night in which Christ was born. The Lord who gives peace, because he himself is peace, was born to command peace. It is the same peace of which the Lord later would say to his disciples, "Peace I leave with you; my peace I give you" (John 14:27). "I have told you these things, so that in me you may have peace. In this world you will have trouble. But take heart! I have overcome the world" (John 16:33).

The Thessalonians claimed this peace, and proved it to be applicable and sufficient in their varied situations. This peace lifted them above their problems. In spite of pressure and adversity, their faith grew so that they became examples to others.

Even today we can draw comfort from the experiences of those who have gone before us. We can try to follow their good example, learn not to lose heart, and nurture hope.

Circumstances in the eighties are far from rosy. The world finds itself in chaos. Many a family is in a crisis. The church is often at a loss for the right answers. Small wonder that our hearts lack peace and are full of uncertainty. But in spite of this we can experience the Lord's peace continually, and in every way.

Peace must be practical and practiced! We best begin each new day with God, reading his Word and praying. Then we can think back to this quiet time throughout the day to claim his peace when unrest and discord are knocking at our door. We must remind ourselves that no situation we find ourselves in is beyond the range of God's interest in us.

Additional Scripture Readings:
Isaiah 26:3–4; James 3:17–18

*Go to page 306 for your next
devotional reading.*

WEEKENDING

RESOLVE

O what a happy soul am I!
  Although I cannot see,
I am resolved that in this world
  Contented I will be;
How many blessings I enjoy
  That other people don't!
To weep and sigh because I'm blind,
  I cannot, and I won't.

– Fanny Crosby

REFLECT

Fanny Crosby wrote this poem when she was
only eight years old. Blinded in infancy, Miss
Crosby spent the ninety-eight years of her life
composing over 9,000 songs, many of which
mention a deeper sight than that of our physical
vision.

REVIVE

Saturday: Philippians 4:10–20
Sunday: Psalm 84:1–12

Go to page 310 for your next devotional reading.

that he may feel ashamed. [15]Yet do not regard him as an enemy, but warn him as a brother.

Final Greetings

[16]Now may the Lord of peace himself give you peace at all times and in every way. The Lord be with all of you.

[17]I, Paul, write this greeting in my own hand, which is the distinguishing mark in all my letters. This is how I write.

[18]The grace of our Lord Jesus Christ be with you all.

PAUL writes this letter to young Timothy, who is serving as a pastor in Ephesus. He instructs him how to organize and run the church and how to deal with false teachers and refute what they say. As you read this book, promise God that you will not stray from true faith.

1 TIMOTHY

1 Paul, an apostle of Christ Jesus by the command of God our Savior and of Christ Jesus our hope,

²To Timothy my true son in the faith:

Grace, mercy and peace from God the Father and Christ Jesus our Lord.

Warning Against False Teachers of the Law

³As I urged you when I went into Macedonia, stay there in Ephesus so that you may command certain men not to teach false doctrines any longer ⁴nor to devote themselves to myths and endless genealogies. These promote controversies rather than God's work—which is by faith. ⁵The goal of this command is love, which comes from a pure heart and a good conscience and a sincere faith. ⁶Some have wandered away from these and turned to meaningless talk. ⁷They

want to be teachers of the law, but they do not know what they are talking about or what they so confidently affirm.

⁸We know that the law is good if one uses it properly. ⁹We also know that law*a* is made not for the righteous but for lawbreakers and rebels, the ungodly and sinful, the unholy and irreligious; for those who kill their fathers or mothers, for murderers, ¹⁰for adulterers and perverts, for slave traders and liars and perjurers—and for whatever else is contrary to the sound doctrine ¹¹that conforms to the glorious gospel of the blessed God, which he entrusted to me.

The Lord's Grace to Paul

¹²I thank Christ Jesus our Lord, who has given me strength, that he considered me faithful, appointing me to his service. ¹³Even though I was once a blasphemer and a persecutor and a violent man, I was

---

*a*9 Or *that the law*

shown mercy because I acted in ignorance and unbelief. [14]The grace of our Lord was poured out on me abundantly, along with the faith and love that are in Christ Jesus.

[15]Here is a trustworthy saying that deserves full acceptance: Christ Jesus came into the world to save sinners — of whom I am the worst. [16]But for that very reason I was shown mercy so that in me, the worst of sinners, Christ Jesus might display his unlimited patience as an example for those who would believe on him and receive eternal life. [17]Now to the King eternal, immortal, invisible, the only God, be honor and glory for ever and ever. Amen.

[18]Timothy, my son, I give you this instruction in keeping with the prophecies once made about you, so that by following them you may fight the good fight, [19]holding on to faith and a good conscience. Some have rejected these and so have shipwrecked their faith. [20]Among them are Hymenaeus and Alexander, whom I have handed over to Satan to be taught not to blaspheme.

Instructions on Worship

2 I urge, then, first of all, that requests, prayers, intercession and thanksgiving be made for everyone — [2]for kings and all those in authority, that we may live peaceful and quiet lives in all godliness and holiness. [3]This is good, and pleases God our Savior, [4]who wants all men to be saved and to come to a knowledge of the truth. [5]For there is one God and one mediator between God and men, the man Christ Jesus, [6]who gave himself as a ransom for all men — the testimony given in its proper time. [7]And for this purpose I was appointed a herald and an apostle — I am telling the truth, I am not lying — and a teacher of the true faith to the Gentiles.

[8]I want men everywhere to lift up holy hands in prayer, without anger or disputing.

[9]I also want women to dress modestly, with decency and propriety, not with braided hair or gold or pearls or expensive clothes, [10]but with good deeds, appropriate for women who profess to worship God.

[11]A woman should learn in quietness and full submission. [12]I do not permit a woman to teach or to have authority over a man; she must be silent. [13]For Adam was formed first, then Eve. [14]And Adam was not the one deceived; it was the woman who was deceived and became a sinner. [15]But women[a] will be saved[b] through childbearing — if they continue in faith, love and holiness with propriety.

Overseers and Deacons

3 Here is a trustworthy saying: If anyone sets his heart on being an overseer,[c] he desires a noble task. [2]Now the overseer must be above reproach, the husband of but one wife, temperate, self-controlled, respectable, hospitable, able to teach, [3]not given to drunkenness, not violent but gentle, not quarrelsome, not a lover of money. [4]He must manage his own family well and see that his children obey him with proper respect. [5](If anyone does not know how to manage his own family, how can he take care of God's church?) [6]He must not be a recent convert, or he may become conceited and fall under the same judgment as the devil. [7]He must also have a good reputation with outsiders, so that he will not fall into disgrace and into the devil's trap.

[8]Deacons, likewise, are to be men worthy of respect, sincere, not indulging in much wine, and not pursuing dishonest gain. [9]They must keep hold of the deep truths of the faith with a clear conscience. [10]They must first be tested; and then if there is nothing against them, let them serve as deacons.

[11]In the same way, their wives[d] are to be women worthy of respect, not malicious talkers but temperate and trustworthy in everything.

[12]A deacon must be the husband of but one wife and must manage his children and his household well. [13]Those who have served well gain an excellent standing and great assurance in their faith in Christ Jesus.

[14]Although I hope to come to you soon, I am writing you these instructions so that, [15]if I am delayed, you will know how people ought to conduct themselves in God's household, which is the church of the living God, the pillar and foundation of the truth. [16]Beyond all question, the mystery of godliness is great:

He[e] appeared in a body,[f]
 was vindicated by the Spirit,

was seen by angels,
was preached among the nations,
was believed on in the world,
was taken up in glory.

Instructions to Timothy

4 The Spirit clearly says that in later times some will abandon the faith and follow deceiving spirits and things taught by demons. [2]Such teachings come through hypocritical liars, whose consciences have been seared as with a hot iron. [3]They forbid people to marry and order them to abstain from certain foods, which God created to be received with thanksgiving by those who believe and who know the truth. [4]For everything God created is good, and nothing is to be rejected if it is received with thanksgiving, [5]because it is consecrated by the word of God and prayer.

[6]If you point these things out to the brothers, you will be a good minister of Christ Jesus, brought up in the truths of the faith and of the good teaching that you have followed. [7]Have nothing to do with godless myths and old wives' tales; rather, train yourself to be godly. [8]For physical training is of some value, but godliness has value for all things, holding promise for both the present life and the life to come.

[9]This is a trustworthy saying that deserves full acceptance [10](and for this we labor and strive), that we have put our hope in the living God, who is the Savior of all men, and especially of those who believe.

[11]Command and teach these things. [12]Don't let anyone look down on you because you are young, but set an example for the believers in speech, in life, in love, in faith and in purity. [13]Until I come, devote yourself to the public reading of

MONDAY

VERSE FOR THE DAY:
1 Timothy 2:1

AUTHOR:
Corrie ten Boom

PASSAGE FOR THE DAY:
1 Timothy 2:1–8

An Important Power

PRAYER is such an important power. In the concentration camp, seven hundred of us lived in a room built for two hundred people. We were all dirty, nervous and tense. One day a horrible fight broke out amongst the prisoners. Betsie began to pray aloud. It was as if a storm laid down, until at last all was quiet. Then Betsie said, "Thank you, Father." A tired old woman was used by the Lord to save the situation for seven hundred fellow prisoners through her prayers.

I urge, then, first of all, that requests, prayers, intercession and thanksgiving be made for everyone (1 Timothy 2:1).

There may be days of darkness and distress,
When sin has power to tempt, and care to press.
Yet in the darkest day I will not fear,
For 'midst the shadows, You will still be near.
Thank You, Lord Jesus.

Additional Scripture Readings:
Colossians 4:2–5; James 5:13–18

Go to page 311 for your next devotional reading.

Scripture, to preaching and to teaching. [14]Do not neglect your gift, which was given you through a prophetic message when the body of elders laid their hands on you.

[15]Be diligent in these matters; give yourself wholly to them, so that everyone may see your progress. [16]Watch your life and doctrine closely. Persevere in them, because if you do, you will save both yourself and your hearers.

Advice About Widows, Elders and Slaves

5 Do not rebuke an older man harshly, but exhort him as if he were your father. Treat younger men as brothers, [2]older women as mothers, and younger women as sisters, with absolute purity.

[3]Give proper recognition to those widows who are really in need. [4]But if a widow has children or grandchildren, these should learn first of all to put their religion into practice by caring for their own family and so repaying their parents and grandparents, for this is pleasing to God. [5]The widow who is really in need and left all alone puts her hope in God and continues night and day to pray and to ask God for help. [6]But the widow who lives for pleasure is dead even while she lives. [7]Give the people these instructions, too, so that no one may be open to blame. [8]If anyone does not provide for his relatives, and especially for his immediate family, he has denied the faith and is worse than an unbeliever.

[9]No widow may be put on the list of widows unless she is over sixty, has been faithful to her husband,[a] [10]and is well known for her good deeds, such as bringing up children, showing hospitality, washing the feet of the saints, helping those in trouble and devoting herself to all kinds of good deeds.

[11]As for younger widows, do not put

---

[a]9 Or *has had but one husband*

TUESDAY

VERSE FOR THE DAY:
1 Timothy 4:16

AUTHOR:
Florence Littauer

PASSAGE FOR THE DAY:
1 Timothy 4:9–16

Cramming for Finals

A NINETY-six-year-old lady was a faithful attendant at my women's club Bible studies. She came with her lessons prepared and knew all the answers. One day a tactless member asked her, "Why do you work so hard on these lessons when you're so old and it doesn't matter?"

Little Bess Elkins looked up and said confidently, "I'm cramming for my finals."

It's never too late to get ready for our finals. Narrow is the way which leads to life and few there be that find it. It takes so little to be above average, but it does take a desire to learn and it does take preparation so when the great target appears we'll be able to hit the bull's-eye.

Additional Scripture Readings:
Psalm 119:33–37; Philippians 3:12–14

Go to page 313 for your next devotional reading.

them on such a list. For when their sensual desires overcome their dedication to Christ, they want to marry. [12]Thus they bring judgment on themselves, because they have broken their first pledge. [13]Besides, they get into the habit of being idle and going about from house to house. And not only do they become idlers, but also gossips and busybodies, saying things they ought not to. [14]So I counsel younger widows to marry, to have children, to manage their homes and to give the enemy no opportunity for slander. [15]Some have in fact already turned away to follow Satan.

[16]If any woman who is a believer has widows in her family, she should help them and not let the church be burdened with them, so that the church can help those widows who are really in need.

[17]The elders who direct the affairs of the church well are worthy of double honor, especially those whose work is preaching and teaching. [18]For the Scripture says, "Do not muzzle the ox while it is treading out the grain,"[a] and "The worker deserves his wages."[b] [19]Do not entertain an accusation against an elder unless it is brought by two or three witnesses. [20]Those who sin are to be rebuked publicly, so that the others may take warning.

[21]I charge you, in the sight of God and Christ Jesus and the elect angels, to keep these instructions without partiality, and to do nothing out of favoritism.

[22]Do not be hasty in the laying on of hands, and do not share in the sins of others. Keep yourself pure.

[23]Stop drinking only water, and use a little wine because of your stomach and your frequent illnesses.

[24]The sins of some men are obvious, reaching the place of judgment ahead of them; the sins of others trail behind them. [25]In the same way, good deeds are obvious, and even those that are not cannot be hidden.

6 All who are under the yoke of slavery should consider their masters worthy of full respect, so that God's name and our teaching may not be slandered. [2]Those who have believing masters are not to show less respect for them because they are brothers. Instead, they are to serve them even better, because those who benefit from their service are believers, and dear to them. These are the things you are to teach and urge on them.

Love of Money

[3]If anyone teaches false doctrines and does not agree to the sound instruction of our Lord Jesus Christ and to godly teaching, [4]he is conceited and understands nothing. He has an unhealthy interest in controversies and quarrels about words that result in envy, strife, malicious talk, evil suspicions [5]and constant friction between men of corrupt mind, who have been robbed of the truth and who think that godliness is a means to financial gain.

[6]But godliness with contentment is great gain. [7]For we brought nothing into the world, and we can take nothing out of it. [8]But if we have food and clothing, we will be content with that. [9]People who want to get rich fall into temptation and a trap and into many foolish and harmful desires that plunge men into ruin and destruction. [10]For the love of money is a root of all kinds of evil. Some people, eager for money, have wandered from the faith and pierced themselves with many griefs.

Paul's Charge to Timothy

[11]But you, man of God, flee from all this, and pursue righteousness, godliness, faith, love, endurance and gentleness. [12]Fight the good fight of the faith. Take hold of the eternal life to which you were called when you made your good confession in the presence of many witnesses. [13]In the sight of God, who gives life to everything, and of Christ Jesus, who while testifying before Pontius Pilate made the good confession, I charge you [14]to keep this command without spot or blame until the appearing of our Lord Jesus Christ, [15]which God will bring about in his own time—God, the blessed and only Ruler, the King of kings and Lord of lords, [16]who alone is immortal and who lives in unapproachable light, whom no one has seen or can see. To him be honor and might forever. Amen.

[17]Command those who are rich in this present world not to be arrogant nor to put their hope in wealth, which is so uncertain, but to put their hope in God, who richly provides us with everything for our enjoyment. [18]Command them to do good, to be rich in good deeds, and to be gen-

a[18] Deut. 25:4   b[18] Luke 10:7

VERSE FOR THE DAY:
1 Timothy 6:9–10

AUTHOR:
Martha Manikas-Foster

PASSAGE FOR THE DAY:
1 Timothy 6:1–21

True Success

I RECLINED on my hospital bed with my two-day-old daughter cuddled on my chest. As she slept I caressed her tiny fingers and wondered how she would use them as she grew up. Would they tap formulas and technical data into a now unimagined computer? Would they intricately stitch wounded human tissue? Or perhaps sculpt or paint using vibrant textures and colors? Although I randomly pictured professions at which she might excel, I focused my prayers then as I focus them now, not on *what* she might be, but on *who* she could be.

I know that one day, probably before she puts away her dolls and crayons, she'll learn that some people measure excellence and success solely by "the bottom line"—the money they take home. Some "put their hope in wealth" (1 Timothy 6:17) and build their lives to accommodate its pursuit.

I trust that by that time we'll have taught her to value many things above money. Scripture teaches not that riches themselves are evil but that the value we place on them can lead to our undoing.

> People who want to get rich fall into temptation and a trap and into many foolish and harmful desires that plunge men into ruin and destruction (1 Timothy 6:9).

On the other hand, "godliness with contentment is great gain" (1 Timothy 6:6). The apostle Paul's charge to young Timothy in 1 Timothy 6:11–16 is to flee from the pursuit of riches and instead pursue godliness. Paul further instructs Timothy to:

> Command those who are rich . . . to put their hope in God . . . . Command them to do good, to be rich in good deeds, and to be generous and willing to share (1 Timothy 6:17–18).

When Connie reaches elementary school and her teachers ask her what she wants to be when she grows up, I expect that she will list "teacher," "firefighter," and perhaps "doctor" among her choices. But my prayer will continue to be that no matter what profession she chooses, at the core she will truly succeed by being a righteous and godly woman, full of "faith, love, endurance and gentleness" (1 Timothy 6:11).

Additional Scripture Readings:
Proverbs 22:1–2; Mark 10:17–25

Go to page 316 for your next devotional reading.

erous and willing to share. [19]In this way they will lay up treasure for themselves as a firm foundation for the coming age, so that they may take hold of the life that is truly life.

[20]Timothy, guard what has been entrusted to your care. Turn away from godless chatter and the opposing ideas of what is falsely called knowledge, [21]which some have professed and in so doing have wandered from the faith.

Grace be with you.

*T*HIS *second letter to Timothy is written by Paul shortly before Paul dies (2 Timothy 4:6–8). Times are difficult, both morally and spiritually, and Paul wants to encourage Timothy to persevere in his Christian faith and life. As you read this book, be sure to find your daily strength in Jesus Christ and in God's inspired word.*

2 TIMOTHY

1 Paul, an apostle of Christ Jesus by the will of God, according to the promise of life that is in Christ Jesus,

²To Timothy, my dear son:

Grace, mercy and peace from God the Father and Christ Jesus our Lord.

Encouragement to Be Faithful

³I thank God, whom I serve, as my forefathers did, with a clear conscience, as night and day I constantly remember you in my prayers. ⁴Recalling your tears, I long to see you, so that I may be filled with joy. ⁵I have been reminded of your sincere faith, which first lived in your grandmother Lois and in your mother Eunice and, I am persuaded, now lives in you also. ⁶For this reason I remind you to fan into flame the gift of God, which is in you through the laying on of my hands. ⁷For God did not give us a spirit of timidity, but a spirit of power, of love and of self-discipline.

⁸So do not be ashamed to testify about our Lord, or ashamed of me his prisoner. But join with me in suffering for the gospel, by the power of God, ⁹who has saved us and called us to a holy life—not because of anything we have done but because of his own purpose and grace. This grace was given us in Christ Jesus before the beginning of time, ¹⁰but it has now been revealed through the appearing of our Savior, Christ Jesus, who has destroyed death and has brought life and immortality to light through the gospel. ¹¹And of this gospel I was appointed a herald and an apostle and a teacher. ¹²That is why I am suffering as I am. Yet I am not ashamed, because I know whom I have believed, and am convinced that he is able to guard what I have entrusted to him for that day.

THURSDAY

VERSE FOR THE DAY:
2 Timothy 1:7

AUTHOR:
Beverly LaHaye

PASSAGE FOR THE DAY:
2 Timothy 1:3–7

Living With Fear

WHEN I was a young minister's wife and new mother, I suffered from a serious case of low self-image and overcautiousness. Perhaps, more accurately, I could have been called fearful and anxious. It was very difficult for me to speak to a group of more than seven or eight ladies. When asked to speak, I would often hide behind my husband's ministerial cloak and say that he was the speaker and I was his "helpmeet." Mainly because I was fearful that I would make a mistake and not be accepted by my listeners, I would refuse an invitation to speak to adults. I was only comfortable working with children in church school and in the music department of our church.

In my heart I admired those who were poised in public and could speak articulately, and often I longed to be able to do so myself. But the more I thought about it, the greater my fear. This anxiety affected other areas of my life as well. I knew that sooner or later I would have to face this fear head-on.

After seventeen years as a minister's wife I came to realize that I did not have to continue like this. Living with fear was a choice I was making.

While attending a church school conference at beautiful Forest Home Christian Camp in California, God used Dr. Henry Brandt, a Christian psychologist, to minister his truth to me. Dr. Brandt used 2 Timothy 1:7 as his text; and that day, for the first time, I began to realize that my fears and anxieties were self-imposed. God's choice for me was to have power, love and self-discipline. God did not give me a spirit of fear! My poor self-image, my anxieties, my fears were all my own doing and my sin because I lacked faith to receive the power, love and self-discipline that God really wanted me to have.

As God began to help me with my fearfulness, my own self-image began to improve. Over a period of weeks, and then months, it began to be obvious that God was changing me.

Now, many years later, I can say "Thank you, Lord" for what he has done in me. I would not want to go back to the former Beverly for anything in the world—and the greatest thing is that God is not finished with me yet!

Additional Scripture Readings:
Psalm 34:4–10; Jeremiah 1:4–8

Go to page 317 for your next devotional reading.

[13]What you heard from me, keep as the pattern of sound teaching, with faith and love in Christ Jesus. [14]Guard the good deposit that was entrusted to you — guard it with the help of the Holy Spirit who lives in us.

[15]You know that everyone in the province of Asia has deserted me, including Phygelus and Hermogenes.

[16]May the Lord show mercy to the household of Onesiphorus, because he often refreshed me and was not ashamed of my chains. [17]On the contrary, when he was in Rome, he searched hard for me until he found me. [18]May the Lord grant that he will find mercy from the Lord on that day! You know very well in how many ways he helped me in Ephesus.

2 You then, my son, be strong in the grace that is in Christ Jesus. [2]And the things you have heard me say in the presence of many witnesses entrust to relia-ble men who will also be qualified to teach others. [3]Endure hardship with us like a good soldier of Christ Jesus. [4]No one serving as a soldier gets involved in civilian affairs — he wants to please his commanding officer. [5]Similarly, if anyone competes as an athlete, he does not receive the victor's crown unless he competes according to the rules. [6]The hardworking farmer should be the first to receive a share of the crops. [7]Reflect on what I am saying, for the Lord will give you insight into all this.

[8]Remember Jesus Christ, raised from the dead, descended from David. This is my gospel, [9]for which I am suffering even to the point of being chained like a criminal. But God's word is not chained. [10]Therefore I endure everything for the sake of the elect, that they too may obtain the salvation that is in Christ Jesus, with eternal glory.

FRIDAY

VERSE FOR THE DAY:
2 Timothy 2:1

AUTHOR:
Doris Haase

PASSAGE FOR THE DAY:
2 Timothy 2:1–13

Be Strong in God's Grace

AFTER a long and terrifying captivity, Iranian hostage Gary Lee was home. It was a Sunday morning in February 1981, and I joined with others in his father's church to welcome him. Celebration filled the air as joyful voices sang "Amazing Grace." From my seat I noticed the bearded young man smile and shake his head as though in wonder at the miracle of his safe return.

Months earlier, however, he had experienced another miracle. Shortly after his capture he was allowed to have a Bible and one day he read Isaiah 43:5: "Do not be afraid, for I am with you; I will bring your children from the east and gather you from the west."

"When I read those words," he told his father later, "I felt God was making me a promise. Somehow I knew I would reach home safely. The whole experience became a lot easier after that."

How much lighter trials become when we realize God's grace is twofold. It is not only the happy ending. It is also the peace we can feel during a painful journey, when we trust in God — all the way.

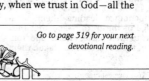

Additional Scripture Readings:
Acts 6:8; 7:55–60; Romans 5:1–5

Go to page 319 for your next devotional reading.

[11]Here is a trustworthy saying:

If we died with him,
　we will also live with him;
[12]if we endure,
　we will also reign with him.
If we disown him,
　he will also disown us;
[13]if we are faithless,
　he will remain faithful,
　for he cannot disown himself.

A Workman Approved by God

[14]Keep reminding them of these things. Warn them before God against quarreling about words; it is of no value, and only ruins those who listen. [15]Do your best to present yourself to God as one approved, a workman who does not need to be ashamed and who correctly handles the word of truth. [16]Avoid godless chatter, because those who indulge in it will become more and more ungodly. [17]Their teaching will spread like gangrene. Among them are Hymenaeus and Philetus, [18]who have wandered away from the truth. They say that the resurrection has already taken place, and they destroy the faith of some. [19]Nevertheless, God's solid foundation stands firm, sealed with this inscription: "The Lord knows those who are his,"[a] and, "Everyone who confesses the name of the Lord must turn away from wickedness."

[20]In a large house there are articles not only of gold and silver, but also of wood and clay; some are for noble purposes and some for ignoble. [21]If a man cleanses himself from the latter, he will be an instrument for noble purposes, made holy, useful to the Master and prepared to do any good work.

[22]Flee the evil desires of youth, and pursue righteousness, faith, love and peace, along with those who call on the Lord out of a pure heart. [23]Don't have anything to do with foolish and stupid arguments, because you know they produce quarrels. [24]And the Lord's servant must not quarrel; instead, he must be kind to everyone, able to teach, not resentful. [25]Those who oppose him he must gently instruct, in the hope that God will grant them repentance leading them to a knowledge of the truth, [26]and that they will come to their senses and escape from the trap of the devil, who has taken them captive to do his will.

Godlessness in the Last Days

3 But mark this: There will be terrible times in the last days. [2]People will be lovers of themselves, lovers of money, boastful, proud, abusive, disobedient to their parents, ungrateful, unholy, [3]without love, unforgiving, slanderous, without self-control, brutal, not lovers of the good, [4]treacherous, rash, conceited, lovers of pleasure rather than lovers of God — [5]having a form of godliness but denying its power. Have nothing to do with them.

[6]They are the kind who worm their way into homes and gain control over weak-willed women, who are loaded down with sins and are swayed by all kinds of evil desires, [7]always learning but never able to acknowledge the truth. [8]Just as Jannes and Jambres opposed Moses, so also these men oppose the truth—men of depraved minds, who, as far as the faith is concerned, are rejected. [9]But they will not get very far because, as in the case of those men, their folly will be clear to everyone.

Paul's Charge to Timothy

[10]You, however, know all about my teaching, my way of life, my purpose, faith, patience, love, endurance, [11]persecutions, sufferings—what kinds of things happened to me in Antioch, Iconium and Lystra, the persecutions I endured. Yet the Lord rescued me from all of them. [12]In fact, everyone who wants to live a godly life in Christ Jesus will be persecuted, [13]while evil men and impostors will go from bad to worse, deceiving and being deceived. [14]But as for you, continue in what you have learned and have become convinced of, because you know those from whom you learned it, [15]and how from infancy you have known the holy Scriptures, which are able to make you wise for salvation through faith in Christ Jesus. [16]All Scripture is God-breathed and is useful for teaching, rebuking, correcting and training in righteousness, [17]so that the man of God may be thoroughly equipped for every good work.

4 In the presence of God and of Christ Jesus, who will judge the living and the dead, and in view of his appearing and his kingdom, I give you this charge: [2]Preach the Word; be prepared in season

[a]19 Num. 16:5 (see Septuagint)

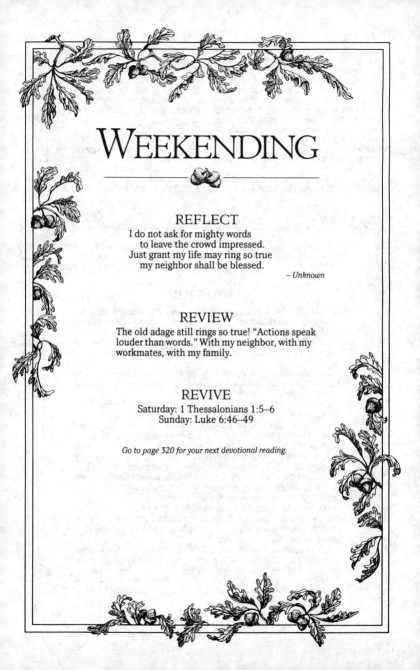

WEEKENDING

REFLECT

I do not ask for mighty words
to leave the crowd impressed.
Just grant my life may ring so true
my neighbor shall be blessed.

– Unknown

REVIEW

The old adage still rings so true! "Actions speak
louder than words." With my neighbor, with my
workmates, with my family.

REVIVE

Saturday: 1 Thessalonians 1:5–6
Sunday: Luke 6:46–49

Go to page 320 for your next devotional reading.

and out of season; correct, rebuke and encourage—with great patience and careful instruction.—³For the time will come when men will not put up with sound doctrine. Instead, to suit their own desires, they will gather around them a great number of teachers to say what their itching ears want to hear. ⁴They will turn their ears away from the truth and turn aside to myths. ⁵But you, keep your head in all situations, endure hardship, do the work of an evangelist, discharge all the duties of your ministry.

⁶For I am already being poured out like a drink offering, and the time has come for my departure. ⁷I have fought the good fight, I have finished the race, I have kept the faith. ⁸Now there is in store for me the crown of righteousness, which the Lord, the righteous Judge, will award to me on that day—and not only to me, but also to all who have longed for his appearing.

Personal Remarks

⁹Do your best to come to me quickly, ¹⁰for Demas, because he loved this world, has deserted me and has gone to Thessalonica. Crescens has gone to Galatia, and Titus to Dalmatia. ¹¹Only Luke is with me. Get Mark and bring him with

MONDAY

VERSE FOR THE DAY:	AUTHOR:	PASSAGE FOR THE DAY:
2 Timothy 3:16–17	Kathryn Hillen	2 Timothy 3:10–17

Tradition

WHEN my sister began keeping house, she immediately removed the handles from her rolling pin! Our mother's rolling pin had lost its handles before we were born, so we grew up using a rolling pin without handles. I seldom use the handles on mine, but I left them intact so that our daughters would learn to use them.

Habit and tradition powerfully influence our actions and beliefs. And this influence goes beyond simple things like handles on rolling pins.

Sometimes it's hard to distinguish our cultural beliefs from Biblical truth. As we grow in the Lord, we must examine our beliefs to make sure they are based on what the Bible says rather than merely on what we were taught. We can *hope* that ideas we were taught will agree with Biblical truth, but we can't be sure unless we examine them. Some concepts we were taught may be prejudices rather than convictions, traditions rather than Biblical truth. If we do not test our beliefs against the Bible, we may perpetuate human opinions rather than God-ordained doctrine, cultural mores rather than Biblical morality.

We need to examine our own beliefs and be responsible for what we teach others, including our children and people in our church. Are we teaching them our opinions and our perspective, or are we teaching them God's?

Growing up in Christ means listening to his voice. We must pray that the Holy Spirit will guide us and lead us into all truth.

Additional Scripture Readings:
Matthew 15:1–6; Colossians 2:8,20–23

Go to page 323 for your next devotional reading.

you, because he is helpful to me in my ministry. [12]I sent Tychicus to Ephesus. [13]When you come, bring the cloak that I left with Carpus at Troas, and my scrolls, especially the parchments.

[14]Alexander the metalworker did me a great deal of harm. The Lord will repay him for what he has done. [15]You too should be on your guard against him, because he strongly opposed our message.

[16]At my first defense, no one came to my support, but everyone deserted me. May it not be held against them. [17]But the Lord stood at my side and gave me strength, so that through me the message might be fully proclaimed and all the Gentiles might hear it. And I was delivered from the lion's mouth. [18]The Lord will rescue me from every evil attack and will bring me safely to his heavenly kingdom. To him be glory for ever and ever. Amen.

Final Greetings

[19]Greet Priscilla[a] and Aquila and the household of Onesiphorus. [20]Erastus stayed in Corinth, and I left Trophimus sick in Miletus. [21]Do your best to get here before winter. Eubulus greets you, and so do Pudens, Linus, Claudia and all the brothers.

[22]The Lord be with your spirit. Grace be with you.

[a]19 Greek *Prisca*, a variant of *Priscilla*

PAUL writes to Titus, a pastor serving in Crete, to advise him both on what to teach the churches and on how to organize them, especially with false teachers around. As you read this book, note God's concern for proper order in the church and for true teaching about Christ.

TITUS

1 Paul, a servant of God and an apostle of Jesus Christ for the faith of God's elect and the knowledge of the truth that leads to godliness— ²a faith and knowledge resting on the hope of eternal life, which God, who does not lie, promised before the beginning of time, ³and at his appointed season he brought his word to light through the preaching entrusted to me by the command of God our Savior,

⁴To Titus, my true son in our common faith:

Grace and peace from God the Father and Christ Jesus our Savior.

Titus' Task on Crete

⁵The reason I left you in Crete was that you might straighten out what was left unfinished and appoint*ᵃ* elders in every town, as I directed you. ⁶An elder must be blameless, the husband of but one wife, a man whose children believe and are not open to the charge of being wild and disobedient. ⁷Since an overseer*ᵇ* is entrusted with God's work, he must be blameless—not overbearing, not quick-tempered, not given to drunkenness, not violent, not pursuing dishonest gain. ⁸Rather he must be hospitable, one who loves what is good, who is self-controlled, upright, holy and disciplined. ⁹He must hold firmly to the trustworthy message as it has been taught, so that he can encourage others by sound doctrine and refute those who oppose it.

¹⁰For there are many rebellious people, mere talkers and deceivers, especially those of the circumcision group. ¹¹They must be silenced, because they are ruining whole households by teaching things they ought not to teach—and that for the sake of dishonest gain. ¹²Even one of their own prophets has said, "Cretans

ᵃ5 Or *ordain*   *ᵇ7* Traditionally *bishop*

are always liars, evil brutes, lazy gluttons." ¹³This testimony is true. Therefore, rebuke them sharply, so that they will be sound in the faith ¹⁴and will pay no attention to Jewish myths or to the commands of those who reject the truth. ¹⁵To the pure, all things are pure, but to those who are corrupted and do not believe, nothing is pure. In fact, both their minds and consciences are corrupted. ¹⁶They claim to know God, but by their actions they deny him. They are detestable, disobedient and unfit for doing anything good.

What Must Be Taught to Various Groups

2 You must teach what is in accord with sound doctrine. ²Teach the older men to be temperate, worthy of respect, self-controlled, and sound in faith, in love and in endurance.

³Likewise, teach the older women to be reverent in the way they live, not to be slanderers or addicted to much wine, but to teach what is good. ⁴Then they can train the younger women to love their husbands and children, ⁵to be self-controlled and pure, to be busy at home, to be kind, and to be subject to their husbands, so that no one will malign the word of God.

⁶Similarly, encourage the young men to be self-controlled. ⁷In everything set them an example by doing what is good. In your teaching show integrity, seriousness ⁸and soundness of speech that cannot be condemned, so that those who oppose you may be ashamed because they have nothing bad to say about us.

⁹Teach slaves to be subject to their masters in everything, to try to please them, not to talk back to them, ¹⁰and not

TUESDAY

VERSE FOR THE DAY: AUTHOR: PASSAGE FOR THE DAY:
Titus 1:13   Doris Haase   Titus 1:5–16

Walk Upright!

ONCE upon a time, in the early days of our country, a weary traveler arrived at the banks of the Mississippi. There was no bridge. It was winter and the water was covered by a layer of ice. Was it strong enough to hold his weight, he wondered? Still, he had to get across before nightfall, and so, terrified, he crept slowly on hands and knees across the frozen surface, certain he would never live to see the other side.

Suddenly he heard the clop, clop of a horse-drawn wagon. As it rattled past, he could hear the driver singing merrily. Unlike himself, the man, obviously familiar with these conditions, had no doubt at all that their glacial road was strong.

I sympathize with that traveler, for I too, am a creeper. I know God has promised no harm will befall me (Psalm 91:10) and that I should cast my cares upon him and he will sustain me (Psalm 55:22). So why do I so often forget that God is one who keeps his promises? He really can bear the weight of my every problem.

Today I resolve to follow the example of that long-ago wagoner. I will believe, walk upright and sing!

Additional Scripture Readings:
Deuteronomy 10:12–22; Psalm 23:4

Go to page 324 for your next devotional reading.

to steal from them, but to show that they can be fully trusted, so that in every way they will make the teaching about God our Savior attractive.

¹¹For the grace of God that brings sal- vation has appeared to all men. ¹²It teaches us to say "No" to ungodliness and worldly passions, and to live self- controlled, upright and godly lives in this present age, ¹³while we wait for the

WEDNESDAY

| VERSE FOR THE DAY:
Titus 2:4–5 | AUTHOR:
Debbie Smith | PASSAGE FOR THE DAY:
Titus 2:1–8 |

Pleasing to God and Family

MY older son at preschool and the baby downstairs with the sit- ter, I settled into bed with my three-year-old daughter for a deli- cious afternoon nap. We giggled quietly, nose-to-nose, covers up to our chins. It was a precious mother-daughter moment that required no words . . . until Whitney spoke up.

"I like this kind of mommy!"

At times like these, I feel like I must be doing something right. Of course, the other side of the coin is obvious: sometimes I am *not* the "kind of mommy" she likes—or deserves!

That thought reminds me that loving children (and husbands) is a learning process. Titus 2:4 confirms that young mothers should be trained by the older women to love their husbands and children.

Interestingly, two Greek words for love are used in the original text. The word for love for husbands connotes nurturing as a friend: "fond of man." The word used here for love for children means maternal love: literally, "fond of one's children."

I am grateful that God addresses on the practical level the daily grind of living as women. Here he makes it clear that he ex- pects holiness in our lives, whatever our ages. The older women are to be exemplary in speech and conduct so that "they can train the younger women" to be the same. Titus 2:5 sets the agenda for young mothers: learn to love family, learn self- control, tend to the home, and be kind and submissive to one's husband.

Running a home, Titus 2:5 implies, requires being a servant. And "if anyone serves, he should do it with the strength God provides, so that in all things God may be praised through Jesus Christ" (1 Peter 4:11).

Such a mommy is pleasing to the Lord . . . and to her children!

Additional Scripture Readings:
Proverbs 31:26–30; 1 Thessalonians 2:7–12

Go to page 327 for your next devotional reading.

blessed hope — the glorious appearing of our great God and Savior, Jesus Christ, [14]who gave himself for us to redeem us from all wickedness and to purify for himself a people that are his very own, eager to do what is good.

[15]These, then, are the things you should teach. Encourage and rebuke with all authority. Do not let anyone despise you.

Doing What Is Good

3 Remind the people to be subject to rulers and authorities, to be obedient, to be ready to do whatever is good, [2]to slander no one, to be peaceable and considerate, and to show true humility toward all men.

[3]At one time we too were foolish, disobedient, deceived and enslaved by all kinds of passions and pleasures. We lived in malice and envy, being hated and hating one another. [4]But when the kindness and love of God our Savior appeared, [5]he saved us, not because of righteous things we had done, but because of his mercy. He saved us through the washing of rebirth and renewal by the Holy Spirit, [6]whom he poured out on us generously through Jesus Christ our Savior, [7]so that, having been justified by his grace, we might become heirs having the hope of eternal life. [8]This is a trustworthy saying. And I want you to stress these things, so that those who have trusted in God may be careful to devote themselves to doing what is good. These things are excellent and profitable for everyone.

[9]But avoid foolish controversies and genealogies and arguments and quarrels about the law, because these are unprofitable and useless. [10]Warn a divisive person once, and then warn him a second time. After that, have nothing to do with him. [11]You may be sure that such a man is warped and sinful; he is self-condemned.

Final Remarks

[12]As soon as I send Artemas or Tychicus to you, do your best to come to me at Nicopolis, because I have decided to winter there. [13]Do everything you can to help Zenas the lawyer and Apollos on their way and see that they have everything they need. [14]Our people must learn to devote themselves to doing what is good, in order that they may provide for daily necessities and not live unproductive lives.

[15]Everyone with me sends you greetings. Greet those who love us in the faith.

Grace be with you all.

*P*AUL *writes this brief letter to ask*
Philemon, a Christian brother living
(probably) in Colosse, to forgive and
take back Onesimus, a runaway slave
who has become a Christian and is
helping Paul in prison. As you read
this book, be willing to forgive others,
no matter what they do to you.

PHILEMON

¹Paul, a prisoner of Christ Jesus, and Timothy our brother,

To Philemon our dear friend and fellow worker, ²to Apphia our sister, to Archippus our fellow soldier and to the church that meets in your home:

³Grace to you and peace from God our Father and the Lord Jesus Christ.

Thanksgiving and Prayer

⁴I always thank my God as I remember you in my prayers, ⁵because I hear about your faith in the Lord Jesus and your love for all the saints. ⁶I pray that you may be active in sharing your faith, so that you will have a full understanding of every good thing we have in Christ. ⁷Your love has given me great joy and encouragement, because you, brother, have refreshed the hearts of the saints.

Paul's Plea for Onesimus

⁸Therefore, although in Christ I could be bold and order you to do what you ought to do, ⁹yet I appeal to you on the basis of love. I then, as Paul—an old man and now also a prisoner of Christ Jesus— ¹⁰I appeal to you for my son Onesimus,ᵃ who became my son while I was in chains. ¹¹Formerly he was useless to you, but now he has become useful both to you and to me.

¹²I am sending him—who is my very heart—back to you. ¹³I would have liked to keep him with me so that he could take your place in helping me while I am in chains for the gospel. ¹⁴But I did not want to do anything without your consent, so that any favor you do will be spontaneous and not forced. ¹⁵Perhaps the reason he was separated from you for a little while was that you might have him back for

ᵃ10 *Onesimus* means *useful.*

good— ¹⁶no longer as a slave, but better than a slave, as a dear brother. He is very dear to me but even dearer to you, both as a man and as a brother in the Lord.

¹⁷So if you consider me a partner, welcome him as you would welcome me. ¹⁸If he has done you any wrong or owes you anything, charge it to me. ¹⁹I, Paul, am writing this with my own hand. I will pay it back—not to mention that you owe me your very self. ²⁰I do wish, brother, that I may have some benefit from you in the Lord; refresh my heart in Christ. ²¹Confi-

dent of your obedience, I write to you, knowing that you will do even more than I ask.

²²And one thing more: Prepare a guest room for me, because I hope to be restored to you in answer to your prayers.

²³Epaphras, my fellow prisoner in Christ Jesus, sends you greetings. ²⁴And so do Mark, Aristarchus, Demas and Luke, my fellow workers.

²⁵The grace of the Lord Jesus Christ be with your spirit.

THURSDAY

VERSE FOR THE DAY:
Philemon 6–7

AUTHOR:
Kathryn Hillen

PASSAGE FOR THE DAY:
Philemon 1–25

Sweetheart

"LET Me Call You Sweetheart—I Can't Remember Your Name."

The pin, almost as big as a saucer, was worn by a middle-aged woman—without doubt, an extrovert. We were at a state PTA convention, encountering many unfamiliar faces. The pin seemed to be her humorous way of saying, "Let's be friends for today, but I'm not even going to attempt to remember your name."

We have many temporary relationships: those beside us on the plane or in the laundromat, the people who camp next to us at a resort, and the neighbors who move in and out with such rapidity. It's up to us to decide if these contacts will be meaningless or significant.

Ask God, "What would you like to say to this person through me?" You may be surprised. He may ask you to speak words of appreciation and encouragement, to witness about Christ, or only to be friendly. When we look a person in the eye and ask about their lives, we show that they are valuable. And even if we never do learn the person's name, we have been a channel through which God can reach him or her. That is both exciting and humbling.

Additional Scripture Readings:
2 Corinthians 5:18–20; Colossians 4:2–6

Go to page 329 for your next devotional reading.

*THE author of this letter encourages
Christians who are being persecuted for
their faith by pointing them to the
greatness of the Son of God who became man. Christ is the full expression
of God's revelation, better than anything in the Old Testament; the author
warns his readers to depend on Christ
alone. As you read this book, commit
yourself firmly to Jesus your Intercessor,
and be sure to persevere and grow daily
in your Christian faith and life.*

HEBREWS

The Son Superior to Angels

1 In the past God spoke to our forefathers through the prophets at many times and in various ways, ²but in these last days he has spoken to us by his Son, whom he appointed heir of all things, and through whom he made the universe. ³The Son is the radiance of God's glory and the exact representation of his being, sustaining all things by his powerful word. After he had provided purification for sins, he sat down at the right hand of the Majesty in heaven. ⁴So he became as much superior to the angels as the name he has inherited is superior to theirs.

⁵For to which of the angels did God ever say,

"You are my Son;
today I have become your
Father*ᵃ* "*ᵇ*?

Or again,

"I will be his Father,
and he will be my Son"*ᶜ*?

⁶And again, when God brings his firstborn into the world, he says,

"Let all God's angels worship him."[a]

[7]In speaking of the angels he says,

"He makes his angels winds,
   his servants flames of fire."[b]

[8]But about the Son he says,

"Your throne, O God, will last for ever
   and ever,
   and righteousness will be the
      scepter of your kingdom.
[9]You have loved righteousness and
      hated wickedness;
   therefore God, your God, has set
      you above your companions

by anointing you with the oil of
   joy."[c]

[10]He also says,

"In the beginning, O Lord, you laid
      the foundations of the earth,
   and the heavens are the work of
      your hands.
[11]They will perish, but you remain;
   they will all wear out like a
      garment.
[12]You will roll them up like a robe;
   like a garment they will be
      changed.

[a]6 Deut. 32:43 (see Dead Sea Scrolls and Septuagint)   [b]7 Psalm 104:4   [c]9 Psalm 45:6,7

FRIDAY

VERSE FOR THE DAY:
Hebrews 1:12

AUTHOR:
Janet C. Jones

PASSAGE FOR THE DAY:
Hebrews 1:1–14

Changes and Choices

RECENTLY my life has been filled with changes and choices. I guess that can be said of all of our lives. Would it not be good if we could choose a period of our lives that was enjoyable and let time stand still? But we cannot. Ecclesiastes 3:11 and 14 tell us, "he has made everything beautiful in its time," and "everything God does will endure forever."

If our childhood was a happy time, we did not want it to end. Everything was new, fresh and meaningful. We wanted our teen years to be over soon so we could be adults. In young adulthood, there were many changes and choices: college, marriage, the birth of children or the choice of a job. In middle age and even in our "golden years," there are still changes and choices.

My parents are in their golden years. Both of them have had severe physical problems. Because of this, I have had to make many choices and to endure a lot of changes. But Christ was and is precious, and his Word has been very real. When it became necessary to consider retirement housing for my mother and father, it was a difficult adjustment for all of us. But each day, as I went to God's Word, he had something just for me. For example, "Now go, lead the people to the place I spoke of, and my angel will go before you" (Exodus 32:34).

Yes, life is filled with changes and choices, but the right choice is Jesus Christ. He will take you through all the changes.

Additional Scripture Readings:
Luke 10:38–42; Hebrews 11:24–26

*Go to page 331 for your next
devotional reading.*

But you remain the same,
and your years will never end."[a]

[13]To which of the angels did God ever say,

"Sit at my right hand
until I make your enemies
a footstool for your feet"[b]?

[14]Are not all angels ministering spirits sent to serve those who will inherit salvation?

Warning to Pay Attention

2 We must pay more careful attention, therefore, to what we have heard, so that we do not drift away. [2]For if the message spoken by angels was binding, and every violation and disobedience received its just punishment, [3]how shall we escape if we ignore such a great salvation? This salvation, which was first announced by the Lord, was confirmed to us by those who heard him. [4]God also testified to it by signs, wonders and various miracles, and gifts of the Holy Spirit distributed according to his will.

Jesus Made Like His Brothers

[5]It is not to angels that he has subjected the world to come, about which we are speaking. [6]But there is a place where someone has testified:

"What is man that you are mindful of
him,
the son of man that you care for
him?
[7]You made him a little[c] lower than
the angels;
you crowned him with glory and
honor
[8]   and put everything under his
feet."[d]

In putting everything under him, God left nothing that is not subject to him. Yet at present we do not see everything subject to him. [9]But we see Jesus, who was made a little lower than the angels, now crowned with glory and honor because he suffered death, so that by the grace of God he might taste death for everyone.

[10]In bringing many sons to glory, it was fitting that God, for whom and through whom everything exists, should make the author of their salvation perfect through suffering. [11]Both the one who makes men

holy and those who are made holy are of the same family. So Jesus is not ashamed to call them brothers. [12]He says,

"I will declare your name to my
brothers;
in the presence of the congregation
I will sing your praises."[e]

[13]And again,

"I will put my trust in him."[f]

And again he says,

"Here am I, and the children God has
given me."[g]

[14]Since the children have flesh and blood, he too shared in their humanity so that by his death he might destroy him who holds the power of death—that is, the devil— [15]and free those who all their lives were held in slavery by their fear of death. [16]For surely it is not angels he helps, but Abraham's descendants. [17]For this reason he had to be made like his brothers in every way, in order that he might become a merciful and faithful high priest in service to God, and that he might make atonement for[h] the sins of the people. [18]Because he himself suffered when he was tempted, he is able to help those who are being tempted.

Jesus Greater Than Moses

3 Therefore, holy brothers, who share in the heavenly calling, fix your thoughts on Jesus, the apostle and high priest whom we confess. [2]He was faithful to the one who appointed him, just as Moses was faithful in all God's house. [3]Jesus has been found worthy of greater honor than Moses, just as the builder of a house has greater honor than the house itself. [4]For every house is built by someone, but God is the builder of everything. [5]Moses was faithful as a servant in all God's house, testifying to what would be said in the future. [6]But Christ is faithful as a son over God's house. And we are his house, if we hold on to our courage and the hope of which we boast.

Warning Against Unbelief

[7]So, as the Holy Spirit says:

"Today, if you hear his voice,
[8]   do not harden your hearts

a12 Psalm 102:25-27   b13 Psalm 110:1   c7 Or him for a little while; also in verse 9
d8 Psalm 8:4-6   e12 Psalm 22:22   f13 Isaiah 8:17   g13 Isaiah 8:18   h17 Or and that he might
turn aside God's wrath, taking away

WEEKENDING

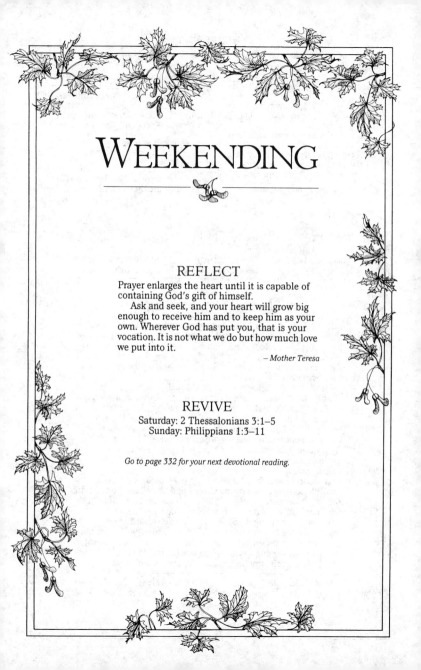

REFLECT

Prayer enlarges the heart until it is capable of containing God's gift of himself.

Ask and seek, and your heart will grow big enough to receive him and to keep him as your own. Wherever God has put you, that is your vocation. It is not what we do but how much love we put into it.

– Mother Teresa

REVIVE

Saturday: 2 Thessalonians 3:1–5
Sunday: Philippians 1:3–11

Go to page 332 for your next devotional reading.

as you did in the rebellion,
  during the time of testing in the
    desert,
[9]where your fathers tested and tried
  me
and for forty years saw what I did.
[10]That is why I was angry with that
    generation,
  and I said, 'Their hearts are always
    going astray,
  and they have not known my ways.'
[11]So I declared on oath in my anger,
  'They shall never enter my rest.' "[a]

[12]See to it, brothers, that none of you

has a sinful, unbelieving heart that turns
away from the living God. [13]But encourage one another daily, as long as it is
called Today, so that none of you may be
hardened by sin's deceitfulness. [14]We
have come to share in Christ if we hold
firmly till the end the confidence we had
at first. [15]As has just been said:

"Today, if you hear his voice,
  do not harden your hearts
  as you did in the rebellion."[b]

[16]Who were they who heard and rebelled? Were they not all those Moses led

---

[a]11 Psalm 95:7-11   [b]15 Psalm 95:7,8

MONDAY

VERSE FOR THE DAY:	AUTHOR:	PASSAGE FOR THE DAY:
Hebrews 3:13	Kathryn Hillen	Hebrews 3:12–19

Encouragement

MR. BARNS, a retired and somewhat senile bachelor, radiated
the love of God and was loved by the people of the church. The
last place I expected to see him was in the church nursery. Yet
there he was, watching as I stuffed my wiggling two-year-old
Paul into his snowsuit. It was Sunday night after the service, and
I was exhausted.

"God has blessed many people through your hands," he said
simply, as if he had come especially to deliver a message. I
thanked him as he turned to go, his shabby, ill-fitting clothes
hanging on his sparse frame. He lived in a basement apartment
with only his books, mementos and meager possessions. He had
no close relatives, no one to care for him except his church family. I often had felt sorry for him, but now he walked with the
pride of someone who had just given away something of great
value—and he had.

His encouragement lessened my exhaustion and eased the
painful memory of the wrong notes I had played on the organ in
that day's services. I even felt better about not being able to sit
with my family, a small sacrifice. I was uplifted.

I have often thought about that humble servant of God, willing to go out of his way to encourage a tired young mother.
Surely he had no way of knowing how I felt or what his words
meant to my lagging spirit. But he was faithful to God's prompting. This is a ministry that can be both yours and mine.

Additional Scripture Readings:
Acts 15:30–34; 1 Thessalonians 3:1–8

*Go to page 334 for your next
devotional reading.*

out of Egypt? [17]And with whom was he angry for forty years? Was it not with those who sinned, whose bodies fell in the desert? [18]And to whom did God swear that they would never enter his rest if not to those who disobeyed[a]? [19]So we see that they were not able to enter, because of their unbelief.

A Sabbath-Rest for the People of God

4 Therefore, since the promise of entering his rest still stands, let us be careful that none of you be found to have fallen short of it. [2]For we also have had the gospel preached to us, just as they did; but the message they heard was of no value to them, because those who heard did not combine it with faith.[b] [3]Now we who have believed enter that rest, just as God has said,

"So I declared on oath in my anger,
    'They shall never enter my rest.' "[c]

And yet his work has been finished since the creation of the world. [4]For somewhere he has spoken about the seventh day in these words: "And on the seventh day God rested from all his work."[d] [5]And again in the passage above he says, "They shall never enter my rest."

[6]It still remains that some will enter that rest, and those who formerly had the gospel preached to them did not go in, because of their disobedience. [7]Therefore God again set a certain day, calling it Today, when a long time later he spoke through David, as was said before:

"Today, if you hear his voice,
    do not harden your hearts."[e]

[8]For if Joshua had given them rest, God would not have spoken later about another day. [9]There remains, then, a Sabbath-rest for the people of God; [10]for anyone who enters God's rest also rests from his own work, just as God did from his. [11]Let us, therefore, make every effort to enter that rest, so that no one will fall by following their example of disobedience.

[12]For the word of God is living and active. Sharper than any double-edged sword, it penetrates even to dividing soul and spirit, joints and marrow; it judges the thoughts and attitudes of the heart. [13]Nothing in all creation is hidden from

God's sight. Everything is uncovered and laid bare before the eyes of him to whom we must give account.

Jesus the Great High Priest

[14]Therefore, since we have a great high priest who has gone through the heavens,[f] Jesus the Son of God, let us hold firmly to the faith we profess. [15]For we do not have a high priest who is unable to sympathize with our weaknesses, but we have one who has been tempted in every way, just as we are — yet was without sin. [16]Let us then approach the throne of grace with confidence, so that we may receive mercy and find grace to help us in our time of need.

5 Every high priest is selected from among men and is appointed to represent them in matters related to God, to offer gifts and sacrifices for sins. [2]He is able to deal gently with those who are ignorant and are going astray, since he himself is subject to weakness. [3]This is why he has to offer sacrifices for his own sins, as well as for the sins of the people.

[4]No one takes this honor upon himself; he must be called by God, just as Aaron was. [5]So Christ also did not take upon himself the glory of becoming a high priest. But God said to him,

"You are my Son;
    today I have become your
        Father.[g]"[h]

[6]And he says in another place,

"You are a priest forever,
    in the order of Melchizedek."[i]

[7]During the days of Jesus' life on earth, he offered up prayers and petitions with loud cries and tears to the one who could save him from death, and he was heard because of his reverent submission. [8]Although he was a son, he learned obedience from what he suffered [9]and, once made perfect, he became the source of eternal salvation for all who obey him [10]and was designated by God to be high priest in the order of Melchizedek.

Warning Against Falling Away

[11]We have much to say about this, but it is hard to explain because you are slow to learn. [12]In fact, though by this time you ought to be teachers, you need someone

VERSE FOR THE DAY:	AUTHOR:	PASSAGE FOR THE DAY:
Hebrews 5:14	Barbara Bush	Hebrews 5:11 — 6:12

The Wise Are Mature

THE writer of the letter to the Hebrews was frustrated. He had many wonderful truths he wanted to impart, but his audience did not want to expend much energy on spiritual growth. They had been Christians for some time, but they knew little more than when they first believed.

Those who feed on and digest the meat of God's Word attain maturity in their Christian lives. They gain the wisdom in speech and action that is the mark of the mature. If we are not mature, the reason is obvious: we have not been workmen but idlers in Bible study. We have not made constant use of the Scriptures to distinguish good from evil. We are still dependent on others for our knowledge, as children are, in danger of being misguided by those who sound knowledgeable but may be as ignorant as we.

This is why there are so few wise people. Those who get all their knowledge of God's Word from an hour or two on Sunday will never have a personal grasp of its content. Paul said that if we want to be wise, if we want to "correctly handle the word of truth," we must be workmen (2 Timothy 2:15). We must do the job ourselves instead of expecting a pastor or teacher to do it all for us. We must read the Bible. We must digest it, meditate on it, memorize it, understand it.

God does not want us to remain spiritually immature. He wants us to:

> . . . become mature, attaining to the whole measure of the fullness of Christ. Then we will no longer be infants, tossed back and forth by the waves, and blown here and there by every wind of teaching and by the cunning and craftiness of men in their deceitful scheming. Instead, speaking the truth in love, we will in all things grow up (Ephesians 4:13–15).

Additional Scripture Readings:
Luke 8:14–15; James 1:2–4

Go to page 335 for your next
devotional reading.

to teach you the elementary truths of God's word all over again. You need milk, not solid food! [13]Anyone who lives on milk, being still an infant, is not acquainted with the teaching about righteousness. [14]But solid food is for the mature, who by constant use have trained themselves to distinguish good from evil.

6 Therefore let us leave the elementary teachings about Christ and go on to maturity, not laying again the foundation of repentance from acts that lead to death,[a] and of faith in God, [2]instruction about baptisms, the laying on of hands, the resurrection of the dead, and eternal judgment. [3]And God permitting, we will do so.

[4]It is impossible for those who have once been enlightened, who have tasted the heavenly gift, who have shared in the Holy Spirit, [5]who have tasted the goodness of the word of God and the powers of

a1 Or from useless rituals

WEDNESDAY

VERSE FOR THE DAY:
Hebrews 6:18

AUTHOR:
Neva Coyle

PASSAGE FOR THE DAY:
Hebrews 6:13–20

Keeping Promises

DID anyone ever tell you that they would do something for you that needed to be done, and then they didn't do it? Did anyone ever promise you something and then break that promise? Were you ever lied to? Did you ever count on someone for support, and then just when you needed it you found that your friend was not in a position to give that support? Did you ever read a brochure about a vacation spot, and when you got there found that the modern cabin in the photograph was the only one at the place and it was occupied? If any of these situations ring a bell with you, then you know what it is like to be disillusioned or deceived.

Deception—what a disabling, evil element. Falsehood, misrepresentation, fabrication, dishonesty, fraud—all synonymous with deception. I have used these words to illustrate what God is not. We tend to be skeptical because of past experiences. We want everything proven to us before we believe. Why? Because we may have believed something once too often, and been deceived one time too many. We are more acquainted with lies than truth.

God knows that we are more apt to be skeptical than believing. Yet we remain gullible and vulnerable. He knows that even with the intense conditioning most of us have had, we want to believe. We need to believe. We are immensely relieved when we find an honest friend whom we can trust. God can be to us that friend. Listen to his words to us from Hebrews 6:18: "It is impossible for God to lie." Think about it—impossible. When God makes a promise, you can count on him to keep it!

Additional Scripture Readings:
Psalm 103:17–18; Isaiah 40:6–8

Go to page 338 for your next devotional reading.

the coming age, [6]if they fall away, to be brought back to repentance, because[a] to their loss they are crucifying the Son of God all over again and subjecting him to public disgrace.

[7]Land that drinks in the rain often falling on it and that produces a crop useful to those for whom it is farmed receives the blessing of God. [8]But land that produces thorns and thistles is worthless and is in danger of being cursed. In the end it will be burned.

[9]Even though we speak like this, dear friends, we are confident of better things in your case—things that accompany salvation. [10]God is not unjust; he will not forget your work and the love you have shown him as you have helped his people and continue to help them. [11]We want each of you to show this same diligence to the very end, in order to make your hope sure. [12]We do not want you to become lazy, but to imitate those who through faith and patience inherit what has been promised.

The Certainty of God's Promise

[13]When God made his promise to Abraham, since there was no one greater for him to swear by, he swore by himself, [14]saying, "I will surely bless you and give you many descendants."[b] [15]And so after waiting patiently, Abraham received what was promised.

[16]Men swear by someone greater than themselves, and the oath confirms what is said and puts an end to all argument. [17]Because God wanted to make the unchanging nature of his purpose very clear to the heirs of what was promised, he confirmed it with an oath. [18]God did this so that, by two unchangeable things in which it is impossible for God to lie, we who have fled to take hold of the hope offered to us may be greatly encouraged. [19]We have this hope as an anchor for the soul, firm and secure. It enters the inner sanctuary behind the curtain, [20]where Jesus, who went before us, has entered on our behalf. He has become a high priest forever, in the order of Melchizedek.

Melchizedek the Priest

7 This Melchizedek was king of Salem and priest of God Most High. He met Abraham returning from the defeat of the kings and blessed him, [2]and Abraham gave him a tenth of everything. First, his name means "king of righteousness"; then also, "king of Salem" means "king of peace." [3]Without father or mother, without genealogy, without beginning of days or end of life, like the Son of God he remains a priest forever.

[4]Just think how great he was: Even the patriarch Abraham gave him a tenth of the plunder! [5]Now the law requires the descendants of Levi who become priests to collect a tenth from the people—that is, their brothers—even though their brothers are descended from Abraham. [6]This man, however, did not trace his descent from Levi, yet he collected a tenth from Abraham and blessed him who had the promises. [7]And without doubt the lesser person is blessed by the greater. [8]In the one case, the tenth is collected by men who die; but in the other case, by him who is declared to be living. [9]One might even say that Levi, who collects the tenth, paid the tenth through Abraham, [10]because when Melchizedek met Abraham, Levi was still in the body of his ancestor.

Jesus Like Melchizedek

[11]If perfection could have been attained through the Levitical priesthood (for on the basis of it the law was given to the people), why was there still need for another priest to come—one in the order of Melchizedek, not in the order of Aaron? [12]For when there is a change of the priesthood, there must also be a change of the law. [13]He of whom these things are said belonged to a different tribe, and no one from that tribe has ever served at the altar. [14]For it is clear that our Lord descended from Judah, and in regard to that tribe Moses said nothing about priests. [15]And what we have said is even more clear if another priest like Melchizedek appears, [16]one who has become a priest not on the basis of a regulation as to his ancestry but on the basis of the power of an indestructible life. [17]For it is declared:

"You are a priest forever,
    in the order of Melchizedek."[c]

[18]The former regulation is set aside because it was weak and useless [19](for the law made nothing perfect), and a better hope is introduced, by which we draw near to God.

[20]And it was not without an oath! Oth-

---

[a]6 Or repentance while   [b]14 Gen. 22:17   [c]17 Psalm 110:4

ers became priests without any oath, [21]but he became a priest with an oath when God said to him:

"The Lord has sworn
    and will not change his mind:
'You are a priest forever.' "[a]

[22]Because of this oath, Jesus has become the guarantee of a better covenant.

[23]Now there have been many of those priests, since death prevented them from continuing in office; [24]but because Jesus lives forever, he has a permanent priesthood. [25]Therefore he is able to save completely[b] those who come to God through him, because he always lives to intercede for them.

[26]Such a high priest meets our need—one who is holy, blameless, pure, set apart from sinners, exalted above the heavens. [27]Unlike the other high priests, he does not need to offer sacrifices day after day, first for his own sins, and then for the sins of the people. He sacrificed for their sins once for all when he offered himself. [28]For the law appoints as high priests men who are weak; but the oath, which came after the law, appointed the Son, who has been made perfect forever.

The High Priest of a New Covenant

8 The point of what we are saying is this: We do have such a high priest, who sat down at the right hand of the throne of the Majesty in heaven, [2]and who serves in the sanctuary, the true tabernacle set up by the Lord, not by man.

[3]Every high priest is appointed to offer both gifts and sacrifices, and so it was necessary for this one also to have something to offer. [4]If he were on earth, he would not be a priest, for there are already men who offer the gifts prescribed by the law. [5]They serve at a sanctuary that is a copy and shadow of what is in heaven. This is why Moses was warned when he was about to build the tabernacle: "See to it that you make everything according to the pattern shown you on the mountain."[c] [6]But the ministry Jesus has received is as superior to theirs as the covenant of which he is mediator is superior to the old one, and it is founded on better promises.

[7]For if there had been nothing wrong with that first covenant, no place would

have been sought for another. [8]But God found fault with the people and said[d]:

"The time is coming, declares the Lord,
    when I will make a new covenant
with the house of Israel
    and with the house of Judah.
[9]It will not be like the covenant
    I made with their forefathers
when I took them by the hand
    to lead them out of Egypt,
because they did not remain faithful
    to my covenant,
    and I turned away from them,
                declares the Lord.
[10]This is the covenant I will make with
        the house of Israel
    after that time, declares the Lord.
I will put my laws in their minds
    and write them on their hearts.
I will be their God,
    and they will be my people.
[11]No longer will a man teach his
        neighbor,
    or a man his brother, saying, 'Know
        the Lord,'
because they will all know me,
    from the least of them to the
        greatest.
[12]For I will forgive their wickedness
    and will remember their sins no
        more."[e]

[13]By calling this covenant "new," he has made the first one obsolete; and what is obsolete and aging will soon disappear.

Worship in the Earthly Tabernacle

9 Now the first covenant had regulations for worship and also an earthly sanctuary. [2]A tabernacle was set up. In its first room were the lampstand, the table and the consecrated bread; this was called the Holy Place. [3]Behind the second curtain was a room called the Most Holy Place, [4]which had the golden altar of incense and the gold-covered ark of the covenant. This ark contained the gold jar of manna, Aaron's staff that had budded, and the stone tablets of the covenant. [5]Above the ark were the cherubim of the Glory, overshadowing the atonement cover.[f] But we cannot discuss these things in detail now.

[6]When everything had been arranged like this, the priests entered regularly

---

[a]21 Psalm 110:4   [b]25 Or *forever*   [c]5 Exodus 25:40   [d]8 Some manuscripts may be translated *fault and said to the people.*   [e]12 Jer. 31:31-34   [f]5 Traditionally *the mercy seat*

into the outer room to carry on their ministry. [7]But only the high priest entered the inner room, and that only once a year, and never without blood, which he offered for himself and for the sins the people had committed in ignorance. [8]The Holy Spirit was showing by this that the way into the Most Holy Place had not yet been disclosed as long as the first tabernacle was still standing. [9]This is an illustration for the present time, indicating that the gifts and sacrifices being offered were not able to clear the conscience of the worshiper. [10]They are only a matter of food and drink and various ceremonial washings—external regulations applying until the time of the new order.

The Blood of Christ

[11]When Christ came as high priest of the good things that are already here,[a] he went through the greater and more perfect tabernacle that is not man-made, that is to say, not a part of this creation. [12]He did not enter by means of the blood of goats and calves; but he entered the Most Holy Place once for all by his own blood, having obtained eternal redemption. [13]The blood of goats and bulls and

[a]11 Some early manuscripts *are to come*

THURSDAY

VERSE FOR THE DAY:
Hebrews 10:23

AUTHOR:
Hannah Whitall Smith

PASSAGE FOR THE DAY:
Hebrews 10:19–25

Turning From Doubting

YOU cannot perhaps hinder the suggestions of doubt from coming to you any more than you can hinder someone in the street from swearing as you go by; consequently you are not sinning in the one case any more than in the other. Just as you can refuse to listen to them or join in their oaths, so can you also refuse to listen to the doubts or join in with them. They are not your doubts until you consent to them and adopt them as true. When they come you must at once turn from them.

Give up your liberty to doubt forever. Put your will in this matter over on the Lord's side and trust him to keep you from falling. Tell him all about your weakness and your long-encouraged habits of doubt and how helpless you are before them. Then commit the whole battle to him. Tell him you will not doubt again, putting forth all your will power on his side and against his enemy and yours. Then "keep your eyes on Jesus" (Hebrews 12:2), looking away from yourself and away from your doubts, holding fast the profession of your faith without wavering, because "he who promised is faithful" (Hebrews 10:23). Rely on his faithfulness, not on your own. You have committed the keeping of your soul to him as the faithful Creator, and you must never again admit the possibility of his being unfaithful.

Cultivate a continuous habit of believing, and sooner or later all of your doubts will vanish in the glory of the absolute faithfulness of God.

Additional Scripture Readings:
Luke 1:11–20; John 20:26–29

Go to page 340 for your next devotional reading.

the ashes of a heifer sprinkled on those who are ceremonially unclean sanctify them so that they are outwardly clean. [14]How much more, then, will the blood of Christ, who through the eternal Spirit offered himself unblemished to God, cleanse our consciences from acts that lead to death,[a] so that we may serve the living God!

[15]For this reason Christ is the mediator of a new covenant, that those who are called may receive the promised eternal inheritance—now that he has died as a ransom to set them free from the sins committed under the first covenant.

[16]In the case of a will,[b] it is necessary to prove the death of the one who made it, [17]because a will is in force only when somebody has died; it never takes effect while the one who made it is living. [18]This is why even the first covenant was not put into effect without blood. [19]When Moses had proclaimed every commandment of the law to all the people, he took the blood of calves, together with water, scarlet wool and branches of hyssop, and sprinkled the scroll and all the people. [20]He said, "This is the blood of the covenant, which God has commanded you to keep."[c] [21]In the same way, he sprinkled with the blood both the tabernacle and everything used in its ceremonies. [22]In fact, the law requires that nearly everything be cleansed with blood, and without the shedding of blood there is no forgiveness.

[23]It was necessary, then, for the copies of the heavenly things to be purified with these sacrifices, but the heavenly things themselves with better sacrifices than these. [24]For Christ did not enter a manmade sanctuary that was only a copy of the true one; he entered heaven itself, now to appear for us in God's presence. [25]Nor did he enter heaven to offer himself again and again, the way the high priest enters the Most Holy Place every year with blood that is not his own. [26]Then Christ would have had to suffer many times since the creation of the world. But now he has appeared once for all at the end of the ages to do away with sin by the sacrifice of himself. [27]Just as man is destined to die once, and after that to face judgment, [28]so Christ was sacrificed once to take away the sins of many people; and he will appear a second time, not to bear

sin, but to bring salvation to those who are waiting for him.

Christ's Sacrifice Once for All

10 The law is only a shadow of the good things that are coming—not the realities themselves. For this reason it can never, by the same sacrifices repeated endlessly year after year, make perfect those who draw near to worship. [2]If it could, would they not have stopped being offered? For the worshipers would have been cleansed once for all, and would no longer have felt guilty for their sins. [3]But those sacrifices are an annual reminder of sins, [4]because it is impossible for the blood of bulls and goats to take away sins.

[5]Therefore, when Christ came into the world, he said:

"Sacrifice and offering you did not
    desire,
  but a body you prepared for me;
[6]with burnt offerings and sin offerings
    you were not pleased.
[7]Then I said, 'Here I am—it is written
    about me in the scroll—
  I have come to do your will,
    O God.' "[d]

[8]First he said, "Sacrifices and offerings, burnt offerings and sin offerings you did not desire, nor were you pleased with them" (although the law required them to be made). [9]Then he said, "Here I am, I have come to do your will." He sets aside the first to establish the second. [10]And by that will, we have been made holy through the sacrifice of the body of Jesus Christ once for all.

[11]Day after day every priest stands and performs his religious duties; again and again he offers the same sacrifices, which can never take away sins. [12]But when this priest had offered for all time one sacrifice for sins, he sat down at the right hand of God. [13]Since that time he waits for his enemies to be made his footstool, [14]because by one sacrifice he has made perfect forever those who are being made holy.

[15]The Holy Spirit also testifies to us about this. First he says:

[16]"This is the covenant I will make with
    them
  after that time, says the Lord.
  I will put my laws in their hearts,

---

[a]14 Or *from useless rituals*   [b]16 Same Greek word as *covenant*; also in verse 17   [c]20 Exodus 24:8
[d]7 Psalm 40:6-8 (see Septuagint)

VERSE FOR THE DAY:
Hebrews 11:39–40

AUTHOR:
Luci Swindoll

PASSAGE FOR THE DAY:
Hebrews 11:23–29,39–40

Moses' Choice—Your Choice

THIS inspiring chapter of Hebrews has been called the Faith Hall of Fame. These noted saints pleased God and were commended by him because, in faith, they trusted God for what they hoped for, even though they could not see the goal at the time.

The most amazing person in this whole bunch is Moses, because of a choice he made. And what did he choose? "He chose to be mistreated along with the people of God." Why would he do that? At that time, Egypt was the loftiest society of the day—rich in beauty, education, art, trade, culture—and the Hebrew people were, by comparison, nothing more than a dung heap on the outskirts of town. Moses, even though he had been reared from babyhood by the daughter of Pharaoh, chose the dung heap. Unbelievable! Instead of staying where things were nice and clean, prestigious and comfortable, he chose mistreatment. I find that thought-provoking.

Would I choose mistreatment? I wonder if I'd have that strength of character. Loving the nicer things in life, I'd have to reach down into that part of me where my values lie. What would it take to make me choose what's best rather than what's easiest? Such a decision would have to come from a sense of direction—from my faith.

By faith, Moses chose wisely and looked at the disgrace and mistreatment as a temporary burden, with his ultimate reward of greater value than what society had to offer. Faith willfully chooses even disgrace or mistreatment because it sees, through an act of trust, the eventual reward that comes from him who is invisible.

You have the same opportunity to choose either a reward that stops here or one that lies ahead in a place that cannot be seen. You have a chance to choose for your sake or for the sake of Christ. It boils down to that. How will you choose? Remember Moses.

Additional Scripture Readings:
Esther 4:6–16; Daniel 3:13–18

Go to page 342 for your next devotional reading.

and I will write them on their minds."[a]

[17]Then he adds:

"Their sins and lawless acts
I will remember no more."[b]

[18]And where these have been forgiven, there is no longer any sacrifice for sin.

A Call to Persevere

[19]Therefore, brothers, since we have confidence to enter the Most Holy Place by the blood of Jesus, [20]by a new and living way opened for us through the curtain, that is, his body, [21]and since we have a great priest over the house of God, [22]let us draw near to God with a sincere heart in full assurance of faith, having our hearts sprinkled to cleanse us from a guilty conscience and having our bodies washed with pure water. [23]Let us hold unswervingly to the hope we profess, for he who promised is faithful. [24]And let us consider how we may spur one another on toward love and good deeds. [25]Let us not give up meeting together, as some are in the habit of doing, but let us encourage one another — and all the more as you see the Day approaching.

[26]If we deliberately keep on sinning after we have received the knowledge of the truth, no sacrifice for sins is left, [27]but only a fearful expectation of judgment and of raging fire that will consume the enemies of God. [28]Anyone who rejected the law of Moses died without mercy on the testimony of two or three witnesses. [29]How much more severely do you think a man deserves to be punished who has trampled the Son of God under foot, who has treated as an unholy thing the blood of the covenant that sanctified him, and who has insulted the Spirit of grace? [30]For we know him who said, "It is mine to avenge; I will repay,"[c] and again, "The Lord will judge his people."[d] [31]It is a dreadful thing to fall into the hands of the living God.

[32]Remember those earlier days after you had received the light, when you stood your ground in a great contest in the face of suffering. [33]Sometimes you were publicly exposed to insult and persecution; at other times you stood side by side with those who were so treated. [34]You sympathized with those in prison and joyfully accepted the confiscation of your property, because you knew that you yourselves had better and lasting possessions.

[35]So do not throw away your confidence; it will be richly rewarded. [36]You need to persevere so that when you have done the will of God, you will receive what he has promised. [37]For in just a very little while,

"He who is coming will come and will not delay.
[38]   But my righteous one[e] will live by faith.
And if he shrinks back,
    I will not be pleased with him."[f]

[39]But we are not of those who shrink back and are destroyed, but of those who believe and are saved.

By Faith

11 Now faith is being sure of what we hope for and certain of what we do not see. [2]This is what the ancients were commended for.

[3]By faith we understand that the universe was formed at God's command, so that what is seen was not made out of what was visible.

[4]By faith Abel offered God a better sacrifice than Cain did. By faith he was commended as a righteous man, when God spoke well of his offerings. And by faith he still speaks, even though he is dead.

[5]By faith Enoch was taken from this life, so that he did not experience death; he could not be found, because God had taken him away. For before he was taken, he was commended as one who pleased God. [6]And without faith it is impossible to please God, because anyone who comes to him must believe that he exists and that he rewards those who earnestly seek him.

[7]By faith Noah, when warned about things not yet seen, in holy fear built an ark to save his family. By his faith he condemned the world and became heir of the righteousness that comes by faith.

[8]By faith Abraham, when called to go to a place he would later receive as his inheritance, obeyed and went, even though he did not know where he was going. [9]By faith he made his home in the promised land like a stranger in a foreign country; he lived in tents, as did Isaac and Jacob,

[a]16 Jer. 31:33   [b]17 Jer. 31:34   [c]30 Deut. 32:35   [d]30 Deut. 32:36; Psalm 135:14   [e]38 One
early manuscript But the righteous   [f]38 Hab. 2:3,4

WEEKENDING

REFLECT

From morning until night
I am busy.
Surely all this motion
is getting me somewhere,
isn't it?

Somewhere . . .
What an indefinite term!
Where am I going?
Am I any closer to being there
than I was yesterday?
I don't know . . .
I've been so busy going,
I haven't thought about
where . . .
Of course, I know.
I want to know God,
Now . . .
as He is revealed in Jesus Christ.

RENEW

Let's check and see if I'm going
ahead,
or backward,
or nowhere . . . .

– Gladis and Gordon DePree

REVIVE

Saturday: 2 Timothy 4:6–8
Sunday: Philippians 3:12–14

Go to page 344 for your next devotional reading.

who were heirs with him of the same promise. [10]For he was looking forward to the city with foundations, whose architect and builder is God.

[11]By faith Abraham, even though he was past age — and Sarah herself was barren — was enabled to become a father because he[a] considered him faithful who had made the promise. [12]And so from this one man, and he as good as dead, came descendants as numerous as the stars in the sky and as countless as the sand on the seashore.

[13]All these people were still living by faith when they died. They did not receive the things promised; they only saw them and welcomed them from a distance. And they admitted that they were aliens and strangers on earth. [14]People who say such things show that they are looking for a country of their own. [15]If they had been thinking of the country they had left, they would have had opportunity to return. [16]Instead, they were longing for a better country — a heavenly one. Therefore God is not ashamed to be called their God, for he has prepared a city for them.

[17]By faith Abraham, when God tested him, offered Isaac as a sacrifice. He who had received the promises was about to sacrifice his one and only son, [18]even though God had said to him, "It is through Isaac that your offspring[b] will be reckoned."[c] [19]Abraham reasoned that God could raise the dead, and figuratively speaking, he did receive Isaac back from death.

[20]By faith Isaac blessed Jacob and Esau in regard to their future.

[21]By faith Jacob, when he was dying, blessed each of Joseph's sons, and worshiped as he leaned on the top of his staff.

[22]By faith Joseph, when his end was near, spoke about the exodus of the Israelites from Egypt and gave instructions about his bones.

[23]By faith Moses' parents hid him for three months after he was born, because they saw he was no ordinary child, and they were not afraid of the king's edict.

[24]By faith Moses, when he had grown up, refused to be known as the son of Pharaoh's daughter. [25]He chose to be mistreated along with the people of God rather than to enjoy the pleasures of sin for a short time. [26]He regarded disgrace for the sake of Christ as of greater value than the treasures of Egypt, because he was looking ahead to his reward. [27]By faith he left Egypt, not fearing the king's anger; he persevered because he saw him who is invisible. [28]By faith he kept the Passover and the sprinkling of blood, so that the destroyer of the firstborn would not touch the firstborn of Israel.

[29]By faith the people passed through the Red Sea[d] as on dry land; but when the Egyptians tried to do so, they were drowned.

[30]By faith the walls of Jericho fell, after the people had marched around them for seven days.

[31]By faith the prostitute Rahab, because she welcomed the spies, was not killed with those who were disobedient.[e]

[32]And what more shall I say? I do not have time to tell about Gideon, Barak, Samson, Jephthah, David, Samuel and the prophets, [33]who through faith conquered kingdoms, administered justice, and gained what was promised; who shut the mouths of lions, [34]quenched the fury of the flames, and escaped the edge of the sword; whose weakness was turned to strength; and who became powerful in battle and routed foreign armies. [35]Women received back their dead, raised to life again. Others were tortured and refused to be released, so that they might gain a better resurrection. [36]Some faced jeers and flogging, while still others were chained and put in prison. [37]They were stoned[f]; they were sawed in two; they were put to death by the sword. They went about in sheepskins and goatskins, destitute, persecuted and mistreated — [38]the world was not worthy of them. They wandered in deserts and mountains, and in caves and holes in the ground.

[39]These were all commended for their faith, yet none of them received what had been promised. [40]God had planned something better for us so that only together with us would they be made perfect.

God Disciplines His Sons

12 Therefore, since we are surrounded by such a great cloud of witnesses, let us throw off everything that hinders and the sin that so easily entangles, and let us run with perseverance the

---

a11 Or By faith even Sarah, who was past age, was enabled to bear children because she   b18 Greek seed   c18 Gen. 21:12   d29 That is, Sea of Reeds   e31 Or unbelieving   f37 Some early manuscripts stoned; they were put to the test;

race marked out for us. ²Let us fix our eyes on Jesus, the author and perfecter of our faith, who for the joy set before him endured the cross, scorning its shame, and sat down at the right hand of the throne of God. ³Consider him who endured such opposition from sinful men, so that you will not grow weary and lose heart.

⁴In your struggle against sin, you have not yet resisted to the point of shedding your blood. ⁵And you have forgotten that word of encouragement that addresses you as sons:

"My son, do not make light of the
     Lord's discipline,
   and do not lose heart when he
     rebukes you,
⁶because the Lord disciplines those he
     loves,
   and he punishes everyone he
     accepts as a son."ᵃ

⁷Endure hardship as discipline; God is

ᵃ6 Prov. 3:11,12

MONDAY

VERSE FOR THE DAY:
Hebrews 12:10

AUTHOR:
Diane Head

PASSAGE FOR THE DAY:
Hebrews 12:1–13

His Discipline

MOST of us have had at least one week when everything seemed to go wrong. The kids knocked down the apple display at the market; the plumbing decided it was time to back up; the furnace died; the car had a flat (with the entire Brownie troop inside); and the stomach flu toppled the whole household.

These events don't always come in groups, but even one at a time they can be mildly irritating and sometimes downright exasperating.

Then there are the more serious events that enter our lives—seemingly without reason. The ones that slice at our very roots: perhaps a lost job or maybe a transfer to another city. Maybe it's the extended illness of a family member or a life-threatening accident or not enough money to go around.

Do you ever wonder about the calamities that meet us head-on in everyday life? Do you ever ask as I do, "Why me, Lord?" Are daily catastrophes just happenstance or is there a reason behind them?

God disciplines us for our good, that we may share in his holiness" (Hebrews 12:10). What a difference it makes in the atmosphere of our homes if we face those calamities with an attitude of joy. Not a fake, pasted-on joy—but a joy that comes from knowing that he is bringing us closer to a sharing in his holiness—through discipline.

So the next time those rough winds sweep through our homes—let's rejoice! It won't be long until we can lift our hearts and laugh in his sunshine . . . in his holiness.

Additional Scripture Readings:
Deuteronomy 8:1–5; Proverbs 3:11–12

Go to page 346 for your next devotional reading.

treating you as sons. For what son is not disciplined by his father? [8]If you are not disciplined (and everyone undergoes discipline), then you are illegitimate children and not true sons. [9]Moreover, we have all had human fathers who disciplined us and we respected them for it. How much more should we submit to the Father of our spirits and live! [10]Our fathers disciplined us for a little while as they thought best; but God disciplines us for our good, that we may share in his holiness. [11]No discipline seems pleasant at the time, but painful. Later on, however, it produces a harvest of righteousness and peace for those who have been trained by it.

[12]Therefore, strengthen your feeble arms and weak knees. [13]"Make level paths for your feet,"[a] so that the lame may not be disabled, but rather healed.

Warning Against Refusing God

[14]Make every effort to live in peace with all men and to be holy; without holiness no one will see the Lord. [15]See to it that no one misses the grace of God and that no bitter root grows up to cause trouble and defile many. [16]See that no one is sexually immoral, or is godless like Esau, who for a single meal sold his inheritance rights as the oldest son. [17]Afterward, as you know, when he wanted to inherit this blessing, he was rejected. He could bring about no change of mind, though he sought the blessing with tears.

[18]You have not come to a mountain that can be touched and that is burning with fire; to darkness, gloom and storm; [19]to a trumpet blast or to such a voice speaking words that those who heard it begged that no further word be spoken to them, [20]because they could not bear what was commanded: "If even an animal touches the mountain, it must be stoned."[b] [21]The sight was so terrifying that Moses said, "I am trembling with fear."[c]

[22]But you have come to Mount Zion, to the heavenly Jerusalem, the city of the living God. You have come to thousands upon thousands of angels in joyful assembly, [23]to the church of the firstborn, whose names are written in heaven. You have come to God, the judge of all men, to the spirits of righteous men made perfect, [24]to Jesus the mediator of a new covenant, and to the sprinkled blood that speaks a better word than the blood of Abel.

[25]See to it that you do not refuse him who speaks. If they did not escape when they refused him who warned them on earth, how much less will we, if we turn away from him who warns us from heaven? [26]At that time his voice shook the earth, but now he has promised, "Once more I will shake not only the earth but also the heavens."[d] [27]The words "once more" indicate the removing of what can be shaken—that is, created things—so that what cannot be shaken may remain.

[28]Therefore, since we are receiving a kingdom that cannot be shaken, let us be thankful, and so worship God acceptably with reverence and awe, [29]for our "God is a consuming fire."[e]

Concluding Exhortations

13 Keep on loving each other as brothers. [2]Do not forget to entertain strangers, for by so doing some people have entertained angels without knowing it. [3]Remember those in prison as if you were their fellow prisoners, and those who are mistreated as if you yourselves were suffering.

[4]Marriage should be honored by all, and the marriage bed kept pure, for God will judge the adulterer and all the sexually immoral. [5]Keep your lives free from the love of money and be content with what you have, because God has said,

"Never will I leave you;
    never will I forsake you."[f]

[6]So we say with confidence,

"The Lord is my helper; I will not be afraid.
    What can man do to me?"[g]

[7]Remember your leaders, who spoke the word of God to you. Consider the outcome of their way of life and imitate their faith. [8]Jesus Christ is the same yesterday and today and forever.

[9]Do not be carried away by all kinds of strange teachings. It is good for our hearts to be strengthened by grace, not by ceremonial foods, which are of no value to those who eat them. [10]We have an altar from which those who minister at the tabernacle have no right to eat.

[11]The high priest carries the blood of

---

[a]13 Prov. 4:26   [b]20 Exodus 19:12,13   [c]21 Deut. 9:19   [d]26 Haggai 2:6   [e]29 Deut. 4:24
[f]5 Deut. 31:6   [g]6 Psalm 118:6,7

VERSE FOR THE DAY:	*AUTHOR:*	*PASSAGE FOR THE DAY:*
Hebrews 13:5	Sue Richards	Hebrews 13:1–6

Uncoupled

MY husband of eight years left me at the beginning of my fourth month of pregnancy. I have never felt more rejected, vulnerable or unloved. I was nauseated, tired, and constantly trying to explain to my two-year-old son that Daddy wasn't coming back home because he didn't love Mommy anymore.

Michigan's howling winter winds, which seemed to seep through even brick walls, only added to my depression as I hauled groceries and toddler up three flights of stairs. We had just moved to Michigan from Virginia, and this was supposed to be our temporary apartment while our house in Virginia was being sold.

No house, no job, no husband, no church. Just an active little boy asking heartbreaking questions, a stomach that gagged at the thought of food, and an empty bed with sheets as cold as the February winds.

Yet, somewhere, there was something else too. It was deep inside my heart. It didn't feel overpowering or dramatic, but it gave me courage to get up each morning and make it through the day.

I knew that God loved me. I wish I could say I laughed in the face of all adversity, but I didn't. I sobbed into my pillow at night, then lay awake unable to breathe through my nose, wondering what would happen to me and my two babies.

I did more than wonder, though. I prayed. I prayed when I did my grocery shopping, when I bathed little Matthew, and when I strained over my ever-protruding belly to trim my toenails.

How reassuring it was for me in those lonely times to read God's words:

> Never will I leave you;
> never will I forsake you.

I held on to those words when I felt totally abandoned, totally alone. In those times, when I was willing to reach out to God and his reassuring words, he faithfully held me up.

Thank you, Lord, for granting me strength to live through the difficult times. And thank you for holding me up, especially in my most vulnerable moments.

Additional Scripture Readings:
Isaiah 40:11; 2 Corinthians 4:7–9

Go to page 349 for your next devotional reading.

animals into the Most Holy Place as a sin offering, but the bodies are burned outside the camp. [12]And so Jesus also suffered outside the city gate to make the people holy through his own blood. [13]Let us, then, go to him outside the camp, bearing the disgrace he bore. [14]For here we do not have an enduring city, but we are looking for the city that is to come.

[15]Through Jesus, therefore, let us continually offer to God a sacrifice of praise —the fruit of lips that confess his name. [16]And do not forget to do good and to share with others, for with such sacrifices God is pleased.

[17]Obey your leaders and submit to their authority. They keep watch over you as men who must give an account. Obey them so that their work will be a joy, not a burden, for that would be of no advantage to you.

[18]Pray for us. We are sure that we have a clear conscience and desire to live honorably in every way. [19]I particularly urge you to pray so that I may be restored to you soon.

[20]May the God of peace, who through the blood of the eternal covenant brought back from the dead our Lord Jesus, that great Shepherd of the sheep, [21]equip you with everything good for doing his will, and may he work in us what is pleasing to him, through Jesus Christ, to whom be glory for ever and ever. Amen.

[22]Brothers, I urge you to bear with my word of exhortation, for I have written you only a short letter.

[23]I want you to know that our brother Timothy has been released. If he arrives soon, I will come with him to see you.

[24]Greet all your leaders and all God's people. Those from Italy send you their greetings.

[25]Grace be with you all.

*J*AMES *(a brother of Jesus) writes this
letter to urge Christians to express their
faith in daily living. He reminds them
of what Jesus said, especially in the
Sermon on the Mount (Matthew 5–7).
As you read this book, ask yourself
whether others can see by what you do
and say that you believe in Jesus.*

JAMES

1 James, a servant of God and of the
Lord Jesus Christ,

To the twelve tribes scattered among
the nations:

Greetings.

Trials and Temptations

²Consider it pure joy, my brothers,
whenever you face trials of many kinds,
³because you know that the testing of
your faith develops perseverance. ⁴Perse-
verance must finish its work so that you
may be mature and complete, not lacking
anything. ⁵If any of you lacks wisdom, he
should ask God, who gives generously to
all without finding fault, and it will be
given to him. ⁶But when he asks, he must
believe and not doubt, because he who
doubts is like a wave of the sea, blown
and tossed by the wind. ⁷That man should
not think he will receive anything from

the Lord; ⁸he is a double-minded man,
unstable in all he does.

⁹The brother in humble circumstances
ought to take pride in his high position.
¹⁰But the one who is rich should take
pride in his low position, because he will
pass away like a wild flower. ¹¹For the sun
rises with scorching heat and withers the
plant; its blossom falls and its beauty is
destroyed. In the same way, the rich man
will fade away even while he goes about
his business.

¹²Blessed is the man who perseveres
under trial, because when he has stood
the test, he will receive the crown of life
that God has promised to those who love
him.

¹³When tempted, no one should say,
"God is tempting me." For God cannot be
tempted by evil, nor does he tempt anyone; ¹⁴but each one is tempted when, by
his own evil desire, he is dragged away
and enticed. ¹⁵Then, after desire has con-

ceived, it gives birth to sin; and sin, when it is full-grown, gives birth to death.

¹⁶Don't be deceived, my dear brothers. ¹⁷Every good and perfect gift is from above, coming down from the Father of the heavenly lights, who does not change like shifting shadows. ¹⁸He chose to give us birth through the word of truth, that we might be a kind of firstfruits of all he created.

Listening and Doing

¹⁹My dear brothers, take note of this: Everyone should be quick to listen, slow to speak and slow to become angry, ²⁰for man's anger does not bring about the righteous life that God desires. ²¹Therefore, get rid of all moral filth and the evil that is so prevalent and humbly accept the word planted in you, which can save you.

²²Do not merely listen to the word, and so deceive yourselves. Do what it says. ²³Anyone who listens to the word but does not do what it says is like a man who looks at his face in a mirror ²⁴and, after looking at himself, goes away and immediately forgets what he looks like. ²⁵But the man who looks intently into the perfect law that gives freedom, and continues to do this, not forgetting what he has heard, but doing it—he will be blessed in what he does.

²⁶If anyone considers himself religious and yet does not keep a tight rein on his tongue, he deceives himself and his religion is worthless. ²⁷Religion that God our Father accepts as pure and faultless is this: to look after orphans and widows in their distress and to keep oneself from being polluted by the world.

Favoritism Forbidden

2 My brothers, as believers in our glorious Lord Jesus Christ, don't show favoritism. ²Suppose a man comes into your meeting wearing a gold ring and fine clothes, and a poor man in shabby clothes also comes in. ³If you show special attention to the man wearing fine

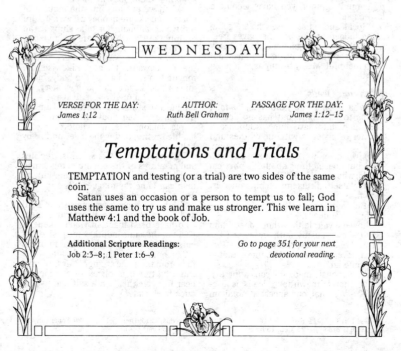

WEDNESDAY

VERSE FOR THE DAY:
James 1:12

AUTHOR:
Ruth Bell Graham

PASSAGE FOR THE DAY:
James 1:12–15

Temptations and Trials

TEMPTATION and testing (or a trial) are two sides of the same coin.

Satan uses an occasion or a person to tempt us to fall; God uses the same to try us and make us stronger. This we learn in Matthew 4:1 and the book of Job.

Additional Scripture Readings:
Job 2:3–8; 1 Peter 1:6–9

Go to page 351 for your next devotional reading.

clothes and say, "Here's a good seat for you," but say to the poor man, "You stand there" or "Sit on the floor by my feet," [4]have you not discriminated among yourselves and become judges with evil thoughts?

[5]Listen, my dear brothers: Has not God chosen those who are poor in the eyes of the world to be rich in faith and to inherit the kingdom he promised those who love him? [6]But you have insulted the poor. Is it not the rich who are exploiting you? Are they not the ones who are dragging you into court? [7]Are they not the ones who are slandering the noble name of him to whom you belong?

[8]If you really keep the royal law found in Scripture, "Love your neighbor as yourself,"[a] you are doing right. [9]But if you show favoritism, you sin and are convicted by the law as lawbreakers. [10]For whoever keeps the whole law and yet stumbles at just one point is guilty of breaking all of it. [11]For he who said, "Do not commit adultery,"[b] also said, "Do not murder."[c] If you do not commit adultery but do commit murder, you have become a lawbreaker.

[12]Speak and act as those who are going to be judged by the law that gives freedom, [13]because judgment without mercy will be shown to anyone who has not been merciful. Mercy triumphs over judgment!

Faith and Deeds

[14]What good is it, my brothers, if a man claims to have faith but has no deeds? Can such faith save him? [15]Suppose a brother or sister is without clothes and daily food. [16]If one of you says to him, "Go, I wish you well; keep warm and well fed," but does nothing about his physical needs, what good is it? [17]In the same way, faith by itself, if it is not accompanied by action, is dead.

[18]But someone will say, "You have faith; I have deeds."

Show me your faith without deeds, and I will show you my faith by what I do. [19]You believe that there is one God. Good! Even the demons believe that—and shudder.

[20]You foolish man, do you want evidence that faith without deeds is useless[d]? [21]Was not our ancestor Abraham considered righteous for what he did when he offered his son Isaac on the altar? [22]You see that his faith and his actions were working together, and his faith was made complete by what he did. [23]And the scripture was fulfilled that says, "Abraham believed God, and it was credited to him as righteousness,"[e] and he was called God's friend. [24]You see that a person is justified by what he does and not by faith alone.

[25]In the same way, was not even Rahab the prostitute considered righteous for what she did when she gave lodging to the spies and sent them off in a different direction? [26]As the body without the spirit is dead, so faith without deeds is dead.

Taming the Tongue

3 Not many of you should presume to be teachers, my brothers, because you know that we who teach will be judged more strictly. [2]We all stumble in many ways. If anyone is never at fault in what he says, he is a perfect man, able to keep his whole body in check.

[3]When we put bits into the mouths of horses to make them obey us, we can turn the whole animal. [4]Or take ships as an example. Although they are so large and are driven by strong winds, they are steered by a very small rudder wherever the pilot wants to go. [5]Likewise the tongue is a small part of the body, but it makes great boasts. Consider what a great forest is set on fire by a small spark. [6]The tongue also is a fire, a world of evil among the parts of the body. It corrupts the whole person, sets the whole course of his life on fire, and is itself set on fire by hell.

[7]All kinds of animals, birds, reptiles and creatures of the sea are being tamed and have been tamed by man, [8]but no man can tame the tongue. It is a restless evil, full of deadly poison.

[9]With the tongue we praise our Lord and Father, and with it we curse men, who have been made in God's likeness. [10]Out of the same mouth come praise and cursing. My brothers, this should not be. [11]Can both fresh water and salt[f] water flow from the same spring? [12]My brothers, can a fig tree bear olives, or a grapevine bear figs? Neither can a salt spring produce fresh water.

[a]8 Lev. 19:18   [b]11 Exodus 20:14; Deut. 5:18   [c]11 Exodus 20:13; Deut. 5:17   [d]20 Some early manuscripts dead   [e]23 Gen. 15:6   [f]11 Greek bitter (see also verse 14)

VERSE FOR THE DAY: AUTHOR: PASSAGE FOR THE DAY:
James 3:13   Luci Swindoll   James 3:13–18

Real Wisdom

ONCE I asked my brother Chuck if he'd rather have wisdom or youth, presupposing the two don't reside in the same person at the same time. Without hesitation he answered, "Oh, wisdom, Sis, hands down. That way I don't keep doing the same dumb things I did as a kid." Then, with a twinkle in his eye, he added, "Of course, I'd really prefer having wisdom in a young body."

Sara Teasdale informs me, in her excellent poem "Wisdom," that when I calmly look life in the eye, having grown wise from beating and flapping against its imperfections, learning to compromise, and accepting the fact that everyone and everything has its shortcomings:

> Life will have given me the truth
> And taken in exchange, my youth.

Inadvertently, one is given up for the other.

There are two kinds of wisdom, the apostle James says: worldly wisdom that is contaminated, ambitious and envious; and heavenly wisdom that is pure, content, merciful and submissive. So to be spiritually wise, a person must exhibit understanding, acceptance and peace.

James also says that the one who is understanding and wise will show it by his "good life." It's taken me over fifty years to learn that the good life is *not* attaining a college degree, succeeding in one's career, owning an expensive car, having money in the bank or vacationing in Hawaii. While that stuff is wonderful and sweet to my worldly tastes, it's not the good life.

The good life is peace—knowing that I was considerate instead of crabby, that I stood by faithfully when all the chips were down for the other guy, that I sacrificially gave to a worthy cause, that I showed impartiality when I really wanted my preference, that I was real in the midst of phonies, that I was forgiving, that I had the courage to defer reward for something better down the road.

Why couldn't I have learned this when I still had a young body?

Additional Scripture Readings: *Go to page 353 for your next*
Proverbs 4:5–7; 1 Corinthians 2:6–13   *devotional reading.*

Two Kinds of Wisdom

[13]Who is wise and understanding among you? Let him show it by his good life, by deeds done in the humility that comes from wisdom. [14]But if you harbor bitter envy and selfish ambition in your hearts, do not boast about it or deny the truth. [15]Such "wisdom" does not come down from heaven but is earthly, unspiritual, of the devil. [16]For where you have envy and selfish ambition, there you find disorder and every evil practice.

[17]But the wisdom that comes from heaven is first of all pure; then peace-loving, considerate, submissive, full of mercy and good fruit, impartial and sincere. [18]Peacemakers who sow in peace raise a harvest of righteousness.

Submit Yourselves to God

4 What causes fights and quarrels among you? Don't they come from your desires that battle within you? [2]You want something but don't get it. You kill and covet, but you cannot have what you want. You quarrel and fight. You do not have, because you do not ask God. [3]When you ask, you do not receive, because you ask with wrong motives, that you may spend what you get on your pleasures.

[4]You adulterous people, don't you know that friendship with the world is hatred toward God? Anyone who chooses to be a friend of the world becomes an enemy of God. [5]Or do you think Scripture says without reason that the spirit he caused to live in us envies intensely?[a] [6]But he gives us more grace. That is why Scripture says:

"God opposes the proud
    but gives grace to the humble."[b]

[7]Submit yourselves, then, to God. Resist the devil, and he will flee from you. [8]Come near to God and he will come near to you. Wash your hands, you sinners, and purify your hearts, you double-minded. [9]Grieve, mourn and wail. Change your laughter to mourning and your joy to gloom. [10]Humble yourselves before the Lord, and he will lift you up.

[11]Brothers, do not slander one another. Anyone who speaks against his brother or judges him speaks against the law and judges it. When you judge the law, you are not keeping it, but sitting in judgment on it. [12]There is only one Lawgiver and Judge, the one who is able to save and destroy. But you—who are you to judge your neighbor?

Boasting About Tomorrow

[13]Now listen, you who say, "Today or tomorrow we will go to this or that city, spend a year there, carry on business and make money." [14]Why, you do not even know what will happen tomorrow. What is your life? You are a mist that appears for a little while and then vanishes. [15]Instead, you ought to say, "If it is the Lord's will, we will live and do this or that." [16]As it is, you boast and brag. All such boasting is evil. [17]Anyone, then, who knows the good he ought to do and doesn't do it, sins.

Warning to Rich Oppressors

5 Now listen, you rich people, weep and wail because of the misery that is coming upon you. [2]Your wealth has rotted, and moths have eaten your clothes. [3]Your gold and silver are corroded. Their corrosion will testify against you and eat your flesh like fire. You have hoarded wealth in the last days. [4]Look! The wages you failed to pay the workmen who mowed your fields are crying out against you. The cries of the harvesters have reached the ears of the Lord Almighty. [5]You have lived on earth in luxury and self-indulgence. You have fattened yourselves in the day of slaughter.[c] [6]You have condemned and murdered innocent men, who were not opposing you.

Patience in Suffering

[7]Be patient, then, brothers, until the Lord's coming. See how the farmer waits for the land to yield its valuable crop and how patient he is for the autumn and spring rains. [8]You too, be patient and stand firm, because the Lord's coming is near. [9]Don't grumble against each other, brothers, or you will be judged. The Judge is standing at the door!

[10]Brothers, as an example of patience in the face of suffering, take the prophets who spoke in the name of the Lord. [11]As you know, we consider blessed those who have persevered. You have heard of Job's perseverance and have seen what the Lord finally brought about. The Lord is full of compassion and mercy.

---

[a]5 Or that God jealously longs for the spirit that he made to live in us; or that the Spirit he caused to live in us longs jealously   [b]6 Prov. 3:34   [c]5 Or yourselves as in a day of feasting

¹²Above all, my brothers, do not swear —not by heaven or by earth or by anything else. Let your "Yes" be yes, and your "No," no, or you will be condemned.

The Prayer of Faith

¹³Is any one of you in trouble? He should pray. Is anyone happy? Let him sing songs of praise. ¹⁴Is any one of you sick? He should call the elders of the church to pray over him and anoint him with oil in the name of the Lord. ¹⁵And the prayer offered in faith will make the sick person well; the Lord will raise him up. If he has sinned, he will be forgiven. ¹⁶Therefore confess your sins to each other and pray for each other so that you may be healed. The prayer of a righteous man is powerful and effective.

¹⁷Elijah was a man just like us. He prayed earnestly that it would not rain,

---

FRIDAY

VERSE FOR THE DAY: AUTHOR: PASSAGE FOR THE DAY:
James 5:16   Karen Burton Mains   James 5:13–20

Women of Prayer

IN one year, Christianity lost three holy women of faith, Agnes Sanford, Corrie ten Boom and Catherine Marshall—as well as countless others whose names are unknown but who nevertheless did the work of God in this world. These are the women who knew what it meant to experience the presence of the unseen, who spent hours on their knees, who wept over the wounds of the world. For them, prayer was a second language. Who will take their place?

Frankly, there are very few candidates from our generation of women—those of us who have lavished hours in front of the television set, in the shopping plazas, in self-indulgence, in not developing a disciplined spiritual life.

Unless—unless, we begin to grow up spiritually. Unless we become convinced that we are the generation of Christian adults ultimately responsible for the spiritual condition of our nation. We must understand that there are increasingly few in that generation ahead of us left to pray over this world. We are coming of age. But are we coming to terms with our lack of spiritual depth and ability?

It is we who must learn the meaning of forbearing.

It is we who must develop the disciplines of spiritual perseverance, not shrinking back from growth but doing the will of God, having faith and keeping our souls.

It is we who must become women of faith and prayer and obedience and service.

It is we who must set a spiritual standard for the next generation.

It is time for us all to grow up.

Additional Scripture Readings:
Ephesians 6:18–20; Colossians 4:12–13

Go to page 354 for your next devotional reading.

WEEKENDING

REJOICE

In heavenly love abiding,
No change my heart shall fear;
And safe is such confiding,
For nothing changes here.
The storm may roar without me,
My heart may low be laid,
But God is round about me,
And can I be dismayed?

Wherever He may guide me,
No fear shall turn me back;
My Shepherd is beside me,
And nothing shall I lack.
His wisdom ever waketh,
His sight is never dim;
He knows the way He taketh,
And I will walk with Him.

Green pastures are before me,
Which yet I have not seen;
Bright skies will soon be o'er me,
Where darkest clouds have been.
My hope I cannot measure,
My path to life is free;
My Savior is my treasure,
And he will walk with me.

— Anna L. Waring

REVIVE

Saturday: Hebrews 13:20–21
Sunday: Psalm 107:1–22

Go to page 357 for your next devotional reading.

Go to page 357 for your next devotional reading.

and it did not rain on the land for three and a half years. [18]Again he prayed, and the heavens gave rain, and the earth produced its crops.

[19]My brothers, if one of you should wander from the truth and someone should bring him back, [20]remember this: Whoever turns a sinner from the error of his way will save him from death and cover over a multitude of sins.

*P*ETER *writes this letter to a group of Christians suffering for their faith, reminding them of how much Jesus suffered. He inspires them with hope for the future and shows them how to grow in their faith. As you read this book, decide to do your best to live a holy life as you look forward to the return of Jesus and to the reward he promises to give his followers.*

1 PETER

1 Peter, an apostle of Jesus Christ,

To God's elect, strangers in the world, scattered throughout Pontus, Galatia, Cappadocia, Asia and Bithynia, ²who have been chosen according to the foreknowledge of God the Father, through the sanctifying work of the Spirit, for obedience to Jesus Christ and sprinkling by his blood:

Grace and peace be yours in abundance.

Praise to God for a Living Hope

³Praise be to the God and Father of our Lord Jesus Christ! In his great mercy he has given us new birth into a living hope through the resurrection of Jesus Christ from the dead, ⁴and into an inheritance that can never perish, spoil or fade—kept in heaven for you, ⁵who through faith are shielded by God's power until the coming of the salvation that is ready to be revealed in the last time. ⁶In this you greatly rejoice, though now for a little while you may have had to suffer grief in all kinds of trials. ⁷These have come so that your faith—of greater worth than gold, which perishes even though refined by fire—may be proved genuine and may result in praise, glory and honor when Jesus Christ is revealed. ⁸Though you have not seen him, you love him; and even though you do not see him now, you believe in him and are filled with an inexpressible and glorious joy, ⁹for you are receiving the goal of your faith, the salvation of your souls.

¹⁰Concerning this salvation, the prophets, who spoke of the grace that was to

come to you, searched intently and with the greatest care, [11]trying to find out the time and circumstances to which the Spirit of Christ in them was pointing when he predicted the sufferings of Christ and the glories that would follow. [12]It was revealed to them that they were not serving themselves but you, when they spoke of the things that have now been told you by those who have preached the gospel to you by the Holy Spirit sent from heaven. Even angels long to look into these things.

Be Holy

[13]Therefore, prepare your minds for action; be self-controlled; set your hope fully on the grace to be given you when Jesus Christ is revealed. [14]As obedient children, do not conform to the evil desires you had when you lived in ignorance. [15]But just as he who called you is holy, so be holy in all

MONDAY

VERSE FOR THE DAY:
1 Peter 1:7

AUTHOR:
Mary Jane Worden

PASSAGE FOR THE DAY:
1 Peter 1:3–12

Faith and Grief

IN the early years of my marriage I had, providentially, read many books about loss and grief, always reminding God that I was willing to help others through their crisis times. But in my prayers I also shared the desire to be spared this anguish in my own life.

For whatever reason, God chose not to spare me this deep pain. After the death of my husband Jim, in those agonizing early days, I knew enough about God's character to be able to say, "Someday I will be able to look back and say even out of this God has brought good." I can't imagine what good or how that could possibly be true; it goes contrary to everything I feel right now. But I choose to believe the truth of what I've been taught all these years about God's character. Someday it will be true.

Four years later, I can see good that God has done in our lives. Had I been given the choice, I would never have chosen this. But I am grateful for the growth that I see in all of us, although I would have wished it to come in another way. What we have learned in these four years about ourselves, about our world, about God is of great value. I feel confident that Jim would like the persons we are becoming.

The Scriptures teach that God will use suffering to build character and to purify our faith (see Romans 5 and 1 Peter 1). I can't presume to know all that he is doing in our lives; that he has allowed us to see a small part of it, I'm grateful.

Those strong words in Isaiah 61:1–3 ring true for me. Change. Growth. Healing. Beauty for ashes. Gladness for mourning. Praise out of despair. But the last phrase is all-important: that it might be to his glory, "for the display of his splendor."

Additional Scripture Readings:
Isaiah 61:1–3; Romans 5:3–5

*Go to page 359 for your next
devotional reading.*

you do; [16]for it is written: "Be holy, because I am holy."[a]

[17]Since you call on a Father who judges each man's work impartially, live your lives as strangers here in reverent fear. [18]For you know that it was not with perishable things such as silver or gold that you were redeemed from the empty way of life handed down to you from your forefathers, [19]but with the precious blood of Christ, a lamb without blemish or defect. [20]He was chosen before the creation of the world, but was revealed in these last times for your sake. [21]Through him you believe in God, who raised him from the dead and glorified him, and so your faith and hope are in God.

[22]Now that you have purified yourselves by obeying the truth so that you have sincere love for your brothers, love one another deeply, from the heart.[b] [23]For you have been born again, not of perishable seed, but of imperishable, through the living and enduring word of God. [24]For,

"All men are like grass,
    and all their glory is like the
        flowers of the field;
the grass withers and the flowers fall,
[25]   but the word of the Lord stands
        forever."[c]

And this is the word that was preached to you.

2 Therefore, rid yourselves of all malice and all deceit, hypocrisy, envy, and slander of every kind. [2]Like newborn babies, crave pure spiritual milk, so that by it you may grow up in your salvation, [3]now that you have tasted that the Lord is good.

The Living Stone and a Chosen People

[4]As you come to him, the living Stone — rejected by men but chosen by God and precious to him— [5]you also, like living stones, are being built into a spiritual house to be a holy priesthood, offering spiritual sacrifices acceptable to God through Jesus Christ. [6]For in Scripture it says:

"See, I lay a stone in Zion,
    a chosen and precious cornerstone,
and the one who trusts in him
    will never be put to shame."[d]

[7]Now to you who believe, this stone is precious. But to those who do not believe,

"The stone the builders rejected
    has become the capstone,[e]"[f]

[8]and,

"A stone that causes men to stumble
    and a rock that makes them fall."[g]

They stumble because they disobey the message—which is also what they were destined for.

[9]But you are a chosen people, a royal priesthood, a holy nation, a people belonging to God, that you may declare the praises of him who called you out of darkness into his wonderful light. [10]Once you were not a people, but now you are the people of God; once you had not received mercy, but now you have received mercy.

[11]Dear friends, I urge you, as aliens and strangers in the world, to abstain from sinful desires, which war against your soul. [12]Live such good lives among the pagans that, though they accuse you of doing wrong, they may see your good deeds and glorify God on the day he visits us.

Submission to Rulers and Masters

[13]Submit yourselves for the Lord's sake to every authority instituted among men: whether to the king, as the supreme authority, [14]or to governors, who are sent by him to punish those who do wrong and to commend those who do right. [15]For it is God's will that by doing good you should silence the ignorant talk of foolish men. [16]Live as free men, but do not use your freedom as a cover-up for evil; live as servants of God. [17]Show proper respect to everyone: Love the brotherhood of believers, fear God, honor the king.

[18]Slaves, submit yourselves to your masters with all respect, not only to those who are good and considerate, but also to those who are harsh. [19]For it is commendable if a man bears up under the pain of unjust suffering because he is conscious of God. [20]But how is it to your credit if you receive a beating for doing wrong and endure it? But if you suffer for doing good and you endure it, this is commendable before God. [21]To this you were called, because Christ suffered for you, leaving you an example, that you should follow in his steps.

a16 Lev. 11:44,45; 19:2; 20:7   *b22* Some early manuscripts *from a pure heart*   *c25* Isaiah 40:6-8
d6 Isaiah 28:16   *e7* Or *cornerstone*   *f7* Psalm 118:22   *g8* Isaiah 8:14

VERSE FOR THE DAY:
1 Peter 1:16

AUTHOR:
June Hunt

PASSAGE FOR THE DAY:
1 Peter 1:13–25

Living a Holy Life

HAVE you had difficulty with this Scripture verse: "Be holy, because I am holy" (Leviticus 11:44; 1 Peter 1:16)? Since most people think being holy is synonymous with being sinless, who could possibly be holy? It's unattainable . . . unimaginable!

A friend once said to me, "I know *holy* means 'set apart,' but I don't want to be set apart. That sounds like being in quarantine for having a constant case of measles!" Some people *do* think of a holy person as one who lives a monkish existence, praying twenty-three hours a day in order to avoid sin. Holiness, however, does not bring isolation but integration. With Christ in you, his character becomes a part of you so that his nature may be expressed through you. In other words, Christlikeness will come out of you *naturally*.

When I was little, my Uncle Jimmy walked me through his watermelon patch in Idabel, Oklahoma. Holding a tiny black seed he said, "These big melons grew from seeds just like this one." That seemed impossible to me! Yet eighty miles from Idabel is Hope, Arkansas, the town where something more "impossible" became reality. Young Jason Bright gave his watermelon seed proper care and the right environment to grow. The result? A world-record 260-pound watermelon! Watermelon seeds simply do what comes naturally to them—they grow. Their seeds are set apart by God for that purpose.

When you are set apart by God, holiness becomes natural. The Father is the gardener; Christ is the seed. With Christ in you, you will grow to be like him. It is explained in 1 John 3:9:

> No one who is born of God will continue to sin, because God's seed remains in him.

It is natural for the Lord not to sin. Therefore, with God's seed in you, it becomes increasingly natural for you not to sin. What seems impossible becomes possible. You will not become instantly sinless, but you will sin less and less and less.

God calls you holy. With his presence inside you, he will produce the impossible through you. Why settle for anything less?

Additional Scripture Readings:
Colossians 3:12–17; Hebrews 12:10–14

Go to page 361 for your next devotional reading.

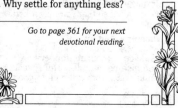

22"He committed no sin,
  and no deceit was found in his
    mouth."*a*

23When they hurled their insults at him, he did not retaliate; when he suffered, he made no threats. Instead, he entrusted himself to him who judges justly. 24He himself bore our sins in his body on the tree, so that we might die to sins and live for righteousness; by his wounds you have been healed. 25For you were like sheep going astray, but now you have returned to the Shepherd and Overseer of your souls.

Wives and Husbands

3 Wives, in the same way be submissive to your husbands so that, if any of them do not believe the word, they may be won over without words by the behavior of their wives, 2when they see the purity and reverence of your lives. 3Your beauty should not come from outward adornment, such as braided hair and the wearing of gold jewelry and fine clothes. 4Instead, it should be that of your inner self, the unfading beauty of a gentle and quiet spirit, which is of great worth in God's sight. 5For this is the way the holy women of the past who put their hope in God used to make themselves beautiful. They were submissive to their own husbands, 6like Sarah, who obeyed Abraham and called him her master. You are her daughters if you do what is right and do not give way to fear.

7Husbands, in the same way be considerate as you live with your wives, and treat them with respect as the weaker partner and as heirs with you of the gracious gift of life, so that nothing will hinder your prayers.

Suffering for Doing Good

8Finally, all of you, live in harmony with one another; be sympathetic, love as brothers, be compassionate and humble. 9Do not repay evil with evil or insult with insult, but with blessing, because to this you were called so that you may inherit a blessing. 10For,

"Whoever would love life
  and see good days
must keep his tongue from evil
  and his lips from deceitful speech.
11He must turn from evil and do good;

he must seek peace and pursue it.
12For the eyes of the Lord are on the
    righteous
  and his ears are attentive to their
    prayer,
but the face of the Lord is against
    those who do evil."*b*

13Who is going to harm you if you are eager to do good? 14But even if you should suffer for what is right, you are blessed. "Do not fear what they fear*c*; do not be frightened."*d* 15But in your hearts set apart Christ as Lord. Always be prepared to give an answer to everyone who asks you to give the reason for the hope that you have. But do this with gentleness and respect, 16keeping a clear conscience, so that those who speak maliciously against your good behavior in Christ may be ashamed of their slander. 17It is better, if it is God's will, to suffer for doing good than for doing evil. 18For Christ died for sins once for all, the righteous for the unrighteous, to bring you to God. He was put to death in the body but made alive by the Spirit, 19through whom*e* also he went and preached to the spirits in prison 20who disobeyed long ago when God waited patiently in the days of Noah while the ark was being built. In it only a few people, eight in all, were saved through water, 21and this water symbolizes baptism that now saves you also — not the removal of dirt from the body but the pledge*f* of a good conscience toward God. It saves you by the resurrection of Jesus Christ, 22who has gone into heaven and is at God's right hand — with angels, authorities and powers in submission to him.

Living for God

4 Therefore, since Christ suffered in his body, arm yourselves also with the same attitude, because he who has suffered in his body is done with sin. 2As a result, he does not live the rest of his earthly life for evil human desires, but rather for the will of God. 3For you have spent enough time in the past doing what pagans choose to do — living in debauchery, lust, drunkenness, orgies, carousing and detestable idolatry. 4They think it strange that you do not plunge with them into the same flood of dissipation, and they heap abuse on you. 5But they will have to give account to him who is ready

a22 Isaiah 53:9   *b12* Psalm 34:12-16   *c14* Or *not fear their threats*   *d14* Isaiah 8:12
e18,19 Or *alive in the spirit,* 19*through which*   *f21* Or *response*

VERSE FOR THE DAY:
1 Peter 3:1

AUTHOR:
Beverly LaHaye

PASSAGE FOR THE DAY:
1 Peter 3:1–6

So They May Be Won Over

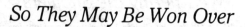

DURING the span of wonderful years of ministry God has given my husband and me, it has been our joy to have helped many couples during times of marital difficulty. Sometimes they were helped by reading one of our books relating to their problem, but often help came through a personal counseling meeting.

One such meeting took place several years ago when a lovely Christian woman came to us with a troubled, broken heart. She was married to a man who had professed Jesus Christ years before but who had turned away from those beliefs. Her story revealed that he was conducting himself in a manner that was disobedient to God's Word, making her miserable also.

The natural reaction for many wives caught in these circumstances is to lash back and to shut her husband out of her life. This woman quickly learned that if she took matters into her own hands there would not be much need for communication. Her heart resisted his role as head of the home.

In her attempt to separate herself from her husband—even though they remained living together—she decided to join an evening Bible study just to get out of the house.

God began to work in her heart and impress upon her that she was disobeying him by the way she lived and conducted herself. She learned through study of the Word that submission to and love for her husband was an outgrowth of spiritual development and a close relationship with the Lord.

As this woman sat before us one evening, pouring out her heart to the Lord, she longed for a close relationship with both God and her husband. We read 1 Peter 3:1–6 to her and challenged her to obey the principles taught there.

Not every wife's story ends on such a happy note, but this lovely woman found that God could change her conduct and give her a gentle and quiet spirit. As a result, her husband changed and began to walk in obedience to God.

Additional Scripture Readings:
Ephesians 5:22–33; Titus 2:3–5

Go to page 362 for your next devotional reading.

VERSE FOR THE DAY:
1 Peter 5:10

AUTHOR:
Beth Donigan Seversen

PASSAGE FOR THE DAY:
1 Peter 5:1–11

Weathering the Showers

THE *Water Garden*, by Claude Monet, is one of my favorite paintings. You will find the original in an impressionist museum, de l'Orangerie, in Paris. It is painted in the round and hangs in a circular room. When you stand in the center of the room you are completely engulfed in a luxuriant water garden!

My print, hanging over the desk in my office, is only a small representation of the delightful, full-scale original. If you study the painting, one of the surprises you will find is that the major part of the canvas is covered in dark shades of black, blue and green. These rather drab colors stand in stark contrast to the delicate pastels. Actually, they serve to highlight the beautiful florals, which appear rich and striking upon the deep, dark waters. At first glance, your eyes are drawn to the colorful petals; then you realize that Monet painted the dark tones to enhance the lighter.

Monet's painting has much to remind me about the water garden of my life, and of its Artist. First, it encourages me that there is a purpose and design to my life, and that perhaps, at times, I focus too exclusively on the darker portions of my painting.

It also reminds me that my Lord, the Artist of my life, has intentionally allowed the blue, green, and, yes, sometimes even the gray and black hues to be brushed on my canvas for a reason. God uses these shadows to make my life richer. Often, when I look back on difficulties, such as my father's death, times when I have been misunderstood by friends or my expectations have been dashed, I can see, now, his handiwork creating a brilliance of color and beauty from pain and suffering. The Artist uses a multitude of techniques in our lives to help us become the people he created us to be.

Finally, I am reminded that just like the water lilies in Monet's masterpiece, God keeps the leaves and petals afloat through the muck, wind and rain that are part of the storms of life. Water gardens survive April showers and worse, and I will too, by God's help and grace.

Additional Scripture Readings:
Matthew 7:24–27; Mark 4:35–41

Go to page 365 for your next devotional reading.

to judge the living and the dead. [6]For this is the reason the gospel was preached even to those who are now dead, so that they might be judged according to men in regard to the body, but live according to God in regard to the spirit.

[7]The end of all things is near. Therefore be clear minded and self-controlled so that you can pray. [8]Above all, love each other deeply, because love covers over a multitude of sins. [9]Offer hospitality to one another without grumbling. [10]Each one should use whatever gift he has received to serve others, faithfully administering God's grace in its various forms. [11]If anyone speaks, he should do it as one speaking the very words of God. If anyone serves, he should do it with the strength God provides, so that in all things God may be praised through Jesus Christ. To him be the glory and the power for ever and ever. Amen.

Suffering for Being a Christian

[12]Dear friends, do not be surprised at the painful trial you are suffering, as though something strange were happening to you. [13]But rejoice that you participate in the sufferings of Christ, so that you may be overjoyed when his glory is revealed. [14]If you are insulted because of the name of Christ, you are blessed, for the Spirit of glory and of God rests on you. [15]If you suffer, it should not be as a murderer or thief or any other kind of criminal, or even as a meddler. [16]However, if you suffer as a Christian, do not be ashamed, but praise God that you bear that name. [17]For it is time for judgment to begin with the family of God; and if it begins with us, what will the outcome be for those who do not obey the gospel of God? [18]And,

"If it is hard for the righteous to be saved,
  what will become of the ungodly and the sinner?"[a]

[19]So then, those who suffer according to God's will should commit themselves to their faithful Creator and continue to do good.

To Elders and Young Men

5 To the elders among you, I appeal as a fellow elder, a witness of Christ's sufferings and one who also will share in the glory to be revealed: [2]Be shepherds of God's flock that is under your care, serving as overseers—not because you must, but because you are willing, as God wants you to be; not greedy for money, but eager to serve; [3]not lording it over those entrusted to you, but being examples to the flock. [4]And when the Chief Shepherd appears, you will receive the crown of glory that will never fade away.

[5]Young men, in the same way be submissive to those who are older. All of you, clothe yourselves with humility toward one another, because,

"God opposes the proud
  but gives grace to the humble."[b]

[6]Humble yourselves, therefore, under God's mighty hand, that he may lift you up in due time. [7]Cast all your anxiety on him because he cares for you.

[8]Be self-controlled and alert. Your enemy the devil prowls around like a roaring lion looking for someone to devour. [9]Resist him, standing firm in the faith, because you know that your brothers throughout the world are undergoing the same kind of sufferings.

[10]And the God of all grace, who called you to his eternal glory in Christ, after you have suffered a little while, will himself restore you and make you strong, firm and steadfast. [11]To him be the power for ever and ever. Amen.

Final Greetings

[12]With the help of Silas,[c] whom I regard as a faithful brother, I have written to you briefly, encouraging you and testifying that this is the true grace of God. Stand fast in it.

[13]She who is in Babylon, chosen together with you, sends you her greetings, and so does my son Mark. [14]Greet one another with a kiss of love.

Peace to all of you who are in Christ.

a18 Prov. 11:31   *b5* Prov. 3:34   *c12* Greek *Silvanus*, a variant of *Silas*

*P*ETER *writes a second letter because false teachers are troubling the church and disturbing the faith of some by their heresy, immorality and greed. He wants Christians to grow in the knowledge of the truth of God's Word. As you read this book, remember that God will eventually win the battle against false teaching, and promise the Lord that you will study to increase your knowledge of the Bible.*

2 PETER

1 Simon Peter, a servant and apostle of Jesus Christ,

To those who through the righteousness of our God and Savior Jesus Christ have received a faith as precious as ours:

²Grace and peace be yours in abundance through the knowledge of God and of Jesus our Lord.

Making One's Calling and Election Sure

³His divine power has given us everything we need for life and godliness through our knowledge of him who called us by his own glory and goodness. ⁴Through these he has given us his very great and precious promises, so that through them you may participate in the divine nature and escape the corruption in the world caused by evil desires.

⁵For this very reason, make every effort to add to your faith goodness; and to goodness, knowledge; ⁶and to knowledge, self-control; and to self-control, perseverance; and to perseverance, godliness; ⁷and to godliness, brotherly kindness; and to brotherly kindness, love. ⁸For if you possess these qualities in increasing measure, they will keep you from being ineffective and unproductive in your knowledge of our Lord Jesus Christ. ⁹But if anyone does not have them, he is nearsighted and blind, and has forgotten that he has been cleansed from his past sins.

¹⁰Therefore, my brothers, be all the more eager to make your calling and elec-

tion sure. For if you do these things, you will never fall, [11]and you will receive a rich welcome into the eternal kingdom of our Lord and Savior Jesus Christ.

Prophecy of Scripture

[12]So I will always remind you of these things, even though you know them and are firmly established in the truth you now have. [13]I think it is right to refresh your memory as long as I live in the tent of this body, [14]because I know that I will soon put it aside, as our Lord Jesus Christ has made clear to me. [15]And I will make every effort to see that after my departure you will always be able to remember these things.

[16]We did not follow cleverly invented stories when we told you about the power and coming of our Lord Jesus Christ, but we were eyewitnesses of his majesty. [17]For he received honor and glory from God the Father when the voice came to him from the Majestic Glory, saying, "This is my Son, whom I love; with him I

FRIDAY

VERSE FOR THE DAY:
2 Peter 1:3

AUTHOR:
Jo Ann Lemon

PASSAGE FOR THE DAY:
2 Peter 1:3–11

Self-sacrifice

THERE were once two porcupines who lived in Alaska. Desiring to get warm, they drew close to each other. As they did, they needled one another. It hurt so much that they pulled apart. But when they did, they got cold again, so they drew close once more, and hurt each other as before. Their predicament—they were either cold or hurting.

All too often this is the situation even in Christian homes. Personality differences are like the quills of the porcupines. They can get tangled and cause hurt. We must work at our relationships so that we will demonstrate the Christlike qualities of love, compassion, self-sacrifice and a forgiving spirit. The motto for our homes should be: "Be completely humble and gentle; be patient, bearing with one another in love" (Ephesians 4:2).

Love demonstrates itself in action. Have we done something today to demonstrate our love for our families? Love takes pleasure in its object. Jesus' example of love and compassion teaches us that it is possible for these qualities to be part of our Christian homes.

Self-sacrifice is against our human nature, yet it should be part of our "new nature." If each of us had an attitude of self-sacrifice, what a change would come about in the atmosphere of our homes. Self-sacrifice is total unselfishness.

Loving unselfishly does not mean making the least of ourselves but making the most of someone else. We view the other person through the eyes of Jesus.

This thought can transform relationships in our homes, especially with our unsaved loved ones!

Additional Scripture Readings:
Romans 12:9–13; 1 John 3:11–18

Go to page 367 for your next devotional reading.

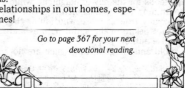

am well pleased."[a] [18]We ourselves heard this voice that came from heaven when we were with him on the sacred mountain.

[19]And we have the word of the prophets made more certain, and you will do well to pay attention to it, as to a light shining in a dark place, until the day dawns and the morning star rises in your hearts. [20]Above all, you must understand that no prophecy of Scripture came about by the prophet's own interpretation. [21]For prophecy never had its origin in the will of man, but men spoke from God as they were carried along by the Holy Spirit.

False Teachers and Their Destruction

2 But there were also false prophets among the people, just as there will be false teachers among you. They will secretly introduce destructive heresies, even denying the sovereign Lord who bought them—bringing swift destruction on themselves. [2]Many will follow their shameful ways and will bring the way of truth into disrepute. [3]In their greed these teachers will exploit you with stories they have made up. Their condemnation has long been hanging over them, and their destruction has not been sleeping.

[4]For if God did not spare angels when they sinned, but sent them to hell,[b] putting them into gloomy dungeons[c] to be held for judgment; [5]if he did not spare the ancient world when he brought the flood on its ungodly people, but protected Noah, a preacher of righteousness, and seven others; [6]if he condemned the cities of Sodom and Gomorrah by burning them to ashes, and made them an example of what is going to happen to the ungodly; [7]and if he rescued Lot, a righteous man, who was distressed by the filthy lives of lawless men [8](for that righteous man, living among them day after day, was tormented in his righteous soul by the lawless deeds he saw and heard)— [9]if this is so, then the Lord knows how to rescue godly men from trials and to hold the unrighteous for the day of judgment, while continuing their punishment.[d] [10]This is especially true of those who follow the corrupt desire of the sinful nature[e] and despise authority.

Bold and arrogant, these men are not afraid to slander celestial beings; [11]yet even angels, although they are stronger and more powerful, do not bring slanderous accusations against such beings in the presence of the Lord. [12]But these men blaspheme in matters they do not understand. They are like brute beasts, creatures of instinct, born only to be caught and destroyed, and like beasts they too will perish.

[13]They will be paid back with harm for the harm they have done. Their idea of pleasure is to carouse in broad daylight. They are blots and blemishes, reveling in their pleasures while they feast with you.[f] [14]With eyes full of adultery, they never stop sinning; they seduce the unstable; they are experts in greed—an accursed brood! [15]They have left the straight way and wandered off to follow the way of Balaam son of Beor, who loved the wages of wickedness. [16]But he was rebuked for his wrongdoing by a donkey—a beast without speech—who spoke with a man's voice and restrained the prophet's madness.

[17]These men are springs without water and mists driven by a storm. Blackest darkness is reserved for them. [18]For they mouth empty, boastful words and, by appealing to the lustful desires of sinful human nature, they entice people who are just escaping from those who live in error. [19]They promise them freedom, while they themselves are slaves of depravity—for a man is a slave to whatever has mastered him. [20]If they have escaped the corruption of the world by knowing our Lord and Savior Jesus Christ and are again entangled in it and overcome, they are worse off at the end than they were at the beginning. [21]It would have been better for them not to have known the way of righteousness, than to have known it and then to turn their backs on the sacred command that was passed on to them. [22]Of them the proverbs are true: "A dog returns to its vomit,"[g] and, "A sow that is washed goes back to her wallowing in the mud."

The Day of the Lord

3 Dear friends, this is now my second letter to you. I have written both of them as reminders to stimulate you to wholesome thinking. [2]I want you to recall the words spoken in the past by the holy

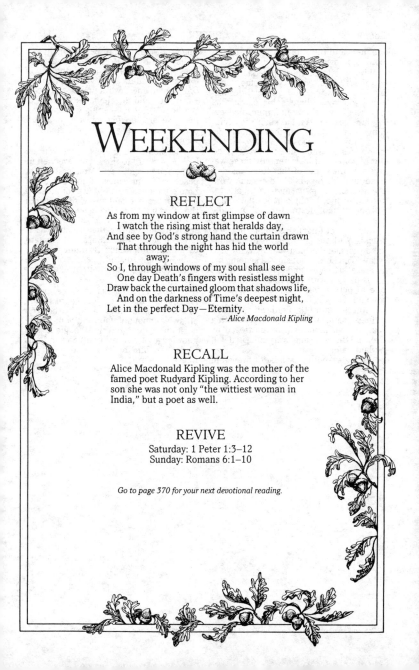

WEEKENDING

REFLECT

As from my window at first glimpse of dawn
  I watch the rising mist that heralds day,
And see by God's strong hand the curtain drawn
  That through the night has hid the world
          away;
So I, through windows of my soul shall see
  One day Death's fingers with resistless might
Draw back the curtained gloom that shadows life,
  And on the darkness of Time's deepest night,
Let in the perfect Day—Eternity.
                    — *Alice Macdonald Kipling*

RECALL

Alice Macdonald Kipling was the mother of the
famed poet Rudyard Kipling. According to her
son she was not only "the wittiest woman in
India," but a poet as well.

REVIVE

Saturday: 1 Peter 1:3–12
Sunday: Romans 6:1–10

Go to page 370 for your next devotional reading.

prophets and the command given by our Lord and Savior through your apostles.

[3]First of all, you must understand that in the last days scoffers will come, scoffing and following their own evil desires. [4]They will say, "Where is this 'coming' he promised? Ever since our fathers died, everything goes on as it has since the beginning of creation." [5]But they deliberately forget that long ago by God's word the heavens existed and the earth was formed out of water and by water. [6]By these waters also the world of that time was deluged and destroyed. [7]By the same word the present heavens and earth are reserved for fire, being kept for the day of judgment and destruction of ungodly men.

[8]But do not forget this one thing, dear friends: With the Lord a day is like a thousand years, and a thousand years are like a day. [9]The Lord is not slow in keeping his promise, as some understand slowness. He is patient with you, not wanting anyone to perish, but everyone to come to repentance.

[10]But the day of the Lord will come like a thief. The heavens will disappear with a roar; the elements will be destroyed by fire, and the earth and everything in it will be laid bare.[a]

[11]Since everything will be destroyed in this way, what kind of people ought you to be? You ought to live holy and godly lives [12]as you look forward to the day of God and speed its coming.[b] That day will bring about the destruction of the heavens by fire, and the elements will melt in the heat. [13]But in keeping with his promise we are looking forward to a new heaven and a new earth, the home of righteousness.

[14]So then, dear friends, since you are looking forward to this, make every effort to be found spotless, blameless and at peace with him. [15]Bear in mind that our Lord's patience means salvation, just as our dear brother Paul also wrote you with the wisdom that God gave him. [16]He writes the same way in all his letters, speaking in them of these matters. His letters contain some things that are hard to understand, which ignorant and unstable people distort, as they do the other Scriptures, to their own destruction.

[17]Therefore, dear friends, since you already know this, be on your guard so that you may not be carried away by the error of lawless men and fall from your secure position. [18]But grow in the grace and knowledge of our Lord and Savior Jesus Christ. To him be glory both now and forever! Amen.

---

[a]10 Some manuscripts be burned up   [b]12 Or as you wait eagerly for the day of God to come

*J*OHN *writes this first letter to emphasize some of the same themes as his Gospel (such as "walking in the light," "knowing the truth," and "loving one another"). He does so because antichrists are promoting false views of the Son of God. As you read this book, realize how much God wants you to fight sin, to love others and to believe in the true Jesus for eternal life.*

1 JOHN

The Word of Life

1 That which was from the beginning, which we have heard, which we have seen with our eyes, which we have looked at and our hands have touched—this we proclaim concerning the Word of life. [2] The life appeared; we have seen it and testify to it, and we proclaim to you the eternal life, which was with the Father and has appeared to us. [3] We proclaim to you what we have seen and heard, so that you also may have fellowship with us. And our fellowship is with the Father and with his Son, Jesus Christ. [4] We write this to make our*a* joy complete.

Walking in the Light

[5] This is the message we have heard from him and declare to you: God is light; in him there is no darkness at all. [6] If we claim to have fellowship with him yet walk in the darkness, we lie and do not live by the truth. [7] But if we walk in the light, as he is in the light, we have fellowship with one another, and the blood of Jesus, his Son, purifies us from all*b* sin.

[8] If we claim to be without sin, we deceive ourselves and the truth is not in us. [9] If we confess our sins, he is faithful and just and will forgive us our sins and purify us from all unrighteousness. [10] If we claim we have not sinned, we make him out to be a liar and his word has no place in our lives.

2 My dear children, I write this to you so that you will not sin. But if anybody does sin, we have one who speaks to

*a*4 Some manuscripts *your*   *b*7 Or *every*

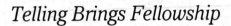

VERSE FOR THE DAY:
1 John 1:3–4

AUTHOR:
Rosemary Jensen

PASSAGE FOR THE DAY:
1 John 1:1–10

Telling Brings Fellowship

IN 1 John 1:3–4 we see John eager to tell his friends and associates what he knows of Jesus—what he has "seen and heard." It seems that he could hardly wait to tell them, because by telling them what he knew of Jesus he would promote fellowship with his friends. True fellowship was what John wanted, and it is what we want too. Fellowship is not just camaraderie; it is what two or more people experience when they have the same goals and desires, when they think alike and communicate in such a way as to actually enter into the other's experience.

John wanted this kind of communication with his friends. It was as if he was saying to them, "Let me tell you what I have seen and heard of Jesus Christ *so that* we may have the same mind about him, the same desire to know him better, the same experience of him." Then he goes on to say that we will have this fellowship because we have fellowship with the same Father and the same Son, Jesus Christ. We fellowship with God (the Father and the Son), and he brings us into fellowship with each other. He is the basis for our fellowship because together we share his life.

Are you eager to declare to your family and friends what you have "seen and heard" of Jesus Christ so that you may enter into true fellowship with them? Telling them about Jesus (and also listening to them tell you!) is the most fulfilling experience you can have with other human beings. Exchanging the knowledge of Jesus Christ with others will bring you greater joy than you can imagine. At least that's what John says in 1 John 1:4: "We write this to make our [and your] joy complete." *Telling brings fellowship and fellowship brings joy.*

Talking with others about Jesus is always risky. They may label you a fanatic. You may risk turning them off. But it is worth the risk, because it will bring that complete joy you desperately desire.

Additional Scripture Readings:
Galatians 2:8–9; 3 John 3–4

*Go to page 373 for your next
devotional reading.*

the Father in our defense—Jesus Christ, the Righteous One. ²He is the atoning sacrifice for our sins, and not only for ours but also for[a] the sins of the whole world.

³We know that we have come to know him if we obey his commands. ⁴The man who says, "I know him," but does not do what he commands is a liar, and the truth is not in him. ⁵But if anyone obeys his word, God's love[b] is truly made complete in him. This is how we know we are in him: ⁶Whoever claims to live in him must walk as Jesus did.

⁷Dear friends, I am not writing you a new command but an old one, which you have had since the beginning. This old command is the message you have heard. ⁸Yet I am writing you a new command; its truth is seen in him and you, because the darkness is passing and the true light is already shining.

⁹Anyone who claims to be in the light but hates his brother is still in the darkness. ¹⁰Whoever loves his brother lives in the light, and there is nothing in him[c] to make him stumble. ¹¹But whoever hates his brother is in the darkness and walks around in the darkness; he does not know where he is going, because the darkness has blinded him.

¹²I write to you, dear children,
    because your sins have been
        forgiven on account of his
        name.
¹³I write to you, fathers,
    because you have known him who
        is from the beginning.
I write to you, young men,
    because you have overcome the evil
        one.
I write to you, dear children,
    because you have known the
        Father.
¹⁴I write to you, fathers,
    because you have known him who
        is from the beginning.
I write to you, young men,
    because you are strong,
    and the word of God lives in you,
    and you have overcome the evil
        one.

Do Not Love the World

¹⁵Do not love the world or anything in the world. If anyone loves the world, the love of the Father is not in him. ¹⁶For ev-
erything in the world—the cravings of sinful man, the lust of his eyes and the boasting of what he has and does—comes not from the Father but from the world. ¹⁷The world and its desires pass away, but the man who does the will of God lives forever.

Warning Against Antichrists

¹⁸Dear children, this is the last hour; and as you have heard that the antichrist is coming, even now many antichrists have come. This is how we know it is the last hour. ¹⁹They went out from us, but they did not really belong to us. For if they had belonged to us, they would have remained with us; but their going showed that none of them belonged to us.

²⁰But you have an anointing from the Holy One, and all of you know the truth.[d] ²¹I do not write to you because you do not know the truth, but because you do know it and because no lie comes from the truth. ²²Who is the liar? It is the man who denies that Jesus is the Christ. Such a man is the antichrist—he denies the Father and the Son. ²³No one who denies the Son has the Father; whoever acknowledges the Son has the Father also.

²⁴See that what you have heard from the beginning remains in you. If it does, you also will remain in the Son and in the Father. ²⁵And this is what he promised us—even eternal life.

²⁶I am writing these things to you about those who are trying to lead you astray. ²⁷As for you, the anointing you received from him remains in you, and you do not need anyone to teach you. But as his anointing teaches you about all things and as that anointing is real, not counterfeit—just as it has taught you, remain in him.

Children of God

²⁸And now, dear children, continue in him, so that when he appears we may be confident and unashamed before him at his coming. ²⁹If you know that he is righteous, you know that everyone who does what is right has been born of him.

3 How great is the love the Father has lavished on us, that we should be called children of God! And that is what we are! The reason the world does not know us is that it did not know him. ²Dear

---

[a]2 Or *He is the one who turns aside God's wrath, taking away our sins, and not only ours but also*
[b]5 Or *word, love for God*   [c]10 Or *it*   [d]20 Some manuscripts *and you know all things*

friends, now we are children of God, and what we will be has not yet been made known. But we know that when he appears,[a] we shall be like him, for we shall see him as he is. [3]Everyone who has this hope in him purifies himself, just as he is pure.

[4]Everyone who sins breaks the law; in fact, sin is lawlessness. [5]But you know that he appeared so that he might take away our sins. And in him is no sin. [6]No one who lives in him keeps on sinning. No one who continues to sin has either seen him or known him.

[7]Dear children, do not let anyone lead you astray. He who does what is right is righteous, just as he is righteous. [8]He who does what is sinful is of the devil, because the devil has been sinning from the beginning. The reason the Son of God appeared was to destroy the devil's work. [9]No one who is born of God will continue to sin, because God's seed remains in him; he cannot go on sinning, because he has been born of God. [10]This is how we know who the children of God are and who the children of the devil are: Anyone who does not do what is right is not a child of God; nor is anyone who does not love his brother.

Love One Another

[11]This is the message you heard from the beginning: We should love one another. [12]Do not be like Cain, who belonged to the evil one and murdered his brother. And why did he murder him? Because his own actions were evil and his brother's were righteous. [13]Do not be surprised, my brothers, if the world hates you. [14]We know that we have passed from death to life, because we love our brothers. Anyone who does not love remains in death. [15]Anyone who hates his brother is a murderer, and you know that no murderer has eternal life in him.

[16]This is how we know what love is: Jesus Christ laid down his life for us. And we ought to lay down our lives for our brothers. [17]If anyone has material possessions and sees his brother in need but has no pity on him, how can the love of God be in him? [18]Dear children, let us not love with words or tongue but with actions and in truth. [19]This then is how we know that we belong to the truth, and how we set our hearts at rest in his presence [20]whenever our hearts condemn us. For God is greater than our hearts, and he knows everything.

[21]Dear friends, if our hearts do not condemn us, we have confidence before God [22]and receive from him anything we ask, because we obey his commands and do what pleases him. [23]And this is his command: to believe in the name of his Son, Jesus Christ, and to love one another as he commanded us. [24]Those who obey his commands live in him, and he in them. And this is how we know that he lives in us: We know it by the Spirit he gave us.

Test the Spirits

4 Dear friends, do not believe every spirit, but test the spirits to see whether they are from God, because many false prophets have gone out into the world. [2]This is how you can recognize the Spirit of God: Every spirit that acknowledges that Jesus Christ has come in the flesh is from God, [3]but every spirit that does not acknowledge Jesus is not from God. This is the spirit of the antichrist, which you have heard is coming and even now is already in the world.

[4]You, dear children, are from God and have overcome them, because the one who is in you is greater than the one who is in the world. [5]They are from the world and therefore speak from the viewpoint of the world, and the world listens to them. [6]We are from God, and whoever knows God listens to us; but whoever is not from God does not listen to us. This is how we recognize the Spirit[b] of truth and the spirit of falsehood.

God's Love and Ours

[7]Dear friends, let us love one another, for love comes from God. Everyone who loves has been born of God and knows God. [8]Whoever does not love does not know God, because God is love. [9]This is how God showed his love among us: He sent his one and only Son[c] into the world that we might live through him. [10]This is love: not that we loved God, but that he loved us and sent his Son as an atoning sacrifice for[d] our sins. [11]Dear friends, since God so loved us, we also ought to love one another. [12]No one has ever seen God; but if we love one another, God lives in us and his love is made complete in us. [13]We know that we live in him and he

---

[a]2 Or when it is made known   [b]6 Or spirit   [c]9 Or his only begotten Son   [d]10 Or as the one who would turn aside his wrath, taking away

VERSE FOR THE DAY:
1 John 5:4

AUTHOR:
Luci Swindoll

PASSAGE FOR THE DAY:
1 John 5:1–12

Real Power

THIS verse, 1 John 5:4, has been a favorite of mine for years; but only lately have I come to realize that the verse is not so much about faith as it is about power. It's not an obvious power like that displayed by bulldozing through a riverbed in a GMC truck or by the ability to lift weights. It's a quiet power, like that inherent in a seed, which causes a plant to pop out of the ground and burst into flower, or in the meaningful words that fly across the airwaves altering convictions and changing hearts for all eternity.

Power. Have you ever been so mad at a person that you wanted to walk out and never talk to her again, but decided instead to hang in there, communicate, and make it right? Or, have you felt tremendously inadequate for an assigned task, found a Scripture of encouragement, and come out a winner? Have you invested love and concern into a person who is basically unlovable and witnessed a transformation in her behavior—primarily because of your sensitivity and acceptance? That's the kind of power I'm talking about.

This verse says that we, the children of God, actually can overcome the world by faithfully believing that we have God's power to effect change. Doesn't that make you want to try it in every area of your life? It does me!

I want to quit worrying about money. I want to lose weight. I want to be a kinder, more gentle person. I want to be supportive, not envious. I want to sing more and gripe less. I want to look for the positive, not dwell on the negative. I want to reach out to those who need me, not wait for them to come to me. I want to relax and laugh. I want to live fully.

Shall I go on? You make your own list, remembering that by faith you've already overcome the world. Claim that. When God commissions, he empowers. That power is absolutely yours, by faith. Take it and head out. The victories are just beginning.

Additional Scripture Readings:
Romans 8:31–39; 1 Corinthians 15:57–58

Go to page 376 for your next devotional reading.

in us, because he has given us of his Spirit. [14]And we have seen and testify that the Father has sent his Son to be the Savior of the world. [15]If anyone acknowledges that Jesus is the Son of God, God lives in him and he in God. [16]And so we know and rely on the love God has for us.

God is love. Whoever lives in love lives in God, and God in him. [17]In this way, love is made complete among us so that we will have confidence on the day of judgment, because in this world we are like him. [18]There is no fear in love. But perfect love drives out fear, because fear has to do with punishment. The one who fears is not made perfect in love.

[19]We love because he first loved us. [20]If anyone says, "I love God," yet hates his brother, he is a liar. For anyone who does not love his brother, whom he has seen, cannot love God, whom he has not seen. [21]And he has given us this command: Whoever loves God must also love his brother.

Faith in the Son of God

5 Everyone who believes that Jesus is the Christ is born of God, and everyone who loves the father loves his child as well. [2]This is how we know that we love the children of God: by loving God and carrying out his commands. [3]This is love for God: to obey his commands. And his commands are not burdensome, [4]for everyone born of God overcomes the world. This is the victory that has overcome the world, even our faith. [5]Who is it that overcomes the world? Only he who believes that Jesus is the Son of God.

[6]This is the one who came by water and blood—Jesus Christ. He did not come by water only, but by water and blood. And it is the Spirit who testifies, because the Spirit is the truth. [7]For there are three that testify: [8]the[a] Spirit, the water and the blood; and the three are in agreement. [9]We accept man's testimony, but God's testimony is greater because it is the testimony of God, which he has given about his Son. [10]Anyone who believes in the Son of God has this testimony in his heart. Anyone who does not believe God has made him out to be a liar, because he has not believed the testimony God has given about his Son. [11]And this is the testimony: God has given us eternal life, and this life is in his Son. [12]He who has the Son has life; he who does not have the Son of God does not have life.

Concluding Remarks

[13]I write these things to you who believe in the name of the Son of God so that you may know that you have eternal life. [14]This is the confidence we have in approaching God: that if we ask anything according to his will, he hears us. [15]And if we know that he hears us—whatever we ask—we know that we have what we asked of him.

[16]If anyone sees his brother commit a sin that does not lead to death, he should pray and God will give him life. I refer to those whose sin does not lead to death. There is a sin that leads to death. I am not saying that he should pray about that. [17]All wrongdoing is sin, and there is sin that does not lead to death.

[18]We know that anyone born of God does not continue to sin; the one who was born of God keeps him safe, and the evil one cannot harm him. [19]We know that we are children of God, and that the whole world is under the control of the evil one. [20]We know also that the Son of God has come and has given us understanding, so that we may know him who is true. And we are in him who is true—even in his Son Jesus Christ. He is the true God and eternal life.

[21]Dear children, keep yourselves from idols.

---

[a]7,8 Late manuscripts of the Vulgate *testify in heaven: the Father, the Word and the Holy Spirit, and these three are one.* [8]*And there are three that testify on earth: the* (not found in any Greek manuscript before the sixteenth century)

*J*OHN *writes this second letter to warn the church to stand firm against false teachers and to keep loving other Christians. As you read this book, learn how to stand up for your Lord whenever you encounter false teachers.*

2 JOHN

¹The elder,

To the chosen lady and her children, whom I love in the truth—and not I only, but also all who know the truth— ²because of the truth, which lives in us and will be with us forever:

³Grace, mercy and peace from God the Father and from Jesus Christ, the Father's Son, will be with us in truth and love.

⁴It has given me great joy to find some of your children walking in the truth, just as the Father commanded us. ⁵And now, dear lady, I am not writing you a new command but one we have had from the beginning. I ask that we love one another. ⁶And this is love: that we walk in obedience to his commands. As you have heard from the beginning, his command is that you walk in love.

⁷Many deceivers, who do not acknowledge Jesus Christ as coming in the flesh, have gone out into the world. Any such person is the deceiver and the antichrist. ⁸Watch out that you do not lose what you have worked for, but that you may be rewarded fully. ⁹Anyone who runs ahead and does not continue in the teaching of Christ does not have God; whoever continues in the teaching has both the Father and the Son. ¹⁰If anyone comes to you and does not bring this teaching, do not take him into your house or welcome him. ¹¹Anyone who welcomes him shares in his wicked work.

¹²I have much to write to you, but I do not want to use paper and ink. Instead, I hope to visit you and talk with you face to face, so that our joy may be complete.

¹³The children of your chosen sister send their greetings.

VERSE FOR THE DAY:	AUTHOR:	PASSAGE FOR THE DAY:
2 John 1,13	Ruth A. Tucker	2 John 1–13

Chosen Ladies

WHO was this "chosen lady" who merited a letter from the apostle John? Where was she from? What was her role in the ministry? How did she come to faith in Christ? How often we wish the Bible offered more details about individuals and events, and in this letter we are left to wonder about an unnamed, unidentified woman and her "chosen sister." Scholars have speculated that these two women were leaders of house churches and that the children mentioned were their spiritual children. As such they may have had an important role in the foundational growth of the early church.

In one sense, it is their lack of identity that allows them to better represent the countless "chosen ladies" from around the world who have faithfully served the Lord through the centuries—women whose names have been lost in the annals of history.

I often wonder where I would be today were it not for two "chosen ladies." Miss Salthammer and Miss Cowan moved to my rural community in northern Wisconsin several years before I was born, and out of their sacrificial church-planting ministry came the Green Grove Alliance Church.

When I was growing up in that little country church, the two women had long since packed their bags and moved on to plant other churches. I know of them through prayer requests offered on their behalf and through their occasional return visits to teach vacation Bible school. As kids, we sometimes laughed at the way they dressed, and we told jokes about how they were paid with a load of potatoes or turnips instead of money. I later learned that when Miss Cowan died she was buried in a pauper's grave.

They were very ordinary women whose span of years has ended and whose names will soon be forgotten. But their ministry lives on through the generations of their spiritual children. They were chosen ladies.

Additional Scripture Readings:
Galatians 6:7–10; Revelation 14:12–13

Go to page 378 for your next devotional reading.

*J*OHN *writes this third letter to commend a church leader for his hospitality and to warn against another one who is unfriendly and even cruel. As you read this book, think how you can act as a friend toward other Christians.*

3 JOHN

[1]The elder,

To my dear friend Gaius, whom I love in the truth.

[2]Dear friend, I pray that you may enjoy good health and that all may go well with you, even as your soul is getting along well. [3]It gave me great joy to have some brothers come and tell about your faithfulness to the truth and how you continue to walk in the truth. [4]I have no greater joy than to hear that my children are walking in the truth.

[5]Dear friend, you are faithful in what you are doing for the brothers, even though they are strangers to you. [6]They have told the church about your love. You will do well to send them on their way in a manner worthy of God. [7]It was for the sake of the Name that they went out, receiving no help from the pagans. [8]We ought therefore to show hospitality to such men so that we may work together for the truth.

[9]I wrote to the church, but Diotrephes, who loves to be first, will have nothing to do with us. [10]So if I come, I will call attention to what he is doing, gossiping maliciously about us. Not satisfied with that, he refuses to welcome the brothers. He also stops those who want to do so and puts them out of the church.

[11]Dear friend, do not imitate what is evil but what is good. Anyone who does what is good is from God. Anyone who does what is evil has not seen God. [12]Demetrius is well spoken of by everyone —and even by the truth itself. We also speak well of him, and you know that our testimony is true.

[13]I have much to write you, but I do not want to do so with pen and ink. [14]I hope to see you soon, and we will talk face to face.

Peace to you. The friends here send their greetings. Greet the friends there by name.

VERSE FOR THE DAY:	AUTHOR:	PASSAGE FOR THE DAY:
3 John 4	Susan L. Lenzkes	3 John 1–14

My Boy

I LOOK at the shiny-shaggy hair
and round, blue-gray eyes;
the small pink tongue struggling
impatiently against tiny white teeth
to form a word,
to convey an exciting new-born thought;
the broad little boy hand
covered with dirt, reaching
to touch my cheek;
and suddenly I realize
the astounding responsibilities
that are mine before that hand
expands to a man's hand.
O God,
hold my son's hand while he crosses
the danger-filled street to manhood.

This was to be my stay-at-home-and-get-a-few-things-done day. That would be just fine, except for one thing: I have a toddler who wants to help.

I finish the washing, and he struggles the piles of clean clothes toward their dresser drawers. I suppose a hundred years from now I won't care that they started the trip neatly folded.

I sweep the floor, and he insists on helping me by emptying the dustpan. In the overall scheme of things, I suppose the fact that he dumped the dirt back onto the floor is relatively unimportant.

I begin mixing ingredients for yeast rolls, and he insists on adding the flour. If I look at the situation optimistically, unbleached white is a good color on me.

I do know he's really trying, Lord. And I know he needs practice to learn. But it would truly be so much easier to simply do it myself.

I watch, filled with apprehension, as he teeters toward me, chubby hands cupping fragile eggs, and I'm suddenly aware that you, God, have entrusted me with the fragile life of this child. Guide me as I help my little helper become your man.

Additional Scripture Readings:
Deuteronomy 6:6–7; Luke 17:1–2

Go to page 380 for your next devotional reading.

*J*UDE *(a brother of Jesus and James)*
writes this short letter to warn Chris-
tians against false teachers in the
church and to urge them to strengthen
their faith and love. As you read this
book, begin to grow in faith and love by
depending on the Father, Son, and
Holy Spirit.

JUDE

¹Jude, a servant of Jesus Christ and a brother of James,

To those who have been called, who are loved by God the Father and kept by*ᵃ* Jesus Christ:

²Mercy, peace and love be yours in abundance.

The Sin and Doom of Godless Men

³Dear friends, although I was very eager to write to you about the salvation we share, I felt I had to write and urge you to contend for the faith that was once for all entrusted to the saints. ⁴For certain men whose condemnation was written about*ᵇ* long ago have secretly slipped in among you. They are godless men, who change the grace of our God into a license for immorality and deny Jesus Christ our only Sovereign and Lord.

⁵Though you already know all this, I want to remind you that the Lord*ᶜ* delivered his people out of Egypt, but later destroyed those who did not believe. ⁶And the angels who did not keep their positions of authority but abandoned their own home—these he has kept in darkness, bound with everlasting chains for judgment on the great Day. ⁷In a similar way, Sodom and Gomorrah and the surrounding towns gave themselves up to sexual immorality and perversion. They serve as an example of those who suffer the punishment of eternal fire.

⁸In the very same way, these dreamers pollute their own bodies, reject authority and slander celestial beings. ⁹But even the archangel Michael, when he was disputing with the devil about the body of Moses, did not dare to bring a slanderous accusation against him, but said, "The

ᵃ1 Or *for; or in Jesus*   *ᵇ4* Or *men who were marked out for condemnation*   *ᶜ5* Some early manuscripts *Jesus*

Lord rebuke you!" [10]Yet these men speak abusively against whatever they do not understand; and what things they do understand by instinct, like unreasoning animals—these are the very things that destroy them.

[11]Woe to them! They have taken the way of Cain; they have rushed for profit into Balaam's error; they have been destroyed in Korah's rebellion.

[12]These men are blemishes at your love feasts, eating with you without the slightest qualm—shepherds who feed only themselves. They are clouds without rain, blown along by the wind; autumn trees, without fruit and uprooted—twice dead. [13]They are wild waves of the sea, foaming up their shame; wandering stars, for whom blackest darkness has been reserved forever.

[14]Enoch, the seventh from Adam, prophesied about these men: "See, the Lord is coming with thousands upon thousands of his holy ones [15]to judge everyone, and to convict all the ungodly of all the ungodly acts they have done in the ungodly way, and of all the harsh words ungodly sinners have spoken against him." [16]These men are grumblers and faultfinders; they follow their own evil de-

FRIDAY

VERSE FOR THE DAY:
Jude 21

AUTHOR:
Ruth Senter

PASSAGE FOR THE DAY:
Jude 17–23

Obstacles and Opportunities

THE story is told of an old Scottish fisherman who was having afternoon tea with some friends in a little tearoom by the sea. As he was describing some of his fishing exploits of the day, his hand accidentally knocked over his cup of tea. An ugly, brown tea stain appeared on the freshly whitewashed wall beside him.

"Never mind about the stain," said a friend as he rose from his chair and drew from his pocket a brown crayon. There emerged from that ugly, brown tea stain a magnificent stag with antlers spread and back arched. The friend of the fisherman was one of England's most famous painters.

Life is full of ugly tea stains that splash against whitewashed walls. Reality often seems to be more obstacle than opportunity, more pain than pleasure, more chaos than calm, more hurt than happiness, more tension than tenderness. But if I interpret Romans 8:28 correctly, I must believe that as God's woman, God is using everything in my life to make me more like himself.

Together, he and I can take the tea stains in my life and make something out of them. We can take the chaos and be calm, take the tensions and be tender, take the hurts and be content, take the obstacles and build opportunities. That is what God offers me from life.

And when God says that's what he can do for me, only my unbelief keeps me from experiencing it. If the Christian life is worth living, then God is worth believing. And if I believe God, there is no end to the possibilities.

Additional Scripture Readings:
Acts 4:28–30; Philippians 1:19–21

Go to page 381 for your next devotional reading.

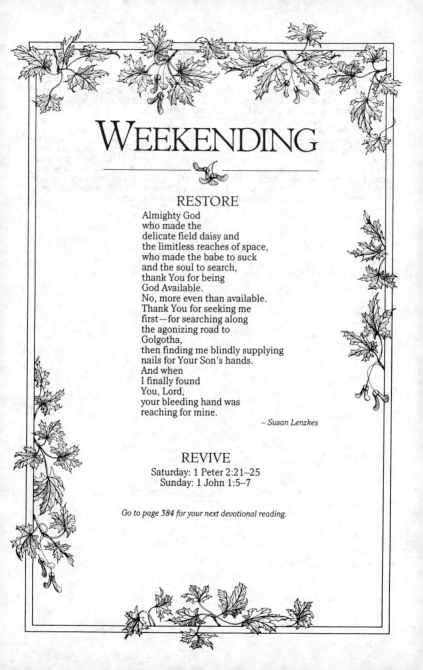

WEEKENDING

RESTORE

Almighty God
who made the
delicate field daisy and
the limitless reaches of space,
who made the babe to suck
and the soul to search,
thank You for being
God Available.
No, more even than available.
Thank You for seeking me
first—for searching along
the agonizing road to
Golgotha,
then finding me blindly supplying
nails for Your Son's hands.
And when
I finally found
You, Lord,
your bleeding hand was
reaching for mine.

– Susan Lenzkes

REVIVE

Saturday: 1 Peter 2:21–25
Sunday: 1 John 1:5–7

Go to page 384 for your next devotional reading.

sires; they boast about themselves and flatter others for their own advantage.

A Call to Persevere

[17]But, dear friends, remember what the apostles of our Lord Jesus Christ foretold. [18]They said to you, "In the last times there will be scoffers who will follow their own ungodly desires." [19]These are the men who divide you, who follow mere natural instincts and do not have the Spirit.

[20]But you, dear friends, build yourselves up in your most holy faith and pray in the Holy Spirit. [21]Keep yourselves in God's love as you wait for the mercy of our Lord Jesus Christ to bring you to eternal life.

[22]Be merciful to those who doubt; [23]snatch others from the fire and save them; to others show mercy, mixed with fear—hating even the clothing stained by corrupted flesh.

Doxology

[24]To him who is able to keep you from falling and to present you before his glorious presence without fault and with great joy— [25]to the only God our Savior be glory, majesty, power and authority, through Jesus Christ our Lord, before all ages, now and forevermore! Amen.

*J*OHN, *banished to the island of Patmos, writes what Christ reveals to him in order to comfort Christians suffering for their faith. Through visions of God in control of both the present and the future, he offers them hope, assuring them that in the end Christ will achieve victory over Satan, who is doomed to eternal punishment. As you read this book, rejoice in the awesome power of Christ, and remember that regardless of what happens now or in the future, nothing can ever separate you from his love.*

REVELATION

Prologue

1 The revelation of Jesus Christ, which God gave him to show his servants what must soon take place. He made it known by sending his angel to his servant John, ²who testifies to everything he saw —that is, the word of God and the testimony of Jesus Christ. ³Blessed is the one who reads the words of this prophecy, and blessed are those who hear it and take to heart what is written in it, because the time is near.

Greetings and Doxology

⁴John,

To the seven churches in the province of Asia:

Grace and peace to you from him who is, and who was, and who is to come, and from the seven spirits*ᵃ* before his throne, ⁵and from Jesus Christ, who is the faithful witness, the firstborn from the dead, and the ruler of the kings of the earth.

ᵃ4 Or *the sevenfold Spirit*

To him who loves us and has freed us from our sins by his blood, [6]and has made us to be a kingdom and priests to serve his God and Father—to him be glory and power for ever and ever! Amen.

[7]Look, he is coming with the clouds,
    and every eye will see him,
    even those who pierced him;
and all the peoples of the earth will
    mourn because of him.
               So shall it be! Amen.

[8]"I am the Alpha and the Omega," says the Lord God, "who is, and who was, and who is to come, the Almighty."

One Like a Son of Man

[9]I, John, your brother and companion in the suffering and kingdom and patient endurance that are ours in Jesus, was on the island of Patmos because of the word of God and the testimony of Jesus. [10]On the Lord's Day I was in the Spirit, and I heard behind me a loud voice like a trumpet, [11]which said: "Write on a scroll what you see and send it to the seven churches:

| MONDAY |

VERSE FOR THE DAY:
Revelation 1:5

AUTHOR:
Marjorie Holmes

PASSAGE FOR THE DAY:
Revelation 1:4–8

God's Eraser

I'LL probably never meet Kara, now four years old. But one day she made a beautiful observation that has helped me.

"We had been standing on the hillside watching the airplane skywriting," her grandmother wrote me one day. "When the words began to disappear, she asked, 'Why, Grandma? Where do they go?'

"Then, as I groped for an answer, her little face brightened and she suddenly exclaimed, 'Maybe Jesus has an eraser!'"

I smiled as I read, but my eyes filled and suddenly I wanted to hug that little girl. For that morning I had been grieving over past mistakes. A cruel thing I had said to my mother the day I left for college. And Dad . . . if only I'd invited him to that luncheon where I was to speak—he'd have been so proud. One tender but painful memory releases others: the time I'd punished a child unfairly, humiliated my husband, let a friend down . . . .

No matter how much we mature as people, grow as Christians, try desperately to compensate, memories of our own failures rise up to haunt us, and sting—how they sting. For me, it's not the unkindnesses of others that hurt so much or last so long, it's the burden of my own. Yes, I ask God to forgive me, and try to believe that I am forgiven. But the memory won't go away. And if I can't forgive myself, how can God?

Then a little girl, in her innocence and wisdom, makes me realize: Like that writing on the sky that simply disappears, Jesus has wiped away all things I so bitterly regret. Jesus does have an eraser.

Additional Scripture Readings:
Psalm 103:11–12; Micah 7:18–19

Go to page 388 for your next
devotional reading.

to Ephesus, Smyrna, Pergamum, Thyatira, Sardis, Philadelphia and Laodicea."

[12]I turned around to see the voice that was speaking to me. And when I turned I saw seven golden lampstands, [13]and among the lampstands was someone "like a son of man,"[a] dressed in a robe reaching down to his feet and with a golden sash around his chest. [14]His head and hair were white like wool, as white as snow, and his eyes were like blazing fire. [15]His feet were like bronze glowing in a furnace, and his voice was like the sound of rushing waters. [16]In his right hand he held seven stars, and out of his mouth came a sharp double-edged sword. His face was like the sun shining in all its brilliance.

[17]When I saw him, I fell at his feet as though dead. Then he placed his right hand on me and said: "Do not be afraid. I am the First and the Last. [18]I am the Living One; I was dead, and behold I am alive for ever and ever! And I hold the keys of death and Hades.

[19]"Write, therefore, what you have seen, what is now and what will take place later. [20]The mystery of the seven stars that you saw in my right hand and of the seven golden lampstands is this: The seven stars are the angels[b] of the seven churches, and the seven lampstands are the seven churches.

To the Church in Ephesus

2 "To the angel[c] of the church in Ephesus write:

These are the words of him who holds the seven stars in his right hand and walks among the seven golden lampstands: [2]I know your deeds, your hard work and your perseverance. I know that you cannot tolerate wicked men, that you have tested those who claim to be apostles but are not, and have found them false. [3]You have persevered and have endured hardships for my name, and have not grown weary.

[4]Yet I hold this against you: You have forsaken your first love. [5]Remember the height from which you have fallen! Repent and do the things you did at first. If you do not repent, I will come to you and remove your lampstand from its place. [6]But you have this in your fa-

vor: You hate the practices of the Nicolaitans, which I also hate.

[7]He who has an ear, let him hear what the Spirit says to the churches. To him who overcomes, I will give the right to eat from the tree of life, which is in the paradise of God.

To the Church in Smyrna

[8]"To the angel of the church in Smyrna write:

These are the words of him who is the First and the Last, who died and came to life again. [9]I know your afflictions and your poverty—yet you are rich! I know the slander of those who say they are Jews and are not, but are a synagogue of Satan. [10]Do not be afraid of what you are about to suffer. I tell you, the devil will put some of you in prison to test you, and you will suffer persecution for ten days. Be faithful, even to the point of death, and I will give you the crown of life.

[11]He who has an ear, let him hear what the Spirit says to the churches. He who overcomes will not be hurt at all by the second death.

To the Church in Pergamum

[12]"To the angel of the church in Pergamum write:

These are the words of him who has the sharp, double-edged sword. [13]I know where you live—where Satan has his throne. Yet you remain true to my name. You did not renounce your faith in me, even in the days of Antipas, my faithful witness, who was put to death in your city— where Satan lives.

[14]Nevertheless, I have a few things against you: You have people there who hold to the teaching of Balaam, who taught Balak to entice the Israelites to sin by eating food sacrificed to idols and by committing sexual immorality. [15]Likewise you also have those who hold to the teaching of the Nicolaitans. [16]Repent therefore! Otherwise, I will soon come to you and will fight against them with the sword of my mouth.

[17]He who has an ear, let him hear what the Spirit says to the churches. To him who overcomes, I will give

some of the hidden manna. I will also give him a white stone with a new name written on it, known only to him who receives it.

To the Church in Thyatira

18"To the angel of the church in Thyatira write:

These are the words of the Son of God, whose eyes are like blazing fire and whose feet are like burnished bronze. 19I know your deeds, your love and faith, your service and perseverance, and that you are now doing more than you did at first.

20Nevertheless, I have this against you: You tolerate that woman Jezebel, who calls herself a prophetess. By her teaching she misleads my servants into sexual immorality and the eating of food sacrificed to idols. 21I have given her time to repent of her immorality, but she is unwilling. 22So I will cast her on a bed of suffering, and I will make those who commit adultery with her suffer intensely, unless they repent of her ways. 23I will strike her children dead. Then all the churches will know that I am he who searches hearts and minds, and I will repay each of you according to your deeds. 24Now I say to the rest of you in Thyatira, to you who do not hold to her teaching and have not learned Satan's so-called deep secrets (I will not impose any other burden on you): 25Only hold on to what you have until I come.

26To him who overcomes and does my will to the end, I will give authority over the nations—

27'He will rule them with an iron scepter;
    he will dash them to pieces
        like pottery'a—

just as I have received authority from my Father. 28I will also give him the morning star. 29He who has an ear, let him hear what the Spirit says to the churches.

To the Church in Sardis

3 "To the angelb of the church in Sardis write:

These are the words of him who holds the seven spiritsc of God and the seven stars. I know your deeds; you have a reputation of being alive, but you are dead. 2Wake up! Strengthen what remains and is about to die, for I have not found your deeds complete in the sight of my God. 3Remember, therefore, what you have received and heard; obey it, and repent. But if you do not wake up, I will come like a thief, and you will not know at what time I will come to you.

4Yet you have a few people in Sardis who have not soiled their clothes. They will walk with me, dressed in white, for they are worthy. 5He who overcomes will, like them, be dressed in white. I will never blot out his name from the book of life, but will acknowledge his name before my Father and his angels. 6He who has an ear, let him hear what the Spirit says to the churches.

To the Church in Philadelphia

7"To the angel of the church in Philadelphia write:

These are the words of him who is holy and true, who holds the key of David. What he opens no one can shut, and what he shuts no one can open. 8I know your deeds. See, I have placed before you an open door that no one can shut. I know that you have little strength, yet you have kept my word and have not denied my name. 9I will make those who are of the synagogue of Satan, who claim to be Jews though they are not, but are liars—I will make them come and fall down at your feet and acknowledge that I have loved you. 10Since you have kept my command to endure patiently, I will also keep you from the hour of trial that is going to come upon the whole world to test those who live on the earth.

11I am coming soon. Hold on to what you have, so that no one will take your crown. 12Him who overcomes I will make a pillar in the temple of my God. Never again will he leave it. I will write on him the name of my God and the name of the city of my God, the new Jerusalem, which is coming down out of heaven from my God; and I will also write on

---

a27 Psalm 2:9   b1 Or *messenger*; also in verses 7 and 14   c1 Or *the sevenfold Spirit* him my new name. [13]He who has an ear, let him hear what the Spirit says to the churches.

To the Church in Laodicea

[14]"To the angel of the church in Laodicea write:

These are the words of the Amen, the faithful and true witness, the ruler of God's creation. [15]I know your deeds, that you are neither cold nor hot. I wish you were either one or the other! [16]So, because you are lukewarm—neither hot nor cold—I am about to spit you out of my mouth. [17]You say, 'I am rich; I have acquired wealth and do not need a thing.' But you do not realize that you are wretched, pitiful, poor, blind and naked. [18]I counsel you to buy from me gold refined in the fire, so you can become rich; and white clothes to wear, so you can cover your shameful nakedness; and salve to put on your eyes, so you can see.

[19]Those whom I love I rebuke and discipline. So be earnest, and repent. [20]Here I am! I stand at the door and knock. If anyone hears my voice and opens the door, I will come in and eat with him, and he with me.

[21]To him who overcomes, I will give the right to sit with me on my throne, just as I overcame and sat down with my Father on his throne. [22]He who has an ear, let him hear what the Spirit says to the churches."

The Throne in Heaven

4 After this I looked, and there before me was a door standing open in heaven. And the voice I had first heard speaking to me like a trumpet said, "Come up here, and I will show you what must take place after this." [2]At once I was in the Spirit, and there before me was a throne in heaven with someone sitting on it. [3]And the one who sat there had the appearance of jasper and carnelian. A rainbow, resembling an emerald, encircled the throne. [4]Surrounding the throne were twenty-four other thrones, and seated on them were twenty-four elders. They were dressed in white and had crowns of gold on their heads. [5]From the throne came flashes of lightning, rumblings and peals

of thunder. Before the throne, seven lamps were blazing. These are the seven spirits[a] of God. [6]Also before the throne there was what looked like a sea of glass, clear as crystal.

In the center, around the throne, were four living creatures, and they were covered with eyes, in front and in back. [7]The first living creature was like a lion, the second was like an ox, the third had a face like a man, the fourth was like a flying eagle. [8]Each of the four living creatures had six wings and was covered with eyes all around, even under his wings. Day and night they never stop saying:

"Holy, holy, holy
　is the Lord God Almighty,
　who was, and is, and is to come."

[9]Whenever the living creatures give glory, honor and thanks to him who sits on the throne and who lives for ever and ever, [10]the twenty-four elders fall down before him who sits on the throne, and worship him who lives for ever and ever. They lay their crowns before the throne and say:

[11]"You are worthy, our Lord and God,
　to receive glory and honor and
　　power,
　for you created all things,
　　and by your will they were created
　　and have their being."

The Scroll and the Lamb

5 Then I saw in the right hand of him who sat on the throne a scroll with writing on both sides and sealed with seven seals. [2]And I saw a mighty angel proclaiming in a loud voice, "Who is worthy to break the seals and open the scroll?" [3]But no one in heaven or on earth or under the earth could open the scroll or even look inside it. [4]I wept and wept because no one was found who was worthy to open the scroll or look inside. [5]Then one of the elders said to me, "Do not weep! See, the Lion of the tribe of Judah, the Root of David, has triumphed. He is able to open the scroll and its seven seals."

[6]Then I saw a Lamb, looking as if it had been slain, standing in the center of the throne, encircled by the four living creatures and the elders. He had seven horns and seven eyes, which are the seven spirits[a] of God sent out into all the earth. [7]He

VERSE FOR THE DAY:	AUTHOR:	PASSAGE FOR THE DAY:
Revelation 3:15–16	Catherine Marshall	Revelation 3:14–22

Author of Creativity

I AM troubled about a quality of blandness in our nation today, a lack of creativity. It's apparent in our leaders. Most gear their lives to television ratings, are afraid to take stands on issues. Movies and stage plays focus on sex and violence, with little originality. Sex so dominates advertising and the arts that it has become commonplace, almost boring.

Jesus lashed out at the spiritless quality in the people of his time:

> I know your deeds, that you are neither cold nor hot. I wish you were either one or the other! So, because you are lukewarm—neither hot nor cold—I am about to spit you out of my mouth (Revelation 3:15–16).

One of our new neighbors is no longer trapped in a bland way of life. Yet for the first twelve years of her marriage, Cynthia felt she was losing her identity in an endless procession of social events and chauffeuring of children.

In a search for answers, Cynthia set aside an hour each day for meditation. As she did this over a period of weeks there came to her the realization that she was being met in this quiet hour, at her point of need, by something more than her own thoughts and her own psyche, by Someone who loved her and who insisted that his love must be passed on to her family and her friends.

"I realized one day that my church had little more meaning for me than did our country club," Cynthia said. "I called our pastor and asked if there was a Bible study."

That's what brought Cynthia and her husband to our house, where eight couples were already meeting twice a month to find ways to relate the Bible to some everyday problems we were all facing. Out of this experience has come a new level of shared concerns for us all and the exciting discovery of answers sought out together.

As I ponder Cynthia's story, I've concluded that we don't have to settle for blandness in life; God, who is the Author of creativity, is ready to make a dull life adventuresome the moment we allow his Holy Spirit to go to work inside us.

Additional Scripture Readings:
1 Thessalonians 5:16–23; 1 Peter 1:3–6

Go to page 391 for your next devotional reading.

came and took the scroll from the right hand of him who sat on the throne. ⁸And when he had taken it, the four living creatures and the twenty-four elders fell down before the Lamb. Each one had a harp and they were holding golden bowls full of incense, which are the prayers of the saints. ⁹And they sang a new song:

"You are worthy to take the scroll
    and to open its seals,
because you were slain,
    and with your blood you purchased
        men for God
    from every tribe and language and
        people and nation.
¹⁰You have made them to be a kingdom
        and priests to serve our God,
    and they will reign on the earth."

¹¹Then I looked and heard the voice of many angels, numbering thousands upon thousands, and ten thousand times ten thousand. They encircled the throne and the living creatures and the elders. ¹²In a loud voice they sang:

"Worthy is the Lamb, who was slain,
to receive power and wealth and
        wisdom and strength
and honor and glory and praise!"

¹³Then I heard every creature in heaven and on earth and under the earth and on the sea, and all that is in them, singing:

"To him who sits on the throne and
        to the Lamb
be praise and honor and glory and
        power,
        for ever and ever!"

¹⁴The four living creatures said, "Amen," and the elders fell down and worshiped.

The Seals

6 I watched as the Lamb opened the first of the seven seals. Then I heard one of the four living creatures say in a voice like thunder, "Come!" ²I looked, and there before me was a white horse! Its rider held a bow, and he was given a crown, and he rode out as a conqueror bent on conquest.

³When the Lamb opened the second seal, I heard the second living creature say, "Come!" ⁴Then another horse came out, a fiery red one. Its rider was given power to take peace from the earth and to

make men slay each other. To him was given a large sword.

⁵When the Lamb opened the third seal, I heard the third living creature say, "Come!" I looked, and there before me was a black horse! Its rider was holding a pair of scales in his hand. ⁶Then I heard what sounded like a voice among the four living creatures, saying, "A quart*a* of wheat for a day's wages,*b* and three quarts of barley for a day's wages,*b* and do not damage the oil and the wine!"

⁷When the Lamb opened the fourth seal, I heard the voice of the fourth living creature say, "Come!" ⁸I looked, and there before me was a pale horse! Its rider was named Death, and Hades was following close behind him. They were given power over a fourth of the earth to kill by sword, famine and plague, and by the wild beasts of the earth.

⁹When he opened the fifth seal, I saw under the altar the souls of those who had been slain because of the word of God and the testimony they had maintained. ¹⁰They called out in a loud voice, "How long, Sovereign Lord, holy and true, until you judge the inhabitants of the earth and avenge our blood?" ¹¹Then each of them was given a white robe, and they were told to wait a little longer, until the number of their fellow servants and brothers who were to be killed as they had been was completed.

¹²I watched as he opened the sixth seal. There was a great earthquake. The sun turned black like sackcloth made of goat hair, the whole moon turned blood red, ¹³and the stars in the sky fell to earth, as late figs drop from a fig tree when shaken by a strong wind. ¹⁴The sky receded like a scroll, rolling up, and every mountain and island was removed from its place.

¹⁵Then the kings of the earth, the princes, the generals, the rich, the mighty, and every slave and every free man hid in caves and among the rocks of the mountains. ¹⁶They called to the mountains and the rocks, "Fall on us and hide us from the face of him who sits on the throne and from the wrath of the Lamb! ¹⁷For the great day of their wrath has come, and who can stand?"

144,000 Sealed

7 After this I saw four angels standing at the four corners of the earth, hold-

---

*a*6 Greek *a choinix* (probably about a liter)   *b*6 Greek *a denarius* ing back the four winds of the earth to prevent any wind from blowing on the land or on the sea or on any tree. [2]Then I saw another angel coming up from the east, having the seal of the living God. He called out in a loud voice to the four angels who had been given power to harm the land and the sea: [3]"Do not harm the land or the sea or the trees until we put a seal on the foreheads of the servants of our God." [4]Then I heard the number of those who were sealed: 144,000 from all the tribes of Israel.

[5]From the tribe of Judah 12,000 were sealed,
  from the tribe of Reuben 12,000,
  from the tribe of Gad 12,000,
[6]from the tribe of Asher 12,000,
  from the tribe of Naphtali 12,000,
  from the tribe of Manasseh 12,000,
[7]from the tribe of Simeon 12,000,
  from the tribe of Levi 12,000,
  from the tribe of Issachar 12,000,
[8]from the tribe of Zebulun 12,000,
  from the tribe of Joseph 12,000,
  from the tribe of Benjamin 12,000.

The Great Multitude in White Robes

[9]After this I looked and there before me was a great multitude that no one could count, from every nation, tribe, people and language, standing before the throne and in front of the Lamb. They were wearing white robes and were holding palm branches in their hands. [10]And they cried out in a loud voice:

"Salvation belongs to our God,
who sits on the throne,
and to the Lamb."

[11]All the angels were standing around the throne and around the elders and the four living creatures. They fell down on their faces before the throne and worshiped God, [12]saying:

"Amen!
Praise and glory
and wisdom and thanks and honor
and power and strength
be to our God for ever and ever.
Amen!"

[13]Then one of the elders asked me, "These in white robes—who are they, and where did they come from?"

[14]I answered, "Sir, you know."

And he said, "These are they who have come out of the great tribulation; they have washed their robes and made them white in the blood of the Lamb. [15]Therefore,

"they are before the throne of God
  and serve him day and night in his temple;
and he who sits on the throne will
  spread his tent over them.
[16]Never again will they hunger;
  never again will they thirst.
The sun will not beat upon them,
  nor any scorching heat.
[17]For the Lamb at the center of the
  throne will be their shepherd;
he will lead them to springs of
  living water.
And God will wipe away every tear
  from their eyes."

The Seventh Seal and the Golden Censer

8 When he opened the seventh seal, there was silence in heaven for about half an hour.

[2]And I saw the seven angels who stand before God, and to them were given seven trumpets.

[3]Another angel, who had a golden censer, came and stood at the altar. He was given much incense to offer, with the prayers of all the saints, on the golden altar before the throne. [4]The smoke of the incense, together with the prayers of the saints, went up before God from the angel's hand. [5]Then the angel took the censer, filled it with fire from the altar, and hurled it on the earth; and there came peals of thunder, rumblings, flashes of lightning and an earthquake.

The Trumpets

[6]Then the seven angels who had the seven trumpets prepared to sound them.

[7]The first angel sounded his trumpet, and there came hail and fire mixed with blood, and it was hurled down upon the earth. A third of the earth was burned up, a third of the trees were burned up, and all the green grass was burned up.

[8]The second angel sounded his trumpet, and something like a huge mountain, all ablaze, was thrown into the sea. A third of the sea turned into blood, [9]a third of the living creatures in the sea died, and a third of the ships were destroyed.

[10]The third angel sounded his trumpet, and a great star, blazing like a torch, fell from the sky on a third of the rivers and on the springs of water— [11]the name of

the star is Wormwood. *a* A third of the waters turned bitter, and many people died from the waters that had become bitter.

¹²The fourth angel sounded his trumpet, and a third of the sun was struck, a third of the moon, and a third of the stars, so that a third of them turned dark. A third of the day was without light, and also a third of the night.

¹³As I watched, I heard an eagle that

was flying in midair call out in a loud voice: "Woe! Woe! Woe to the inhabitants of the earth, because of the trumpet blasts about to be sounded by the other three angels!"

9 The fifth angel sounded his trumpet, and I saw a star that had fallen from the sky to the earth. The star was given the key to the shaft of the Abyss. ²When he opened the Abyss, smoke rose from it

a11 That is, Bitterness

WEDNESDAY

VERSE FOR THE DAY:
Revelation 7:9

AUTHOR:
Wanda K. Jones

PASSAGE FOR THE DAY:
Revelation 7:9–17

Among the Great Multitude

ONE of the rewards of reading the Bible in its entirety is to see that our walk with Christ ends in joy and victory! Through the eyes of the apostle John in Revelation 7, we see a God-given picture of the joyful culmination of our journey here on earth.

Over the years, as I have listened to the sermons of godly men and women and as I have sat under professors who expounded the Word of God, it was with joy and expectancy that I visualized the great multitude that will eventually gather to worship the Lord. The throng will be so great that no one will be able to count its members. People "from every nation, tribe, people and language, standing before the throne and in front of the Lamb" (Revelation 7:9). Each time I visualized this glorious band of the redeemed, I thought, "Oh, how wonderful! I'm going to be among them!" I still feel that way. What a triumphant future for every believer!

Revelation 7 tells us that we will be rewarded by serving and loving the Lord. We have many opportunities to serve. In this land, and in many other countries, people are hungry and thirsty, homeless and with no one who really cares about them. Others may be well cared for physically and financially, but they carry many burdens both day and night.

Are you included among those who carry many burdens? Or are you numbered in the throng of believers? Will the final chapter of your life close in defeat or victory? If you have not asked Jesus to take your burden of sin, ask him to "wipe away every tear" (Revelation 7:17) from your eyes, to cleanse you in his blood. Then one day you will be a member of that great multitude that no one can number!

Additional Scripture Readings:
Matthew 24:10–14; Hebrews 10:35–39

Go to page 396 for your next devotional reading.

like the smoke from a gigantic furnace. The sun and sky were darkened by the smoke from the Abyss. ³And out of the smoke locusts came down upon the earth and were given power like that of scorpions of the earth. ⁴They were told not to harm the grass of the earth or any plant or tree, but only those people who did not have the seal of God on their foreheads. ⁵They were not given power to kill them, but only to torture them for five months. And the agony they suffered was like that of the sting of a scorpion when it strikes a man. ⁶During those days men will seek death, but will not find it; they will long to die, but death will elude them.

⁷The locusts looked like horses prepared for battle. On their heads they wore something like crowns of gold, and their faces resembled human faces. ⁸Their hair was like women's hair, and their teeth were like lions' teeth. ⁹They had breastplates like breastplates of iron, and the sound of their wings was like the thundering of many horses and chariots rushing into battle. ¹⁰They had tails and stings like scorpions, and in their tails they had power to torment people for five months. ¹¹They had as king over them the angel of the Abyss, whose name in Hebrew is Abaddon, and in Greek, Apollyon.ᵃ

¹²The first woe is past; two other woes are yet to come.

¹³The sixth angel sounded his trumpet, and I heard a voice coming from the hornsᵇ of the golden altar that is before God. ¹⁴It said to the sixth angel who had the trumpet, "Release the four angels who are bound at the great river Euphrates." ¹⁵And the four angels who had been kept ready for this very hour and day and month and year were released to kill a third of mankind. ¹⁶The number of the mounted troops was two hundred million. I heard their number.

¹⁷The horses and riders I saw in my vision looked like this: Their breastplates were fiery red, dark blue, and yellow as sulfur. The heads of the horses resembled the heads of lions, and out of their mouths came fire, smoke and sulfur. ¹⁸A third of mankind was killed by the three plagues of fire, smoke and sulfur that came out of their mouths. ¹⁹The power of the horses was in their mouths and in their tails; for their tails were like snakes, having heads with which they inflict injury.

²⁰The rest of mankind that were not killed by these plagues still did not repent of the work of their hands; they did not stop worshiping demons, and idols of gold, silver, bronze, stone and wood—idols that cannot see or hear or walk. ²¹Nor did they repent of their murders, their magic arts, their sexual immorality or their thefts.

The Angel and the Little Scroll

10 Then I saw another mighty angel coming down from heaven. He was robed in a cloud, with a rainbow above his head; his face was like the sun, and his legs were like fiery pillars. ²He was holding a little scroll, which lay open in his hand. He planted his right foot on the sea and his left foot on the land, ³and he gave a loud shout like the roar of a lion. When he shouted, the voices of the seven thunders spoke. ⁴And when the seven thunders spoke, I was about to write; but I heard a voice from heaven say, "Seal up what the seven thunders have said and do not write it down."

⁵Then the angel I had seen standing on the sea and on the land raised his right hand to heaven. ⁶And he swore by him who lives for ever and ever, who created the heavens and all that is in them, the earth and all that is in it, and the sea and all that is in it, and said, "There will be no more delay! ⁷But in the days when the seventh angel is about to sound his trumpet, the mystery of God will be accomplished, just as he announced to his servants the prophets."

⁸Then the voice that I had heard from heaven spoke to me once more: "Go, take the scroll that lies open in the hand of the angel who is standing on the sea and on the land."

⁹So I went to the angel and asked him to give me the little scroll. He said to me, "Take it and eat it. It will turn your stomach sour, but in your mouth it will be as sweet as honey." ¹⁰I took the little scroll from the angel's hand and ate it. It tasted as sweet as honey in my mouth, but when I had eaten it, my stomach turned sour. ¹¹Then I was told, "You must prophesy again about many peoples, nations, languages and kings."

The Two Witnesses

11 I was given a reed like a measuring rod and was told, "Go and meas-

---

ᵃ11 *Abaddon* and *Apollyon* mean *Destroyer.*　　　ᵇ13 That is, projections ure the temple of God and the altar, and count the worshipers there. ²But exclude the outer court; do not measure it, because it has been given to the Gentiles. They will trample on the holy city for 42 months. ³And I will give power to my two witnesses, and they will prophesy for 1,260 days, clothed in sackcloth." ⁴These are the two olive trees and the two lampstands that stand before the Lord of the earth. ⁵If anyone tries to harm them, fire comes from their mouths and devours their enemies. This is how anyone who wants to harm them must die. ⁶These men have power to shut up the sky so that it will not rain during the time they are prophesying; and they have power to turn the waters into blood and to strike the earth with every kind of plague as often as they want.

⁷Now when they have finished their testimony, the beast that comes up from the Abyss will attack them, and overpower and kill them. ⁸Their bodies will lie in the street of the great city, which is figuratively called Sodom and Egypt, where also their Lord was crucified. ⁹For three and a half days men from every people, tribe, language and nation will gaze on their bodies and refuse them burial. ¹⁰The inhabitants of the earth will gloat over them and will celebrate by sending each other gifts, because these two prophets had tormented those who live on the earth.

¹¹But after the three and a half days a breath of life from God entered them, and they stood on their feet, and terror struck those who saw them. ¹²Then they heard a loud voice from heaven saying to them, "Come up here." And they went up to heaven in a cloud, while their enemies looked on.

¹³At that very hour there was a severe earthquake and a tenth of the city collapsed. Seven thousand people were killed in the earthquake, and the survivors were terrified and gave glory to the God of heaven.

¹⁴The second woe has passed; the third woe is coming soon.

The Seventh Trumpet

¹⁵The seventh angel sounded his trumpet, and there were loud voices in heaven, which said:

"The kingdom of the world has
    become the kingdom of our
    Lord and of his Christ,

and he will reign for ever and ever."

¹⁶And the twenty-four elders, who were seated on their thrones before God, fell on their faces and worshiped God, ¹⁷saying:

"We give thanks to you, Lord God
    Almighty,
    the One who is and who was,
because you have taken your great
    power
    and have begun to reign.
¹⁸The nations were angry;
    and your wrath has come.
The time has come for judging the
    dead,
    and for rewarding your servants the
    prophets
and your saints and those who
    reverence your name,
    both small and great—
and for destroying those who destroy
    the earth."

¹⁹Then God's temple in heaven was opened, and within his temple was seen the ark of his covenant. And there came flashes of lightning, rumblings, peals of thunder, an earthquake and a great hailstorm.

The Woman and the Dragon

12 A great and wondrous sign appeared in heaven: a woman clothed with the sun, with the moon under her feet and a crown of twelve stars on her head. ²She was pregnant and cried out in pain as she was about to give birth. ³Then another sign appeared in heaven: an enormous red dragon with seven heads and ten horns and seven crowns on his heads. ⁴His tail swept a third of the stars out of the sky and flung them to the earth. The dragon stood in front of the woman who was about to give birth, so that he might devour her child the moment it was born. ⁵She gave birth to a son, a male child, who will rule all the nations with an iron scepter. And her child was snatched up to God and to his throne. ⁶The woman fled into the desert to a place prepared for her by God, where she might be taken care of for 1,260 days.

⁷And there was war in heaven. Michael and his angels fought against the dragon, and the dragon and his angels fought back. ⁸But he was not strong enough, and they lost their place in heaven. ⁹The great dragon was hurled down—that ancient serpent called the devil, or Satan, who

leads the whole world astray. He was hurled to the earth, and his angels with him.

¹⁰Then I heard a loud voice in heaven say:

> "Now have come the salvation and
>> the power and the kingdom of
>> our God,
> and the authority of his Christ.
> For the accuser of our brothers,
>> who accuses them before our God
>> day and night,
>> has been hurled down.
¹¹They overcame him
>> by the blood of the Lamb
>> and by the word of their testimony;
> they did not love their lives so much
>> as to shrink from death.
¹²Therefore rejoice, you heavens
>> and you who dwell in them!
> But woe to the earth and the sea,
>> because the devil has gone down to
>> you!
> He is filled with fury,
>> because he knows that his time is
>> short."

¹³When the dragon saw that he had been hurled to the earth, he pursued the woman who had given birth to the male child. ¹⁴The woman was given the two wings of a great eagle, so that she might fly to the place prepared for her in the desert, where she would be taken care of for a time, times and half a time, out of the serpent's reach. ¹⁵Then from his mouth the serpent spewed water like a river, to overtake the woman and sweep her away with the torrent. ¹⁶But the earth helped the woman by opening its mouth and swallowing the river that the dragon had spewed out of his mouth. ¹⁷Then the dragon was enraged at the woman and went off to make war against the rest of her offspring—those who obey God's commandments and hold to the testimo-

13 ny of Jesus. ¹And the dragon[a] stood on the shore of the sea.

The Beast out of the Sea

And I saw a beast coming out of the sea. He had ten horns and seven heads, with ten crowns on his horns, and on each head a blasphemous name. ²The beast I saw resembled a leopard, but had feet like those of a bear and a mouth like that of a lion. The dragon gave the beast his power and his throne and great authority. ³One of the heads of the beast seemed to have had a fatal wound, but the fatal wound had been healed. The whole world was astonished and followed the beast. ⁴Men worshiped the dragon because he had given authority to the beast, and they also worshiped the beast and asked, "Who is like the beast? Who can make war against him?"

⁵The beast was given a mouth to utter proud words and blasphemies and to exercise his authority for forty-two months. ⁶He opened his mouth to blaspheme God, and to slander his name and his dwelling place and those who live in heaven. ⁷He was given power to make war against the saints and to conquer them. And he was given authority over every tribe, people, language and nation. ⁸All inhabitants of the earth will worship the beast—all whose names have not been written in the book of life belonging to the Lamb that was slain from the creation of the world.[b]

⁹He who has an ear, let him hear.

> ¹⁰If anyone is to go into captivity,
>> into captivity he will go.
> If anyone is to be killed[c] with the
>> sword,
>> with the sword he will be killed.

This calls for patient endurance and faithfulness on the part of the saints.

The Beast out of the Earth

¹¹Then I saw another beast, coming out of the earth. He had two horns like a lamb, but he spoke like a dragon. ¹²He exercised all the authority of the first beast on his behalf, and made the earth and its inhabitants worship the first beast, whose fatal wound had been healed. ¹³And he performed great and miraculous signs, even causing fire to come down from heaven to earth in full view of men. ¹⁴Because of the signs he was given power to do on behalf of the first beast, he deceived the inhabitants of the earth. He ordered them to set up an image in honor of the beast who was wounded by the sword and yet lived. ¹⁵He was given power to give breath to the image of the first beast, so that it could speak and cause all who refused to worship the image to be killed. ¹⁶He also forced everyone, small and great, rich and

---

a1 Some late manuscripts And I belonging to the Lamb that was slain   *b8 Or written from the creation of the world in the book of life*   *c10 Some manuscripts anyone kills* poor, free and slave, to receive a mark on his right hand or on his forehead, [17]so that no one could buy or sell unless he had the mark, which is the name of the beast or the number of his name.

[18]This calls for wisdom. If anyone has insight, let him calculate the number of the beast, for it is man's number. His number is 666.

The Lamb and the 144,000

14 Then I looked, and there before me was the Lamb, standing on Mount Zion, and with him 144,000 who had his name and his Father's name written on their foreheads. [2]And I heard a sound from heaven like the roar of rushing waters and like a loud peal of thunder. The sound I heard was like that of harpists playing their harps. [3]And they sang a new song before the throne and before the four living creatures and the elders. No one could learn the song except the 144,000 who had been redeemed from the earth. [4]These are those who did not defile themselves with women, for they kept themselves pure. They follow the Lamb wherever he goes. They were purchased from among men and offered as firstfruits to God and the Lamb. [5]No lie was found in their mouths; they are blameless.

The Three Angels

[6]Then I saw another angel flying in midair, and he had the eternal gospel to proclaim to those who live on the earth—to every nation, tribe, language and people. [7]He said in a loud voice, "Fear God and give him glory, because the hour of his judgment has come. Worship him who made the heavens, the earth, the sea and the springs of water."

[8]A second angel followed and said, "Fallen! Fallen is Babylon the Great, which made all the nations drink the maddening wine of her adulteries."

[9]A third angel followed them and said in a loud voice: "If anyone worships the beast and his image and receives his mark on the forehead or on the hand, [10]he, too, will drink of the wine of God's fury, which has been poured full strength into the cup of his wrath. He will be tormented with burning sulfur in the presence of the holy angels and of the Lamb. [11]And the smoke of their torment rises for ever and ever. There is no rest day or night for those who worship the beast and his image, or for anyone who receives the mark of his name." [12]This calls for patient endurance on the part of the saints who obey God's commandments and remain faithful to Jesus.

[13]Then I heard a voice from heaven say, "Write: Blessed are the dead who die in the Lord from now on."

"Yes," says the Spirit, "they will rest from their labor, for their deeds will follow them."

The Harvest of the Earth

[14]I looked, and there before me was a white cloud, and seated on the cloud was one "like a son of man"[a] with a crown of gold on his head and a sharp sickle in his hand. [15]Then another angel came out of the temple and called in a loud voice to him who was sitting on the cloud, "Take your sickle and reap, because the time to reap has come, for the harvest of the earth is ripe." [16]So he who was seated on the cloud swung his sickle over the earth, and the earth was harvested.

[17]Another angel came out of the temple in heaven, and he too had a sharp sickle. [18]Still another angel, who had charge of the fire, came from the altar and called in a loud voice to him who had the sharp sickle, "Take your sharp sickle and gather the clusters of grapes from the earth's vine, because its grapes are ripe." [19]The angel swung his sickle on the earth, gathered its grapes and threw them into the great winepress of God's wrath. [20]They were trampled in the winepress outside the city, and blood flowed out of the press, rising as high as the horses' bridles for a distance of 1,600 stadia.[b]

Seven Angels With Seven Plagues

15 I saw in heaven another great and marvelous sign: seven angels with the seven last plagues—last, because with them God's wrath is completed. [2]And I saw what looked like a sea of glass mixed with fire and, standing beside the sea, those who had been victorious over the beast and his image and over the number of his name. They held harps given them by God [3]and sang the song of Moses the servant of God and the song of the Lamb:

"Great and marvelous are your deeds,
     Lord God Almighty.

---

[a]14 Daniel 7:13   [b]20 That is, about 180 miles (about 300 kilometers)

Just and true are your ways,
    King of the ages.
[4]Who will not fear you, O Lord,
    and bring glory to your name?
For you alone are holy.
All nations will come
    and worship before you,
for your righteous acts have been
    revealed."

[5]After this I looked and in heaven the temple, that is, the tabernacle of the Testimony, was opened. [6]Out of the temple came the seven angels with the seven plagues. They were dressed in clean,

shining linen and wore golden sashes around their chests. [7]Then one of the four living creatures gave to the seven angels seven golden bowls filled with the wrath of God, who lives for ever and ever. [8]And the temple was filled with smoke from the glory of God and from his power, and no one could enter the temple until the seven plagues of the seven angels were completed.

The Seven Bowls of God's Wrath

16 Then I heard a loud voice from the temple saying to the seven angels,

THURSDAY

VERSE FOR THE DAY: AUTHOR: PASSAGE FOR THE DAY:
Revelation 14:13   Gien Karssen   Revelation 14:6–13

Rest and Reward

THE Bible leaves no doubt that there is life after death. Humanity is created for eternity. The earthly life is but an overture, a prelude of the reality to come. Blessed—happy, to be envied —are the dead "who die in the Lord." They are people who during their earthly life believed in Jesus Christ as their Savior and Lord. When they exchange the temporal for the eternal, their work is done forever. They finally have rest. All the troubles and tensions of their earthly existence are behind them. They have arrived at their eternal destination. They are HOME!

The Scriptures paint a frightening alternative for people who do not seek God during their lifetime: "And the smoke of their torment rises for ever and ever. There is no rest day or night" (Revelation 14:11).

What a contrast!

The dead who die in the Lord not only enjoy eternally the absence of unrest, pain and sorrow, but they also are rewarded: "Their deeds will follow them."

Human beings are free to live their lives according to their own choices. But they have to keep in mind that there will be a future settling of accounts. All will—justly—be rewarded according to their deeds. The measuring staff will be administered according to their attitude toward the Lord Jesus Christ.

True rest awaits only those who during their life on earth took God seriously. Without him there is no real rest, in the present or in the future.

Additional Scripture Readings:
Matthew 25:31–46; Luke 16:19–26

Go to page 402 for your next devotional reading.

"Go, pour out the seven bowls of God's wrath on the earth."

[2]The first angel went and poured out his bowl on the land, and ugly and painful sores broke out on the people who had the mark of the beast and worshiped his image.

[3]The second angel poured out his bowl on the sea, and it turned into blood like that of a dead man, and every living thing in the sea died.

[4]The third angel poured out his bowl on the rivers and springs of water, and they became blood. [5]Then I heard the angel in charge of the waters say:

"You are just in these judgments,
    you who are and who were, the
        Holy One,
    because you have so judged;
[6]for they have shed the blood of your
        saints and prophets,
    and you have given them blood to
        drink as they deserve."

[7]And I heard the altar respond:

"Yes, Lord God Almighty,
    true and just are your judgments."

[8]The fourth angel poured out his bowl on the sun, and the sun was given power to scorch people with fire. [9]They were seared by the intense heat and they cursed the name of God, who had control over these plagues, but they refused to repent and glorify him.

[10]The fifth angel poured out his bowl on the throne of the beast, and his kingdom was plunged into darkness. Men gnawed their tongues in agony [11]and cursed the God of heaven because of their pains and their sores, but they refused to repent of what they had done.

[12]The sixth angel poured out his bowl on the great river Euphrates, and its water was dried up to prepare the way for the kings from the East. [13]Then I saw three evil[a] spirits that looked like frogs; they came out of the mouth of the dragon, out of the mouth of the beast and out of the mouth of the false prophet. [14]They are spirits of demons performing miraculous signs, and they go out to the kings of the whole world, to gather them for the battle on the great day of God Almighty.

[15]"Behold, I come like a thief! Blessed is he who stays awake and keeps his clothes with him, so that he may not go naked and be shamefully exposed."

[16]Then they gathered the kings together to the place that in Hebrew is called Armageddon.

[17]The seventh angel poured out his bowl into the air, and out of the temple came a loud voice from the throne, saying, "It is done!" [18]Then there came flashes of lightning, rumblings, peals of thunder and a severe earthquake. No earthquake like it has ever occurred since man has been on earth, so tremendous was the quake. [19]The great city split into three parts, and the cities of the nations collapsed. God remembered Babylon the Great and gave her the cup filled with the wine of the fury of his wrath. [20]Every island fled away and the mountains could not be found. [21]From the sky huge hailstones of about a hundred pounds each fell upon men. And they cursed God on account of the plague of hail, because the plague was so terrible.

The Woman on the Beast

17 One of the seven angels who had the seven bowls came and said to me, "Come, I will show you the punishment of the great prostitute, who sits on many waters. [2]With her the kings of the earth committed adultery and the inhabitants of the earth were intoxicated with the wine of her adulteries."

[3]Then the angel carried me away in the Spirit into a desert. There I saw a woman sitting on a scarlet beast that was covered with blasphemous names and had seven heads and ten horns. [4]The woman was dressed in purple and scarlet, and was glittering with gold, precious stones and pearls. She held a golden cup in her hand, filled with abominable things and the filth of her adulteries. [5]This title was written on her forehead:

MYSTERY
BABYLON THE GREAT
THE MOTHER OF PROSTITUTES
AND OF THE ABOMINATIONS OF THE EARTH.

[6]I saw that the woman was drunk with the blood of the saints, the blood of those who bore testimony to Jesus.

When I saw her, I was greatly astonished. [7]Then the angel said to me: "Why are you astonished? I will explain to you the mystery of the woman and of the beast she rides, which has the seven heads and ten horns. [8]The beast, which you saw, once was, now is not, and will

---

[a]13 Greek unclean

come up out of the Abyss and go to his destruction. The inhabitants of the earth whose names have not been written in the book of life from the creation of the world will be astonished when they see the beast, because he once was, now is not, and yet will come.

9"This calls for a mind with wisdom. The seven heads are seven hills on which the woman sits. 10They are also seven kings. Five have fallen, one is, the other has not yet come; but when he does come, he must remain for a little while. 11The beast who once was, and now is not, is an eighth king. He belongs to the seven and is going to his destruction.

12"The ten horns you saw are ten kings who have not yet received a kingdom, but who for one hour will receive authority as kings along with the beast. 13They have one purpose and will give their power and authority to the beast. 14They will make war against the Lamb, but the Lamb will overcome them because he is Lord of lords and King of kings—and with him will be his called, chosen and faithful followers."

15Then the angel said to me, "The waters you saw, where the prostitute sits, are peoples, multitudes, nations and languages. 16The beast and the ten horns you saw will hate the prostitute. They will bring her to ruin and leave her naked; they will eat her flesh and burn her with fire. 17For God has put it into their hearts to accomplish his purpose by agreeing to give the beast their power to rule, until God's words are fulfilled. 18The woman you saw is the great city that rules over the kings of the earth."

The Fall of Babylon

18 After this I saw another angel coming down from heaven. He had great authority, and the earth was illuminated by his splendor. 2With a mighty voice he shouted:

"Fallen! Fallen is Babylon the Great!
   She has become a home for demons
and a haunt for every evil*a* spirit,
   a haunt for every unclean and detestable bird.
3For all the nations have drunk
   the maddening wine of her adulteries.

The kings of the earth committed
   adultery with her,
and the merchants of the earth
   grew rich from her excessive luxuries."

4Then I heard another voice from heaven say:

"Come out of her, my people,
   so that you will not share in her sins,
   so that you will not receive any of her plagues;
5for her sins are piled up to heaven,
   and God has remembered her crimes.
6Give back to her as she has given;
   pay her back double for what she has done.
   Mix her a double portion from her own cup.
7Give her as much torture and grief
   as the glory and luxury she gave herself.
In her heart she boasts,
   'I sit as queen; I am not a widow,
   and I will never mourn.'
8Therefore in one day her plagues will overtake her:
   death, mourning and famine.
She will be consumed by fire,
   for mighty is the Lord God who judges her.

9"When the kings of the earth who committed adultery with her and shared her luxury see the smoke of her burning, they will weep and mourn over her. 10Terrified at her torment, they will stand far off and cry:

" 'Woe! Woe, O great city,
   O Babylon, city of power!
In one hour your doom has come!'

11"The merchants of the earth will weep and mourn over her because no one buys their cargoes any more— 12cargoes of gold, silver, precious stones and pearls; fine linen, purple, silk and scarlet cloth; every sort of citron wood, and articles of every kind made of ivory, costly wood, bronze, iron and marble; 13cargoes of cinnamon and spice, of incense, myrrh and frankincense, of wine and olive oil, of fine flour and wheat; cattle and sheep; horses and carriages; and bodies and souls of men.

14"They will say, 'The fruit you longed

a2 Greek *unclean*

for is gone from you. All your riches and splendor have vanished, never to be recovered.' ¹⁵The merchants who sold these things and gained their wealth from her will stand far off, terrified at her torment. They will weep and mourn ¹⁶and cry out:

" 'Woe! Woe, O great city,
     dressed in fine linen, purple and
          scarlet,
     and glittering with gold, precious
          stones and pearls!
¹⁷In one hour such great wealth has
     been brought to ruin!'

"Every sea captain, and all who travel by ship, the sailors, and all who earn their living from the sea, will stand far off. ¹⁸When they see the smoke of her burning, they will exclaim, 'Was there ever a city like this great city?' ¹⁹They will throw dust on their heads, and with weeping and mourning cry out:

" 'Woe! Woe, O great city,
     where all who had ships on the sea
          became rich through her wealth!
In one hour she has been brought to
     ruin!
²⁰Rejoice over her, O heaven!
     Rejoice, saints and apostles and
          prophets!
God has judged her for the way she
     treated you.' "

²¹Then a mighty angel picked up a boulder the size of a large millstone and threw it into the sea, and said:

"With such violence
     the great city of Babylon will be
          thrown down,
     never to be found again.
²²The music of harpists and musicians,
          flute players and trumpeters,
     will never be heard in you again.
No workman of any trade
     will ever be found in you again.
The sound of a millstone
     will never be heard in you again.
²³The light of a lamp
     will never shine in you again.
The voice of bridegroom and bride
     will never be heard in you again.
Your merchants were the world's great
     men.
By your magic spell all the nations
     were led astray.
²⁴In her was found the blood of
     prophets and of the saints,

and of all who have been killed on
     the earth."

Hallelujah!

19 After this I heard what sounded like the roar of a great multitude in heaven shouting:

"Hallelujah!
Salvation and glory and power belong
     to our God,
² for true and just are his judgments.
He has condemned the great
          prostitute
     who corrupted the earth by her
          adulteries.
He has avenged on her the blood of
     his servants."

³And again they shouted:

"Hallelujah!
The smoke from her goes up for ever
     and ever."

⁴The twenty-four elders and the four living creatures fell down and worshiped God, who was seated on the throne. And they cried:

"Amen, Hallelujah!"

⁵Then a voice came from the throne, saying:

"Praise our God,
     all you his servants,
you who fear him,
     both small and great!"

⁶Then I heard what sounded like a great multitude, like the roar of rushing waters and like loud peals of thunder, shouting:

"Hallelujah!
     For our Lord God Almighty reigns.
⁷Let us rejoice and be glad
     and give him glory!
For the wedding of the Lamb has
          come,
     and his bride has made herself
          ready.
⁸Fine linen, bright and clean,
     was given her to wear."
(Fine linen stands for the righteous acts of the saints.)

⁹Then the angel said to me, "Write: 'Blessed are those who are invited to the wedding supper of the Lamb!' " And he added, "These are the true words of God."
¹⁰At this I fell at his feet to worship him. But he said to me, "Do not do it! I

am a fellow servant with you and with your brothers who hold to the testimony of Jesus. Worship God! For the testimony of Jesus is the spirit of prophecy."

The Rider on the White Horse

¹¹I saw heaven standing open and there before me was a white horse, whose rider is called Faithful and True. With justice he judges and makes war. ¹²His eyes are like blazing fire, and on his head are many crowns. He has a name written on him that no one knows but he himself. ¹³He is dressed in a robe dipped in blood, and his name is the Word of God. ¹⁴The armies of heaven were following him, riding on white horses and dressed in fine linen, white and clean. ¹⁵Out of his mouth comes a sharp sword with which to strike down the nations. "He will rule them with an iron scepter."ᵃ He treads the winepress of the fury of the wrath of God Almighty. ¹⁶On his robe and on his thigh he has this name written:

KING OF KINGS AND LORD OF LORDS.

¹⁷And I saw an angel standing in the sun, who cried in a loud voice to all the birds flying in midair, "Come, gather together for the great supper of God, ¹⁸so that you may eat the flesh of kings, generals, and mighty men, of horses and their riders, and the flesh of all people, free and slave, small and great."

¹⁹Then I saw the beast and the kings of the earth and their armies gathered together to make war against the rider on the horse and his army. ²⁰But the beast was captured, and with him the false prophet who had performed the miraculous signs on his behalf. With these signs he had deluded those who had received the mark of the beast and worshiped his image. The two of them were thrown alive into the fiery lake of burning sulfur. ²¹The rest of them were killed with the sword that came out of the mouth of the rider on the horse, and all the birds gorged themselves on their flesh.

The Thousand Years

20 And I saw an angel coming down out of heaven, having the key to the Abyss and holding in his hand a great chain. ²He seized the dragon, that ancient serpent, who is the devil, or Satan, and bound him for a thousand years. ³He threw him into the Abyss, and locked and

sealed it over him, to keep him from deceiving the nations anymore until the thousand years were ended. After that, he must be set free for a short time.

⁴I saw thrones on which were seated those who had been given authority to judge. And I saw the souls of those who had been beheaded because of their testimony for Jesus and because of the word of God. They had not worshiped the beast or his image and had not received his mark on their foreheads or their hands. They came to life and reigned with Christ a thousand years. ⁵(The rest of the dead did not come to life until the thousand years were ended.) This is the first resurrection. ⁶Blessed and holy are those who have part in the first resurrection. The second death has no power over them, but they will be priests of God and of Christ and will reign with him for a thousand years.

Satan's Doom

⁷When the thousand years are over, Satan will be released from his prison ⁸and will go out to deceive the nations in the four corners of the earth—Gog and Magog—to gather them for battle. In number they are like the sand on the seashore. ⁹They marched across the breadth of the earth and surrounded the camp of God's people, the city he loves. But fire came down from heaven and devoured them. ¹⁰And the devil, who deceived them, was thrown into the lake of burning sulfur, where the beast and the false prophet had been thrown. They will be tormented day and night for ever and ever.

The Dead Are Judged

¹¹Then I saw a great white throne and him who was seated on it. Earth and sky fled from his presence, and there was no place for them. ¹²And I saw the dead, great and small, standing before the throne, and books were opened. Another book was opened, which is the book of life. The dead were judged according to what they had done as recorded in the books. ¹³The sea gave up the dead that were in it, and death and Hades gave up the dead that were in them, and each person was judged according to what he had done. ¹⁴Then death and Hades were thrown into the lake of fire. The lake of fire is the second death. ¹⁵If anyone's

ᵃ15 Psalm 2:9

name was not found written in the book of life, he was thrown into the lake of fire.

The New Jerusalem

21 Then I saw a new heaven and a new earth, for the first heaven and the first earth had passed away, and there was no longer any sea. ²I saw the Holy City, the new Jerusalem, coming down out of heaven from God, prepared as a bride beautifully dressed for her husband. ³And I heard a loud voice from the throne saying, "Now the dwelling of God is with men, and he will live with them. They will be his people, and God himself will be with them and be their God. ⁴He will wipe every tear from their eyes. There will be no more death or mourning or crying or pain, for the old order of things has passed away."

⁵He who was seated on the throne said, "I am making everything new!" Then he said, "Write this down, for these words are trustworthy and true."

⁶He said to me: "It is done. I am the Alpha and the Omega, the Beginning and the End. To him who is thirsty I will give to drink without cost from the spring of the water of life. ⁷He who overcomes will inherit all this, and I will be his God and he will be my son. ⁸But the cowardly, the unbelieving, the vile, the murderers, the sexually immoral, those who practice magic arts, the idolaters and all liars — their place will be in the fiery lake of burning sulfur. This is the second death."

⁹One of the seven angels who had the seven bowls full of the seven last plagues came and said to me, "Come, I will show you the bride, the wife of the Lamb." ¹⁰And he carried me away in the Spirit to a mountain great and high, and showed me the Holy City, Jerusalem, coming down out of heaven from God. ¹¹It shone with the glory of God, and its brilliance was like that of a very precious jewel, like a jasper, clear as crystal. ¹²It had a great, high wall with twelve gates, and with twelve angels at the gates. On the gates were written the names of the twelve tribes of Israel. ¹³There were three gates on the east, three on the north, three on the south and three on the west. ¹⁴The wall of the city had twelve foundations, and on them were the names of the twelve apostles of the Lamb.

¹⁵The angel who talked with me had a measuring rod of gold to measure the city, its gates and its walls. ¹⁶The city was laid out like a square, as long as it was wide. He measured the city with the rod and found it to be 12,000 stadia[a] in length, and as wide and high as it is long. ¹⁷He measured its wall and it was 144 cubits[b] thick,[c] by man's measurement, which the angel was using. ¹⁸The wall was made of jasper, and the city of pure gold, as pure as glass. ¹⁹The foundations of the city walls were decorated with every kind of precious stone. The first foundation was jasper, the second sapphire, the third chalcedony, the fourth emerald, ²⁰the fifth sardonyx, the sixth carnelian, the seventh chrysolite, the eighth beryl, the ninth topaz, the tenth chrysoprase, the eleventh jacinth, and the twelfth amethyst.[d] ²¹The twelve gates were twelve pearls, each gate made of a single pearl. The great street of the city was of pure gold, like transparent glass.

²²I did not see a temple in the city, because the Lord God Almighty and the Lamb are its temple. ²³The city does not need the sun or the moon to shine on it, for the glory of God gives it light, and the Lamb is its lamp. ²⁴The nations will walk by its light, and the kings of the earth will bring their splendor into it. ²⁵On no day will its gates ever be shut, for there will be no night there. ²⁶The glory and honor of the nations will be brought into it. ²⁷Nothing impure will ever enter it, nor will anyone who does what is shameful or deceitful, but only those whose names are written in the Lamb's book of life.

The River of Life

22 Then the angel showed me the river of the water of life, as clear as crystal, flowing from the throne of God and of the Lamb ²down the middle of the great street of the city. On each side of the river stood the tree of life, bearing twelve crops of fruit, yielding its fruit every month. And the leaves of the tree are for the healing of the nations. ³No longer will there be any curse. The throne of God and of the Lamb will be in the city, and his servants will serve him. ⁴They will see his face, and his name will be on their foreheads. ⁵There will be no more night. They will not need the light of a lamp or the light of the sun, for the Lord God will

---

a16 That is, about 1,400 miles (about 2,200 kilometers)   *b17* That is, about 200 feet (about 65 meters)   *c17* Or *high*   *d20* The precise identification of some of these precious stones is uncertain.

give them light. And they will reign for ever and ever.

⁶The angel said to me, "These words are trustworthy and true. The Lord, the God of the spirits of the prophets, sent his angel to show his servants the things that must soon take place."

Jesus Is Coming

⁷"Behold, I am coming soon! Blessed is he who keeps the words of the prophecy in this book."

⁸I, John, am the one who heard and saw these things. And when I had heard and seen them, I fell down to worship at the feet of the angel who had been showing them to me. ⁹But he said to me, "Do not do it! I am a fellow servant with you and with your brothers the prophets and of all who keep the words of this book. Worship God!"

¹⁰Then he told me, "Do not seal up the words of the prophecy of this book, because the time is near. ¹¹Let him who does wrong continue to do wrong; let him who is vile continue to be vile; let him who does right continue to do right; and let him who is holy continue to be holy."

¹²"Behold, I am coming soon! My reward is with me, and I will give to everyone according to what he has done. ¹³I am the Alpha and the Omega, the First and the Last, the Beginning and the End.

FRIDAY

VERSE FOR THE DAY: AUTHOR: PASSAGE FOR THE DAY:
Revelation 22:16   Marilyn Morgan Helleberg   Revelation 22:7–16

Morning Star

"I AM . . . the bright Morning Star" (Revelation 22:16).

These words of the risen Christ correspond with a statement once made by a nineteen-year-old youth named Abe Lincoln: "I never behold the stars that I do not feel that I am looking into the face of God."

Stars! What is it about them that so kindles our sense of wonder? Scientists tell us that, when we look up at the night sky, we are seeing light that left some of those faraway stars thousands of light years ago. Tonight, if the sky is clear, you and I might actually see light rays that left some distant star on the night Jesus was born! That makes me aware that our lives touch eternity.

I need the stars. I need them because of my craving for beauty and my longing for perfection in this less-than-beautiful, imperfect world. I need them because I often buy security at the cost of my sense of enchantment, and the price is much too high. I need them to deepen my experience of awe and wonder, to remind me of the kingdom and the power and the glory of God and of his creation.

If the sky is clear tonight, let's step outside and look at the stars. Perhaps, like Abe Lincoln, we'll sense that we're looking into the face of God.

Additional Scripture Readings:
Psalm 19:1–6; Isaiah 40:25–26

Go to page 403 for your next devotional reading.

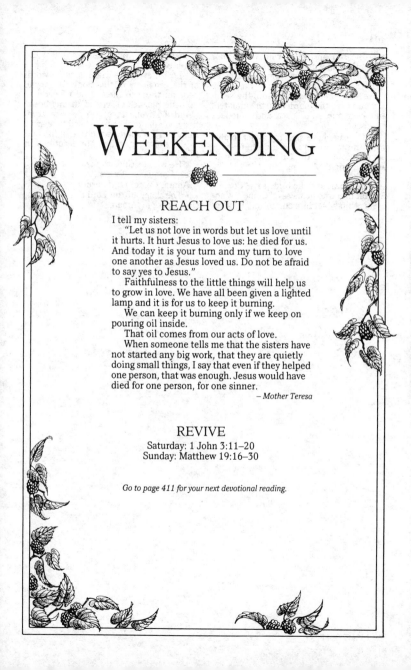

WEEKENDING

REACH OUT

I tell my sisters:
    "Let us not love in words but let us love until
it hurts. It hurt Jesus to love us: he died for us.
And today it is your turn and my turn to love
one another as Jesus loved us. Do not be afraid
to say yes to Jesus."
    Faithfulness to the little things will help us
to grow in love. We have all been given a lighted
lamp and it is for us to keep it burning.
    We can keep it burning only if we keep on
pouring oil inside.
    That oil comes from our acts of love.
    When someone tells me that the sisters have
not started any big work, that they are quietly
doing small things, I say that even if they helped
one person, that was enough. Jesus would have
died for one person, for one sinner.

– Mother Teresa

REVIVE

Saturday: 1 John 3:11–20
Sunday: Matthew 19:16–30

Go to page 411 for your next devotional reading.

[14]"Blessed are those who wash their robes, that they may have the right to the tree of life and may go through the gates into the city. [15]Outside are the dogs, those who practice magic arts, the sexually immoral, the murderers, the idolaters and everyone who loves and practices falsehood.

[16]"I, Jesus, have sent my angel to give you[a] this testimony for the churches. I am the Root and the Offspring of David, and the bright Morning Star."

[17]The Spirit and the bride say, "Come!" And let him who hears say, "Come!" Whoever is thirsty, let him come; and whoever wishes, let him take the free gift of the water of life.

[18]I warn everyone who hears the words of the prophecy of this book: If anyone adds anything to them, God will add to him the plagues described in this book. [19]And if anyone takes words away from this book of prophecy, God will take away from him his share in the tree of life and in the holy city, which are described in this book.

[20]He who testifies to these things says, "Yes, I am coming soon."

Amen. Come, Lord Jesus.

[21]The grace of the Lord Jesus be with God's people. Amen.

---

[a]16 The Greek is plural.

PSALMS
PROVERBS

DAVID, the shepherd boy and Israel's greatest king, writes most of the psalms. Together these 150 songs form the greatest collection of prayers ever written. A wide range of human emotion is expressed—joy, excitement, compassion, love, anger, grief, depression. As you read this book, remember that no matter what you are feeling, God wants to hear about it in your prayers to him. He promises to listen to all your concerns and to answer them for Jesus' sake.

PSALMS

BOOK I

Psalms 1–41

Psalm 1

¹Blessed is the man
   who does not walk in the counsel
      of the wicked
 or stand in the way of sinners
   or sit in the seat of mockers.
²But his delight is in the law of the
      LORD,
   and on his law he meditates day
      and night.

³He is like a tree planted by streams
      of water,
   which yields its fruit in season
 and whose leaf does not wither.
   Whatever he does prospers.

⁴Not so the wicked!
   They are like chaff
      that the wind blows away.
⁵Therefore the wicked will not stand in
      the judgment,
   nor sinners in the assembly of the
      righteous.

⁶For the LORD watches over the way of
      the righteous,

but the way of the wicked will
     perish.

Psalm 2

[1] Why do the nations conspire[a]
     and the peoples plot in vain?
[2] The kings of the earth take their
          stand
     and the rulers gather together
against the LORD
     and against his Anointed One.[b]
[3] "Let us break their chains," they say,
     "and throw off their fetters."

[4] The One enthroned in heaven laughs;
     the Lord scoffs at them.
[5] Then he rebukes them in his anger
     and terrifies them in his wrath,
          saying,
[6] "I have installed my King[c]
     on Zion, my holy hill."

[7] I will proclaim the decree of the LORD:

He said to me, "You are my Son[d];
     today I have become your Father.[e]
[8] Ask of me,
     and I will make the nations your
          inheritance,
     the ends of the earth your
          possession.
[9] You will rule them with an iron
          scepter[f];
     you will dash them to pieces like
          pottery."

[10] Therefore, you kings, be wise;
     be warned, you rulers of the earth.
[11] Serve the LORD with fear
     and rejoice with trembling.
[12] Kiss the Son, lest he be angry
     and you be destroyed in your way,
for his wrath can flare up in a
          moment.
     Blessed are all who take refuge in
          him.

Psalm 3

A psalm of David. When he fled from
     his son Absalom.

[1] O LORD, how many are my foes!
     How many rise up against me!
[2] Many are saying of me,
     "God will not deliver him." *Selah*[g]

[3] But you are a shield around me,
          O LORD;
     you bestow glory on me and lift[h]
          up my head.
[4] To the LORD I cry aloud,
     and he answers me from his holy
          hill.   *Selah*

[5] I lie down and sleep;
     I wake again, because the LORD
          sustains me.
[6] I will not fear the tens of thousands
     drawn up against me on every side.

[7] Arise, O LORD!
     Deliver me, O my God!
Strike all my enemies on the jaw;
     break the teeth of the wicked.

[8] From the LORD comes deliverance.
     May your blessing be on your
          people.   *Selah*

Psalm 4

For the director of music. With stringed
     instruments. A psalm of David.

[1] Answer me when I call to you,
          O my righteous God.
Give me relief from my distress;
     be merciful to me and hear my
          prayer.

[2] How long, O men, will you turn my
          glory into shame[i]?
How long will you love delusions
     and seek false gods[j]?   *Selah*
[3] Know that the LORD has set apart the
          godly for himself;
     the LORD will hear when I call to
          him.

[4] In your anger do not sin;
     when you are on your beds,
     search your hearts and be silent.
                                   Selah

[5] Offer right sacrifices
     and trust in the LORD.

[6] Many are asking, "Who can show us
          any good?"
     Let the light of your face shine
          upon us, O LORD.
[7] You have filled my heart with greater
          joy
     than when their grain and new wine
          abound.
[8] I will lie down and sleep in peace,

---

[a]1 Hebrew; Septuagint *rage*   [b]2 Or *anointed one*   [c]6 Or *king*   [d]7 Or *son; also in verse 12*
[e]7 Or *have begotten you*   [f]9 Or *will break them with a rod of iron*   [g]2 A word of uncertain meaning,
occurring frequently in the Psalms; possibly a musical term   [h]3 Or LORD, / *my Glorious One, who lifts*
[i]2 Or *you dishonor my Glorious One*   [j]2 Or *seek lies*

for you alone, O Lord,
make me dwell in safety.

Psalm 5

*For the director of music. For flutes.
A psalm of David.*

[1]Give ear to my words, O Lord,
consider my sighing.
[2]Listen to my cry for help,
my King and my God,
for to you I pray.
[3]In the morning, O Lord, you hear my
voice;
in the morning I lay my requests
before you
and wait in expectation.

[4]You are not a God who takes pleasure
in evil;
with you the wicked cannot dwell.
[5]The arrogant cannot stand in your
presence;
you hate all who do wrong.
[6]You destroy those who tell lies;
bloodthirsty and deceitful men
the Lord abhors.

[7]But I, by your great mercy,
will come into your house;
in reverence will I bow down
toward your holy temple.
[8]Lead me, O Lord, in your
righteousness
because of my enemies—
make straight your way before me.

[9]Not a word from their mouth can be
trusted;
their heart is filled with
destruction.
Their throat is an open grave;
with their tongue they speak deceit.
[10]Declare them guilty, O God!
Let their intrigues be their
downfall.
Banish them for their many sins,
for they have rebelled against you.

[11]But let all who take refuge in you be
glad;
let them ever sing for joy.
Spread your protection over them,
that those who love your name may
rejoice in you.
[12]For surely, O Lord, you bless the
righteous;
you surround them with your favor
as with a shield.

Psalm 6

*For the director of music. With stringed
instruments. According to* sheminith. [a]
A psalm of David.

[1]O Lord, do not rebuke me in your
anger
or discipline me in your wrath.
[2]Be merciful to me, Lord, for I am
faint;
O Lord, heal me, for my bones are
in agony.
[3]My soul is in anguish.
How long, O Lord, how long?

[4]Turn, O Lord, and deliver me;
save me because of your unfailing
love.
[5]No one remembers you when he is
dead.
Who praises you from the grave[b]?

[6]I am worn out from groaning;
all night long I flood my bed with
weeping
and drench my couch with tears.
[7]My eyes grow weak with sorrow;
they fail because of all my foes.

[8]Away from me, all you who do evil,
for the Lord has heard my weeping.
[9]The Lord has heard my cry for mercy;
the Lord accepts my prayer.
[10]All my enemies will be ashamed and
dismayed;
they will turn back in sudden
disgrace.

Psalm 7

A shiggaion[c] *of David, which he sang to
the Lord concerning Cush, a Benjamite.*

[1]O Lord my God, I take refuge in you;
save and deliver me from all who
pursue me,
[2]or they will tear me like a lion
and rip me to pieces with no one to
rescue me.

[3]O Lord my God, if I have done this
and there is guilt on my hands—
[4]if I have done evil to him who is at
peace with me
or without cause have robbed my
foe—
[5]then let my enemy pursue and
overtake me;
let him trample my life to the
ground

---

[a]Title: Probably a musical term   [b]5 Hebrew *Sheol*   [c]Title: Probably a literary or musical term

and make me sleep in the dust.
Selah

⁶Arise, O Lord, in your anger;
rise up against the rage of my
enemies.
Awake, my God; decree justice.
⁷Let the assembled peoples gather
around you.
Rule over them from on high;
⁸ let the Lord judge the peoples.
Judge me, O Lord, according to my
righteousness,
according to my integrity, O Most
High.
⁹O righteous God,
who searches minds and hearts,
bring to an end the violence of the
wicked
and make the righteous secure.

¹⁰My shield*ᵃ* is God Most High,
who saves the upright in heart.
¹¹God is a righteous judge,
a God who expresses his wrath
every day.
¹²If he does not relent,
he*ᵇ* will sharpen his sword;
he will bend and string his bow.
¹³He has prepared his deadly weapons;
he makes ready his flaming arrows.

¹⁴He who is pregnant with evil
and conceives trouble gives birth to
disillusionment.
¹⁵He who digs a hole and scoops it out
falls into the pit he has made.
¹⁶The trouble he causes recoils on
himself;
his violence comes down on his
own head.

¹⁷I will give thanks to the Lord because
of his righteousness
and will sing praise to the name of
the Lord Most High.

Psalm 8

For the director of music. According to
gittith.ᶜ A psalm of David.

¹O Lord, our Lord,
how majestic is your name in all
the earth!

You have set your glory
above the heavens.

²From the lips of children and infants
you have ordained praise*ᵈ*
because of your enemies,
to silence the foe and the avenger.

³When I consider your heavens,
the work of your fingers,
the moon and the stars,
which you have set in place,
⁴what is man that you are mindful of
him,
the son of man that you care for
him?
⁵You made him a little lower than the
heavenly beings*ᵉ*
and crowned him with glory and
honor.

⁶You made him ruler over the works of
your hands;
you put everything under his feet:
⁷all flocks and herds,
and the beasts of the field,
⁸the birds of the air,
and the fish of the sea,
all that swim the paths of the seas.

⁹O Lord, our Lord,
how majestic is your name in all
the earth!

Psalm 9*ᶠ*

For the director of music. To the tune
of, "The Death of the Son." A psalm
of David.

¹I will praise you, O Lord, with all my
heart;
I will tell of all your wonders.
²I will be glad and rejoice in you;
I will sing praise to your name,
O Most High.

³My enemies turn back;
they stumble and perish before you.
⁴For you have upheld my right and my
cause;
you have sat on your throne,
judging righteously.
⁵You have rebuked the nations and
destroyed the wicked;
you have blotted out their name for
ever and ever.
⁶Endless ruin has overtaken the
enemy,

ᵃ10 Or *sovereign*   *ᵇ12* Or *If a man does not repent, / God*   *ᶜTitle:* Probably a musical term   *ᵈ2* Or *strength*   *ᵉ5* Or *than God*   *ᶠPsalms* 9 and 10 may have been originally a single acrostic poem, the stanzas of which begin with the successive letters of the Hebrew alphabet. In the Septuagint they constitute one psalm.

VERSE FOR THE DAY:	AUTHOR:	PASSAGE FOR THE DAY:
Psalm 8:1	Debbie Smith	Psalm 8:1–9

How Majestic Is Your Name

MICHAEL and I fell in love and into marriage almost before we knew what happened! We both considered ourselves rational, logical twenty-three-year-olds; but within three weeks of laying eyes on each other, we were engaged. Five months later, after many hours of prayer and counsel, we made our life commitment—to get to know each other!

Part of getting acquainted included writing songs together. God had planned that in advance, because it had never crossed my mind that I would marry a musician, much less write songs with him! Early in our marriage, we spent some of our favorite moments in the evenings at the piano, a kerosene lamp flickering and the Bible opened to the Psalms.

One evening we turned to Psalm 8. What an expression of joy from a man who understood the majesty of creation . . . and that God had entrusted man to rule over it! Furthermore, the psalmist David affirms our worth in this psalm. No room for poor self-image here!

Michael began searching for a tune to the Scriptural line:

> O LORD, our Lord,
> how majestic is your name in all the earth!
> (Psalm 8:1).

Fingers busy on the keyboard, he stopped, midmelody. Turning to me, he pointed to a large, framed poster hanging in our den. It lists all the names of Jesus found in the Bible. Reading down the list, my husband chose a few that fit the tune, and the song "How Majestic Is Your Name" was born!

> O Lord our Lord, how majestic is your name
> in all the earth.
> O Lord our Lord, how majestic is your name
> in all the earth.
> O Lord, we praise your name.
> O Lord, we magnify your name . . .
> Prince of Peace, Mighty God, O Lord God
> Almighty!*

Michael and I discovered that not only did our musical collaboration bring us closer together, it also brought us closer to our majestic God.

Additional Scripture Readings:
Ephesians 5:19–20; Philippians 2:9–11

Go to page 414 for your next devotional reading.

you have uprooted their cities;
even the memory of them has
    perished.

⁷The Lord reigns forever;
he has established his throne for
    judgment.
⁸He will judge the world in
    righteousness;
he will govern the peoples with
    justice.
⁹The Lord is a refuge for the
    oppressed,
a stronghold in times of trouble.
¹⁰Those who know your name will trust
    in you,
for you, Lord, have never forsaken
    those who seek you.

¹¹Sing praises to the Lord, enthroned in
    Zion;
proclaim among the nations what
    he has done.
¹²For he who avenges blood remembers;
he does not ignore the cry of the
    afflicted.

¹³O Lord, see how my enemies
    persecute me!
Have mercy and lift me up from the
    gates of death,
¹⁴that I may declare your praises
in the gates of the Daughter of
    Zion
and there rejoice in your salvation.
¹⁵The nations have fallen into the pit
    they have dug;
their feet are caught in the net they
    have hidden.
¹⁶The Lord is known by his justice;
the wicked are ensnared by the
    work of their hands. *Higgaion.* ᵃ
                                    Selah
¹⁷The wicked return to the grave,ᵇ
all the nations that forget
    God.
¹⁸But the needy will not always be
    forgotten,
nor the hope of the afflicted ever
    perish.

¹⁹Arise, O Lord, let not man triumph;
let the nations be judged in your
    presence.
²⁰Strike them with terror, O Lord;
let the nations know they are but
    men.   *Selah*

Psalm 10ᶜ

¹Why, O Lord, do you stand far off?
Why do you hide yourself in times
    of trouble?

²In his arrogance the wicked man
    hunts down the weak,
who are caught in the schemes he
    devises.
³He boasts of the cravings of his heart;
he blesses the greedy and reviles
    the Lord.
⁴In his pride the wicked does not seek
    him;
in all his thoughts there is no room
    for God.
⁵His ways are always prosperous;
he is haughty and your laws are far
    from him;
he sneers at all his enemies.
⁶He says to himself, "Nothing will
    shake me;
I'll always be happy and never have
    trouble."
⁷His mouth is full of curses and lies
    and threats;
trouble and evil are under his
    tongue.
⁸He lies in wait near the villages;
from ambush he murders the
    innocent,
watching in secret for his victims.
⁹He lies in wait like a lion in cover;
he lies in wait to catch the
    helpless;
he catches the helpless and drags
    them off in his net.
¹⁰His victims are crushed, they
    collapse;
they fall under his strength.
¹¹He says to himself, "God has
    forgotten;
he covers his face and never sees."

¹²Arise, Lord! Lift up your hand, O God.
Do not forget the helpless.
¹³Why does the wicked man revile
    God?
Why does he say to himself,
    "He won't call me to account"?
¹⁴But you, O God, do see trouble and
    grief;
you consider it to take it in hand.
The victim commits himself to you;
you are the helper of the fatherless.

ᵃ16 Or *Meditation*; possibly a musical notation   ᵇ17 Hebrew *Sheol*   ᶜPsalms 9 and 10 may have
been originally a single acrostic poem, the stanzas of which begin with the successive letters of the
Hebrew alphabet. In the Septuagint they constitute one psalm.

¹⁵Break the arm of the wicked and evil
   man;
   call him to account for his
      wickedness
   that would not be found out.

¹⁶The Lord is King for ever and ever;
   the nations will perish from his
      land.
¹⁷You hear, O Lord, the desire of the
      afflicted;
   you encourage them, and you listen
      to their cry,
¹⁸defending the fatherless and the
      oppressed,
   in order that man, who is of the
      earth, may terrify no more.

Psalm 11

For the director of music. Of David.

¹In the Lord I take refuge.
   How then can you say to me:
   "Flee like a bird to your mountain.
²For look, the wicked bend their bows;
   they set their arrows against the
      strings
 to shoot from the shadows
   at the upright in heart.
³When the foundations are being
      destroyed,
   what can the righteous do*ᵃ*?"

⁴The Lord is in his holy temple;
   the Lord is on his heavenly throne.
 He observes the sons of men;
   his eyes examine them.
⁵The Lord examines the righteous,
   but the wicked*ᵇ* and those who
      love violence
   his soul hates.
⁶On the wicked he will rain
   fiery coals and burning sulfur;
   a scorching wind will be their
      lot.

⁷For the Lord is righteous,
   he loves justice;
   upright men will see his face.

Psalm 12

For the director of music. According to
sheminith. *ᶜ* A psalm of David.

¹Help, Lord, for the godly are no more;
   the faithful have vanished from
      among men.

²Everyone lies to his neighbor;
   their flattering lips speak with
      deception.
³May the Lord cut off all flattering lips
   and every boastful tongue
⁴that says, "We will triumph with our
      tongues;
   we own our lips*ᵈ*—who is our
      master?"

⁵"Because of the oppression of the
      weak
   and the groaning of the needy,
 I will now arise," says the Lord.
   "I will protect them from those who
      malign them."
⁶And the words of the Lord are
      flawless,
   like silver refined in a furnace of
      clay,
   purified seven times.

⁷O Lord, you will keep us safe
   and protect us from such people
      forever.
⁸The wicked freely strut about
   when what is vile is honored among
      men.

Psalm 13

For the director of music. A psalm
of David.

¹How long, O Lord? Will you forget me
      forever?
   How long will you hide your face
      from me?
²How long must I wrestle with my
      thoughts
   and every day have sorrow in my
      heart?
   How long will my enemy triumph
      over me?

³Look on me and answer, O Lord my
      God.
   Give light to my eyes, or I will
      sleep in death;
⁴my enemy will say, "I have overcome
      him,"
   and my foes will rejoice when
      I fall.

⁵But I trust in your unfailing love;
   my heart rejoices in your salvation.
⁶I will sing to the Lord,
   for he has been good to me.

ᵃ3 Or *what is the Righteous One doing*   *ᵇ5* Or *The Lord, the Righteous One, examines the wicked, /*
*ᶜ*Title: Probably a musical term   *ᵈ4* Or */ our lips are our plowshares*

Psalm 14

For the director of music. Of David.

¹The fool[a] says in his heart,
  "There is no God."
They are corrupt, their deeds are vile;
  there is no one who does good.

²The LORD looks down from heaven
  on the sons of men
to see if there are any who
    understand,
  any who seek God.

³All have turned aside,
  they have together become corrupt;
there is no one who does good,
  not even one.

⁴Will evildoers never learn—
  those who devour my people as
    men eat bread
and who do not call on the LORD?
⁵There they are, overwhelmed with
    dread,

for God is present in the company
  of the righteous.
⁶You evildoers frustrate the plans of
    the poor,
  but the LORD is their refuge.

⁷Oh, that salvation for Israel would
    come out of Zion!
When the LORD restores the
    fortunes of his people,
  let Jacob rejoice and Israel be glad!

Psalm 15

A psalm of David.

¹LORD, who may dwell in your
    sanctuary?
  Who may live on your holy hill?

²He whose walk is blameless
  and who does what is righteous,
  who speaks the truth from his heart
³ and has no slander on his tongue,
  who does his neighbor no wrong

a1 The Hebrew words rendered *fool* in Psalms denote one who is morally deficient.

TUESDAY

| VERSE FOR THE DAY: | AUTHOR: | PASSAGE FOR THE DAY: |
| Psalm 14:1 | Ruth Bell Graham | Psalm 14:1–7 |

The Fools

"THE fool says in his heart, 'There is no God.' " This designa-
tion goes for those who doubt God's sovereignty as well as those
who deny Him. Either He is sovereign, or He is not God. Therefore, when we become so preoccupied with and dismayed by circumstances and certain people that we doubt God's ability to
handle things in His own way, and in His own time, then we,
too, are fools.

Additional Scripture Readings: Go to page 419 for your next
1 Kings 19:1–18; Luke 24:17–25   devotional reading.

and casts no slur on his fellowman,
[4]who despises a vile man
  but honors those who fear the LORD,
who keeps his oath
  even when it hurts,
[5]who lends his money without usury
  and does not accept a bribe against
    the innocent.

He who does these things
  will never be shaken.

Psalm 16

A miktam [a] of David.

[1]Keep me safe, O God,
  for in you I take refuge.

[2]I said to the LORD, "You are my Lord;
  apart from you I have no good
    thing." ·
[3]As for the saints who are in the land,
  they are the glorious ones in whom
    is all my delight. [b]
[4]The sorrows of those will increase
  who run after other gods.
I will not pour out their libations of
    blood
  or take up their names on my lips.

[5]LORD, you have assigned me my
    portion and my cup;
  you have made my lot secure.
[6]The boundary lines have fallen for me
    in pleasant places;
  surely I have a delightful
    inheritance.

[7]I will praise the LORD, who counsels
    me;
  even at night my heart instructs
    me.
[8]I have set the LORD always before me.
  Because he is at my right hand,
  I will not be shaken.

[9]Therefore my heart is glad and my
    tongue rejoices;
  my body also will rest secure,
[10]because you will not abandon me to
    the grave, [c]
  nor will you let your Holy One [d] see
    decay.
[11]You have made [e] known to me the
    path of life;
  you will fill me with joy in your
    presence,

with eternal pleasures at your right
    hand.

Psalm 17

A prayer of David.

[1]Hear, O LORD, my righteous plea;
  listen to my cry.
Give ear to my prayer—
  it does not rise from deceitful lips.
[2]May my vindication come from you;
  may your eyes see what is right.

[3]Though you probe my heart and
    examine me at night,
  though you test me, you will find
    nothing;
  I have resolved that my mouth will
    not sin.
[4]As for the deeds of men—
  by the word of your lips
I have kept myself
  from the ways of the violent. [b]
[5]My steps have held to your paths;
  my feet have not slipped.

[6]I call on you, O God, for you will
    answer me;
  give ear to me and hear my prayer.
[7]Show the wonder of your great love,
  you who save by your right hand
  those who take refuge in you from
    their foes.
[8]Keep me as the apple of your eye;
  hide me in the shadow of your
    wings
[9]from the wicked who assail me,
  from my mortal enemies who
    surround me.

[10]They close up their callous hearts,
  and their mouths speak with
    arrogance.
[11]They have tracked me down, they
    now surround me,
  with eyes alert, to throw me to the
    ground.
[12]They are like a lion hungry for prey,
  like a great lion crouching in cover.

[13]Rise up, O LORD, confront them, bring
    them down;
  rescue me from the wicked by your
    sword.
[14]O LORD, by your hand save me from
    such men,

---

[a]Title: Probably a literary or musical term   [b]3 Or *As for the pagan priests who are in the land / and the nobles in whom all delight, I said:*   [c]10 Hebrew *Sheol*   [d]10 Or *your faithful one*   [e]11 Or *You will make*

from men of this world whose
reward is in this life.

You still the hunger of those you
cherish;
their sons have plenty,
and they store up wealth for their
children.
¹⁵And I—in righteousness I will see
your face;
when I awake, I will be satisfied
with seeing your likeness.

Psalm 18

For the director of music. Of David the
servant of the LORD. He sang to the LORD
the words of this song when the LORD
delivered him from the hand of all
his enemies and from the hand
of Saul. He said:

¹I love you, O LORD, my strength.

²The LORD is my rock, my fortress and
my deliverer;
my God is my rock, in whom I take
refuge.
He is my shield and the hornᵃ of
my salvation, my stronghold.
³I call to the LORD, who is worthy of
praise,
and I am saved from my enemies.

⁴The cords of death entangled me;
the torrents of destruction
overwhelmed me.
⁵The cords of the graveᵇ coiled around
me;
the snares of death confronted me.
⁶In my distress I called to the LORD;
I cried to my God for help.
From his temple he heard my voice;
my cry came before him, into his
ears.

⁷The earth trembled and quaked,
and the foundations of the
mountains shook;
they trembled because he was
angry.
⁸Smoke rose from his nostrils;
consuming fire came from his
mouth,
burning coals blazed out of it.
⁹He parted the heavens and came
down;
dark clouds were under his feet.
¹⁰He mounted the cherubim and flew;

he soared on the wings of the wind.
¹¹He made darkness his covering, his
canopy around him—
the dark rain clouds of the sky.
¹²Out of the brightness of his presence
clouds advanced,
with hailstones and bolts of
lightning.
¹³The LORD thundered from heaven;
the voice of the Most High
resounded.ᶜ
¹⁴He shot his arrows and scattered the
enemies,
great bolts of lightning and routed
them.
¹⁵The valleys of the sea were exposed
and the foundations of the earth
laid bare
at your rebuke, O LORD,
at the blast of breath from your
nostrils.

¹⁶He reached down from on high and
took hold of me;
he drew me out of deep waters.
¹⁷He rescued me from my powerful
enemy,
from my foes, who were too strong
for me.
¹⁸They confronted me in the day of my
disaster,
but the LORD was my support.
¹⁹He brought me out into a spacious
place;
he rescued me because he
delighted in me.

²⁰The LORD has dealt with me according
to my righteousness;
according to the cleanness of my
hands he has rewarded me.
²¹For I have kept the ways of the LORD;
I have not done evil by turning
from my God.
²²All his laws are before me;
I have not turned away from his
decrees.
²³I have been blameless before him
and have kept myself from sin.
²⁴The LORD has rewarded me according
to my righteousness,
according to the cleanness of my
hands in his sight.

²⁵To the faithful you show yourself
faithful,
to the blameless you show yourself
blameless,

ᵃ2 *Horn* here symbolizes strength.   ᵇ5 Hebrew *Sheol*   ᶜ13 Some Hebrew manuscripts and
Septuagint (see also 2 Samuel 22:14); most Hebrew manuscripts *resounded, / amid hailstones and bolts of
lightning*

²⁶to the pure you show yourself pure,
but to the crooked you show
yourself shrewd.
²⁷You save the humble
but bring low those whose eyes are
haughty.
²⁸You, O LORD, keep my lamp burning;
my God turns my darkness into
light.
²⁹With your help I can advance against
a troop^a;
with my God I can scale a wall.

³⁰As for God, his way is perfect;
the word of the LORD is flawless.
He is a shield
for all who take refuge in him.
³¹For who is God besides the LORD?
And who is the Rock except our
God?
³²It is God who arms me with strength
and makes my way perfect.
³³He makes my feet like the feet of a
deer;
he enables me to stand on the
heights.
³⁴He trains my hands for battle;
my arms can bend a bow of bronze.
³⁵You give me your shield of victory,
and your right hand sustains me;
you stoop down to make me great.
³⁶You broaden the path beneath me,
so that my ankles do not turn.

³⁷I pursued my enemies and overtook
them;
I did not turn back till they were
destroyed.
³⁸I crushed them so that they could not
rise;
they fell beneath my feet.
³⁹You armed me with strength for
battle;
you made my adversaries bow at my
feet.
⁴⁰You made my enemies turn their
backs in flight,
and I destroyed my foes.
⁴¹They cried for help, but there was no
one to save them—
to the LORD, but he did not answer.
⁴²I beat them as fine as dust borne on
the wind;
I poured them out like mud in the
streets.

⁴³You have delivered me from the
attacks of the people;

you have made me the head of
nations;
people I did not know are subject
to me.
⁴⁴As soon as they hear me, they obey
me;
foreigners cringe before me.
⁴⁵They all lose heart;
they come trembling from their
strongholds.

⁴⁶The LORD lives! Praise be to my Rock!
Exalted be God my Savior!
⁴⁷He is the God who avenges me,
who subdues nations under me,
⁴⁸ who saves me from my enemies.
You exalted me above my foes;
from violent men you rescued me.
⁴⁹Therefore I will praise you among the
nations, O LORD;
I will sing praises to your name.
⁵⁰He gives his king great victories;
he shows unfailing kindness to his
anointed,
to David and his descendants
forever.

Psalm 19

For the director of music. A psalm
of David.

¹The heavens declare the glory of God;
the skies proclaim the work of his
hands.
²Day after day they pour forth speech;
night after night they display
knowledge.
³There is no speech or language
where their voice is not heard.^b
⁴Their voice^c goes out into all the
earth,
their words to the ends of the
world.

In the heavens he has pitched a tent
for the sun,
⁵ which is like a bridegroom coming
forth from his pavilion,
like a champion rejoicing to run his
course.
⁶It rises at one end of the heavens
and makes its circuit to the other;
nothing is hidden from its heat.

⁷The law of the LORD is perfect,
reviving the soul.
The statutes of the LORD are
trustworthy,

^a29 Or can run through a barricade   ^b3 Or They have no speech, there are no words; / no sound is heard
from them   ^c4 Septuagint, Jerome and Syriac; Hebrew line

making wise the simple.
⁸The precepts of the Lᴏʀᴅ are right,
   giving joy to the heart.
The commands of the Lᴏʀᴅ are
      radiant,
   giving light to the eyes.
⁹The fear of the Lᴏʀᴅ is pure,
   enduring forever.
The ordinances of the Lᴏʀᴅ are sure
   and altogether righteous.
¹⁰They are more precious than gold,
   than much pure gold;
they are sweeter than honey,
   than honey from the comb.
¹¹By them is your servant warned;
   in keeping them there is great
      reward.

¹²Who can discern his errors?
   Forgive my hidden faults.
¹³Keep your servant also from willful
      sins;
   may they not rule over me.
Then will I be blameless,
   innocent of great transgression.

¹⁴May the words of my mouth and the
      meditation of my heart
   be pleasing in your sight,
   O Lᴏʀᴅ, my Rock and my
      Redeemer.

Psalm 20

For the director of music. A psalm
of David.

¹May the Lᴏʀᴅ answer you when you
      are in distress;
   may the name of the God of Jacob
      protect you.
²May he send you help from the
      sanctuary
   and grant you support from Zion.
³May he remember all your sacrifices
   and accept your burnt offerings.
                              Selah
⁴May he give you the desire of your
      heart
   and make all your plans succeed.
⁵We will shout for joy when you are
      victorious
   and will lift up our banners in the
      name of our God.
May the Lᴏʀᴅ grant all your requests.

⁶Now I know that the Lᴏʀᴅ saves his
      anointed;
   he answers him from his holy
      heaven

with the saving power of his right
      hand.
⁷Some trust in chariots and some in
      horses,
   but we trust in the name of the
      Lᴏʀᴅ our God.
⁸They are brought to their knees and
      fall,
   but we rise up and stand firm.

⁹O Lᴏʀᴅ, save the king!
   Answer*ᵃ* us when we call!

Psalm 21

For the director of music. A psalm
of David.

¹O Lᴏʀᴅ, the king rejoices in your
      strength.
   How great is his joy in the victories
      you give!
²You have granted him the desire of
      his heart
   and have not withheld the request
      of his lips.   *Selah*
³You welcomed him with rich blessings
   and placed a crown of pure gold on
      his head.
⁴He asked you for life, and you gave it
      to him—
   length of days, for ever and ever.
⁵Through the victories you gave, his
      glory is great;
   you have bestowed on him splendor
      and majesty.
⁶Surely you have granted him eternal
      blessings
   and made him glad with the joy of
      your presence.
⁷For the king trusts in the Lᴏʀᴅ;
   through the unfailing love of the
      Most High
he will not be shaken.

⁸Your hand will lay hold on all your
      enemies;
   your right hand will seize your foes.
⁹At the time of your appearing
   you will make them like a fiery
      furnace.
In his wrath the Lᴏʀᴅ will swallow
      them up,
   and his fire will consume them.
¹⁰You will destroy their descendants
      from the earth,
   their posterity from mankind.
¹¹Though they plot evil against you

ᵃ9 Or save! / O King, answer

VERSE FOR THE DAY:
Psalm 19:1

AUTHOR:
Gloria Gaither

PASSAGE FOR THE DAY:
Psalm 19:1–14

I Declare

IT was the sun pouring through the kitchen window at 7:00 A.M., for the first time after the long winter, that made me turn to Psalm 19 instead of the chapter in Colossians we had been reading that week to the kids at the breakfast table. I was reading it for the kids, right? So they would focus on the glorious, first sunny morning of early spring.

But as I read, I became overwhelmed with the way this fellow-poet had reached from the circumstances of his life into mine.

The psalm opened with the familiar verse:

> The heavens declare the glory of God;
> the skies proclaim the work of his hands.

The psalmist then moves on to list the all-encompassing, beautiful declarations of God's law. These declarations so powerfully bring into focus what life should be about, so speak to our human frailties, so heal our broken dreams, so reassure our lost confidences, so pinpoint our areas of weakness, that the psalmist literally falls to his knees in repentance.

His error and hidden faults, his smallness and willful sins are all exposed. And more than that, he begins to ask himself, "If we are supposed to be the most articulate of all God's creatures, what are our lives saying? What are we making as the declaration of our days?"

Shamed by the articulate heavens, we hear our own voices praying aloud with the psalmist in repentance and supplication:

> May the words of my mouth and the meditation
> of my heart
> be pleasing in your sight,
> O LORD, my Rock and my Redeemer
> (Psalm 19:14).

The children were very silent as I, overwhelmed by what I had read, sobbed through these final words of the psalm. Then together we prayed, "Jesus, this day let our actions and attitudes be in sync with all creation. May we articulate praise with the moments we are given today. Amen."

(As a result of this experience, Gloria wrote: "Praise You; I Will Praise You," "Anthem," "What Are the Words?" "I'd Say 'I Love You' in a Thousand Ways," and "Hallelu—Hallelujah!")

Additional Scripture Readings:
Proverbs 4:23–27; Matthew 5:14–16

Go to page 421 for your next devotional reading.

and devise wicked schemes, they
cannot succeed;
[12]for you will make them turn their
backs
when you aim at them with drawn
bow.

[13]Be exalted, O Lord, in your strength;
we will sing and praise your might.

Psalm 22

For the director of music. To the tune
of, "The Doe of the Morning." A psalm
of David.

[1]My God, my God, why have you
forsaken me?
Why are you so far from saving me,
so far from the words of my
groaning?
[2]O my God, I cry out by day, but you
do not answer,
by night, and am not silent.

[3]Yet you are enthroned as the Holy
One;
you are the praise of Israel. [a]
[4]In you our fathers put their trust;
they trusted and you delivered
them.
[5]They cried to you and were saved;
in you they trusted and were not
disappointed.

[6]But I am a worm and not a man,
scorned by men and despised by
the people.
[7]All who see me mock me;
they hurl insults, shaking their
heads:
[8]"He trusts in the Lord;
let the Lord rescue him.
Let him deliver him,
since he delights in him."

[9]Yet you brought me out of the womb;
you made me trust in you
even at my mother's breast.
[10]From birth I was cast upon you;
from my mother's womb you have
been my God.
[11]Do not be far from me,
for trouble is near
and there is no one to help.

[12]Many bulls surround me;
strong bulls of Bashan encircle me.
[13]Roaring lions tearing their prey

open their mouths wide against me.
[14]I am poured out like water,
and all my bones are out of joint.
My heart has turned to wax;
it has melted away within me.
[15]My strength is dried up like a
potsherd,
and my tongue sticks to the roof of
my mouth;
you lay me [b] in the dust of death.
[16]Dogs have surrounded me;
a band of evil men has encircled
me,
they have pierced [c] my hands and
my feet.
[17]I can count all my bones;
people stare and gloat over me.
[18]They divide my garments among them
and cast lots for my clothing.

[19]But you, O Lord, be not far off;
O my Strength, come quickly to
help me.
[20]Deliver my life from the sword,
my precious life from the power of
the dogs.
[21]Rescue me from the mouth of the
lions;
save [d] me from the horns of the
wild oxen.

[22]I will declare your name to my
brothers;
in the congregation I will praise
you.
[23]You who fear the Lord, praise him!
All you descendants of Jacob,
honor him!
Revere him, all you descendants of
Israel!
[24]For he has not despised or disdained
the suffering of the afflicted one;
he has not hidden his face from him
but has listened to his cry for help.

[25]From you comes the theme of my
praise in the great assembly;
before those who fear you [e] will I
fulfill my vows.
[26]The poor will eat and be satisfied;
they who seek the Lord will praise
him—
may your hearts live forever!
[27]All the ends of the earth
will remember and turn to the
Lord,
and all the families of the nations
will bow down before him,

---

[a]3 Or Yet you are holy, / enthroned on the praises of Israel   [b]15 Or / I am laid   [c]16 Some Hebrew
manuscripts, Septuagint and Syriac; most Hebrew manuscripts / like the lion,   [d]21 Or / you have heard
[e]25 Hebrew him

VERSE FOR THE DAY:
Psalm 22:11

AUTHOR:
Susan L. Lenzkes

PASSAGE FOR THE DAY:
Psalm 22:1–24

Teen Trouble

SOME days should never be recorded, repeated or remembered.

Take today, for instance. After a morning of upheaval with my daughter, she confided in me that she was in the absolute pits of a mood (she could have saved the trouble of making the announcement). Then she needed my complete attention for the next hour to gripe about everything and anything that has ever touched her nineteen-year-old world. She said she didn't know what's the matter with her lately, and I have a permanent crease across my tongue from resisting the urge to tell her!

She finally left for work, and my number-one son must have thought I'd be lonely for disaster, so he proceeded to erupt. He became incensed over some infraction to his personal sense of justice and shoved a bike at his brother, nearly wiping out his ability to father succeeding generations.

After tending to the offended, I tried to deal with the offender and got a verbal volley that could knock any mother off her Nikes. An impartial jury surely would have labeled it "mother abuse" and given him a few years in solitary.

So in the middle of this—I mean in the very middle of this scene, not knowing whether to laugh or to cry because this five-foot-ten-inch kid is exhibiting every characteristic of the "terrible twos" in outsized triplicate—a man called and asked if he had reached the Lenzkes' residence . . . the Susan L. Lenzkes' residence.

It seems he had discovered my book *When the Handwriting on the Wall Is in Brown Crayon* in, of all places, a doctor's waiting room, and he and his wife were so taken by it that they had headed straight for a bookstore and bought one.

At the bookstore they found out where I live. Then they found my phone number in the directory and called to tell me what a blessing my life was to them! (The Lord's timing is most humbling!)

But, I know that our Lord is faithful. He promised we could pick up snakes with our bare hands and drink deadly poison, and live with teenagers (well, that last addition seems to fit nicely here) and not be hurt at all!

Additional Scripture Readings:
Mark 16:14–18; Philippians 2:1–4

Go to page 426 for your next devotional reading.

28for dominion belongs to the LORD
   and he rules over the nations.

29All the rich of the earth will feast and
      worship;
   all who go down to the dust will
      kneel before him—
   those who cannot keep themselves
      alive.
30Posterity will serve him;
   future generations will be told
      about the Lord.
31They will proclaim his righteousness
   to a people yet unborn—
   for he has done it.

Psalm 23

A psalm of David.

1The LORD is my shepherd, I shall not
   be in want.
2   He makes me lie down in green
      pastures,
   he leads me beside quiet waters,
3   he restores my soul.
   He guides me in paths of
      righteousness
   for his name's sake.
4Even though I walk
   through the valley of the shadow of
      death,*a*
   I will fear no evil,
   for you are with me;
   your rod and your staff,
   they comfort me.

5You prepare a table before me
   in the presence of my enemies.
   You anoint my head with oil;
   my cup overflows.
6Surely goodness and love will follow
      me
   all the days of my life,
   and I will dwell in the house of the
      LORD
   forever.

Psalm 24

Of David. A psalm.

1The earth is the LORD's, and
      everything in it,
   the world, and all who live in it;
2for he founded it upon the seas
   and established it upon the waters.

3Who may ascend the hill of the LORD?
   Who may stand in his holy place?
4He who has clean hands and a pure
      heart,
   who does not lift up his soul to an
      idol
   or swear by what is false.*b*
5He will receive blessing from the LORD
   and vindication from God his
      Savior.
6Such is the generation of those who
      seek him,
   who seek your face, O God of
      Jacob.*c*   *Selah*

7Lift up your heads, O you gates;
   be lifted up, you ancient doors,
   that the King of glory may come in.
8Who is this King of glory?
   The LORD strong and mighty,
   the LORD mighty in battle.
9Lift up your heads, O you gates;
   lift them up, you ancient doors,
   that the King of glory may come in.
10Who is he, this King of glory?
   The LORD Almighty—
   he is the King of glory.   *Selah*

Psalm 25*d*

Of David.

1To you, O LORD, I lift up my soul;
2   in you I trust, O my God.
   Do not let me be put to shame,
   nor let my enemies triumph over
      me.
3No one whose hope is in you
   will ever be put to shame,
   but they will be put to shame
   who are treacherous without
      excuse.

4Show me your ways, O LORD,
   teach me your paths;
5guide me in your truth and teach me,
   for you are God my Savior,
   and my hope is in you all day long.
6Remember, O LORD, your great mercy
      and love,
   for they are from of old.
7Remember not the sins of my youth
   and my rebellious ways;
   according to your love remember me,
   for you are good, O LORD.

8Good and upright is the LORD;

a4 Or *through the darkest valley*   *b4* Or *swear falsely*   *c6* Two Hebrew manuscripts and Syriac (see
also Septuagint); most Hebrew manuscripts *face, Jacob*   *d*This psalm is an acrostic poem, the verses of
which begin with the successive letters of the Hebrew alphabet.

therefore he instructs sinners in his
ways.
9He guides the humble in what is right
and teaches them his way.
10All the ways of the Lord are loving
and faithful
for those who keep the demands of
his covenant.
11For the sake of your name, O Lord,
forgive my iniquity, though it is
great.
12Who, then, is the man that fears the
Lord?
He will instruct him in the way
chosen for him.
13He will spend his days in prosperity,
and his descendants will inherit the
land.
14The Lord confides in those who fear
him;
he makes his covenant known to
them.
15My eyes are ever on the Lord,
for only he will release my feet
from the snare.

16Turn to me and be gracious to me,
for I am lonely and afflicted.
17The troubles of my heart have
multiplied;
free me from my anguish.
18Look upon my affliction and my
distress
and take away all my sins.
19See how my enemies have increased
and how fiercely they hate me!
20Guard my life and rescue me;
let me not be put to shame,
for I take refuge in you.
21May integrity and uprightness protect
me,
because my hope is in you.

22Redeem Israel, O God,
from all their troubles!

Psalm 26

Of David.

1Vindicate me, O Lord,
for I have led a blameless life;
I have trusted in the Lord
without wavering.
2Test me, O Lord, and try me,
examine my heart and my mind;
3for your love is ever before me,
and I walk continually in your
truth.

4I do not sit with deceitful men,
nor do I consort with hypocrites;
5I abhor the assembly of evildoers
and refuse to sit with the wicked.
6I wash my hands in innocence,
and go about your altar, O Lord,
7proclaiming aloud your praise
and telling of all your wonderful
deeds.
8I love the house where you live,
O Lord,
the place where your glory dwells.

9Do not take away my soul along with
sinners,
my life with bloodthirsty men,
10in whose hands are wicked schemes,
whose right hands are full of bribes.
11But I lead a blameless life;
redeem me and be merciful to me.

12My feet stand on level ground;
in the great assembly I will praise
the Lord.

Psalm 27

Of David.

1The Lord is my light and my
salvation—
whom shall I fear?
The Lord is the stronghold of my
life—
of whom shall I be afraid?
2When evil men advance against me
to devour my flesh,a
when my enemies and my foes attack
me,
they will stumble and fall.
3Though an army besiege me,
my heart will not fear;
though war break out against me,
even then will I be confident.

4One thing I ask of the Lord,
this is what I seek:
that I may dwell in the house of the
Lord
all the days of my life,
to gaze upon the beauty of the Lord
and to seek him in his temple.
5For in the day of trouble
he will keep me safe in his
dwelling;
he will hide me in the shelter of his
tabernacle
and set me high upon a rock.
6Then my head will be exalted

a2 Or to slander me

above the enemies who surround
  me;
at his tabernacle will I sacrifice with
  shouts of joy;
  I will sing and make music to the
    LORD.

[7]Hear my voice when I call, O LORD;
  be merciful to me and answer me.
[8]My heart says of you, "Seek his[a]
  face!"
  Your face, LORD, I will seek.
[9]Do not hide your face from me,
  do not turn your servant away in
    anger;
  you have been my helper.
Do not reject me or forsake me,
  O God my Savior.
[10]Though my father and mother forsake
  me,
  the LORD will receive me.
[11]Teach me your way, O LORD;
  lead me in a straight path
  because of my oppressors.
[12]Do not turn me over to the desire of
  my foes,
  for false witnesses rise up against
    me,
  breathing out violence.

[13]I am still confident of this:
  I will see the goodness of the LORD
  in the land of the living.
[14]Wait for the LORD;
  be strong and take heart
  and wait for the LORD.

Psalm 28

Of David.

[1]To you I call, O LORD my Rock;
  do not turn a deaf ear to me.
For if you remain silent,
  I will be like those who have gone
    down to the pit.
[2]Hear my cry for mercy
  as I call to you for help,
as I lift up my hands
  toward your Most Holy Place.

[3]Do not drag me away with the
  wicked,
  with those who do evil,
who speak cordially with their
  neighbors
  but harbor malice in their hearts.
[4]Repay them for their deeds
  and for their evil work;

repay them for what their hands have
  done
  and bring back upon them what
    they deserve.
[5]Since they show no regard for the
  works of the LORD
  and what his hands have done,
he will tear them down
  and never build them up again.

[6]Praise be to the LORD,
  for he has heard my cry for mercy.
[7]The LORD is my strength and my
  shield;
  my heart trusts in him, and I am
    helped.
My heart leaps for joy
  and I will give thanks to him in
    song.

[8]The LORD is the strength of his
  people,
  a fortress of salvation for his
    anointed one.
[9]Save your people and bless your
  inheritance;
  be their shepherd and carry them
    forever.

Psalm 29

A psalm of David.

[1]Ascribe to the LORD, O mighty ones,
  ascribe to the LORD glory and
    strength.
[2]Ascribe to the LORD the glory due his
  name;
  worship the LORD in the splendor of
    his[b] holiness.

[3]The voice of the LORD is over the
  waters;
  the God of glory thunders,
  the LORD thunders over the mighty
    waters.
[4]The voice of the LORD is powerful;
  the voice of the LORD is majestic.
[5]The voice of the LORD breaks the
  cedars;
  the LORD breaks in pieces the
    cedars of Lebanon.
[6]He makes Lebanon skip like a calf,
  Sirion[c] like a young wild ox.
[7]The voice of the LORD strikes
  with flashes of lightning.
[8]The voice of the LORD shakes the
  desert;

---

[a]8 Or To you, O my heart, he has said, "Seek my   [b]2 Or LORD with the splendor of   [c]6 That is,
Mount Hermon

the LORD shakes the Desert of
      Kadesh.
9The voice of the LORD twists the
      oaks*a*
and strips the forests bare.
And in his temple all cry, "Glory!"

10The LORD sits*b* enthroned over the
      flood;
   the LORD is enthroned as King
      forever.
11The LORD gives strength to his people;
   the LORD blesses his people with
      peace.

Psalm 30

A psalm. A song. For the dedication of
      the temple.*c* Of David.

1I will exalt you, O LORD,
   for you lifted me out of the depths
   and did not let my enemies gloat
      over me.
2O LORD my God, I called to you for
      help
   and you healed me.
3O LORD, you brought me up from the
      grave*d*;
   you spared me from going down
      into the pit.

4Sing to the LORD, you saints of his;
   praise his holy name.
5For his anger lasts only a moment,
   but his favor lasts a lifetime;
weeping may remain for a night,
   but rejoicing comes in the morning.

6When I felt secure, I said,
   "I will never be shaken."
7O LORD, when you favored me,
   you made my mountain*e* stand
      firm;
but when you hid your face,
   I was dismayed.

8To you, O LORD, I called;
   to the Lord I cried for mercy:
9"What gain is there in my
      destruction,*f*
   in my going down into the pit?
Will the dust praise you?
   Will it proclaim your faithfulness?
10Hear, O LORD, and be merciful to me;
   O LORD, be my help."

11You turned my wailing into dancing;
   you removed my sackcloth and
      clothed me with joy,

12that my heart may sing to you and
      not be silent.
O LORD my God, I will give you
      thanks forever.

Psalm 31

For the director of music. A psalm
      of David.

1In you, O LORD, I have taken refuge;
   let me never be put to shame;
   deliver me in your righteousness.
2Turn your ear to me,
   come quickly to my rescue;
be my rock of refuge,
   a strong fortress to save me.
3Since you are my rock and my
      fortress,
   for the sake of your name lead and
      guide me.
4Free me from the trap that is set for
      me,
   for you are my refuge.
5Into your hands I commit my spirit;
   redeem me, O LORD, the God of
      truth.

6I hate those who cling to worthless
      idols;
   I trust in the LORD.
7I will be glad and rejoice in your
      love,
   for you saw my affliction
   and knew the anguish of my soul.
8You have not handed me over to the
      enemy
   but have set my feet in a spacious
      place.

9Be merciful to me, O LORD, for I am
      in distress;
   my eyes grow weak with sorrow,
   my soul and my body with grief.
10My life is consumed by anguish
   and my years by groaning;
my strength fails because of my
      affliction,*g*
   and my bones grow weak.
11Because of all my enemies,
   I am the utter contempt of my
      neighbors;
I am a dread to my friends—
   those who see me on the street flee
      from me.
12I am forgotten by them as though I
      were dead;
   I have become like broken pottery.

---

a9 Or LORD *makes the deer give birth*   *b10* Or *sat*   *c*Title: Or *palace*   *d3* Hebrew *Sheol*   *e7* Or
hill country   *f9* Or *there if I am silenced*   *g10* Or *guilt*

¹³For I hear the slander of many;
    there is terror on every side;
they conspire against me
    and plot to take my life.

¹⁴But I trust in you, O Lord;
    I say, "You are my God."
¹⁵My times are in your hands;
    deliver me from my enemies

and from those who pursue me.
¹⁶Let your face shine on your servant;
    save me in your unfailing love.
¹⁷Let me not be put to shame, O Lord,
    for I have cried out to you;
but let the wicked be put to shame
    and lie silent in the grave.^a
¹⁸Let their lying lips be silenced,
    for with pride and contempt

^a17 Hebrew *Sheol*

FRIDAY

VERSE FOR THE DAY: *AUTHOR:*   *PASSAGE FOR THE DAY:*
Psalm 30:5   Mary Jane Worden   Psalm 30:1–12

Night Weeping

AS I walked past the kitchen bulletin board I glanced, as usual,
at our family picture. I was surprised by the sudden intense
pain, the almost doubling-over kind from those first days of
grief, after my husband Jim's death. Somehow there aren't
enough words (in my vocabulary at least) to describe the great
varieties of pain. Today it was the stomach-turning kind, pro-
ducing that urge to bolt, to run or somehow try to squirm away
from the source of pain. Impossible—like trying to crawl out
from under the labor contractions of childbirth. Agonizing, but
necessary I guess, and (sometimes to my disappointment) sur-
vivable. Just there, and unavoidable, at least for this moment.
Do I need to learn to work with it, sort of "riding" it rather than
fighting it, as they taught us in childbirth classes? Sometimes
the evil behind death peers through, and it seems such a horror.
It makes me wish I were a screamer. Instead the silent tears slip
down my cheeks. Tonight the pain and sadness are specific and
profound, not just the vague weeping of fatigue.

As I read back in my journals I find myself almost relieved to
see the variety of feelings. One big component of the pain is
fear—a fear that this experience of pain may not be momentary
but might settle down on me as a permanent condition, an in-
curable disease, an overwhelming and unmoving cloud cover.
This time it's got me and it may never let me go. I need to keep
reminding myself, in the midst of the pain, that I can acknowledge it and give in to it because it isn't a life sentence.

> Weeping may remain for a night,
>   but rejoicing comes in the morning
>   (Psalm 30:5).

Additional Scripture Readings:
Matthew 5:4; Revelation 21:3–4

*Go to page 428 for your next
devotional reading.*

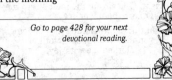

they speak arrogantly against the
righteous.

¹⁹How great is your goodness,
    which you have stored up for those
        who fear you,
    which you bestow in the sight of men
        on those who take refuge in you.
²⁰In the shelter of your presence you
        hide them
    from the intrigues of men;
    in your dwelling you keep them safe
        from accusing tongues.

²¹Praise be to the LORD,
    for he showed his wonderful love to
        me
    when I was in a besieged city.
²²In my alarm I said,
    "I am cut off from your sight!"
    Yet you heard my cry for mercy
        when I called to you for help.

²³Love the LORD, all his saints!
    The LORD preserves the faithful,
    but the proud he pays back in full.
²⁴Be strong and take heart,
    all you who hope in the LORD.

Psalm 32

Of David. A *maskil.* ᵃ

¹Blessed is he
    whose transgressions are forgiven,
    whose sins are covered.
²Blessed is the man
    whose sin the LORD does not count
        against him
    and in whose spirit is no deceit.

³When I kept silent,
    my bones wasted away
    through my groaning all day long.
⁴For day and night
    your hand was heavy upon me;
    my strength was sapped
        as in the heat of summer.   *Selah*
⁵Then I acknowledged my sin to you
    and did not cover up my iniquity.
I said, "I will confess
    my transgressions to the LORD"—
    and you forgave
        the guilt of my sin.   *Selah*

⁶Therefore let everyone who is godly
        pray to you
    while you may be found;
    surely when the mighty waters rise,
        they will not reach him.
⁷You are my hiding place;

you will protect me from trouble
    and surround me with songs of
        deliverance.   *Selah*

⁸I will instruct you and teach you in
        the way you should go;
    I will counsel you and watch over
        you.
⁹Do not be like the horse or the mule,
    which have no understanding
    but must be controlled by bit and
        bridle
    or they will not come to you.
¹⁰Many are the woes of the wicked,
    but the LORD's unfailing love
    surrounds the man who trusts in
        him.

¹¹Rejoice in the LORD and be glad, you
        righteous;
    sing, all you who are upright in
        heart!

Psalm 33

¹Sing joyfully to the LORD, you
        righteous;
    it is fitting for the upright to praise
        him.
²Praise the LORD with the harp;
    make music to him on the
        ten-stringed lyre.
³Sing to him a new song;
    play skillfully, and shout for joy.

⁴For the word of the LORD is right and
        true;
    he is faithful in all he does.
⁵The LORD loves righteousness and
        justice;
    the earth is full of his unfailing
        love.

⁶By the word of the LORD were the
        heavens made,
    their starry host by the breath of
        his mouth.
⁷He gathers the waters of the sea into
        jarsᵇ;
    he puts the deep into storehouses.
⁸Let all the earth fear the LORD;
    let all the people of the world
        revere him.
⁹For he spoke, and it came to be;
    he commanded, and it stood firm.
¹⁰The LORD foils the plans of the
        nations;
    he thwarts the purposes of the
        peoples.

ᵃTitle: Probably a literary or musical term   ᵇ7 Or *sea as into a heap*

WEEKENDING

RELATE

In the late 1800's Mrs. Louisa M.R. Stead watched as her husband died while trying to save a drowning boy. This familiar hymn was written as a response to her struggle with the "why?" questions she asked God during that difficult time.

RESPOND

'Tis so sweet to trust in Jesus,
Just to take Him at His word,
Just to rest upon His promise,
Just to know, "Thus saith the Lord."

I'm so glad I learned to trust Thee,
Precious Jesus, Savior, Friend;
And I know that Thou art with me,
Wilt be with me to the end.

Jesus, Jesus, how I trust Him!
How I've proved Him o'er and o'er!
Jesus, Jesus, precious Jesus!
O for grace to trust Him more!

– Louisa M.R. Stead

REVIVE

Saturday: Psalm 125:1–5
Sunday: John 14:1–4

Go to page 430 for your next devotional reading.

¹¹But the plans of the LORD stand firm
forever,
the purposes of his heart through
all generations.

¹²Blessed is the nation whose God is
the LORD,
the people he chose for his
inheritance.
¹³From heaven the LORD looks down
and sees all mankind;
¹⁴from his dwelling place he watches
all who live on earth—
¹⁵he who forms the hearts of all,
who considers everything they do.
¹⁶No king is saved by the size of his
army;
no warrior escapes by his great
strength.
¹⁷A horse is a vain hope for deliverance;
despite all its great strength it
cannot save.
¹⁸But the eyes of the LORD are on those
who fear him,
on those whose hope is in his
unfailing love,
¹⁹to deliver them from death
and keep them alive in famine.

²⁰We wait in hope for the LORD;
he is our help and our shield.
²¹In him our hearts rejoice,
for we trust in his holy name.
²²May your unfailing love rest upon us,
O LORD,
even as we put our hope in you.

Psalm 34ᵃ

Of David. When he pretended to be
insane before Abimelech, who drove
him away, and he left.

¹I will extol the LORD at all times;
his praise will always be on my lips.
²My soul will boast in the LORD;
let the afflicted hear and rejoice.
³Glorify the LORD with me;
let us exalt his name together.

⁴I sought the LORD, and he answered
me;
he delivered me from all my fears.
⁵Those who look to him are radiant;
their faces are never covered with
shame.
⁶This poor man called, and the LORD
heard him;

he saved him out of all his
troubles.
⁷The angel of the LORD encamps
around those who fear him,
and he delivers them.

⁸Taste and see that the LORD is good;
blessed is the man who takes
refuge in him.
⁹Fear the LORD, you his saints,
for those who fear him lack
nothing.
¹⁰The lions may grow weak and hungry,
but those who seek the LORD lack
no good thing.

¹¹Come, my children, listen to me;
I will teach you the fear of the
LORD.
¹²Whoever of you loves life
and desires to see many good days,
¹³keep your tongue from evil
and your lips from speaking lies.
¹⁴Turn from evil and do good;
seek peace and pursue it.

¹⁵The eyes of the LORD are on the
righteous
and his ears are attentive to their
cry;
¹⁶the face of the LORD is against those
who do evil,
to cut off the memory of them from
the earth.

¹⁷The righteous cry out, and the LORD
hears them;
he delivers them from all their
troubles.
¹⁸The LORD is close to the
brokenhearted
and saves those who are crushed in
spirit.

¹⁹A righteous man may have many
troubles,
but the LORD delivers him from
them all;
²⁰he protects all his bones,
not one of them will be broken.

²¹Evil will slay the wicked;
the foes of the righteous will be
condemned.
²²The LORD redeems his servants;
no one will be condemned who
takes refuge in him.

ᵃThis psalm is an acrostic poem, the verses of which begin with the successive letters of the Hebrew
alphabet.

Psalm 35

Of David.

¹Contend, O Lᴏʀᴅ, with those who
contend with me;
fight against those who fight
against me.
²Take up shield and buckler;

arise and come to my aid.
³Brandish spear and javelin*a*
against those who pursue me.
Say to my soul,
"I am your salvation."

⁴May those who seek my life
be disgraced and put to shame;
may those who plot my ruin

a3 Or and block the way

MONDAY

VERSE FOR THE DAY:
Psalm 34:6

AUTHOR:
Wanda K. Jones

PASSAGE FOR THE DAY:
Psalm 34:1–22

The Lord Hears

PSALM 34 has been a source of strength and encouragement
ever since I drank from the "living waters" of eternal salvation in
Jesus Christ. Praising, glorifying and honoring the Lord as David
did has proven to be a great blessing even in extremely difficult
circumstances.

As a young Christian in college I was often on my knees asking
the Lord to help with college fees and even incidentals—stock-
ings, underwear, notebook paper and a warm scarf. The wonderful thing was that when I sought him in prayer, he answered!

The main building on our college campus was perched on a
hill overlooking the Hudson River. The setting was beautiful.
Maneuvering was more difficult. It was easy going when we
walked down into the town but coming back was the struggle.
Groups of students often stopped along the way to rest.

I learned and quoted Psalm 34 on those walks up the hillside.
I had no problem with verse 6:

> This poor man called, and the Lᴏʀᴅ heard him;
> he saved him out of all his troubles.

I knew then, as I know now, that anyone—man, woman,
young, old, rich, poor, black or white—can call on the Lord, and
he will answer and meet the need.

If you have been going through a difficult period in your life, if
you have been crushed by some unkind deed, or if you have lost
a loved one and are feeling the pangs of loneliness, remember:
the psalmist said that "the Lᴏʀᴅ is close to the brokenhearted"
(Psalm 34:18).

Why not take refuge in him?

Additional Scripture Readings:
Isaiah 41:17–20; 2 Thessalonians 2:11–12

Go to page 433 for your next
devotional reading.

be turned back in dismay.
⁵May they be like chaff before the
wind,
with the angel of the LORD driving
them away;
⁶may their path be dark and slippery,
with the angel of the LORD pursuing
them.
⁷Since they hid their net for me
without cause
and without cause dug a pit for me,
⁸may ruin overtake them by surprise—
may the net they hid entangle
them,
may they fall into the pit, to their
ruin.
⁹Then my soul will rejoice in the LORD
and delight in his salvation.
¹⁰My whole being will exclaim,
"Who is like you, O LORD?
You rescue the poor from those too
strong for them,
the poor and needy from those who
rob them."

¹¹Ruthless witnesses come forward;
they question me on things I know
nothing about.
¹²They repay me evil for good
and leave my soul forlorn.
¹³Yet when they were ill, I put on
sackcloth
and humbled myself with fasting.
When my prayers returned to me
unanswered,
¹⁴ I went about mourning
as though for my friend or brother.
I bowed my head in grief
as though weeping for my mother.
¹⁵But when I stumbled, they gathered
in glee;
attackers gathered against me when
I was unaware.
They slandered me without ceasing.
¹⁶Like the ungodly they maliciously
mocked*ᵃ*;
they gnashed their teeth at me.
¹⁷O Lord, how long will you look on?
Rescue my life from their ravages,
my precious life from these lions.
¹⁸I will give you thanks in the great
assembly;
among throngs of people I will
praise you.

¹⁹Let not those gloat over me
who are my enemies without
cause;

let not those who hate me without
reason
maliciously wink the eye.
²⁰They do not speak peaceably,
but devise false accusations
against those who live quietly in
the land.
²¹They gape at me and say, "Aha! Aha!
With our own eyes we have seen
it."

²²O LORD, you have seen this; be not
silent.
Do not be far from me, O Lord.
²³Awake, and rise to my defense!
Contend for me, my God and Lord.
²⁴Vindicate me in your righteousness,
O LORD my God;
do not let them gloat over me.
²⁵Do not let them think, "Aha, just
what we wanted!"
or say, "We have swallowed him
up."

²⁶May all who gloat over my distress
be put to shame and confusion;
may all who exalt themselves over me
be clothed with shame and
disgrace.
²⁷May those who delight in my
vindication
shout for joy and gladness;
may they always say, "The LORD be
exalted,
who delights in the well-being of
his servant."
²⁸My tongue will speak of your
righteousness
and of your praises all day long.

Psalm 36

For the director of music. Of David the
servant of the LORD.

¹An oracle is within my heart
concerning the sinfulness of the
wicked:*ᵇ*
There is no fear of God
before his eyes.
²For in his own eyes he flatters
himself
too much to detect or hate his sin.
³The words of his mouth are wicked
and deceitful;
he has ceased to be wise and to do
good.
⁴Even on his bed he plots evil;

ᵃ16 Septuagint; Hebrew may mean *ungodly circle of mockers.*   ᵇ1 Or *heart: / Sin proceeds from the*
wicked.

he commits himself to a sinful
course
and does not reject what is wrong.

⁵Your love, O LORD, reaches to the
heavens,
your faithfulness to the skies.
⁶Your righteousness is like the mighty
mountains,
your justice like the great deep.
O LORD, you preserve both man and
beast.
⁷   How priceless is your unfailing love!
Both high and low among men
find*a* refuge in the shadow of your
wings.
⁸They feast on the abundance of your
house;
you give them drink from your river
of delights.
⁹For with you is the fountain of life;
in your light we see light.

¹⁰Continue your love to those who
know you,
your righteousness to the upright in
heart.
¹¹May the foot of the proud not come
against me,
nor the hand of the wicked drive
me away.
¹²See how the evildoers lie fallen—
thrown down, not able to rise!

Psalm 37*b*

Of David.

¹Do not fret because of evil men
or be envious of those who do
wrong;
²for like the grass they will soon
wither,
like green plants they will soon die
away.

³Trust in the LORD and do good;
dwell in the land and enjoy safe
pasture.
⁴Delight yourself in the LORD
and he will give you the desires of
your heart.

⁵Commit your way to the LORD;
trust in him and he will do this:
⁶He will make your righteousness
shine like the dawn,
the justice of your cause like the
noonday sun.

⁷Be still before the LORD and wait
patiently for him;
do not fret when men succeed in
their ways,
when they carry out their wicked
schemes.

⁸Refrain from anger and turn from
wrath;
do not fret—it leads only to evil.
⁹For evil men will be cut off,
but those who hope in the LORD
will inherit the land.

¹⁰A little while, and the wicked will be
no more;
though you look for them, they will
not be found.
¹¹But the meek will inherit the land
and enjoy great peace.

¹²The wicked plot against the righteous
and gnash their teeth at them;
¹³but the Lord laughs at the wicked,
for he knows their day is coming.

¹⁴The wicked draw the sword
and bend the bow
to bring down the poor and needy,
to slay those whose ways are
upright.
¹⁵But their swords will pierce their own
hearts,
and their bows will be broken.

¹⁶Better the little that the righteous
have
than the wealth of many wicked;
¹⁷for the power of the wicked will be
broken,
but the LORD upholds the righteous.

¹⁸The days of the blameless are known
to the LORD,
and their inheritance will endure
forever.
¹⁹In times of disaster they will not
wither;
in days of famine they will enjoy
plenty.

²⁰But the wicked will perish:
The LORD's enemies will be like the
beauty of the fields,
they will vanish—vanish like
smoke.

²¹The wicked borrow and do not repay,
but the righteous give generously;
²²those the LORD blesses will inherit the
land,

a7 Or *love, O God! / Men find*; or *love! / Both heavenly beings and men / find*   *b*This psalm is an acrostic
poem, the stanzas of which begin with the successive letters of the Hebrew alphabet.

VERSE FOR THE DAY:
Psalm 37:5

AUTHOR:
Ruth Bell Graham

PASSAGE FOR THE DAY:
Psalm 37:1–7

Commit to God

THE Amplified Bible pictures us committing our load to God by rolling it onto Him. It is helpful to note that we can roll something that is too heavy to carry or to cast.

What are we to commit—to trust—to God?

Ourselves. Psalm 22:8:

> He trusts in the LORD;
>   let the LORD rescue him.
> Let him deliver him, since he delights in him.

Our Burden. Psalm 55:22:

> Cast your cares on the LORD
>   and he will sustain you;
>   he will never let the righteous fall.

Our Souls. 1 Peter 4:19:

So then, those who suffer according to God's will should commit themselves to their faithful Creator and continue to do good.

Our Way. Psalm 37:5:

> Commit your way to the LORD;
>   trust in him.

Our Cause. 1 Peter 2:23:

When they hurled their insults at him, he did not retaliate; when he suffered, he made no threats. Instead, he entrusted himself to him who judges justly.

Our Works. Proverbs 16:3:

> Commit to the LORD whatever you do,
>   and your plans will succeed.

Additional Scripture Readings:
1 Samuel 7:2–4; Acts 14:23–26

Go to page 434 for your next
devotional reading.

but those he curses will be cut
off.

²³If the LORD delights in a man's
way,
he makes his steps firm;
²⁴though he stumble, he will not fall,
for the LORD upholds him with his
hand.

²⁵I was young and now I am old,
yet I have never seen the righteous
forsaken
or their children begging bread.
²⁶They are always generous and lend
freely;
their children will be blessed.

²⁷Turn from evil and do good;
then you will dwell in the land
forever.
²⁸For the LORD loves the just
and will not forsake his faithful
ones.

They will be protected forever,
but the offspring of the wicked will
be cut off;

²⁹the righteous will inherit the land
and dwell in it forever.

³⁰The mouth of the righteous man
utters wisdom,
and his tongue speaks what is just.
³¹The law of his God is in his heart;
his feet do not slip.

³²The wicked lie in wait for the
righteous,
seeking their very lives;
³³but the LORD will not leave them in
their power
or let them be condemned when
brought to trial.

³⁴Wait for the LORD
and keep his way.
He will exalt you to inherit the land;
when the wicked are cut off, you
will see it.

³⁵I have seen a wicked and ruthless
man
flourishing like a green tree in its
native soil,

WEDNESDAY

VERSE FOR THE DAY:	AUTHOR:	PASSAGE FOR THE DAY:
Psalm 37:12–13	Ruth Bell Graham	Psalm 37:10–17

Don't Fret

WHEN "the wicked plot . . . the LORD laughs" (also see Psalm
2:4).
When he prospers, don't fret (Psalm 39:6–7).
When he persecutes:

Rejoice and be glad (Matthew 5:12).
Love your enemies (Matthew 5:44).
Bless them (Romans 12:14).
Do good to them (Luke 6:27).
Pray for them (Matthew 5:44).

Additional Scripture Readings:
Genesis 50:15–20; Psalm 73:2,21–24

*Go to page 440 for your next
devotional reading.*

³⁶but he soon passed away and was no
more;
though I looked for him, he could
not be found.

³⁷Consider the blameless, observe the
upright;
there is a future*ᵃ* for the man of
peace.
³⁸But all sinners will be destroyed;
the future*ᵇ* of the wicked will be
cut off.

³⁹The salvation of the righteous comes
from the Lᴏʀᴅ;
he is their stronghold in time of
trouble.
⁴⁰The Lᴏʀᴅ helps them and delivers
them;
he delivers them from the wicked
and saves them,
because they take refuge in him.

Psalm 38

A psalm of David. A petition.

¹O Lᴏʀᴅ, do not rebuke me in your
anger
or discipline me in your wrath.
²For your arrows have pierced me,
and your hand has come down
upon me.
³Because of your wrath there is no
health in my body;
my bones have no soundness
because of my sin.
⁴My guilt has overwhelmed me
like a burden too heavy to bear.

⁵My wounds fester and are loathsome
because of my sinful folly.
⁶I am bowed down and brought very
low;
all day long I go about mourning.
⁷My back is filled with searing pain;
there is no health in my body.
⁸I am feeble and utterly crushed;
I groan in anguish of heart.

⁹All my longings lie open before you,
O Lᴏʀᴅ;
my sighing is not hidden from you.
¹⁰My heart pounds, my strength fails
me;
even the light has gone from my
eyes.
¹¹My friends and companions avoid me
because of my wounds;
my neighbors stay far away.

¹²Those who seek my life set their
traps,
those who would harm me talk of
my ruin;
all day long they plot deception.

¹³I am like a deaf man, who cannot
hear,
like a mute, who cannot open his
mouth;
¹⁴I have become like a man who does
not hear,
whose mouth can offer no reply.
¹⁵I wait for you, O Lᴏʀᴅ;
you will answer, O Lord my God.
¹⁶For I said, "Do not let them gloat
or exalt themselves over me when
my foot slips."

¹⁷For I am about to fall,
and my pain is ever with me.
¹⁸I confess my iniquity;
I am troubled by my sin.
¹⁹Many are those who are my vigorous
enemies;
those who hate me without reason
are numerous.
²⁰Those who repay my good with evil
slander me when I pursue what is
good.

²¹O Lᴏʀᴅ, do not forsake me;
be not far from me, O my God.
²²Come quickly to help me,
O Lord my Savior.

Psalm 39

For the director of music. For Jeduthun.
A psalm of David.

¹I said, "I will watch my ways
and keep my tongue from sin;
I will put a muzzle on my mouth
as long as the wicked are in my
presence."
²But when I was silent and still,
not even saying anything good,
my anguish increased.
³My heart grew hot within me,
and as I meditated, the fire burned;
then I spoke with my tongue:

⁴"Show me, O Lᴏʀᴅ, my life's end
and the number of my days;
let me know how fleeting is my life.
⁵You have made my days a mere
handbreadth;
the span of my years is as nothing
before you.

ᵃ37 Or *there will be posterity*   *ᵇ38* Or *posterity*

Each man's life is but a breath.
                                    Selah

⁶Man is a mere phantom as he goes to
    and fro:
  He bustles about, but only in vain;
  he heaps up wealth, not knowing
    who will get it.

⁷"But now, Lord, what do I look for?
  My hope is in you.
⁸Save me from all my transgressions;
  do not make me the scorn of fools.
⁹I was silent; I would not open my
    mouth,
  for you are the one who has done
    this.
¹⁰Remove your scourge from me;
  I am overcome by the blow of your
    hand.
¹¹You rebuke and discipline men for
    their sin;
  you consume their wealth like a
    moth—
  each man is but a breath.   *Selah*

¹²"Hear my prayer, O LORD,
  listen to my cry for help;
  be not deaf to my weeping.
  For I dwell with you as an alien,
  a stranger, as all my fathers were.
¹³Look away from me, that I may
    rejoice again
  before I depart and am no more."

Psalm 40

For the director of music. Of David.
A psalm.

¹I waited patiently for the LORD;
  he turned to me and heard my cry.
²He lifted me out of the slimy pit,
  out of the mud and mire;
  he set my feet on a rock
  and gave me a firm place to stand.
³He put a new song in my mouth,
  a hymn of praise to our God.
  Many will see and fear
  and put their trust in the LORD.

⁴Blessed is the man
  who makes the LORD his trust,
  who does not look to the proud,
  to those who turn aside to false
    gods.[a]
⁵Many, O LORD my God,
  are the wonders you have done.
  The things you planned for us
  no one can recount to you;

were I to speak and tell of them,
  they would be too many to declare.

⁶Sacrifice and offering you did not
    desire,
  but my ears you have pierced[b, c];
  burnt offerings and sin offerings
  you did not require.
⁷Then I said, "Here I am, I have
    come—
  it is written about me in the
    scroll.[d]
⁸I desire to do your will, O my God;
  your law is within my heart."

⁹I proclaim righteousness in the great
    assembly;
  I do not seal my lips,
  as you know, O LORD.
¹⁰I do not hide your righteousness in
    my heart;
  I speak of your faithfulness and
    salvation.
  I do not conceal your love and your
    truth
  from the great assembly.

¹¹Do not withhold your mercy from me,
    O LORD;
  may your love and your truth
  always protect me.
¹²For troubles without number
    surround me;
  my sins have overtaken me, and I
    cannot see.
  They are more than the hairs of my
    head,
  and my heart fails within me.

¹³Be pleased, O LORD, to save me;
  O LORD, come quickly to help me.
¹⁴May all who seek to take my life
  be put to shame and confusion;
  may all who desire my ruin
  be turned back in disgrace.
¹⁵May those who say to me, "Aha!
    Aha!"
  be appalled at their own shame.
¹⁶But may all who seek you
  rejoice and be glad in you;
  may those who love your salvation
    always say,
  "The LORD be exalted!"

¹⁷Yet I am poor and needy;
  may the Lord think of me.
  You are my help and my deliverer;
  O my God, do not delay.

---

a4 Or *to falsehood*   *b6* Hebrew; Septuagint *but a body you have prepared for me* (see also Symmachus
and Theodotion)   *c6* Or *opened*   *d7* Or *come / with the scroll written for me*

Psalm 41

For the director of music. A psalm
of David.

[1]Blessed is he who has regard for the
weak;
    the Lord delivers him in times of
trouble.
[2]The Lord will protect him and
preserve his life;
    he will bless him in the land
    and not surrender him to the desire
of his foes.
[3]The Lord will sustain him on his
sickbed
    and restore him from his bed of
illness.

[4]I said, "O Lord, have mercy on me;
    heal me, for I have sinned against
you."
[5]My enemies say of me in malice,
    "When will he die and his name
perish?"
[6]Whenever one comes to see me,
    he speaks falsely, while his heart
gathers slander;
    then he goes out and spreads it
abroad.

[7]All my enemies whisper together
against me;
    they imagine the worst for me,
saying,
[8]"A vile disease has beset him;
    he will never get up from the place
where he lies."
[9]Even my close friend, whom I trusted,
    he who shared my bread,
    has lifted up his heel against me.

[10]But you, O Lord, have mercy on
me;
    raise me up, that I may repay
them.
[11]I know that you are pleased with
me,
    for my enemy does not triumph
over me.
[12]In my integrity you uphold me
    and set me in your presence
forever.

[13]Praise be to the Lord, the God of
Israel,
    from everlasting to everlasting.
    Amen and Amen.

BOOK II

Psalms 42–72

Psalm 42 [a]

For the director of music. A *maskil* [b] of
the Sons of Korah.

[1]As the deer pants for streams of
water,
    so my soul pants for you, O God.
[2]My soul thirsts for God, for the living
God.
    When can I go and meet with God?
[3]My tears have been my food
day and night,
    while men say to me all day long,
    "Where is your God?"
[4]These things I remember
    as I pour out my soul:
how I used to go with the multitude,
    leading the procession to the house
of God,
with shouts of joy and thanksgiving
    among the festive throng.

[5]Why are you downcast, O my soul?
    Why so disturbed within me?
Put your hope in God,
    for I will yet praise him,
    my Savior and [6]my God.

My [c] soul is downcast within me;
    therefore I will remember you
from the land of the Jordan,
    the heights of Hermon—from
Mount Mizar.
[7]Deep calls to deep
    in the roar of your waterfalls;
all your waves and breakers
    have swept over me.

[8]By day the Lord directs his love,
    at night his song is with me—
    a prayer to the God of my life.

[9]I say to God my Rock,
    "Why have you forgotten me?
Why must I go about mourning,
    oppressed by the enemy?"
[10]My bones suffer mortal agony
    as my foes taunt me,
saying to me all day long,
    "Where is your God?"

[11]Why are you downcast, O my soul?
    Why so disturbed within me?
Put your hope in God,

---

[a]In many Hebrew manuscripts Psalms 42 and 43 constitute one psalm.   [b]Title: Probably a literary or musical term   [c]5,6 A few Hebrew manuscripts, Septuagint and Syriac; most Hebrew manuscripts *praise him for his saving help. / [6]O my God, my*

for I will yet praise him,
my Savior and my God.

Psalm 43[a]

[1]Vindicate me, O God,
    and plead my cause against an
        ungodly nation;
    rescue me from deceitful and
        wicked men.
[2]You are God my stronghold.
    Why have you rejected me?
Why must I go about mourning,
    oppressed by the enemy?
[3]Send forth your light and your truth,
    let them guide me;
    let them bring me to your holy
        mountain,
    to the place where you dwell.
[4]Then will I go to the altar of God,
    to God, my joy and my delight.
I will praise you with the harp,
    O God, my God.

[5]Why are you downcast, O my soul?
    Why so disturbed within me?
Put your hope in God,
    for I will yet praise him,
    my Savior and my God.

Psalm 44

For the director of music. Of the Sons
of Korah. A *maskil.*[b]

[1]We have heard with our ears, O God;
    our fathers have told us
what you did in their days,
    in days long ago.
[2]With your hand you drove out the
        nations
    and planted our fathers;
you crushed the peoples
    and made our fathers flourish.
[3]It was not by their sword that they
        won the land,
    nor did their arm bring them
        victory;
it was your right hand, your arm,
    and the light of your face, for you
        loved them.

[4]You are my King and my God,
    who decrees[c] victories for Jacob.
[5]Through you we push back our
        enemies;
    through your name we trample our
        foes.
[6]I do not trust in my bow,

my sword does not bring me
    victory;
[7]but you give us victory over our
        enemies,
    you put our adversaries to shame.
[8]In God we make our boast all day
        long,
    and we will praise your name
        forever.   *Selah*

[9]But now you have rejected and
        humbled us;
    you no longer go out with our
        armies.
[10]You made us retreat before the
        enemy,
    and our adversaries have plundered
        us.
[11]You gave us up to be devoured like
        sheep
    and have scattered us among the
        nations.
[12]You sold your people for a pittance,
    gaining nothing from their sale.

[13]You have made us a reproach to our
        neighbors,
    the scorn and derision of those
        around us.
[14]You have made us a byword among
        the nations;
    the peoples shake their heads at us.
[15]My disgrace is before me all day long,
    and my face is covered with shame
[16]at the taunts of those who reproach
        and revile me,
    because of the enemy, who is bent
        on revenge.

[17]All this happened to us,
    though we had not forgotten you
    or been false to your covenant.
[18]Our hearts had not turned back;
    our feet had not strayed from your
        path.
[19]But you crushed us and made us a
        haunt for jackals
    and covered us over with deep
        darkness.

[20]If we had forgotten the name of our
        God
    or spread out our hands to a
        foreign god,
[21]would not God have discovered it,
    since he knows the secrets of the
        heart?
[22]Yet for your sake we face death all
        day long;

---

[a]In many Hebrew manuscripts Psalms 42 and 43 constitute one psalm.   [b]Title: Probably a literary or
musical term   [c]4 Septuagint, Aquila and Syriac; Hebrew *King, O God; / command*

we are considered as sheep to be
    slaughtered.

²³Awake, O Lord! Why do you sleep?
    Rouse yourself! Do not reject us
    forever.
²⁴Why do you hide your face
    and forget our misery and
      oppression?

²⁵We are brought down to the dust;
    our bodies cling to the ground.
²⁶Rise up and help us;
    redeem us because of your
      unfailing love.

Psalm 45

For the director of music. To the tune
of, "Lilies." Of the Sons of Korah. A
maskil. ᵃ A wedding song.

¹My heart is stirred by a noble theme
    as I recite my verses for the king;
    my tongue is the pen of a skillful
      writer.

²You are the most excellent of men
    and your lips have been anointed
      with grace,
    since God has blessed you forever.
³Gird your sword upon your side,
    O mighty one;
    clothe yourself with splendor and
      majesty.
⁴In your majesty ride forth victoriously
    in behalf of truth, humility and
      righteousness;
    let your right hand display awesome
      deeds.
⁵Let your sharp arrows pierce the
      hearts of the king's enemies;
    let the nations fall beneath your
      feet.
⁶Your throne, O God, will last for ever
    and ever;
    a scepter of justice will be the
      scepter of your kingdom.
⁷You love righteousness and hate
      wickedness;
    therefore God, your God, has set
      you above your companions
    by anointing you with the oil of joy.
⁸All your robes are fragrant with myrrh
      and aloes and cassia;
    from palaces adorned with ivory
    the music of the strings makes you
      glad.

⁹Daughters of kings are among your
      honored women;
    at your right hand is the royal bride
      in gold of Ophir.

¹⁰Listen, O daughter, consider and give
      ear:
    Forget your people and your
      father's house.
¹¹The king is enthralled by your beauty;
    honor him, for he is your lord.
¹²The Daughter of Tyre will come with
    a gift, ᵇ
    men of wealth will seek your favor.

¹³All glorious is the princess within her
      chamber,;
    her gown is interwoven with gold.
¹⁴In embroidered garments she is led to
      the king;
    her virgin companions follow her
    and are brought to you.
¹⁵They are led in with joy and gladness;
    they enter the palace of the king.

¹⁶Your sons will take the place of your
      fathers;
    you will make them princes
      throughout the land.
¹⁷I will perpetuate your memory
      through all generations;
    therefore the nations will praise you
      for ever and ever.

Psalm 46

For the director of music. Of the Sons
of Korah. According to *alamoth.* ᶜ
A song.

¹God is our refuge and strength,
    an ever-present help in trouble.
²Therefore we will not fear, though the
      earth give way
    and the mountains fall into the
      heart of the sea,
³though its waters roar and foam
    and the mountains quake with their
      surging.   *Selah*

⁴There is a river whose streams make
      glad the city of God,
    the holy place where the Most High
      dwells.
⁵God is within her, she will not fall;
    God will help her at break of day.
⁶Nations are in uproar, kingdoms fall;
    he lifts his voice, the earth melts.

⁷The LORD Almighty is with us;

ᵃTitle: Probably a literary or musical term   ᵇ12 Or *A Tyrian robe is among the gifts*   ᶜTitle: Probably
a musical term

the God of Jacob is our fortress.
Selah

⁸Come and see the works of the Lord,
the desolations he has brought on
the earth.
⁹He makes wars cease to the ends of
the earth;
he breaks the bow and shatters the
spear,
he burns the shields*ᵃ* with fire.
¹⁰"Be still, and know that I am God;
I will be exalted among the nations,
I will be exalted in the earth."

¹¹The Lord Almighty is with us;
the God of Jacob is our fortress.
Selah

ᵃ9 Or *chariots*

Psalm 47

For the director of music. Of the Sons
of Korah. A psalm.

¹Clap your hands, all you nations;
shout to God with cries of joy.
²How awesome is the Lord Most High,
the great King over all the earth!
³He subdued nations under us,
peoples under our feet.
⁴He chose our inheritance for us,
the pride of Jacob, whom he loved.
Selah

⁵God has ascended amid shouts of joy,
the Lord amid the sounding of
trumpets.

THURSDAY

VERSE FOR THE DAY: AUTHOR: PASSAGE FOR THE DAY:
Psalm 46:10   Hannah Whitall Smith   Psalm 46:1–11

Resting, Not Worrying

AMONG the peaks of the Sierra Nevada mountains, not far from the busy whirl of San Francisco, lies Lake Tahoe. It is twenty-three miles long, ten miles wide, and so deep that a line dropped nineteen hundred feet does not touch bottom; and it lies five thousand feet above the neighboring ocean. Storms come and go in waters that are lower down the mountains, but this lake is so still and clear that the eye can penetrate, it is said, a hundred feet into its depths. Around its mild verdant sides are the mountains, ever crowned with snow. The sky above is as calm as the motionless water. Nature loses scarcely anything of its clear outline as it is reflected there. Here the soul may learn something of what rest is, as day after day one opens one's heart to let the sweet influence of nature's sabbath enter and reign. This is but a faint type of what we may find in Christ.

In the pressure of the greatest responsibilities, in the worry of the smallest cares, in the perplexities of life's moments of crisis, we may have the Lake Tahoe rest in the security of God's will. Learn to live in this rest. In the calmness of spirit it will give, your soul will reflect, as in a mirror, the beauty of the Lord; and the tumult of men's lives will be calmed in your presence, as your tumults have been calmed in his presence.

Additional Scripture Readings:
Psalm 131:1–3; Philippians 4:4–7

Go to page 444 for your next
devotional reading.

⁶Sing praises to God, sing praises;
    sing praises to our King, sing
        praises.

⁷For God is the King of all the earth;
    sing to him a psalm*a* of praise.
⁸God reigns over the nations;
    God is seated on his holy throne.
⁹The nobles of the nations assemble
        as the people of the God of
        Abraham,
for the kings*b* of the earth belong to
        God;
    he is greatly exalted.

Psalm 48

A song. A psalm of the Sons of Korah.

¹Great is the LORD, and most worthy of
        praise,
    in the city of our God, his holy
        mountain.
²It is beautiful in its loftiness,
    the joy of the whole earth.
Like the utmost heights of Zaphon*c*
        is Mount Zion,
    the*d* city of the Great King.
³God is in her citadels;
    he has shown himself to be her
        fortress.

⁴When the kings joined forces,
    when they advanced together,
⁵they saw ,her, and were astounded;
    they fled in terror.
⁶Trembling seized them there,
    pain like that of a woman in labor.
⁷You destroyed them like ships of
        Tarshish
    shattered by an east wind.

⁸As we have heard,
    so have we seen
in the city of the LORD Almighty,
    in the city of our God:
    God makes her secure forever.
                                Selah

⁹Within your temple, O God,
    we meditate on your unfailing love.
¹⁰Like your name, O God,
    your praise reaches to the ends of
        the earth;
    your right hand is filled with
        righteousness.
¹¹Mount Zion rejoices,
    the villages of Judah are glad

because of your judgments.

¹²Walk about Zion, go around her,
    count her towers,
¹³consider well her ramparts,
    view her citadels,
    that you may tell of them to the
        next generation.
¹⁴For this God is our God for ever and
        ever;
    he will be our guide even to the
        end.

Psalm 49

For the director of music. Of the Sons
of Korah. A psalm.

¹Hear this, all you peoples;
    listen, all who live in this world,
²both low and high,
    rich and poor alike:
³My mouth will speak words of
        wisdom;
    the utterance from my heart will
        give understanding.
⁴I will turn my ear to a proverb;
    with the harp I will expound my
        riddle:

⁵Why should I fear when evil days
        come,
    when wicked deceivers surround
        me—
⁶those who trust in their wealth
    and boast of their great riches?
⁷No man can redeem the life of
        another
    or give to God a ransom for him—
⁸the ransom for a life is costly,
    no payment is ever enough—
⁹that he should live on forever
    and not see decay.

¹⁰For all can see that wise men die;
    the foolish and the senseless alike
        perish
    and leave their wealth to others.
¹¹Their tombs will remain their houses*e*
        forever,
    their dwellings for endless
        generations,
    though they had*f* named lands
        after themselves.

¹²But man, despite his riches, does not
        endure;
    he is*g* like the beasts that perish.

---

*a*7 Or *a maskil* (probably a literary or musical term)   *b*9 Or *shields*   *c*2 *Zaphon* can refer to a sacred
mountain or the direction north.   *d*2 Or *earth, / Mount Zion, on the northern side / of the*
*e*11 Septuagint and Syriac; Hebrew *In their thoughts their houses will remain*   *f*11 Or / *for they have*
*g*12 Hebrew; Septuagint and Syriac read verse 12 the same as verse 20.

[13]This is the fate of those who trust in
themselves,
and of their followers, who approve
their sayings.   *Selah*
[14]Like sheep they are destined for the
grave,[a]
and death will feed on them.
The upright will rule over them in the
morning;
their forms will decay in the
grave,[a]
far from their princely mansions.
[15]But God will redeem my life[b] from
the grave;
he will surely take me to himself.
Selah

[16]Do not be overawed when a man
grows rich,
when the splendor of his house
increases;
[17]for he will take nothing with him
when he dies,
his splendor will not descend with
him.
[18]Though while he lived he counted
himself blessed—
and men praise you when you
prosper—
[19]he will join the generation of his
fathers,
who will never see the light of life.

[20]A man who has riches without
understanding
is like the beasts that perish.

Psalm 50

A psalm of Asaph.

[1]The Mighty One, God, the LORD,
speaks and summons the earth
from the rising of the sun to the
place where it sets.
[2]From Zion, perfect in beauty,
God shines forth.
[3]Our God comes and will not be silent;
a fire devours before him,
and around him a tempest rages.
[4]He summons the heavens above,
and the earth, that he may judge
his people:
[5]"Gather to me my consecrated ones,
who made a covenant with me by
sacrifice."
[6]And the heavens proclaim his
righteousness,
for God himself is judge.   *Selah*

[7]"Hear, O my people, and I will speak,
O Israel, and I will testify against
you:
I am God, your God.
[8]I do not rebuke you for your sacrifices
or your burnt offerings, which are
ever before me.
[9]I have no need of a bull from your
stall
or of goats from your pens,
[10]for every animal of the forest is mine,
and the cattle on a thousand hills.
[11]I know every bird in the mountains,
and the creatures of the field are
mine.
[12]If I were hungry I would not tell
you,
for the world is mine, and all that
is in it.
[13]Do I eat the flesh of bulls
or drink the blood of goats?
[14]Sacrifice thank offerings to God,
fulfill your vows to the Most High,
[15]and call upon me in the day of
trouble;
I will deliver you, and you will
honor me."

[16]But to the wicked, God says:

"What right have you to recite my
laws
or take my covenant on your
lips?
[17]You hate my instruction
and cast my words behind you.
[18]When you see a thief, you join with
him;
you throw in your lot with
adulterers.
[19]You use your mouth for evil
and harness your tongue to deceit.
[20]You speak continually against your
brother
and slander your own mother's
son.
[21]These things you have done and I
kept silent;
you thought I was altogether[c] like
you.
But I will rebuke you
and accuse you to your face.

[22]"Consider this, you who forget God,
or I will tear you to pieces, with
none to rescue:
[23]He who sacrifices thank offerings
honors me,
and he prepares the way

---

a14 Hebrew *Sheol*; also in verse 15   *b15* Or *soul*   *c21* Or *thought the 'I AM' was*

so that I may show him[a] the
salvation of God."

Psalm 51

For the director of music. A psalm of
David. When the prophet Nathan came
to him after David had committed
adultery with Bathsheba.

[1]Have mercy on me, O God,
　　according to your unfailing love;
according to your great compassion
　　blot out my transgressions.
[2]Wash away all my iniquity
　　and cleanse me from my sin.

[3]For I know my transgressions,
　　and my sin is always before me.
[4]Against you, you only, have I sinned
　　and done what is evil in your sight,
so that you are proved right when you
　　speak
　　and justified when you judge.
[5]Surely I was sinful at birth,
　　sinful from the time my mother
　　conceived me.
[6]Surely you desire truth in the inner
　　parts[b];
　　you teach[c] me wisdom in the
　　inmost place.

[7]Cleanse me with hyssop, and I will be
　　clean;
　　wash me, and I will be whiter than
　　snow.
[8]Let me hear joy and gladness;
　　let the bones you have crushed
　　rejoice.
[9]Hide your face from my sins
　　and blot out all my iniquity.

[10]Create in me a pure heart, O God,
　　and renew a steadfast spirit within
　　me.
[11]Do not cast me from your presence
　　or take your Holy Spirit from me.
[12]Restore to me the joy of your
　　salvation
　　and grant me a willing spirit, to
　　sustain me.

[13]Then I will teach transgressors your
　　ways,
　　and sinners will turn back to you.
[14]Save me from bloodguilt, O God,
　　the God who saves me,
　　and my tongue will sing of your
　　righteousness.

[15]O Lord, open my lips,
　　and my mouth will declare your
　　praise.
[16]You do not delight in sacrifice, or I
　　would bring it;
　　you do not take pleasure in burnt
　　offerings.
[17]The sacrifices of God are[d] a broken
　　spirit;
　　a broken and contrite heart,
　　O God, you will not despise.

[18]In your good pleasure make Zion
　　prosper;
　　build up the walls of Jerusalem.
[19]Then there will be righteous
　　sacrifices,
　　whole burnt offerings to delight
　　you;
　　then bulls will be offered on your
　　altar.

Psalm 52

For the director of music. A maskil[e]
of David. When Doeg the Edomite had
gone to Saul and told him: "David has
gone to the house of Ahimelech."

[1]Why do you boast of evil, you mighty
　　man?
　　Why do you boast all day long,
　　you who are a disgrace in the eyes
　　of God?
[2]Your tongue plots destruction;
　　it is like a sharpened razor,
　　you who practice deceit.
[3]You love evil rather than good,
　　falsehood rather than speaking the
　　truth.   Selah
[4]You love every harmful word,
　　O you deceitful tongue!

[5]Surely God will bring you down to
　　everlasting ruin:
　　He will snatch you up and tear you
　　from your tent;
　　he will uproot you from the land of
　　the living.   Selah
[6]The righteous will see and fear;
　　they will laugh at him, saying,
[7]"Here now is the man
　　who did not make God his
　　stronghold
　　but trusted in his great wealth
　　and grew strong by destroying
　　others!"

[a]23 Or and to him who considers his way / I will show
is uncertain.   [c]6 Or you desired . . . ; / you taught
Probably a literary or musical term

[b]6 The meaning of the Hebrew for this phrase
[d]17 Or My sacrifice, O God, is   [e]Title:

FRIDAY

VERSE FOR THE DAY: AUTHOR: PASSAGE FOR THE DAY:
Psalm 51:3–4   Gini Andrews   Psalm 51:1–19

Losing the Way

FROM top to bottom, our society is success oriented, however one may define that in terms of one's own goals. Christians are not immune; "Everything comes out okay for Christians," "The King's kids are always winners" are misleading slogans to live by. We develop unrealistic expectations of the Christian life and of ourselves; and then when our wings get broken, we think failure ends our usefulness.

For those of us who know too well the salt taste of failure, it helps to remember that even the great ones of the faith failed, yet God continued to use them, often in a deeper way *after* their fall.

Some of David's greatest psalms came after his greatest mistakes. God called him "a man after his own heart" (1 Samuel 13:14). Abraham lied, perhaps to save his skin, yet he is the towering example of faith for three major religions and is called "God's friend" (James 2:23).

It is those who have plumbed the depths of failure to whom God invariably gives the call to shepherd others. This is not a call given only to the gifted, the highly trained, or the polished as such. Without a bitter experience of their own inadequacy and poverty, they are quite unfitted to bear the burden of spiritual ministry. It takes a person who has discovered something of the measure of his own weakness to be patient with the foibles of others.

Too often we live in a quid-pro-quo relationship with God: "I've been faithful to you, I've worked hard, so please give me this or that." Or, "I've failed again; I can't expect any blessing." We forget that the whole of our life is grace.

Too many sincere Christians, facing their failures, berate themselves unmercifully and keep asking God for forgiveness. Each of us should memorize, hang on the mirror, and make forever our own the ringing truth: "There is now no [repeat *no*] condemnation for those who are in Christ Jesus" (Romans 8:1).

Not only does he not condemn us; he even brings blessings from the ashes of our failures.

Additional Scripture Readings: *Go to page 447 for your next*
John 18:15–27; 21:15–17; Acts 9:1–6,15–16   *devotional reading.*

[8]But I am like an olive tree
   flourishing in the house of God;
I trust in God's unfailing love
   for ever and ever.
[9]I will praise you forever for what you
      have done;
   in your name I will hope, for your
      name is good.
   I will praise you in the presence of
      your saints.

Psalm 53

For the director of music. According to
mahalath. [a] A *maskil* [b] of David.

[1]The fool says in his heart,
   "There is no God."
They are corrupt, and their ways are
      vile;
   there is no one who does good.

[2]God looks down from heaven
   on the sons of men
to see if there are any who
      understand,
   any who seek God.
[3]Everyone has turned away,
   they have together become corrupt;
there is no one who does good,
   not even one.

[4]Will the evildoers never learn—
   those who devour my people as
      men eat bread
   and who do not call on God?
[5]There they were, overwhelmed with
      dread,
   where there was nothing to dread.
God scattered the bones of those who
      attacked you;
   you put them to shame, for God
      despised them.

[6]Oh, that salvation for Israel would
      come out of Zion!
   When God restores the fortunes of
      his people,
   let Jacob rejoice and Israel be glad!

Psalm 54

For the director of music. With stringed
instruments. A *maskil* [b] of David. When
the Ziphites had gone to Saul and said,
"Is not David hiding among us?"

[1]Save me, O God, by your name;
   vindicate me by your might.

[2]Hear my prayer, O God;
   listen to the words of my mouth.

[3]Strangers are attacking me;
   ruthless men seek my life—
   men without regard for God.   *Selah*

[4]Surely God is my help;
   the Lord is the one who sustains
      me.

[5]Let evil recoil on those who slander
      me;
   in your faithfulness destroy them.

[6]I will sacrifice a freewill offering to
      you;
   I will praise your name, O LORD,
   for it is good.
[7]For he has delivered me from all my
      troubles,
   and my eyes have looked in
      triumph on my foes.

Psalm 55

For the director of music. With stringed
instruments. A *maskil* [b] of David.

[1]Listen to my prayer, O God,
   do not ignore my plea;
[2] hear me and answer me.
My thoughts trouble me and I am
      distraught
[3] at the voice of the enemy,
   at the stares of the wicked;
for they bring down suffering upon
      me
   and revile me in their anger.

[4]My heart is in anguish within me;
   the terrors of death assail me.
[5]Fear and trembling have beset me;
   horror has overwhelmed me.
[6]I said, "Oh, that I had the wings of a
      dove!
   I would fly away and be at rest—
[7]I would flee far away
   and stay in the desert;   *Selah*
[8]I would hurry to my place of shelter,
   far from the tempest and storm."

[9]Confuse the wicked, O Lord,
      confound their speech,
   for I see violence and strife in the
      city.
[10]Day and night they prowl about on its
      walls;
   malice and abuse are within it.

---

[a]Title: Probably a musical term   [b]Title: Probably a literary or musical term

11Destructive forces are at work in the
    city;
    threats and lies never leave its
        streets.

12If an enemy were insulting me,
    I could endure it;
if a foe were raising himself against
        me,
    I could hide from him.
13But it is you, a man like myself,
    my companion, my close friend,
14with whom I once enjoyed sweet
        fellowship
    as we walked with the throng at the
        house of God.

15Let death take my enemies by
        surprise;
    let them go down alive to the
        grave,ᵃ
    for evil finds lodging among
        them.

16But I call to God,
    and the LORD saves me.
17Evening, morning and noon
    I cry out in distress,
    and he hears my voice.
18He ransoms me unharmed
    from the battle waged against me,
    even though many oppose me.
19God, who is enthroned forever,
    will hear them and afflict them—
                                    Selah

men who never change their ways
    and have no fear of God.

20My companion attacks his friends;
    he violates his covenant.
21His speech is smooth as butter,
    yet war is in his heart;
his words are more soothing than
        oil,
    yet they are drawn swords.

22Cast your cares on the LORD
    and he will sustain you;
    he will never let the righteous
        fall.
23But you, O God, will bring down
        the wicked
    into the pit of corruption;
bloodthirsty and deceitful men
    will not live out half their
        days.

But as for me, I trust in you.

Psalm 56

For the director of music. To the tune
of, "A Dove on Distant Oaks." Of David.
A miktam. ᵇ When the Philistines had
seized him in Gath.

1Be merciful to me, O God, for men
        hotly pursue me;
    all day long they press their attack.
2My slanderers pursue me all day long;
    many are attacking me in their
        pride.

3When I am afraid,
    I will trust in you.
4In God, whose word I praise,
    in God I trust; I will not be afraid.
    What can mortal man do to me?

5All day long they twist my words;
    they are always plotting to harm
        me.
6They conspire, they lurk,
    they watch my steps,
    eager to take my life.

7On no account let them escape;
    in your anger, O God, bring down
        the nations.
8Record my lament;
    list my tears on your scrollᶜ—
    are they not in your record?

9Then my enemies will turn back
    when I call for help.
    By this I will know that God is for
        me.
10In God, whose word I praise,
    in the LORD, whose word I praise—
11in God I trust; I will not be afraid.
    What can man do to me?

12I am under vows to you, O God;
    I will present my thank offerings to
        you.
13For you have delivered meᵈ from
        death
    and my feet from stumbling,
that I may walk before God
    in the light of life.ᵉ

Psalm 57

For the director of music. To the tune
of, "Do Not Destroy." Of David. A
miktam. ᵇ When he had fled from Saul
into the cave.

1Have mercy on me, O God, have
        mercy on me,

ᵃ15 Hebrew Sheol   ᵇTitle: Probably a literary or musical term   ᶜ8 Or I put my tears in your wineskin
ᵈ13 Or my soul   ᵉ13 Or the land of the living

WEEKENDING

RENEW

My moments of being most complete, most
integrated, have come either in complete
solitude or when I am being part of a body made
up of many people going in the same direction.
A vivid example is a great symphony orchestra,
where each instrument is completely necessary
for the whole; a violin cannot take the place of a
trombone, nor cymbals of the harp; and there
are even times when the lowly triangle is the
focus of the music.

– Madeleine L'Engle

REFLECT

Take a bit of time to examine yourself. When are
you "most complete, most integrated"? Return
to that place, that situation, to regain the
healthy sense of self that is so easily lost in our
world's clamor and activity.

REVIVE
Saturday: Psalm 131:1–3
Sunday: 1 Corinthians 12:14–27

Go to page 451 for your next devotional reading.

for in you my soul takes refuge.
I will take refuge in the shadow of
    your wings
until the disaster has passed.

[2]I cry out to God Most High,
    to God, who fulfills his purpose for
        me.
[3]He sends from heaven and saves me,
    rebuking those who hotly pursue
        me;   *Selah*
God sends his love and his
    faithfulness.

[4]I am in the midst of lions;
    I lie among ravenous beasts—
men whose teeth are spears and
    arrows,
    whose tongues are sharp swords.

[5]Be exalted, O God, above the
    heavens;
    let your glory be over all the earth.

[6]They spread a net for my feet—
    I was bowed down in distress.
They dug a pit in my path—
    but they have fallen into it
        themselves.   *Selah*

[7]My heart is steadfast, O God,
    my heart is steadfast;
    I will sing and make music.
[8]Awake, my soul!
    Awake, harp and lyre!
    I will awaken the dawn.

[9]I will praise you, O Lord, among the
    nations;
    I will sing of you among the
        peoples.
[10]For great is your love, reaching to the
    heavens;
    your faithfulness reaches to the
        skies.

[11]Be exalted, O God, above the
    heavens;
    let your glory be over all the earth.

Psalm 58

For the director of music. To the tune
of, "Do Not Destroy." Of David.
A *miktam.* [a]

[1]Do you rulers indeed speak justly?
    Do you judge uprightly among
        men?
[2]No, in your heart you devise injustice,
    and your hands mete out violence
        on the earth.

[3]Even from birth the wicked go astray;
    from the womb they are wayward
        and speak lies.
[4]Their venom is like the venom of a
    snake,
    like that of a cobra that has
        stopped its ears,
[5]that will not heed the tune of the
    charmer,
    however skillful the enchanter may
        be.

[6]Break the teeth in their mouths,
    O God;
    tear out, O LORD, the fangs of the
        lions!
[7]Let them vanish like water that flows
    away;
    when they draw the bow, let their
        arrows be blunted.
[8]Like a slug melting away as it moves
    along,
    like a stillborn child, may they not
        see the sun.

[9]Before your pots can feel the heat of
    the thorns—
    whether they be green or dry—the
        wicked will be swept away.[b]
[10]The righteous will be glad when they
    are avenged,
    when they bathe their feet in the
        blood of the wicked.
[11]Then men will say,
    "Surely the righteous still are
        rewarded;
    surely there is a God who judges
        the earth."

Psalm 59

For the director of music. To the tune
of, "Do Not Destroy." Of David. A
miktam. [a] When Saul had sent men to
watch David's house in order
to kill him.

[1]Deliver me from my enemies, O God;
    protect me from those who rise up
        against me.
[2]Deliver me from evildoers
    and save me from bloodthirsty men.

[3]See how they lie in wait for me!
    Fierce men conspire against me
    for no offense or sin of mine,
        O LORD.
[4]I have done no wrong, yet they are
    ready to attack me.

[a]Title: Probably a literary or musical term   [b]9 The meaning of the Hebrew for this verse is uncertain.

Arise to help me; look on my
  plight!
⁵O LORD God Almighty, the God of
    Israel,
  rouse yourself to punish all the
    nations;
  show no mercy to wicked traitors.
                                        Selah

⁶They return at evening,
  snarling like dogs,
  and prowl about the city.
⁷See what they spew from their
    mouths —
  they spew out swords from their
    lips,
  and they say, "Who can hear us?"
⁸But you, O LORD, laugh at them;
  you scoff at all those nations.

⁹O my Strength, I watch for you;
  you, O God, are my fortress, ¹⁰my
    loving God.

God will go before me
  and will let me gloat over those
    who slander me.
¹¹But do not kill them, O Lord our
    shield,ᵃ
  or my people will forget.
In your might make them wander
    about,
  and bring them down.
¹²For the sins of their mouths,
  for the words of their lips,
  let them be caught in their pride.
For the curses and lies they utter,
¹³ consume them in wrath,
  consume them till they are no
    more.
Then it will be known to the ends of
    the earth
  that God rules over Jacob.   *Selah*

¹⁴They return at evening,
  snarling like dogs,
  and prowl about the city.
¹⁵They wander about for food
  and howl if not satisfied.
¹⁶But I will sing of your strength,
  in the morning I will sing of your
    love;
  for you are my fortress,
  my refuge in times of trouble.

¹⁷O my Strength, I sing praise to you;
  you, O God, are my fortress, my
    loving God.

Psalm 60

For the director of music. To the tune
of, "The Lily of the Covenant." A
*miktam*ᵇ of David. For teaching. When
he fought Aram Naharaimᶜ and Aram
Zobah,ᵈ and when Joab returned and
struck down twelve thousand Edomites
in the Valley of Salt.

¹You have rejected us, O God, and
    burst forth upon us;
  you have been angry — now restore
    us!
²You have shaken the land and torn it
    open;
  mend its fractures, for it is
    quaking.
³You have shown your people
    desperate times;
  you have given us wine that makes
    us stagger.

⁴But for those who fear you, you have
    raised a banner
  to be unfurled against the bow.
                                        Selah

⁵Save us and help us with your right
    hand,
  that those you love may be
    delivered.
⁶God has spoken from his sanctuary:
  "In triumph I will parcel out
    Shechem
  and measure off the Valley of
    Succoth.
⁷Gilead is mine, and Manasseh is
    mine;
  Ephraim is my helmet,
  Judah my scepter.
⁸Moab is my washbasin,
  upon Edom I toss my sandal;
  over Philistia I shout in
    triumph."

⁹Who will bring me to the fortified
    city?
  Who will lead me to Edom?
¹⁰Is it not you, O God, you who have
    rejected us
  and no longer go out with our
    armies?
¹¹Give us aid against the enemy,
  for the help of man is worthless.
¹²With God we will gain the
    victory,
  and he will trample down our
    enemies.

ᵃ11 Or *sovereign*   ᵇTitle: Probably a literary or musical term   ᶜTitle: That is, Arameans of Northwest
Mesopotamia   ᵈTitle: That is, Arameans of central Syria

Psalm 61

For the director of music. With stringed
instruments. Of David.

[1] Hear my cry, O God;
    listen to my prayer.

[2] From the ends of the earth I call to
    you,
    I call as my heart grows faint;
    lead me to the rock that is higher
      than I.
[3] For you have been my refuge,
    a strong tower against the foe.

[4] I long to dwell in your tent forever
    and take refuge in the shelter of
      your wings.   *Selah*
[5] For you have heard my vows, O God;
    you have given me the heritage of
      those who fear your name.

[6] Increase the days of the king's life,
    his years for many generations.
[7] May he be enthroned in God's
      presence forever;
    appoint your love and faithfulness
      to protect him.

[8] Then will I ever sing praise to your
      name
    and fulfill my vows day after day.

Psalm 62

For the director of music. For Jeduthun.
A psalm of David.

[1] My soul finds rest in God alone;
    my salvation comes from him.
[2] He alone is my rock and my salvation;
    he is my fortress, I will never be
      shaken.

[3] How long will you assault a man?
    Would all of you throw him down—
    this leaning wall, this tottering
      fence?
[4] They fully intend to topple him
    from his lofty place;
    they take delight in lies.
With their mouths they bless,
    but in their hearts they curse. *Selah*

[5] Find rest, O my soul, in God alone;
    my hope comes from him.
[6] He alone is my rock and my salvation;
    he is my fortress, I will not be
      shaken.
[7] My salvation and my honor depend
    on God[a];

---

a7 Or *God Most High is my salvation and my honor*

he is my mighty rock, my refuge.
[8] Trust in him at all times, O people;
    pour out your hearts to him,
    for God is our refuge.   *Selah*

[9] Lowborn men are but a breath,
    the highborn are but a lie;
if weighed on a balance, they are
      nothing;
    together they are only a breath.
[10] Do not trust in extortion
    or take pride in stolen goods;
though your riches increase,
    do not set your heart on them.

[11] One thing God has spoken,
    two things have I heard:
    that you, O God, are strong,
[12]   and that you, O Lord, are loving.
Surely you will reward each person
    according to what he has done.

Psalm 63

A psalm of David. When he was in the
Desert of Judah.

[1] O God, you are my God,
    earnestly I seek you;
    my soul thirsts for you,
    my body longs for you,
in a dry and weary land
    where there is no water.

[2] I have seen you in the sanctuary
    and beheld your power and your
      glory.
[3] Because your love is better than life,
    my lips will glorify you.
[4] I will praise you as long as I live,
    and in your name I will lift up my
      hands.
[5] My soul will be satisfied as with the
      richest of foods;
    with singing lips my mouth will
      praise you.

[6] On my bed I remember you;
    I think of you through the watches
      of the night.
[7] Because you are my help,
    I sing in the shadow of your wings.
[8] My soul clings to you;
    your right hand upholds me.

[9] They who seek my life will be
      destroyed;
    they will go down to the depths of
      the earth.
[10] They will be given over to the sword
    and become food for jackals.

VERSE FOR THE DAY: AUTHOR: PASSAGE FOR THE DAY:
Psalm 63:1   Rosalind Rinker   Psalm 63:1–11

A Spring of Living Water

O GOD, you are my God,
   earnestly I seek you;
my soul thirsts for you . . .
   in a dry and weary land
      where there is no water (Psalm 63:1).

The book of Psalms is a book of prayer that embraces every experience possible to human beings. As we read Psalm 63, we see that David was a fugitive in the desert of Judah. He was greatly distressed. He thirsted after God.

We can identify with David's great thirst, but that may be where the parallel ends. Unlike David, who fought on the side of God, often our enemies are the result of our personal failures.

The thirst that we have in common with David is worth looking into. We thirst for different things at different times: recognition, friends, a life-mate, a home, children, a home church, an education, a job and money, and gifts to serve our Lord (wisdom, insight, courage). But most of all we thirst to love and be loved.

In John 4, Jesus used earthly water to introduce living water, which alone can quench our thirsty hearts, no matter who we are. When Jesus asked for a drink from the Samaritan woman, he did so even though the request broke all Jewish religious, racial, and sexual laws. These laws and customs, however, were not as important to Jesus as his desire to offer the woman living water.

Today the invitation still stands: "Everyone who drinks this water will be thirsty again, but whoever drinks the water I give him will never thirst. Indeed, the water I give him will become in him a spring of water welling up to eternal life" (John 4:13–14).

Psalm 63 joyfully proclaims the blessings David received when he cried out to God; they can be yours also: to see the glory of God, to know God's love is better than life, to praise him with singing lips, to meditate on him when sleepless, and to stay close to him because his right hand upholds you.

We serve a risen Savior who has given us his Holy Spirit (John 7:37–39) as "living water," which becomes like an artesian well within us. He invites us: If anyone thirsts, let her ask, "for everyone who asks receives" (Matthew 7:7–9).

Additional Scripture Readings:
Isaiah 55:1–3; Matthew 5:6

Go to page 457 for your next devotional reading.

[11]But the king will rejoice in God;
    all who swear by God's name will
        praise him,
    while the mouths of liars will be
        silenced.

Psalm 64

For the director of music. A psalm
of David.

[1]Hear me, O God, as I voice my
        complaint;
    protect my life from the threat of
        the enemy.
[2]Hide me from the conspiracy of the
        wicked,
    from that noisy crowd of evildoers.

[3]They sharpen their tongues like
        swords
    and aim their words like deadly
        arrows.
[4]They shoot from ambush at the
        innocent man;
    they shoot at him suddenly,
        without fear.

[5]They encourage each other in evil
        plans,
    they talk about hiding their snares;
    they say, "Who will see them[a]?"
[6]They plot injustice and say,
    "We have devised a perfect plan!"
    Surely the mind and heart of man
        are cunning.

[7]But God will shoot them with arrows;
    suddenly they will be struck down.
[8]He will turn their own tongues
        against them
    and bring them to ruin;
    all who see them will shake their
        heads in scorn.

[9]All mankind will fear;
    they will proclaim the works of God
    and ponder what he has done.
[10]Let the righteous rejoice in the Lord
    and take refuge in him;
    let all the upright in heart praise
        him!

Psalm 65

For the director of music. A psalm
of David. A song.

[1]Praise awaits[b] you, O God, in Zion;
    to you our vows will be fulfilled.

[2]O you who hear prayer,
    to you all men will come.
[3]When we were overwhelmed by sins,
    you forgave[c] our transgressions.
[4]Blessed are those you choose
    and bring near to live in your
        courts!
We are filled with the good things of
        your house,
    of your holy temple.

[5]You answer us with awesome deeds of
        righteousness,
    O God our Savior,
the hope of all the ends of the earth
    and of the farthest seas,
[6]who formed the mountains by your
        power,
    having armed yourself with
        strength,
[7]who stilled the roaring of the seas,
    the roaring of their waves,
    and the turmoil of the nations.
[8]Those living far away fear your
        wonders;
    where morning dawns and evening
        fades
    you call forth songs of joy.

[9]You care for the land and water it;
    you enrich it abundantly.
The streams of God are filled with
        water
    to provide the people with grain,
    for so you have ordained it.[d]
[10]You drench its furrows
    and level its ridges;
    you soften it with showers
    and bless its crops.
[11]You crown the year with your bounty,
    and your carts overflow with
        abundance.
[12]The grasslands of the desert overflow;
    the hills are clothed with gladness.
[13]The meadows are covered with flocks
    and the valleys are mantled with
        grain;
    they shout for joy and sing.

Psalm 66

For the director of music. A song.
A psalm.

[1]Shout with joy to God, all the earth!
[2] Sing the glory of his name;
    make his praise glorious!

a5 Or us   b1 Or befits; the meaning of the Hebrew for this word is uncertain.   c3 Or made
atonement for   d9 Or for that is how you prepare the land

³Say to God, "How awesome are your
  deeds!
    So great is your power
    that your enemies cringe before
      you.
⁴All the earth bows down to you;
    they sing praise to you,
    they sing praise to your name."
                                    Selah

⁵Come and see what God has done,
    how awesome his works in man's
      behalf!
⁶He turned the sea into dry land,
    they passed through the waters on
      foot—
    come, let us rejoice in him.
⁷He rules forever by his power,
    his eyes watch the nations—
    let not the rebellious rise up
      against him.   *Selah*

⁸Praise our God, O peoples,
    let the sound of his praise be
      heard;
⁹he has preserved our lives
    and kept our feet from slipping.
¹⁰For you, O God, tested us;
    you refined us like silver.
¹¹You brought us into prison
    and laid burdens on our backs.
¹²You let men ride over our heads;
    we went through fire and water,
    but you brought us to a place of
      abundance.

¹³I will come to your temple with burnt
      offerings
    and fulfill my vows to you—
¹⁴vows my lips promised and my mouth
      spoke
    when I was in trouble.
¹⁵I will sacrifice fat animals to you
    and an offering of rams;
    I will offer bulls and goats.   *Selah*

¹⁶Come and listen, all you who fear
      God;
    let me tell you what he has done
      for me.
¹⁷I cried out to him with my mouth;
    his praise was on my tongue.
¹⁸If I had cherished sin in my heart,
    the Lord would not have listened;
¹⁹but God has surely listened
    and heard my voice in prayer.
²⁰Praise be to God,
    who has not rejected my prayer
    or withheld his love from me!

Psalm 67

*For the director of music. With stringed
instruments. A psalm. A song.*

¹May God be gracious to us and bless
    us
    and make his face shine upon us,
                                    Selah
²that your ways may be known on
      earth,
    your salvation among all nations.

³May the peoples praise you, O God;
    may all the peoples praise you.
⁴May the nations be glad and sing for
      joy,
    for you rule the peoples justly
    and guide the nations of the earth.
                                    Selah
⁵May the peoples praise you, O God;
    may all the peoples praise you.

⁶Then the land will yield its harvest,
    and God, our God, will bless us.
⁷God will bless us,
    and all the ends of the earth will
      fear him.

Psalm 68

*For the director of music. Of David.
A psalm. A song.*

¹May God arise, may his enemies be
      scattered;
    may his foes flee before him.
²As smoke is blown away by the wind,
    may you blow them away;
    as wax melts before the fire,
    may the wicked perish before God.
³But may the righteous be glad
    and rejoice before God;
    may they be happy and joyful.

⁴Sing to God, sing praise to his name,
    extol him who rides on the
      clouds[a]—
    his name is the LORD—
    and rejoice before him.
⁵A father to the fatherless, a defender
      of widows,
    is God in his holy dwelling.
⁶God sets the lonely in families,[b]
    he leads forth the prisoners with
      singing;
    but the rebellious live in a
      sun-scorched land.

⁷When you went out before your
      people, O God,

---

[a]4 Or / *prepare the way for him who rides through the deserts*   [b]6 Or *the desolate in a homeland*

when you marched through the
wasteland,   *Selah*
[8]the earth shook,
the heavens poured down rain,
before God, the One of Sinai,
before God, the God of Israel.
[9]You gave abundant showers, O God;
you refreshed your weary
inheritance.
[10]Your people settled in it,
and from your bounty, O God, you
provided for the poor.

[11]The Lord announced the word,
and great was the company of those
who proclaimed it:
[12]"Kings and armies flee in haste;
in the camps men divide the
plunder.
[13]Even while you sleep among the
campfires,[a]
the wings of my dove are sheathed
with silver,
its feathers with shining gold."
[14]When the Almighty[b] scattered the
kings in the land,
it was like snow fallen on Zalmon.

[15]The mountains of Bashan are
majestic mountains;
rugged are the mountains of Bashan.
[16]Why gaze in envy, O rugged
mountains,
at the mountain where God chooses
to reign,
where the LORD himself will dwell
forever?
[17]The chariots of God are tens of
thousands
and thousands of thousands;
the Lord has come from Sinai into
his sanctuary.
[18]When you ascended on high,
you led captives in your train;
you received gifts from men,
even from[c] the rebellious—
that you,[d] O LORD God, might dwell
there.

[19]Praise be to the Lord, to God our
Savior,
who daily bears our burdens.   *Selah*
[20]Our God is a God who saves;
from the Sovereign LORD comes
escape from death.
[21]Surely God will crush the heads of his
enemies,

the hairy crowns of those who go
on in their sins.
[22]The Lord says, "I will bring them
from Bashan;
I will bring them from the depths of
the sea,
[23]that you may plunge your feet in the
blood of your foes,
while the tongues of your dogs have
their share."

[24]Your procession has come into view,
O God,
the procession of my God and King
into the sanctuary.
[25]In front are the singers, after them
the musicians;
with them are the maidens playing
tambourines.
[26]Praise God in the great congregation;
praise the LORD in the assembly of
Israel.
[27]There is the little tribe of Benjamin,
leading them,
there the great throng of Judah's
princes,
and there the princes of Zebulun
and of Naphtali.

[28]Summon your power, O God[e];
show us your strength, O God, as
you have done before.
[29]Because of your temple at Jerusalem
kings will bring you gifts.
[30]Rebuke the beast among the reeds,
the herd of bulls among the calves
of the nations.
Humbled, it may bring bars of silver.
Scatter the nations who delight in
war.
[31]Envoys will come from Egypt;
Cush[f] will submit herself to God.

[32]Sing to God, O kingdoms of the earth,
sing praise to the Lord,   *Selah*
[33]to him who rides the ancient skies
above,
who thunders with mighty voice.
[34]Proclaim the power of God,
whose majesty is over Israel,
whose power is in the skies.
[35]You are awesome, O God, in your
sanctuary;
the God of Israel gives power and
strength to his people.
Praise be to God!

a13 Or *saddlebags*   *b14* Hebrew *Shaddai*   *c18* Or *gifts for men, / even*   *d18* Or *they*   *e28* Many
Hebrew manuscripts, Septuagint and Syriac; most Hebrew manuscripts *Your God has summoned power for
you*   *f31* That is, the upper Nile region

Psalm 69

For the director of music. To the tune of, "Lilies." Of David.

[1]Save me, O God,
    for the waters have come up to my
        neck.
[2]I sink in the miry depths,
    where there is no foothold.
I have come into the deep waters;
    the floods engulf me.
[3]I am worn out calling for help;
    my throat is parched.
My eyes fail,
    looking for my God.
[4]Those who hate me without reason
    outnumber the hairs of my head;
many are my enemies without cause,
    those who seek to destroy me.
I am forced to restore
    what I did not steal.

[5]You know my folly, O God;
    my guilt is not hidden from you.

[6]May those who hope in you
    not be disgraced because of me,
    O Lord, the LORD Almighty;
may those who seek you
    not be put to shame because of me,
    O God of Israel.
[7]For I endure scorn for your sake,
    and shame covers my face.
[8]I am a stranger to my brothers,
    an alien to my own mother's sons;
[9]for zeal for your house consumes me,
    and the insults of those who insult
        you fall on me.
[10]When I weep and fast,
    I must endure scorn;
[11]when I put on sackcloth,
    people make sport of me.
[12]Those who sit at the gate mock me,
    and I am the song of the drunkards.

[13]But I pray to you, O LORD,
    in the time of your favor;
in your great love, O God,
    answer me with your sure salvation.
[14]Rescue me from the mire,
    do not let me sink;
deliver me from those who hate me,
    from the deep waters.
[15]Do not let the floodwaters engulf
    me
    or the depths swallow me up
    or the pit close its mouth over
        me.

[16]Answer me, O LORD, out of the
        goodness of your love;
    in your great mercy turn to me.
[17]Do not hide your face from your
        servant;
    answer me quickly, for I am in
        trouble.
[18]Come near and rescue me;
    redeem me because of my foes.

[19]You know how I am scorned,
        disgraced and shamed;
    all my enemies are before you.
[20]Scorn has broken my heart
        and has left me helpless;
    I looked for sympathy, but there was
        none,
    for comforters, but I found none.
[21]They put gall in my food
    and gave me vinegar for my thirst.

[22]May the table set before them
        become a snare;
    may it become retribution and[a] a
        trap.
[23]May their eyes be darkened so they
        cannot see,
    and their backs be bent forever.
[24]Pour out your wrath on them;
    let your fierce anger overtake them.
[25]May their place be deserted;
    let there be no one to dwell in their
        tents.
[26]For they persecute those you wound
    and talk about the pain of those
        you hurt.
[27]Charge them with crime upon crime;
    do not let them share in your
        salvation.
[28]May they be blotted out of the book
        of life
    and not be listed with the
        righteous.

[29]I am in pain and distress;
    may your salvation, O God, protect
        me.

[30]I will praise God's name in song
    and glorify him with thanksgiving.
[31]This will please the LORD more than
        an ox,
    more than a bull with its horns and
        hoofs.
[32]The poor will see and be glad—
    you who seek God, may your hearts
        live!
[33]The LORD hears the needy
    and does not despise his captive
        people.

[a]22 Or snare / and their fellowship become

³⁴Let heaven and earth praise him,
  the seas and all that move in them,
³⁵for God will save Zion
  and rebuild the cities of Judah.
Then people will settle there and
    possess it;
³⁶ the children of his servants will
      inherit it,
  and those who love his name will
    dwell there.

Psalm 70

*For the director of music. Of David.
A petition.*

¹Hasten, O God, to save me;
  O Lord, come quickly to help me.
²May those who seek my life
  be put to shame and confusion;
may all who desire my ruin
  be turned back in disgrace.
³May those who say to me, "Aha!
    Aha!"
  turn back because of their shame.
⁴But may all who seek you
  rejoice and be glad in you;
may those who love your salvation
  always say,
  "Let God be exalted!"

⁵Yet I am poor and needy;
  come quickly to me, O God.
You are my help and my deliverer;
  O Lord, do not delay.

Psalm 71

¹In you, O Lord, I have taken refuge;
  let me never be put to shame.
²Rescue me and deliver me in your
    righteousness;
  turn your ear to me and save me.
³Be my rock of refuge,
  to which I can always go;
give the command to save me,
  for you are my rock and my
    fortress.
⁴Deliver me, O my God, from the hand
    of the wicked,
  from the grasp of evil and cruel
    men.

⁵For you have been my hope,
  O Sovereign Lord,
  my confidence since my youth.
⁶From birth I have relied on you;
  you brought me forth from my
    mother's womb.
  I will ever praise you.
⁷I have become like a portent to many,
  but you are my strong refuge.
⁸My mouth is filled with your praise,
  declaring your splendor all day
    long.

⁹Do not cast me away when I am old;
  do not forsake me when my
    strength is gone.
¹⁰For my enemies speak against me;
  those who wait to kill me conspire
    together.
¹¹They say, "God has forsaken him;
  pursue him and seize him,
  for no one will rescue him."
¹²Be not far from me, O God;
  come quickly, O my God, to help
    me.
¹³May my accusers perish in shame;
  may those who want to harm me
  be covered with scorn and disgrace.

¹⁴But as for me, I will always have
    hope;
  I will praise you more and more.
¹⁵My mouth will tell of your
    righteousness,
  of your salvation all day long,
  though I know not its measure.
¹⁶I will come and proclaim your mighty
    acts, O Sovereign Lord;
  I will proclaim your righteousness,
    yours alone.
¹⁷Since my youth, O God, you have
    taught me,
  and to this day I declare your
    marvelous deeds.
¹⁸Even when I am old and gray,
  do not forsake me, O God,
till I declare your power to the next
    generation,
  your might to all who are to come.

¹⁹Your righteousness reaches to the
    skies, O God,
  you who have done great things.
  Who, O God, is like you?
²⁰Though you have made me see
    troubles, many and bitter,
  you will restore my life again;
from the depths of the earth
  you will again bring me up.
²¹You will increase my honor
  and comfort me once again.

²²I will praise you with the harp
  for your faithfulness, O my God;
I will sing praise to you with the lyre,
  O Holy One of Israel.
²³My lips will shout for joy
  when I sing praise to you—
  I, whom you have redeemed.

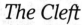
VERSE FOR THE DAY:
Psalm 71:3

AUTHOR:
Gloria Gaither

PASSAGE FOR THE DAY:
Psalm 71:1–24

The Cleft

SO that is what a "cleft of the rock" looks like! I thought of the Fanny Crosby hymn "He Hideth My Soul" as I looked at this place "overshadowed" by a desert mountain, which is nothing more than a "towering" rock. I've heard all these words and phrases in hymns and ancient poetry. Yet, having grown up in Michigan, I more easily related to "the ageless billows roll," or having sins buried in "the depths" never to be remembered again. I could easily visualize the Master warning the man "who puts his hand to the plow and looks back " (Luke 9:62). Or Jesus taking in his hand a mustard seed, planting it in the moist black soil, then pointing to a matured plant so big "that the birds of the air come and perch in its branches" (Matthew 13:32).

I could relate to "shifting sand," for I've seen the "waves" of the sand dunes, or the "shelter from the storm," for I've been caught in the fury of a Midwestern thunderstorm. I've experienced the eye of a tornado, the area that is peaceful and quiet while the circle around it rages and destroys.

But clefts. I'd never really thought much of hiding in the cleft of a rock. Yet, here above me is exactly that: a "cleft of the rock." All around this indentation made eons ago are rugged surfaces exposed constantly to the fury and heat of the desert climate. Yet, inside this cleft the rock is its original pink color, unspoiled and protected. I realize that if the "storm in fury beat around me" I'd want to be in the solid rock, halfway up the mountain, hiding in the fortress made by nature itself, in the cleft of the rock. Perhaps it was about such a place that Fanny Crosby wrote:

> A wonderful Savior is Jesus My Lord,
> A wonderful Savior to me;
> He hideth my soul in the cleft of the rock,
> Where rivers of pleasure I see.
>
> He hideth my soul in the cleft of the rock
> That shadows a dry, thirsty land;
> He hideth my life in the depths of His love,
> And covers me there with His hand,
> And covers me there with His hand.

Additional Scripture Readings:
Exodus 33:18–23; Colossians 3:1–3

Go to page 467 for your next devotional reading.

24My tongue will tell of your righteous
    acts
    all day long,
for those who wanted to harm me
    have been put to shame and
    confusion.

Psalm 72

Of Solomon.

1Endow the king with your justice,
    O God,
    the royal son with your
    righteousness.
2He will*a* judge your people in
    righteousness,
    your afflicted ones with justice.
3The mountains will bring prosperity
    to the people,
    the hills the fruit of righteousness.
4He will defend the afflicted among
    the people
    and save the children of the needy;
    he will crush the oppressor.

5He will endure*b* as long as the sun,
    as long as the moon, through all
    generations.
6He will be like rain falling on a mown
    field,
    like showers watering the earth.
7In his days the righteous will flourish;
    prosperity will abound till the moon
    is no more.

8He will rule from sea to sea
    and from the River*c* to the ends of
    the earth.*d*
9The desert tribes will bow before him
    and his enemies will lick the dust.
10The kings of Tarshish and of distant
    shores
    will bring tribute to him;
    the kings of Sheba and Seba
    will present him gifts.
11All kings will bow down to him
    and all nations will serve him.

12For he will deliver the needy who cry
    out,
    the afflicted who have no one to
    help.
13He will take pity on the weak and the
    needy
    and save the needy from death.
14He will rescue them from oppression
    and violence,

for precious is their blood in his
    sight.

15Long may he live!
    May gold from Sheba be given him.
May people ever pray for him
    and bless him all day long.
16Let grain abound throughout the
    land;
    on the tops of the hills may it sway.
Let its fruit flourish like Lebanon;
    let it thrive like the grass of the
    field.
17May his name endure forever;
    may it continue as long as the sun.

All nations will be blessed through
    him,
    and they will call him blessed.

18Praise be to the LORD God, the God of
    Israel,
    who alone does marvelous deeds.
19Praise be to his glorious name forever;
    may the whole earth be filled with
    his glory.
        Amen and Amen.

20This concludes the prayers of David
    son of Jesse.

BOOK III

Psalms 73–89

Psalm 73

A psalm of Asaph.

1Surely God is good to Israel,
    to those who are pure in heart.

2But as for me, my feet had almost
    slipped;
    I had nearly lost my foothold.
3For I envied the arrogant
    when I saw the prosperity of the
    wicked.

4They have no struggles;
    their bodies are healthy and
    strong.*e*
5They are free from the burdens
    common to man;
    they are not plagued by human ills.
6Therefore pride is their necklace;
    they clothe themselves with
    violence.

a2 Or *May he*; similarly in verses 3-11 and 17   *b5* Septuagint; Hebrew *You will be feared*   *c8* That
is, the Euphrates   *d8* Or *the end of the land*   *e4* With a different word division of the Hebrew;
Masoretic Text *struggles at their death; / their bodies are healthy*

7From their callous hearts comes
iniquity[a];
  the evil conceits of their minds
know no limits.
8They scoff, and speak with malice;
  in their arrogance they threaten
oppression.
9Their mouths lay claim to heaven,
  and their tongues take possession
of the earth.
10Therefore their people turn to them
  and drink up waters in
abundance.[b]
11They say, "How can God know?
  Does the Most High have
knowledge?"

12This is what the wicked are like—
  always carefree, they increase in
wealth.

13Surely in vain have I kept my heart
pure;
  in vain have I washed my hands in
innocence.
14All day long I have been plagued;
  I have been punished every
morning.

15If I had said, "I will speak thus,"
  I would have betrayed your
children.
16When I tried to understand all this,
  it was oppressive to me
17till I entered the sanctuary of God;
  then I understood their final
destiny.

18Surely you place them on slippery
ground;
  you cast them down to ruin.
19How suddenly are they destroyed,
  completely swept away by terrors!
20As a dream when one awakes,
  so when you arise, O Lord,
  you will despise them as fantasies.

21When my heart was grieved
  and my spirit embittered,
22I was senseless and ignorant;
  I was a brute beast before you.

23Yet I am always with you;
  you hold me by my right hand.
24You guide me with your counsel,
  and afterward you will take me into
glory.
25Whom have I in heaven but you?
  And earth has nothing I desire
besides you.

26My flesh and my heart may fail,
  but God is the strength of my heart
  and my portion forever.

27Those who are far from you will
perish;
  you destroy all who are unfaithful
to you.
28But as for me, it is good to be near
God.
  I have made the Sovereign LORD my
refuge;
  I will tell of all your deeds.

Psalm 74

A *maskil*[c] of Asaph.

1Why have you rejected us forever,
O God?
  Why does your anger smolder
  against the sheep of your
pasture?
2Remember the people you purchased
of old,
  the tribe of your inheritance, whom
you redeemed—
  Mount Zion, where you dwelt.
3Turn your steps toward these
everlasting ruins,
  all this destruction the enemy has
brought on the sanctuary.

4Your foes roared in the place where
you met with us;
  they set up their standards as signs.
5They behaved like men wielding axes
  to cut through a thicket of trees.
6They smashed all the carved paneling
  with their axes and hatchets.
7They burned your sanctuary to the
ground;
  they defiled the dwelling place of
your Name.
8They said in their hearts, "We will
crush them completely!"
  They burned every place where God
was worshiped in the land.
9We are given no miraculous signs;
  no prophets are left,
  and none of us knows how long
this will be.

10How long will the enemy mock you,
O God?
  Will the foe revile your name
forever?
11Why do you hold back your hand,
  your right hand?

[a]7 Syriac (see also Septuagint); Hebrew *Their eyes bulge with fat*   [b]10 The meaning of the Hebrew for this verse is uncertain.   [c]Title: Probably a literary or musical term

Take it from the folds of your
    garment and destroy them!

12But you, O God, are my king from of
        old;
    you bring salvation upon the earth.
13It was you who split open the sea by
        your power;
    you broke the heads of the monster
        in the waters.
14It was you who crushed the heads of
        Leviathan
    and gave him as food to the
        creatures of the desert.
15It was you who opened up springs
        and streams;
    you dried up the ever flowing rivers.
16The day is yours, and yours also the
        night;
    you established the sun and moon.
17It was you who set all the boundaries
        of the earth;
    you made both summer and winter.

18Remember how the enemy has
        mocked you, O LORD,
    how foolish people have reviled
        your name.
19Do not hand over the life of your dove
        to wild beasts;
    do not forget the lives of your
        afflicted people forever.
20Have regard for your covenant,
    because haunts of violence fill the
        dark places of the land.
21Do not let the oppressed retreat in
        disgrace;
    may the poor and needy praise your
        name.

22Rise up, O God, and defend your
        cause;
    remember how fools mock you all
        day long.
23Do not ignore the clamor of your
        adversaries,
    the uproar of your enemies, which
        rises continually.

Psalm 75

For the director of music. To the tune
of, "Do Not Destroy." A psalm of Asaph.
A song.

1We give thanks to you, O God,
    we give thanks, for your Name is
        near;
    men tell of your wonderful deeds.

2You say, "I choose the appointed
        time;

it is I who judge uprightly.
3When the earth and all its people
        quake,
    it is I who hold its pillars firm.
                                    Selah

4To the arrogant I say, 'Boast no
        more,'
    and to the wicked, 'Do not lift up
        your horns.
5Do not lift your horns against heaven;
    do not speak with outstretched
        neck.' "

6No one from the east or the west
    or from the desert can exalt a man.
7But it is God who judges:
    He brings one down, he exalts
        another.
8In the hand of the LORD is a cup
    full of foaming wine mixed with
        spices;
    he pours it out, and all the wicked of
        the earth
    drink it down to its very dregs.

9As for me, I will declare this forever;
    I will sing praise to the God of
        Jacob.
10I will cut off the horns of all the
        wicked,
    but the horns of the righteous will
        be lifted up.

Psalm 76

For the director of music. With stringed
instruments. A psalm of Asaph. A song.

1In Judah God is known;
    his name is great in Israel.
2His tent is in Salem,
    his dwelling place in Zion.
3There he broke the flashing arrows,
    the shields and the swords, the
        weapons of war.   Selah

4You are resplendent with light,
    more majestic than mountains rich
        with game.
5Valiant men lie plundered,
    they sleep their last sleep;
not one of the warriors
    can lift his hands.
6At your rebuke, O God of Jacob,
    both horse and chariot lie still.
7You alone are to be feared.
    Who can stand before you when
        you are angry?
8From heaven you pronounced
        judgment,

and the land feared and was
    quiet—
⁹when you, O God, rose up to judge,
    to save all the afflicted of the land.
                                    Selah

¹⁰Surely your wrath against men brings
    you praise,
    and the survivors of your wrath are
    restrained.*ᵃ*

¹¹Make vows to the LORD your God and
    fulfill them;
    let all the neighboring lands
    bring gifts to the One to be feared.
¹²He breaks the spirit of rulers;
    he is feared by the kings of the
    earth.

Psalm 77

For the director of music. For Jeduthun.
Of Asaph. A psalm.

¹I cried out to God for help;
    I cried out to God to hear me.
²When I was in distress, I sought the
    Lord;
    at night I stretched out untiring
    hands
    and my soul refused to be
    comforted.

³I remembered you, O God, and I
    groaned;
    I mused, and my spirit grew faint.
                                    Selah

⁴You kept my eyes from closing;
    I was too troubled to speak.
⁵I thought about the former days,
    the years of long ago;
⁶I remembered my songs in the night.
    My heart mused and my spirit
    inquired:

⁷"Will the Lord reject forever?
    Will he never show his favor again?
⁸Has his unfailing love vanished
    forever?
    Has his promise failed for all time?
⁹Has God forgotten to be merciful?
    Has he in anger withheld his
    compassion?"   *Selah*

¹⁰Then I thought, "To this I will appeal:
    the years of the right hand of the
    Most High."
¹¹I will remember the deeds of the
    LORD;

yes, I will remember your miracles
    of long ago.
¹²I will meditate on all your works
    and consider all your mighty deeds.

¹³Your ways, O God, are holy.
    What god is so great as our God?
¹⁴You are the God who performs
    miracles;
    you display your power among the
    peoples.
¹⁵With your mighty arm you redeemed
    your people,
    the descendants of Jacob and
    Joseph.   *Selah*

¹⁶The waters saw you, O God,
    the waters saw you and writhed;
    the very depths were convulsed.
¹⁷The clouds poured down water,
    the skies resounded with thunder;
    your arrows flashed back and forth.
¹⁸Your thunder was heard in the
    whirlwind,
    your lightning lit up the world;
    the earth trembled and quaked.
¹⁹Your path led through the sea,
    your way through the mighty
    waters,
    though your footprints were not
    seen.

²⁰You led your people like a flock
    by the hand of Moses and Aaron.

Psalm 78

A *maskil*ᵇ of Asaph.

¹O my people, hear my teaching;
    listen to the words of my mouth.
²I will open my mouth in parables,
    I will utter hidden things, things
    from of old—
³what we have heard and known,
    what our fathers have told us.
⁴We will not hide them from their
    children;
    we will tell the next generation
    the praiseworthy deeds of the LORD,
    his power, and the wonders he has
    done.
⁵He decreed statutes for Jacob
    and established the law in Israel,
    which he commanded our forefathers
    to teach their children,
⁶so the next generation would know
    them,
    even the children yet to be born,

ᵃ10 Or *Surely the wrath of men brings you praise, / and with the remainder of wrath you arm yourself*
ᵇTitle: Probably a literary or musical term

and they in turn would tell their
children.
⁷Then they would put their trust in
God
and would not forget his deeds
but would keep his commands.
⁸They would not be like their
forefathers—
a stubborn and rebellious
generation,
whose hearts were not loyal to God,
whose spirits were not faithful to
him.

⁹The men of Ephraim, though armed
with bows,
turned back on the day of battle;
¹⁰they did not keep God's covenant
and refused to live by his law.
¹¹They forgot what he had done,
the wonders he had shown them.
¹²He did miracles in the sight of their
fathers
in the land of Egypt, in the region
of Zoan.
¹³He divided the sea and led them
through;
he made the water stand firm like a
wall.
¹⁴He guided them with the cloud by
day
and with light from the fire all
night.
¹⁵He split the rocks in the desert
and gave them water as abundant
as the seas;
¹⁶he brought streams out of a rocky
crag
and made water flow down like
rivers.

¹⁷But they continued to sin against
him,
rebelling in the desert against the
Most High.
¹⁸They willfully put God to the test
by demanding the food they craved.
¹⁹They spoke against God, saying,
"Can God spread a table in the
desert?
²⁰When he struck the rock, water
gushed out,
and streams flowed abundantly.
But can he also give us food?
Can he supply meat for his
people?"
²¹When the LORD heard them, he was
very angry;
his fire broke out against Jacob,
and his wrath rose against Israel,
²²for they did not believe in God

or trust in his deliverance.
²³Yet he gave a command to the skies
above
and opened the doors of the
heavens;
²⁴he rained down manna for the people
to eat,
he gave them the grain of heaven.
²⁵Men ate the bread of angels;
he sent them all the food they
could eat.
²⁶He let loose the east wind from the
heavens
and led forth the south wind by his
power.
²⁷He rained meat down on them like
dust,
flying birds like sand on the
seashore.
²⁸He made them come down inside
their camp,
all around their tents.
²⁹They ate till they had more than
enough,
for he had given them what they
craved.
³⁰But before they turned from the food
they craved,
even while it was still in their
mouths,
³¹God's anger rose against them;
he put to death the sturdiest
among them,
cutting down the young men of
Israel.

³²In spite of all this, they kept on
sinning;
in spite of his wonders, they did
not believe.
³³So he ended their days in futility
and their years in terror.
³⁴Whenever God slew them, they would
seek him;
they eagerly turned to him again.
³⁵They remembered that God was their
Rock,
that God Most High was their
Redeemer.
³⁶But then they would flatter him with
their mouths,
lying to him with their tongues;
³⁷their hearts were not loyal to him,
they were not faithful to his
covenant.
³⁸Yet he was merciful;
he forgave their iniquities
and did not destroy them.
Time after time he restrained his
anger

and did not stir up his full wrath.
³⁹He remembered that they were but flesh,
a passing breeze that does not return.

⁴⁰How often they rebelled against him in the desert
and grieved him in the wasteland!
⁴¹Again and again they put God to the test;
they vexed the Holy One of Israel.
⁴²They did not remember his power—
the day he redeemed them from the oppressor,
⁴³the day he displayed his miraculous signs in Egypt,
his wonders in the region of Zoan.
⁴⁴He turned their rivers to blood;
they could not drink from their streams.
⁴⁵He sent swarms of flies that devoured them,
and frogs that devastated them.
⁴⁶He gave their crops to the grasshopper,
their produce to the locust.
⁴⁷He destroyed their vines with hail
and their sycamore-figs with sleet.
⁴⁸He gave over their cattle to the hail,
their livestock to bolts of lightning.
⁴⁹He unleashed against them his hot anger,
his wrath, indignation and hostility—
a band of destroying angels.
⁵⁰He prepared a path for his anger;
he did not spare them from death
but gave them over to the plague.
⁵¹He struck down all the firstborn of Egypt,
the firstfruits of manhood in the tents of Ham.
⁵²But he brought his people out like a flock;
he led them like sheep through the desert.
⁵³He guided them safely, so they were unafraid;
but the sea engulfed their enemies.
⁵⁴Thus he brought them to the border of his holy land,
to the hill country his right hand had taken.
⁵⁵He drove out nations before them
and allotted their lands to them as an inheritance;
he settled the tribes of Israel in their homes.

⁵⁶But they put God to the test
and rebelled against the Most High;
they did not keep his statutes.
⁵⁷Like their fathers they were disloyal and faithless,
as unreliable as a faulty bow.
⁵⁸They angered him with their high places;
they aroused his jealousy with their idols.
⁵⁹When God heard them, he was very angry;
he rejected Israel completely.
⁶⁰He abandoned the tabernacle of Shiloh,
the tent he had set up among men.
⁶¹He sent the ark of his might into captivity,
his splendor into the hands of the enemy.
⁶²He gave his people over to the sword;
he was very angry with his inheritance.
⁶³Fire consumed their young men,
and their maidens had no wedding songs;
⁶⁴their priests were put to the sword,
and their widows could not weep.

⁶⁵Then the Lord awoke as from sleep,
as a man wakes from the stupor of wine.
⁶⁶He beat back his enemies;
he put them to everlasting shame.
⁶⁷Then he rejected the tents of Joseph,
he did not choose the tribe of Ephraim;
⁶⁸but he chose the tribe of Judah,
Mount Zion, which he loved.
⁶⁹He built his sanctuary like the heights,
like the earth that he established forever.
⁷⁰He chose David his servant
and took him from the sheep pens;
⁷¹from tending the sheep he brought him
to be the shepherd of his people Jacob,
of Israel his inheritance.
⁷²And David shepherded them with integrity of heart;
with skillful hands he led them.

Psalm 79

A psalm of Asaph.

¹O God, the nations have invaded your inheritance;
they have defiled your holy temple,

they have reduced Jerusalem to
rubble.
²They have given the dead bodies of
your servants
as food to the birds of the air,
the flesh of your saints to the
beasts of the earth.
³They have poured out blood like
water
all around Jerusalem,
and there is no one to bury the
dead.
⁴We are objects of reproach to our
neighbors,
of scorn and derision to those
around us.

⁵How long, O LORD? Will you be angry
forever?
How long will your jealousy burn
like fire?
⁶Pour out your wrath on the
nations
that do not acknowledge you,
on the kingdoms
that do not call on your name;
⁷for they have devoured Jacob
and destroyed his homeland.
⁸Do not hold against us the sins of the
fathers;
may your mercy come quickly to
meet us,
for we are in desperate need.

⁹Help us, O God our Savior,
for the glory of your name;
deliver us and forgive our sins
for your name's sake.
¹⁰Why should the nations say,
"Where is their God?"
Before our eyes, make known among
the nations
that you avenge the outpoured
blood of your servants.
¹¹May the groans of the prisoners come
before you;
by the strength of your arm
preserve those condemned to
die.

¹²Pay back into the laps of our
neighbors seven times
the reproach they have hurled at
you, O Lord.
¹³Then we your people, the sheep of
your pasture,
will praise you forever;
from generation to generation
we will recount your praise.

Psalm 80

For the director of music. To the tune
of, "The Lilies of the Covenant."
Of Asaph. A psalm.

¹Hear us, O Shepherd of Israel,
you who lead Joseph like a flock;
you who sit enthroned between the
cherubim, shine forth
²   before Ephraim, Benjamin and
Manasseh.
Awaken your might;
come and save us.

³Restore us, O God;
make your face shine upon us,
that we may be saved.

⁴O LORD God Almighty,
how long will your anger smolder
against the prayers of your people?
⁵You have fed them with the bread of
tears;
you have made them drink tears by
the bowlful.
⁶You have made us a source of
contention to our neighbors,
and our enemies mock us.

⁷Restore us, O God Almighty;
make your face shine upon us,
that we may be saved.

⁸You brought a vine out of Egypt;
you drove out the nations and
planted it.
⁹You cleared the ground for it,
and it took root and filled the land.
¹⁰The mountains were covered with its
shade,
the mighty cedars with its
branches.
¹¹It sent out its boughs to the Sea,ᵃ
its shoots as far as the River.ᵇ

¹²Why have you broken down its walls
so that all who pass by pick its
grapes?
¹³Boars from the forest ravage it
and the creatures of the field feed
on it.
¹⁴Return to us, O God Almighty!
Look down from heaven and see!
Watch over this vine,
¹⁵   the root your right hand has
planted,
the sonᶜ you have raised up for
yourself.

ᵃ11 Probably the Mediterranean   ᵇ11 That is, the Euphrates   ᶜ15 Or branch

¹⁶Your vine is cut down, it is burned
with fire;
  at your rebuke your people perish.
¹⁷Let your hand rest on the man at
your right hand,
  the son of man you have raised up
for yourself.
¹⁸Then we will not turn away from you;
  revive us, and we will call on your
name.

¹⁹Restore us, O LORD God Almighty;
  make your face shine upon us,
  that we may be saved.

Psalm 81

For the director of music. According to
gittith. ᵃ Of Asaph.

¹Sing for joy to God our strength;
  shout aloud to the God of Jacob!
²Begin the music, strike the
tambourine,
  play the melodious harp and lyre.

³Sound the ram's horn at the New
Moon,
  and when the moon is full, on the
day of our Feast;
⁴this is a decree for Israel,
  an ordinance of the God of Jacob.
⁵He established it as a statute for
Joseph
  when he went out against Egypt,
  where we heard a language we did
not understand.ᵇ

⁶He says, "I removed the burden from
their shoulders;
  their hands were set free from the
basket.
⁷In your distress you called and I
rescued you,
  I answered you out of a
thundercloud;
  I tested you at the waters of
Meribah.   Selah

⁸"Hear, O my people, and I will warn
you —
  if you would but listen to me,
O Israel!
⁹You shall have no foreign god among
you;
  you shall not bow down to an alien
god.
¹⁰I am the LORD your God,
  who brought you up out of Egypt.

Open wide your mouth and I will
fill it.

¹¹"But my people would not listen to
me;
  Israel would not submit to me.
¹²So I gave them over to their stubborn
hearts
  to follow their own devices.

¹³"If my people would but listen to me,
  if Israel would follow my ways,
¹⁴how quickly would I subdue their
enemies
  and turn my hand against their
foes!
¹⁵Those who hate the LORD would
cringe before him,
  and their punishment would last
forever.
¹⁶But you would be fed with the finest
of wheat;
  with honey from the rock I would
satisfy you."

Psalm 82

A psalm of Asaph.

¹God presides in the great assembly;
  he gives judgment among the
"gods":

²"How long will youᶜ defend the
unjust
  and show partiality to the wicked?
                                    Selah
³Defend the cause of the weak and
fatherless;
  maintain the rights of the poor and
oppressed.
⁴Rescue the weak and needy;
  deliver them from the hand of the
wicked.

⁵"They know nothing, they understand
nothing.
  They walk about in darkness;
  all the foundations of the earth are
shaken.

⁶"I said, 'You are "gods";
  you are all sons of the Most High.'
⁷But you will die like mere men;
  you will fall like every other ruler."

⁸Rise up, O God, judge the earth,
  for all the nations are your
inheritance.

ᵃTitle: Probably a musical term   ᵇ5 Or / and we heard a voice we had not known   ᶜ2 The Hebrew is
plural.

Psalm 83

A song. A psalm of Asaph.

[1] O God, do not keep silent;
  be not quiet, O God, be not
    still.
[2] See how your enemies are astir,
  how your foes rear their heads.
[3] With cunning they conspire against
    your people;
  they plot against those you cherish.
[4] "Come," they say, "let us destroy
    them as a nation,
  that the name of Israel be
    remembered no more."

[5] With one mind they plot together;
  they form an alliance against
    you—
[6] the tents of Edom and the
    Ishmaelites,
  of Moab and the Hagrites,
[7] Gebal,[a] Ammon and Amalek,
  Philistia, with the people of Tyre.
[8] Even Assyria has joined them
  to lend strength to the descendants
    of Lot.   *Selah*

[9] Do to them as you did to Midian,
  as you did to Sisera and Jabin at
    the river Kishon,
[10] who perished at Endor
  and became like refuse on the
    ground.
[11] Make their nobles like Oreb and
    Zeeb,
  all their princes like Zebah and
    Zalmunna,
[12] who said, "Let us take possession
  of the pasturelands of God."

[13] Make them like tumbleweed, O my
    God,
  like chaff before the wind.
[14] As fire consumes the forest
  or a flame sets the mountains
    ablaze,
[15] so pursue them with your tempest
  and terrify them with your storm.
[16] Cover their faces with shame
  so that men will seek your name,
    O LORD.

[17] May they ever be ashamed and
    dismayed;
  may they perish in disgrace.
[18] Let them know that you, whose name
    is the LORD—

that you alone are the Most High
  over all the earth.

Psalm 84

For the director of music. According to gittith.[b] Of the Sons of Korah. A psalm.

[1] How lovely is your dwelling place,
  O LORD Almighty!
[2] My soul yearns, even faints,
  for the courts of the LORD;
my heart and my flesh cry out
  for the living God.

[3] Even the sparrow has found a home,
  and the swallow a nest for herself,
  where she may have her young—
a place near your altar,
  O LORD Almighty, my King and my
    God.
[4] Blessed are those who dwell in your
    house;
  they are ever praising you.   *Selah*

[5] Blessed are those whose strength is in
    you,
  who have set their hearts on
    pilgrimage.
[6] As they pass through the Valley of
    Baca,
  they make it a place of springs;
  the autumn rains also cover it with
    pools.[c]
[7] They go from strength to strength,
  till each appears before God in
    Zion.

[8] Hear my prayer, O LORD God
    Almighty;
  listen to me, O God of Jacob. *Selah*
[9] Look upon our shield,[d] O God;
  look with favor on your anointed
    one.

[10] Better is one day in your courts
  than a thousand elsewhere;
I would rather be a doorkeeper in the
    house of my God
  than dwell in the tents of the
    wicked.
[11] For the LORD God is a sun and shield;
  the LORD bestows favor and honor;
no good thing does he withhold
  from those whose walk is
    blameless.

[12] O LORD Almighty,
  blessed is the man who trusts in
    you.

---

a7 That is, Byblos   *b*Title: Probably a musical term   *c6* Or *blessings*   *d9* Or *sovereign*

VERSE FOR THE DAY:
Psalm 84:3

AUTHOR:
Debby Boone

PASSAGE FOR THE DAY:
Psalm 84:1–12

I Will Meet All Their Needs

I READ Psalm 84:3 one morning while on an airplane flying across the country, after I'd left my family for a few days to sing in different churches. As I read the verse, I knew that the Lord wanted to use this Scripture to teach me something about raising children. I took out my journal to record some thoughts about this "nest" where I could lay down my own young: 1. A nest is a place of security, rest and provision. 2. It is a place to lay my children on God's altar daily. 3. It will take a sacrifice of time to seek knowledge and wisdom for my young.

I closed my journal, feeling a sense of accomplishment and great motivation to begin building the perfect nest for my four children.

The next morning I was on another plane headed for one more concert when I read the psalm again. This time the second verse jumped out at me:

> My soul yearns, even faints,
> for the courts of the Lord;
> my heart and my flesh cry out
> for the living God.

I was overwhelmed by this expression of great love and desire to be with the Lord. Yet it did not match the uneasy feeling in my own heart. My feeling of impending failure. The feeling that, sure, I can make a great list of how to raise my kids, but can I live up to it? Instead of seeking God's presence, I wanted to hide from him and avoid facing my own discouragement and his disappointment.

Then I felt the Lord speak gently to my heart: "Debby, this nest is not made up of *your* sacrifices. It is made up of *mine.* I have made every sacrifice necessary to provide a place for your family to dwell. There I will meet all their needs. Come to my courts and be reminded of my love for you and all that that love has made available to you."

Joseph Scriven's hymn "What a Friend We Have in Jesus" came to my heart as the plane started to descend. I now knew that I could trust. Not in the nest I could build, but in the Lord's altar.

Additional Scripture Readings:
Psalm 23:5–6; John 14:1–4

*Go to page 473 for your next
devotional reading.*

Psalm 85

For the director of music. Of the Sons
of Korah. A psalm.

¹You showed favor to your land,
O LORD;
  you restored the fortunes of Jacob.
²You forgave the iniquity of your
people
  and covered all their sins.   *Selah*
³You set aside all your wrath
  and turned from your fierce anger.

⁴Restore us again, O God our Savior,
  and put away your displeasure
    toward us.
⁵Will you be angry with us forever?
  Will you prolong your anger through
    all generations?
⁶Will you not revive us again,
  that your people may rejoice in
    you?
⁷Show us your unfailing love, O LORD,
  and grant us your salvation.

⁸I will listen to what God the LORD will
say;
  he promises peace to his people,
    his saints —
  but let them not return to folly.
⁹Surely his salvation is near those who
fear him,
  that his glory may dwell in our
    land.

¹⁰Love and faithfulness meet together;
  righteousness and peace kiss each
    other.
¹¹Faithfulness springs forth from the
earth,
  and righteousness looks down from
    heaven.
¹²The LORD will indeed give what is
good,
  and our land will yield its harvest.
¹³Righteousness goes before him
  and prepares the way for his steps.

Psalm 86

A prayer of David.

¹Hear, O LORD, and answer me,
  for I am poor and needy.
²Guard my life, for I am devoted to
you.
  You are my God; save your servant
    who trusts in you.

³Have mercy on me, O Lord,
  for I call to you all day long.
⁴Bring joy to your servant,
  for to you, O Lord,
    I lift up my soul.

⁵You are forgiving and good, O Lord,
  abounding in love to all who call to
    you.
⁶Hear my prayer, O LORD;
  listen to my cry for mercy.
⁷In the day of my trouble I will call to
you,
  for you will answer me.

⁸Among the gods there is none like
you, O Lord;
  no deeds can compare with
    yours.
⁹All the nations you have made
  will come and worship before you,
    O Lord;
  they will bring glory to your
    name.
¹⁰For you are great and do marvelous
deeds;
  you alone are God.

¹¹Teach me your way, O LORD,
  and I will walk in your truth;
  give me an undivided heart,
    that I may fear your name.
¹²I will praise you, O Lord my God,
  with all my heart;
  I will glorify your name forever.
¹³For great is your love toward me;
  you have delivered me from the
    depths of the grave.ᵃ

¹⁴The arrogant are attacking me,
O God;
  a band of ruthless men seeks my
    life —
  men without regard for you.
¹⁵But you, O Lord, are a compassionate
    and gracious God,
  slow to anger, abounding in love
    and faithfulness.
¹⁶Turn to me and have mercy on
me;
  grant your strength to your
    servant
  and save the son of your
    maidservant.ᵇ
¹⁷Give me a sign of your goodness,
  that your enemies may see it and be
    put to shame,
  for you, O LORD, have helped me
    and comforted me.

ᵃ13 Hebrew *Sheol*   ᵇ16 Or *save your faithful son*

Psalm 87

Of the Sons of Korah. A psalm. A song.

[1]He has set his foundation on the holy
    mountain;
[2] the LORD loves the gates of Zion
    more than all the dwellings of
    Jacob.
[3]Glorious things are said of you,
    O city of God: *Selah*
[4]"I will record Rahab[g] and Babylon
    among those who acknowledge
    me—
  Philistia too, and Tyre, along with
    Cush[b]—
  and will say, 'This[c] one was born
    in Zion.' "

[5]Indeed, of Zion it will be said,
    "This one and that one were born
    in her,
    and the Most High himself will
    establish her."
[6]The LORD will write in the register of
    the peoples:
    "This one was born in Zion." *Selah*
[7]As they make music they will sing,
    "All my fountains are in you."

Psalm 88

A song. A psalm of the Sons of Korah.
For the director of music. According to
mahalath leannoth.[d] A *maskil*[e] of
Heman the Ezrahite.

[1]O LORD, the God who saves me,
    day and night I cry out before you.
[2]May my prayer come before you;
    turn your ear to my cry.

[3]For my soul is full of trouble
    and my life draws near the grave.[f]
[4]I am counted among those who go
    down to the pit;
    I am like a man without strength.
[5]I am set apart with the dead,
    like the slain who lie in the grave,
  whom you remember no more,
    who are cut off from your care.

[6]You have put me in the lowest pit,
    in the darkest depths.
[7]Your wrath lies heavily upon me;
    you have overwhelmed me with all
    your waves.   *Selah*

[8]You have taken from me my closest
    friends
    and have made me repulsive to
    them.
  I am confined and cannot escape;
[9] my eyes are dim with grief.

I call to you, O LORD, every day;
    I spread out my hands to you.
[10]Do you show your wonders to the
    dead?
    Do those who are dead rise up and
    praise you?   *Selah*
[11]Is your love declared in the grave,
    your faithfulness in Destruction[g]?
[12]Are your wonders known in the place
    of darkness,
    or your righteous deeds in the land
    of oblivion?

[13]But I cry to you for help, O LORD;
    in the morning my prayer comes
    before you.
[14]Why, O LORD, do you reject me
    and hide your face from me?

[15]From my youth I have been afflicted
    and close to death;
    I have suffered your terrors and am
    in despair.
[16]Your wrath has swept over me;
    your terrors have destroyed me.
[17]All day long they surround me like a
    flood;
    they have completely engulfed me.
[18]You have taken my companions and
    loved ones from me;
    the darkness is my closest friend.

Psalm 89

A *maskil*[e] of Ethan the Ezrahite.

[1]I will sing of the LORD's great love
    forever;
    with my mouth I will make your
    faithfulness known through all
    generations.
[2]I will declare that your love stands
    firm forever,
    that you established your
    faithfulness in heaven itself.

[3]You said, "I have made a covenant
    with my chosen one,
    I have sworn to David my servant,
[4]I will establish your line forever

and make your throne firm through
all generations.' "   *Selah*

⁵The heavens praise your wonders,
  O LORD,
  your faithfulness too, in the
    assembly of the holy ones.
⁶For who in the skies above can
    compare with the LORD?
  Who is like the LORD among the
    heavenly beings?
⁷In the council of the holy ones God is
    greatly feared;
  he is more awesome than all who
    surround him.
⁸O LORD God Almighty, who is like
    you?
  You are mighty, O LORD, and your
    faithfulness surrounds you.

⁹You rule over the surging sea;
  when its waves mount up, you still
    them.
¹⁰You crushed Rahab like one of the
    slain;
  with your strong arm you scattered
    your enemies.
¹¹The heavens are yours, and yours also
    the earth;
  you founded the world and all that
    is in it.
¹²You created the north and the south;
  Tabor and Hermon sing for joy at
    your name.
¹³Your arm is endued with power;
  your hand is strong, your right hand
    exalted.

¹⁴Righteousness and justice are the
    foundation of your throne;
  love and faithfulness go before you.
¹⁵Blessed are those who have learned to
    acclaim you,
  who walk in the light of your
    presence, O LORD.
¹⁶They rejoice in your name all day
    long;
  they exult in your righteousness.
¹⁷For you are their glory and strength,
  and by your favor you exalt our
    horn.ᵃ
¹⁸Indeed, our shieldᵇ belongs to the
    LORD,
  our king to the Holy One of Israel.

¹⁹Once you spoke in a vision,
  to your faithful people you said:
"I have bestowed strength on a
    warrior;

I have exalted a young man from
    among the people.
²⁰I have found David my servant;
  with my sacred oil I have anointed
    him.
²¹My hand will sustain him;
  surely my arm will strengthen him.
²²No enemy will subject him to tribute;
  no wicked man will oppress him.
²³I will crush his foes before him
  and strike down his adversaries.
²⁴My faithful love will be with him,
  and through my name his hornᶜ
    will be exalted.
²⁵I will set his hand over the sea,
  his right hand over the rivers.
²⁶He will call out to me, 'You are my
    Father,
  my God, the Rock my Savior.'
²⁷I will also appoint him my firstborn,
  the most exalted of the kings of the
    earth.
²⁸I will maintain my love to him
    forever,
  and my covenant with him will
    never fail.
²⁹I will establish his line forever,
  his throne as long as the heavens
    endure.

³⁰"If his sons forsake my law
  and do not follow my statutes,
³¹if they violate my decrees
  and fail to keep my commands,
³²I will punish their sin with the rod,
  their iniquity with flogging;
³³but I will not take my love from him,
  nor will I ever betray my
    faithfulness.
³⁴I will not violate my covenant
  or alter what my lips have uttered.
³⁵Once for all, I have sworn by my
    holiness—
  and I will not lie to David—
³⁶that his line will continue forever
  and his throne endure before me
    like the sun;
³⁷it will be established forever like the
    moon,
  the faithful witness in the sky."   *Selah*

³⁸But you have rejected, you have
    spurned,
  you have been very angry with your
    anointed one.
³⁹You have renounced the covenant
    with your servant

ᵃ17 *Horn* here symbolizes strong one.   ᵇ18 Or *sovereign*   ᶜ24 *Horn* here symbolizes strength.

and have defiled his crown in the
    dust.
⁴⁰You have broken through all his walls
    and reduced his strongholds to
        ruins.
⁴¹All who pass by have plundered him;
    he has become the scorn of his
        neighbors.
⁴²You have exalted the right hand of his
        foes;
    you have made all his enemies
        rejoice.
⁴³You have turned back the edge of his
        sword
    and have not supported him in
        battle.
⁴⁴You have put an end to his splendor
    and cast his throne to the ground.
⁴⁵You have cut short the days of his
        youth;
    you have covered him with a
        mantle of shame.   *Selah*

⁴⁶How long, O LORD? Will you hide
        yourself forever?
    How long will your wrath burn like
        fire?
⁴⁷Remember how fleeting is my life.
    For what futility you have created
        all men!
⁴⁸What man can live and not see death,
    or save himself from the power of
        the grave*ᵃ*?   *Selah*
⁴⁹O Lord, where is your former great
        love,
    which in your faithfulness you
        swore to David?
⁵⁰Remember, Lord, how your servant
        has*ᵇ* been mocked,
    how I bear in my heart the taunts
        of all the nations,
⁵¹the taunts with which your enemies
        have mocked, O LORD,
    with which they have mocked every
        step of your anointed one.

⁵²Praise be to the LORD forever!
    Amen and Amen.

BOOK IV

Psalms 90–106

Psalm 90

A prayer of Moses the man of God.

¹Lord, you have been our dwelling
        place

throughout all generations.
²Before the mountains were born
    or you brought forth the earth and
        the world,
    from everlasting to everlasting you
        are God.

³You turn men back to dust,
    saying, "Return to dust, O sons of
        men."
⁴For a thousand years in your sight
    are like a day that has just gone by,
    or like a watch in the night.
⁵You sweep men away in the sleep of
        death;
    they are like the new grass of the
        morning—
⁶though in the morning it springs up
        new,
    by evening it is dry and withered.

⁷We are consumed by your anger
    and terrified by your indignation.
⁸You have set our iniquities before
        you,
    our secret sins in the light of your
        presence.
⁹All our days pass away under your
        wrath;
    we finish our years with a moan.
¹⁰The length of our days is seventy
        years—
    or eighty, if we have the strength;
    yet their span*ᶜ* is but trouble and
        sorrow,
    for they quickly pass, and we fly
        away.

¹¹Who knows the power of your anger?
    For your wrath is as great as the
        fear that is due you.
¹²Teach us to number our days aright,
    that we may gain a heart of
        wisdom.

¹³Relent, O LORD! How long will it be?
    Have compassion on your servants.
¹⁴Satisfy us in the morning with your
        unfailing love,
    that we may sing for joy and be
        glad all our days.
¹⁵Make us glad for as many days as you
        have afflicted us,
    for as many years as we have seen
        trouble.
¹⁶May your deeds be shown to your
        servants,
    your splendor to their children.

ᵃ48 Hebrew *Sheol*   *ᵇ50* Or *your servants have*   *ᶜ10* Or *yet the best of them*

17May the favor*a* of the Lord our God
    rest upon us;
  establish the work of our hands for
    us —
  yes, establish the work of our
    hands.

Psalm 91

1He who dwells in the shelter of the
    Most High
  will rest in the shadow of the
    Almighty.*b*
2I will say*c* of the Lord, "He is my
    refuge and my fortress,
  my God, in whom I trust."

3Surely he will save you from the
    fowler's snare
  and from the deadly pestilence.
4He will cover you with his feathers,
  and under his wings you will find
    refuge;
  his faithfulness will be your shield
    and rampart.
5You will not fear the terror of night,
  nor the arrow that flies by day,
6nor the pestilence that stalks in the
    darkness,
  nor the plague that destroys at
    midday.
7A thousand may fall at your side,
  ten thousand at your right hand,
  but it will not come near you.
8You will only observe with your eyes
  and see the punishment of the
    wicked.

9If you make the Most High your
    dwelling—
  even the Lord, who is my refuge—
10then no harm will befall you,
  no disaster will come near your
    tent.
11For he will command his angels
    concerning you
  to guard you in all your ways;
12they will lift you up in their hands,
  so that you will not strike your foot
    against a stone.
13You will tread upon the lion and the
    cobra;
  you will trample the great lion and
    the serpent.

14"Because he loves me," says the Lord,
  "I will rescue him;
  I will protect him, for he
    acknowledges my name.
15He will call upon me, and I will
    answer him;
  I will be with him in trouble,
  I will deliver him and honor him.
16With long life will I satisfy him
  and show him my salvation."

Psalm 92

A psalm. A song. For the Sabbath day.

1It is good to praise the Lord
  and make music to your name,
    O Most High,
2to proclaim your love in the morning
  and your faithfulness at night,
3to the music of the ten-stringed lyre
  and the melody of the harp.

4For you make me glad by your deeds,
    O Lord;
  I sing for joy at the works of your
    hands.
5How great are your works, O Lord,
  how profound your thoughts!
6The senseless man does not know,
  fools do not understand,
7that though the wicked spring up like
    grass
  and all evildoers flourish,
  they will be forever destroyed.

8But you, O Lord, are exalted forever.

9For surely your enemies, O Lord,
  surely your enemies will perish;
  all evildoers will be scattered.
10You have exalted my horn*d* like that
    of a wild ox;
  fine oils have been poured upon
    me.
11My eyes have seen the defeat of my
    adversaries;
  my ears have heard the rout of my
    wicked foes.

12The righteous will flourish like a palm
    tree,
  they will grow like a cedar of
    Lebanon;
13planted in the house of the Lord,
  they will flourish in the courts of
    our God.
14They will still bear fruit in old age,
  they will stay fresh and green,
15proclaiming, "The Lord is upright;
  he is my Rock, and there is no
    wickedness in him."

---

a17 Or *beauty*   *b1* Hebrew *Shaddai*   *c2* Or *He says*   *d10* *Horn* here symbolizes strength.

THURSDAY

VERSE FOR THE DAY:
Psalm 91:2

AUTHOR:
Hope MacDonald

PASSAGE FOR THE DAY:
Psalm 91:1–16

Our Dwelling Place

THE other night I took care of my grandchildren. Six-year-old Shane woke up crying. He had been dreaming of goblins and other childhood terrors. After he quieted down, he showed me the well-worn Bible his grandfather had given him. Shane always keeps it under his pillow. As I left the room, he said, "You know, Grandma, when you sleep with your Bible, it's almost like sleeping with Jesus!" And he lay down like a little lamb and went to sleep. He was resting in the shadow of the Almighty. Later I found myself asking, "Is this where I'm resting today?"

Try reading Psalm 91 every day for the next month. Your life will be changed, as mine was, because this is a triumphant song of faith. In it we learn that God is our dwelling place. It's under his wings that we find refuge, even in the midst of the universal evil that surrounds us.

We all face dangers and heartaches in life because we live in a lost and fallen world. But in the midst of these difficulties we can be absolutely confident that we are not left alone to deal with them. God's faithfulness is our constant shield. We are covered by the shadow of the Almighty! Oh, the security that is ours in God's promise that he will be with us in trouble (Psalm 91:15)!

These unchanging promises are for those who choose, by an act of their will, to put themselves under the care and protection of the living God. These promises are for those who dwell within the shelter of the Most High, who make their home with Jesus.

Why is this a psalm of irrepressible beauty? Because in it we are given a fresh glimpse into all that is ours through Jesus Christ our Lord. We come away from this psalm with an overwhelming sense of awe and wonder at God's continual provision for us.

Additional Scripture Readings:
Psalm 121:1–8; Lamentations 3:19–26

Go to page 479 for your next devotional reading.

Psalm 93

[1]The LORD reigns, he is robed in
majesty;
the LORD is robed in majesty
and is armed with strength.
The world is firmly established;
it cannot be moved.
[2]Your throne was established long
ago;
you are from all eternity.

[3]The seas have lifted up, O LORD,
the seas have lifted up their voice;
the seas have lifted up their
pounding waves.
[4]Mightier than the thunder of the great
waters,
mightier than the breakers of the
sea—
the LORD on high is mighty.

[5]Your statutes stand firm;
holiness adorns your house
for endless days, O LORD.

Psalm 94

[1]O LORD, the God who avenges,
O God who avenges, shine forth.
[2]Rise up, O Judge of the earth;
pay back to the proud what they
deserve.
[3]How long will the wicked, O LORD,
how long will the wicked be
jubilant?

[4]They pour out arrogant words;
all the evildoers are full of boasting.
[5]They crush your people, O LORD;
they oppress your inheritance.
[6]They slay the widow and the alien;
they murder the fatherless.
[7]They say, "The LORD does not see;
the God of Jacob pays no heed."

[8]Take heed, you senseless ones among
the people;
you fools, when will you become
wise?
[9]Does he who implanted the ear not
hear?
Does he who formed the eye not
see?
[10]Does he who disciplines nations not
punish?
Does he who teaches man lack
knowledge?
[11]The LORD knows the thoughts of man;
he knows that they are futile.

[12]Blessed is the man you discipline,
O LORD,

the man you teach from your law;
[13]you grant him relief from days of
trouble,
till a pit is dug for the wicked.
[14]For the LORD will not reject his
people;
he will never forsake his
inheritance.
[15]Judgment will again be founded on
righteousness,
and all the upright in heart will
follow it.

[16]Who will rise up for me against the
wicked?
Who will take a stand for me
against evildoers?
[17]Unless the LORD had given me help,
I would soon have dwelt in the
silence of death.
[18]When I said, "My foot is slipping,"
your love, O LORD, supported me.
[19]When anxiety was great within me,
your consolation brought joy to my
soul.

[20]Can a corrupt throne be allied with
you—
one that brings on misery by its
decrees?
[21]They band together against the
righteous
and condemn the innocent to
death.
[22]But the LORD has become my fortress,
and my God the rock in whom I
take refuge.
[23]He will repay them for their sins
and destroy them for their
wickedness;
the LORD our God will destroy them.

Psalm 95

[1]Come, let us sing for joy to the LORD;
let us shout aloud to the Rock of
our salvation.
[2]Let us come before him with
thanksgiving
and extol him with music and song.

[3]For the LORD is the great God,
the great King above all gods.
[4]In his hand are the depths of the
earth,
and the mountain peaks belong to
him.
[5]The sea is his, for he made it,
and his hands formed the dry land.

[6]Come, let us bow down in worship,

let us kneel before the Lord our
  Maker;
[7]for he is our God
  and we are the people of his
    pasture,
  the flock under his care.

Today, if you hear his voice,
[8] do not harden your hearts as you
    did at Meribah,[a]
  as you did that day at Massah[b] in
    the desert,
[9]where your fathers tested and tried
    me,
  though they had seen what I did.
[10]For forty years I was angry with that
    generation;
  I said, "They are a people whose
    hearts go astray,
  and they have not known my ways."
[11]So I declared on oath in my anger,
  "They shall never enter my rest."

Psalm 96

[1]Sing to the Lord a new song;
  sing to the Lord, all the earth.
[2]Sing to the Lord, praise his name;
  proclaim his salvation day after day.
[3]Declare his glory among the nations,
  his marvelous deeds among all
    peoples.

[4]For great is the Lord and most worthy
    of praise;
  he is to be feared above all gods.
[5]For all the gods of the nations are
    idols,
  but the Lord made the heavens.
[6]Splendor and majesty are before him;
  strength and glory are in his
    sanctuary.

[7]Ascribe to the Lord, O families of
    nations,
  ascribe to the Lord glory and
    strength.
[8]Ascribe to the Lord the glory due his
    name;
  bring an offering and come into his
    courts.
[9]Worship the Lord in the splendor of
    his[c] holiness;
  tremble before him, all the earth.

[10]Say among the nations, "The Lord
    reigns."
  The world is firmly established, it
    cannot be moved;

he will judge the peoples with
  equity.
[11]Let the heavens rejoice, let the earth
    be glad;
  let the sea resound, and all that is
    in it;
[12] let the fields be jubilant, and
    everything in them.
  Then all the trees of the forest will
    sing for joy;
[13] they will sing before the Lord, for
    he comes,
  he comes to judge the earth.
  He will judge the world in
    righteousness
  and the peoples in his truth.

Psalm 97

[1]The Lord reigns, let the earth be glad;
  let the distant shores rejoice.

[2]Clouds and thick darkness surround
    him;
  righteousness and justice are the
    foundation of his throne.
[3]Fire goes before him
  and consumes his foes on every
    side.
[4]His lightning lights up the world;
  the earth sees and trembles.
[5]The mountains melt like wax before
    the Lord,
  before the Lord of all the earth.
[6]The heavens proclaim his
    righteousness,
  and all the peoples see his glory.

[7]All who worship images are put to
    shame,
  those who boast in idols—
  worship him, all you gods!

[8]Zion hears and rejoices
  and the villages of Judah are glad
  because of your judgments, O Lord.
[9]For you, O Lord, are the Most High
    over all the earth;
  you are exalted far above all gods.

[10]Let those who love the Lord hate evil,
  for he guards the lives of his
    faithful ones
  and delivers them from the hand of
    the wicked.
[11]Light is shed upon the righteous
  and joy on the upright in heart.
[12]Rejoice in the Lord, you who are
    righteous,
  and praise his holy name.

---

[a]8 Meribah means quarreling.   [b]8 Massah means testing.   [c]9 Or Lord with the splendor of

Psalm 98

A psalm.

[1]Sing to the LORD a new song,
  for he has done marvelous things;
his right hand and his holy arm
  have worked salvation for him.
[2]The LORD has made his salvation
    known
  and revealed his righteousness to
    the nations.
[3]He has remembered his love
  and his faithfulness to the house of
    Israel;
all the ends of the earth have seen
  the salvation of our God.

[4]Shout for joy to the LORD, all the
    earth,
  burst into jubilant song with music;
[5]make music to the LORD with the
    harp,
  with the harp and the sound of
    singing,
[6]with trumpets and the blast of the
    ram's horn—
  shout for joy before the LORD, the
    King.

[7]Let the sea resound, and everything
    in it,
  the world, and all who live in it.
[8]Let the rivers clap their hands,
  let the mountains sing together for
    joy;
[9]let them sing before the LORD,
  for he comes to judge the earth.
He will judge the world in
    righteousness
  and the peoples with equity.

Psalm 99

[1]The LORD reigns,
  let the nations tremble;
he sits enthroned between the
    cherubim,
  let the earth shake.
[2]Great is the LORD in Zion;
  he is exalted over all the nations.
[3]Let them praise your great and
      awesome name—
  he is holy.

[4]The King is mighty, he loves justice—
  you have established equity;
in Jacob you have done
  what is just and right.
[5]Exalt the LORD our God

and worship at his footstool;
  he is holy.

[6]Moses and Aaron were among his
    priests,
  Samuel was among those who
    called on his name;
they called on the LORD
  and he answered them.
[7]He spoke to them from the pillar of
    cloud;
  they kept his statutes and the
    decrees he gave them.

[8]O LORD our God,
  you answered them;
you were to Israel[a] a forgiving God,
  though you punished their
    misdeeds.[b]
[9]Exalt the LORD our God
  and worship at his holy mountain,
  for the LORD our God is holy.

Psalm 100

A psalm. For giving thanks.

[1]Shout for joy to the LORD, all the
    earth.
[2] Worship the LORD with gladness;
  come before him with joyful songs.
[3]Know that the LORD is God.
  It is he who made us, and we are
    his[c];
  we are his people, the sheep of his
    pasture.

[4]Enter his gates with thanksgiving
  and his courts with praise;
  give thanks to him and praise his
    name.
[5]For the LORD is good and his love
    endures forever;
  his faithfulness continues through
    all generations.

Psalm 101

Of David. A psalm.

[1]I will sing of your love and justice;
  to you, O LORD, I will sing praise.
[2]I will be careful to lead a blameless
    life—
  when will you come to me?

I will walk in my house
  with blameless heart.
[3]I will set before my eyes
  no vile thing.

---

a8 Hebrew *them*   *b8* Or *l an avenger of the wrongs done to them*   *c3* Or *and not we ourselves*

The deeds of faithless men I hate;
  they will not cling to me.
[4]Men of perverse heart shall be far
    from me;
  I will have nothing to do with evil.

[5]Whoever slanders his neighbor in
    secret,
  him will I put to silence;
whoever has haughty eyes and a
    proud heart,
  him will I not endure.

[6]My eyes will be on the faithful in the
    land,
  that they may dwell with me;
he whose walk is blameless
  will minister to me.

[7]No one who practices deceit
  will dwell in my house;
no one who speaks falsely
  will stand in my presence.

[8]Every morning I will put to silence
  all the wicked in the land;
I will cut off every evildoer
  from the city of the LORD.

Psalm 102

*A prayer of an afflicted man. When he is
faint and pours out his lament before
the LORD.*

[1]Hear my prayer, O LORD;
  let my cry for help come to you.
[2]Do not hide your face from me
  when I am in distress.
Turn your ear to me;
  when I call, answer me quickly.

[3]For my days vanish like smoke;
  my bones burn like glowing embers.
[4]My heart is blighted and withered like
    grass;
  I forget to eat my food.
[5]Because of my loud groaning
  I am reduced to skin and bones.
[6]I am like a desert owl,
  like an owl among the ruins.
[7]I lie awake; I have become
  like a bird alone on a roof.
[8]All day long my enemies taunt me;
  those who rail against me use my
    name as a curse.
[9]For I eat ashes as my food
  and mingle my drink with tears
[10]because of your great wrath,
  for you have taken me up and
    thrown me aside.

[11]My days are like the evening shadow;
  I wither away like grass.

[12]But you, O LORD, sit enthroned
    forever;
  your renown endures through all
    generations.
[13]You will arise and have compassion
    on Zion,
  for it is time to show favor to her;
  the appointed time has come.
[14]For her stones are dear to your
    servants;
  her very dust moves them to pity.
[15]The nations will fear the name of the
    LORD,
  all the kings of the earth will revere
    your glory.
[16]For the LORD will rebuild Zion
  and appear in his glory.
[17]He will respond to the prayer of the
    destitute;
  he will not despise their plea.

[18]Let this be written for a future
    generation,
  that a people not yet created may
    praise the LORD:
[19]"The LORD looked down from his
    sanctuary on high,
  from heaven he viewed the earth,
[20]to hear the groans of the prisoners
  and release those condemned to
    death."
[21]So the name of the LORD will be
    declared in Zion
  and his praise in Jerusalem
[22]when the peoples and the kingdoms
  assemble to worship the LORD.

[23]In the course of my life[a] he broke my
    strength;
  he cut short my days.
[24]So I said:
  "Do not take me away, O my God,
    in the midst of my days;
  your years go on through all
    generations.
[25]In the beginning you laid the
    foundations of the earth,
  and the heavens are the work of
    your hands.
[26]They will perish, but you remain;
  they will all wear out like a
    garment.
Like clothing you will change them
  and they will be discarded.
[27]But you remain the same,
  and your years will never end.

[a]23 Or *By his power*

28The children of your servants will live
in your presence;
their descendants will be
established before you."

Psalm 103

Of David.

1Praise the LORD, O my soul;
all my inmost being, praise his holy
name.
2Praise the LORD, O my soul,
and forget not all his benefits—
3who forgives all your sins
and heals all your diseases,
4who redeems your life from the pit
and crowns you with love and
compassion,
5who satisfies your desires with good
things
so that your youth is renewed like
the eagle's.

6The LORD works righteousness
and justice for all the oppressed.

7He made known his ways to Moses,
his deeds to the people of Israel:
8The LORD is compassionate and
gracious,
slow to anger, abounding in love.
9He will not always accuse,
nor will he harbor his anger forever;
10he does not treat us as our sins
deserve
or repay us according to our
iniquities.
11For as high as the heavens are above
the earth,
so great is his love for those who
fear him;
12as far as the east is from the west,
so far has he removed our
transgressions from us.
13As a father has compassion on his
children,
so the LORD has compassion on
those who fear him;
14for he knows how we are formed,
he remembers that we are dust.
15As for man, his days are like grass,
he flourishes like a flower of the
field;
16the wind blows over it and it is gone,
and its place remembers it no
more.
17But from everlasting to everlasting

the LORD's love is with those who
fear him,
and his righteousness with their
children's children—
18with those who keep his covenant
and remember to obey his precepts.

19The LORD has established his throne
in heaven,
and his kingdom rules over all.

20Praise the LORD, you his angels,
you mighty ones who do his
bidding,
who obey his word.
21Praise the LORD, all his heavenly
hosts,
you his servants who do his will.
22Praise the LORD, all his works
everywhere in his dominion.

Praise the LORD, O my soul.

Psalm 104

1Praise the LORD, O my soul.

O LORD my God, you are very great;
you are clothed with splendor and
majesty.
2He wraps himself in light as with a
garment;
he stretches out the heavens like a
tent
3 and lays the beams of his upper
chambers on their waters.
He makes the clouds his chariot
and rides on the wings of the wind.
4He makes winds his messengers,a
flames of fire his servants.

5He set the earth on its foundations;
it can never be moved.
6You covered it with the deep as with
a garment;
the waters stood above the
mountains.
7But at your rebuke the waters fled,
at the sound of your thunder they
took to flight;
8they flowed over the mountains,
they went down into the valleys,
to the place you assigned for them.
9You set a boundary they cannot cross;
never again will they cover the
earth.

10He makes springs pour water into the
ravines;
it flows between the mountains.

a4 Or angels

VERSE FOR THE DAY:
Psalm 103:3

AUTHOR:
Janice Kempe

PASSAGE FOR THE DAY:
Psalm 103:1–22

Time With Daddy

KEVIN and I walked Krista to kindergarten today. Her school is up and over a large hill and through a woods, so we noticed each flower and green leaf that told us spring was near and listened to the birds that had returned after a long, cold winter.

After the good-by kisses Kevin and I began our walk back up and over the big hill. He was fascinated by the selection of rocks and sticks and immediately began gathering a collection. Our progress was slow because we had to stop every few steps to retrieve dropped treasures. The capacity of his two hands just wasn't enough to accommodate the desires of his curious little mind! He had no more time for noticing birds and flowers. With grim determination, he tended to the safe passage of his wonderful new collection.

I couldn't understand why each stone was so special, nor why he needed so many sticks, but he guarded them with great care and knew instantly if he had dropped one.

Upon reaching our front door, Kevin and I were both exhausted!

He struggled up the front steps through the front door. But suddenly he let go of his precious treasures, and they fell to the front hall floor. His determined scowl melted into a wide grin. He ran off as if the things he had struggled to bring home had lost their value. Kevin had seen something far more important, and immediately his focus had changed to a new center of attention—Daddy!

I long to keep in mind that picture of my little boy dropping his burdensome treasures to run to his father. I too get burdened down by my treasures. My house, my belongings, my responsibilities, and all the things I've spent so much time and energy acquiring seem to take me over sometimes. I find myself attending to their care with an overwhelming single-mindedness. Sometimes I need to see God and do more than just acknowledge his presence. I need to drop everything else and run to him. I need to forsake the housework, the shopping, and the thousand other things that occupy my time, and go to him for a time of togetherness.

Additional Scripture Readings:
Luke 10:38–42; John 21:4–7

*Go to page 484 for your next
devotional reading.*

11They give water to all the beasts of
the field;
the wild donkeys quench their
thirst.
12The birds of the air nest by the
waters;
they sing among the branches.
13He waters the mountains from his
upper chambers;
the earth is satisfied by the fruit of
his work.
14He makes grass grow for the cattle,
and plants for man to cultivate—
bringing forth food from the earth:
15wine that gladdens the heart of man,
oil to make his face shine,
and bread that sustains his heart.
16The trees of the LORD are well
watered,
the cedars of Lebanon that he
planted.
17There the birds make their nests;
the stork has its home in the pine
trees.
18The high mountains belong to the
wild goats;
the crags are a refuge for the
coneys.*a*

19The moon marks off the seasons,
and the sun knows when to go
down.
20You bring darkness, it becomes night,
and all the beasts of the forest
prowl.
21The lions roar for their prey
and seek their food from God.
22The sun rises, and they steal away;
they return and lie down in their
dens.
23Then man goes out to his work,
to his labor until evening.

24How many are your works, O LORD!
In wisdom you made them all;
the earth is full of your creatures.
25There is the sea, vast and spacious,
teeming with creatures beyond
number—
living things both large and small.
26There the ships go to and fro,
and the leviathan, which you
formed to frolic there.

27These all look to you
to give them their food at the
proper time.
28When you give it to them,
they gather it up;
when you open your hand,
they are satisfied with good things.
29When you hide your face,
they are terrified;
when you take away their breath,
they die and return to the dust.
30When you send your Spirit,
they are created,
and you renew the face of the
earth.

31May the glory of the LORD endure
forever;
may the LORD rejoice in his works—
32he who looks at the earth, and it
trembles,
who touches the mountains, and
they smoke.

33I will sing to the LORD all my life;
I will sing praise to my God as long
as I live.
34May my meditation be pleasing to
him,
as I rejoice in the LORD.
35But may sinners vanish from the earth
and the wicked be no more.

Praise the LORD, O my soul.

Praise the LORD.*b*

Psalm 105

1Give thanks to the LORD, call on his
name;
make known among the nations
what he has done.
2Sing to him, sing praise to him;
tell of all his wonderful acts.
3Glory in his holy name;
let the hearts of those who seek the
LORD rejoice.
4Look to the LORD and his strength;
seek his face always.

5Remember the wonders he has done,
his miracles, and the judgments he
pronounced,
6O descendants of Abraham his
servant,
O sons of Jacob, his chosen ones.
7He is the LORD our God;
his judgments are in all the earth.

8He remembers his covenant forever,
the word he commanded, for a
thousand generations,
9the covenant he made with Abraham,

a18 That is, the hyrax or rock badger   *b35* Hebrew *Hallelu Yah;* in the Septuagint this line stands at
the beginning of Psalm 105.

the oath he swore to Isaac.
[10]He confirmed it to Jacob as a decree,
   to Israel as an everlasting covenant:
[11]"To you I will give the land of Canaan
   as the portion you will inherit."

[12]When they were but few in number,
   few indeed, and strangers in it,
[13]they wandered from nation to nation,
   from one kingdom to another.
[14]He allowed no one to oppress them;
   for their sake he rebuked kings:
[15]"Do not touch my anointed ones;
   do my prophets no harm."

[16]He called down famine on the land
   and destroyed all their supplies of
      food;
[17]and he sent a man before them—
   Joseph, sold as a slave.
[18]They bruised his feet with shackles,
   his neck was put in irons,
[19]till what he foretold came to pass,
   till the word of the LORD proved
      him true.
[20]The king sent and released him,
   the ruler of peoples set him free.
[21]He made him master of his
      household,
   ruler over all he possessed,
[22]to instruct his princes as he pleased
   and teach his elders wisdom.

[23]Then Israel entered Egypt;
   Jacob lived as an alien in the land
      of Ham.
[24]The LORD made his people very
      fruitful;
   he made them too numerous for
      their foes,
[25]whose hearts he turned to hate his
      people,
   to conspire against his servants.
[26]He sent Moses his servant,
   and Aaron, whom he had chosen.
[27]They performed his miraculous signs
      among them,
   his wonders in the land of Ham.
[28]He sent darkness and made the land
      dark—
   for had they not rebelled against
      his words?
[29]He turned their waters into blood,
   causing their fish to die.
[30]Their land teemed with frogs,
   which went up into the bedrooms
      of their rulers.
[31]He spoke, and there came swarms of
      flies,

and gnats throughout their country.
[32]He turned their rain into hail,
   with lightning throughout their
      land;
[33]he struck down their vines and fig
      trees
   and shattered the trees of their
      country.
[34]He spoke, and the locusts came,
   grasshoppers without number;
[35]they ate up every green thing in their
      land,
   ate up the produce of their soil.
[36]Then he struck down all the firstborn
      in their land,
   the firstfruits of all their manhood.

[37]He brought out Israel, laden with
      silver and gold,
   and from among their tribes no one
      faltered.
[38]Egypt was glad when they left,
   because dread of Israel had fallen
      on them.
[39]He spread out a cloud as a covering,
   and a fire to give light at night.
[40]They asked, and he brought them
      quail
   and satisfied them with the bread
      of heaven.
[41]He opened the rock, and water
      gushed out;
   like a river it flowed in the desert.

[42]For he remembered his holy promise
   given to his servant Abraham.
[43]He brought out his people with
      rejoicing,
   his chosen ones with shouts of joy;
[44]he gave them the lands of the
      nations,
   and they fell heir to what others
      had toiled for—
[45]that they might keep his precepts
   and observe his laws.

Praise the LORD.[a]

Psalm 106

[1]Praise the LORD.[b]

Give thanks to the LORD, for he is
      good;
   his love endures forever.
[2]Who can proclaim the mighty acts of
      the LORD
   or fully declare his praise?
[3]Blessed are they who maintain
      justice,

---

[a]45 Hebrew *Hallelu Yah*   [b]1 Hebrew *Hallelu Yah*; also in verse 48

who constantly do what is right.
⁴Remember me, O Lᴏʀᴅ, when you
show favor to your people,
come to my aid when you save
them,
⁵that I may enjoy the prosperity of
your chosen ones,
that I may share in the joy of your
nation
and join your inheritance in giving
praise.

⁶We have sinned, even as our fathers
did;
we have done wrong and acted
wickedly.
⁷When our fathers were in Egypt,
they gave no thought to your
miracles;
they did not remember your many
kindnesses,
and they rebelled by the sea, the
Red Sea.ᵃ
⁸Yet he saved them for his name's
sake,
to make his mighty power known.
⁹He rebuked the Red Sea, and it dried
up;
he led them through the depths as
through a desert.
¹⁰He saved them from the hand of the
foe;
from the hand of the enemy he
redeemed them.
¹¹The waters covered their adversaries;
not one of them survived.
¹²Then they believed his promises
and sang his praise.

¹³But they soon forgot what he had
done
and did not wait for his counsel.
¹⁴In the desert they gave in to their
craving;
in the wasteland they put God to
the test.
¹⁵So he gave them what they asked for,
but sent a wasting disease upon
them.
¹⁶In the camp they grew envious of
Moses
and of Aaron, who was consecrated
to the Lᴏʀᴅ.
¹⁷The earth opened up and swallowed
Dathan;
it buried the company of Abiram.
¹⁸Fire blazed among their followers;

a flame consumed the wicked.

¹⁹At Horeb they made a calf
and worshiped an idol cast from
metal.
²⁰They exchanged their Glory
for an image of a bull, which eats
grass.
²¹They forgot the God who saved them,
who had done great things in
Egypt,
²²miracles in the land of Ham
and awesome deeds by the Red
Sea.
²³So he said he would destroy them—
had not Moses, his chosen one,
stood in the breach before him
to keep his wrath from destroying
them.

²⁴Then they despised the pleasant land;
they did not believe his promise.
²⁵They grumbled in their tents
and did not obey the Lᴏʀᴅ.
²⁶So he swore to them with uplifted
hand
that he would make them fall in
the desert,
²⁷make their descendants fall among
the nations
and scatter them throughout the
lands.

²⁸They yoked themselves to the Baal of
Peor
and ate sacrifices offered to lifeless
gods;
²⁹they provoked the Lᴏʀᴅ to anger by
their wicked deeds,
and a plague broke out among
them.
³⁰But Phinehas stood up and
intervened,
and the plague was checked.
³¹This was credited to him as
righteousness
for endless generations to come.

³²By the waters of Meribah they
angered the Lᴏʀᴅ,
and trouble came to Moses because
of them;
³³for they rebelled against the Spirit of
God,
and rash words came from Moses'
lips.ᵇ

³⁴They did not destroy the peoples
as the Lᴏʀᴅ had commanded them,

ᵃ7 Hebrew Yam Suph; that is, Sea of Reeds; also in verses 9 and 22   ᵇ33 Or against his spirit, / and
rash words came from his lips

35but they mingled with the nations
  and adopted their customs.
36They worshiped their idols,
  which became a snare to them.
37They sacrificed their sons
  and their daughters to demons.
38They shed innocent blood,
  the blood of their sons and
    daughters,
whom they sacrificed to the idols of
    Canaan,
  and the land was desecrated by
    their blood.
39They defiled themselves by what they
    did;
  by their deeds they prostituted
    themselves.

40Therefore the Lord was angry with his
    people
  and abhorred his inheritance.
41He handed them over to the nations,
  and their foes ruled over them.
42Their enemies oppressed them
  and subjected them to their power.
43Many times he delivered them,
  but they were bent on rebellion
  and they wasted away in their sin.

44But he took note of their distress
  when he heard their cry;
45for their sake he remembered his
    covenant
  and out of his great love he
    relented.
46He caused them to be pitied
  by all who held them captive.

47Save us, O Lord our God,
  and gather us from the nations,
that we may give thanks to your holy
    name
  and glory in your praise.

48Praise be to the Lord, the God of
    Israel,
  from everlasting to everlasting.
Let all the people say, "Amen!"

Praise the Lord.

BOOK V

Psalms 107–150

Psalm 107

1Give thanks to the Lord, for he is
    good;
  his love endures forever.

2Let the redeemed of the Lord say
    this—
  those he redeemed from the hand
    of the foe,
3those he gathered from the lands,
  from east and west, from north and
    south. *a*

4Some wandered in desert wastelands,
  finding no way to a city where they
    could settle.
5They were hungry and thirsty,
  and their lives ebbed away.
6Then they cried out to the Lord in
    their trouble,
  and he delivered them from their
    distress.
7He led them by a straight way
  to a city where they could settle.
8Let them give thanks to the Lord for
    his unfailing love
  and his wonderful deeds for men,
9for he satisfies the thirsty
  and fills the hungry with good
    things.

10Some sat in darkness and the deepest
    gloom,
  prisoners suffering in iron chains,
11for they had rebelled against the
    words of God
  and despised the counsel of the
    Most High.
12So he subjected them to bitter labor;
  they stumbled, and there was no
    one to help.
13Then they cried to the Lord in their
    trouble,
  and he saved them from their
    distress.
14He brought them out of darkness and
    the deepest gloom
  and broke away their chains.
15Let them give thanks to the Lord for
    his unfailing love
  and his wonderful deeds for men,
16for he breaks down gates of bronze
  and cuts through bars of iron.

17Some became fools through their
    rebellious ways
  and suffered affliction because of
    their iniquities.
18They loathed all food
  and drew near the gates of death.
19Then they cried to the Lord in their
    trouble,
  and he saved them from their
    distress.

a 3 Hebrew north and the sea

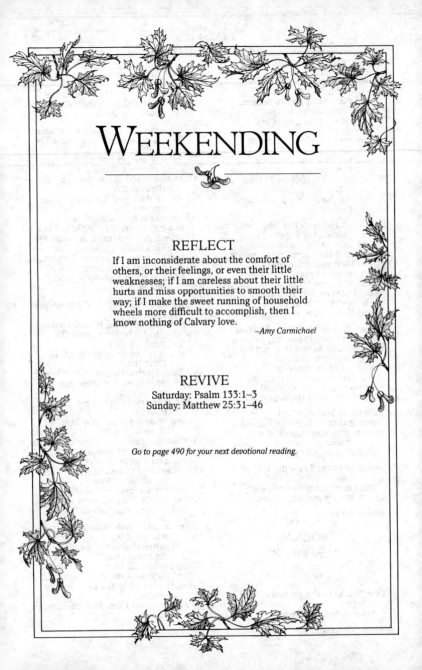

WEEKENDING

REFLECT

If I am inconsiderate about the comfort of others, or their feelings, or even their little weaknesses; if I am careless about their little hurts and miss opportunities to smooth their way; if I make the sweet running of household wheels more difficult to accomplish, then I know nothing of Calvary love.

–Amy Carmichael

REVIVE

Saturday: Psalm 133:1–3
Sunday: Matthew 25:31–46

Go to page 490 for your next devotional reading.

²⁰He sent forth his word and healed
them;
  he rescued them from the grave.
²¹Let them give thanks to the LORD for
his unfailing love
  and his wonderful deeds for men.
²²Let them sacrifice thank offerings
  and tell of his works with songs of
joy.

²³Others went out on the sea in ships;
  they were merchants on the mighty
waters.
²⁴They saw the works of the LORD,
  his wonderful deeds in the deep.
²⁵For he spoke and stirred up a tempest
  that lifted high the waves.
²⁶They mounted up to the heavens and
went down to the depths;
  in their peril their courage melted
away.
²⁷They reeled and staggered like
drunken men;
  they were at their wits' end.
²⁸Then they cried out to the LORD in
their trouble,
  and he brought them out of their
distress.
²⁹He stilled the storm to a whisper;
  the waves of the sea were hushed.
³⁰They were glad when it grew calm,
  and he guided them to their desired
haven.
³¹Let them give thanks to the LORD for
his unfailing love
  and his wonderful deeds for men.
³²Let them exalt him in the assembly
of the people
  and praise him in the council of
the elders.

³³He turned rivers into a desert,
  flowing springs into thirsty ground,
³⁴and fruitful land into a salt waste,
  because of the wickedness of those
who lived there.
³⁵He turned the desert into pools of
water
  and the parched ground into
flowing springs;
³⁶there he brought the hungry to live,
  and they founded a city where they
could settle.
³⁷They sowed fields and planted
vineyards
  that yielded a fruitful harvest;
³⁸he blessed them, and their numbers
greatly increased,
  and he did not let their herds
diminish.

³⁹Then their numbers decreased, and
they were humbled
  by oppression, calamity and sorrow;
⁴⁰he who pours contempt on nobles
  made them wander in a trackless
waste.
⁴¹But he lifted the needy out of their
affliction
  and increased their families like
flocks.
⁴²The upright see and rejoice,
  but all the wicked shut their
mouths.

⁴³Whoever is wise, let him heed these
things
  and consider the great love of the
LORD.

Psalm 108

A song. A psalm of David.

¹My heart is steadfast, O God;
  I will sing and make music with all
my soul.
²Awake, harp and lyre!
  I will awaken the dawn.
³I will praise you, O LORD, among the
nations;
  I will sing of you among the
peoples.
⁴For great is your love, higher than the
heavens;
  your faithfulness reaches to the
skies.
⁵Be exalted, O God, above the
heavens,
  and let your glory be over all the
earth.

⁶Save us and help us with your right
hand,
  that those you love may be
delivered.
⁷God has spoken from his sanctuary:
  "In triumph I will parcel out
Shechem
  and measure off the Valley of
Succoth.
⁸Gilead is mine, Manasseh is mine;
  Ephraim is my helmet,
  Judah my scepter.
⁹Moab is my washbasin,
  upon Edom I toss my sandal;
  over Philistia I shout in triumph."

¹⁰Who will bring me to the fortified
city?
  Who will lead me to Edom?

11Is it not you, O God, you who have
    rejected us
  and no longer go out with our
    armies?
12Give us aid against the enemy,
  for the help of man is worthless.
13With God we will gain the victory,
  and he will trample down our
    enemies.

Psalm 109

For the director of music. Of David.
A psalm.

1O God, whom I praise,
  do not remain silent,
2for wicked and deceitful men
  have opened their mouths against
    me;
  they have spoken against me with
    lying tongues.
3With words of hatred they surround
    me;
  they attack me without cause.
4In return for my friendship they
    accuse me,
  but I am a man of prayer.
5They repay me evil for good,
  and hatred for my friendship.

6Appoint[a] an evil man[b] to oppose
    him;
  let an accuser[c] stand at his right
    hand.
7When he is tried, let him be found
    guilty,
  and may his prayers condemn him.
8May his days be few;
  may another take his place of
    leadership.
9May his children be fatherless
  and his wife a widow.
10May his children be wandering
    beggars;
  may they be driven[d] from their
    ruined homes.
11May a creditor seize all he has;
  may strangers plunder the fruits of
    his labor.
12May no one extend kindness to him
  or take pity on his fatherless
    children.
13May his descendants be cut off,
  their names blotted out from the
    next generation.
14May the iniquity of his fathers be
  remembered before the LORD;

may the sin of his mother never be
    blotted out.
15May their sins always remain before
    the LORD,
  that he may cut off the memory of
    them from the earth.

16For he never thought of doing a
    kindness,
  but hounded to death the poor
  and the needy and the
    brokenhearted.
17He loved to pronounce a curse—
  may it[e] come on him;
  he found no pleasure in blessing—
  may it be[f] far from him.
18He wore cursing as his garment;
  it entered into his body like water,
  into his bones like oil.
19May it be like a cloak wrapped about
    him,
  like a belt tied forever around him.
20May this be the LORD's payment to my
    accusers,
  to those who speak evil of me.

21But you, O Sovereign LORD,
  deal well with me for your name's
    sake;
  out of the goodness of your love,
    deliver me.
22For I am poor and needy,
  and my heart is wounded within
    me.
23I fade away like an evening shadow;
  I am shaken off like a locust.
24My knees give way from fasting;
  my body is thin and gaunt.
25I am an object of scorn to my
    accusers;
  when they see me, they shake their
    heads.

26Help me, O LORD my God;
  save me in accordance with your
    love.
27Let them know that it is your hand,
  that you, O LORD, have done it.
28They may curse, but you will bless;
  when they attack they will be put
    to shame,
  but your servant will rejoice.
29My accusers will be clothed with
    disgrace
  and wrapped in shame as in a
    cloak.

30With my mouth I will greatly extol
  the LORD;

---

a6 Or *They say:, "Appoint* (with quotation marks at the end of verse 19)   b6 Or *the Evil One*   c6 Or
let Satan   d10 Septuagint; Hebrew *sought*   e17 Or *curse, / and it has*   f17 Or *blessing, / and it is*

in the great throng I will praise
  him.
³¹For he stands at the right hand of the
    needy one,
  to save his life from those who
    condemn him.

Psalm 110

Of David. A psalm.

¹The Lord says to my Lord:
  "Sit at my right hand
until I make your enemies
  a footstool for your feet."

²The Lord will extend your mighty
    scepter from Zion;
  you will rule in the midst of your
    enemies.
³Your troops will be willing
  on your day of battle.
Arrayed in holy majesty,
  from the womb of the dawn
  you will receive the dew of your
    youth.^a

⁴The Lord has sworn
  and will not change his mind:
"You are a priest forever,
  in the order of Melchizedek."

⁵The Lord is at your right hand;
  he will crush kings on the day of
    his wrath.
⁶He will judge the nations, heaping up
    the dead
  and crushing the rulers of the
    whole earth.
⁷He will drink from a brook beside the
    way^b;
  therefore he will lift up his head.

Psalm 111^c

¹Praise the Lord.^d

I will extol the Lord with all my heart
  in the council of the upright and in
    the assembly.

²Great are the works of the Lord;
  they are pondered by all who
    delight in them.
³Glorious and majestic are his deeds,
  and his righteousness endures
    forever.

⁴He has caused his wonders to be
    remembered;
  the Lord is gracious and
    compassionate.
⁵He provides food for those who fear
    him;
  he remembers his covenant forever.
⁶He has shown his people the power of
    his works,
  giving them the lands of other
    nations.
⁷The works of his hands are faithful
    and just;
  all his precepts are trustworthy.
⁸They are steadfast for ever and ever,
    done in faithfulness and
    uprightness.
⁹He provided redemption for his
    people;
  he ordained his covenant forever—
  holy and awesome is his name.

¹⁰The fear of the Lord is the beginning
    of wisdom;
  all who follow his precepts have
    good understanding.
  To him belongs eternal praise.

Psalm 112^c

¹Praise the Lord.^d

Blessed is the man who fears the
    Lord,
  who finds great delight in his
    commands.

²His children will be mighty in the
    land;
  the generation of the upright will
    be blessed.
³Wealth and riches are in his house,
  and his righteousness endures
    forever.
⁴Even in darkness light dawns for the
    upright,
  for the gracious and compassionate
    and righteous man.^e
⁵Good will come to him who is
    generous and lends freely,
  who conducts his affairs with
    justice.
⁶Surely he will never be shaken;
  a righteous man will be
    remembered forever.
⁷He will have no fear of bad news;

---

^a3 Or / your young men will come to you like the dew   ^b7 Or / The One who grants succession will set
him in authority   ^cThis psalm is an acrostic poem, the lines of which begin with the successive letters
of the Hebrew alphabet.   ^d1 Hebrew Hallelu Yah   ^e4 Or / for ,the Lord, is gracious and
compassionate and righteous

his heart is steadfast, trusting in
the Lord.
8His heart is secure, he will have no
fear;
in the end he will look in triumph
on his foes.
9He has scattered abroad his gifts to
the poor,
his righteousness endures forever;
his horn*a* will be lifted high in
honor.

10The wicked man will see and be
vexed,
he will gnash his teeth and waste
away;
the longings of the wicked will
come to nothing.

Psalm 113

1Praise the Lord.*b*

Praise, O servants of the Lord,
praise the name of the Lord.
2Let the name of the Lord be praised,
both now and forevermore.
3From the rising of the sun to the
place where it sets,
the name of the Lord is to be
praised.

4The Lord is exalted over all the
nations,
his glory above the heavens.
5Who is like the Lord our God,
the One who sits enthroned on
high,
6who stoops down to look
on the heavens and the earth?

7He raises the poor from the dust
and lifts the needy from the ash
heap;
8he seats them with princes,
with the princes of their people.
9He settles the barren woman in her
home
as a happy mother of children.

Praise the Lord.

Psalm 114

1When Israel came out of Egypt,
the house of Jacob from a people
of foreign tongue,
2Judah became God's sanctuary,
Israel his dominion.

3The sea looked and fled,

the Jordan turned back;
4the mountains skipped like rams,
the hills like lambs.

5Why was it, O sea, that you fled,
O Jordan, that you turned back,
6you mountains, that you skipped like
rams,
you hills, like lambs?

7Tremble, O earth, at the presence of
the Lord,
at the presence of the God of
Jacob,
8who turned the rock into a pool,
the hard rock into springs of water.

Psalm 115

1Not to us, O Lord, not to us
but to your name be the glory,
because of your love and
faithfulness.

2Why do the nations say,
"Where is their God?"
3Our God is in heaven;
he does whatever pleases him.
4But their idols are silver and gold,
made by the hands of men.
5They have mouths, but cannot speak,
eyes, but they cannot see;
6they have ears, but cannot hear,
noses, but they cannot smell;
7they have hands, but cannot feel,
feet, but they cannot walk;
nor can they utter a sound with
their throats.
8Those who make them will be like
them,
and so will all who trust in them.

9O house of Israel, trust in the Lord—
he is their help and shield.
10O house of Aaron, trust in the Lord—
he is their help and shield.
11You who fear him, trust in the Lord—
he is their help and shield.

12The Lord remembers us and will bless
us:
He will bless the house of Israel,
he will bless the house of Aaron,
13he will bless those who fear the
Lord—
small and great alike.

14May the Lord make you increase,
both you and your children.
15May you be blessed by the Lord,
the Maker of heaven and earth.

*a*9 *Horn* here symbolizes dignity.   *b*1 Hebrew *Hallelu Yah;* also in verse 9

[16]The highest heavens belong to the
    LORD,
  but the earth he has given to man.
[17]It is not the dead who praise the
    LORD,
  those who go down to silence;
[18]it is we who extol the LORD,
  both now and forevermore.

Praise the LORD. [a]

Psalm 116

[1]I love the LORD, for he heard my
    voice;
  he heard my cry for mercy.
[2]Because he turned his ear to me,
  I will call on him as long as I live.

[3]The cords of death entangled me,
  the anguish of the grave[b] came
    upon me;
  I was overcome by trouble and
    sorrow.
[4]Then I called on the name of the
    LORD:
  "O LORD, save me!"

[5]The LORD is gracious and righteous;
  our God is full of compassion.
[6]The LORD protects the simplehearted;
  when I was in great need, he saved
    me.

[7]Be at rest once more, O my soul,
  for the LORD has been good to you.

[8]For you, O LORD, have delivered my
    soul from death,
  my eyes from tears,
  my feet from stumbling,
[9]that I may walk before the LORD
  in the land of the living.
[10]I believed; therefore[c] I said,
  "I am greatly afflicted."
[11]And in my dismay I said,
  "All men are liars."

[12]How can I repay the LORD
  for all his goodness to me?
[13]I will lift up the cup of salvation
  and call on the name of the LORD.
[14]I will fulfill my vows to the LORD
  in the presence of all his people.

[15]Precious in the sight of the LORD
  is the death of his saints.
[16]O LORD, truly I am your servant;
  I am your servant, the son of your
    maidservant[d];
  you have freed me from my chains.

[17]I will sacrifice a thank offering to you
  and call on the name of the LORD.
[18]I will fulfill my vows to the LORD
  in the presence of all his people,
[19]in the courts of the house of the
    LORD—
  in your midst, O Jerusalem.

Praise the LORD. [a]

Psalm 117

[1]Praise the LORD, all you nations;
  extol him, all you peoples.
[2]For great is his love toward us,
  and the faithfulness of the LORD
    endures forever.

Praise the LORD. [a]

Psalm 118

[1]Give thanks to the LORD, for he is
    good;
  his love endures forever.

[2]Let Israel say:
  "His love endures forever."
[3]Let the house of Aaron say:
  "His love endures forever."
[4]Let those who fear the LORD say:
  "His love endures forever."

[5]In my anguish I cried to the LORD,
  and he answered by setting me free.
[6]The LORD is with me; I will not be
    afraid.
  What can man do to me?
[7]The LORD is with me; he is my helper.
  I will look in triumph on my
    enemies.

[8]It is better to take refuge in the LORD
  than to trust in man.
[9]It is better to take refuge in the LORD
  than to trust in princes.

[10]All the nations surrounded me,
  but in the name of the LORD I cut
    them off.
[11]They surrounded me on every side,
  but in the name of the LORD I cut
    them off.
[12]They swarmed around me like bees,
  but they died out as quickly as
    burning thorns;
  in the name of the LORD I cut them
    off.

[13]I was pushed back and about to fall,
  but the LORD helped me.

---

[a]18,19,2 Hebrew *Hallelu Yah*   [b]3 Hebrew *Sheol*   [c]10 Or *believed even when*   [d]16 Or *servant, your
faithful son*

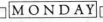
MONDAY

VERSE FOR THE DAY:
Psalm 116:3

AUTHOR:
Carol L. Baldwin

PASSAGE FOR THE DAY:
Psalm 116:1–19

Comfort in Bereavement

"I FEEL like I could cry forever. I miss him so much that I actually hurt inside. Will my life ever be the same?"

Have you felt the deep sorrow of the mourning widow? If you have lost a child, parent, close relative or friend, perhaps you have also felt comfortless. Is there anyone who can minister to you when you feel overwhelmed with grief?

The psalmist shows that he identifies with the pain of the bereaved:

> The cords of death entangled me,
>> the anguish of the grave came upon me;
>> I was overcome by trouble and sorrow
>>> (Psalm 116:3).

Enveloped by emptiness, loneliness and stress, who does the psalmist turn to?

> I called on the name of the LORD:
>> "O LORD, save me!' (Psalm 116:4).

He turns to the only one who will dry all of our tears (Isaiah 25:8); the one who carries all of our sorrows (Isaiah 53:4); the man acquainted with grief (Isaiah 53:3).

Likewise, we must turn to God and his Word for comfort in our times of sorrow. Without denying our pain, Scripture gives us a proper perspective, something we can easily lose in times of emotional trauma and crisis.

God's Word gives hope when we feel utterly alone and hopeless. We can take comfort in knowing that God does not allow a trial in our lives that is too great for us to bear (1 Corinthians 10:13). We can also be assured that death does not conquer those who die in Christ (1 Corinthians 15:22,53-56).

God is in charge of all things. Even the terrible destruction and the traumatic aftermath of death for those who mourn are under his lordship. God's Word and Spirit can comfort our grieving hearts so that we will be able to say with the psalmist:

> I may walk before the LORD
>> in the land of the living . . .
> I am [his] servant. . . .
> Praise the LORD (Psalm 116:9,16,19).

Additional Scripture Readings:
2 Corinthians 1:3–4; 1 Thessalonians 4:13–18

Go to page 498 for your next devotional reading.

¹⁴The Lord is my strength and my song;
   he has become my salvation.

¹⁵Shouts of joy and victory
   resound in the tents of the
     righteous:
"The Lord's right hand has done
   mighty things!
¹⁶ The Lord's right hand is lifted high;
   the Lord's right hand has done
   mighty things!"

¹⁷I will not die but live,
   and will proclaim what the Lord
   has done.
¹⁸The Lord has chastened me severely,
   but he has not given me over to
   death.

¹⁹Open for me the gates of
   righteousness;
   I will enter and give thanks to the
   Lord.
²⁰This is the gate of the Lord
   through which the righteous may
   enter.
²¹I will give you thanks, for you
   answered me;
   you have become my salvation.

²²The stone the builders rejected
   has become the capstone;
²³the Lord has done this,
   and it is marvelous in our eyes.
²⁴This is the day the Lord has made;
   let us rejoice and be glad in it.

²⁵O Lord, save us;
   O Lord, grant us success.
²⁶Blessed is he who comes in the name
   of the Lord.
   From the house of the Lord we
   bless you.ᵃ
²⁷The Lord is God,
   and he has made his light shine
   upon us.
With boughs in hand, join in the
   festal procession
upᵇ to the horns of the altar.

²⁸You are my God, and I will give you
   thanks;
   you are my God, and I will exalt
   you.

²⁹Give thanks to the Lord, for he is
   good;
   his love endures forever.

Psalm 119ᶜ

א Aleph

¹Blessed are they whose ways are
   blameless,
   who walk according to the law of
   the Lord.
²Blessed are they who keep his
   statutes
   and seek him with all their heart.
³They do nothing wrong;
   they walk in his ways.
⁴You have laid down precepts
   that are to be fully obeyed.
⁵Oh, that my ways were steadfast
   in obeying your decrees!
⁶Then I would not be put to shame
   when I consider all your
   commands.
⁷I will praise you with an upright heart
   as I learn your righteous laws.
⁸I will obey your decrees;
   do not utterly forsake me.

ב Beth

⁹How can a young man keep his way
   pure?
   By living according to your word.
¹⁰I seek you with all my heart;
   do not let me stray from your
   commands.
¹¹I have hidden your word in my heart
   that I might not sin against you.
¹²Praise be to you, O Lord;
   teach me your decrees.
¹³With my lips I recount
   all the laws that come from your
   mouth.
¹⁴I rejoice in following your statutes
   as one rejoices in great riches.
¹⁵I meditate on your precepts
   and consider your ways.
¹⁶I delight in your decrees;
   I will not neglect your word.

ג Gimel

¹⁷Do good to your servant, and I will
   live;
   I will obey your word.
¹⁸Open my eyes that I may see
   wonderful things in your law.
¹⁹I am a stranger on earth;
   do not hide your commands from
   me.
²⁰My soul is consumed with longing
   for your laws at all times.

ᵃ26 The Hebrew is plural. ᵇ27 Or *Bind the festal sacrifice with ropes / and take it* ᶜThis psalm is
an acrostic poem; the verses of each stanza begin with the same letter of the Hebrew alphabet.

²¹You rebuke the arrogant, who are
    cursed
    and who stray from your
       commands.
²²Remove from me scorn and contempt,
    for I keep your statutes.
²³Though rulers sit together and slander
       me,
    your servant will meditate on your
       decrees.
²⁴Your statutes are my delight;
    they are my counselors.

ד   Daleth

²⁵I am laid low in the dust;
    preserve my life according to your
       word.
²⁶I recounted my ways and you
       answered me;
    teach me your decrees.
²⁷Let me understand the teaching of
       your precepts;
    then I will meditate on your
       wonders.
²⁸My soul is weary with sorrow;
    strengthen me according to your
       word.
²⁹Keep me from deceitful ways;
    be gracious to me through your law.
³⁰I have chosen the way of truth;
    I have set my heart on your laws.
³¹I hold fast to your statutes, O Lord;
    do not let me be put to shame.
³²I run in the path of your commands,
    for you have set my heart free.

ה   He

³³Teach me, O Lord, to follow your
       decrees;
    then I will keep them to the end.
³⁴Give me understanding, and I will
       keep your law
    and obey it with all my heart.
³⁵Direct me in the path of your
       commands,
    for there I find delight.
³⁶Turn my heart toward your statutes
    and not toward selfish gain.
³⁷Turn my eyes away from worthless
       things;
    preserve my life according to your
       word.ᵃ
³⁸Fulfill your promise to your servant,
    so that you may be feared.
³⁹Take away the disgrace I dread,
    for your laws are good.
⁴⁰How I long for your precepts!

Preserve my life in your
    righteousness.

ו   Waw

⁴¹May your unfailing love come to me,
       O Lord,
    your salvation according to your
       promise;
⁴²then I will answer the one who taunts
       me,
    for I trust in your word.
⁴³Do not snatch the word of truth from
       my mouth,
    for I have put my hope in your
       laws.
⁴⁴I will always obey your law,
    for ever and ever.
⁴⁵I will walk about in freedom,
    for I have sought out your precepts.
⁴⁶I will speak of your statutes before
       kings
    and will not be put to shame,
⁴⁷for I delight in your commands
    because I love them.
⁴⁸I lift up my hands toᵇ your
       commands, which I love,
    and I meditate on your decrees.

ז   Zayin

⁴⁹Remember your word to your servant,
    for you have given me hope.
⁵⁰My comfort in my suffering is this:
    Your promise preserves my life.
⁵¹The arrogant mock me without
       restraint,
    but I do not turn from your law.
⁵²I remember your ancient laws,
       O Lord,
    and I find comfort in them.
⁵³Indignation grips me because of the
       wicked,
    who have forsaken your law.
⁵⁴Your decrees are the theme of my
       song
    wherever I lodge.
⁵⁵In the night I remember your name,
       O Lord,
    and I will keep your law.
⁵⁶This has been my practice:
    I obey your precepts.

ח   Heth

⁵⁷You are my portion, O Lord;
    I have promised to obey your
       words.
⁵⁸I have sought your face with all my
       heart;

ᵃ37 Two manuscripts of the Masoretic Text and Dead Sea Scrolls; most manuscripts of the Masoretic
Text *life in your way*   ᵇ48 Or *for*

be gracious to me according to your
promise.
59I have considered my ways
and have turned my steps to your
statutes.
60I will hasten and not delay
to obey your commands.
61Though the wicked bind me with
ropes,
I will not forget your law.
62At midnight I rise to give you thanks
for your righteous laws.
63I am a friend to all who fear you,
to all who follow your precepts.
64The earth is filled with your love,
O LORD;
teach me your decrees.

ט Teth

65Do good to your servant
according to your word, O LORD.
66Teach me knowledge and good
judgment,
for I believe in your commands.
67Before I was afflicted I went astray,
but now I obey your word.
68You are good, and what you do is
good;
teach me your decrees.
69Though the arrogant have smeared
me with lies,
I keep your precepts with all my
heart.
70Their hearts are callous and
unfeeling,
but I delight in your law.
71It was good for me to be afflicted
so that I might learn your decrees.
72The law from your mouth is more
precious to me
than thousands of pieces of silver
and gold.

י Yodh

73Your hands made me and formed me;
give me understanding to learn your
commands.
74May those who fear you rejoice when
they see me,
for I have put my hope in your
word.
75I know, O LORD, that your laws are
righteous,
and in faithfulness you have
afflicted me.
76May your unfailing love be my
comfort,
according to your promise to your
servant.

77Let your compassion come to me that
I may live,
for your law is my delight.
78May the arrogant be put to shame for
wronging me without cause;
but I will meditate on your
precepts.
79May those who fear you turn to me,
those who understand your
statutes.
80May my heart be blameless toward
your decrees,
that I may not be put to shame.

כ Kaph

81My soul faints with longing for your
salvation,
but I have put my hope in your
word.
82My eyes fail, looking for your promise;
I say, "When will you comfort me?"
83Though I am like a wineskin in the
smoke,
I do not forget your decrees.
84How long must your servant wait?
When will you punish my
persecutors?
85The arrogant dig pitfalls for me,
contrary to your law.
86All your commands are trustworthy;
help me, for men persecute me
without cause.
87They almost wiped me from the earth,
but I have not forsaken your
precepts.
88Preserve my life according to your
love,
and I will obey the statutes of your
mouth.

ל Lamedh

89Your word, O LORD, is eternal;
it stands firm in the heavens.
90Your faithfulness continues through
all generations;
you established the earth, and it
endures.
91Your laws endure to this day,
for all things serve you.
92If your law had not been my delight,
I would have perished in my
affliction.
93I will never forget your precepts,
for by them you have preserved my
life.
94Save me, for I am yours;
I have sought out your precepts.
95The wicked are waiting to destroy me,
but I will ponder your statutes.
96To all perfection I see a limit;

but your commands are boundless.

מ Mem

⁹⁷Oh, how I love your law!
I meditate on it all day long.
⁹⁸Your commands make me wiser than
my enemies,
for they are ever with me.
⁹⁹I have more insight than all my
teachers,
for I meditate on your statutes.
¹⁰⁰I have more understanding than the
elders,
for I obey your precepts.
¹⁰¹I have kept my feet from every evil
path
so that I might obey your word.
¹⁰²I have not departed from your laws,
for you yourself have taught me.
¹⁰³How sweet are your words to my
taste,
sweeter than honey to my mouth!
¹⁰⁴I gain understanding from your
precepts;
therefore I hate every wrong path.

נ Nun

¹⁰⁵Your word is a lamp to my feet
and a light for my path.
¹⁰⁶I have taken an oath and confirmed
it,
that I will follow your righteous
laws.
¹⁰⁷I have suffered much;
preserve my life, O LORD, according
to your word.
¹⁰⁸Accept, O LORD, the willing praise of
my mouth,
and teach me your laws.
¹⁰⁹Though I constantly take my life in
my hands,
I will not forget your law.
¹¹⁰The wicked have set a snare for me,
but I have not strayed from your
precepts.
¹¹¹Your statutes are my heritage forever;
they are the joy of my heart.
¹¹²My heart is set on keeping your
decrees
to the very end.

ס Samekh

¹¹³I hate double-minded men,
but I love your law.
¹¹⁴You are my refuge and my shield;
I have put my hope in your word.
¹¹⁵Away from me, you evildoers,
that I may keep the commands of
my God!

¹¹⁶Sustain me according to your
promise, and I will live;
do not let my hopes be dashed.
¹¹⁷Uphold me, and I will be delivered;
I will always have regard for your
decrees.
¹¹⁸You reject all who stray from your
decrees,
for their deceitfulness is in vain.
¹¹⁹All the wicked of the earth you
discard like dross;
therefore I love your statutes.
¹²⁰My flesh trembles in fear of you;
I stand in awe of your laws.

ע Ayin

¹²¹I have done what is righteous and
just;
do not leave me to my oppressors.
¹²²Ensure your servant's well-being;
let not the arrogant oppress me.
¹²³My eyes fail, looking for your
salvation,
looking for your righteous promise.
¹²⁴Deal with your servant according to
your love
and teach me your decrees.
¹²⁵I am your servant; give me
discernment
that I may understand your
statutes.
¹²⁶It is time for you to act, O LORD;
your law is being broken.
¹²⁷Because I love your commands
more than gold, more than pure
gold,
¹²⁸and because I consider all your
precepts right,
I hate every wrong path.

פ Pe

¹²⁹Your statutes are wonderful;
therefore I obey them.
¹³⁰The unfolding of your words gives
light;
it gives understanding to the
simple.
¹³¹I open my mouth and pant,
longing for your commands.
¹³²Turn to me and have mercy on me,
as you always do to those who love
your name.
¹³³Direct my footsteps according to
your word;
let no sin rule over me.
¹³⁴Redeem me from the oppression of
men,
that I may obey your precepts.
¹³⁵Make your face shine upon your
servant

and teach me your decrees.
¹³⁶Streams of tears flow from my eyes,
for your law is not obeyed.

צ Tsadhe

¹³⁷Righteous are you, O LORD,
and your laws are right.
¹³⁸The statutes you have laid down are righteous;
they are fully trustworthy.
¹³⁹My zeal wears me out,
for my enemies ignore your words.
¹⁴⁰Your promises have been thoroughly tested,
and your servant loves them.
¹⁴¹Though I am lowly and despised,
I do not forget your precepts.
¹⁴²Your righteousness is everlasting
and your law is true.
¹⁴³Trouble and distress have come upon me,
but your commands are my delight.
¹⁴⁴Your statutes are forever right;
give me understanding that I may live.

ק Qoph

¹⁴⁵I call with all my heart; answer me, O LORD,
and I will obey your decrees.
¹⁴⁶I call out to you; save me
and I will keep your statutes.
¹⁴⁷I rise before dawn and cry for help;
I have put my hope in your word.
¹⁴⁸My eyes stay open through the watches of the night,
that I may meditate on your promises.
¹⁴⁹Hear my voice in accordance with your love;
preserve my life, O LORD, according to your laws.
¹⁵⁰Those who devise wicked schemes are near,
but they are far from your law.
¹⁵¹Yet you are near, O LORD,
and all your commands are true.
¹⁵²Long ago I learned from your statutes
that you established them to last forever.

ר Resh

¹⁵³Look upon my suffering and deliver me,
for I have not forgotten your law.
¹⁵⁴Defend my cause and redeem me;
preserve my life according to your promise.
¹⁵⁵Salvation is far from the wicked,
for they do not seek out your decrees.
¹⁵⁶Your compassion is great, O LORD;
preserve my life according to your laws.
¹⁵⁷Many are the foes who persecute me,
but I have not turned from your statutes.
¹⁵⁸I look on the faithless with loathing,
for they do not obey your word.
¹⁵⁹See how I love your precepts;
preserve my life, O LORD, according to your love.
¹⁶⁰All your words are true;
all your righteous laws are eternal.

ש Sin and Shin

¹⁶¹Rulers persecute me without cause,
but my heart trembles at your word.
¹⁶²I rejoice in your promise
like one who finds great spoil.
¹⁶³I hate and abhor falsehood
but I love your law.
¹⁶⁴Seven times a day I praise you
for your righteous laws.
¹⁶⁵Great peace have they who love your law,
and nothing can make them stumble.
¹⁶⁶I wait for your salvation, O LORD,
and I follow your commands.
¹⁶⁷I obey your statutes,
for I love them greatly.
¹⁶⁸I obey your precepts and your statutes,
for all my ways are known to you.

ת Taw

¹⁶⁹May my cry come before you, O LORD;
give me understanding according to your word.
¹⁷⁰May my supplication come before you;
deliver me according to your promise.
¹⁷¹May my lips overflow with praise,
for you teach me your decrees.
¹⁷²May my tongue sing of your word,
for all your commands are righteous.
¹⁷³May your hand be ready to help me,
for I have chosen your precepts.
¹⁷⁴I long for your salvation, O LORD,
and your law is my delight.
¹⁷⁵Let me live that I may praise you,
and may your laws sustain me.
¹⁷⁶I have strayed like a lost sheep.
Seek your servant,

for I have not forgotten your
commands.

Psalm 120

A song of ascents.

[1] I call on the LORD in my distress,
and he answers me.
[2] Save me, O LORD, from lying lips
and from deceitful tongues.

[3] What will he do to you,
and what more besides, O deceitful
tongue?
[4] He will punish you with a warrior's
sharp arrows,
with burning coals of the broom
tree.

[5] Woe to me that I dwell in Meshech,
that I live among the tents of
Kedar!
[6] Too long have I lived
among those who hate peace.
[7] I am a man of peace;
but when I speak, they are for war.

Psalm 121

A song of ascents.

[1] I lift up my eyes to the hills—
where does my help come from?
[2] My help comes from the LORD,
the Maker of heaven and earth.

[3] He will not let your foot slip—
he who watches over you will not
slumber;
[4] indeed, he who watches over Israel
will neither slumber nor sleep.

[5] The LORD watches over you—
the LORD is your shade at your right
hand;
[6] the sun will not harm you by day,
nor the moon by night.

[7] The LORD will keep you from all
harm—
he will watch over your life;
[8] the LORD will watch over your coming
and going
both now and forevermore.

Psalm 122

A song of ascents. Of David.

[1] I rejoiced with those who said to me,
"Let us go to the house of the
LORD."

[2] Our feet are standing
in your gates, O Jerusalem.

[3] Jerusalem is built like a city
that is closely compacted together.
[4] That is where the tribes go up,
the tribes of the LORD,
to praise the name of the LORD
according to the statute given to
Israel.
[5] There the thrones for judgment stand,
the thrones of the house of David.

[6] Pray for the peace of Jerusalem:
"May those who love you be secure.
[7] May there be peace within your walls
and security within your citadels."
[8] For the sake of my brothers and
friends,
I will say, "Peace be within you."
[9] For the sake of the house of the LORD
our God,
I will seek your prosperity.

Psalm 123

A song of ascents.

[1] I lift up my eyes to you,
to you whose throne is in heaven.
[2] As the eyes of slaves look to the hand
of their master,
as the eyes of a maid look to the
hand of her mistress,
so our eyes look to the LORD our God,
till he shows us his mercy.

[3] Have mercy on us, O LORD, have
mercy on us,
for we have endured much
contempt.
[4] We have endured much ridicule from
the proud,
much contempt from the arrogant.

Psalm 124

A song of ascents. Of David.

[1] If the LORD had not been on our
side—
let Israel say—
[2] if the LORD had not been on our side
when men attacked us,
[3] when their anger flared against us,
they would have swallowed us alive;
[4] the flood would have engulfed us,
the torrent would have swept over
us,
[5] the raging waters
would have swept us away.

⁶Praise be to the LORD,
    who has not let us be torn by their
      teeth.
⁷We have escaped like a bird
    out of the fowler's snare;
 the snare has been broken,
    and we have escaped.
⁸Our help is in the name of the LORD,
    the Maker of heaven and earth.

Psalm 125

A song of ascents.

¹Those who trust in the LORD are like
    Mount Zion,
    which cannot be shaken but
      endures forever.
²As the mountains surround
    Jerusalem,
 so the LORD surrounds his people
    both now and forevermore.

³The scepter of the wicked will not
    remain
    over the land allotted to the
      righteous,
 for then the righteous might use
    their hands to do evil.

⁴Do good, O LORD, to those who are
    good,
    to those who are upright in heart.
⁵But those who turn to crooked ways
    the LORD will banish with the
      evildoers.

Peace be upon Israel.

Psalm 126

A song of ascents.

¹When the LORD brought back the
    captives to ᵃ Zion,
 we were like men who dreamed.ᵇ
²Our mouths were filled with laughter,
    our tongues with songs of joy.
 Then it was said among the nations,
    "The LORD has done great things for
      them."
³The LORD has done great things for us,
    and we are filled with joy.

⁴Restore our fortunes,ᶜ O LORD,
    like streams in the Negev.
⁵Those who sow in tears
    will reap with songs of joy.
⁶He who goes out weeping,
    carrying seed to sow,

    will return with songs of joy,
    carrying sheaves with him.

Psalm 127

A song of ascents. Of Solomon.

¹Unless the LORD builds the house,
    its builders labor in vain.
 Unless the LORD watches over the city,
    the watchmen stand guard in vain.
²In vain you rise early
    and stay up late,
 toiling for food to eat—
    for he grants sleep toᵈ those he
      loves.

³Sons are a heritage from the LORD,
    children a reward from him.
⁴Like arrows in the hands of a warrior
    are sons born in one's youth.
⁵Blessed is the man
    whose quiver is full of them.
 They will not be put to shame
    when they contend with their
      enemies in the gate.

Psalm 128

A song of ascents.

¹Blessed are all who fear the LORD,
    who walk in his ways.
²You will eat the fruit of your labor;
    blessings and prosperity will be
      yours.
³Your wife will be like a fruitful vine
    within your house;
 your sons will be like olive shoots
    around your table.
⁴Thus is the man blessed
    who fears the LORD.

⁵May the LORD bless you from Zion
    all the days of your life;
 may you see the prosperity of
    Jerusalem,
⁶ and may you live to see your
    children's children.

Peace be upon Israel.

Psalm 129

A song of ascents.

¹They have greatly oppressed me from
    my youth—
    let Israel say—

ᵃ1 Or LORD restored the fortunes of   ᵇ1 Or men restored to health   ᶜ4 Or Bring back our captives
ᵈ2 Or eat— / for while they sleep he provides for

VERSE FOR THE DAY:	AUTHOR:	PASSAGE FOR THE DAY:
Psalm 126:5	Ruth A. Tucker	Psalm 126:1–6

Sowing in Tears

SO often it is assumed that someone who is going through difficult times is incapable of effectively ministering to someone
else. Indeed, as we are counseling those who are depressed and
struggling with personal problems, it never seems to occur to us
to encourage them to reach out to minister to others rather than
focus exclusively on themselves. How insightful the psalmist
was in writing:

> He who goes out weeping,
>   carrying seed to sow,
> will return with songs of joy,
>   carrying sheaves with him (Psalm 126:6).

It was during a very stressful period in my own life a few years
ago that I was thrust suddenly into a care-giving situation. I had
promised a friend that I would be a "daughter" to her mother
while she and her husband fulfilled a two-year mission commitment in Africa. I might have had second thoughts about my new
role had I realized that the day after my friend would leave, her
mother would enter the hospital where her condition would utterly bewilder the doctors until she died several weeks later.

I was in no condition to minister to someone else—so I
thought. But as I began making those daily hospital visits to
Clara, I discovered that instead of adding to my stress, my time
with her was rejuvenating. As I identified with her needs, my
own problems paled into insignificance. And as I served her and
focused on her well-being, I felt better about myself. Clara certainly was not passive in the care-giving process. She responded
to my love and gave back to me far more than I gave her. She
helped me make it through a very tough time in my life, and I
will always have the sweet memories of being close to her during
her final days, when I went out weeping and returned with songs
of joy.

Additional Scripture Readings:
Isaiah 61:1–3; 2 Timothy 1:6–12

*Go to page 500 for your next
devotional reading.*

²they have greatly oppressed me from
  my youth,
  but they have not gained the victory
    over me.
³Plowmen have plowed my back
  and made their furrows long.
⁴But the Lᴏʀᴅ is righteous;
  he has cut me free from the cords
    of the wicked.

⁵May all who hate Zion
  be turned back in shame.
⁶May they be like grass on the roof,
  which withers before it can grow;
⁷with it the reaper cannot fill his
    hands,
  nor the one who gathers fill his
    arms.
⁸May those who pass by not say,
  "The blessing of the Lᴏʀᴅ be upon
    you;
  we bless you in the name of the
    Lᴏʀᴅ."

Psalm 130

A song of ascents.

¹Out of the depths I cry to you,
  O Lᴏʀᴅ;
²   O Lord, hear my voice.
Let your ears be attentive
  to my cry for mercy.

³If you, O Lᴏʀᴅ, kept a record of sins,
  O Lord, who could stand?
⁴But with you there is forgiveness;
  therefore you are feared.

⁵I wait for the Lᴏʀᴅ, my soul waits,
  and in his word I put my hope.
⁶My soul waits for the Lord
  more than watchmen wait for the
    morning,
  more than watchmen wait for the
    morning.

⁷O Israel, put your hope in the Lᴏʀᴅ,
  for with the Lᴏʀᴅ is unfailing love
  and with him is full redemption.
⁸He himself will redeem Israel
  from all their sins.

Psalm 131

A song of ascents. Of David.

¹My heart is not proud, O Lᴏʀᴅ,
  my eyes are not haughty;

I do not concern myself with great
  matters
  or things too wonderful for me.
²But I have stilled and quieted my
  soul;
  like a weaned child with its mother,
  like a weaned child is my soul
    within me.

³O Israel, put your hope in the Lᴏʀᴅ
  both now and forevermore.

Psalm 132

A song of ascents.

¹O Lᴏʀᴅ, remember David
  and all the hardships he endured.

²He swore an oath to the Lᴏʀᴅ
  and made a vow to the Mighty One
    of Jacob:
³"I will not enter my house
  or go to my bed—
⁴I will allow no sleep to my eyes,
  no slumber to my eyelids,
⁵till I find a place for the Lᴏʀᴅ,
  a dwelling for the Mighty One of
    Jacob."

⁶We heard it in Ephrathah,
  we came upon it in the fields of
    Jaar*ᵃ*ᵇ
⁷"Let us go to his dwelling place;
  let us worship at his footstool—
⁸arise, O Lᴏʀᴅ, and come to your
    resting place,
  you and the ark of your might.
⁹May your priests be clothed with
    righteousness;
  may your saints sing for joy."

¹⁰For the sake of David your servant,
  do not reject your anointed one.

¹¹The Lᴏʀᴅ swore an oath to David,
  a sure oath that he will not revoke:
"One of your own descendants
  I will place on your throne—
¹²if your sons keep my covenant
  and the statutes I teach them,
then their sons will sit
  on your throne for ever and ever."

¹³For the Lᴏʀᴅ has chosen Zion,
  he has desired it for his dwelling:
¹⁴"This is my resting place for ever and
    ever;
  here I will sit enthroned, for I have
    desired it—

ᵃ6 That is, Kiriath Jearim   ᵇ6 Or *heard of it in Ephrathah, / we found it in the fields of Jaar.* (And no
quotes around verses 7-9)

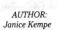
| VERSE FOR THE DAY:
Psalm 130:1–2 | AUTHOR:
Janice Kempe | PASSAGE FOR THE DAY:
Psalm 130:1–8 |

Out of the Depths

I'LL bet I've washed that dish a million times! My kitchen sink seems like a hole that I keep falling into and can't escape from. I wonder how many spoons and forks I've washed in the last ten years? And the laundry basket. It's perpetually full! I'll bet I could go to the dryer any time, day or night, and find at least ten ragged towels, six wrinkled shirts, and twenty-three socks, five of which have no mate. Who cares?

> Out of the depths I cry to you, O Lord;
>   O Lord, hear my voice.
> Let your ears be attentive
>   to my cry for mercy (Psalm 130:1–2)

Am I in the depths? Is this utter despair? I don't think so, but it is definitely uncomfortable. I'm having the blahs.

"Out of my blahs I cry to you, O Lord. Lord, hear my voice; Let your ears be attentive to my cry for mercy" (Kempe 1983).

That's my translation! Sometimes I have trouble relating to the trials and tragedies that drove God's people of the Old Testament to cry to him for deliverance. They make my own trial seem unimportant in comparison. But today I think God is telling me to stop comparing and to realize that the depressions and setbacks I experience are just as important to him as the conflicts and moral dilemmas faced by people in Bible times. They were his children, and he heard their voices and led them out of the depths. I also am his child, and he hears my voice and will lead me out of my depths. God is as eager to hear my pleas as he was to hear theirs.

My Lord cares! He cares when I feel like a failure. He cares when I feel as if all my education and training have led me to nothing but a sinkful of dishes. I think he smiles when I mop up spilled milk at each meal. I think he smiles when he hears a resounding "Yuck" in response to a new recipe I tried. He smiles and gives me gentle words of encouragement.

Additional Scripture Readings:
Numbers 11:10–23; Hebrews 4:14–16

*Go to page 504 for your next
devotional reading.*

¹⁵I will bless her with abundant
     provisions;
   her poor will I satisfy with food.
¹⁶I will clothe her priests with
     salvation,
   and her saints will ever sing for joy.

¹⁷"Here I will make a horn[a] grow for
     David
   and set up a lamp for my anointed
     one.
¹⁸I will clothe his enemies with shame,
   but the crown on his head will be
     resplendent."

Psalm 133

A song of ascents. Of David.

¹How good and pleasant it is
   when brothers live together in
     unity!
²It is like precious oil poured on the
     head,
   running down on the beard,
 running down on Aaron's beard,
   down upon the collar of his robes.
³It is as if the dew of Hermon
   were falling on Mount Zion.
 For there the LORD bestows his
     blessing,
   even life forevermore.

Psalm 134

A song of ascents.

¹Praise the LORD, all you servants of
     the LORD
   who minister by night in the house
     of the LORD.
²Lift up your hands in the sanctuary
   and praise the LORD.

³May the LORD, the Maker of heaven
     and earth,
   bless you from Zion.

Psalm 135

¹Praise the LORD.[b]

 Praise the name of the LORD;
   praise him, you servants of the
     LORD,
²you who minister in the house of the
     LORD,
   in the courts of the house of our
     God.

³Praise the LORD, for the LORD is good;

   sing praise to his name, for that is
     pleasant.
⁴For the LORD has chosen Jacob to be
     his own,
   Israel to be his treasured
     possession.

⁵I know that the LORD is great,
   that our Lord is greater than all
     gods.
⁶The LORD does whatever pleases him,
   in the heavens and on the earth,
   in the seas and all their depths.
⁷He makes clouds rise from the ends
     of the earth;
   he sends lightning with the rain
   and brings out the wind from his
     storehouses.

⁸He struck down the firstborn of
     Egypt,
   the firstborn of men and animals.
⁹He sent his signs and wonders into
     your midst, O Egypt,
   against Pharaoh and all his
     servants.
¹⁰He struck down many nations
   and killed mighty kings—
¹¹Sihon king of the Amorites,
   Og king of Bashan
   and all the kings of Canaan—
¹²and he gave their land as an
     inheritance,
   an inheritance to his people Israel.

¹³Your name, O LORD, endures forever,
   your renown, O LORD, through all
     generations.
¹⁴For the LORD will vindicate his people
   and have compassion on his
     servants.

¹⁵The idols of the nations are silver and
     gold,
   made by the hands of men.
¹⁶They have mouths, but cannot speak,
   eyes, but they cannot see;
¹⁷they have ears, but cannot hear,
   nor is there breath in their mouths.
¹⁸Those who make them will be like
     them,
   and so will all who trust in them.

¹⁹O house of Israel, praise the LORD;
   O house of Aaron, praise the LORD;
²⁰O house of Levi, praise the LORD;
   you who fear him, praise the LORD.
²¹Praise be to the LORD from Zion,
   to him who dwells in Jerusalem.

 Praise the LORD.

---

[a]17 Horn here symbolizes strong one, that is, king.   [b]1 Hebrew Hallelu Yah; also in verses 3 and 21

Psalm 136

¹Give thanks to the LORD, for he is
good.
> *His love endures forever.*
²Give thanks to the God of gods.
> *His love endures forever.*
³Give thanks to the Lord of lords:
> *His love endures forever.*

⁴to him who alone does great wonders,
> *His love endures forever.*
⁵who by his understanding made the
heavens,
> *His love endures forever.*
⁶who spread out the earth upon the
waters,
> *His love endures forever.*
⁷who made the great lights —
> *His love endures forever.*
⁸the sun to govern the day,
> *His love endures forever.*
⁹the moon and stars to govern the
night;
> *His love endures forever.*

¹⁰to him who struck down the firstborn
of Egypt
> *His love endures forever.*
¹¹and brought Israel out from among
them
> *His love endures forever.*
¹²with a mighty hand and outstretched
arm;
> *His love endures forever.*

¹³to him who divided the Red Sea*ᵃ*
asunder
> *His love endures forever.*
¹⁴and brought Israel through the midst
of it,
> *His love endures forever.*
¹⁵but swept Pharaoh and his army into
the Red Sea;
> *His love endures forever.*

¹⁶to him who led his people through
the desert,
> *His love endures forever.*
¹⁷who struck down great kings,
> *His love endures forever.*
¹⁸and killed mighty kings —
> *His love endures forever.*
¹⁹Sihon king of the Amorites
> *His love endures forever.*
²⁰and Og king of Bashan —
> *His love endures forever.*
²¹and gave their land as an inheritance,
> *His love endures forever.*

²²an inheritance to his servant Israel;
> *His love endures forever.*

²³to the One who remembered us in
our low estate
> *His love endures forever.*
²⁴and freed us from our enemies,
> *His love endures forever.*
²⁵and who gives food to every creature.
> *His love endures forever.*

²⁶Give thanks to the God of heaven.
> *His love endures forever.*

Psalm 137

¹By the rivers of Babylon we sat and
wept
when we remembered Zion.
²There on the poplars
we hung our harps,
³for there our captors asked us for
songs,
our tormentors demanded songs of
joy;
they said, "Sing us one of the songs
of Zion!"

⁴How can we sing the songs of the
LORD
while in a foreign land?
⁵If I forget you, O Jerusalem,
may my right hand forget ,its skill,.
⁶May my tongue cling to the roof of
my mouth
if I do not remember you,
if I do not consider Jerusalem
my highest joy.

⁷Remember, O LORD, what the
Edomites did
on the day Jerusalem fell.
"Tear it down," they cried,
"tear it down to its foundations!"

⁸O Daughter of Babylon, doomed to
destruction,
happy is he who repays you
for what you have done to us —
⁹he who seizes your infants
and dashes them against the rocks.

Psalm 138

Of David.

¹I will praise you, O LORD, with all my
heart;
before the "gods" I will sing your
praise.

ᵃ13 Hebrew Yam Suph; that is, Sea of Reeds; also in verse 15

²I will bow down toward your holy
  temple
    and will praise your name
  for your love and your faithfulness,
for you have exalted above all things
    your name and your word.
³When I called, you answered me;
    you made me bold and
      stouthearted.

⁴May all the kings of the earth praise
    you, O LORD,
  when they hear the words of your
    mouth.
⁵May they sing of the ways of the
    LORD,
  for the glory of the LORD is great.

⁶Though the LORD is on high, he looks
    upon the lowly,
  but the proud he knows from afar.
⁷Though I walk in the midst of
    trouble,
  you preserve my life;
you stretch out your hand against the
    anger of my foes,
  with your right hand you save me.
⁸The LORD will fulfill his purpose for
    me;
  your love, O LORD, endures
    forever—
  do not abandon the works of your
    hands.

Psalm 139

For the director of music. Of David.
A psalm.

¹O LORD, you have searched me
    and you know me.
²You know when I sit and when I rise;
    you perceive my thoughts from afar.
³You discern my going out and my
    lying down;
  you are familiar with all my ways.
⁴Before a word is on my tongue
    you know it completely, O LORD.

⁵You hem me in—behind and before;
    you have laid your hand upon me.
⁶Such knowledge is too wonderful for
    me,
  too lofty for me to attain.

⁷Where can I go from your Spirit?
  Where can I flee from your
    presence?
⁸If I go up to the heavens, you are
    there;

if I make my bed in the depths,ᵃ
  you are there.
⁹If I rise on the wings of the dawn,
  if I settle on the far side of the sea,
¹⁰even there your hand will guide me,
    your right hand will hold me fast.

¹¹If I say, "Surely the darkness will hide
    me
  and the light become night around
    me,"
¹²even the darkness will not be dark to
    you;
  the night will shine like the day,
  for darkness is as light to you.

¹³For you created my inmost being;
    you knit me together in my
      mother's womb.
¹⁴I praise you because I am fearfully
    and wonderfully made;
  your works are wonderful,
    I know that full well.
¹⁵My frame was not hidden from you
    when I was made in the secret
      place.
  When I was woven together in the
      depths of the earth,
¹⁶   your eyes saw my unformed body.
  All the days ordained for me
    were written in your book
    before one of them came to be.

¹⁷How precious toᵇ me are your
    thoughts, O God!
  How vast is the sum of them!
¹⁸Were I to count them,
    they would outnumber the grains of
      sand.
  When I awake,
    I am still with you.

¹⁹If only you would slay the wicked,
    O God!
  Away from me, you bloodthirsty
    men!
²⁰They speak of you with evil intent;
    your adversaries misuse your name.
²¹Do I not hate those who hate you,
    O LORD,
  and abhor those who rise up
    against you?
²²I have nothing but hatred for them;
    I count them my enemies.

²³Search me, O God, and know my
    heart;
  test me and know my anxious
    thoughts.

ᵃ8 Hebrew Sheol   ᵇ17 Or concerning

VERSE FOR THE DAY:
Psalm 139:1

AUTHOR:
Hope MacDonald

PASSAGE FOR THE DAY:
Psalm 139:1–24

God's Active Presence

"OH! If only I could take this big tummy and set it on a chair for just one hour," sighed my eight-month-pregnant daughter. But we both knew that she couldn't. That little life went with her wherever she went, day or night.

I thought about that as I read this psalm today. I believe it is one of the most personal passages in all of Scripture. It is a psalm about God's continual, active presence with me wherever I go, day or night.

Christ in me means that God knows everything about me. He knows when I sit down and when I stand up (Psalm 139:2). He knows my name (Isaiah 43:1). He knows how many hairs I have on my head (Luke 12:7)! He knows my words completely, even before they are spoken (Psalm 139:4)! In fact, he saw me when I was being formed in my mother's womb. He was there, knitting me together (Psalm 139:13–16)! Indeed, such knowledge is too wonderful, too lofty for any of us to fully comprehend (Psalm 139:6).

Not only do we learn about God's eternal presence *with* us every moment, but we also get a tiny glimpse into the absolute holiness of God and his unconditional love for us. We are reminded that God knows and understands us better than anyone else ever will. His love for us is everlasting and personal. St. Augustine said, "God loves each one of us as though there were only one of us to love." What a treasure this truth is. Because of it, we can live in the certainty that his grace is sufficient for us today, regardless of our circumstances.

Just as my daughter could not set aside that little life she was carrying, not even for an hour, neither can we, who have received Jesus as Savior, ever be without him. We are bonded together in love. His Spirit is at work within us, making us more like Jesus with each passing day. We are each an everlasting child of God.

Additional Scripture Readings:
Jeremiah 1:4–8; Ephesians 1:17–21

Go to page 507 for your next devotional reading.

²⁴See if there is any offensive way in
me,
and lead me in the way everlasting.

Psalm 140

For the director of music. A psalm
of David.

¹Rescue me, O LORD, from evil men;
protect me from men of violence,
²who devise evil plans in their hearts
and stir up war every day.
³They make their tongues as sharp as
a serpent's;
the poison of vipers is on their lips.
Selah

⁴Keep me, O LORD, from the hands of
the wicked;
protect me from men of violence
who plan to trip my feet.
⁵Proud men have hidden a snare for
me;
they have spread out the cords of
their net
and have set traps for me along my
path.   *Selah*

⁶O LORD, I say to you, "You are my
God."
Hear, O LORD, my cry for mercy.
⁷O Sovereign LORD, my strong deliverer,
who shields my head in the day of
battle—
⁸do not grant the wicked their desires,
O LORD;
do not let their plans succeed,
or they will become proud.   *Selah*

⁹Let the heads of those who surround
me
be covered with the trouble their
lips have caused.
¹⁰Let burning coals fall upon them;
may they be thrown into the fire,
into miry pits, never to rise.
¹¹Let slanderers not be established in
the land;
may disaster hunt down men of
violence.

¹²I know that the LORD secures justice
for the poor
and upholds the cause of the
needy.
¹³Surely the righteous will praise your
name
and the upright will live before you.

Psalm 141

A psalm of David.

¹O LORD, I call to you; come quickly to
me.
Hear my voice when I call to you.
²May my prayer be set before you like
incense;
may the lifting up of my hands be
like the evening sacrifice.

³Set a guard over my mouth, O LORD;
keep watch over the door of my
lips.
⁴Let not my heart be drawn to what is
evil,
to take part in wicked deeds
with men who are evildoers;
let me not eat of their delicacies.

⁵Let a righteous man*ᵃ* strike me—it is
a kindness;
let him rebuke me—it is oil on my
head.
My head will not refuse it.

Yet my prayer is ever against the
deeds of evildoers;
6 their rulers will be thrown down
from the cliffs,
and the wicked will learn that my
words were well spoken.
⁷They will say,, "As one plows and
breaks up the earth,
so our bones have been scattered at
the mouth of the grave.*ᵇ*"

⁸But my eyes are fixed on you,
O Sovereign LORD;
in you I take refuge—do not give
me over to death.
⁹Keep me from the snares they have
laid for me,
from the traps set by evildoers.
¹⁰Let the wicked fall into their own
nets,
while I pass by in safety.

Psalm 142

A *maskil*ᶜ of David. When he was in the
cave. A prayer.

¹I cry aloud to the LORD;
I lift up my voice to the LORD for
mercy.
²I pour out my complaint before him;
before him I tell my trouble.

³When my spirit grows faint within me,

ᵃ5 Or *Let the Righteous One*   ᵇ7 Hebrew *Sheol*   ᶜTitle: Probably a literary or musical term

it is you who know my way.
In the path where I walk
   men have hidden a snare for me.
4Look to my right and see;
   no one is concerned for me.
I have no refuge;
   no one cares for my life.

5I cry to you, O LORD;
   I say, "You are my refuge,
   my portion in the land of the
      living."
6Listen to my cry,
   for I am in desperate need;
rescue me from those who pursue me,
   for they are too strong for me.
7Set me free from my prison,
   that I may praise your name.

Then the righteous will gather about
   me
   because of your goodness to me.

Psalm 143

A psalm of David.

1O LORD, hear my prayer,
   listen to my cry for mercy;
in your faithfulness and righteousness
   come to my relief.
2Do not bring your servant into
      judgment,
   for no one living is righteous before
      you.

3The enemy pursues me,
   he crushes me to the ground;
he makes me dwell in darkness
   like those long dead.
4So my spirit grows faint within me;
   my heart within me is dismayed.

5I remember the days of long ago;
   I meditate on all your works
and consider what your hands have
      done.
6I spread out my hands to you;
   my soul thirsts for you like a
      parched land.   *Selah*

7Answer me quickly, O LORD;
   my spirit fails.
Do not hide your face from me
   or I will be like those who go down
      to the pit.
8Let the morning bring me word of
   your unfailing love,
   for I have put my trust in you.
Show me the way I should go,

for to you I lift up my soul.
9Rescue me from my enemies, O LORD,
   for I hide myself in you.
10Teach me to do your will,
   for you are my God;
may your good Spirit
   lead me on level ground.

11For your name's sake, O LORD,
      preserve my life;
in your righteousness, bring me out
      of trouble.
12In your unfailing love, silence my
      enemies;
   destroy all my foes,
   for I am your servant.

Psalm 144

Of David.

1Praise be to the LORD my Rock,
   who trains my hands for war,
   my fingers for battle.
2He is my loving God and my fortress,
   my stronghold and my deliverer,
my shield, in whom I take refuge,
   who subdues peoples*a* under me.

3O LORD, what is man that you care for
      him,
   the son of man that you think of
      him?
4Man is like a breath;
   his days are like a fleeting shadow.

5Part your heavens, O LORD, and come
      down;
   touch the mountains, so that they
      smoke.
6Send forth lightning and scatter the
      enemies;
   shoot your arrows and rout them.
7Reach down your hand from on high;
   deliver me and rescue me
from the mighty waters,
   from the hands of foreigners
8whose mouths are full of lies,
   whose right hands are deceitful.

9I will sing a new song to you, O God;
   on the ten-stringed lyre I will make
      music to you,
10to the One who gives victory to kings,
   who delivers his servant David from
      the deadly sword.

11Deliver me and rescue me
   from the hands of foreigners
whose mouths are full of lies,

a2 Many manuscripts of the Masoretic Text, Dead Sea Scrolls, Aquila, Jerome and Syriac; most
manuscripts of the Masoretic Text *subdues my people*

FRIDAY

VERSE FOR THE DAY:
Psalm 145:18

AUTHOR:
Debbie Smith

PASSAGE FOR THE DAY:
Psalm 145:1–21

The Lord Is Faithful

"CAROL has gone into labor. She's at the hospital now . . . but they think the baby is dead!"

How could Carol, a friend who had suffered through three miscarriages, be asked to endure this tragedy? I hung up the phone, only to pick it up again to dial friends and family with a plea for prayer. God in his power could save that child!

The afternoon stretched on, and I remember praying almost constantly. "The LORD is near to all who call on him" (Psalm 145:18). I felt his presence, knowing that Carol and Bill surely felt it too.

Responding to a nudge to go to the hospital, I left the children with a sitter and set out on the thirty-minute drive, both desiring to "be there" for my friends and dreading what I might have to face.

By the time I reached the hospital the baby had been born, dead. Our pastor emerged from the room, assuring those of us waiting outside that Carol and Bill were taking their loss well, resting on faith. I wept with my friends, then listened as they spoke of the faith and comfort that God was providing. They recognized that God was in control, and they insisted that the prayers of believers had eased the pain. His peace was on their faces and in their words.

I left, numbed by the ordeal, yet strangely consoled. Driving home, I thanked my "gracious and compassionate" Lord (Psalm 145:8) for guiding my steps to that hospital room. The experience seemed an answer to many prayers for courage—for myself. For years I had struggled to believe that "the LORD watches over all who love him" (Psalm 145:20)—that he would be enough in any crisis I might have to face. My doubts were put to rest in five minutes inside that room.

The song Michael and I had written years before became vibrant again for me:

> Great is the Lord, he is holy and just;
> By his power we trust in his love.*

Yes. God is sufficient.

Additional Scripture Readings:
1 Corinthians 1:4–9; 1 Peter 1:3–9

*Go to page 509 for your next
devotional reading.*

whose right hands are deceitful.

¹²Then our sons in their youth
  will be like well-nurtured plants,
and our daughters will be like pillars
  carved to adorn a palace.
¹³Our barns will be filled
  with every kind of provision.
Our sheep will increase by thousands,
  by tens of thousands in our fields;
¹⁴ our oxen will draw heavy loads.ᵃ
There will be no breaching of walls,
  no going into captivity,
  no cry of distress in our streets.

¹⁵Blessed are the people of whom this
    is true;
  blessed are the people whose God
    is the LORD.

Psalm 145ᵇ

A psalm of praise. Of David.

¹I will exalt you, my God the King;
  I will praise your name for ever and
    ever.
²Every day I will praise you
  and extol your name for ever and
    ever.

³Great is the LORD and most worthy of
    praise;
  his greatness no one can fathom.
⁴One generation will commend your
    works to another;
  they will tell of your mighty acts.
⁵They will speak of the glorious
    splendor of your majesty,
  and I will meditate on your
    wonderful works.ᶜ
⁶They will tell of the power of your
    awesome works,
  and I will proclaim your great
    deeds.
⁷They will celebrate your abundant
    goodness
  and joyfully sing of your
    righteousness.

⁸The LORD is gracious and
    compassionate,
  slow to anger and rich in love.
⁹The LORD is good to all;
  he has compassion on all he has
    made.

¹⁰All you have made will praise you,
    O LORD;
  your saints will extol you.
¹¹They will tell of the glory of your
    kingdom
  and speak of your might,
¹²so that all men may know of your
    mighty acts
  and the glorious splendor of your
    kingdom.
¹³Your kingdom is an everlasting
    kingdom,
  and your dominion endures through
    all generations.

  The LORD is faithful to all his
    promises
  and loving toward all he has
    made.ᵈ
¹⁴The LORD upholds all those who fall
  and lifts up all who are bowed
    down.
¹⁵The eyes of all look to you,
  and you give them their food at the
    proper time.
¹⁶You open your hand
  and satisfy the desires of every
    living thing.

¹⁷The LORD is righteous in all his ways
  and loving toward all he has made.
¹⁸The LORD is near to all who call on
    him,
  to all who call on him in truth.
¹⁹He fulfills the desires of those who
    fear him;
  he hears their cry and saves them.
²⁰The LORD watches over all who love
    him,
  but all the wicked he will destroy.

²¹My mouth will speak in praise of the
    LORD.
  Let every creature praise his holy
    name
  for ever and ever.

Psalm 146

¹Praise the LORD.ᵉ

  Praise the LORD, O my soul.
² I will praise the LORD all my life;
  I will sing praise to my God as long
    as I live.

ᵃ14 Or *our chieftains will be firmly established*   ᵇThis psalm is an acrostic poem, the verses of which
(including verse 13b) begin with the successive letters of the Hebrew alphabet.   ᶜ5 Dead Sea Scrolls
and Syriac (see also Septuagint); Masoretic Text *On the glorious splendor of your majesty / and on your
wonderful works I will meditate*   ᵈ13 One manuscript of the Masoretic Text, Dead Sea Scrolls and
Syriac (see also Septuagint); most manuscripts of the Masoretic Text do not have the last two lines of
verse 13.   ᵉ1 Hebrew *Hallelu Yah*; also in verse 10

WEEKENDING

REJOICE

Each day, upon my daily round,
I find myself on holy ground —
The morning-glories on my fence
Inspire quiet reverence.
Just one small, tender seedling grew,
And now, this miracle in blue.
A robin in the apple tree
Sings out his glad doxology.
I hear the pure, unsullied joy
Of laughter from a little boy;
I bow before the firm belief
And faith of one who lives with grief;
I watch a jet plane skim the skies
And marvel at man's enterprise;
I look upon a field of wheat
And thank God for the bread we eat;
I watch the benedictive rain
On low-bowed heads of flower and grain.
A friend drops in, a neighbor calls,
The lamps are lit, night gently falls;
Contentment settles with the sun
In labors of the day well done.
So many little altars there,
So many simple calls to prayer,
So many reasons for thanksgiving —
The sacraments of daily living.

— Helen Lowrie Marshall

REVIVE

Saturday: Psalm 135:1–21
Sunday: Exodus 3:1–22

Go to page 511 for your next devotional reading.

[3]Do not put your trust in princes,
　　in mortal men, who cannot save.
[4]When their spirit departs, they return
　　　to the ground;
　　on that very day their plans come
　　　to nothing.

[5]Blessed is he whose help is the God
　　　of Jacob,
　　whose hope is in the LORD his God,
[6]the Maker of heaven and earth,
　　the sea, and everything in them—
　　the LORD, who remains faithful
　　　forever.
[7]He upholds the cause of the
　　　oppressed
　　and gives food to the hungry.
　The LORD sets prisoners free,
[8]　the LORD gives sight to the blind,
　the LORD lifts up those who are bowed
　　　down,
　　the LORD loves the righteous.
[9]The LORD watches over the alien
　　and sustains the fatherless and the
　　　widow,
　　but he frustrates the ways of the
　　　wicked.

[10]The LORD reigns forever,
　　your God, O Zion, for all
　　　generations.

　Praise the LORD.

Psalm 147

[1]Praise the LORD.[a]

How good it is to sing praises to our
　　　God,
　　how pleasant and fitting to praise
　　　him!

[2]The LORD builds up Jerusalem;
　　he gathers the exiles of Israel.
[3]He heals the brokenhearted
　　and binds up their wounds.

[4]He determines the number of the
　　　stars
　　and calls them each by name.
[5]Great is our Lord and mighty in
　　　power;
　　his understanding has no limit.
[6]The LORD sustains the humble
　　but casts the wicked to the ground.

[7]Sing to the LORD with thanksgiving;
　　make music to our God on the
　　　harp.
[8]He covers the sky with clouds;

he supplies the earth with rain
　　and makes grass grow on the hills.
[9]He provides food for the cattle
　　and for the young ravens when they
　　　call.

[10]His pleasure is not in the strength of
　　　the horse,
　　nor his delight in the legs of a man;
[11]the LORD delights in those who fear
　　　him,
　　who put their hope in his unfailing
　　　love.

[12]Extol the LORD, O Jerusalem;
　　praise your God, O Zion,
[13]for he strengthens the bars of your
　　　gates
　　and blesses your people within you.
[14]He grants peace to your borders
　　and satisfies you with the finest of
　　　wheat.

[15]He sends his command to the earth;
　　his word runs swiftly.
[16]He spreads the snow like wool
　　and scatters the frost like ashes.
[17]He hurls down his hail like pebbles.
　　Who can withstand his icy blast?
[18]He sends his word and melts them;
　　he stirs up his breezes, and the
　　　waters flow.

[19]He has revealed his word to Jacob,
　　his laws and decrees to Israel.
[20]He has done this for no other nation;
　　they do not know his laws.

　Praise the LORD.

Psalm 148

[1]Praise the LORD.[b]

Praise the LORD from the heavens,
　　praise him in the heights above.
[2]Praise him, all his angels,
　　praise him, all his heavenly hosts.
[3]Praise him, sun and moon,
　　praise him, all you shining stars.
[4]Praise him, you highest heavens
　　and you waters above the skies.
[5]Let them praise the name of the
　　　LORD,
　　for he commanded and they were
　　　created.
[6]He set them in place for ever and
　　　ever;
　　he gave a decree that will never
　　　pass away.

[a]1 Hebrew *Hallelu Yah*; also in verse 20　　[b]1 Hebrew *Hallelu Yah*; also in verse 14

VERSE FOR THE DAY:
Psalm 147:10

AUTHOR:
Debbie Smith

PASSAGE FOR THE DAY:
Psalm 147:7–11

Delight Only in Him

I AM convinced that there is no insignificant verse in the Bible. Surely the Holy Spirit has used them all to convict, correct, encourage and edify. When I recall a very difficult time in my life, I also remember how he showed me an important, though unlikely, verse in his Word:

> His pleasure is not in the strength of the horse,
> *nor his delight in the legs of a man* (Psalm
> 147:10, italics mine).

I was struggling with anorexia nervosa when that verse jumped out of the page and hit my heart. I had been obsessed with the size of legs, arms, waist—with *everything* about my physical appearance. Here, God tells me that the condition of my heart is important to him, much more important than the condition of my body. David goes on to say:

> The LORD delights in those who fear him,
> who put their hope in his unfailing love
> (Psalm 147:11).

I realized that I had feared the opinions of others; I had feared that I would not measure up. I had placed my hope, not in God's unconditional love, but in controlling my weight.

What began in the eighth grade as a week-long diet with a friend became seven years of starvation for me. For some deep psychological, emotional and spiritual reasons, I kept losing weight. By my senior year of high school, I was five feet, three inches tall and all of seventy-nine pounds.

When I sank below eighty pounds, my internal battle intensified. I was a Christian, desiring to serve God, yet enslaved to food. I was miserable. Night after night I sobbed into my pillow, pleading that God would make me normal.

He answered those prayers slowly and gently. First, he showed me my sin and forgave me. He gave me caring friends to talk to, reassurance from his Word, and a wonderful husband. Michael loves *me*, not my dress size!

And, as confirmation that my healing is complete, God has given us three beautiful children—our three miracles, we call them, since I was told I would never be able to bear children as a result of my anorexia.

Now I desire only to fear God and put my hope in his love . . . and through his strength, I will delight only in him!

Additional Scripture Readings:
Jeremiah 17:5–8; 1 Peter 3:3–4

*Go to page 516 for your next
devotional reading.*

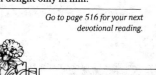

7Praise the LORD from the earth,
   you great sea creatures and all
     ocean depths,
8lightning and hail, snow and clouds,
   stormy winds that do his bidding,
9you mountains and all hills,
   fruit trees and all cedars,
10wild animals and all cattle,
   small creatures and flying birds,
11kings of the earth and all nations,
   you princes and all rulers on earth,
12young men and maidens,
   old men and children.

13Let them praise the name of the
     LORD,
   for his name alone is exalted;
   his splendor is above the earth and
     the heavens.
14He has raised up for his people a
     horn,[a]
   the praise of all his saints,
   of Israel, the people close to his
     heart.

Praise the LORD.

Psalm 149

1Praise the LORD.[b]

Sing to the LORD a new song,
   his praise in the assembly of the
     saints.
2Let Israel rejoice in their Maker;
   let the people of Zion be glad in
     their King.
3Let them praise his name with
     dancing
   and make music to him with
     tambourine and harp.
4For the LORD takes delight in his
     people;

he crowns the humble with
     salvation.
5Let the saints rejoice in this honor
   and sing for joy on their beds.

6May the praise of God be in their
     mouths
   and a double-edged sword in their
     hands,
7to inflict vengeance on the nations
   and punishment on the peoples,
8to bind their kings with fetters,
   their nobles with shackles of iron,
9to carry out the sentence written
     against them.
   This is the glory of all his saints.

Praise the LORD.

Psalm 150

1Praise the LORD.[c]

Praise God in his sanctuary;
   praise him in his mighty heavens.
2Praise him for his acts of power;
   praise him for his surpassing
     greatness.
3Praise him with the sounding of the
     trumpet,
   praise him with the harp and lyre,
4praise him with tambourine and
     dancing,
   praise him with the strings and
     flute,
5praise him with the clash of cymbals,
   praise him with resounding
     cymbals.

6Let everything that has breath praise
     the LORD.

Praise the LORD.

---

[a]14 Horn here symbolizes strong one, that is, king.   [b]1 Hebrew Hallelu Yah; also in verse 9
[c]1 Hebrew Hallelu Yah; also in verse 6

SOLOMON *"spoke three thousand proverbs" (1 Kings 4:32), many of which are collected in this book. These wise sayings describe patterns that operate in everyday life, offering us advice on how to conduct ourselves in various situations. Solomon's fundamental instruction is to fear and trust the Lord. As you read this book, remember that God has something to say about every aspect of your life; seek his wisdom in the decisions you must make each day.*

PROVERBS

Prologue: Purpose and Theme

1 The proverbs of Solomon son of David, king of Israel:

²for attaining wisdom and discipline;
    for understanding words of insight;
³for acquiring a disciplined and
        prudent life,
    doing what is right and just and
        fair;
⁴for giving prudence to the simple,
    knowledge and discretion to the
        young—

⁵let the wise listen and add to their
        learning,
    and let the discerning get
        guidance—
⁶for understanding proverbs and
        parables,
    the sayings and riddles of the
        wise.

⁷The fear of the LORD is the beginning
        of knowledge,
    but fools*ᵃ* despise wisdom and
        discipline.

ᵃ7 The Hebrew words rendered *fool* in Proverbs, and often elsewhere in the Old Testament, denote one who is morally deficient.

Exhortations to Embrace Wisdom

Warning Against Enticement

[8]Listen, my son, to your father's instruction
  and do not forsake your mother's teaching.
[9]They will be a garland to grace your head
  and a chain to adorn your neck.

[10]My son, if sinners entice you,
  do not give in to them.
[11]If they say, "Come along with us;
  let's lie in wait for someone's blood,
  let's waylay some harmless soul;
[12]let's swallow them alive, like the grave,[a]
  and whole, like those who go down to the pit;
[13]we will get all sorts of valuable things
  and fill our houses with plunder;
[14]throw in your lot with us,
  and we will share a common purse"—
[15]my son, do not go along with them,
  do not set foot on their paths;
[16]for their feet rush into sin,
  they are swift to shed blood.
[17]How useless to spread a net
  in full view of all the birds!
[18]These men lie in wait for their own blood;
  they waylay only themselves!
[19]Such is the end of all who go after ill-gotten gain;
  it takes away the lives of those who get it.

Warning Against Rejecting Wisdom

[20]Wisdom calls aloud in the street,
  she raises her voice in the public squares;
[21]at the head of the noisy streets[b] she cries out,
  in the gateways of the city she makes her speech:

[22]"How long will you simple ones[c] love your simple ways?
  How long will mockers delight in mockery
  and fools hate knowledge?
[23]If you had responded to my rebuke,
  I would have poured out my heart to you

and made my thoughts known to you.
[24]But since you rejected me when I called
  and no one gave heed when I stretched out my hand,
[25]since you ignored all my advice
  and would not accept my rebuke,
[26]I in turn will laugh at your disaster;
  I will mock when calamity overtakes you—
[27]when calamity overtakes you like a storm,
  when disaster sweeps over you like a whirlwind,
  when distress and trouble overwhelm you.

[28]"Then they will call to me but I will not answer;
  they will look for me but will not find me.
[29]Since they hated knowledge
  and did not choose to fear the LORD,
[30]since they would not accept my advice
  and spurned my rebuke,
[31]they will eat the fruit of their ways
  and be filled with the fruit of their schemes.
[32]For the waywardness of the simple will kill them,
  and the complacency of fools will destroy them;
[33]but whoever listens to me will live in safety
  and be at ease, without fear of harm."

Moral Benefits of Wisdom

2 My son, if you accept my words
  and store up my commands within you,
[2]turning your ear to wisdom
  and applying your heart to understanding,
[3]and if you call out for insight
  and cry aloud for understanding,
[4]and if you look for it as for silver
  and search for it as for hidden treasure,
[5]then you will understand the fear of the LORD
  and find the knowledge of God.
[6]For the LORD gives wisdom,

---

[a]12 Hebrew Sheol   [b]21 Hebrew; Septuagint / on the tops of the walls   [c]22 The Hebrew word rendered simple in Proverbs generally denotes one without moral direction and inclined to evil.

and from his mouth come
   knowledge and understanding.
[7]He holds victory in store for the
   upright,
   he is a shield to those whose walk
      is blameless,
[8]for he guards the course of the just
   and protects the way of his faithful
      ones.

[9]Then you will understand what is
   right and just
   and fair—every good path.
[10]For wisdom will enter your heart,
   and knowledge will be pleasant to
      your soul.
[11]Discretion will protect you,
   and understanding will guard you.

[12]Wisdom will save you from the ways
      of wicked men,
   from men whose words are
      perverse,
[13]who leave the straight paths
   to walk in dark ways,
[14]who delight in doing wrong
   and rejoice in the perverseness of
      evil,
[15]whose paths are crooked
   and who are devious in their ways.

[16]It will save you also from the
      adulteress,
   from the wayward wife with her
      seductive words,
[17]who has left the partner of her youth
   and ignored the covenant she made
      before God.[a]
[18]For her house leads down to death
   and her paths to the spirits of the
      dead.
[19]None who go to her return
   or attain the paths of life.

[20]Thus you will walk in the ways of
      good men
   and keep to the paths of the
      righteous.
[21]For the upright will live in the land,
   and the blameless will remain in it;
[22]but the wicked will be cut off from
      the land,
   and the unfaithful will be torn from
      it.

Further Benefits of Wisdom

3 My son, do not forget my teaching,
   but keep my commands in your
      heart,

[2]for they will prolong your life many
      years
   and bring you prosperity.

[3]Let love and faithfulness never leave
      you;
   bind them around your neck,
   write them on the tablet of your
      heart.
[4]Then you will win favor and a good
      name
   in the sight of God and man.

[5]Trust in the LORD with all your heart
   and lean not on your own
      understanding;
[6]in all your ways acknowledge him,
   and he will make your paths
      straight.[b]

[7]Do not be wise in your own eyes;
   fear the LORD and shun evil.
[8]This will bring health to your body
   and nourishment to your bones.

[9]Honor the LORD with your wealth,
   with the firstfruits of all your crops;
[10]then your barns will be filled to
      overflowing,
   and your vats will brim over with
      new wine.

[11]My son, do not despise the LORD's
      discipline
   and do not resent his rebuke,
[12]because the LORD disciplines those he
      loves,
   as a father[c] the son he delights in.

[13]Blessed is the man who finds wisdom,
   the man who gains understanding,
[14]for she is more profitable than silver
   and yields better returns than gold.
[15]She is more precious than rubies;
   nothing you desire can compare
      with her.
[16]Long life is in her right hand;
   in her left hand are riches and
      honor.
[17]Her ways are pleasant ways,
   and all her paths are peace.
[18]She is a tree of life to those who
      embrace her;
   those who lay hold of her will be
      blessed.

[19]By wisdom the LORD laid the earth's
      foundations,
   by understanding he set the
      heavens in place;

---

[a]17 Or *covenant of her God*   [b]6 Or *will direct your paths*   [c]12 Hebrew; Septuagint / *and he punishes*

VERSE FOR THE DAY:	AUTHOR:	PASSAGE FOR THE DAY:
Proverbs 3:5–6	ann kiemel anderson	Proverbs 3:1–8

trust

THIS is another verse with a command: "TRUST . . . LEAN NOT on your own understanding"; and a promise: "he WILL make your paths straight" (caps mine).

trust is such a lovely word in a world thoroughly self-indulged and complicated. it is quiet. simple. it represents freedom. rest. letting go.

a favorite, old hymn my father would often sing was, "tis so sweet to trust in Jesus, just to take him at his word . . . just to REST upon his promise. . . . " most of us are too busy and noisy to hear the "still, small voice." to identify it. to trust in its power above our human strivings.

friends of ours, who had been down the battered road of infertility, longed for another baby. a perfect situation came about. a young birth mother who felt the only answer for her baby was adoption.

a precious baby girl was born. i loved the birth mother and knew that this was a very painful decision. the adoptive couple came from another city to meet the birth mother and to take their new baby home. it was thanksgiving week. relatives had flown in for a family celebration. the birth mother signed the papers, releasing the baby from the hospital. but in the courtroom, days later, she broke down. she just couldn't give up her baby. she drove hundreds of miles on thanksgiving day to take back her baby.

the couple's celebration turned to heartbreak. immediately, they began to trust. not to figure it all out, or judge the birth mother. they waited quietly. in a year, twin girls were born and theirs was the chosen family. they lost one, and God gave them back two.

there are very many unknowns in life. a husband's job. our children's struggles. a tentative move. critical talk behind our backs. a search for our own identity. bills to pay. aged parents to look after.

let go completely. trust. live with it all in an open hand before God. Jesus promises he WILL work it all out. i do believe for you, always . . . a new sunrise.

Additional Scripture Readings:
Isaiah 26:3–14; Romans 15:13

Go to page 525 for your next devotional reading.

²⁰by his knowledge the deeps were
    divided,
  and the clouds let drop the dew.

²¹My son, preserve sound judgment and
    discernment,
  do not let them out of your sight;
²²they will be life for you,
  an ornament to grace your neck.
²³Then you will go on your way in
    safety,
  and your foot will not stumble;
²⁴when you lie down, you will not be
    afraid;
  when you lie down, your sleep will
    be sweet.
²⁵Have no fear of sudden disaster
  or of the ruin that overtakes the
    wicked,
²⁶for the Lord will be your confidence
  and will keep your foot from being
    snared.

²⁷Do not withhold good from those who
    deserve it,
  when it is in your power to act.
²⁸Do not say to your neighbor,
  "Come back later; I'll give it
    tomorrow"—
  when you now have it with you.

²⁹Do not plot harm against your
    neighbor,
  who lives trustfully near you.
³⁰Do not accuse a man for no reason—
  when he has done you no harm.

³¹Do not envy a violent man
  or choose any of his ways,
³²for the Lord detests a perverse man
  but takes the upright into his
    confidence.

³³The Lord's curse is on the house of
    the wicked,
  but he blesses the home of the
    righteous.
³⁴He mocks proud mockers
  but gives grace to the humble.
³⁵The wise inherit honor,
  but fools he holds up to shame.

Wisdom Is Supreme

4 Listen, my sons, to a father's
    instruction;
  pay attention and gain
    understanding.
²I give you sound learning,
  so do not forsake my teaching.

³When I was a boy in my father's
    house,
  still tender, and an only child of my
    mother,
⁴he taught me and said,
  "Lay hold of my words with all your
    heart;
  keep my commands and you will
    live.
⁵Get wisdom, get understanding;
  do not forget my words or swerve
    from them.
⁶Do not forsake wisdom, and she will
    protect you;
  love her, and she will watch over
    you.
⁷Wisdom is supreme; therefore get
    wisdom.
  Though it cost all you have,ᵃ get
    understanding.
⁸Esteem her, and she will exalt you;
  embrace her, and she will honor
    you.
⁹She will set a garland of grace on
    your head
  and present you with a crown of
    splendor."

¹⁰Listen, my son, accept what I say,
  and the years of your life will be
    many.
¹¹I guide you in the way of wisdom
  and lead you along straight paths.
¹²When you walk, your steps will not be
    hampered;
  when you run, you will not
    stumble.
¹³Hold on to instruction, do not let it
    go;
  guard it well, for it is your life.
¹⁴Do not set foot on the path of the
    wicked
  or walk in the way of evil men.
¹⁵Avoid it, do not travel on it;
  turn from it and go on your way.
¹⁶For they cannot sleep till they do evil;
  they are robbed of slumber till they
    make someone fall.
¹⁷They eat the bread of wickedness
  and drink the wine of violence.

¹⁸The path of the righteous is like the
    first gleam of dawn,
  shining ever brighter till the full
    light of day.
¹⁹But the way of the wicked is like
    deep darkness;
  they do not know what makes them
    stumble.

ᵃ7 Or *Whatever else you get*

20My son, pay attention to what I say;
   listen closely to my words.
21Do not let them out of your sight,
   keep them within your heart;
22for they are life to those who find
      them
   and health to a man's whole body.
23Above all else, guard your heart,
   for it is the wellspring of life.
24Put away perversity from your mouth;
   keep corrupt talk far from your lips.
25Let your eyes look straight ahead,
   fix your gaze directly before you.
26Make level*a* paths for your feet
   and take only ways that are firm.
27Do not swerve to the right or the left;
   keep your foot from evil.

Warning Against Adultery

5 My son, pay attention to my
   wisdom,
   listen well to my words of insight,
2that you may maintain discretion
   and your lips may preserve
      knowledge.
3For the lips of an adulteress drip
      honey,
   and her speech is smoother than
      oil;
4but in the end she is bitter as gall,
   sharp as a double-edged sword.
5Her feet go down to death;
   her steps lead straight to the
      grave.*b*
6She gives no thought to the way of
      life;
   her paths are crooked, but she
      knows it not.

7Now then, my sons, listen to me;
   do not turn aside from what I say.
8Keep to a path far from her,
   do not go near the door of her
      house,
9lest you give your best strength to
      others
   and your years to one who is cruel,
10lest strangers feast on your wealth
   and your toil enrich another man's
      house.
11At the end of your life you will groan,
   when your flesh and body are
      spent.
12You will say, "How I hated discipline!
   How my heart spurned correction!
13I would not obey my teachers
   or listen to my instructors.
14I have come to the brink of utter ruin

in the midst of the whole
      assembly."

15Drink water from your own cistern,
   running water from your own well.
16Should your springs overflow in the
      streets,
   your streams of water in the public
      squares?
17Let them be yours alone,
   never to be shared with strangers.
18May your fountain be blessed,
   and may you rejoice in the wife of
      your youth.
19A loving doe, a graceful deer—
   may her breasts satisfy you always,
   may you ever be captivated by her
      love.
20Why be captivated, my son, by an
      adulteress?
   Why embrace the bosom of another
      man's wife?

21For a man's ways are in full view of
      the LORD,
   and he examines all his paths.
22The evil deeds of a wicked man
      ensnare him;
   the cords of his sin hold him fast.
23He will die for lack of discipline,
   led astray by his own great folly.

Warnings Against Folly

6 My son, if you have put up security
   for your neighbor,
   if you have struck hands in pledge
      for another,
2if you have been trapped by what you
      said,
   ensnared by the words of your
      mouth,
3then do this, my son, to free yourself,
   since you have fallen into your
      neighbor's hands:
   Go and humble yourself;
   press your plea with your neighbor!
4Allow no sleep to your eyes,
   no slumber to your eyelids.
5Free yourself, like a gazelle from the
      hand of the hunter,
   like a bird from the snare of the
      fowler.

6Go to the ant, you sluggard;
   consider its ways and be wise!
7It has no commander,
   no overseer or ruler,
8yet it stores its provisions in summer
   and gathers its food at harvest.

a26 Or Consider the   b5 Hebrew Sheol

⁹How long will you lie there, you
  sluggard?
  When will you get up from your
    sleep?
¹⁰A little sleep, a little slumber,
  a little folding of the hands to
    rest—
¹¹and poverty will come on you like a
    bandit
  and scarcity like an armed man.ᵃ

¹²A scoundrel and villain,
  who goes about with a corrupt
    mouth,
¹³ who winks with his eye,
  signals with his feet
  and motions with his fingers,
¹⁴ who plots evil with deceit in his
    heart—
  he always stirs up dissension.
¹⁵Therefore disaster will overtake him
    in an instant;
  he will suddenly be
    destroyed—without remedy.

¹⁶There are six things the LORD hates,
  seven that are detestable to him:
¹⁷   haughty eyes,
     a lying tongue,
     hands that shed innocent blood,
¹⁸   a heart that devises wicked
       schemes,
     feet that are quick to rush into
       evil,
¹⁹   a false witness who pours out lies
     and a man who stirs up
       dissension among brothers.

Warning Against Adultery

²⁰My son, keep your father's commands
  and do not forsake your mother's
    teaching.
²¹Bind them upon your heart forever;
  fasten them around your neck.
²²When you walk, they will guide you;
  when you sleep, they will watch
    over you;
  when you awake, they will speak to
    you.
²³For these commands are a lamp,
  this teaching is a light,
  and the corrections of discipline
  are the way to life,
²⁴keeping you from the immoral
    woman,
  from the smooth tongue of the
    wayward wife.
²⁵Do not lust in your heart after her
    beauty

  or let her captivate you with her
    eyes,
²⁶for the prostitute reduces you to a
    loaf of bread,
  and the adulteress preys upon your
    very life.
²⁷Can a man scoop fire into his lap
  without his clothes being burned?
²⁸Can a man walk on hot coals
  without his feet being scorched?
²⁹So is he who sleeps with another
    man's wife;
  no one who touches her will go
    unpunished.

³⁰Men do not despise a thief if he
    steals
  to satisfy his hunger when he is
    starving.
³¹Yet if he is caught, he must pay
    sevenfold,
  though it costs him all the wealth
    of his house.
³²But a man who commits adultery
    lacks judgment;
  whoever does so destroys himself.
³³Blows and disgrace are his lot,
  and his shame will never be wiped
    away;
³⁴for jealousy arouses a husband's fury,
  and he will show no mercy when he
    takes revenge.
³⁵He will not accept any compensation;
  he will refuse the bribe, however
    great it is.

Warning Against the Adulteress

7 My son, keep my words
  and store up my commands within
    you.
²Keep my commands and you will live;
  guard my teachings as the apple of
    your eye.
³Bind them on your fingers;
  write them on the tablet of your
    heart.
⁴Say to wisdom, "You are my sister,"
  and call understanding your
    kinsman;
⁵they will keep you from the
    adulteress,
  from the wayward wife with her
    seductive words.

⁶At the window of my house
  I looked out through the lattice.
⁷I saw among the simple,
  I noticed among the young men,
  a youth who lacked judgment.

ᵃ*11 Or like a vagrant / and scarcity like a beggar*

⁸He was going down the street near
    her corner,
  walking along in the direction of
      her house
⁹at twilight, as the day was fading,
    as the dark of night set in.

¹⁰Then out came a woman to meet
    him,
  dressed like a prostitute and with
      crafty intent.
¹¹(She is loud and defiant,
    her feet never stay at home;
¹²now in the street, now in the squares,
    at every corner she lurks.)
¹³She took hold of him and kissed him
  and with a brazen face she said:

¹⁴"I have fellowship offerings[a] at home;
    today I fulfilled my vows.
¹⁵So I came out to meet you;
    I looked for you and have found
      you!
¹⁶I have covered my bed
    with colored linens from Egypt.
¹⁷I have perfumed my bed
    with myrrh, aloes and cinnamon.
¹⁸Come, let's drink deep of love till
    morning;
  let's enjoy ourselves with love!
¹⁹My husband is not at home;
    he has gone on a long journey.
²⁰He took his purse filled with money
    and will not be home till full
      moon."

²¹With persuasive words she led him
    astray;
  she seduced him with her smooth
      talk.
²²All at once he followed her
    like an ox going to the slaughter,
  like a deer[b] stepping into a noose[c]
²³   till an arrow pierces his liver,
  like a bird darting into a snare,
    little knowing it will cost him his
      life.

²⁴Now then, my sons, listen to me;
    pay attention to what I say.
²⁵Do not let your heart turn to her ways
    or stray into her paths.
²⁶Many are the victims she has brought
    down;
  her slain are a mighty throng.
²⁷Her house is a highway to the grave,[d]
    leading down to the chambers of
      death.

Wisdom's Call

8 Does not wisdom call out?
    Does not understanding raise her
      voice?
²On the heights along the way,
    where the paths meet, she takes
      her stand;
³beside the gates leading into the city,
    at the entrances, she cries aloud:
⁴"To you, O men, I call out;
    I raise my voice to all mankind.
⁵You who are simple, gain prudence;
    you who are foolish, gain
      understanding.
⁶Listen, for I have worthy things to
    say;
  I open my lips to speak what is
      right.
⁷My mouth speaks what is true,
    for my lips detest wickedness.
⁸All the words of my mouth are just;
    none of them is crooked or
      perverse.
⁹To the discerning all of them are
    right;
  they are faultless to those who have
      knowledge.
¹⁰Choose my instruction instead of
    silver,
  knowledge rather than choice gold,
¹¹for wisdom is more precious than
    rubies,
  and nothing you desire can
      compare with her.

¹²"I, wisdom, dwell together with
    prudence;
  I possess knowledge and discretion.
¹³To fear the LORD is to hate evil;
    I hate pride and arrogance,
  evil behavior and perverse speech.
¹⁴Counsel and sound judgment are
    mine;
  I have understanding and power.
¹⁵By me kings reign
    and rulers make laws that are just;
¹⁶by me princes govern,
    and all nobles who rule on earth.[e]
¹⁷I love those who love me,
    and those who seek me find me.
¹⁸With me are riches and honor,
    enduring wealth and prosperity.
¹⁹My fruit is better than fine gold;
    what I yield surpasses choice silver.
²⁰I walk in the way of righteousness,
    along the paths of justice,

---

a14 Traditionally *peace offerings*   b22 Syriac (see also Septuagint); Hebrew *fool*   c22 The meaning
of the Hebrew for this line is uncertain.   d27 Hebrew *Sheol*   e16 Many Hebrew manuscripts and
Septuagint; most Hebrew manuscripts *and nobles—all righteous rulers*

21bestowing wealth on those who love
me
and making their treasuries full.

22"The Lord brought me forth as the
first of his works,[a, b]
before his deeds of old;
23I was appointed[c] from eternity,
from the beginning, before the
world began.
24When there were no oceans, I was
given birth,
when there were no springs
abounding with water;
25before the mountains were settled in
place,
before the hills, I was given birth,
26before he made the earth or its fields
or any of the dust of the world.
27I was there when he set the heavens
in place,
when he marked out the horizon on
the face of the deep,
28when he established the clouds above
and fixed securely the fountains of
the deep,
29when he gave the sea its boundary
so the waters would not overstep
his command,
and when he marked out the
foundations of the earth.
30 Then I was the craftsman at his
side.
I was filled with delight day after day,
rejoicing always in his presence,
31rejoicing in his whole world
and delighting in mankind.

32"Now then, my sons, listen to me;
blessed are those who keep my
ways.
33Listen to my instruction and be wise;
do not ignore it.
34Blessed is the man who listens to me,
watching daily at my doors,
waiting at my doorway.
35For whoever finds me finds life
and receives favor from the Lord.
36But whoever fails to find me harms
himself;
all who hate me love death."

Invitations of Wisdom and of Folly

9 Wisdom has built her house;
she has hewn out its seven pillars.
2She has prepared her meat and mixed
her wine;
she has also set her table.

3She has sent out her maids, and she
calls
from the highest point of the
city.
4"Let all who are simple come in
here!"
she says to those who lack
judgment.
5"Come, eat my food
and drink the wine I have mixed.
6Leave your simple ways and you will
live;
walk in the way of understanding.

7"Whoever corrects a mocker invites
insult;
whoever rebukes a wicked man
incurs abuse.
8Do not rebuke a mocker or he will
hate you;
rebuke a wise man and he will love
you.
9Instruct a wise man and he will be
wiser still;
teach a righteous man and he will
add to his learning.

10"The fear of the Lord is the beginning
of wisdom,
and knowledge of the Holy One is
understanding.
11For through me your days will be
many,
and years will be added to your
life.
12If you are wise, your wisdom will
reward you;
if you are a mocker, you alone will
suffer."

13The woman Folly is loud;
she is undisciplined and without
knowledge.
14She sits at the door of her house,
on a seat at the highest point of
the city,
15calling out to those who pass by,
who go straight on their way.
16"Let all who are simple come in
here!"
she says to those who lack
judgment.
17"Stolen water is sweet;
food eaten in secret is delicious!"
18But little do they know that the dead
are there,
that her guests are in the depths of
the grave.[d]

---

a22 Or way; or dominion   b22 Or The Lord possessed me at the beginning of his work; or The Lord
brought me forth at the beginning of his work   c23 Or fashioned   d18 Hebrew Sheol

Proverbs of Solomon

10 The proverbs of Solomon:

A wise son brings joy to his
father,
but a foolish son grief to his
mother.

2Ill-gotten treasures are of no value,
but righteousness delivers from
death.

3The Lord does not let the righteous
go hungry
but he thwarts the craving of the
wicked.

4Lazy hands make a man poor,
but diligent hands bring wealth.

5He who gathers crops in summer is a
wise son,
but he who sleeps during harvest is
a disgraceful son.

6Blessings crown the head of the
righteous,
but violence overwhelms the mouth
of the wicked. *a*

7The memory of the righteous will be a
blessing,
but the name of the wicked will
rot.

8The wise in heart accept commands,
but a chattering fool comes to ruin.

9The man of integrity walks securely,
but he who takes crooked paths
will be found out.

10He who winks maliciously causes
grief,
and a chattering fool comes to ruin.

11The mouth of the righteous is a
fountain of life,
but violence overwhelms the mouth
of the wicked.

12Hatred stirs up dissension,
but love covers over all wrongs.

13Wisdom is found on the lips of the
discerning,
but a rod is for the back of him
who lacks judgment.

14Wise men store up knowledge,
but the mouth of a fool invites
ruin.

15The wealth of the rich is their
fortified city,

but poverty is the ruin of the poor.

16The wages of the righteous bring
them life,
but the income of the wicked
brings them punishment.

17He who heeds discipline shows the
way to life,
but whoever ignores correction
leads others astray.

18He who conceals his hatred has lying
lips,
and whoever spreads slander is a
fool.

19When words are many, sin is not
absent,
but he who holds his tongue is
wise.

20The tongue of the righteous is choice
silver,
but the heart of the wicked is of
little value.

21The lips of the righteous nourish
many,
but fools die for lack of judgment.

22The blessing of the Lord brings
wealth,
and he adds no trouble to it.

23A fool finds pleasure in evil conduct,
but a man of understanding
delights in wisdom.

24What the wicked dreads will overtake
him;
what the righteous desire will be
granted.

25When the storm has swept by, the
wicked are gone,
but the righteous stand firm
forever.

26As vinegar to the teeth and smoke to
the eyes,
so is a sluggard to those who send
him.

27The fear of the Lord adds length to
life,
but the years of the wicked are cut
short.

28The prospect of the righteous is joy,
but the hopes of the wicked come
to nothing.

29The way of the Lord is a refuge for
the righteous,

---

a6 Or but the mouth of the wicked conceals violence; also in verse 11

but it is the ruin of those who do
evil.

30The righteous will never be uprooted,
but the wicked will not remain in
the land.

31The mouth of the righteous brings
forth wisdom,
but a perverse tongue will be cut
out.

32The lips of the righteous know what
is fitting,
but the mouth of the wicked only
what is perverse.

11 The Lord abhors dishonest
scales,
but accurate weights are his
delight.

2When pride comes, then comes
disgrace,
but with humility comes wisdom.

3The integrity of the upright guides
them,
but the unfaithful are destroyed by
their duplicity.

4Wealth is worthless in the day of
wrath,
but righteousness delivers from
death.

5The righteousness of the blameless
makes a straight way for them,
but the wicked are brought down
by their own wickedness.

6The righteousness of the upright
delivers them,
but the unfaithful are trapped by
evil desires.

7When a wicked man dies, his hope
perishes;
all he expected from his power
comes to nothing.

8The righteous man is rescued from
trouble,
and it comes on the wicked
instead.

9With his mouth the godless destroys
his neighbor,
but through knowledge the
righteous escape.

10When the righteous prosper, the city
rejoices;
when the wicked perish, there are
shouts of joy.

11Through the blessing of the upright a
city is exalted,
but by the mouth of the wicked it
is destroyed.

12A man who lacks judgment derides
his neighbor,
but a man of understanding holds
his tongue.

13A gossip betrays a confidence,
but a trustworthy man keeps a
secret.

14For lack of guidance a nation falls,
but many advisers make victory
sure.

15He who puts up security for another
will surely suffer,
but whoever refuses to strike hands
in pledge is safe.

16A kindhearted woman gains respect,
but ruthless men gain only wealth.

17A kind man benefits himself,
but a cruel man brings trouble on
himself.

18The wicked man earns deceptive
wages,
but he who sows righteousness
reaps a sure reward.

19The truly righteous man attains life,
but he who pursues evil goes to his
death.

20The Lord detests men of perverse
heart
but he delights in those whose
ways are blameless.

21Be sure of this: The wicked will not
go unpunished,
but those who are righteous will go
free.

22Like a gold ring in a pig's snout
is a beautiful woman who shows no
discretion.

23The desire of the righteous ends only
in good,
but the hope of the wicked only in
wrath.

24One man gives freely, yet gains even
more;
another withholds unduly, but
comes to poverty.

25A generous man will prosper;
he who refreshes others will himself
be refreshed.

²⁶People curse the man who hoards
grain,
but blessing crowns him who is
willing to sell.

²⁷He who seeks good finds goodwill,
but evil comes to him who searches
for it.

²⁸Whoever trusts in his riches will fall,
but the righteous will thrive like a
green leaf.

²⁹He who brings trouble on his family
will inherit only wind,
and the fool will be servant to the
wise.

³⁰The fruit of the righteous is a tree of
life,
and he who wins souls is wise.

³¹If the righteous receive their due on
earth,
how much more the ungodly and
the sinner!

12 Whoever loves discipline loves
knowledge,
but he who hates correction is
stupid.

²A good man obtains favor from the
LORD,
but the LORD condemns a crafty
man.

³A man cannot be established through
wickedness,
but the righteous cannot be
uprooted.

⁴A wife of noble character is her
husband's crown,
but a disgraceful wife is like decay
in his bones.

⁵The plans of the righteous are just,
but the advice of the wicked is
deceitful.

⁶The words of the wicked lie in wait
for blood,
but the speech of the upright
rescues them.

⁷Wicked men are overthrown and are
no more,
but the house of the righteous
stands firm.

⁸A man is praised according to his
wisdom,
but men with warped minds are
despised.

⁹Better to be a nobody and yet have a
servant
than pretend to be somebody and
have no food.

¹⁰A righteous man cares for the needs
of his animal,
but the kindest acts of the wicked
are cruel.

¹¹He who works his land will have
abundant food,
but he who chases fantasies lacks
judgment.

¹²The wicked desire the plunder of evil
men,
but the root of the righteous
flourishes.

¹³An evil man is trapped by his sinful
talk,
but a righteous man escapes
trouble.

¹⁴From the fruit of his lips a man is
filled with good things
as surely as the work of his hands
rewards him.

¹⁵The way of a fool seems right to him,
but a wise man listens to advice.

¹⁶A fool shows his annoyance at once,
but a prudent man overlooks an
insult.

¹⁷A truthful witness gives honest
testimony,
but a false witness tells lies.

¹⁸Reckless words pierce like a sword,
but the tongue of the wise brings
healing.

¹⁹Truthful lips endure forever,
but a lying tongue lasts only a
moment.

²⁰There is deceit in the hearts of those
who plot evil,
but joy for those who promote
peace.

²¹No harm befalls the righteous,
but the wicked have their fill of
trouble.

²²The LORD detests lying lips,
but he delights in men who are
truthful.

²³A prudent man keeps his knowledge
to himself,
but the heart of fools blurts out
folly.

²⁴Diligent hands will rule,
  but laziness ends in slave labor.

²⁵An anxious heart weighs a man down,
  but a kind word cheers him up.

²⁶A righteous man is cautious in
    friendship,ᵃ
  but the way of the wicked leads
    them astray.

²⁷The lazy man does not roastᵇ his
    game,
  but the diligent man prizes his
    possessions.

²⁸In the way of righteousness there is
    life;
  along that path is immortality.

13 A wise son heeds his father's
    instruction,

but a mocker does not listen to
    rebuke.

²From the fruit of his lips a man
    enjoys good things,
  but the unfaithful have a craving
    for violence.

³He who guards his lips guards his life,
  but he who speaks rashly will come
    to ruin.

⁴The sluggard craves and gets nothing,
  but the desires of the diligent are
    fully satisfied.

⁵The righteous hate what is false,
  but the wicked bring shame and
    disgrace.

⁶Righteousness guards the man of
    integrity,

ᵃ26 Or *man is a guide to his neighbor*   ᵇ27 The meaning of the Hebrew for this word is uncertain.

| WEDNESDAY |

VERSE FOR THE DAY: *AUTHOR:*   *PASSAGE FOR THE DAY:*
Proverbs 12:16   Pamela Reeve   *Proverbs 12:14–28*

Relationships: Why Bother

THE other morning I was studying the section of Proverbs that
says:

  A fool shows his annoyance at once,
    but a prudent man overlooks an insult
      (Proverbs 12:16).

  I said to the Lord, "You know, that's great, that's tremendous!
That's where I want to be, Lord. That's for me today." Within
two hours after I arrived at my office, I did not ignore what I saw
as an insult. I showed my annoyance immediately!
  All of the good spiritual input that we receive and enjoy is put
to the test as we relate to other people. My real growth that
morning did not take place as I was reading the Bible verse and
thinking, "Isn't that marvelous?" The real growth came from
blowing it and realizing I had really blown it. "Lord, forgive me.
Wrong way. No good. Bring me another test and help me respond properly." That is growth.

Additional Scripture Readings: *Go to page 527 for your next*
James 1:22–25; 1 John 2:1–6   *devotional reading.*

but wickedness overthrows the
sinner.

⁷One man pretends to be rich, yet has
   nothing;
   another pretends to be poor, yet
   has great wealth.

⁸A man's riches may ransom his life,
   but a poor man hears no threat.

⁹The light of the righteous shines
   brightly,
   but the lamp of the wicked is
   snuffed out.

¹⁰Pride only breeds quarrels,
   but wisdom is found in those who
   take advice.

¹¹Dishonest money dwindles away,
   but he who gathers money little by
   little makes it grow.

¹²Hope deferred makes the heart sick,
   but a longing fulfilled is a tree of
   life.

¹³He who scorns instruction will pay for
   it,
   but he who respects a command is
   rewarded.

¹⁴The teaching of the wise is a fountain
   of life,
   turning a man from the snares of
   death.

¹⁵Good understanding wins favor,
   but the way of the unfaithful is
   hard.ᵃ

¹⁶Every prudent man acts out of
   knowledge,
   but a fool exposes his folly.

¹⁷A wicked messenger falls into trouble,
   but a trustworthy envoy brings
   healing.

¹⁸He who ignores discipline comes to
   poverty and shame,
   but whoever heeds correction is
   honored.

¹⁹A longing fulfilled is sweet to the
   soul,
   but fools detest turning from evil.

²⁰He who walks with the wise grows
   wise,
   but a companion of fools suffers
   harm.

²¹Misfortune pursues the sinner,

but prosperity is the reward of the
   righteous.

²²A good man leaves an inheritance for
   his children's children,
   but a sinner's wealth is stored up
   for the righteous.

²³A poor man's field may produce
   abundant food,
   but injustice sweeps it away.

²⁴He who spares the rod hates his son,
   but he who loves him is careful to
   discipline him.

²⁵The righteous eat to their hearts'
   content,
   but the stomach of the wicked goes
   hungry.

14 The wise woman builds her
   house,
   but with her own hands the foolish
   one tears hers down.

²He whose walk is upright fears the
   Lord,
   but he whose ways are devious
   despises him.

³A fool's talk brings a rod to his back,
   but the lips of the wise protect
   them.

⁴Where there are no oxen, the manger
   is empty,
   but from the strength of an ox
   comes an abundant harvest.

⁵A truthful witness does not deceive,
   but a false witness pours out lies.

⁶The mocker seeks wisdom and finds
   none,
   but knowledge comes easily to the
   discerning.

⁷Stay away from a foolish man,
   for you will not find knowledge on
   his lips.

⁸The wisdom of the prudent is to give
   thought to their ways,
   but the folly of fools is deception.

⁹Fools mock at making amends for sin,
   but goodwill is found among the
   upright.

¹⁰Each heart knows its own bitterness,
   and no one else can share its joy.

¹¹The house of the wicked will be
   destroyed,

VERSE FOR THE DAY:
Proverbs 13:3

AUTHOR:
Susan L. Lenzkes

PASSAGE FOR THE DAY:
Proverbs 13:1–5

That's a Mouthful!

DON'T look now, Lord!
I don't want You
to see me
standing here with
my big foot
crammed in my mouth.

Don't worry, child.
If I didn't love you
just as much with your
foot in your mouth,
I'd hardly ever get a
chance to love you.

Mothers are often forced to utter things other people wouldn't even think. One day I actually heard myself yelling in my hands-on-hips tone of voice, "All right! Who put the fire truck in the toilet?"

A lot of motherly queries seem to be preceded by the weary word, "Who put the . . . ," and end with a scramble of objects so strange they could be a mad Parker Brothers' game of chance.

Over the years, anyone who happened to be in the wrong place at the right time could have heard me asking who put: the cereal behind the couch? (the ants found it first); the pine cones in my purse? (I discovered them during church); the lemon pudding mix in the wading pool? (it was gelling in the corners); the toothpaste on the wall? (it looked like a fluoridated Picasso); the toy dish in the oven? (the flames were leaping out the vent).

Actually, parents should be taught not to ask questions, because either no one did it, or the other guy did it. And if you ever do manage to pin the culprit, you tend to ask why. "*Why* did you put the rock in the refrigerator?" And then you get an answer: "Because I wanted a cold rock."

It's obvious that parenthood requires carloads of patience. And I could feel reasonably righteous about boisterously losing that patience when the going gets rough, if it weren't for the fact that God has to lavish so much of it on me.

Occasionally, after I've lost my temper at the children, I've heard my heavenly Father patiently asking, "Who put the foot in the mouth?"

Additional Scripture Readings:
Ephesians 5:29; James 1:19–21

*Go to page 529 for your next
devotional reading.*

but the tent of the upright will
flourish.

¹²There is a way that seems right to a
man,
but in the end it leads to death.

¹³Even in laughter the heart may ache,
and joy may end in grief.

¹⁴The faithless will be fully repaid for
their ways,
and the good man rewarded for his.

¹⁵A simple man believes anything,
but a prudent man gives thought to
his steps.

¹⁶A wise man fears the LORD and shuns
evil,
but a fool is hotheaded and
reckless.

¹⁷A quick-tempered man does foolish
things,
and a crafty man is hated.

¹⁸The simple inherit folly,
but the prudent are crowned with
knowledge.

¹⁹Evil men will bow down in the
presence of the good,
and the wicked at the gates of the
righteous.

²⁰The poor are shunned even by their
neighbors,
but the rich have many friends.

²¹He who despises his neighbor sins,
but blessed is he who is kind to the
needy.

²²Do not those who plot evil go astray?
But those who plan what is good
find*a* love and faithfulness.

²³All hard work brings a profit,
but mere talk leads only to poverty.

²⁴The wealth of the wise is their crown,
but the folly of fools yields folly.

²⁵A truthful witness saves lives,
but a false witness is deceitful.

²⁶He who fears the LORD has a secure
fortress,
and for his children it will be a
refuge.

²⁷The fear of the LORD is a fountain of
life,
turning a man from the snares of
death.

²⁸A large population is a king's glory,
but without subjects a prince is
ruined.

²⁹A patient man has great
understanding,
but a quick-tempered man displays
folly.

³⁰A heart at peace gives life to the
body,
but envy rots the bones.

³¹He who oppresses the poor shows
contempt for their Maker,
but whoever is kind to the needy
honors God.

³²When calamity comes, the wicked are
brought down,
but even in death the righteous
have a refuge.

³³Wisdom reposes in the heart of the
discerning
and even among fools she lets
herself be known.*b*

³⁴Righteousness exalts a nation,
but sin is a disgrace to any people.

³⁵A king delights in a wise servant,
but a shameful servant incurs his
wrath.

15 A gentle answer turns away
wrath,
but a harsh word stirs up anger.

²The tongue of the wise commends
knowledge,
but the mouth of the fool gushes
folly.

³The eyes of the LORD are everywhere,
keeping watch on the wicked and
the good.

⁴The tongue that brings healing is a
tree of life,
but a deceitful tongue crushes the
spirit.

⁵A fool spurns his father's discipline,
but whoever heeds correction shows
prudence.

⁶The house of the righteous contains
great treasure,
but the income of the wicked
brings them trouble.

⁷The lips of the wise spread
knowledge;

_____
*a*22 Or *show*   *b*33 Hebrew; Septuagint and Syriac / *but in the heart of fools she is not known*

not so the hearts of fools.

⁸The LORD detests the sacrifice of the
    wicked,
    but the prayer of the upright
        pleases him.

⁹The LORD detests the way of the
    wicked
    but he loves those who pursue
        righteousness.

¹⁰Stern discipline awaits him who
    leaves the path;
    he who hates correction will die.

¹¹Death and Destruction^a lie open
    before the LORD—
    how much more the hearts of men!

¹²A mocker resents correction;
    he will not consult the wise.

¹³A happy heart makes the face
        cheerful,
    but heartache crushes the spirit.

¹⁴The discerning heart seeks
        knowledge,
    but the mouth of a fool feeds on
        folly.

¹⁵All the days of the oppressed are
        wretched,
    but the cheerful heart has a
        continual feast.

¹⁶Better a little with the fear of the
    LORD

^a11 Hebrew *Sheol and Abaddon*

FRIDAY

VERSE FOR THE DAY: AUTHOR: PASSAGE FOR THE DAY:
Proverbs 15:13,15,30   Marjorie Holmes   Proverbs 15:13–33

It's Been a Good Day

IT'S been a good day, Lord. Yes, a very good day.

I didn't realize it while it was happening. There were many
frustrations. I was very discouraged when the letter I was praying for didn't come. Then the telephone rang, bringing good
news.

When a child was carried home from the playground hurt and
we rushed him to the hospital, you knew my awful fears. But to
learn that it wasn't really serious brought a sense of heightened
joy. (Sheer relief can generate sheer bliss.)

So now the child is asleep, with the bandage slipped rather
comically from his head. My husband stands in the yard, leaning
on his rake as he visits with a neighbor.

Other children come spilling across the yard. The sun is a
golden glory behind the trees. I can smell the pot roast mingling
with the tangy fragrance of burning leaves.

I look back on this day with its usual ups and downs. Its moments of anguish, its moments of gratefulness and joy. And now
that it's ending, an aching awareness fills me. I realize that it's
been a good day, Lord. A very good day.

For it's been filled with life. The life you have given me to
cope with, and to contribute to. And I wouldn't want to have
missed it, not a single moment of it.

Thank you, God, for this good day.

Additional Scripture Readings: *Go to page 532 for your next*
Psalm 118:24; Matthew 6:33–34   *devotional reading.*

than great wealth with turmoil.

¹⁷Better a meal of vegetables where
there is love
than a fattened calf with hatred.

¹⁸A hot-tempered man stirs up
dissension,
but a patient man calms a quarrel.

¹⁹The way of the sluggard is blocked
with thorns,
but the path of the upright is a
highway.

²⁰A wise son brings joy to his father,
but a foolish man despises his
mother.

²¹Folly delights a man who lacks
judgment,
but a man of understanding keeps a
straight course.

²²Plans fail for lack of counsel,
but with many advisers they
succeed.

²³A man finds joy in giving an apt
reply—
and how good is a timely word!

²⁴The path of life leads upward for the
wise
to keep him from going down to
the grave.ᵃ

²⁵The LORD tears down the proud man's
house
but he keeps the widow's
boundaries intact.

²⁶The LORD detests the thoughts of the
wicked,
but those of the pure are pleasing
to him.

²⁷A greedy man brings trouble to his
family,
but he who hates bribes will live.

²⁸The heart of the righteous weighs its
answers,
but the mouth of the wicked
gushes evil.

²⁹The LORD is far from the wicked
but he hears the prayer of the
righteous.

³⁰A cheerful look brings joy to the
heart,
and good news gives health to the
bones.

³¹He who listens to a life-giving rebuke
will be at home among the wise.

³²He who ignores discipline despises
himself,
but whoever heeds correction gains
understanding.

³³The fear of the LORD teaches a man
wisdom,ᵇ
and humility comes before honor.

16

To man belong the plans of the
heart,
but from the LORD comes the reply
of the tongue.

²All a man's ways seem innocent to
him,
but motives are weighed by the
LORD.

³Commit to the LORD whatever you do,
and your plans will succeed.

⁴The LORD works out everything for his
own ends—
even the wicked for a day of
disaster.

⁵The LORD detests all the proud of
heart.
Be sure of this: They will not go
unpunished.

⁶Through love and faithfulness sin is
atoned for;
through the fear of the LORD a man
avoids evil.

⁷When a man's ways are pleasing to
the LORD,
he makes even his enemies live at
peace with him.

⁸Better a little with righteousness
than much gain with injustice.

⁹In his heart a man plans his course,
but the LORD determines his steps.

¹⁰The lips of a king speak as an oracle,
and his mouth should not betray
justice.

¹¹Honest scales and balances are from
the LORD;
all the weights in the bag are of his
making.

¹²Kings detest wrongdoing,
for a throne is established through
righteousness.

¹³Kings take pleasure in honest lips;

ᵃ24 Hebrew Sheol   ᵇ33 Or Wisdom teaches the fear of the LORD

they value a man who speaks the
truth.

[14]A king's wrath is a messenger of
death,
but a wise man will appease it.

[15]When a king's face brightens, it
means life;
his favor is like a rain cloud in
spring.

[16]How much better to get wisdom than
gold,
to choose understanding rather
than silver!

[17]The highway of the upright avoids
evil;
he who guards his way guards his
life.

[18]Pride goes before destruction,
a haughty spirit before a fall.

[19]Better to be lowly in spirit and among
the oppressed
than to share plunder with the
proud.

[20]Whoever gives heed to instruction
prospers,
and blessed is he who trusts in the
LORD.

[21]The wise in heart are called
discerning,
and pleasant words promote
instruction.[a]

[22]Understanding is a fountain of life to
those who have it,
but folly brings punishment to
fools.

[23]A wise man's heart guides his mouth,
and his lips promote instruction.[b]

[24]Pleasant words are a honeycomb,
sweet to the soul and healing to
the bones.

[25]There is a way that seems right to a
man,
but in the end it leads to death.

[26]The laborer's appetite works for him;
his hunger drives him on.

[27]A scoundrel plots evil,
and his speech is like a scorching
fire.

[28]A perverse man stirs up dissension,

and a gossip separates close
friends.

[29]A violent man entices his neighbor
and leads him down a path that is
not good.

[30]He who winks with his eye is plotting
perversity;
he who purses his lips is bent on
evil.

[31]Gray hair is a crown of splendor;
it is attained by a righteous life.

[32]Better a patient man than a warrior,
a man who controls his temper
than one who takes a city.

[33]The lot is cast into the lap,
but its every decision is from the
LORD.

17 Better a dry crust with peace and
quiet
than a house full of feasting,[c] with
strife.

[2]A wise servant will rule over a
disgraceful son,
and will share the inheritance as
one of the brothers.

[3]The crucible for silver and the furnace
for gold,
but the LORD tests the heart.

[4]A wicked man listens to evil lips;
a liar pays attention to a malicious
tongue.

[5]He who mocks the poor shows
contempt for their Maker;
whoever gloats over disaster will
not go unpunished.

[6]Children's children are a crown to the
aged,
and parents are the pride of their
children.

[7]Arrogant[d] lips are unsuited to a
fool—
how much worse lying lips to a
ruler!

[8]A bribe is a charm to the one who
gives it;
wherever he turns, he succeeds.

[9]He who covers over an offense
promotes love,
but whoever repeats the matter
separates close friends.

---

[a]21 Or words make a man persuasive   [b]23 Or mouth / and makes his lips persuasive   [c]1 Hebrew
sacrifices   [d]7 Or Eloquent

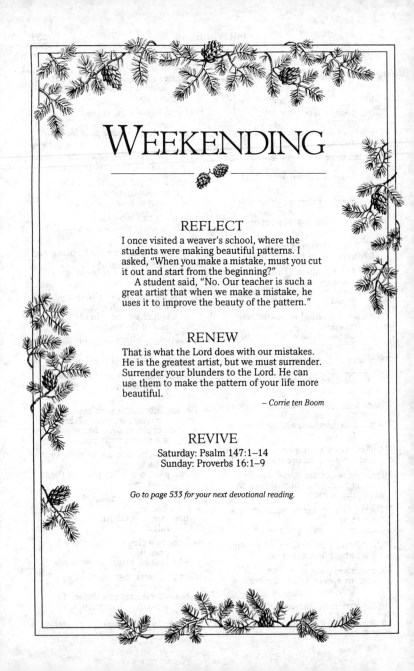

WEEKENDING

REFLECT

I once visited a weaver's school, where the
students were making beautiful patterns. I
asked, "When you make a mistake, must you cut
it out and start from the beginning?"

A student said, "No. Our teacher is such a
great artist that when we make a mistake, he
uses it to improve the beauty of the pattern."

RENEW

That is what the Lord does with our mistakes.
He is the greatest artist, but we must surrender.
Surrender your blunders to the Lord. He can
use them to make the pattern of your life more
beautiful.

— Corrie ten Boom

REVIVE

Saturday: Psalm 147:1–14
Sunday: Proverbs 16:1–9

Go to page 533 for your next devotional reading.

¹⁰A rebuke impresses a man of
      discernment
  more than a hundred lashes a fool.

¹¹An evil man is bent only on rebellion;
  a merciless official will be sent
      against him.

¹²Better to meet a bear robbed of her
      cubs
  than a fool in his folly.

¹³If a man pays back evil for good,
  evil will never leave his house.

¹⁴Starting a quarrel is like breaching a
      dam;
  so drop the matter before a dispute
      breaks out.

¹⁵Acquitting the guilty and condemning
      the innocent—
  the LORD detests them both.

¹⁶Of what use is money in the hand of
  a fool,

since he has no desire to get
      wisdom?

¹⁷A friend loves at all times,
  and a brother is born for adversity.

¹⁸A man lacking in judgment strikes
      hands in pledge
  and puts up security for his
      neighbor.

¹⁹He who loves a quarrel loves sin;
  he who builds a high gate invites
      destruction.

²⁰A man of perverse heart does not
      prosper;
  he whose tongue is deceitful falls
      into trouble.

²¹To have a fool for a son brings grief;
  there is no joy for the father of a
      fool.

²²A cheerful heart is good medicine,
  but a crushed spirit dries up the
      bones.

MONDAY

| VERSE FOR THE DAY: | AUTHOR: | PASSAGE FOR THE DAY: |
| Proverbs 17:17 | Susan L. Lenzkes | Proverbs 17:14–22 |

A Friend in Need

FRIENDSHIP gives license to show up at the door of need without asking, "When would you like me to come?" or "What would you like me to do?" Nor does friendship call out, "Just let me know if you need anything."

Practiced friendship whispers, "I'll be there" and promptly steps through the door with sensitivity, respect, and understanding.

But what about honoring the right to invite? Those who wait for parchment invitations wait long, for need rarely throws a party—rarely even has a voice.

Yet need has its own needs. It needs protection from strangers tromping in with work boots and good intentions. And it needs relief from acquaintances wearing the spiked heels of advice and pat answers.

Need waits with longing for the familiar entrance of dear ones who pad barefoot through the soul on ordinary days.

Additional Scripture Readings:
Ruth 1:11–18; Mark 2:1–5

*Go to page 536 for your next
devotional reading.*

23A wicked man accepts a bribe in
secret
to pervert the course of justice.

24A discerning man keeps wisdom in
view,
but a fool's eyes wander to the
ends of the earth.

25A foolish son brings grief to his father
and bitterness to the one who bore
him.

26It is not good to punish an innocent
man,
or to flog officials for their integrity.

27A man of knowledge uses words with
restraint,
and a man of understanding is
even-tempered.

28Even a fool is thought wise if he
keeps silent,
and discerning if he holds his
tongue.

18 An unfriendly man pursues
selfish ends;
he defies all sound judgment.

2A fool finds no pleasure in
understanding
but delights in airing his own
opinions.

3When wickedness comes, so does
contempt,
and with shame comes disgrace.

4The words of a man's mouth are deep
waters,
but the fountain of wisdom is a
bubbling brook.

5It is not good to be partial to the
wicked
or to deprive the innocent of
justice.

6A fool's lips bring him strife,
and his mouth invites a beating.

7A fool's mouth is his undoing,
and his lips are a snare to his soul.

8The words of a gossip are like choice
morsels;
they go down to a man's inmost
parts.

9One who is slack in his work
is brother to one who destroys.

10The name of the LORD is a strong
tower;
the righteous run to it and are safe.

11The wealth of the rich is their
fortified city;
they imagine it an unscalable wall.

12Before his downfall a man's heart is
proud,
but humility comes before honor.

13He who answers before listening—
that is his folly and his shame.

14A man's spirit sustains him in
sickness,
but a crushed spirit who can bear?

15The heart of the discerning acquires
knowledge;
the ears of the wise seek it out.

16A gift opens the way for the giver
and ushers him into the presence
of the great.

17The first to present his case seems
right,
till another comes forward and
questions him.

18Casting the lot settles disputes
and keeps strong opponents apart.

19An offended brother is more
unyielding than a fortified city,
and disputes are like the barred
gates of a citadel.

20From the fruit of his mouth a man's
stomach is filled;
with the harvest from his lips he is
satisfied.

21The tongue has the power of life and
death,
and those who love it will eat its
fruit.

22He who finds a wife finds what is
good
and receives favor from the LORD.

23A poor man pleads for mercy,
but a rich man answers harshly.

24A man of many companions may
come to ruin,
but there is a friend who sticks
closer than a brother.

19 Better a poor man whose walk is
blameless
than a fool whose lips are perverse.

2It is not good to have zeal without
knowledge,
nor to be hasty and miss the way.

3A man's own folly ruins his life,
yet his heart rages against the LORD.

⁴Wealth brings many friends,
  but a poor man's friend deserts
  him.

⁵A false witness will not go
  unpunished,
  and he who pours out lies will not
  go free.

⁶Many curry favor with a ruler,
  and everyone is the friend of a man
  who gives gifts.

⁷A poor man is shunned by all his
  relatives—
  how much more do his friends
  avoid him!
 Though he pursues them with
  pleading,
  they are nowhere to be found. ᵃ

⁸He who gets wisdom loves his own
  soul;
  he who cherishes understanding
  prospers.

⁹A false witness will not go
  unpunished,
  and he who pours out lies will
  perish.

¹⁰It is not fitting for a fool to live in
  luxury—
  how much worse for a slave to rule
  over princes!

¹¹A man's wisdom gives him patience;
  it is to his glory to overlook an
  offense.

¹²A king's rage is like the roar of a lion,
  but his favor is like dew on the
  grass.

¹³A foolish son is his father's ruin,
  and a quarrelsome wife is like a
  constant dripping.

¹⁴Houses and wealth are inherited from
  parents,
  but a prudent wife is from the
  LORD.

¹⁵Laziness brings on deep sleep,
  and the shiftless man goes hungry.

¹⁶He who obeys instructions guards his
  life,
  but he who is contemptuous of his
  ways will die.

¹⁷He who is kind to the poor lends to
  the LORD,

and he will reward him for what he
  has done.

¹⁸Discipline your son, for in that there
  is hope;
  do not be a willing party to his
  death.

¹⁹A hot-tempered man must pay the
  penalty;
  if you rescue him, you will have to
  do it again.

²⁰Listen to advice and accept
  instruction,
  and in the end you will be wise.

²¹Many are the plans in a man's heart,
  but it is the LORD's purpose that
  prevails.

²²What a man desires is unfailing love ᵇ;
  better to be poor than a liar.

²³The fear of the LORD leads to life:
  Then one rests content, untouched
  by trouble.

²⁴The sluggard buries his hand in the
  dish;
  he will not even bring it back to his
  mouth!

²⁵Flog a mocker, and the simple will
  learn prudence;
  rebuke a discerning man, and he
  will gain knowledge.

²⁶He who robs his father and drives out
  his mother
  is a son who brings shame and
  disgrace.

²⁷Stop listening to instruction, my son,
  and you will stray from the words
  of knowledge.

²⁸A corrupt witness mocks at justice,
  and the mouth of the wicked gulps
  down evil.

²⁹Penalties are prepared for mockers,
  and beatings for the backs of fools.

20 Wine is a mocker and beer a
       brawler;
  whoever is led astray by them is not
  wise.

²A king's wrath is like the roar of a
  lion;
  he who angers him forfeits his life.

³It is to a man's honor to avoid strife,
  but every fool is quick to quarrel.

ᵃ7 The meaning of the Hebrew for this sentence is uncertain.   ᵇ22 Or *A man's greed is his shame*

⁴A sluggard does not plow in season;
  so at harvest time he looks but
    finds nothing.

⁵The purposes of a man's heart are
    deep waters,
  but a man of understanding draws
    them out.

⁶Many a man claims to have unfailing
    love,

but a faithful man who can
    find?

⁷The righteous man leads a blameless
    life;
  blessed are his children after him.

⁸When a king sits on his throne to
    judge,
  he winnows out all evil with his
    eyes.

TUESDAY

VERSE FOR THE DAY:
Proverbs 19:21

AUTHOR:
Marlene Obie

PASSAGE FOR THE DAY:
Proverbs 19:21–29

I Got It!

I CAN'T believe I got the job, Lord.

Well, I can too believe it. What's the matter with my faith anyway? No matter how often you answer my prayers, I always do a double take when I get the answer.

I asked for your guidance about whether or not to go to work and where I should work. Thank you for showing me your will.

Now I'm really in trouble. My wardrobe is straight out of the frumpville collection. Except for my combination interview-banquet-church outfit, I honestly have nothing decent to wear. I know my closet is crammed with material that resembles clothing. However half of these pieces have some permanent spot on them. And the other half doesn't match. Help me to figure something out, Lord. I can't afford to buy anything new right now. I'll have to make do.

I have a few days to try to organize our family schedules and duties, but I'm afraid my faith is weak here, too. If I couldn't get it together in the last twenty years, can I reasonably assume I'll do it in the next two days? Some people say that working outside the home forces you to be more organized. I hope that's true.

My feelings are jumbled. I'm glad I got the job and feel both confident and nervous about my competence. I wonder what my bosses and co-workers will really be like. Will they accept me? Will the job be exciting and challenging? Can I handle juggling a career with being a wife and mother?

Lord, keep me from these needless questions and worries. I know you led me to this job, and I know that you'll walk with me. Because I know this is your plan, I can face anything—even a new job.

Additional Scripture Readings:
Matthew 7:7–11; 1 John 5:14–15

Go to page 541 for your next
devotional reading.

⁹Who can say, "I have kept my heart
   pure;
   I am clean and without sin"?

¹⁰Differing weights and differing
   measures—
   the LORD detests them both.

¹¹Even a child is known by his actions,
   by whether his conduct is pure and
   right.

¹²Ears that hear and eyes that see—
   the LORD has made them both.

¹³Do not love sleep or you will grow
   poor;
   stay awake and you will have food
   to spare.

¹⁴"It's no good, it's no good!" says the
   buyer;
   then off he goes and boasts about
   his purchase.

¹⁵Gold there is, and rubies in
   abundance,
   but lips that speak knowledge are a
   rare jewel.

¹⁶Take the garment of one who puts up
   security for a stranger;
   hold it in pledge if he does it for a
   wayward woman.

¹⁷Food gained by fraud tastes sweet to
   a man,
   but he ends up with a mouth full of
   gravel.

¹⁸Make plans by seeking advice;
   if you wage war, obtain guidance.

¹⁹A gossip betrays a confidence;
   so avoid a man who talks too
   much.

²⁰If a man curses his father or mother,
   his lamp will be snuffed out in
   pitch darkness.

²¹An inheritance quickly gained at the
   beginning
   will not be blessed at the end.

²²Do not say, "I'll pay you back for this
   wrong!"
   Wait for the LORD, and he will
   deliver you.

²³The LORD detests differing weights,
   and dishonest scales do not please
   him.

²⁴A man's steps are directed by the
   LORD.
   How then can anyone understand
   his own way?

²⁵It is a trap for a man to dedicate
   something rashly
   and only later to consider his vows.

²⁶A wise king winnows out the wicked;
   he drives the threshing wheel over
   them.

²⁷The lamp of the LORD searches the
   spirit of a man[a];
   it searches out his inmost being.

²⁸Love and faithfulness keep a king
   safe;
   through love his throne is made
   secure.

²⁹The glory of young men is their
   strength,
   gray hair the splendor of the old.

³⁰Blows and wounds cleanse away evil,
   and beatings purge the inmost
   being.

21 The king's heart is in the hand
   of the LORD;
   he directs it like a watercourse
   wherever he pleases.

²All a man's ways seem right to him,
   but the LORD weighs the heart.

³To do what is right and just
   is more acceptable to the LORD than
   sacrifice.

⁴Haughty eyes and a proud heart,
   the lamp of the wicked, are sin!

⁵The plans of the diligent lead to
   profit
   as surely as haste leads to poverty.

⁶A fortune made by a lying tongue
   is a fleeting vapor and a deadly
   snare.[b]

⁷The violence of the wicked will drag
   them away,
   for they refuse to do what is right.

⁸The way of the guilty is devious,
   but the conduct of the innocent is
   upright.

⁹Better to live on a corner of the roof
   than share a house with a
   quarrelsome wife.

---

[a]27 Or *The spirit of man is the LORD's lamp*   [b]6 Some Hebrew manuscripts, Septuagint and Vulgate;
most Hebrew manuscripts *vapor for those who seek death*

¹⁰The wicked man craves evil;
  his neighbor gets no mercy from
  him.

¹¹When a mocker is punished, the
  simple gain wisdom;
  when a wise man is instructed, he
  gets knowledge.

¹²The Righteous One*a* takes note of the
  house of the wicked
  and brings the wicked to ruin.

¹³If a man shuts his ears to the cry of
  the poor,
  he too will cry out and not be
  answered.

¹⁴A gift given in secret soothes anger,
  and a bribe concealed in the cloak
  pacifies great wrath.

¹⁵When justice is done, it brings joy to
  the righteous
  but terror to evildoers.

¹⁶A man who strays from the path of
  understanding
  comes to rest in the company of
  the dead.

¹⁷He who loves pleasure will become
  poor;
  whoever loves wine and oil will
  never be rich.

¹⁸The wicked become a ransom for the
  righteous,
  and the unfaithful for the upright.

¹⁹Better to live in a desert
  than with a quarrelsome and
  ill-tempered wife.

²⁰In the house of the wise are stores of
  choice food and oil,
  but a foolish man devours all he
  has.

²¹He who pursues righteousness and
  love
  finds life, prosperity*b* and honor.

²²A wise man attacks the city of the
  mighty
  and pulls down the stronghold in
  which they trust.

²³He who guards his mouth and his
  tongue
  keeps himself from calamity.

²⁴The proud and arrogant
  man—"Mocker" is his name;

he behaves with overweening pride.

²⁵The sluggard's craving will be the
  death of him,
  because his hands refuse to work.

²⁶All day long he craves for more,
  but the righteous give without
  sparing.

²⁷The sacrifice of the wicked is
  detestable—
  how much more so when brought
  with evil intent!

²⁸A false witness will perish,
  and whoever listens to him will be
  destroyed forever.*c*

²⁹A wicked man puts up a bold front,
  but an upright man gives thought
  to his ways.

³⁰There is no wisdom, no insight, no
  plan
  that can succeed against the LORD.

³¹The horse is made ready for the day
  of battle,
  but victory rests with the LORD.

22 A good name is more desirable
  than great riches;
  to be esteemed is better than silver
  or gold.

²Rich and poor have this in common:
  The LORD is the Maker of them all.

³A prudent man sees danger and takes
  refuge,
  but the simple keep going and
  suffer for it.

⁴Humility and the fear of the LORD
  bring wealth and honor and life.

⁵In the paths of the wicked lie thorns
  and snares,
  but he who guards his soul stays far
  from them.

⁶Train*d* a child in the way he should
  go,
  and when he is old he will not turn
  from it.

⁷The rich rule over the poor,
  and the borrower is servant to the
  lender.

⁸He who sows wickedness reaps
  trouble,
  and the rod of his fury will be
  destroyed.

---

a12 Or *The righteous man*   *b21* Or *righteousness*   *c28* Or / *but the words of an obedient man will live*
on   *d6* Or *Start*

⁹A generous man will himself be
blessed,
  for he shares his food with the
  poor.

¹⁰Drive out the mocker, and out goes
strife;
  quarrels and insults are ended.

¹¹He who loves a pure heart and whose
speech is gracious
  will have the king for his friend.

¹²The eyes of the Lord keep watch over
knowledge,
  but he frustrates the words of the
  unfaithful.

¹³The sluggard says, "There is a lion
outside!"
  or, "I will be murdered in the
  streets!"

¹⁴The mouth of an adulteress is a deep
pit;
  he who is under the Lord's wrath
  will fall into it.

¹⁵Folly is bound up in the heart of a
child,
  but the rod of discipline will drive
  it far from him.

¹⁶He who oppresses the poor to
increase his wealth
  and he who gives gifts to the
  rich—both come to poverty.

Sayings of the Wise

¹⁷Pay attention and listen to the
sayings of the wise;
  apply your heart to what I teach,
¹⁸for it is pleasing when you keep them
in your heart
  and have all of them ready on your
  lips.
¹⁹So that your trust may be in the Lord,
  I teach you today, even you.
²⁰Have I not written thirty*ᵃ* sayings for
you,
  sayings of counsel and knowledge,
²¹teaching you true and reliable words,
  so that you can give sound answers
  to him who sent you?

²²Do not exploit the poor because they
are poor
  and do not crush the needy in
  court,
²³for the Lord will take up their case

and will plunder those who plunder
them.

²⁴Do not make friends with a
hot-tempered man,
  do not associate with one easily
  angered,
²⁵or you may learn his ways
  and get yourself ensnared.

²⁶Do not be a man who strikes hands in
pledge
  or puts up security for debts;
²⁷if you lack the means to pay,
  your very bed will be snatched from
  under you.

²⁸Do not move an ancient boundary
stone
  set up by your forefathers.

²⁹Do you see a man skilled in his work?
He will serve before kings;
  he will not serve before obscure
  men.

23 When you sit to dine with a
ruler,
  note well whatᵇ is before you,
²and put a knife to your throat
  if you are given to gluttony.
³Do not crave his delicacies,
  for that food is deceptive.

⁴Do not wear yourself out to get rich;
  have the wisdom to show restraint.
⁵Cast but a glance at riches, and they
are gone,
  for they will surely sprout wings
  and fly off to the sky like an eagle.

⁶Do not eat the food of a stingy man,
  do not crave his delicacies;
⁷for he is the kind of man
  who is always thinking about the
  cost.ᶜ
"Eat and drink," he says to you,
  but his heart is not with you.
⁸You will vomit up the little you have
eaten
  and will have wasted your
  compliments.

⁹Do not speak to a fool,
  for he will scorn the wisdom of
  your words.

¹⁰Do not move an ancient boundary
stone
  or encroach on the fields of the
  fatherless,

ᵃ20 Or *not formerly written;* or *not written excellent*   *ᵇ1* Or *who*   *ᶜ7* Or *for as he thinks within*
himself, / so he is; or *for as he puts on a feast, / so he is*

¹¹for their Defender is strong;
  he will take up their case against
    you.

¹²Apply your heart to instruction
  and your ears to words of
    knowledge.

¹³Do not withhold discipline from a
    child;
  if you punish him with the rod, he
    will not die.
¹⁴Punish him with the rod
  and save his soul from death.^a

¹⁵My son, if your heart is wise,
  then my heart will be glad;
¹⁶my inmost being will rejoice
  when your lips speak what is right.

¹⁷Do not let your heart envy sinners,
  but always be zealous for the fear
    of the LORD.
¹⁸There is surely a future hope for you,
  and your hope will not be cut off.

¹⁹Listen, my son, and be wise,
  and keep your heart on the right
    path.
²⁰Do not join those who drink too
    much wine
  or gorge themselves on meat,
²¹for drunkards and gluttons become
    poor,
  and drowsiness clothes them in
    rags.

²²Listen to your father, who gave you
    life,
  and do not despise your mother
    when she is old.
²³Buy the truth and do not sell it;
  get wisdom, discipline and
    understanding.
²⁴The father of a righteous man has
    great joy;
  he who has a wise son delights in
    him.
²⁵May your father and mother be glad;
  may she who gave you birth rejoice!

²⁶My son, give me your heart
  and let your eyes keep to my ways,
²⁷for a prostitute is a deep pit
  and a wayward wife is a narrow
    well.
²⁸Like a bandit she lies in wait,
  and multiplies the unfaithful among
    men.

²⁹Who has woe? Who has sorrow?

Who has strife? Who has
    complaints?
Who has needless bruises? Who has
    bloodshot eyes?
³⁰Those who linger over wine,
  who go to sample bowls of mixed
    wine.
³¹Do not gaze at wine when it is red,
  when it sparkles in the cup,
  when it goes down smoothly!
³²In the end it bites like a snake
  and poisons like a viper.
³³Your eyes will see strange sights
  and your mind imagine confusing
    things.
³⁴You will be like one sleeping on the
    high seas,
  lying on top of the rigging.
³⁵"They hit me," you will say, "but I'm
    not hurt!
  They beat me, but I don't feel it!
When will I wake up
  so I can find another drink?"

24 Do not envy wicked men,
  do not desire their company;
²for their hearts plot violence,
  and their lips talk about making
    trouble.

³By wisdom a house is built,
  and through understanding it is
    established;
⁴through knowledge its rooms are
    filled
  with rare and beautiful treasures.

⁵A wise man has great power,
  and a man of knowledge increases
    strength;
⁶for waging war you need guidance,
  and for victory many advisers.

⁷Wisdom is too high for a fool;
  in the assembly at the gate he has
    nothing to say.

⁸He who plots evil
  will be known as a schemer.
⁹The schemes of folly are sin,
  and men detest a mocker.

¹⁰If you falter in times of trouble,
  how small is your strength!

¹¹Rescue those being led away to death;
  hold back those staggering toward
    slaughter.
¹²If you say, "But we knew nothing
    about this,"

^a14 Hebrew *Sheol*

does not he who weighs the heart
perceive it?
Does not he who guards your life
know it?
Will he not repay each person
according to what he has done?

[13]Eat honey, my son, for it is good;
honey from the comb is sweet to
your taste.
[14]Know also that wisdom is sweet to
your soul;

if you find it, there is a future hope
for you,
and your hope will not be cut off.

[15]Do not lie in wait like an outlaw
against a righteous man's
house,
do not raid his dwelling place;
[16]for though a righteous man falls seven
times, he rises again,
but the wicked are brought down
by calamity.

WEDNESDAY

VERSE FOR THE DAY: Proverbs 23:25	*AUTHOR:* Shirley Dobson	*PASSAGE FOR THE DAY:* Proverbs 23:17–25

Sunshine of My Life

THE gift was not one that you would expect to receive from an eight-year-old boy. He had bought me a lovely desk set. The ostrich-feathered white pen looked like an old fashioned quill that Ben Franklin might have used to sign the Declaration of Independence. The stand was padded in matching white, with a spray of pink flowers delicately painted around the edges. I was so touched that my eyes brimmed with tears as I hugged and thanked my son for such an extravagant gift. It has been five years since that day and the pen still sits on the nightstand near my bed as a reminder of Ryan's spontaneous gift of love.

There are times in our lives when the cost of parenting seems staggeringly high! No matter how you look at it, children are emotionally exhausting, time-consuming, sometimes frustrating, and always maddeningly complex. In fact, their developmental years are governed entirely by "Murphy's Law." For example, if they drop a slice of bread on the carpet, it will inevitably land buttered side down. And when they catch the flu, they never vomit in the bathroom. They turn up their noses at their oatmeal and gag at the sight of their eggs, but enthusiastically drink the dog's water and float their rubber duckies in the toilet. I'm sure you could add to this list of childhood "Murphyisms."

But in moments when you are touched by the soul of a child, as I was through Ryan's act of love, you suddenly realize the eternal significance of these precious years. Then, no other task on earth seems quite as important or meaningful as raising and training and guiding him through his developmental experiences.

Additional Scripture Readings:
2 Kings 4:1–7; Luke 2:51–52

*Go to page 549 for your next
devotional reading.*

[17]Do not gloat when your enemy falls;
    when he stumbles, do not let your
        heart rejoice,
[18]or the LORD will see and disapprove
    and turn his wrath away from him.

[19]Do not fret because of evil men
    or be envious of the wicked,
[20]for the evil man has no future hope,
    and the lamp of the wicked will be
        snuffed out.

[21]Fear the LORD and the king, my son,
    and do not join with the rebellious,
[22]for those two will send sudden
        destruction upon them,
    and who knows what calamities
        they can bring?

Further Sayings of the Wise

[23]These also are sayings of the wise:

To show partiality in judging is not
        good:
[24]Whoever says to the guilty, "You are
        innocent"—
    peoples will curse him and nations
        denounce him.
[25]But it will go well with those who
        convict the guilty,
    and rich blessing will come upon
        them.

[26]An honest answer
    is like a kiss on the lips.

[27]Finish your outdoor work
    and get your fields ready;
    after that, build your house.

[28]Do not testify against your neighbor
        without cause,
    or use your lips to deceive.
[29]Do not say, "I'll do to him as he has
        done to me;
    I'll pay that man back for what he
        did."

[30]I went past the field of the sluggard,
    past the vineyard of the man who
        lacks judgment;
[31]thorns had come up everywhere,
    the ground was covered with weeds,
    and the stone wall was in ruins.
[32]I applied my heart to what I observed
    and learned a lesson from what I
        saw:
[33]A little sleep, a little slumber,
    a little folding of the hands to
        rest—

[34]and poverty will come on you like a
        bandit
    and scarcity like an armed man.[a]

More Proverbs of Solomon

25 These are more proverbs of Solo-
    mon, copied by the men of Hezeki-
ah king of Judah:

[2]It is the glory of God to conceal a
        matter;
    to search out a matter is the glory
        of kings.

[3]As the heavens are high and the earth
        is deep,
    so the hearts of kings are
        unsearchable.

[4]Remove the dross from the silver,
    and out comes material for[b] the
        silversmith;
[5]remove the wicked from the king's
        presence,
    and his throne will be established
        through righteousness.

[6]Do not exalt yourself in the king's
        presence,
    and do not claim a place among
        great men;
[7]it is better for him to say to you,
        "Come up here,"
    than for him to humiliate you
        before a nobleman.

What you have seen with your eyes
[8]   do not bring[c] hastily to court,
    for what will you do in the end
        if your neighbor puts you to shame?

[9]If you argue your case with a
        neighbor,
    do not betray another man's
        confidence,
[10]or he who hears it may shame you
    and you will never lose your bad
        reputation.

[11]A word aptly spoken
    is like apples of gold in settings of
        silver.

[12]Like an earring of gold or an
        ornament of fine gold
    is a wise man's rebuke to a
        listening ear.

[13]Like the coolness of snow at harvest
        time

---

[a]34 Or like a vagrant / and scarcity like a beggar
whom you had set your eyes. / [8]Do not go

[b]4 Or comes a vessel from   [c]7,8 Or nobleman / on

is a trustworthy messenger to those
    who send him;
he refreshes the spirit of his
    masters.

¹⁴Like clouds and wind without rain
    is a man who boasts of gifts he
    does not give.

¹⁵Through patience a ruler can be
    persuaded,
    and a gentle tongue can break a
    bone.

¹⁶If you find honey, eat just enough—
    too much of it, and you will vomit.

¹⁷Seldom set foot in your neighbor's
    house—
    too much of you, and he will hate
    you.

¹⁸Like a club or a sword or a sharp
    arrow
    is the man who gives false
    testimony against his neighbor.

¹⁹Like a bad tooth or a lame foot
    is reliance on the unfaithful in
    times of trouble.

²⁰Like one who takes away a garment
    on a cold day,
    or like vinegar poured on soda,
    is one who sings songs to a heavy
    heart.

²¹If your enemy is hungry, give him
    food to eat;
    if he is thirsty, give him water to
    drink.

²²In doing this, you will heap burning
    coals on his head,
    and the LORD will reward you.

²³As a north wind brings rain,
    so a sly tongue brings angry looks.

²⁴Better to live on a corner of the roof
    than share a house with a
    quarrelsome wife.

²⁵Like cold water to a weary soul
    is good news from a distant land.

²⁶Like a muddied spring or a polluted
    well
    is a righteous man who gives way to
    the wicked.

²⁷It is not good to eat too much honey,
    nor is it honorable to seek one's
    own honor.

²⁸Like a city whose walls are broken
    down
    is a man who lacks self-control.

26 Like snow in summer or rain in
    harvest,
    honor is not fitting for a fool.

²Like a fluttering sparrow or a darting
    swallow,
    an undeserved curse does not come
    to rest.

³A whip for the horse, a halter for the
    donkey,
    and a rod for the backs of fools!

⁴Do not answer a fool according to his
    folly,
    or you will be like him yourself.

⁵Answer a fool according to his folly,
    or he will be wise in his own eyes.

⁶Like cutting off one's feet or drinking
    violence
    is the sending of a message by the
    hand of a fool.

⁷Like a lame man's legs that hang
    limp
    is a proverb in the mouth of a fool.

⁸Like tying a stone in a sling
    is the giving of honor to a fool.

⁹Like a thornbush in a drunkard's
    hand
    is a proverb in the mouth of a fool.

¹⁰Like an archer who wounds at
    random
    is he who hires a fool or any
    passer-by.

¹¹As a dog returns to its vomit,
    so a fool repeats his folly.

¹²Do you see a man wise in his own
    eyes?
    There is more hope for a fool than
    for him.

¹³The sluggard says, "There is a lion in
    the road,
    a fierce lion roaming the streets!"

¹⁴As a door turns on its hinges,
    so a sluggard turns on his bed.

¹⁵The sluggard buries his hand in the
    dish;
    he is too lazy to bring it back to his
    mouth.

¹⁶The sluggard is wiser in his own eyes
    than seven men who answer
    discreetly.

¹⁷Like one who seizes a dog by the ears
    is a passer-by who meddles in a
    quarrel not his own.

¹⁸Like a madman shooting
firebrands or deadly arrows
¹⁹is a man who deceives his neighbor
and says, "I was only joking!"

²⁰Without wood a fire goes out;
without gossip a quarrel dies down.

²¹As charcoal to embers and as wood to
fire,
so is a quarrelsome man for
kindling strife.

²²The words of a gossip are like choice
morsels;
they go down to a man's inmost
parts.

²³Like a coating of glaze*a* over
earthenware
are fervent lips with an evil heart.

²⁴A malicious man disguises himself
with his lips,
but in his heart he harbors deceit.
²⁵Though his speech is charming, do
not believe him,
for seven abominations fill his
heart.
²⁶His malice may be concealed by
deception,
but his wickedness will be exposed
in the assembly.
²⁷If a man digs a pit, he will fall into it;
if a man rolls a stone, it will roll
back on him.
²⁸A lying tongue hates those it hurts,
and a flattering mouth works ruin.

27 Do not boast about tomorrow,
for you do not know what a day
may bring forth.

²Let another praise you, and not your
own mouth;
someone else, and not your own
lips.

³Stone is heavy and sand a burden,
but provocation by a fool is heavier
than both.

⁴Anger is cruel and fury overwhelming,
but who can stand before jealousy?

⁵Better is open rebuke
than hidden love.

⁶Wounds from a friend can be trusted,
but an enemy multiplies kisses.

⁷He who is full loathes honey,
but to the hungry even what is
bitter tastes sweet.

⁸Like a bird that strays from its nest
is a man who strays from his home.

⁹Perfume and incense bring joy to the
heart,
and the pleasantness of one's friend
springs from his earnest
counsel.

¹⁰Do not forsake your friend and the
friend of your father,
and do not go to your brother's
house when disaster strikes
you—
better a neighbor nearby than a
brother far away.

¹¹Be wise, my son, and bring joy to my
heart;
then I can answer anyone who
treats me with contempt.

¹²The prudent see danger and take
refuge,
but the simple keep going and
suffer for it.

¹³Take the garment of one who puts up
security for a stranger;
hold it in pledge if he does it for a
wayward woman.

¹⁴If a man loudly blesses his neighbor
early in the morning,
it will be taken as a curse.

¹⁵A quarrelsome wife is like
a constant dripping on a rainy day;
¹⁶restraining her is like restraining the
wind
or grasping oil with the hand.

¹⁷As iron sharpens iron,
so one man sharpens another.

¹⁸He who tends a fig tree will eat its
fruit,
and he who looks after his master
will be honored.

¹⁹As water reflects a face,
so a man's heart reflects the man.

²⁰Death and Destruction*b* are never
satisfied,
and neither are the eyes of man.

²¹The crucible for silver and the furnace
for gold,

a23 With a different word division of the Hebrew; Masoretic Text *of silver dross*   *b20* Hebrew *Sheol and Abaddon*

but man is tested by the praise he
receives.

²²Though you grind a fool in a mortar,
  grinding him like grain with a
    pestle,
  you will not remove his folly from
    him.

²³Be sure you know the condition of
    your flocks,
  give careful attention to your herds;
²⁴for riches do not endure forever,
  and a crown is not secure for all
    generations.
²⁵When the hay is removed and new
    growth appears
  and the grass from the hills is
    gathered in,
²⁶the lambs will provide you with
    clothing,
  and the goats with the price of a
    field.
²⁷You will have plenty of goats' milk
  to feed you and your family
  and to nourish your servant girls.

28

The wicked man flees though no
  one pursues,
  but the righteous are as bold as a
    lion.

²When a country is rebellious, it has
    many rulers,
  but a man of understanding and
    knowledge maintains order.

³A ruler^a who oppresses the poor
  is like a driving rain that leaves no
    crops.

⁴Those who forsake the law praise the
    wicked,
  but those who keep the law resist
    them.

⁵Evil men do not understand justice,
  but those who seek the Lord
    understand it fully.

⁶Better a poor man whose walk is
    blameless
  than a rich man whose ways are
    perverse.

⁷He who keeps the law is a discerning
    son,
  but a companion of gluttons
    disgraces his father.

⁸He who increases his wealth by
    exorbitant interest

amasses it for another, who will be
  kind to the poor.

⁹If anyone turns a deaf ear to the law,
  even his prayers are detestable.

¹⁰He who leads the upright along an
    evil path
  will fall into his own trap,
  but the blameless will receive a
    good inheritance.

¹¹A rich man may be wise in his own
    eyes,
  but a poor man who has
    discernment sees through him.

¹²When the righteous triumph, there is
    great elation;
  but when the wicked rise to power,
    men go into hiding.

¹³He who conceals his sins does not
    prosper,
  but whoever confesses and
    renounces them finds mercy.

¹⁴Blessed is the man who always fears
    the Lord,
  but he who hardens his heart falls
    into trouble.

¹⁵Like a roaring lion or a charging bear
  is a wicked man ruling over a
    helpless people.

¹⁶A tyrannical ruler lacks judgment,
  but he who hates ill-gotten gain
    will enjoy a long life.

¹⁷A man tormented by the guilt of
    murder
  will be a fugitive till death;
  let no one support him.

¹⁸He whose walk is blameless is kept
    safe,
  but he whose ways are perverse will
    suddenly fall.

¹⁹He who works his land will have
    abundant food,
  but the one who chases fantasies
    will have his fill of poverty.

²⁰A faithful man will be richly blessed,
  but one eager to get rich will not
    go unpunished.

²¹To show partiality is not good—
  yet a man will do wrong for a piece
    of bread.

²²A stingy man is eager to get rich

---

^a3 Or *A poor man*

and is unaware that poverty awaits
him.

²³He who rebukes a man will in the
end gain more favor
than he who has a flattering
tongue.

²⁴He who robs his father or mother
and says, "It's not wrong" —
he is partner to him who destroys.

²⁵A greedy man stirs up dissension,
but he who trusts in the LORD will
prosper.

²⁶He who trusts in himself is a fool,
but he who walks in wisdom is kept
safe.

²⁷He who gives to the poor will lack
nothing,
but he who closes his eyes to them
receives many curses.

²⁸When the wicked rise to power,
people go into hiding;
but when the wicked perish, the
righteous thrive.

29 A man who remains stiff-necked
after many rebukes
will suddenly be
destroyed — without remedy.

²When the righteous thrive, the people
rejoice;
when the wicked rule, the people
groan.

³A man who loves wisdom brings joy
to his father,
but a companion of prostitutes
squanders his wealth.

⁴By justice a king gives a country
stability,
but one who is greedy for bribes
tears it down.

⁵Whoever flatters his neighbor
is spreading a net for his feet.

⁶An evil man is snared by his own sin,
but a righteous one can sing and be
glad.

⁷The righteous care about justice for
the poor,
but the wicked have no such
concern.

⁸Mockers stir up a city,
but wise men turn away anger.

⁹If a wise man goes to court with a
fool,
the fool rages and scoffs, and there
is no peace.

¹⁰Bloodthirsty men hate a man of
integrity
and seek to kill the upright.

¹¹A fool gives full vent to his anger,
but a wise man keeps himself
under control.

¹²If a ruler listens to lies,
all his officials become wicked.

¹³The poor man and the oppressor have
this in common:
The LORD gives sight to the eyes of
both.

¹⁴If a king judges the poor with
fairness,
his throne will always be secure.

¹⁵The rod of correction imparts wisdom,
but a child left to himself disgraces
his mother.

¹⁶When the wicked thrive, so does sin,
but the righteous will see their
downfall.

¹⁷Discipline your son, and he will give
you peace;
he will bring delight to your soul.

¹⁸Where there is no revelation, the
people cast off restraint;
but blessed is he who keeps the
law.

¹⁹A servant cannot be corrected by
mere words;
though he understands, he will not
respond.

²⁰Do you see a man who speaks in
haste?
There is more hope for a fool than
for him.

²¹If a man pampers his servant from
youth,
he will bring grief[a] in the end.

²²An angry man stirs up dissension,
and a hot-tempered one commits
many sins.

²³A man's pride brings him low,
but a man of lowly spirit gains
honor.

ᵃ21 The meaning of the Hebrew for this word is uncertain.

²⁴The accomplice of a thief is his own
    enemy;
  he is put under oath and dare not
    testify.

²⁵Fear of man will prove to be a snare,
  but whoever trusts in the LORD is
    kept safe.

²⁶Many seek an audience with a ruler,
  but it is from the LORD that man
    gets justice.

²⁷The righteous detest the dishonest;
  the wicked detest the upright.

Sayings of Agur

30 The sayings of Agur son of
  Jakeh—an oracle^a:

This man declared to Ithiel,
  to Ithiel and to Ucal:^b

²"I am the most ignorant of men;
  I do not have a man's
    understanding.
³I have not learned wisdom,
  nor have I knowledge of the Holy
    One.
⁴Who has gone up to heaven and come
    down?
  Who has gathered up the wind in
    the hollow of his hands?
  Who has wrapped up the waters in his
    cloak?
  Who has established all the ends of
    the earth?
  What is his name, and the name of
    his son?
  Tell me if you know!

⁵"Every word of God is flawless;
  he is a shield to those who take
    refuge in him.
⁶Do not add to his words,
  or he will rebuke you and prove you
    a liar.

⁷"Two things I ask of you, O LORD;
  do not refuse me before I die:
⁸Keep falsehood and lies far from me;
  give me neither poverty nor riches,
  but give me only my daily bread.
⁹Otherwise, I may have too much and
    disown you
  and say, 'Who is the LORD?'
  Or I may become poor and steal,
  and so dishonor the name of my
    God.

¹⁰"Do not slander a servant to his
    master,
  or he will curse you, and you will
    pay for it.

¹¹"There are those who curse their
    fathers
  and do not bless their mothers;
¹²those who are pure in their own eyes
  and yet are not cleansed of their
    filth;
¹³those whose eyes are ever so haughty,
  whose glances are so disdainful;
¹⁴those whose teeth are swords
  and whose jaws are set with knives
  to devour the poor from the earth,
    the needy from among mankind.

¹⁵"The leech has two daughters.
  'Give! Give!' they cry.

  "There are three things that are never
    satisfied,
  four that never say, 'Enough!':
¹⁶the grave,^c the barren womb,
  land, which is never satisfied with
    water,
  and fire, which never says,
    'Enough!'

¹⁷"The eye that mocks a father,
  that scorns obedience to a mother,
  will be pecked out by the ravens of
    the valley,
  will be eaten by the vultures.

¹⁸"There are three things that are too
    amazing for me,
  four that I do not understand:
¹⁹the way of an eagle in the sky,
  the way of a snake on a rock,
  the way of a ship on the high seas,
    and the way of a man with a
      maiden.

²⁰"This is the way of an adulteress:
  She eats and wipes her mouth
  and says, 'I've done nothing wrong.'

²¹"Under three things the earth
    trembles,
  under four it cannot bear up:
²²a servant who becomes king,
  a fool who is full of food,
²³an unloved woman who is married,
  and a maidservant who displaces
    her mistress.

²⁴"Four things on earth are small,
  yet they are extremely wise:
²⁵Ants are creatures of little strength,

^a1 Or *Jakeh of Massa*   ^b1 Masoretic Text; with a different word division of the Hebrew *declared, "I am
weary, O God; / I am weary, O God, and faint.*   ^c16 Hebrew *Sheol*

yet they store up their food in the
summer;
26coneys[a] are creatures of little power,
yet they make their home in the
crags;
27locusts have no king,
yet they advance together in ranks;
28a lizard can be caught with the hand,
yet it is found in kings' palaces.

29"There are three things that are
stately in their stride,
four that move with stately bearing:
30a lion, mighty among beasts,
who retreats before nothing;
31a strutting rooster, a he-goat,
and a king with his army around
him.[b]

32"If you have played the fool and
exalted yourself,
or if you have planned evil,
clap your hand over your mouth!
33For as churning the milk produces
butter,
and as twisting the nose produces
blood,
so stirring up anger produces
strife."

Sayings of King Lemuel

31 The sayings of King Lemuel—an
oracle[c] his mother taught him:

2"O my son, O son of my womb,
O son of my vows,[d]
3do not spend your strength on
women,
your vigor on those who ruin kings.

4"It is not for kings, O Lemuel—
not for kings to drink wine,
not for rulers to crave beer,
5lest they drink and forget what the
law decrees,
and deprive all the oppressed of
their rights.
6Give beer to those who are perishing,
wine to those who are in anguish;
7let them drink and forget their
poverty
and remember their misery no
more.

8"Speak up for those who cannot
speak for themselves,
for the rights of all who are
destitute.

9Speak up and judge fairly;
defend the rights of the poor and
needy."

Epilogue: The Wife of Noble Character

10[e]A wife of noble character who can
find?
She is worth far more than rubies.
11Her husband has full confidence in
her
and lacks nothing of value.
12She brings him good, not harm,
all the days of her life.
13She selects wool and flax
and works with eager hands.
14She is like the merchant ships,
bringing her food from afar.
15She gets up while it is still dark;
she provides food for her family
and portions for her servant girls.
16She considers a field and buys it;
out of her earnings she plants a
vineyard.
17She sets about her work vigorously;
her arms are strong for her tasks.
18She sees that her trading is profitable,
and her lamp does not go out at
night.
19In her hand she holds the distaff
and grasps the spindle with her
fingers.
20She opens her arms to the poor
and extends her hands to the
needy.
21When it snows, she has no fear for
her household;
for all of them are clothed in
scarlet.
22She makes coverings for her bed;
she is clothed in fine linen and
purple.
23Her husband is respected at the city
gate,
where he takes his seat among the
elders of the land.
24She makes linen garments and sells
them,
and supplies the merchants with
sashes.
25She is clothed with strength and
dignity;
she can laugh at the days to
come.
26She speaks with wisdom,

---

[a]26 That is, the hyrax or rock badger   [b]31 Or king secure against revolt   [c]1 Or of Lemuel king of
Massa, which   [d]2 Or / the answer to my prayers   [e]10 Verses 10-31 are an acrostic, each verse
beginning with a successive letter of the Hebrew alphabet.

VERSE FOR THE DAY:	AUTHOR:	PASSAGE FOR THE DAY:
Proverbs 31:30–31	Dorothy Patterson	Proverbs 31:10–31

Strength in Wisdom

THE Sabbath service in the Jewish home unashamedly reveals the high position of women in Israel from Biblical times until the present. Sabbath is primarily a home-centered, family celebration, which makes it only natural that the mother of the home receive the honor of welcoming the Sabbath by lighting of the candles. Traditionally, the husband recites what is without doubt the most eloquent tribute to a godly woman that has ever been penned.*

Proverbs 31:10–31 presents the divine challenge for womanhood—diligent homemaker, valuable helper, nurturing mother, upright and God-fearing woman. The "wife of noble character" receives a reward for faithfulness because she is not dependent on the temporary, superficial, deceptive façade of "charm," which is a mere outward varnish easily scarred and marred by people and circumstances, and "beauty," which can depart like an unfaithful friend to make room for wrinkles and blemishes. Rather she crowns an enduring, satisfying fear of the Lord with a reverent and obedient spirit that makes her worthy of praise and honor from her family and the Creator himself (Proverbs 31:30).

Homemaking is unique in combining the most menial jobs with the most meaningful tasks: it is a challenge to accommodate others without losing one's own identity: it is a demanding pursuit, but the fringe benefits are terrific!

William Booth, the founder of the Salvation Army, gave this glowing tribute of his wife Catherine at the time of her death:

> To me she has been made of God, never-failing sympathy, reliable wisdom, and unvarnished truth—in short, all that is noble and good; and consequently a tower of strength, a mine of wealth, and an everflowing fountain of comfort and joy.†

With "undistracted devotion to the Lord" Catherine Booth was a woman to be praised because she feared the Lord.

Additional Scripture Readings:
Genesis 2:18–24; Luke 1:39–49

*Go to page 550 for your next
devotional reading.*

*Hyman E. Goldin, *The Jewish Woman and Her Home*, New York: Hebrew Publishing Company, 1941, pp. 124-131.
† T. Stead, *Catherine Booth*, Oakville, Canada: Triumph Press, pp. 119, 120-121.

and faithful instruction is on her
tongue.
²⁷She watches over the affairs of her
household
and does not eat the bread of
idleness.
²⁸Her children arise and call her
blessed;
her husband also, and he praises
her:

²⁹"Many women do noble things,
but you surpass them all."
³⁰Charm is deceptive, and beauty is
fleeting;
but a woman who fears the LORD is
to be praised.
³¹Give her the reward she has
earned,
and let her works bring her praise
at the city gate.

FRIDAY

VERSE FOR THE DAY:
Proverbs 31:31

AUTHOR:
Marlene Obie

PASSAGE FOR THE DAY:
Proverbs 31:25–31

With No Apologies

SHOULD I apologize for liking my career, Lord?

I've had inklings that I'm expected to dislike working. Some women pity me because my house and yard resemble a junk shop and I can't attend the neighborhood coffees and luncheons. They shake their heads at my time-clock schedule. They think I couldn't possibly enjoy such an existence.

Sure, I have days when everything goes wrong and I question whether this is a calling or a sentence in a forced labor camp. However, when the boss is grumpy, customers are unreasonable and auditors are looking over my shoulder, I remember comparable days when I worked solely at home. Those days were not without disasters, interruptions and stresses.

Thank you for showing me the joys of each of the different businesses I've worked in. I especially appreciate the way I'm treated by my peers. (My family would be surprised to know that I'm respected at the office.) Requests for my assistance are made politely and are addressed to my given name. I feel like a member of a team and not a quarterback without anyone to pass to.

No, I won't apologize for liking my careers. I feel my work as a wife, a mother, a homemaker, a writer, and a secretary are all important.

Lord, thank you for giving me gifts to use in these various capacities. What I have I must use, and no matter what anyone else thinks, I won't apologize. I like who I am and what I do at least ninety percent of the time.

Additional Scripture Readings:
Judges 4:4–10; 1 Thessalonians 4:11–12

*Go to page 5 for your next
devotional reading.*

INDEXES
READING PLANS

The figures of the table are calculated on the basis of a shekel equaling 11.5 grams, a cubit equaling 18 inches and an ephah equaling 22 liters. The quart referred to is either a dry quart (slightly larger than a liter) or a liquid quart (slightly smaller than a liter), whichever is applicable. The ton referred to in the footnotes is the American ton of 2,000 pounds.

This table is based upon the best available information, but it is not intended to be mathematically precise; like the measurement equivalents in the footnotes, it merely gives approximate amounts and distances. Weights and measures differed somewhat at various times and places in the ancient world. There is uncertainty particularly about the ephah and the bath; further discoveries may give more light on these units of capacity.

	BIBLICAL UNIT		APPROXIMATE AMERICAN EQUIVALENT	APPROXIMATE METRIC EQUIVALENT
WEIGHTS	talent	(60 minas)	75 pounds	34 kilograms
	mina	(50 shekels)	1 1/4 pounds	0.6 kilogram
	shekel	(2 bekas)	2/5 ounce	11.5 grams
	pim	(2/3 shekel)	1/3 ounce	7.6 grams
	beka	(10 gerahs)	1/5 ounce	5.5 grams
	gerah		1/50 ounce	0.6 gram
LENGTH	cubit		18 inches	0.5 meter
	span		9 inches	23 centimeters
	handbreadth		3 inches	8 centimeters
CAPACITY **Dry Measure**	cor [homer]	(10 ephahs)	6 bushels	220 liters
	lethek	(5 ephahs)	3 bushels	110 liters
	ephah	(10 omers)	3/5 bushel	22 liters
	seah	(1/3 ephah)	7 quarts	7.3 liters
	omer	(1/10 ephah)	2 quarts	2 liters
	cab	(1/18 ephah)	1 quart	1 liter
Liquid Measure	bath	(1 ephah)	6 gallons	22 liters
	hin	(1/6 bath)	4 quarts	4 liters
	log	(1/72 bath)	1/3 quart	0.3 liter

ACKNOWLEDGMENTS INDEX

Page 5: Taken from WOMEN IN GOD'S PRESENCE compiled by Delores Taylor. Copyright © 1988 by Christian Publications, Camphill, PA. Used by permission.

Page 8: By Beth Donigan Seversen. Copyright © 1990 by The Zondervan Corporation.

Page 12: Reprinted with permission from Daily Guideposts 1987. Copyright © 1986 by Guideposts Associates, Inc., Carmel, NY 10512.

Page 14: By Jill Briscoe. Copyright © 1990 by The Zondervan Corporation.

Page 16: Taken from COME TO THE WATERS by Diane Head. Copyright © 1985 by Diane Head. Published by Zondervan Publishing House. Used by permission.

Page 20: Taken from SITTING BY MY LAUGHING FIRE by Ruth Bell Graham. Copyright © 1977 by Ruth Bell Graham. Published by Word, Inc., Irving, TX. Used by permission.

Page 24: Taken from A CLOSER WALK by Catherine Marshall. Copyright © 1986 by Calen, Inc. Published by Chosen Books, Fleming H. Revell Company. Used by permission.

Page 26: By Rosalind Rinker. Copyright © 1990 by The Zondervan Corporation.

Page 35: By Hope MacDonald. Copyright © 1990 by The Zondervan Corporation.

Page 37: By Sue Richards. Copyright © 1990 by The Zondervan Corporation.

Page 39: By Carol L. Baldwin. Copyright © 1990 by The Zondervan Corporation.

Page 41: Taken from EXPERIENCE GOD'S FORGIVENESS by Luis Palau. Copyright © 1984 by Multnomah Press. Used by permission.

Page 43: Taken from LISTENING TO GOD by Janice Kempe. Copyright © 1985 by The Zondervan Corporation. Used by permission.

Page 47: By Jill Briscoe. Copyright © 1990 by The Zondervan Corporation.

Page 52: By Wanda K. Jones. Copyright © 1990 by The Zondervan Corporation.

Page 55: From the book ON ASKING GOD WHY by Elisabeth Elliot. Copyright © (1898) by Fleming H. Revell. Used by permission of Fleming H. Revell Company.

Page 60: From the book PASSION AND PURITY by Elisabeth Elliot. Copyright © (1984) by Fleming H. Revell. Used by permission of Fleming H. Revell Company.

Page 62: By Rosalind Rinker. Copyright © 1990 by The Zondervan Corporation.

Page 64: By Ruth A. Tucker. Copyright © 1990 by The Zondervan Corporation.

Page 66: By Hope MacDonald. Copyright © 1990 by The Zondervan Corporation.

Page 72: By Anne Ortlund. Copyright © 1968 by Anne Ortlund. Used by permission.

Page 76: By Anne Ortlund. Copyright © 1982 by Anne Ortlund. Used by permission.

Page 78: Excerpt from GIVE US THIS DAY OUR DAILY BREAD by Colleen Townsend Evans, copyright © (1981) by Colleen Townsend Evans and Laura Hobe. Used by permission of Doubleday, a division of Bantam, Doubleday, Dell Publishing Group, Inc.

Page 81: By Rosemary Jensen. Copyright © 1990 by The Zondervan Corporation.

Page 85: Taken from A VIOLENT GRACE by Gini Andrews. Copyright © 1986 by Gini Andrews. Used by permission of Zondervan Publishing House.

Page 93: Taken from RISE AND SHINE by Alma Barkman. Copyright © 1987. Moody Bible Institute of Chicago. Moody Press. Used by permission.

Page 95: By Jill Briscoe. Copyright © 1990 by The Zondervan Corporation.

Page 97: Taken from THE QUIET HEART by June Masters Bacher. Copyright © 1988 by Harvest House Publishers, Eugene, OR 97402. Used by permission

Page 100: Taken from STARTLED BY SILENCE by Ruth Senter. Copyright © 1987 by Ruth Senter. Used by permission of Zondervan Publishing House.

Page 102: By Jill Briscoe. Copyright © 1990 by The Zondervan Corporation.

Page 104: By Joni Eareckson Tada. Copyright © 1990 by The Zondervan Corporation.

Page 106: By Rosalind Rinker. Copyright © 1990 by The Zondervan Corporation.

Page 110: From the book EACH NEW DAY by Corrie ten Boom. Copyright © 1977 by Corrie ten Boom. Used by permission of Fleming H. Revell Company.

Page 113: By Jill Briscoe. Copyright © 1990 by The Zondervan Corporation.

Page 115: Copyright © 1987, CRC Publications, a Ministry of the Christian Reformed Church. Reprinted from *The Banner* (April 6, 1987) with permission.

Page 117: From the book WITH MY WHOLE HEART by Karen Burton Mains. Copyright © 1987 by Multnomah Press. Published by Multnomah Press, Portland, Oregon 97266. Used by permission.

Page 119: Taken from A WOMAN'S CHOICE by Eugenia Price. Copyright © 1962 by Eugenia Price. Published by Zondervan Bible Publishers. Used by permission.

Page 124: By Rosemary Jensen. Copyright © 1990 by The Zondervan Corporation.

Page 127: Taken from MEMORIES by Kathryn Hillen. Copyright © 1987 by Kathryn Hillen. Used by permission of Zondervan Publishing House.

Page 129: By Jill Briscoe. Copyright © 1990 by The Zondervan Corporation.

Page 131: Taken from Luke 1:46–50.

Page 132: Taken from BE STILL AND KNOW by Millie Stamm. Copyright © 1978 by Millie Stamm. Used by permission of Zondervan Publishing House.

Page 135: By Rosalind Rinker. Copyright © 1990 by The Zondervan Corporation.

Page 145: By Gloria Gaither. Copyright © 1990 by Gloria Gaither.

Page 147: By Carol L. Baldwin. Copyright © 1990 by The Zondervan Corporation.

Page 148: Taken from KINDRED SPIRITS by Kathy Narramore and Alice Hill. Copyright © 1985 by The Zondervan Corporation. Used by permission.

Page 396: Taken from BESIDE STILL WATERS by Gien Karssen. Copyright © 1985 by Gien Karssen. Used by permission of NavPress.

Page 402: Reprinted with permission from Daily Guideposts 1989. Copyright © 1988 by Guideposts Associates, Inc., Carmel, NY 10512.

Page 403: Taken from MY LIFE FOR THE POOR by Mother Teresa of Calcutta. Copyright © 1985 by Jose Gonzalez-Balado and Janet N. Playfoot. Published by Harper & Row, Publishers, Inc. Used by permission.

Page 411: By Debbie Smith. Copyright © 1990 by The Zondervan Corporation.

Page 414: By Ruth Bell Graham. Copyright © 1990 by Ruth Bell Graham.

Page 419: By Gloria Gaither. Copyright © 1990 by Gloria Gaither.

Page 421: Taken from A SILVER PEN FOR CLOUDY DAYS by Susan L. Lenzkes. Copyright © 1987 by Susan L. Lenzkes. Used by permission of Zondervan Publishing House.

Page 426: Taken from EARLY WIDOW by Mary Jane Worden. Copyright © 1989 by Mary Jane Worden. Used by permission of InterVarsity Press, P.O. Box 1400, Downers Grove, IL 60515.

Page 428: Taken from 101 MORE HYMN STORIES by Kenneth W. Osbeck. Copyright © 1985 by KREGEL PUBLICAIONS, P.O. Box 2607, Grand Rapids, MI 49501. Used by permission.

Page 430: By Wanda K. Jones. Copyright © 1990 by The Zondervan Corporation.

Page 433: By Ruth Bell Graham. Copyright © 1990 by Ruth Bell Graham.

Page 434: By Ruth Bell Graham. Copyright © 1990 by Ruth Bell Graham.

Page 440: Taken from GOD IS ENOUGH by Hannah Whitall Smith. Published by Zondervan Publishing House.

Page 444: Taken from A VIOLENT GRACE by Gini Andrews. Copyright © 1986 by Gini Andrews. Used by permission of Zondervan Publishing House.

Page 447: Taken from THE IRRATIONAL SEASON by Madeleine L'Engle. Copyright © 1977 by Crosswicks, Ltd. Published by Harper & Row Publishers, Inc. Used by permission.

Page 451: By Roslind Rinker. Copyright © 1990 by The Zondervan Corporation.

Page 457: By Gloria Gaither. Copyright © 1990 by Gloria Gaither.

Page 467: By Debby Boone. Copyright © 1990 by The Zondervan Corporation.

Page 473: By Hope MacDonald. Copyright © 1990 by The Zondervan Corporation.

Page 479: Taken from LISTENING TO GOD by Janice Kempe. Copyright © 1985 by The Zondervan Corporation. Used by permission.

Page 484: Taken from IF by Amy Carmichael. Copyright © 1980 by The Zondervan Corporation. Used by permission.

Page 490: By Carol L. Baldwin. Copyright © 1990 by The Zondervan Corporation.

Page 498: By Ruth A. Tucker. Copyright © 1990 by The Zondervan Corporation.

Page 500: Taken from LISTENING TO GOD by Janice Kempe. Copyright © 1985 by The Zondervan Corporation. Used by permission.

Page 504: By Hope MacDonald. Copyright © 1990 by The Zondervan Corporation.

Page 507: By Debbie Smith. Copyright © 1990 by The Zondervan Corporation.

Page 509: "Sacraments of Daily Living" taken from CLOSE TO THE HEART by Helen Lowrie Marshall. Copyright © 1958 by Helen Lowrie Marshall (renewed 1986). Used by permission.

Page 511: By Debbie Smith. Copyright © 1990 by The Zondervan Corporation.

Page 516: By Ann Kiemel Anderson. Copyright © 1990 by The Zondervan Corporation.

Page 525: From the booklet RELATIONSHIPS by Pamela Reeve. Copyright © 1982 by Multnomah Press. Published by Multnomah Press, Portland, Oregon 97266. Used by permission.

Page 527: Taken from WHEN THE HANDWRITING ON THE WALL IS IN BROWN CRAYON by Susan L. Lenzkes. Copyright © 1981 by Susan L. Lenzkes. Used by permission of Zondervan Publishing House.

Page 529: Excerpt from WHO AM I GOD? by Marjorie Holmes. Copyright © 1970, 1971 by Marjorie Holmes Mighell. Used by permission of Doubleday, a division of Bantam, Doubleday, Dell Publishing Group, Inc.

Page 532: From the book EACH NEW DAY by Corrie ten Boom. Copyright © 1977 by Corrie ten Boom. Used by permission of Fleming H. Revell Company.

Page 533: Taken from A SILVER PEN FOR CLOUDY DAYS by Susan L. Lenzkes. Copyright © 1987 by Susan L. Lenzkes. Used by permission of Zondervan Publishing House.

Page 536: Taken from WHAT COLOR IS MY COLLAR? by Marlene Obie. Copyright © 1985 by The Zondervan Corporation. Used by permission.

Page 541: Taken from LET'S MAKE A MEMORY by Gloria Gaither and Shirley Dobson. Copyright © 1983 by Gloria Gaither, Shirley Dobson, and James Dobson, Inc. Published by Word, Inc., Dallas, Texas. Used by permission.

Page 549: By Dorothy Patterson. Copyright © 1990 by The Zondervan Corporation.

Page 550: Taken from WHAT COLOR IS MY COLLAR? by Marlene Obie. Copyright © 1985 by The Zondervan Corporation. Used by permission.

Every effort has been made to give proper credit for each devotion used in this Women's Devotional Bible. If any error or inaccuracy is noted, please inform the publishers.

READING PLAN

God's Word is full of promises, encouragement and guidance for you. This reading plan gives you a simple structure for reading through the New Testament, Psalms and Proverbs in one year.

DATE	PASSAGE	DATE	PASSAGE
January 1	Matthew 1 Proverbs 1:1–7	January 24	Matthew 24:1–44 Proverbs 7:6–23
January 2	Matthew 2 Proverbs 1:8–19	January 25	Matthew 24:45–25:30 Proverbs 7:24–27
January 3	Matthew 3 Proverbs 1:20–33	January 26	Matthew 25:31–26:16 Proverbs 8:1–11
January 4	Matthew 4 Proverbs 2:1–11	January 27	Matthew 26:17–56 Proverbs 8:12–21
January 5	Matthew 5 Proverbs 2:12–22	January 28	Matthew 26:57–75 Proverbs 8:22–36
January 6	Matthew 6 Proverbs 3:1–4	January 29	Matthew 27:1–31 Proverbs 9:1–6
January 7	Matthew 7 Proverbs 3:5–10	January 30	Matthew 27:32–66 Proverbs 9:7–12
January 8	Matthew 8 Proverbs 3:11–18	January 31	Matthew 28 Proverbs 9:13–18
January 9	Matthew 9 Proverbs 3:19–26	February 1	Mark 1:1–20 Proverbs 10:1–5
January 10	Matthew 10 Proverbs 3:27–35	February 2	Mark 1:21–45 Proverbs 10:6–11
January 11	Matthew 11 Proverbs 4:1–9	February 3	Mark 2 Proverbs 10:12–16
January 12	Matthew 12 Proverbs 4:10–19	February 4	Mark 3:1–19 Proverbs 10:17–23
January 13	Matthew 13:1–52 Proverbs 4:20–27	February 5	Mark 3:20–35 Proverbs 10:24–27
January 14	Matthew 13:53–14:36 Proverbs 5:1–6	February 6	Mark 4:1–34 Proverbs 10:28–32
January 15	Matthew 15 Proverbs 5:7–14	February 7	Mark 4:35–5:20 Proverbs 11:1–4
January 16	Matthew 16 Proverbs 5:15–23	February 8	Mark 5:21–43 Proverbs 11:5–9
January 17	Matthew 17 Proverbs 6:1–5	February 9	Mark 6:1–13 Proverbs 11:10–14
January 18	Matthew 18 Proverbs 6:6–11	February 10	Mark 6:14–29 Proverbs 11:15–19
January 19	Matthew 19:1–20:16 Proverbs 6:12–15	February 11	Mark 6:30–56 Proverbs 11:20–26
January 20	Matthew 20:17–21:17 Proverbs 6:16–19	February 12	Mark 7:1–23 Proverbs 11:27–31
January 21	Matthew 21:18–46 Proverbs 6:20–29	February 13	Mark 7:24–37 Proverbs 12:1–6
January 22	Matthew 22:1–40 Proverbs 6:30–35	February 14	Mark 8:1–21 Proverbs 12:7–10
January 23	Matthew 22:41–23:38 Proverbs 7:1–5	February 15	Mark 8:22–9:13 Proverbs 12:11–14

AUTHOR BIOGRAPHIES

Many gifted women contributed their insights to this Women's Devotional New Testament. This index gives you information about each author and tells you where her contributions can be found.

Ann Kiemel Anderson is the author of ten books, including *I'm Out to Change My World*, and *I Love the Word Impossible*. Formerly a school teacher, a youth director and a college dean of women, she now devotes her time primarily to being a wife and the mother of four young sons. *Devotions by this author can be found on pages 216, 516.*

Gini Andrews has written several best-selling books that reflect in a personal way her walk with God. As a single Christian woman she wrote *Your Half of the Apple*. In *A Violent Grace* she shares her failures and heartache after marriage. She also wrote *Sons of Freedom* and *Esther*. *Devotions by this author can be found on pages 35, 444.*

June Masters Bacher taught elementary school and English until her retirement several years ago. She has written several books, including *Quiet Moments for Women* and a series of pioneer romance novels. June and her husband George live in California. *Devotions by this author can be found on pages 97, 182, 185, 270.*

Carol L. Baldwin is a marriage, group and individual counselor and the author of the book *Friendship Counseling*. Much of the material in her devotional readings developed from the trauma of being widowed at age twenty-seven. She is now married again and lives with her husband and their four daughters. *Devotions by this author can be found on pages 39, 147, 204, 301, 490.*

Alma Barkman is the mother of four children, living in Manitoba. As a free-lance writer she is the author of numerous articles and several books. *Devotions by this author can be found on pages 93, 238.*

Mary Beckwith, an editor, enjoys traveling, teaching, organizing and correspondence. She has written and conducted a variety of workshops for women, young girls and writers. She lives in California with her husband Clint and their three children. *A devotion by this author can be found on page 177.*

Debby Boone is a popular recording artist, performer, actress and author. Debby's recording of the song "You Light Up My Life" won her the Grammy Award for the best new artist in 1977. She has since recorded ten albums and has won two additional Grammy Awards. She is the author of *Debby Boone—So Far*, and two children's books. She and her husband Gabriel have four children. *Devotions by this author can be found on pages 273, 467.*

Jill Briscoe is the coordinator of women's ministries at Elmbrook Church in Waukesha, Wisconsin and the director of "Telling the Truth" media ministries. She is the author of numerous books, including *There's a Snake in My Garden*, *Prime Rib and Apple*, and *Thank You for Being a Friend*. She and her husband Stuart have three children. *Devotions by this author can be found on pages 14, 47, 95, 102, 113, 129.*

Barbara Bush, a pastor's wife and mother of four children, has written several books including *Ask Adam* and *I Can't Stand Cindy, Lord*. She enjoys her writing as well as sewing, stitchery, music and travel. *Devotions by this author can be found on pages 248, 334.*

Amy Carmichael (1867–1951) worked for many years in South India, rescuing children who had been "married to the gods" in nearby temples. Her brilliant style has made the stories of these children and the ministry of Dohnavur Fellowship known around the world. *A devotion by this author can be found on page 484.*

Marie Chapian has written twenty-four books, including the *A Heart for God* devotional series, *Mothers and Daughters*, and *Am I the Only One Here With Faded Jeans?* for which she won a Campus Life Gold Medallion award in 1988. Marie studied at Moody Bible Institute, Metropolitan State University and the University of Minnesota (where she received her Ph.D.). She is the mother of two daughters. *Devotions by this author can be found on pages 219, 260, 293.*

Mrs. Charles E. Cowman and her husband served as pioneer missionaries in Japan and China from 1901 to 1917. Mr. Cowman's poor health forced them to return to the U.S., and Mrs. Cowman nursed him until his death six years later. Mrs. Cowman's devotional books, *Streams in the Desert*, have been popular for more than sixty years. *A devotion by this author can be found on page 58.*

Neva Coyle was educated in Minnesota and California, where she now lives with her husband and three children. As president and founder of Overeaters Victorious, she lectures and leads her "Free to Be Thin" seminars. *A devotion by this author can be found on page 335.*

Fanny Crosby (1820–1915) was blinded in infancy supposedly by the ministrations of a "quack" physician called in to look at her eye infection. The hymns she wrote in her lifetime, over 9,000, have influenced thousands throughout the years. *A devotion by this author can be found on page 306.*

Gladis and Gordon DePree are the authors of several books, including *A Blade of Grass* and *Faces of God*. Gladis also wrote *Festival*, a book about life on Hong Kong Island. The DePrees live and work in the Middle East. *Devotions by this author can be found on page 342.*

Shirley Dobson is an author, homemaker, wife, and mother of a daughter and a son. She has served as a Bible Study Fellowship leader and as director for her church's ministry to women. She and her husband Dr. James Dobson often have appeared together on radio and television. *Devotions by this author can be found on page 541.*

Elisabeth Elliot was a young missionary wife and mother when her husband and four other men were killed while attempting to reach the Auca Indians. She is the author of many books, including *Through Gates of Splendor*, *Shadow of the Almighty* and *These Strange Ashes*. *Devotions by this author can be found on pages 55, 60.*

Colleen Townsend Evans lives with her husband in the Washington, D.C., area where he pastors the National Presbyterian Church. They have four children. She is a best-selling author of many books, including *A Deeper Joy* and *Make Me Like You, Lord*. *Devotions by this author can be found on page 78.*

Gloria Gaither is a lyricist, teacher, speaker, wife and mother. With the Bill Gaither Trio, Gloria has recorded over forty albums and is the coauthor of close to five hundred songs. Her ten books include *We Have This Moment*, and *Hands Across the Seasons*. She has won many awards, including the 1986 Dove Award for songwriter of the year. She and her husband Bill have three children. *Devotions by this author can be found on pages 145, 275, 419, 457.*

Ruth Bell Graham is the daughter of missionaries to China, the wife of evangelist Billy Graham, the mother of five, a grandmother to eighteen, and now a great-grandmother as well. She is the author of *Our Christmas Story*, *It's My Turn*, *Legacy of a Pack Rat*, and a collection of poems titled *Sitting by My Laughing Fire*. *Devotions by this author can be found on pages 20, 186, 349, 414, 433, 434.*

June Gunden graduated from Goshen College with a degree in English. She taught that subject for several years on the junior high level. She now works as a free-lance Bible editor and proofreader. She and her husband Doug have two sons, Troy and Benjamin. *Devotions by this author can be found on page 169.*

Doris Haase lives in California where she is part of a support group that reaches out to troubled people. She tries daily to put into practice one of her favorite Biblical principles found in Psalm 39:1–2: "I will . . . keep my tongue from sin." *Devotions by this author can be found on pages 317, 323.*

Diane Head is a homemaker, free-lance writer and illustrator. She has written two books, *Come to the Waters* and *A Precious Bit of Forever*. In 1980 she was selected as an "Outstanding Young Woman of America" in recognition of her personal and professional accomplishments. She and her husband have two daughters. *Devotions by this author can be found on pages 16, 344.*

Marilyn Morgan Helleberg began a lifelong career in writing when her first-grade teacher set a poem to music and taught it to the class. She has filled thirty-five notebooks over the past fifteen years and looks at them as a chronicle of her life with God. *Devotions by this author can be found on page 402.*

Alice Hill attended Asbury College, where her friendship with Kathy Narramore began, culminating in their book *Kindred Spirits*. Alice has also written *Help!* She enjoys running and classical music. Alice and her husband Dick have two children. *Devotions by this author can be found on pages 148, 268.*

Kathryn Hillen retired several years ago from her profession as an executive secretary to pursue a degree in Biblical literature. She and her husband have four grown children. Her book credits include *There Came Unto Him . . . Women* and *Memories*. *Devotions by this author can be found on pages 127, 320, 327, 332.*

Phyllis Hobe, a full-time writer, now makes her home in the country, after living most of her life in the city. The dog and cat who live with her are finding the free and open country lifestyle as enjoyable as she does. *A devotion by this author can be found on page 12.*

Marjorie Holmes first gained national attention as an author for her book of prayers, *I've Got to Talk to Somebody, God*. She has also written seven novels. Now living in Pennsylvania with her husband George, their four children and their families gather at her lakefront home in Virginia every Christmas. *Devotions by this author can be found on pages 384, 529.*

Gladys Hunt is the author of fifteen books, including *Honey for a Child's Heart*, and *We Need Each Other: The Miracle of Relationships*. Because inductive Bible study is one of her principle interests, she is active in small group Bible studies and is the author of eight Fisherman Bible Study guides. She is an enthusiastic wife, mother and grandmother. *Devotions by this author can be found on pages 207, 209.*

June Hunt is a speaker, singer, author and the host of the award-winning national radio program "Hope for the Heart." Through three music albums and her devotional book *Seeing Yourself Through God's Eyes*, she is committed to unraveling the difficult "heart" issues of life with practical help and Biblical hope. *Devotions by this author can be found on pages 229, 236, 265, 359.*

Rosemary Jensen is the executive director of Bible Study Fellowship, with headquarters in San Antonio, Texas. Prior to taking the post in 1980 she served as a high school teacher, medical specialist, business woman and Bible teacher. Together with her husband, Dr. Robert T. Jensen, she served as a missionary to Tanzania, Africa, for nine years. Rosemary and her husband have three daughters and six grandchildren. *Devotions by this author can be found on pages 81, 124, 370.*

Janet C. Jones was born into a Christian family and graduated from Nyack College in 1953. That same year she married Rev. George Jones. They raised three children, have cared for five foster children, and now minister to and nurture other people's children. *A devotion by this author can be found on page 329.*

Wanda K. Jones is a popular teacher and seminar speaker and the coordinator of Christian Family Outreach, Inc. She and her husband Howard, the first black evangelist on the Billy Graham Crusade staff, have been married over forty-five years. They enjoy five children and six grandchildren. While serving as missionaries in Africa they preached, taught and became well-known personalities on radio station ELWA. *Devotions by this author can be found on pages 62, 257, 391, 430.*

Gien Karssen served on the Navigator's staff at The Hague in the Netherlands. She started the work of the Navigators in the Netherlands as well as Europe. Gien pursues a writing ministry and is the author of eight books. *Devotions by this author can be found on pages 305, 396.*

Janice Kempe is a writer and homemaker. She and her husband are parents of two sons and one daughter. Janice has taught elementary school and has written two books, *Listening to God* and *Growing Up Together. Devotions by this author can be found on pages 479, 500.*

Sue Monk Kidd has written many articles for *Guideposts* magazine as well as one book *God's Joyful Surprise.* She and her husband Sandy have two teenagers, Bob and Ann. *Devotions by this author can be found on page 193.*

Alice Macdonald Kipling, who died in 1910, was the mother of famed poet Rudyard Kipling. *A devotion by this author can be found on page 367.*

Beverly LaHaye is the founder and president of Concerned Women for America and is an advocate, author and spokesperson on women's and family issues. She has written the books *The Restless Woman* and *Who But a Woman,* and she is the coauthor of *The Act of Marriage.* She and her husband have four children and eight grandchildren. *Devotions by this author can be found on pages 280, 316, 361.*

Elizabeth Larsen has written one novel and enjoys reading, needlepoint, cooking and writing. She and her husband Jerry have one son. *A devotion by this author can be found on page 188.*

Judith Lechman is a workshop leader and speaker. She has published over one hundred short stories as well as two books, *The World of Emily Howland* and *Yielding to Courage. Devotions by this author can be found on pages 223, 266.*

JoAnn Lemon and her husband Stan served as missionaries to Viet Nam from 1958–1972. In 1980 they returned overseas to serve in a church in Kowloon, Hong Kong for eight years. During these various ministries JoAnn was actively involved in women's ministries as well as music ministries. JoAnn and her husband have three children and four grandchildren. *A devotion by this author can be found on page 365.*

Madeleine L'Engle is a graduate of Smith College and Columbia University. She has been active in theater, as a teacher, lecturer and writer. Her books for children (and those who are children at heart) have won many awards. Probably the best known is *A Wrinkle in Time. Devotions by this author can be found on pages 240, 447.*

Susan L. Lenzkes lives and writes in California with her three children and her husband Herb. She is the author of *A Silver Pen for Cloudy Days* and *When the Writing on the Wall Is in Brown Crayon.* Susan enjoys singing in choirs and trios and ensembles, teaching Bible studies, and arranging flowers. *Devotions by this author can be found on pages 232, 378, 381, 421, 527, 533.*

Florence Littauer graduated with honors from the University of Massachusetts and is the founder of C.L.A.S.S. (Christian Leaders and Speakers Seminars). She has authored many books, including *Hope for Hurting People* and *After Every Wedding Comes a Marriage.* She makes frequent guest appearances on radio and television and has spoken to groups all over the world. *Devotions by this author can be found on page 311.*

Jeanette Lockerbie and her husband have retired in Florida. Before retiring she worked as an editor for *Psychology for Living.* As a free-lance writer she has published many books, including *Salt in My Kitchen* and *Time Out for Coffee. Devotions by this author can be found on page 212.*

Hope MacDonald has written articles for *Partnership, Today's Christian Woman* and *Faith at Work,* and is the author of *Discovering How to Pray, Discovering the Joy of Obedience* and *When Angels Appear.* Hope and her husband have been married forty-one years and have three children and six grandchildren. *Devotions by this author can be found on pages 35, 66, 287, 473, 504.*

Karen Burton Mains lives and ministers in the Chicago area, with her husband David co-hosting and speaking on The Chapel of the Air radio program. Karen wrote the best-selling book, *Open Heart, Open Home.* Her other book credits include *Karen, Karen, Making Sunday Special* and *The Fragile Curtain. Devotions by this author can be found on pages 117, 252, 353.*

Martha Manikas-Foster is a book editor and free-lance writer who studied at Houghton College and the University of Iowa. She worked as a newspaper reporter before entering book publishing in 1983. She has written articles for *Bookstore Journal* and *Paraplegia News.* She and her husband David have one daughter. *Devotions by this author can be found on pages 295, 299, 313.*

Catherine Marshall wrote many books before her death in 1983. They include: *A Man Called Peter, To Live Again,* and *Meeting God at Every Turn. Devotions by this author can be found on pages 24, 388.*

Helen Lowrie Marshall's (1904–1975) first book of poetry was printed and bound by hand in the home of her brother. She wrote many poems for use in Hallmark cards. A wife and mother of two sons, she was active in church and civic groups, and was in demand as a lecturer. *A devotion by this author can be found on page 509.*

Joan Rae Mills, married and the mother of two young children, is a free-lance writer and former English teacher. She enjoys restoring antiques, reading, writing and decorating. *Devotions by this author can be found on page 115.*

Kathy Narramore, a teacher and speaker, was born in Peking and lived her childhood years in several Chinese cities and the island of Taiwan. She graduated from Asbury College. Kathy and her husband Bruce live in California and are the parents of two children. *Devotions by this author can be found on pages 148, 268.*

Marlene Obie spends her time as a homemaker, free-lance writer, secretary, wife, and mother of three. She is the author of *What's a Mother to Do?* and *What Color Is My Collar?* Her articles have appeared in many Christian periodicals. *Devotions by this author can be found on pages 536, 550.*

Anne Ortlund is an award-winning musician and the author of seven books including *Building a Great Marriage,* and *Children Are Wet Cement,* which won the Christy Award as the best marriage-family book of 1982. She and her husband Ray are the coauthors of four additional books. Anne and Ray minister together through Renewal Ministries. They have four children. *Devotions by this author can be found on pages 72, 76, 153, 285.*

Luis Palau's story about Clara Barton, founder of the Red Cross, appears in his book *Experiencing God's Forgiveness*. He has written several other books on the Christian walk. *A devotion by this author can be found on page 41.*

Dorothy Patterson is a homemaker, author, conference speaker and adjunct professor of Christian Marriage and Family at the Criswell College in Dallas, Texas. She holds several degrees and is a member of the Council for Biblical Manhood and Womanhood, the Advisory Board of Concerned Women for America, and the Board of Directors for the Religious Roundtable Issue and Answers. She and her husband Dr. Paige Patterson have two children. *Devotions by this author can be found on page 549.*

Rebecca Manley Pippert, has spoken on four continents and written several books. They include *Out of the Saltshaker*, which has been translated into more than ten languages, *Hope Has Its Reasons* and *Pizza Parlor Evangelism*. She and her husband Wesley have two children. *Devotions by this author can be found on pages 161, 231, 263.*

Elizabeth Prentiss (1818–1878) early in life showed an ability for writing both prose and poetry. She taught school in Massachusetts and Virginia before marrying a minister in 1845. She wrote *Stepping Heavenward*, a popular book in her time. *A devotion by this author can be found on page 291.*

Eugenia Price is the author of twenty-two books, which have been translated into eleven languages. She holds the Georgia Distinguished Service Award and numerous fiction awards from the Dixie Council of Authors and the Georgia Writer's Association. Her manuscripts and letters make up a special collection at Boston University's Mugar Library. *Devotions by this author can be found on page 119.*

Pamela Reeve graduated from New York University with a degree in architecture. After several year's work in that field, she felt God's call to build people rather than things. That change, and further education, finally led her to a position as Dean of Women for Multnomah School of the Bible. She has now retired but continues to advise, teach part-time and speak at conferences and retreats. *A devotion by this author can be found on page 525.*

Sue Richards has lived in seven states as well as West Germany. She and her two children and husband Larry now live in Florida. Sue teaches eleventh-grade English and enjoys tennis and fishing. She has written one book, *Ministry to the Divorced*. *Devotions by this author can be found on pages 37, 151, 214, 346.*

Rosalind Rinker served for fourteen years as a missionary in China and then worked for twelve years with college students as a staff counselor with InterVarsity Christian Fellowship. She is active in a Mandarin-speaking Chinese church and teaches among Chinese churches in the Los Angeles area. For the past thirty years she has been a free-lance writer and speaker. Her fifteen books include *Prayer: Conversing With God*. *Devotions by this author can be found on pages 26, 62, 106, 135, 451.*

Dale Evans Rogers has traveled nationwide, appearing on radio and television as an actress, singer and speaker. She has written over a dozen books, including *Angel Unaware* and *Dearest Debbie*. She and her husband, Roy Rogers, live in California. *Devotions by this author can be found on page 211.*

Ruth Senter is a pastor's daughter and a pastor's wife, and therefore is uniquely capable of writing a book called *So You're the Pastor's Wife*. She has been involved in many aspects of book, periodical and curriculum publishing. She and her husband Mark have two children. *Devotions by this author can be found on pages 100, 380.*

Beth Donigan Seversen earned her master of divinity degree from Trinity Evangelical Divinity School and serves as the Associate pastor of Women's Ministries at Elmbrook Church, Waukesha, Wisconsin. She is also Jill Briscoe's writing assistant and in this capacity has written four inductive Bible studies. She and her husband have one daughter. *Devotions by this author can be found on pages 8, 250, 362.*

Linda Ching Sledge teaches at Westchester, New York, Community College. She lives there with her husband Gary and two sons. All the family enjoy trips to New York's Museum of Natural History to see the dinosaur exhibit. One of her hobbies is reading detective novels. *Devotions by this author can be found on pages 165, 258.*

Debbie Smith has written over one hundred songs with her husband, musician and recording artist Michael W. Smith. During her college years at Wheaton she spent six months in Haiti, where she helped establish a nutrition clinic. She now devotes most of her energies to her three children. *Devotions by this author can be found on pages 290, 324, 411, 507, 511.*

Hannah Whithall Smith (1832–1911) and her husband, Robert Pearsall Smith, were popular Bible conference leaders for many years. Personal tragedy led Mrs. Smith to write several books on suffering and obedience to the will of God, including *The Christian's Secret of a Happy Life* and *The God of All Comfort*. *Devotions by this author can be found on pages 338, 440.*

Millie Stamm has worked for many years directing Meditation Moments, a prayer ministry to Christian women. Her concern for Christian women in all walks of life has shown itself in her writing and speaking ministry. She has published two popular devotional books, *Meditation Moments* and *Be Still and Know*. *A devotion by this author can be found on page 132.*

Louisa Stead (1850–1917) heard the call of God to missionary service while still a child. After the death of her first husband, Mrs. Stead and her daughter served as missionaries in South Africa. While there Mrs. Stead married a South African native and worked on the mission field there until her death. *A devotion by this author can be found on page 428.*

Charlotte Stemple and her husband spent ten years as missionaries in Viet Nam in church planting and nursing ministries. The Stemples now live in the U.S. where Charlotte is involved in women's ministries. They have two sons. *A devotion by this author can be found on page 5.*

Luci Swindoll chose to retire early from her thirty-year career with the Mobil Oil Corporation to join Insight for Living, an international radio ministry where she is the vice president of public relations. Luci is a nationwide speaker and the author of seven books. *Devotions by this author can be found on pages 276, 340, 351, 373.*

Jean E. Syswerda, an editor with Zondervan Bible Publishers, keeps busy with her work, her family, with her church's ministry to teens, and with reading, gardening and decorating with antiques. She and her husband and three children enjoy country life in West Michigan. *A devotion by this author can be found on page 174.*

Joni Eareckson Tada is an internationally known mouth artist and author who developed her artistic talents after a diving accident in 1967 left her paralyzed below her shoulders. Her eleven books include her autobiography *Joni* and *Choices . . . Changes.* She works for the disabled as the founder and president of Joni and Friends. She also serves on the National Council for Disability, to which she was appointed by President Reagan in 1987. *A devotion by this author can be found on page 104.*

Delores Taylor, a singer and songwriter, has over fifty gospel songs to her credit. She graduated from Nyack College in Nyack, New York, and spent the next fifteen years touring and singing with the Alliance Trio. Delores and her husband Roy live in Virginia, where she now operates a dress shop and is president of her church's Women's Missionary Prayer Fellowship. *A devotion by this author can be found on page 243.*

Gigi Graham Tchividjian, daughter of Dr. Billy Graham, is first of all a wife and mother. She and her husband are the parents of seven children whose ages span twenty years. She is the author of *A Woman's Quest for Serenity* and *Sincerely, Gigi. Devotions by this author can be found on pages 221, 283.*

Rebecca Tempest works at present in a research laboratory at the University of Michigan in Ann Arbor, Michigan. She is a writer, mainly of poetry, and has had several of her poems published. *A devotion by this author can be found on page 149.*

Betsie ten Boom, the sister of writer and speaker Corrie ten Boom, died during World War II in a Nazi concentration camp. She and her sister ministered to many during the Nazi occupation of the Netherlands, hiding Jews in their home and providing encouragement to fellow prisoners in the camps. *A devotion by this author can be found on page 254.*

Corrie ten Boom, as a single Dutch woman, courageously hid Jews in her home during the Nazi occupation of World War II. She related her experiences in her most famous book *The Hiding Place.* After the war until her death she traveled and spoke, making people aware of the strength and contentment available in a close walk with God. *Devotions by this author can be found on pages 110, 278, 310, 532.*

Mother Theresa was born and raised in Albania. Her early religious training as a Sister of Loreto and her years of teaching in India were followed by the founding of her own order, the Sisters of Charity, to work with the poorest of the poor. Her work with the poor in India won her the Nobel Peace Prize. *Devotions by this author can be found on pages 167, 331, 403.*

Ruth A. Tucker earned her doctorate in history from Northern Illinois University and is a visiting professor at Trinity Evangelical Divinity School and a teacher at Moffat College of Bible in Kenya. She is the author of eight books and has won Gold Medallion Awards for *First Ladies of the Parish* (1989) and *From Jerusalem to Irian Jaya* (1984). She has one son. *Devotions by this author can be found on pages 64, 157, 376, 498.*

Shirley Pope Waite's writing career began back in high school when a teacher encouraged her to use those abilities. She has been a free-lance writer for many years and teaches courses on writing at a nearby college. She and husband Kyle raised six children. *A devotion by this author can be found on page 242.*

Anna L. Waring (1820–1910) was a Welsh poet. Several of her poems were set to music and became familiar and popular hymns. *A devotion by this author can be found on page 354.*

Mary Jane Worden and her husband Jim worked as staff members of Inter-Varsity Christian Fellowship until his death in a car accident in 1983. Out of those experiences came her book *Early Widow.* With her three children, Jane now lives and works in Nairobi, Kenya. *Devotions by this author can be found on pages 357, 426.*

SUBJECT INDEX

The subjects covered in the devotions are many and varied. This subject index will help you locate material on just about any topic or issue of interest, or about any problem confronting you.

NOTES

NOTES

NOTES